STATE & LOCAL PUBLIC FINANCE 3E

RONALD C. FISHER

Department of Economics
Michigan State University

THOMSON
SOUTH-WESTERN

Australia · Brazil · Canada · Mexico · Singapore · Spain · United Kingdom · United States

THOMSON

SOUTH-WESTERN

State and Local Public Finance, Third Edition
Ronald C. Fisher

VP/Editorial Director:
Jack W. Calhoun

Editor-in-Chief:
Alex von Rosenberg

Publisher:
Steve Momper

Associate Developmental Editor:
Michael Guendelsberger

Editorial Assistant:
Jessica Hartmann

Senior Marketing Manager:
Brian Joyner

Production Project Manager:
Tamborah E. Moore

Manager of Technology, Editorial:
Vicky True

Technology Project Editor:
Dana Cowden

Web Coordinator:
Karen L. Schaffer

Senior Manufacturing Coordinator:
Sandee Milewski

Production House:
Interactive Composition Corporation

Printer:
RRD Crawfordsville
Crawfordsville, Indiana

Art Director:
Michelle Kunkler

Internal Designer:
Trish Knopke, Cincinnati

Cover Designer:
Trish Knopke, Cincinnati

Cover Images:
© Getty Images, Inc.

Photography Manager:
John Hill

Photo Researcher:
Rose Alcorn

Library of Congress Control
Number: 2005929434

For more information about
our products, contact us at:

Thomson Learning
Academic Resource Center

1-800-423-0563

Thomson Higher Education
5191 Natorp Boulevard
Mason, OH 45040
USA

To my students

PREFACE

State and Local Public Finance provides an examination and analysis of public finance practices and problems in a federal fiscal system, focusing on the behavior and policies of state and local governments. The text presents detailed descriptions of significant institutions where appropriate, applies modern economic theory to the way these institutions are used to produce and finance services, and evaluates alternative policies. Although the emphasis is on American institutions and issues, much of the economic analysis applies generally to any federal system.

In the first edition, it seemed necessary to justify why a book devoted to state and local government was necessary. But with a global trend toward decentralization, political changes in the United States favoring more reliance on states, and concern about education and economic development often leading the news, the importance of state–local government now almost seems obvious. Still, the argument from that first edition bears repeating for any remaining skeptics.

A book devoted solely to state and local government fiscal issues continues to be appropriate for at least three reasons. First, the subnational government sector is a substantial component of the U.S. economy, with spending that accounts for nearly 14 percent of gross domestic product and more than half of public domestic expenditure. Second, of all services provided through the public sector, those provided by state and local governments—education, transportation, health and welfare, public safety, sanitation—are the most familiar to individuals and have the greatest effect on day-to-day life. Third, the information and knowledge available about state–local policy issues continues to grow and evolve.

The book is intended to be ideal for undergraduates who are studying public finance and have some knowledge of economic principles. The text provides complete coverage for courses specializing in state and local government. For one-semester or yearlong courses on public finance in general, two approaches are possible: the book may be used to supplement a general text, or it may become the basis for the course, with the general theory illustrated by state–local examples. For instance, the general equilibrium analysis of capital taxes can be illustrated just as well—and perhaps more interestingly—by the property tax as by the corporate income tax. The book is also useful to undergraduate students studying political science, public administration, journalism, or prelaw; to students in master's degree programs in public policy analysis, public administration, or planning; and to government officials and applied economists in government and consulting. Additionally, graduate students in economics may also use the book as both a survey of and reference to the economics literature on state–local finance issues.

STRUCTURE OF THE THIRD EDITION

This new edition retains what users identified as positive features in the past. Relatively sophisticated economic and policy analysis is presented, albeit using basic tools. Complicated and controversial economic and political issues are examined using institutional knowledge and basic economic concepts. Readers are expected to know basic microeconomics at the introductory level, but they do not have to know the theoretical tools usually associated with intermediate-level microeconomics. (In the few cases where these techniques add to the understanding of the material, they are presented in appendices.) Students should learn economists' conclusions and rationale even if they do not have a detailed understanding of the underlying theory or the econometrics from which those conclusions were derived. The intent of *State and Local Public Finance* remains to represent fairly the thinking of economists about state–local issues.

This new edition incorporates a number of changes. On a general level, the numerous visuals presenting fiscal data have been updated. The most recent information, including from the 2002 Census of Governments, has been incorporated into an expanded set of charts and tables depicting the current fiscal state of subnational governments. The "Headlines" vignettes at the beginning of each chapter presenting practical cases of state–local finance reported in the media have been updated to reflect current issues and illustrations. The "International Comparisons" sections have been expanded and enhanced. Citations to important books and papers in the literature regarding state and local government finance and policy have been updated, so that the volume remains a relatively comprehensive reference source.

On a substantive level, the four main policy chapters covering education (19), transportation (20), health and welfare (21), and economic development (22), as well as the chapter coving budgets (11) have been completely revised to reflect the substantial changes in the policy environment of each area in the past decade. These include (a) the changes to the entire structure of the welfare system with the adoption of Temporary Assistance to Needy Families in 1996 and subsequent revisions; (b) continuing changes by both the federal government and states to Medicaid, coupled with continuing increases in health-care costs; (c) the growing role for state governments in financing and assessing education, now in the environment of the federal No Child Left Behind initiative; (d) the growing degree of traffic congestion and responses of states; and (e) the continuing budget problems for many states as a consequence of changes in the national economy and political constraints.

Part I continues to present an overview of the state–local sector, discussion of the economic role for subnational governments, and a review of the microeconomic reasons for government provision in general. The basic fiscal institutions and core economic theory are presented in Parts II–IV. Following discussion of the interplay between the structure of subnational governments and their fiscal role in Part II, the provision of services in Part III—including the roles of costs, user charges, grants, and borrowing—are examined before analysis of the various state–local taxes in Part IV. These core chapters can be covered in any order using cross-references to material in other chapters. In Part V, the institutional information and economic analyses from the core sections are applied to four key policy issues. Each chapter concludes with both discussion questions and a list of relevant additional readings.

ACKNOWLEDGMENTS

I am particularly happy to thank the many students at Michigan State University—undergraduates and graduate students alike—who over the years have contributed to my career and this project in so many ways. Their questions, comments, and suggestions have contributed to both my knowledge of state–local finance and my understanding of how important economic concepts can be illustrated and conveyed in interesting and effective ways. Particular thanks for fine research assistance for this edition goes to Eric Becker, Kristen Brinkley, Douglas Harris, and Thomas Keller. The project also benefited greatly from a leave from my administrative duties provided by the university.

I have also been fortunate in my career in having a number of influential and inspiring teachers and mentors. The late Walter Adams, Byron Brown, the late Daniel Saks, and Milton Taylor at Michigan State University and Vernon Henderson and Allen Feldman at Brown University were instrumental in introducing economics to me and showing me how it could profitably be employed in understanding public-sector issues. John Shannon of the Advisory Commission on Intergovernmental Relations helped me in the early years of my career to learn how to bridge the gap between theory and policy, and Robert A. Bowman, while State Treasurer of Michigan, gave me the opportunity later to practice what I had learned.

This and prior editions have benefited greatly from the careful, detailed, and helpful comments, criticisms, and suggestions from many users and reviewers. For their valued assistance, I owe special gratitude and appreciation to

John E. Anderson
University of Nebraska

John H. Beck
Gonzaga University

Jeff E. Biddle
Michigan State University

R. Bruce Billings
University of Arizona

William T. Bogart
York College of Pennsylvania

Kenneth D. Boyer
Michigan State University

Byron W. Brown
Michigan State University

Jeffrey I. Chapman
Arizona State University

Dennis C. Coates
University of Maryland—Baltimore County

Susan Crosby
Hagan School of Business, Iona College

Robert B. Fischer
California State University, Chico

William F. Fox
University of Tennessee

Wayland D. Gardner
Western Michigan University

Gerald S. Goldstein
Office of the Superintendent of Financial Institutions, Canada

Beth Honadle
University of Cincinnati

Larry E. Huckins
Baruch College

Oded Izraeli
Oakland University

Craig Johnson
Indiana University

Dudley Johnson
Kibble & Prentice

Stephen E. Lile
Western Kentucky University

William A. McEachern
University of Connecticut

Sharon B. Megdal
University of Arizona

Peter Mieszkowski
Rice University

Pamela Moomau
Joint Committee on Taxation

Edward V. Murphy
Southwest Texas State University

Dick Netzer
New York University

Jun Peng
University of Arizona

Donald J. Reeb
State University of New York, Albany

Timothy Ryan
University of New Orleans

Rexford E. Santerre
University of Connecticut

Daniel B. Suits
Michigan State University

M. Kathleen Thomas
Mississippi State University

Charles Wagoner
Delta State University

Robert W. Wassmer
California State University, Sacramento

William White
Cornell University

David F. Wihry
University of Maine

Douglas Wills
Sweet Briar College

Michael J. Wolkoff
University of Rochester

James H. Wycoff
State University of New York, Albany

John Yinger
Syracuse University

Kurt Zorn
Indiana University

I am extremely pleased about the interest that Thomson Learning South-Western has shown in this project, including the patience, encouragement, and support of Peter Adams, Steve Momper, Michael Guendelsberger, and Jessica Hartmann: the acquisitions editor, publisher, developmental editor, and editorial assistant for economics, respectively. Tamborah Moore has been helpful and encouraging as she attended to various details as Production Project Manager. Nidhi Khanna and the staff at Interactive Composition Corporation were excellent and efficient partners in accommodating my unusual production schedule. Additionally, I thank Julie McNamee, the project copyeditor, for her efforts at helping to produce an easily readable volume.

Ronald C. Fisher

CONTENTS

PART V APPLICATIONS AND POLICY ANALYSIS 493

INTRODUCTION

EVERY PERSON HAS SOME FAMILIARITY WITH STATE AND LOCAL GOVERNMENT FISCAL POLICIES. We attend public schools; travel on streets, highways, and buses; receive clean water and dispose of dirty water; have our trash collected; enjoy the security of police and fire protection; use public hospitals; vacation at parks and public beaches; support the less fortunate with services and income maintenance; and we pay for these services. We pay property, income, and sales taxes; excise taxes on a variety of commodities such as alcohol, tobacco, and gasoline; a number of different user fees; and we buy lottery tickets. All this encompasses state and local government finance. In this book, we will do more than reiterate personal experience, however. The task is to combine knowledge of the institutional details of fiscal policy with an analytical framework so that policy issues can be better understood.

The task begins in Chapter 1 by first providing a general overall view of those institutional facts. How large is the state and local government sector and how has that size changed? What is the role of state and local governments compared to the federal government? What services do state and local governments provide, and how are those services financed? How are state and local governments organized? How representative is your experience, the way it is done in your state and community?

The tools to analyze the institutional details are presented in Chapter 2. Because this is an economics book, these facts are to be analyzed using standard economics methods. What is the economic role of government generally, and where do state and local governments fit in? What is meant by equity and efficiency, the traditional criteria for evaluating economic policy? What economic tools can state and local governments use to carry out their economic responsibilities in an equitable and efficient manner? From the general overview in this introductory section, the book proceeds to specific analysis of separate pieces of state and local finance and then returns, at the end, to more general analysis of broad policy issues.

CHAPTER I

WHY STUDY STATE AND LOCAL GOVERNMENT FINANCE?

. . . It has become evident in recent years that the serious business of governing the United States is largely being done in the States.[1]
—THE WALL STREET JOURNAL

HEADLINES

IN A 1999 SURVEY OF PUBLIC ATTITUDES TOWARDS GOVERNMENTS THAT CONTINUED A LONG SERIES BEGUN BY THE US ADVISORY COMMISSION ON INTERGOVERNMENTAL RELATIONS, RESPONDENTS WERE ASKED... "FROM WHICH LEVEL OF GOVERNMENT DO YOU FEEL YOU GET THE MOST FOR YOUR MONEY?"

LOCAL AND STATE GOVERNMENTS DREW THE HIGHEST NUMBER OF RESPONSES, CONSISTENTLY OUTDRAWING THE FEDERAL GOVERNMENT BEGINNING IN THE 1980S.

A SECOND QUESTION ASKED ABOUT "TRUST AND CONFIDENCE" IN GOVERNMENT TO "DO A GOOD JOB." MUCH HIGHER PERCENTAGES TRUSTED THE LOCAL AND STATE GOVERNMENTS THAN THE FEDERAL GOVERNMENT TO DO A GOOD JOB "A GREAT DEAL OF THE TIME" OR "A FAIR AMOUNT OF THE TIME."[2]

THE PUBLIC'S 1999 RATINGS OF FEDERAL, STATE, AND LOCAL GOVERNMENTS

Government	Most for Money (percentage)	Do a Good Job (percentage)
FEDERAL	23	56
STATE	29	67
LOCAL	31	69

[1]Editorial. "Traverse City Whacks Washington." *Wall Street Journal*, 28 July 1987.

[2]Cole, Richard L. and John Kincaid. "Public Opinion and American Federalism: Perspectives on Taxes, Spending, and Trust." *Spectrum: The Journal of State Government*, Summer 2001.

The economic issues involved in the financing of state–local governments deserve and demand separate attention for four primary reasons: (1) the state–local government sector is a substantial part of the U.S. economy, with its spending representing nearly 14 percent of Gross Domestic Product (GDP) and comprising more than half of total government domestic expenditure; (2) the major services provided by state–local governments—education, transportation, social services, and public safety—are those that most affect residents on a day-to-day basis; (3) state–local government experiences, experiments, and policies often form the basis for subsequent programs or policy changes by the federal government or even by governments in other countries; and (4) because of the *diversity* of state–local governments and the ease of *mobility* among them, the analysis of many economic issues is substantially different in the state and local arenas than for the federal government.

The importance of diversity and mobility for state–local government finance cannot be overemphasized. As you will learn in this book, tremendous diversity exists both in the structure of subnational government in different states and in the magnitude and mix of revenues and expenditures. In 2002, there were about 87,275 different state–local governments in the United States, each with independent functional responsibilities and revenue sources. Besides the 50 states, these included about 39,000 general-purpose local governments (counties, municipalities, and townships) and about 48,600 special-purpose local governments (school and other special districts). Because the boundaries of many of these jurisdictions overlap, any individual is a member or resident of at least two subnational governments (a state and a locality) and more likely a resident of four or more (state, county, municipality, or township, and at least one special district), each with separate elected officials and separate taxes and services.

The complicated relationship among local jurisdictions is illustrated in Figure 1.1, which depicts the cities, townships, and school districts for one county (of 83) in Michigan. Residents of the area covered by the map obviously are part of (that is, elect officials, pay taxes to, and receive services from) the State of Michigan and Ingham County (shown in gray). Within the county, the fine solid lines identify cities (Dansville, East Lansing, Lansing, Leslie, Mason, Stockbridge, Webberville, Williamston, and so on). Townships are shown as the regular square-shaped areas outlined in dotted lines that cover the entire county, with township names printed in italics. School districts (shown by the thicker, jagged lines) cross city, township, and even county boundaries. As an illustration, residents of the Williamston School District also could reside in Williamston City or Williamston, Locke, Leroy, Wheatfield, Alaiedon, or Meridian Townships. Thus, residents in this area are members of at least four state and local jurisdictions.

The division of responsibility among these different types or levels of subnational government varies substantially by state or region, however. In some states, such as Alaska, Arkansas, Delaware, Hawaii, New Mexico, and Vermont, local governments play a relatively limited role with the state government being dominant. In others, such as Colorado, Florida, New York, and Texas, local governments account for the majority of state–local expenditures. The division of responsibility within the local sector also varies by state. In Maryland, for example, counties are the dominant form of local government, collecting about 70 percent of local own-source revenue and making about 74 percent of all local government

Figure 1.1

Overlapping local government boundaries-Ingham County

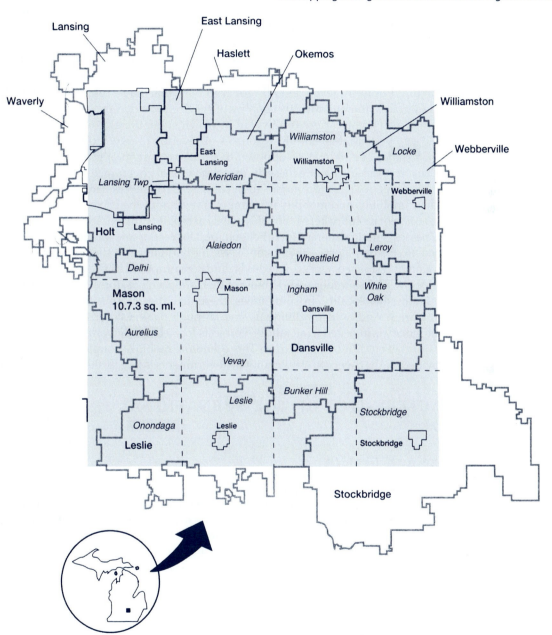

expenditures. At the opposite end of the spectrum, counties have no fiscal role at all in Connecticut where local government services are provided primarily by 179 separate and nonoverlapping "towns." Michigan represents a more common or typical structure where counties account for about 21 percent of local expenditures, municipalities and townships about 32 percent, and the rest by special districts, especially independent school districts.

In short, it can be very misleading to talk about "the services" provided by states, counties, cities, or local governments in general because there is no single structure. Similarly, even among governments that have responsibility for the same services, the quantity and quality of service provided can vary substantially. There is also great variety in the way in which subnational governments finance those services—that is, on which sources of revenue to rely. Indeed, this diversity is the essence of a federal, as opposed to a unitary, system of government.

The *ease of mobility* among these diverse subnational governments, however, causes the diversity to have economic implications. Diversity is largely uninteresting without mobility, and mobility is unimportant without the choice diversity creates. The notion of mobility here is not only physical mobility (the location of residences or businesses among different jurisdictions) but also economic mobility (the choice of where to consume or invest). In many cases, individuals can independently select the location of residence, work, investment, and consumption. Many individuals live in one city, work in another, and do most of their shopping at stores or a shopping mall in still another locality. In some cases, these activities cross state as well as local boundaries. And, when individuals save through bank accounts or mutual funds, their money is invested in all kinds of projects located in many different states, localities, and even different countries. This economic mobility coupled with the choice provided by the diversity of subnational governments is largely the topic of this book.

FISCAL CHARACTERISTICS OF THE SUBNATIONAL PUBLIC SECTOR

Size and Growth

In 2003, state–local governments spent more than $1,160 billion of resources collected from their own sources (that is, excluding spending financed by federal aid), which represented almost 11 percent of GDP (see Table 1.1). When spending financed by federal grants is included, state–local expenditures represent nearly 14 percent of GDP. It is also interesting to compare the state–local sector to the federal government alone. For every dollar collected from its own sources and spent by the federal government in 2003, state–local governments collected and spent about $0.51. In per-capita terms, state–local governments collected and spent about $4,040 per person in 2002, whereas the federal government collected and spent (including grants to state–local governments) about $7,860. If comparison is limited to spending for domestic programs by all levels of government, state–local governments collected more than 40 percent of those funds and were responsible for spending about 53 percent. Finally, as depicted in Figure 1.2, state and local governments account for more than 80 percent of all government employees, a share

Table 1.1

The Relative Size of Federal and State—Local Government, 2003

Type of Expenditure	Federal Government		State and Local Government	
	Amount (billions)	Percentage of GDP	Amount (billions)	Percentage of GDP
Expenditures from own sources	$2,263.9	20.6%	$1,162.5	10.6%
Expenditures after grants	1,924.9	17.5	1,501.5	13.7
Domestic expenditures, own sources	1,581.8	14.4	1,069.2	9.7
Domestic expenditures, after grants	1,243	11.3	1,408.1	12.8

NOTE: Domestic expenditures include nondefense purchases, transfer payments to persons and governments, and net subsidies of government enterprises

SOURCE: Department of Commerce, Bureau of Economic Analysis

Figure 1.2

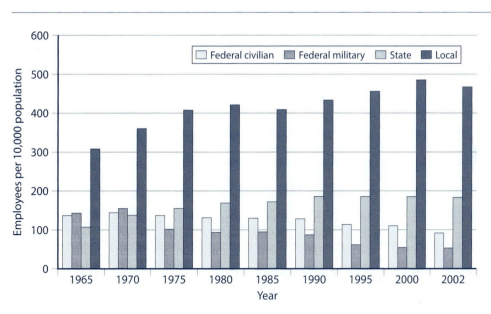

Government employment relative to population

that has been increasing over time. By any of these measures, state–local governments are both an important component of the U.S. economy and a very large fraction of the entire government sector.

Another interesting way to evaluate the magnitude of state–local economic activity is to think of the states as business firms—taking in revenue and producing services—and compare the states based on general revenue to the largest corporations based on sales revenue. All the state governments are large enough to be part of the Fortune 500 list of largest firms, 9 states are among the 50 largest (by revenue) of these entities, and California is fifth largest, exceeded only by Wal-Mart Stores, Exxon-Mobil, General Motors, and Ford.

Figure 1.3

State–local
expenditures (as a
percentage of
personal income)

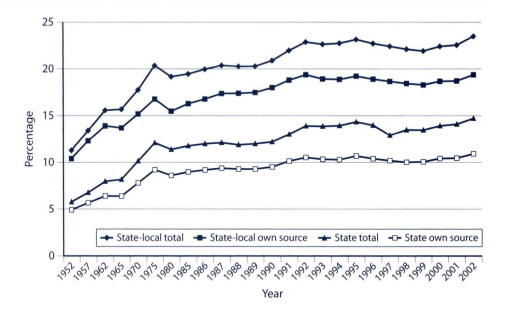

The current substantial relative size of the subnational government sector arose initially from a roughly 25-year period of sustained rapid growth between 1950 and 1975. Using National Income Accounts data, state–local expenditures grew from about 6 percent of GDP in 1950 to about 12 percent in 1975, implying that state–local spending increased at roughly twice the rate of the national economy. Using Census data, the growth of total state–local government expenditures (either including or excluding spending financed by grants), both relative to personal income and in real per-capita dollars, is depicted in Figure 1.3. In 1952, total state–local spending from all sources represented slightly more than 11 percent of personal income, but, by 1975, state–local spending had grown to about 20 percent of income. Even excluding federal grants, state–local spending from own sources increased from about 10 percent of income in 1952 to about 17 percent in 1975. A similar pattern of growth is shown by per-capita, 2000 dollars, indicating that state–local spending also increased faster than population growth and prices during this period. Not surprisingly, the pattern of growth in spending by state governments alone parallels the pattern for the entire state–local sector rather closely.

The relative growth of the state–local sector in this period is usually attributed to three factors. First, income in the United States increased rather substantially in these years; this caused an increase in demand for many different types of goods and services, some of which were provided largely by subnational governments. Second, growth in population and change in the composition of the population (especially the postwar baby boom) also lead to an increase in demand for state–local services (especially education). Third, substantial increases in

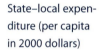

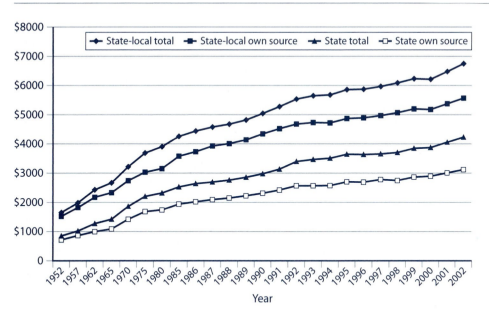

State–local expenditure (per capita in 2000 dollars)

manufacturing-labor productivity and thus manufacturing wages during this period created pressures to increase wages of state and local employees as well. This caused an increase in the relative cost of providing those services. In essence, spending rose faster than the economy grew because the population to be served (especially children) was rising relatively fast, because the costs of providing state–local services were rising faster than average, and because consumers were demanding new or improved services from subnational governments.

The relative size of the state–local government sector has not changed nearly as substantially since the middle 1970s, however. State–local spending has continued to grow relative to personal income since 1975, but at a much more modest pace than previously. Over this period, state–local spending has increased from a little more than 20 percent of income to slightly above 23 percent, hardly dramatic change over a 25-year period. A similar slowdown in the growth of state–local government spending beginning in the latter 1970s is reflected by the graph of real per-capita spending in Figure 1.4. Whereas state–local government spending has continued to increase faster than the combination of population growth and inflation, the growth rate in the last 25 years of the century (168 percent) was substantially less than in the earlier 25 year period (230 percent). Similarly, the change in spending by state governments alone parallels the pattern for the entire state–local sector rather closely. Thus, the past 25 years have seen little substantial change in the relative fiscal magnitude of state and local government, at least at the macro level.

In general, the reduction in the relative growth of the fiscal size of state and local government during the last quarter of the past century simply reflected a reversal of all those factors that had been operating since 1950. Income did not grow as fast in those years as previously, partly because the economy experienced four national recessions between 1974 and 2002. Demand for educational services lessened as the baby boomers completed school and delayed starting their own families. State–local government costs, especially wages, did not increase relatively as fast in this period as previously, in part due to slower growth of private productivity nationally. Federal grants to state–local governments did not grow in this period anywhere near as fast as in the previous period, although state–local spending from own sources also follows the same pattern of slowing growth. Finally, it has been suggested that the slowdown reflects a change in the tastes or preferences of consumers for government services, as reflected by the coordinated opposition to state–local taxes in the late 1970s and 1980s, which has come to be called the "tax revolt." This change in the political environment seems to have persisted. Whatever the combination of factors, it is clear that the past 25 years have represented a very different environment for state–local finance than in the preceding 25-year period of substantial growth.

The growth in state–local spending that has occurred has been influenced by several factors, including increasing health care costs, increasing corrections expenditures by states, slower growth of federal grants, and services that state–local governments are mandated to provide by the national government. Research by Gramlich (1991) suggested that the increased state–local spending in real or relative terms in the 1980s was explained mainly by three factors: (1) rising costs of producing services (especially for health care), (2) increased demand for services (particularly due to more prisons, a growing prison population, as well as an increase in the number of school children), and (3) a small effect from new federal government requirements for state–local spending. Most recently, since 2000 state–local spending has increased relatively substantially again, measured both relative to personal income and in real, per-capita terms. This recent growth seems driven by continuing increases in health care costs, growth in the number of elderly people and school-age children, and public safety issues, including corrections and efforts to prevent terrorism. At the time this is being written, therefore, it is an open question whether this recent growth is a temporary phenomenon or the start of another long period of relative fiscal expansion for the state–local sector.

Although not apparent in Figure 1.4, an important distinction exists between the roles of state and local governments. In 2002, state governments collected 59 percent of state–local taxes and 55 percent of own-source state–local revenue; however, state governments only were responsible for about 45 percent of direct spending. The difference represents the importance of state aid to local governments. To put it another way, local governments are responsible for about 55 percent of state–local spending, but collect only about 41 percent of taxes, a differential that has been growing.

Expenditure Categories

More than half of the money spent by state and local governments in aggregate provides education or income maintenance services, as shown in Figure 1.5. In

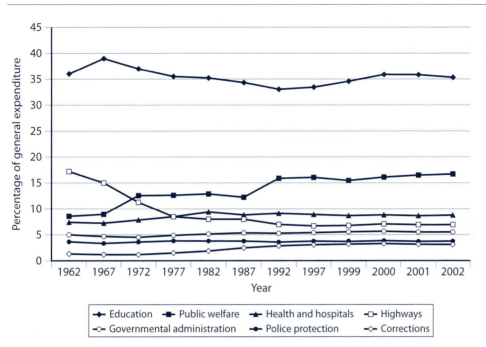

Figure 1.5

Distribution of
state–local general
expenditure

2002, these categories accounted for nearly 52 percent of total state–local general spending, with education accounting for about 36 percent and public welfare about 16 percent. Expenditures for highways and health and hospitals, the other main direct consumer services, represent about 7 to 9 percent of state–local spending, whereas expenditures on police services and corrections represent only about 3 to 4 percent. After a 25-year decline, the share of spending for education has increased in the past 10 years. Expenditure for public welfare and health and hospitals has continued to increase, while the highways have become a smaller fraction of state–local spending in aggregate.

The distribution of spending by category for state–local governments together masks important differences between states and local governments, on average. The distribution of **general expenditure** for states and localities are shown separately in Figure 1.6. (According to the Census definition, general expenditure includes all expenditures except those for government utilities, liquor stores, and employee retirement funds.) Education is by the far the largest category of spending for both states and localities (31 percent for states, including higher education spending and state grants for schools, and 44 percent for localities). States also spend a relatively large fraction of their expenditures on welfare, transportation, and health and hospital services, whereas the other major expenditure categories for local governments are environment and housing, transportation, health and hospitals, and public safety.

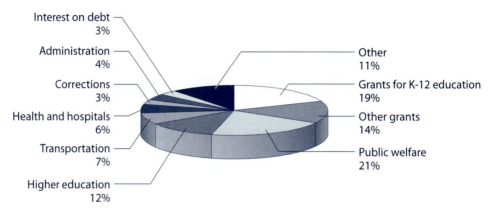

General expenditure, state governments, 2002 (total: $1.109 trillion);

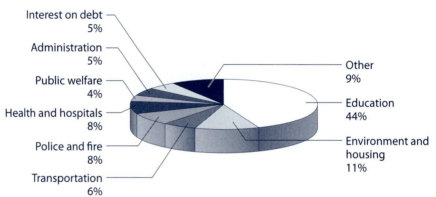

General expenditure, local governments, 2002 (total: $997.6 billion)

Revenue Sources

State–local governments receive revenues from a variety of different sources, including a number of types of taxes, as shown in Figure 1.7. When all revenues to all state–local governments are added together, the five major sources, all of roughly equal importance, are charges and miscellaneous revenue (24.9 percent of the total), sales taxes (19.2 percent), property taxes (16.6 percent), federal grants (21.4 percent), and income taxes (12.0 percent). In contrast, the predominant source of revenue for the federal government is income taxes, including the personal and corporate income taxes and the social security payroll tax. There have been no sustained trends in revenue shares over the past 10 years, although the share from federal aid has started to increase again in the past several years and the share from charges has continued to increase modestly.

The composition of revenues differs between states and local governments even more than the difference in expenditure patterns, as shown by Figure 1.8. Restricting the comparison to **general revenue** (excluding utility, liquor store, and employee retirement revenue), states get nearly 75 percent of their revenue from sales taxes (about 25 percent), income taxes (about 20 percent from individual and corporate

Figure 1.7

Distribution of
state–local general
revenue

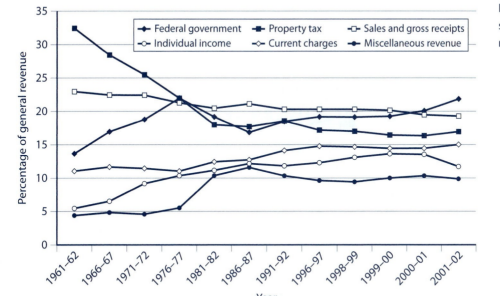

Figure 1.8

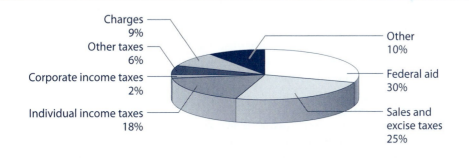

General revenue,
state govern-
ments, 2002 (total:
$1.062 trillion);

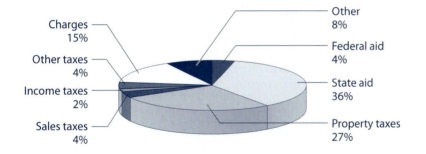

General revenue,
local governments,
2002 (total:
$995.9 billion)

taxes), and federal grants (30 percent). The two dominant sources of general revenue for local governments accounting for about 63 percent of the total are state grants (about 36 percent) and property taxes (27 percent). From another perspective, grants from both the federal and state government provide about 40 percent of local government general revenue. It is worth noting that these are averages for all local governments; substantial variation exists both by type of local government and state.

DIVERSITY OF SUBNATIONAL GOVERNMENTS

Although the statistics presented earlier for both the level and mix of expenditures and revenues characterize the overall state–local sector, they do not necessarily represent the fiscal picture in any individual state and local jurisdiction. As noted, diversity is the norm in subnational finance. Accordingly, the data in Tables 1.2–1.4 show some comparison of the fiscal environment in different states. Comparing the level of expenditures or revenues among states is not enough; instead, it is necessary to standardize the data because of the different sizes and characteristics of the states. The two most common ways of standardizing are to compare the data in per-capita terms (per person) or as a percentage of income. However, suppose that one state has higher per-capita expenditures than another or that expenditures take a larger fraction of income in one state than another. Do these mean that services are greater in one state than the other? Not necessarily.

The rationale for per-capita comparisons is that it may require more expenditure and revenue to provide equal services to a larger population than to a smaller one. The degree to which that is true for different state–local services is not clear, however. If the production of state–local services exhibits **constant returns to scale,** that is, if the average cost of providing a unit of service to one consumer is constant, then total cost will increase proportionately to population. Equal per-capita amounts are then consistent with equal services, *if* all other factors are the same between the jurisdictions being compared. On the other hand, the production of some services may exhibit **increasing returns to scale,** which means that cost per person falls as the number of people served rises. In that case, equal services are consistent with lower per-capita expenditures in the larger jurisdictions, *if* all else is the same.

A similar analysis applies to interjurisdictional comparisons based on the fraction of income taken by state–local expenditures and revenues. One might expect that two states, one rich and one poor, would have the same *percentage* of their income going to government services. This is true only if the income elasticity of demand for those government services is one; that is, if demand for service increases proportionately with income. If not (that is, if demand for state–local services increases slower or faster than income), then equal percentages of income going to state–local expenditures are not expected. In addition, this analysis requires that factors other than income be the same between the jurisdictions being compared.

In general, differences in state–local expenditures or revenues among states may arise because of (1) different decisions about what services to provide through the public sector as opposed to the private sector in different states; (2) differences in input prices (especially labor) among the states; (3) differences in environment such as area, population density, or weather, which affect the cost of producing services; and (4) differences in demand for services from either population differences, income differences, or differences in tastes. Standardization in per-capita terms may offset only the population effects, and standardization by state-income level offsets only the income effect on demand. With either standardization, differences in spending or taxes can remain, which do not reflect service differences. As a result, extreme caution is necessary in making interstate fiscal comparisons. A higher level of revenues and expenditures in one state may mean there are more services in that state, may reflect higher production costs in that state, or may mean that residents of that state have decided to provide some service (hospitals, for instance) through the government rather than privately.

Expenditures

With the preceding cautions in mind, the differences in state–local expenditure among the states are shown in Table 1.2. In 2002, state–local governments spent an average of $6,166 per person or about 19.9 percent of individuals' personal incomes. Seven states spent more than $7,000 per person—Alaska ($13,466), Delaware ($10,808), New York ($8,523), Wyoming ($7,801), Connecticut ($7,105), Minnesota ($7,102), and California ($7,041)—and eight states spent less than $5,300 per person—Arkansas ($4,889), Arizona ($4922), Tennessee ($5,089), New Hampshire ($5,132), South Dakota ($5,145), Missouri ($5,192), Idaho ($5,258), and Oklahoma ($5,273). A similar range exists in the fraction of income taken by state–local expenditures, from 41.9 percent in Alaska and 25.9 percent in New Mexico to 14.9 percent in New Hampshire and 16.4 percent in Connecticut and New Jersey. There is also very little of a regional pattern in the level of expenditures. Although per-capita spending is consistently below average in the Southeast and above average in the Far West, substantial variation occurs within regions in the other cases.

Although a general correspondence exists between the rankings of states by per-capita spending and spending as a percentage of income, some important differences stand out. In California, for example, per-capita spending is 14 percent greater than the national average, but spending relative to income is only slightly above the average. California's apparently high per-capita spending might be attributed to its above-average income. On the other hand, Arkansas is the lowest state in per-capita spending, but its spending relative to income is above average. Here the relatively low income in the state may be holding per-capita spending down. And per-capita spending in both Maryland and Maine is very close to the national average, but spending relative to income is about 16 percent below the national average in Maryland and 14 percent above average in Oregon.

By either measure, spending is way above average in Alaska. The explanation primarily lies in two factors: high costs for producing services and the collection of substantial amounts of oil-extraction revenue, which is distributed as royalties paid to residents.

The last two columns of Table 1.2 show the fraction of state–local expenditures, both before and after transfers, made by the state government in each state. The only obvious regional pattern is the relatively strong role played by state governments in New England (with the exception of New Hampshire). Otherwise, there

Table 1.2

State and Local Government General Expenditure by State, 2002[a]

State and Region	Per Capita State–Local Expenditure	State–Local Expenditure as a Percentage of Personal Income	State Government Share of State–Local Direct Expenditure, Before Transfers[b]	State Government Share of State–Local Direct Expenditure, After Transfers
United States	$6,166	19.9%	56%	45%
New England				
Connecticut	7,105	16.4	66	59
Maine	6,262	22.7	64	61
Massachusetts	6,698	17.1	69	52
New Hampshire	5,132	14.9	56	52
Rhode Island	6,474	21.1	64	63
Vermont	6,264	21.4	78	62
Mideast				
Delaware	6,834	20.9	77	64
District of Columbia	10,804	24.3	na	na
Maryland	6,004	16.6	58	51
New Jersey	6,473	16.4	55	51
New York	8,523	23.8	45	41
Pennsylvania	5,999	19.8	59	49
Great Lakes				
Illinois	5,944	18.1	51	41
Indiana	5,394	19.5	53	43
Michigan	6,116	20.3	62	43
Ohio	5,906	20.6	55	47
Wisconsin	6,339	21.4	55	44
Plains				
Iowa	5,888	21.6	58	49
Kansas	5,534	19.2	56	46
Minnesota	7,102	21.5	63	46
Missouri	5,192	18.5	53	48
Nebraska	5,704	19.8	53	38
North Dakota	6,053	23.6	63	58
South Dakota	5,145	19.1	54	53
Southeast				
Alabama	5,533	22.2	55	49
Arkansas	4,889	21.0	75	58
Florida	5,449	18.2	49	38
Georgia	5,491	18.6	52	41
Kentucky	5,342	21.3	68	60
Louisiana	5,442	22.0	57	51
Mississippi	5,407	24.5	60	54
North Carolina	5,534	19.7	57	46
South Carolina	5,937	23.4	60	56
Tennessee	5,089	18.7	51	42
Virginia	5,547	16.8	58	45
West Virginia	5,447	23.5	71	67

Table 1.2

(continued)

State and Region	Per Capita State–Local Expenditure	State–Local Expenditure as a Percentage of Personal Income	State Government Share of State–Local Direct Expenditure, Before Transfers[b]	State Government Share of State–Local Direct Expenditure, After Transfers
Southwest				
Arizona	4,922	18.2	53	36
New Mexico	6,287	25.9	75	58
Oklahoma	5,273	20.2	62	55
Texas	5,352	18.0	46	41
Rocky Mountain				
Colorado	6,301	17.7	46	39
Idaho	5,258	20.6	62	51
Montana	5,601	22.7	65	60
Utah	5,760	22.8	67	51
Wyoming	7,801	25.6	50	46
Far West				
Alaska	13,466	41.9	75	68
California	7,041	21.0	59	38
Hawaii	6,851	23.7	79	78
Nevada	5,893	18.2	51	35
Oregon	6,720	23.3	58	50
Washington	6,559	19.9	62	47

[a]General expenditure includes all expenditures other than utility, liquor store, and employee retirement expenditures.

[b]State direct general expenditure less intergovernmental revenue plus state aid to local government as a fraction of state–local direct general expenditure less federal aid

SOURCE: US Bureau of the Census, Census of Governments, *State and Local Government Finances, 2002*

is much variation within regions. State governments take a dominant role in Hawaii (79 percent of own-source expenditure), Vermont (78 percent), Delaware (77 percent), Alaska (75 percent), Arkansas (75 percent), New Mexico (75 percent), West Virginia (71 percent), Massachusetts (69 percent), Kentucky (68 percent), and Utah (67 percent). Local governments provide the majority of own-source funds in New York (45 percent of own-source expenditures by the state), Colorado (46 percent), Texas (46 percent), and Florida (49 percent).

Revenues

State levels of state–local revenues and taxes, both per capita and relative to income, are shown in Table 1.3. The relative state rankings in revenues are, not surprisingly, generally similar to the relative state positions in expenditures. Thus, the regional pattern shows relatively low revenues and taxes in the Southeast and substantial variation within most other regions. Besides taxes, state–local general

Table 1.3

State and Local Government Per Capita Revenue, by State, 2002

State & Region	General Revenue	Federal Aid	Taxes
United States	$5,987	$1,281	$3,216
New England			
Connecticut	6,696	1,186	4,441
Maine	6,335	1,491	3,562
Massachusetts	6,143	973	3,764
New Hampshire	5,183	1,048	2,912
Rhode Island	6,332	1,685	3,456
Vermont	6,334	1,785	3,227
Middle Atlantic			
Delaware	7,143	1,223	3,427
District of Columbia	12,102	4,965	5,643
Maryland	6,103	1,119	3,753
New Jersey	6,567	1,064	4,116
New York	8,197	1,907	4,684
Pennsylvania	5,860	1,305	3,064
Great Lakes			
Illinois	5,564	1,024	3,347
Indiana	5,323	1,033	2,794
Michigan	5,830	1,262	3,084
Ohio	5,775	1,221	3,186
Wisconsin	6,069	1,204	3,469
Plains			
Iowa	5,766	1,239	2,847
Kansas	5,445	1,153	2,967
Minnesota	6,748	1,238	3,752
Missouri	5,194	1,310	2,703
Nebraska	5,740	1,153	3,107
North Dakota	6,221	1,801	2,693
South Dakota	5,168	1,524	2,439
Southeast			
Alabama	5,339	1,408	2,185
Arkansas	4,961	1,364	2,417
Florida	5,423	936	2,806
Georgia	5,419	1,143	2,939
Kentucky	5,253	1,339	2,667
Louisiana	5,828	1,451	2,726
Mississippi	5,375	1,626	2,293
North Carolina	5,487	1,272	2,805
South Carolina	5,294	1,329	2,431
Tennessee	4,831	1,337	2,281
Virginia	5,513	881	3,126
West Virginia	5,592	1,659	2,567
Southwest			
Arizona	4,974	1,115	2,810
New Mexico	5,975	1,717	2,681

Table 1.3

(continued)

State & Region	General Revenue	Federal Aid	Taxes
Oklahoma	5,234	1,279	2,545
Texas	5,233	1,099	2,829
Rocky Mountain			
Colorado	6,055	992	3,232
Idaho	5,116	1,094	2,543
Montana	5,679	1,763	2,367
Utah	5,598	1,170	2,699
Wyoming	8,577	2,403	3,681
Far West			
Alaska	11,497	2,854	3,301
California	6,691	1,424	3,555
Hawaii	6,129	1,277	3,498
Nevada	5,714	817	3,220
Oregon	6,321	1,882	2,632
Washington	6,166	1,195	3,311

SOURCE: Bureau of the Census, *State and Local Government Finances, 2002*

revenue includes grants from the federal government as well as charges and fees. Generally, the level of taxes and level of general revenue is correlated, but not necessarily. A state with an unusually large amount of federal aid or charges may have average or above-average revenue, but below-average taxes. For instance, Delaware, which receives substantial revenue from corporate license fees, has a relatively high level of general revenue but about average taxes.

It is important to note that these data refer to revenue and tax collections, *not* burdens. To the extent that states collect revenue from nonresidents (severance taxes, some sales taxes, some business taxes, property taxes on nonresident property owners), the taxes or fees do not represent a burden on residents. In those cases, standardizing by the resident population or income does not provide an accurate or useful picture.

Substantial diversity also exists in the **mix of revenue sources** used in different states, as shown in Table 1.4. The five major state–local revenue sources identified— property taxes, sales taxes, income taxes, federal grants, and user charges—account for more than three-quarters of state–local government general revenue on average, with each accounting for between 12 and 21 percent of revenue. The aggregate picture thus shows a diversified and balanced state–local revenue structure; however, the picture is very different in some individual states. Most obviously, the general sales and individual income tax shares are zero in some cases. In a few states, these five revenue sources in aggregate represent a substantially smaller share of revenue than the average, indicating that there are some other substantial sources of funds in those special cases. For instance, these five sources account for only about 48 percent of revenue in Alaska (which receives substantial revenue from oil leases and severance taxes), for 54 percent in Delaware (which generates substantial corporate

Table 1.4

State—Local Revenue Sources by State, 2002

Percentage of State–Local General Revenue from

State & Region	Federal Aid	Property Tax	General Sales Tax	Individual Income Tax	User Charges
United States	21.4%	16.6%	13.2%	12.0%	15.0%
New England					
Connecticut	17.7	26.3	13.3	16.2	7.7
Maine	23.5	23.7	10.4	13.3	9.9
Massachusetts	15.8	22.4	9.5	20.3	9.8
New Hampshire	20.2	33.9	nt	1.1	12.6
Rhode Island	26.6	20.0	11.0	12.4	8.4
Vermont	28.2	21.4	5.6	10.6	11.3
Middle Atlantic					
Delaware	17.1	7.1	nt	13.6	16.2
District of Columbia	41.0	11.6	8.1	13.7	4.4
Maryland	18.3	16.7	8.3	23.7	12.1
New Jersey	16.2	29.0	10.9	12.4	12.3
New York	23.3	17.2	10.7	19.4	11.7
Pennsylvania	22.3	15.2	10.4	13.2	15.4
Great Lakes					
Illinois	18.4	23.0	10.9	10.8	11.4
Indiana	19.4	18.5	11.7	12.7	17.8
Michigan	21.6	16.9	13.4	11.4	16.1
Ohio	21.1	16.2	11.7	18.0	13.9
Wisconsin	19.8	19.9	12.0	15.3	14.9
Plains					
Iowa	21.5	17.1	12.0	10.8	19.5
Kansas	21.2	17.3	15.7	12.7	14.2
Minnesota	18.3	15.7	11.4	16.4	14.7
Missouri	25.2	13.4	14.6	13.5	13.4
Nebraska	20.1	17.8	13.1	11.7	14.6
North Dakota	28.9	13.3	9.9	5.0	17.7
South Dakota	29.5	17.1	17.2	nt	10.9
Southeast					
Alabama	26.4	6.2	12.5	9.0	25.2
Arkansas	27.5	7.6	19.2	11.8	14.8
Florida	17.3	18.2	17.3	nt	17.3
Georgia	21.1	15.0	16.9	14.6	15.7
Kentucky	25.5	9.3	10.9	16.5	13.3
Louisiana	24.9	7.4	18.6	6.9	17.0
Mississippi	30.2	10.8	15.3	6.4	20.1
North Carolina	23.2	12.3	11.1	16.5	19.3
South Carolina	25.1	14.6	11.5	11.1	21.6
Tennessee	27.7	12.6	21.3	0.5	18.7
Virginia	16.0	17.2	9.2	17.2	16.7
West Virginia	29.7	8.9	9.5	10.2	13.0

Table 1.4

(continued)

State & Region	Percentage of State–Local General Revenue from				
	Federal Aid	Property Tax	General Sales Tax	Individual Income Tax	User Charges
Southwest					
Arizona	22.4	16.7	22.7	8.2	11.3
New Mexico	28.7	7.0	16.2	9.0	11.3
Oklahoma	24.4	8.2	14.4	12.7	18.1
Texas	21.0	22.5	16.8	nt	14.8
Rocky Mountain					
Colorado	16.4	16.0	15.9	13.3	17.7
Idaho	21.4	14.5	12.0	12.7	19.6
Montana	31.0	16.6	nt	10.1	14.6
Utah	20.9	11.4	15.8	12.8	20.0
Wyoming	28.0	16.3	13.7	nt	16.4
Far West					
Alaska	24.8	11.5	1.7	nt	9.7
California	21.3	13.3	13.8	14.6	15.9
Hawaii	20.8	8.3	21.7	15.0	14.0
Nevada	14.3	14.9	19.4	nt	19.2
Oregon	29.8	14.5	nt	17.0	18.0
Washington	19.4	15.9	25.4	nt	18.2

SOURCE: US Bureau of the Census, Census of Governments, *State and Local Government Finances, 2002*

license fees as the official legal "home" state for many of the largest corporations), and for about 68 percent in Nevada (which receives substantial gambling revenue).

More of a regional pattern exists in the reliance on different revenue sources than in the level of taxes and expenditures. For instance, most of the New England states rely on property taxes more than average and the Southeastern states (except Florida and Virginia) rely on property taxes less than average. General sales taxes tend to be relied on more than average in the Southeast and Southwest, individual income taxes tend to be used to a relatively small degree in the Southwestern states, and the use of user charges is relatively low in New England and the Middle Atlantic states but relatively high in the Rocky Mountain, Southeastern, and Far West states. In some cases, these regional patterns result (1) from the relative fiscal importance of state as opposed to local governments, (2) from the nature of the economies in these states and regions, or (3) from historical factors coupled with inertia.

Geographic or regional competitive factors influencing revenue structures are often not decisive, however, as reflected by a number of regional anomalies— similar states located together with different revenue structures. For instance, Oregon has no general sales tax and accordingly relatively high reliance on individual income taxes, whereas neighboring Washington has no individual income tax and high reliance on the sales tax. Among other similar cases, New Jersey relies heavily on property taxes and little on sales taxes, whereas Delaware has little reliance on property taxes, but heavy reliance on income taxes. New Hampshire has very high reliance on property taxes, no sales tax, and a very limited income tax; Maine and Vermont's tax structures are more similar to the national average with more balanced use of income taxes, sales taxes, and user charges. Finally, in two states dominated by the oil industry, property tax reliance is low in Oklahoma and income tax use about average, whereas there is no individual income tax and high property tax reliance in Texas.

Although reflecting the great diversity in the world of state–local finance, these differences in revenue structure also raise the issue of whether there are any economic, as opposed to historical or institutional, explanations for these different fiscal decisions by various states. The economic argument consistently offered to explain the choice of revenue structures is the opportunity to "export" tax and other revenue burdens to nonresidents. For instance, an analysis by Mary Gade and Lee Adkins (1990) of state government (only) revenue structures supports the idea that differences in the opportunity to export taxes go a long way toward explaining states' choices of tax structure. For instance, Gade and Adkins' analysis shows that severance taxes are relied on heavily by states with an immobile resource base, and that taxes deductible against the federal income tax are used more intensively by states where a substantial number of taxpayers itemize deductions and face relatively high federal tax rates. (Through the deduction, state taxpayers lower their federal taxes forcing other federal taxpayers to pay a greater share.) On the other hand, they report that states tend not to try to export tax burden by taxing manufacturing goods heavily, even if they are to be exported, apparently because of a fear of inducing a relocation of those manufacturing activities.

Interstate Variation

During the past 20 years, fiscal differences have narrowed substantially among the states. The changes in the distribution of state–local per-capita direct general expenditure are shown in Table 1.5. If all states and the District of Columbia are considered, the coefficient of variation for per-capita spending fell by half between

Table 1.5

Variation in Per Capita State–Local General Expenditure

		Mean	Coefficient of Variation	Maximum	Minimum	Max to Min Ratio
1982	All states	$1,992	0.47	$7,958	$1,345	5.9
1992	All states	3,900	0.30	9,893	2,751	3.6
1998	All states	5,224	0.23	11,502	4,037	2.9
2002	All states	6,221	0.23	13,466	4,889	2.8
1982	Excl. AK & DC	1,841	0.19	3,157	1,345	2.3
1992	Excl. AK & DC	3,708	0.17	7,788	2,751	2.1
1998	Excl. AK & DC	5,025	0.12	7,351	4,037	1.8
2002	Excl. AK & DC	5,797	0.12	8,491	4,889	1.7

SOURCE: Department of Commerce, Bureau of the Census

1982 and 2002, from .47 to .23. Similarly, the ratio of the highest to lowest spending state fell from 5.9 to 2.8. Even if the two outlying jurisdictions of Alaska and the District of Columbia are excluded from the analysis, an important decline in interstate variation in spending is still apparent. Not surprisingly, there has also been a similar decrease in interstate variation in per-capita revenue. Interstate variation in per-capita revenue is slightly greater than the variation in per-capita spending, which reflects the equalizing role played by federal aid. Some of the narrowing of fiscal differences over this period is the result of growth and changes in the structure of intergovernmental grants. The other major factor is the narrowing of regional economic differences (that is, convergence of state personal income), which has translated into a corresponding narrowing of fiscal differences as well.

INTERNATIONAL COMPARISON

Government Spending in Selected Industrialized Nations

Government spending relative to the size of the nation's economy is smaller in the United States than for most other major industrialized nations, as shown in Figure 1.9. Total (federal, state, and local) government spending in the United States is about 35 percent of GDP, about the same as in Australia, slightly less than in Japan, and substantially less than in Canada, France, Germany, the United Kingdom, or the average of all industrialized nations (the nations in the Organization for Economic Cooperation and Development). Total government receipts as a

Figure 1.9

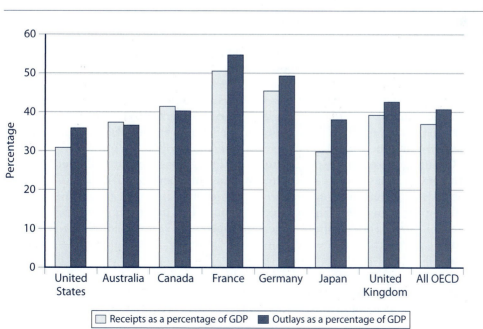

Public sector size, selected nations, 2003

Receipts as a percentage of GDP   Outlays as a percentage of GDP

Figure 1.10

Federal government role, federal nations, 2002

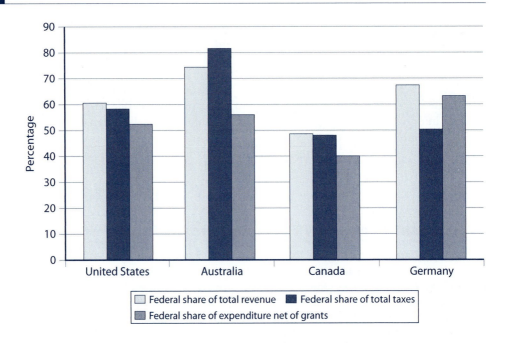

percentage of GDP are lowest in the U.S. among these seven nations (except for Japan). It is interesting to note, as well, that at least in 2003, the total public sector was operating a budget deficit in these nations—outlays are greater than receipts—except for Australia and Canada.

Three of these other nations—Australia, Canada, and Germany—have federal systems of government similar to that in the United States. Each of these nations has separate federal, state, and local governments. Although the structure is similar, the relative role for subnational government compared to the federal government is quite different among these nations, as shown in Figure 1.10. In terms of total government revenue, Australia has the most centralized system and Canada the least, with the federal government's role falling between those two extremes in Germany and the United States.

Central government expenditure, excluding grants paid from the federal government to states and localities, tells a different story. In Australia, for instance, the federal government accounts for only about 55 percent of direct spending, although it generates 75 percent of revenue. The difference represents federal grants to states and localities, which are substantial in the Australian system. The federal government is most dominant in Germany, where it accounts for more than 60 percent of direct public spending. In contrast, the central government accounts for only 40 percent of direct public expenditure in Canada. By this measure, then, states and localities are most important in Canada, where they account for about 60 percent of direct government expenditure (purchases of goods and services).

FISCAL ROLE OF SUBNATIONAL GOVERNMENTS

What is the appropriate economic role for subnational governments in a federal system? Which responsibilities are better handled by the federal government, by the subnational governments, and can be shared among them? In what ways do the main characteristics of that sector—mobility and diversity—influence that role? Richard Musgrave (1959) has identified three traditional economic functions for government: (1) maintaining economic stabilization, (2) altering the distribution of resources, and (3) obtaining an efficient allocation of society's resources. The conventional wisdom has been that state–local governments are limited in achieving the first two principally by the ease of mobility among them. Despite the fact that this notion suggests that stabilization and distribution are more appropriately federal government functions, it is apparent that many state–local services have substantial distributional implications and that the sheer size of the subnational government sector means that it may have macroeconomic effects. Thus, the conventional wisdom and some recent challenges to that wisdom are considered next.

Stabilization Policy

Stabilization policy refers to the role of the government in maintaining employment, price stability, and economic growth through fiscal and monetary policy. The conventional position is that state and local governments are inherently limited in influencing the economic conditions in each specific subnational jurisdiction; that is, a single state or municipality has little control over prices, employment, and the general level of economic activity in that jurisdiction. One reason is that state–local governments do not have any monetary authority (which rests with the Federal Reserve Board). Moreover, it is usually argued that states should not have monetary authority because separate state monetary decisions would increase the costs of transactions over boundaries and because each state would have an incentive to pay for trade by expanding its own "money supply," a large portion of which would be held by nonresidents.

A second factor is that the general openness of state–local jurisdiction economies restricts the opportunity for fiscal policy to be effective. Imagine a state or city attempting to expand economic activity by the traditional expansive fiscal policies-lowering local taxes, providing cash grants to residents, or expanding government purchases. As a result, residents are likely to increase consumption spending, but the ultimate effect of a substantial part of that consumption increase will occur in other jurisdictions where the goods and services are sold or produced. If your city borrowed $100 per resident and then gave each resident $100 "free" to spend in any way, it is no different than if each resident borrowed $100. If the residents use the money to buy shirts, for example, the economic gain goes to the producers of shirts (and suppliers of their inputs), which may not be in your city. In addition, of course, the borrowed funds used to finance the expansive fiscal policy eventually must be repaid with a substantial portion of the funds (perhaps even all) having been borrowed from nonresidents.

Edward Gramlich (1987) challenges this conventional wisdom about the importance of state–local stabilization policy by arguing that changes in the economy as well as past misperceptions may make subnational fiscal policies more potent than believed, and even necessary. Gramlich first notes evidence that individuals may not move between states in many cases for economic reasons and that a growing share of expenditures is for services purchased locally. If these types of mobility are less than previously believed, then subnational fiscal policies can have greater effects within the jurisdiction. In addition, Gramlich argues that, increasingly, macroeconomic problems are regional rather than national, resulting from economic factors affecting specific industries. In that case, regional or state fiscal policy might be necessary, with some regions conducting expansionary policy while others are pursuing contractionary policies.

There is a totally different stabilization issue as well, whether the aggregate fiscal position (taxes and spending) of the subnational sector influences the overall national economy. With subnational government spending accounting for 11 to 14 percent of the national economy, the expectation is that this sector does have an impact on national macroeconomic conditions. This factor has been noted most in two contexts. First, the state–local sector has had an aggregate budget surplus in many years that partly offsets the federal government budget deficits that have been common since 1970. In effect, the investment of surplus funds by state and local governments is a source of finance for both the federal government deficit and private-sector borrowing.

Second, some are concerned that state–local fiscal changes during national economic recessions or expansions might contribute to the national economic cycle. For instance, subnational government policy would be procyclical if states and localities reduce expenditures because a recession causes state–local revenues to decline (or increase less than was anticipated), thereby further reducing aggregate demand and slowing the economy more. A number of studies of this issue generally show that this does not occur, and that state–local government fiscal policies tend to be countercyclical—states and localities respond to the revenue decrease caused by a recession by spending from reserves or by raising tax rates (Bahl, 1984). The maintenance of state–local spending during a national economic contraction has a moderate countercyclical effect. Similarly, during economic expansions, state–local governments often build up reserves, thereby moderating the increase in aggregate demand. It is important to note that this conclusion applies to the aggregate state–local sector and not necessarily to every subnational jurisdiction, and that the magnitude of this state–local countercyclical effect will vary for different recessions and expansions, depending on their length and other characteristics.

The conclusions seem to be that while individual states and localities have been considered limited in their capability to influence aggregate demand in their own jurisdictions, that case may be overstated. In fact, regional macroeconomic problems may demand and even require regional policies. The collective fiscal decisions of states and localities do have an impact on national economic conditions, however. It is incorrect, therefore, to focus only on the federal government's fiscal behavior when evaluating the macroeconomic implications of the public sector.

Distribution Policy

Distribution policy refers to the role of the government in obtaining and maintaining the socially preferred distribution of resources or income, in most cases by redistributing resources from rich to poor (there have been no serious claims that the economy, absent government intervention, generates too much income equality). The conventional wisdom has been very similar to the issue of stabilization. State–local governments are limited in their capability to redistribute resources because different jurisdictions select different amounts of redistribution and individuals and firms can easily move among the jurisdictions to frustrate any intended redistribution. If that is the case, then redistribution is also more appropriately carried out by the federal government (at least if international mobility is less than interjurisdictional mobility within the United States).

The conventional thought can be easily illustrated. Suppose your city proposed to tax all families or individuals with income above $50,000 and to use the revenue to provide cash grants to individuals and families with income below $50,000. Such a pure redistributive policy would create an incentive both for higher-income taxpayers (those above $50,000) to move to a different city where such a redistributive tax did not exist and for lower-income individuals and families (those below $50,000) to move to your city to receive the grants. Paradoxically, if such moves occur, the program does result in a more equal income distribution in your city, but little redistribution from rich to poor. The existence of the incentive does not mean that all individuals will actually respond in this way—moving is costly and other locational factors may offset these redistributional incentives—but if some respond in this way, part of the program's intent is mitigated. The incentive will be greatest for very high- and very low-income individuals and when mobility is easiest. Moving among localities within the same area to avoid or take advantage of a local government redistribution program is expected in most cases to be easier or less costly than moving among states, and similarly moving among nations is more costly than moving among states. For these reasons, it has been argued that redistribution is best handled at the national level, and if not, at the states.

This conventional position flies in the face of several important facts, however. State governments administer the major health and welfare programs (especially Medicaid), which are inherently redistributive. Other services provided by state–local governments, especially education, have important distributional implications. Finally, distributional concerns affect many state–local fiscal decisions, including the choice of tax structure. In the cases of explicit redistribution, substantial diversity exists in the levels of support selected in different states even though the federal government typically pays about half the cost through a system of matching grants with higher matching rates for lower-income states. Similar differences occur in education services offered in different states and localities. Thus, despite the conventional notion that redistribution is best handled by the federal government, the actual fiscal structure leaves a substantial amount of redistribution to the subnational sector.

What accounts for the continuing distributional responsibility of subnational government and what are its effects? One possibility is that society has decided that redistribution should be a subnational government responsibility. This is reasonable if individuals only care about the welfare of other individuals who reside in their jurisdiction and if there is little mobility in response to redistributional policies. In that case, redistribution would be similar to, say, waste collection, and would be best handled at the local level where individual preferences could be satisfied. On the other hand, if individuals care about the welfare of lower-income individuals in the society regardless of what state or city they live in or if mobility frustrates local decisions, then some federal government involvement in redistribution policy is called for.

The federal government is involved in the redistribution decisions of states through the federal grants for those programs. In theory, those grants could correct for the difficulties created by migration by reducing the cost of engaging in redistribution to residents who do not move. In effect, having federal grants pay for part of subnational government redistribution prevents higher-income individuals from avoiding some contribution. The available evidence seems to show, however, that few transfer recipients—on the order of 1 to 2 percent—actually do move to other states to receive higher welfare benefits annually (Gramlich, 1985b). However, the cumulative effect of a small number of moves in each year can be a substantial change in the geographic distribution of welfare recipients over time if the interstate pattern of benefits does not change. Even so, Gramlich's analysis shows that the degree of mobility of recipients alone is not sufficient to justify the relatively large federal government share in welfare-program grants.

The conclusions, then, are that mobility of taxpayers among jurisdictions is not so severe as to preclude subnational redistributive policies, but that even with generous federal grants, many states (representing about half of welfare recipients) choose very low welfare-benefit levels. In Gramlich's (1985b, p. 43) words, "voters in these low-benefit states appear to have little taste for redistribution...." The issue about the appropriate level of government to carry out redistribution policy depends on our attitudes about this variation in benefit levels. If the variation is tolerable, then the current structure (with perhaps less generous federal grants) is acceptable; if a more uniform standard for benefit levels is desired, then a direct federal income-redistribution program or at least a minimum benefit standard imposed by the federal government is called for. These issues are considered in more detail in Chapter 21.

Allocation Policy

Government intervention in the market also may be necessary to ensure that society achieves its desired allocation of resources—that is, for specific goods and services to be produced in the desired quantities. Here the objective of government, at all levels, is to maintain market competition and to provide those goods and services directly that the private market fails to provide efficiently. The practical issues focus on what specific responsibilities fall into the category of private-market failure, how large government should be to meet those responsibilities, how the government's resources should be generated, and on what mix of services should those resources be spent. Because the government is providing these services as a result of the market's failure to do so in an efficient or equitable way, it is important to consider how government can most efficiently provide those services and whether government can do a better job than the market. If a good or service is best provided through government, then the subsequent issue is which level or type of government—federal, state, or local—can best carry out that responsibility.

Given the conventional wisdom that state–local governments are inherently limited in carrying out stabilization and distribution policy, it is not surprising that the focus of economic analysis and research has been on the allocative role of subnational governments—their role, methods, and effectiveness in directly providing goods and services. That, too, is the primary focus of the rest of this book. Because of the importance traditionally assigned to the allocative role of subnational governments, the economic principles about market efficiency and market failure are first reviewed in Chapter 2 to provide a theoretical framework within which the institutions and practice of state–local government finance can be analyzed and evaluated.

SUMMARY

Economic mobility coupled with the choice provided by the diversity of subnational governments makes analysis of state–local government finance interesting and different from that of the federal government.

The current substantial relative size of the subnational government sector—40 percent of the total public sector in the United States—arose from a roughly 25-year period of sustained rapid growth between the early 1950s and mid-1970s. Since the mid-1970s, however, the relative size of the state–local government sector has not increased substantially until the past few years, when relative growth has increased again.

More than half the money spent by state–local governments in aggregate provides education or income maintenance services, with transportation and health and hospitals being the next two largest categories of spending on direct consumer services. To finance these services, state–local governments receive revenue from five major sources, all of roughly equal importance: charges and fees (24.9 percent of the total), federal grants (21.4 percent), sales taxes (19.2 percent), property taxes (16.6 percent), and income taxes (12.0 percent).

The conventional wisdom has been that state–local governments are inherently limited in carrying out stabilization and distribution policy. Therefore, the focus of economic analysis and research has been on the allocative role of subnational governments—their role, methods, and effectiveness in directly providing goods and services. Although individual states and localities may be limited in their capability to influence aggregate demand in their own jurisdictions, regional policies may be preferred to national stabilization policies in some cases. The collective fiscal decisions of states and localities have an effect on national macroeconomic conditions as well. The mobility of taxpayers among jurisdictions is not so severe as to completely offset subnational redistributive policies, but even with generous federal grants, many states (representing about half of welfare recipients) choose to provide a small amount of income redistribution.

DISCUSSION QUESTIONS

1. "The state–local government sector stopped growing relative to the size of the economy in the late 1970s because of a decline in the amount of federal aid to states and localities." Do you think this is correct and why?

2. The recent growth (since 1999) in state and local spending relative to income, population, and prices is still not as fast as growth that occurred in the 1952 to 1975 period. Discuss the reasons why state–local spending increased so fast in the earlier period and consider what might be different in the recent period of growth.

3. Although the diversity of subnational governments means that the notion of "typical" behavior is often not meaningful, it is still common in presentations of data, news reports, and political debate to compare a state or locality to the "national average." How does the state–local sector in your state compare to that average in terms of (1) the structure of localities, (2) the level of expenditure, (3) the pattern of services provided, and (4) the mix of revenue sources? Do you know of any reasons why your case might differ from the national average?

4. Some surveys show that citizens usually are aware of services provided by local governments, but often not certain of the services provided by state governments. Make a list of five services provided by your city/township and five provided by your state that *directly* benefit you. After thinking about how you directly pay for those services, do you believe you get your money's worth?

SELECTED READING

Bahl, Roy. "The Growing Fiscal and Economic Importance of State and Local Governments." In *Financing State and Local Governments in the 1980s*, 7–32. New York: Oxford University Press, 1984.

Giertz, J. Fred and Seth Giertz. "The 2002 Downturn in State Revenues: A Comparative Review and Analysis." *National Tax Journal* 57, 1 (March 2004): 111–132.

Oates, Wallace. "An Economic Approach to Federalism." In *Fiscal Federalism*, 3–30. New York: Harcourt Brace Jovanovich, 1972.

Rivlin, Alice. *Reviving the American Dream: The Economy, the States, and the Federal Government*. Washington, DC: Brookings Institution, 1992.

Sjoquist, David L., ed. *State and Local Finances Under Pressure*. Northampton, MA: Edward Elgar, 2003.

CHAPTER 2

MICROECONOMIC ANALYSIS: MARKET EFFICIENCY AND MARKET FAILURE

The economic function left to state and local governments in the United States system is the allocation function, i.e., the determination of the amount and mix of local public services to be offered.[1]

—ROY BAHL

"FROM THE DAYS OF ADAM SMITH, ECONOMISTS HAVE RECOGNIZED THAT A SYSTEM OF PERFECTLY COMPETITIVE MARKETS ENHANCES ECONOMIC WELL-BEING IN SEVERAL WAYS: BY PERMITTING RESOURCES, PRODUCTS, AND SERVICES TO GO TO THOSE WHO VALUE THEM MOST; BY PROVIDING INCENTIVES FOR COST SAVINGS AND INNOVATION IN THE PRODUCTION AND DISTRIBUTION OF GOODS AND SERVICES; AND BY FOSTERING LOW PRICES. YET, LIKE ADAM SMITH, TODAY'S ECONOMISTS ALSO RECOGNIZE THAT UNDER SOME LIMITED BUT IMPORTANT CIRCUMSTANCES, MARKETS DO NOT ALWAYS ACHIEVE THESE DESIRABLE ENDS. WHEN THEY DO NOT, APPROPRIATE GOVERNMENT ACTION CAN IMPROVE MARKETS' FUNCTIONING AND SO INCREASE ECONOMIC WELL-BEING. . . .

ADAM SMITH PUBLISHED *THE WEALTH OF NATIONS* IN 1776, THE SAME YEAR THOMAS JEFFERSON WROTE THE DECLARATION OF INDEPENDENCE. SINCE THAT TIME . . . GOVERNMENT HAS WORKED IN PARTNERSHIP WITH THE PRIVATE SECTOR TO PROMOTE COMPETITION, DISCOURAGE EXTERNALITIES, AND PROVIDE PUBLIC GOODS.[2]"

---

[1] Bahl, Roy. *Financing State and Local Governments in the 1980s.* Oxford, England: Oxford University Press, 1984, 25.

[2] *Economic Report of the President.* Washington, DC: February 1995, p. 129.

An important issue of microeconomics is when and why collective action, such as that by government, may be preferable to separate economic decision making by individual consumers and producers, usually referred to as the private market. In short, what is the economic rationale for government provision of some goods and services, and how can microeconomic tools be applied to evaluating the relative merits of government and private provision? As noted in Chapter 1, Richard Musgrave has argued that government's economic role may include attaining a more efficient use of society's resources, altering the distribution of resources, and achieving macroeconomic stabilization. However, the focus of microeconomic analysis and research concerning state and local governments has been on the first role—their effectiveness in directly providing goods and services.

Before the potential for government provision can be evaluated against society's goals, you must understand the nature of economic efficiency and the reasons why government intervention may improve upon the results of private-market provision. This chapter reviews the basic microeconomic principles of market operation and economic efficiency, including why private markets may be efficient, the conditions under which private markets will not generate efficiency, the potential distributional concerns from private provision, and the ways government involvement generally in an economy (and not just state–local government) may improve efficiency or resource distribution compared to private markets.

THE EFFICIENCY OF THE MARKET

The concept of economic efficiency most often used in economics is called **Pareto efficiency** or optimality (named after the Italian economist Vilfredo Pareto [1848–1923] who proposed the definition), which states that an economy is efficient if it is not possible to make at least one person better off without making someone else worse off. This concept of economic efficiency is broader than the everyday use of the word efficiency. Economic efficiency includes the idea of technical or engineering efficiency, requiring that goods be produced at lowest cost, while also requiring that the type and quantity of goods and services are consistent with society's desires.

The test for efficiency, then, is to search for changes to the current economic situation that can improve the welfare or economic conditions of some people, but not decrease the welfare of any others. The efficiency definition requires only that it be *possible* to make some consumers better off without hurting anyone and does not address the issue of how any change actually is to be accomplished. If, in fact, no one will be hurt by a change, then those who gain from that change have to compensate those who lose. This requires that the aggregate benefit be greater than the aggregate cost, so the net benefit can be used to compensate anyone who is hurt initially.

If such changes are possible, the economy is not efficient; if those changes are not possible, then the original situation is efficient. If the gain to society from one small change is called the **marginal social benefit** and the cost of the change is the

marginal social cost, then a general efficiency rule for evaluating changes can be stated as follows:

> *If marginal social benefit equals marginal social cost, then the economy is efficient because there is no net gain from any change. If marginal social benefit is greater or less than marginal social cost, the economy is not efficient, and the proposed change would improve economic efficiency.*

Suppose, for example, that it is possible to produce more goods with the same resources by changing to a different (more efficient) production process. With more goods, the welfare of some (or even all) consumers could be improved at no cost to society. That economy was not producing goods efficiently. By "welfare," economists mean the utility or satisfaction consumers receive from consumption. Because a consumer's utility depends on preferences—individual likes and dislikes—each consumer is the sole judge of his or her own welfare. To put it another way, more goods will not improve a consumer's welfare if that consumer does not like those goods.

As another example, suppose that society decides to allocate fewer resources to the military and to use the freed-up resources to produce more education. If consumers in aggregate value the increased amount of education more than the reduced military structure, the economy was not producing an efficient mix of consumer goods. The marginal benefit from providing more education is greater than the marginal cost. At least some consumers are made better off by the change, and any consumers who might be made worse off by the loss of military service could be compensated (and thus not hurt) because the gain to consumers in aggregate is positive.

This notion of economic efficiency has several advantages and one apparent weakness. The advantages are that value judgments about how much society "cares" for different types of consumers are not necessary and that no consumer need be opposed to changes to an inefficient economy. These both follow from the fact that if an economy is not Pareto efficient, no one need be hurt by a change to an efficient situation. The weakness of the definition is the narrow view of inefficiency. If a potential economic change must hurt even one consumer while making all others better off, by the Pareto definition that situation *is* efficient. Because of that narrowness of definition, achieving Pareto efficiency would not resolve all social issues, but there appears to be no shortage of situations that could be improved even by this narrow definition.

How do competitive markets satisfy this definition of efficiency? Although elegant mathematics is required to "prove" the efficiency of competitive equilibrium, the underlying principles are easily demonstrated. The long-run equilibrium of a competitive market is depicted in Figure 2.1a. The market demand for the product approximates the marginal benefit to consumers consuming this good or service; if producers act to maximize profits, the market supply corresponds to the marginal cost of producing the good or service. At the market equilibrium, the marginal cost of producing one more unit equals the marginal benefit—all the possible aggregate social gains from producing this good or service have been achieved. The equilibrium price P^* is equal to both the marginal cost and the marginal benefit.

From the point of view of a typical firm in this competitive market, the equilibrium price also equals the lowest possible production cost per unit—that is, the

Figure 2.1

Competitive market equilibrium

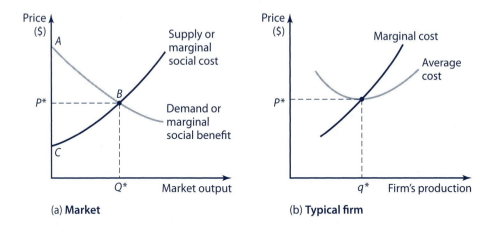

(a) **Market**   (b) **Typical firm**

minimum of the average cost function (Figure 2.1b). At that price, firms are earning normal profits—that is, rates of return equal to those available elsewhere in the economy. Because investors are doing exactly as well in this business as they could in any other, there is no incentive for changes in output or prices.

The dollar magnitude of the gains to society from producing this good or service also can be approximated in Figure 2.1. **Consumer's surplus** is defined as the difference between the marginal benefit to consumers from a unit of the product and the market price they actually pay, which is represented by area ABP^* in Figure 2.1a. **Producer's surplus** is defined as the difference between the price charged for the product and the marginal cost of producing a unit of the product, which is similarly represented by area CBP^* in Figure 2.1a. The net gain to society from producing Q^* units of this good or service can be measured by the sum of the producer's and consumer's surplus. This is nothing more than the difference between the marginal cost and marginal benefit for each unit, summed for all the units produced.

If marginal social cost does not equal marginal social benefit for the amount of a good or service provided, then the outcome is not efficient, as depicted in Figure 2.2. If 100 units of this product are produced and consumed, the marginal benefit or gain to society from unit 101 is $10, whereas the cost to society of producing unit 101 is only $5. Producing one more unit of this product (beyond 100) would provide society a net gain in welfare worth $5. Conversely, if the market fails to provide that unit 101, society effectively loses or foregoes that potential $5 welfare gain—the outcome is not efficient. Similarly, the marginal benefit is greater than the marginal cost for all the potential units of output between 100 and 200. If output and consumption is restricted to 100 units rather the efficient quantity of 200, the welfare loss or welfare foregone by society can be measured by area DEFG, the sum of producer's and consumer's surplus.[3]

---

[3]Area DEFG is approximately equal to $250. DEFG is approximately a triangle, the area of which is ½ (base)(height) or ½ (5)(100) in this case.

Figure 2.2

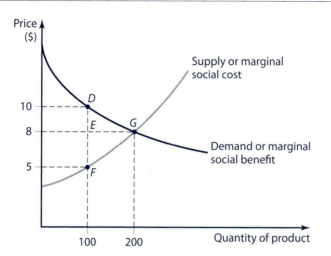

Efficiency requires equal marginal social cost and benefit

The results in a competitive market when producers act to get the highest possible profits and consumers act to get the greatest possible satisfaction are as follows:

1. Marginal cost equals marginal benefit, with both equal to price.

2. Price equals the lowest possible production cost and producers earn normal profits.

3. Because price equals both marginal cost and marginal benefit in all competitive markets—that is, $P_{A*} = MC_A = MB_A$ and $P_{B*} = MC_B = MB_B$—it follows that the relative prices of different products reflect the relative production costs and relative marginal benefits in consumption or

$$\frac{P_{A*}}{P_{B*}} = \frac{MC_A}{MC_B} = \frac{MB_A}{MB_B}$$

WHEN MARKETS ARE NOT EFFICIENT

What might prevent provision through the private-market system from achieving economic efficiency? One possibility is that the marginal cost faced by producers does not reflect all the costs to society from additional production or that an individual consumer's marginal benefit does not equal society's benefit. If benefits accrue to other than the direct consumer or if private production costs do not reflect total social costs, then the competitive market choices may not be socially efficient choices. Although the competitive market sets marginal cost equal to marginal benefit, the costs and benefits are not properly measured. A second possibility is that a lack of competition, such as if economies of scale are present or entry of firms is blocked, may prevent the market from reaching the "marginal cost equals marginal benefit" equilibrium.

Externalities

One problem arises if consumption or production causes **external effects**—that is, if one person's consumption or one firm's production imposes costs or benefits on other consumers or producers. In essence, an **externality** exists if one economic agent's action (consumption or production) affects another agent's welfare outside of changes in market prices or quantities. For instance, in the course of production, one firm (a steel mill) may discharge pollutants into a river, thereby increasing production costs for a downstream firm (a brewer) who must clean the water before using it in production. The pollution is an external effect because it is outside of the steel market—that cost is involuntarily transferred from the steel producer and consumers to the beer producer and consumers. In essence, no market or other mechanism exists to assign a price for river pollution to be paid by the polluter.

Externalities create an efficiency problem because the external costs or benefits usually are not taken into account by the consumer or producer causing the external effect. If an activity creates external costs, then the producer or consumer underestimates the social cost of the activity and chooses too much of that activity from society's viewpoint. If consumption or production generates benefits for others that are not considered, then the consumer or producer underestimates social benefits and chooses too little of that economic activity.

This issue is illustrated in Figure 2.3, which shows an individual's marginal benefit (demand) and marginal cost (price) from consuming a particular good or service. Constant marginal cost is assumed only to simplify the illustration. The quantity selected by consumers who equate marginal cost to marginal private benefits (their benefits) is Q^1. Because each unit of this good purchased by one consumer generates benefits for others as well, the marginal benefit to society is greater than to the direct consumers alone. In that case, the efficient amount of consumption is Q^*, where marginal private cost equals marginal social benefit. Because the direct consumers underestimated benefits, an inefficiently low amount of consumption is selected from society's viewpoint. When externalities are present, private choices by consumers and firms in private markets generally will not provide an economically efficient result. In this particular case, the benefits to other than direct consumers as a result of increasing consumption from Q^1 to Q^* are represented by area HIJK. The net gain to society from increasing consumption from Q^1 to the efficient amount is represented by the area HIK, which is the difference between marginal social benefit and marginal cost.

Government may be able to intervene and create incentives so that private choices of consumers and firms will be efficient in the presence of externalities, however. If there are external costs, a tax equal to the marginal external cost will force the consumer or firm to include all costs in the economic decision, and thus the efficient quantity will be selected. Similarly, inefficiencies caused by external benefits can be corrected by a government subsidy equal to the marginal external

Figure 2.3

Market efficiency
with externalities

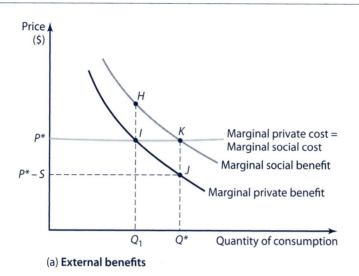

(a) **External benefits**

(b) **External costs**

benefit. If a consumer underestimates benefits by not considering those that accrue to others and thus chooses too little consumption, the subsidy will reduce private cost and induce an increase in consumption to the efficient amount. Returning to Figure 2.3, if marginal costs are reduced to $P^* - S$ by a subsidy of $S per unit, then the consumer is induced to choose consumption level Q^*. The externality has been eliminated, and the private market choice of the consumer is efficient.[4]

[4]This is precisely the rationale for many intergovernmental grants, to correct the externality that arises when state or locally provided public services provide benefits to nonresidents as well.

Externalities are common among the goods and services provided by state and local governments. Education, police and fire protection, transportation, and sanitation services all have benefits that accrue to those who are not direct consumers and to nonresidents of the communities providing those services. Negative externalities also are important for state and local governments because tax payments do not respect political boundaries. Nonresidents not only enjoy the benefits of services provided by a local government but also may pay part of that local government's costs through taxes.

Public Goods

The term **public goods** is used classically to refer to goods or services that exhibit two properties. Public goods are *nonrival*, meaning that one additional person can consume the good without reducing any other consumer's benefit; after the good or service is produced, the marginal cost of an additional consumer is zero. Public goods often are also said to be *nonexcludable*, meaning that it is not possible (at least at reasonable cost) to exclude consumers who do not pay the price from consuming the good or service. The traditional example of a good said to exhibit both properties is national defense. After a region is defended, there is no extra cost from adding one person to that region nor can any individual in the region be excluded from protection. Another example is a lighthouse. After a lighthouse is operating, an additional ship can be guided by the light while others are using it, and it could be very expensive to enforce a "lighthouse use fee" on ships that come in view of the light.[5]

If a good is nonrival, the marginal social cost of adding another consumer is zero, so efficiency requires a zero price. A zero price obviously does not provide revenue to cover any fixed costs, so these goods are not provided in an efficient amount by private firms. Examples of nonrival goods include several usually provided by state–local governments, such as an uncrowded street, bridge, or park. If a park is not crowded, then another person can enter and use the park without reducing the enjoyment or benefit of any other user. To charge a fee to enter a park in that case is not efficient because the fee might induce some people not to use the park. Because the resources (mostly land) for the park already have been set aside, use of that resource at less than capacity is wasteful or inefficient from the viewpoint of the entire society. Of course, the problem remains of deciding on the amount of park services to provide and paying for acquiring those services.

The potential for government involvement in providing nonrival goods seems obvious. The task is to collect revenue to cover the fixed costs of a service (the cost of acquiring and operating the park) while maintaining the price for each use of the service equal to zero, that is, equal to the marginal cost. Government can use general taxes to pay the fixed costs, and because those general taxes do not depend on a taxpayer's use of the service, the price for each use is zero.

It is worth noting that nonrival or public goods may be thought of as a special externality case. A nonrival good for which another consumer may be added at no

---

[5]Coase (1974) provides evidence contradicting this example, suggesting that lighthouses are not good examples of nonexcludable goods. As discussed in the application at the end of this chapter, the possibility of market failure is only one aspect of potential government involvement in an economy.

cost to others is simply a good with a substantial benefit externality. Everyone can benefit if only one consumer provides a nonrival good, so the external benefits are large compared to the private benefits that go only to the buyer. From this viewpoint, the major difference in an efficiency sense between a nonrival good and an external benefit is the *degree* of public impact as compared to private impact.

If a good exhibits the nonexclusion property so that it is not feasible to charge a price for consumption, then private firms also are unable to collect revenue to cover costs. The tax power of government is needed to finance provision of these goods. If a commodity is both nonrival and nonexcludable, then individual consumers have no incentive to reveal their true demand for that good. Instead they can be **free riders,** benefiting, without paying, from the amount of goods purchased by others. Because all individuals have this incentive to understate their true demand, the quantity of these goods provided usually is inefficiently low. Even if the efficient quantity of these goods can be determined, efficient use of the goods may require prices that preclude private provision, as noted previously.

Increasing Returns to Scale

A final efficiency problem for competitive markets occurs if production of some commodities exhibits **increasing returns to scale**—that is, if a proportional change in all production inputs causes a greater than proportional change in output. For instance, if doubling the labor, land, and capital cause output to more than double, then average production costs decrease as output increases. If

$$\text{Total Cost} = (\text{Price}_{\text{Labor}})\,\text{Labor} + (\text{Price}_{\text{Land}})\,\text{Land} + (\text{Price}_{\text{Capital}})\,\text{Capital}$$

and

$$\text{Average Cost} = \frac{\text{Total Cost}}{\text{Output}}$$

and the amounts of labor, land, and capital are doubled, then total cost doubles; but if twice as much of each input causes output to more than double, average cost falls.

A cost function reflecting increasing returns to scale is depicted in Figure 2.4. If average cost is decreasing, then marginal cost must be less than average cost at all output amounts (because average cost is decreased by more production if the extra cost of producing one more unit is less than the existing average cost). The usual explanation for this type of cost structure is the existence of fixed costs that are large compared to variable costs. Because fixed costs must be paid regardless of the level of output, a larger output allows those costs to be spread over more units, causing a decrease in cost per unit. This situation often applies to public utilities, including communications, electricity, natural gas, water, sewer, or transit services, all of which have large capital requirements even to serve a few customers. Industries with increasing returns to scale are often called **natural monopolies** because it makes sense to have only one producer rather than multiple producers duplicating the required infrastructure. Why have two separate but parallel water pipes if one is sufficient?

When increasing returns to scale exists, producers cannot earn a positive profit if price is equal to marginal cost (which is required for efficiency). With the

Figure 2.4

Increasing returns
to scale

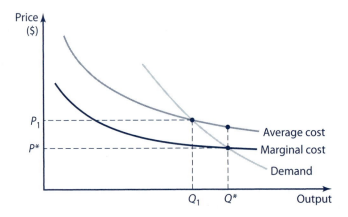

demand for the product as shown in Figure 2.4, efficiency requires a price equal to P^1. However, at that price and the resulting output Q^1, cost per unit is greater than revenue per unit, so the producer earns negative profits (that is, losses), and no firms would stay in business. In contrast, a price equal to average cost of P^2 allows producers to earn a normal profit or rate of return on investment, but output Q^2 is not efficient because too little of society's resources are applied toward producing this good. The inescapable problem is that with increasing returns to scale, a price equal to marginal cost cannot generate enough revenue to cover total costs.

Government intervention may resolve this difficulty. One option is to have government become the producer. This is often done for water, sewer, and transit services, but less often for communications or electricity and gas production. The government can charge consumers a price equal to marginal cost and make up the revenue shortfall with general tax receipts. Also, sometimes more complicated pricing schemes can be used to cover the production-cost deficit while allowing the marginal price to equal marginal cost. This topic is expanded on in Chapter 8 by discussing how governments can set efficient user charges. An alternative to government production of goods with increasing returns to scale is regulated monopoly production, with government as the regulator. In that instance, government grants a firm a monopoly in the sale of the good and attempts to regulate the price so that the producer earns normal profits. In either case, the outcome cannot be efficient because the taxes or regulation create other efficiency problems, so the preferable choice depends on whether government production or regulation works better practically.

DISTRIBUTIONAL CONCERNS

The standard competitive market analysis also can be used to explain the distribution of resources. The markets determine the prices of various types of labor, land, and capital goods, and those prices together with the quantities of the inputs supplied by individuals determine the resources available for market consumption by each individual. If society values highly the ability to pass a football effectively and that skill is in short supply, then individuals with the skill will earn high wages and be able to enjoy substantial consumption. Of course, the same argument applies to other types of (more ordinary) skills as well. If individuals have different abilities and if the financial resources for and incentives to acquire skills are not the same for all, then substantial differences in income and welfare can arise.

If society is not satisfied with the distribution of resources that results from that process, the alternatives are either to alter it directly through transfer payments or subsidies or to reject the market as a means of allocating consumer goods either by altering prices or substituting an entirely different allocation mechanism. Of course, governments do all these things. State governments coordinate major transfer programs, such as Medicaid and food stamps, whereas the national government coordinates others, such as social security. Many states subsidize higher education services through public colleges and offer scholarships to needy students. In some states, nonmarket, public systems provide health-care services for lower income individuals.

These distributional concerns with the outcome of markets provide another reason for government activity. If society is unhappy with the resource distribution (income or wealth) among individuals, then the efficient prices for commodities may not be attractive. Theoretically, efficiency concerns should not dominate equity considerations, so the efficiency criterion may be relevant only if the socially desired distribution is achieved. The traditional economic solution is to transfer resources among individuals to attain the desired resource distribution and then allow markets to allocate goods. If the process of redistribution does not have any costs, then that path may be preferable. Redistribution is not without cost, however, because the taxes used to generate revenue and the receipt of transfer payments may alter behavior and create inefficiency, and because the institution for redistribution, usually government, is costly itself.

An alternative is to have the government provide these goods and services and to alter their prices. As Peter Steiner (1983) has noted, even if it is practical to charge fees for park use, school bus transportation, and school lunches, it may not be desirable if society desires to alter the pattern of consumption as well as increase the level of consumption for some individuals. In addition to these equity reasons, the society may want to alter the pattern of consumption for efficiency reasons because of the externalities involved.

EFFICIENT PROVISION OF PUBLIC GOODS

The rule for efficient provision of goods is that the marginal social cost should equal the marginal social benefit. For externalities or public goods, social costs and benefits will differ from the costs and benefits of the direct consumers. Because all individuals consume a pure public good simultaneously, the **efficiency rule for**

Figure 2.5

Efficient quantity
of a public good

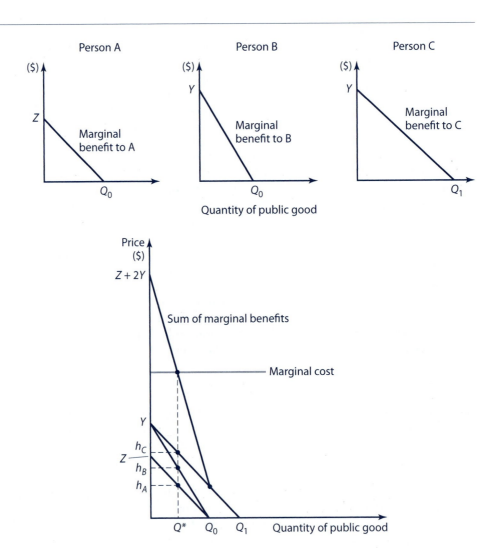

public goods is that the marginal costs to society should equal the sum of the marginal benefits of all consumers, which is the marginal social benefit.

To illustrate the application of this rule, consider a society with three different individuals (or groups of consumers), each with a different demand for the public good, as shown in Figure 2.5. Person A represents a small demand, Person B a medium demand, and Person C a high demand for this public good. A demand function for an individual shows the quantity demanded of *every* price, given that individual's tastes and income and the prices of substitute and complementary goals. The benefits to society equal the benefits to all three consumers together. In the bottom part of Figure 2.5, the marginal benefits of individuals A, B, and C have been added together to give the sum of marginal benefits for all three, labeled $\Sigma_i MB_i$, which means $MB_A + MB_B + MB_C$.

In calculating this aggregate marginal benefit function, the individuals' marginal benefits are added *vertically*. For example, the demand by Person A shows that the marginal benefit of the first unit is $\$Z$; the first unit of national defense, police protection, or whatever provides $\$Z$ worth of benefit to Person A. Similarly, the marginal benefit of the first unit of public good is $\$Y$ for both Persons B and C. The marginal benefit of the first unit to all three individuals (that is, society) is therefore $\$(Z + 2Y)$. The aggregate marginal benefit curve is calculated in that way for every unit of the public good. Although all three consumers receive the same level of public good, only Person C values additional units between Q^0 and Q^1.

The efficient amount of this public good is Q^*, for which the marginal cost to society equals the sum of individuals' marginal benefits. It is implicit in this rule that the marginal cost includes all the costs to the society, including opportunity costs generated by production (such as pollution). This rule is often called the **Samuelson rule** or Samuelson public goods equilibrium, reflecting economist Paul Samuelson's work in deriving the condition. Although the rule was illustrated for a pure public good, the rule also applies to any good involving externalities (recall that public goods are just special cases of external benefits). If consumption of a good by an individual imposes costs on or creates benefits for other individuals, those costs and benefits must be included to satisfy the efficiency rule that marginal social costs must equal marginal social benefits.

Methods of Government Provision

An important topic of this book (and one to which we will return often) is how government might be able to achieve or provide for an efficient use of resources. Government can intervene in private markets in at least three ways: (1) by directly providing goods and services, (2) by creating incentives to alter economic decisions through the use of taxes and subsidies, and (3) by regulating private economic activity. Government in the United States, including state and local government, uses all three methods. Government is essentially the sole producer of some goods and services such as streets and highways and a parallel producer with the private sector of other services such as education, police and fire protection, and waste collection and disposal. A variety of taxes and subsidies are used in an attempt to curtail or expand different activities in view of their external effects. For example, intergovernmental grants, offered by states to localities and by the federal government to the state–local sector, are subsidies in the state–local government arena. In other cases, regulations are imposed on activities of the private sector, such as state regulation of public utilities or private schools, or on the activities of a different level of government, such as state regulation of local police agencies or local schools.

Every attempt by subnational governments to improve economic efficiency, however, may not be successful. Government provision involves substantial transaction costs, including the administrative costs of the government structure itself; the compliance costs to taxpayers and voters of making economic decisions collectively through government; and the information problems facing government in discerning the "public interest." As Peter Steiner (1983) and Richard Nelson (1987) have argued, the fact that private markets fail to provide goods or services efficiently may be of little relevance if government also cannot provide them efficiently. In that case, a different or at least broader analytical framework than the basic microeconomics reviewed in this chapter is necessary to evaluate the role of government. Society would select government to provide some goods and services if government could better serve the public interest, which is not defined solely by economic efficiency. Private provision may be selected for some goods even though the market is inefficient if government provision would be too costly or create other problems; government provision may be selected in other cases even if private-market inefficiencies are insignificant or nonexistent if society seeks another objective, such as fairness or security.

Given these cautions about the emphasis on efficiency, one special government fiscal structure may generate the efficient outcome. At the efficient amount of output shown previously in Figure 2.5, Q^*, the marginal benefits to Persons A, B, and C are labeled h_A, h_B, and h_C, respectively. If these individuals were charged a "price" for this public good equal to h_A, h_B, and h_C, the amount of public good demanded by each individual is Q^*, the efficient amount. Every consumer demands the same amount of government service, which is the efficient amount.

The particular characteristic of this situation that generates the efficient result is that each consumer is being charged a price equal to marginal benefit at the efficient quantity. Although user fees equal to marginal benefits could perhaps accomplish this, it is more common in the provision of government goods for the "price" to be the taxes a consumer pays. In that case, each consumer's taxes must equal marginal benefit, or at least the *share of taxes* paid by each individual should equal that person's *share of marginal benefits*. The shares for each consumer are

$$S_A = h_A/(h_A + h_B + h_C)$$

$$S_B = h_B/(h_A + h_B + h_C)$$

$$S_C = h_C/(h_A + h_B + h_C)$$

$$S_A + S_B + S_C = 1.$$

These tax shares are much like prices because they show the amount each person must pay to increase government spending by $1. For example, if $h_A = 20$ percent, $h_B = 30$ percent, $h_C = 50$ percent, and spending is to increase $1, taxes must also increase by $1, with Person A paying $.20 more, Person B $.30 more, and Person C $.50 more. The price to Person C for another dollar's worth of government service is $.50. If the shares equal marginal benefits, then each is willing to pay the price up to the efficient amount. This situation, with charges or tax shares equal to marginal benefit shares, is called a **Lindahl equilibrium** after the Swedish economist Erik Lindahl (1919–58). If consumers' marginal costs reflect their marginal benefits, then the efficient amount of public good will be demanded. Of course, it is not a simple matter to implement that solution.

First, marginal benefits must be measured and assigned to individuals or at least groups of individuals. This may be an impossible or expensive task in part because consumers have little incentive to reveal their true demand. What, for instance, are the marginal benefits by income class of increasing police service spending by $1? Second, as previously noted, it may not be appropriate to charge marginal prices if the marginal cost of another user is zero. Third, it may not be feasible to exclude consumers from use if they refuse to pay the price set by the government. The Lindahl equilibrium does offer the possibility of efficiency by converting taxes into a form of user charge with tax shares determined by benefit. This idea of benefit taxation and its efficiency properties is raised again in Chapters 5 and 14 concerning property taxes and in Chapter 8 with a more complete discussion of user charges.

APPLICATION TO STATE AND LOCAL GOVERNMENTS

The problems of public goods, externalities, and increasing returns to scale provide reasons for government action to improve the efficiency of the economy, and many, although certainly not all, state–local government activities can be explained by these reasons. On the other hand, state and local government intervention is not used for all local goods or services that involve externalities or public-good properties. Redistribution of society's resources also can be a legitimate and explicit objective of government policy, and although state and local governments may be limited in carrying out redistribution programs, it seems clear that distribution and equity concerns influence many (if not most) state–local government fiscal decisions.

Despite these qualifications, the framework outlined in this chapter offers some explanation for the common fiscal activities and behavior of many state–local governments. Why is government, particularly state and local government, deeply involved in the education business? (As explained in Chapter 1, education is by far the largest subnational government budget category.) First, education produces external benefits such as the gains to all from a literate and educated populous and the information generated by research at educational institutions (which is usually considered a public good). Second, education has the potential to be an important mechanism for income redistribution by affecting earnings potential. Third, education benefits cannot generally be confined to a particular geographic area or industrial sector, so intergovernmental arrangements may be called for. The education case also may illustrate reasons for government provision other than the classic economic efficiency arguments. Public education may be a way of implementing a basic notion of fairness—equal opportunity for all—and it has been a primary way society transmits social values and informal rules of behavior.

Similar arguments can be made about police and fire protection. These services are, to a large degree, nonrival and to a somewhat lesser degree, nonexcludable. Substantial interjurisdictional externalities (or spillovers) also occur in the provision of these goods. Accordingly, almost every municipality or township in the United States provides services of this type. These services also are provided privately, however, in the form of private security guards at businesses, private security patrols in some neighborhoods, and privately purchased and owned equipment such as locks, burglar alarms, smoke detectors, and fire extinguishers.

Yet all these activities also generate external effects. Largely for the economic reasons, government takes a central but not an exclusive role in providing these services (see Application 2.1).

Transportation provides a final illustration. State and local governments finance, own, and operate transportation facilities such as streets and highways, airports, and public-transit systems. The economic efficiency arguments again provide some explanation. If uncrowded, these goods are nonrival, requiring a zero price for efficiency. Benefit spillovers among different jurisdictions providing the facilities also are common, requiring some coordinating mechanism. Although state and local governments provide these facilities, they seldom produce them; rather, governments usually contract with or buy from private firms, thereby taking advantage of any economies of scale in production.

Application 2.1

PUBLIC AND PRIVATE PROVISION OF PUBLIC SAFETY

Although the discussion in this chapter may seem to suggest that goods and services are provided either privately *or* by the public sector, in fact, it is more common for individuals and firms to purchase goods or services in the private market to complement services provided by government. In some cases, state and local governments purchase services from private firms to augment similar services the government produces directly. Public safety or police service is one area where joint public-private action is common.

Public provision of police services is usually called for because of substantial social (as opposed to private) benefits from the service (externalities), the difficulty of forcing consumers to pay for public safety benefits other than through government taxes (nonexclusion), and economies of scale in producing services. Certainly all these factors are important and help explain why most local and state governments in the United

States provide police and other public safety services.

Some forms of public safety services do not meet these conditions; rather, the benefits are mostly private, exclusion is direct, and scale economies are minor, if they exist at all. Thus, individuals and firms privately purchase locks, safes, security lights, and alarm systems, all of which are private goods, providing benefits to the direct consumers. That doesn't mean there is no connection between these goods and publicly provided police services, however, as they seem to complement each other. A security alarm is not likely to deter illegal entry or theft unless the criminal believes that the alarm will attract public safety officers with the power to make an arrest. On the other hand, locks, safes, video surveillance equipment, private neighborhood patrols, and other security devices may reduce the demand for publicly provided police service, freeing up resources for other public safety matters or even other government responsibilities.[6]

[6]For more discussion of these types of security expenditures and the economic relationship to public police services, see Clotfelter (1977).

Application 2.1—Public and Private Provision of Public Safety

The relationship between public police and private security workers is one important aspect of this issue. In fact, private security forces seem to outnumber public law enforcement staff (Sklansky, 1999). Based on 2002 Census data, approximately 575,000 private security guards worked in companies that specialize in providing security services and another 75,000 people worked as private investigators and employees of armored car services. In addition, there are an estimated 450,000 to 500,000 "in-house" security guards—workers hired solely for that purpose by firms or property owners—and about 120,000 employees of firms that install and monitor security and alarm systems. In contrast, the Department of Justice reported a total of about 700,000 state and local government police officers in 2000. So, the number of private security guards (1.2 to 1.3 million) is at least 70 to 80 percent greater than the number of public police officers.

Private security services may both complement and substitute for public safety services, depending on type. For instance, uses of private security guards to guard specific buildings or parking lots is similar in effect to locks and alarm systems installed by private owners, providing mostly private benefits to the direct users of the service. These uses complement but do not really replace public police.

Increasingly, however, private security forces are being used to substitute for or augment public police services, as well. In some cases, groups of individuals or businesses are contracting with private security firms to provide services in addition to those of local police. Such services commonly include patrolling, monitoring behavior, and providing information to public police, but usually do not include arrests or criminal investigation. For instance, businesses in Philadelphia's commercial downtown did just that in 1991. Similarly, homeowners in some neighborhoods (often through a neighborhood association) hire private guards to patrol the neighborhood or staff entry centers, a trend that seems to be increasing partly due to the growth of gated communities. Sklansky (1999) reports that more than 800 private security guards patrol neighborhoods within the city boundaries of Los Angeles (a number equal to about one-tenth of the size of the LAPD). In an economic sense, one can think of the public police as providing a general social benefit, with the additional private service satisfying additional marginal private benefits (demand).

The growth of private security services and expenditures—both for traditional services such as alarm systems and for newer private security guards and patrols—also creates a number of challenges for public police agencies. False alarms are one major problem. *Governing Magazine* (1998) reports that there are about 7 million private electronic security systems in the United States that average about two alarms each per year. But 98 percent of those alarms are false, creating substantial direct costs for public police who respond to the alarm and diverting the time and attention of the public police away from actual criminal activity. Competition for workers is another issue. The growth of private security guards and patrols has made it more difficult for public police agencies to attract and retain police officers, driving up public safety costs.

In a few instances, private security guards or firms are actually replacing public police, at least for some services. Some public police agencies are hiring private guards or security

Application 2.1—Public and Private Provision of Public Safety

firms, without true police power, to provide such functions as patrolling parks, transporting prisoners, directing traffic, enforcing parking rules, or providing a security presence in government buildings. In essence, public police agencies that do this are changing the way public safety services are produced similar to the way in which other services (such as medicine) divide tasks among specialized groups of workers (physicians, physicians' assistants, nurses). Such changes often reflect pressures to produce public services at lower cost, as discussed in Chapter 7.

In a few other cases, private security forces may completely replace public police. Sussex, N.J. replaced its local police force in 1993 with private security guards under contract to the city. Although driven partly by cost considerations, such complete privatization moves also create new issues for government to resolve—how to specify the contracted-for service, monitor the performance of the private supplier, and enforce details of the contract if the contractor fails to comply.

The increasing private provision of public safety services challenges the conventional economic efficiency arguments used to support government provision. If police services really are nonrival and nonexcludable, then why do businesses or individuals voluntarily offer to pay for such services? Interestingly, in a historical sense, private security provision and private security forces once were the norm. In the United States, it was only in the late 1800s and early part of this century that serious civil liberty concerns were raised about private security forces, fueling an increase in public police services. Clifford Shearing (1992) notes that private police began to be perceived as protecting the private interests of the firms that employed them—particularly as a result of the role of private security forces in violent conflicts with emerging labor unions—rather than some general public interest. Since the 1960s, however, such concerns seem to have become less important, at the same time that cost considerations and demand for security have become more important. As a result, private security services have grown in importance again.

SUMMARY

Some important aspects of microeconomics are reviewed in this chapter. An economy is Pareto efficient if it is not possible to make at least one person better off without making someone else worse off. Market efficiency requires that marginal social benefits equal marginal social costs.

Public goods are nonrival, meaning that one additional person can consume the good without reducing any other consumer's benefit. After a nonrival good is produced, the marginal social cost of another consumer is zero, so efficiency requires a zero price.

An externality exists if one economic agent's action (consumption or production) affects another agent's welfare outside of the market. When externalities are present, private choices by consumers and firms in private markets generally will not provide an economically efficient result. Government may be able to intervene and create incentives through the use of taxes, subsidies, or regulations so that private choices of consumers and firms will be efficient in the presence of externalities.

If production of some commodities exhibits increasing returns to scale, it is impossible to have a single price equal to marginal cost (which is required for efficiency) and have the producer earn a profit. Government may resolve this difficulty either by becoming the producer or by regulating monopoly production.

Many, although not all, state–local government activities can be explained by the problems of public goods, externalities, and increasing returns to scale. Redistribution of society's resources also can be a legitimate and explicit objective of government policy.

DISCUSSION QUESTIONS

1. In parts of the country where snow is a regular occurrence, local government almost always provides snow removal from public streets, but seldom provides snow removal from public sidewalks. Sidewalk clearing is either left to individual choice or regulated by the government, perhaps by requiring that property owners clear the walks along their property. Yet the theoretical aspects of these two services are the same. What factors might explain why local governments typically do not plow sidewalks or, from the other point of view, why localities do not simply require property owners to clear snow from streets along their property? What does this imply about the standard externality/public goods argument justifying government intervention?

2. "For an efficient amount of a public good to be provided, the marginal cost of producing another unit of that good must equal the marginal benefit to each individual who consumes the good." Is this statement true or false, and why?

3. Suppose your university is considering building new parking lots on campus. The following table shows the marginal benefit to students, faculty/staff, and visitors for one to five new lots. The table also gives the total cost of acquiring/constructing those lots.

	Marginal Benefits			
No. of Lots	**Students**	**Faculty/Staff**	**Visitors**	**Total Cost**
1	$75,000	$37,500	$12,500	$30,000
2	60,000	35,000	5,000	70,000
3	45,000	30,000	0	120,000
4	25,000	25,000	0	180,000
5	5,000	20,000	0	250,000

Assuming that the lots will not be completely full so that students, staff, and visitors can use them simultaneously, derive the aggregate demand curve or social marginal benefit for parking lots. What is the efficient number of additional lots? If this university builds the efficient number of lots, how should the costs be divided among students, faculty/staff, and visitors?

4. Explain why the existence of benefit spillovers across jurisdiction boundaries could lead the jurisdictions to provide too little of that service from society's viewpoint. If the service in question is public safety, what might be the nature of common benefit spillovers?

SELECTED READING

Bator, Francis M. "The Anatomy of Market Failure." *Quarterly Journal of Economics* 72 (August 1958): 351–79.

Samuelson, Paul A. "Diagrammatic Exposition of a Theory of Public Expenditure." *Review of Economics and Statistics* 37 (1955): 350–56.

Steiner, Peter. "The Public Sector and the Public Interest." In *Public Expenditure and Policy Analysis*, edited by R. Haveman and J. Margolis, 3–41. Boston: Houghton Mifflin, 1983.

PUBLIC CHOICE AND FISCAL FEDERALISM

AS COMPARED TO A CENTRALIZED GOVERNMENT, THE MOST IMPORTANT AND DISTINGUISHING FEATURE OF SUBNA-TIONAL GOVERNMENTS IS THEIR SHEER NUMBER AND THE EASE OF MOVING AMONG THEM. These physical differences have economic implications, however, and perhaps none so important as the implications for tax and expenditure choice by those same subnational governments. That is the general topic of Chapters 3 through 6.

The desire for services by consumer/voters is fundamental to the choice of tax and expenditure by government. Thus, one important issue is how prices of goods and services, incomes, and personal characteristics affect the demand for government services by voters. Important questions include the following: How sensitive is consumption of, say education, to changes in the price of that service? Does the desired consumption of state and local government services increase or decrease as consumers' incomes rise, and by how much? What does demand imply about the benefits from state–local government services?

Given consumer demands, the existing structure of a fiscal federalism— the comparative number and fiscal characteristics of cities, counties, and special-purpose districts—must also influence the fiscal choices of each subnational government. The most obvious examples of this influence include the way communities compete for new businesses by offering tax incentives and compete for new residents by offering services. Given any existing federal structure, the issue is whether the fiscal choices of govern-ments are likely to be efficient, and if not, whether realigning fiscal respon-sibilities within that structure would cause improvement. For example, given a set of local governments in a metropolitan area, should one service, say police protection, be transferred from city to county government?

Alternatively, knowing the types and characteristics of the services that will be provided may help determine the best federal structure to provide those services. In that case, the issue is how many governments there should be, or, equivalently, how big those governments should be. At one end of the spectrum, some services may require only one government, which would cover the entire nation. In contrast, some services may be provided better by many small governments.

The issue then is the optimal design of subnational governments or the optimal allocation of fiscal responsibilities among existing subnational governments. In the following four chapters, we will use economic analysis to explore how individual choice about the activities of government affects the best structure for government.

CHAPTER 3

PUBLIC CHOICE WITHOUT MOBILITY: VOTING

> *. . . The measurement of the preferences for [public] goods . . . cannot be subjected to individual consumer choice. The closest substitute for consumer choice is voting.*[1]
> —HOWARD R. BOWEN

HEADLINES

". . . VOTERS HAVE APPROVED MONEY FOR PROGRAMS THAT HELP KIDS IN TROUBLE.

WITH ALL PRECINCTS REPORTING . . . , THE JUVENILE JUSTICE MILLAGE PASSED 27,159 TO 23,024. . . .

"THE NEW MILLAGE IS EXPECTED TO RAISE ABOUT $1.5 MILLION A YEAR FOR EACH OF THE NEXT FIVE YEARS," SAID THE COUNTY'S CIRCUIT AND PROBATE COURT ADMINISTRATOR.

THE OWNERS OF A HOUSE VALUED AT $100,000 WITH A TAXABLE VALUE OF $50,000 WILL PAY AN EXTRA $20 A YEAR IN PROPERTY TAXES.

MOST OF THE MONEY . . . WILL BE USED TO DEVELOP COUNTY PROGRAMS THAT HELP JUVE-NILE DELINQUENTS WITH PROBLEMS SUCH AS ALCOHOL ADDICTION, WHICH HE SAID ARE LESS EXPENSIVE THAN PLACING KIDS IN STATE PROGRAMS.[2]"

---

[1]"The Interpretation of Voting in the Allocation of Economic Resources." *The Quarterly Journal of Economics.* 58 (Nov. 1943): 33.

[2]Grasha, Kevin. "Eaton County Passes Juvenile Millage." *Lansing State Journal.* November 3, 2004.

FISCAL CHOICES

State and local governments face three fundamental fiscal choices. The first is the choice of revenue or tax structure—that is, determining which different types of revenue sources should be used and in what relative mix. The second choice is the level of total spending and thus the total amount of revenue required. Given a choice of tax structure, adjustments in the level of spending can be accomplished by moving all tax rates up or down as required without changing that basic revenue structure. Finally, the government must choose how to allocate total spending among the various goods and services demanded by voters. This is the decision of which services to provide in what quantity within the total spending goal.

Do not assume that these choices are made separately because the level of spending desired by an individual usually depends on how the individual believes the money will be spent. That is, the desired level of spending may depend on the mix of services provided. The level of spending desired also depends on the choice of revenue structure because the tax and charge system determines the cost or price of government spending to each individual. A person who is exempt from local taxes, for example, is likely to be more supportive of increased local spending than a person who expects to pay the resulting higher taxes.

It appears, however, that governments make some of these decisions more often than others. The level of spending and taxes usually changes each year, sometimes more often, and commonly by a substantial amount; however, the mix of government services may change only in a more gradual way as incremental adjustments are made in each budget cycle. Over a 10-year period, a city may find itself spending more of its budget on public safety and less on education, but it is unlikely for that total change to have occurred in any one year. Finally, the revenue structure may be the most stable of all. Adopting new taxes or fees or major structural changes to increase reliance on one tax at the expense of another is relatively rare. More commonly, rates are adjusted for each budget to provide revenues sufficient for the spending plan.[3] Therefore, although these three fiscal decisions are interrelated, it may be worthwhile to separate them in order to get the analysis started.

One important way that these fundamental state and local government fiscal decisions are made is by voting. Because these goods and services are not being sold in a traditional market, it is impossible for individuals to select and pay for the quantities they desire. Unlike the choice of two hamburgers, fries, and a drink for $3.65, the city resident cannot order two police patrols per hour, a high school education emphasizing science, and one (unlimited) garbage collection per week for $1,200 per year. Those choices are made collectively with the other city residents (or voters). The use of voting to make these choices suggests that not all residents agree, so voting becomes a method of resolving different desires.

---

[3]It is an old debate in public finance whether governments "tax to spend," in which case all revenues generated by the existing structure are spent, or "spend to tax," in which case tax rates are set to fund the selected spending level. The characterization of three separate fiscal decisions for analytical purposes does not presume the answer to the debate nor which decisions "come first."

These differences in desired local government fiscal activity can be resolved in another way that is similar to individual shopping in private markets. If many localities are available for residential choice, individuals may select among them based on the package of taxes and services provided. For purposes of the current discussion, assume that individuals are not mobile, and that they must make fiscal decisions for the community in which they reside. The alternative to voting created by the mobility of residents is explored in detail in Chapter 5.

In this chapter, the economic implications of several types of voting on fiscal decisions are examined. We begin by examining the most common method, majority voting, and then consider how the outcome of majority voting may depend on the political characteristics of the government. This line of inquiry, which bridges economics and political science, is now almost a separate discipline called the *study of public choice*. Obviously, all public-choice issues cannot be covered in one chapter, so the concentration is on those basic results that are most often applied to analyzing state and local government actions.

Desired Government Spending

It is almost axiomatic that not everyone wants the same things from government. To an economist, this suggests that individuals have different demand functions for government services. Individuals may have different demands for the same government service either because they have different incomes or because they value the service differently, that is, they have different tastes for that service.

To illustrate different demands, the example from Chapter 2 of three individuals (or groups), each with a different demand for government services, continues in Figure 3.1. Assuming all three have the same tastes, income differences would be a reason for the different demands. If state and local government services are normal goods (which is usually the case), demand increases with income. For the example in Figure 3.1, it would require that $Income_A < Income_B < Income_C$. Alternatively, if Persons A, B, and C all have the same income, then demand differs because the three value the service differently, with Person C getting the greatest benefit from the service. Of course, it is also possible for demand to differ because both income and tastes vary among individuals.[4]

Even when an individual's demand function is known, to determine the desired amount or quantity of the government service, one must know that individual's price. Individuals "buy" government services with the taxes and fees that they pay, so the tax structure determines each individual's price. Here we assume that this government has selected a tax structure that is not changed depending on the level of spending. The government adjusts the tax rates to generate more or less revenue as required, but the tax mix—the share of revenue from each source—remains the same.

---

[4]It is useful to remember that because mechanisms to induce individuals to reveal their true demand for public goods are generally absent, these demands are not known. Thus, public officials cannot directly compute the desired level of services; voting is a mechanism for individuals to reveal their desires. More details about demand for state–local services appear in Chapter 4.

Figure 3.1

Demand for a
public good

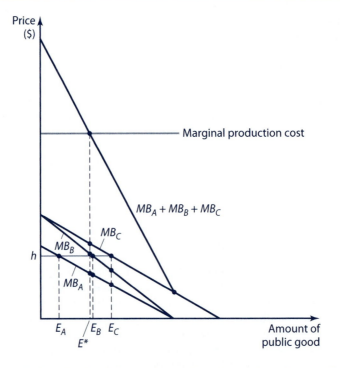

The price to each individual then is his or her share of total taxes. For instance, if the government finances services by a property tax, each individual's tax is equal to the tax rate times the property value, or

$$\text{Rate} \cdot \text{Value}_i.$$

Each individual's share of taxes is equal to

$$\text{Rate} \cdot \text{Value}_i / \Sigma_i \, \text{Rate} \cdot \text{Value}_i,$$

which reduces to

$$\text{Value}_i / \text{Sum of Values}$$

This is the share of taxes paid by person i. Similar tax shares can be defined for any given tax structure.

To carry through the example, assume the simplest tax structure in which each individual pays the same tax so that each has an equal tax share. In the example with three individuals, each pays one-third of the taxes collected by the government. In other words, the price to each individual of buying another dollar's worth of government service is $.333.[5]

---

[5]If incomes differ among the taxpayers, this is a regressive tax system because tax as a fraction of income would decline as income increased (see Chapter 12).

Given these different demands and the assumed tax shares, the price charged each person is one-third of marginal production cost, or h. The desired quantities of government service are E_A, E_B, and E_C, respectively. Because all taxpayers face the same tax price in this example, the differences in desired quantities are determined entirely by the differences in demand.

The problem for the government is choosing among the different desired quantities of government service that result from the combination of demand and tax shares. Because the nature of government goods is that one quantity is provided to all consumers, some compromise is decided by voting. We turn now to a comparison of various voting methods.

MAJORITY VOTING

The most common voting method is majority voting. Sometimes voting is directly on budget issues such as in local government property tax-rate elections, and sometimes voting is for officials who then make the allocation decisions for the constituents. The victorious position or candidate in a majority vote is supported by at least 50 percent plus one of the votes.

Returning now to the example in Figure 3.1, suppose that this government uses majority voting to choose among the three spending levels. Which one, if any, will receive majority support? If the government selects between E_A and E_B, Person A will vote for E_A, the preferred amount of spending, while Person B will vote for E_B. Of these two options, understanding that neither is the first choice, which will Person C select? Because Person C prefers an even greater amount of spending than either A or B, we expect that C will support level E_B because it is closer to the desired amount than E_A. Therefore, spending level E_B receives two votes and is selected by the community over Person A's preferred amount.

How does the community view E_B compared to the higher level E_C? Again, a majority vote would find Person B supporting E_B and Person C supporting E_C, whereas Person A would support B over C because spending level E_B is closer to the low level A prefers. Spending level E_B would be selected as the winner of the majority vote.

This simple example illustrates an important point about majority voting that is often misunderstood. Spending level E_B was selected not because a majority of the voters preferred it, but because it was the only choice that *could* receive majority support. If a low-spending level was proposed, Persons B and C could band together to defeat it, while A and B could similarly prevent the high-spending level from being selected. As a result of this majority vote, both Persons A and C are forced to compromise and accept a spending amount different from what they prefer. Only Person B is perfectly happy with the outcome. The results of this example can be, and have been, generalized.

Will There Be Only One Winner of a Majority Vote?

One concern about majority voting is that there may not be a clear-cut winner or that the winner will be different depending on the order in which the choices are considered. This problem may occur if each voter does not have **single-peaked preferences**—that is, each voter does not have a clearly preferred alternative and does not continually get less satisfaction as he or she moves away from that alternative in either direction.

The potential difficulty with majority voting when preferences are not single-peaked is shown with this example. Again, suppose the three possible spending levels are denoted by E_1, E_2, and E_3, from low to high. Preferences toward those spending levels are as follows:

Person	First Choice	Second Choice	Third Choice
A	E_1	E_2	E_3
B	E_2	E_3	E_1
C	E_3	E_1	E_2

Person C wants a high level of government spending most, but a low level is C's second choice; the medium amount of spending is least preferred. In a vote between levels 1 and 2, 1 receives two votes (from A and C) and wins. Similarly, in a vote between levels 1 and 3, 3 receives two votes (from B and C) and wins. It appears that spending level E_3 has been selected by majority vote and is most preferred. However, suppose level E_3 is compared with E_2 in a vote. Surprisingly, 2 receives two votes (from A and B) and wins. The voting results are not consistent. Level 3 beats 1, level 1 beats 2, but level 2 beats 3. The implication is that the winner depends on the order in which the votes are taken. Level 3 wins if 1 is first put against 2 and the winner put against level 3, but level 1 wins if 2 is first put against 3 and the winner put against 1.

This result occurs because Person C's preferences are not single-peaked. As spending is decreased from the most preferred high level, Person C becomes less and less happy until spending becomes very low, and then C's happiness increases again. Person C is an extremist who is least happy with moderate positions. If preferences exhibit this property, then majority voting *may* be inconsistent (that is, the results are not transitive).

The potential for inconsistency may be a theoretical but not real problem in using majority voting to select amounts of government spending because standard downward-sloping demand curves imply single-peaked preferences. With the demand curve and individual price shown in Figure 3.2, Q_0 is the desired quantity. The consumer has consumer surplus—the difference between the maximum amount the consumer is willing to pay and the price—equal to the area ADP_0. As this consumer moves away from Q_0, the consumer's surplus, and thus the consumer's happiness, continually decreases. At Q_1, the surplus is represented by the area $ACEP_0$; at the lower-quantity Q_2, the surplus is even smaller, represented as $ABFP_0$. If the quantity is increased from Q_0 to Q_3, consumer's surplus also decreases, being equal to area ADP_0 minus area DGH. In short, the desired quantity may be small or large, but if demand is always downward sloping, then consumer

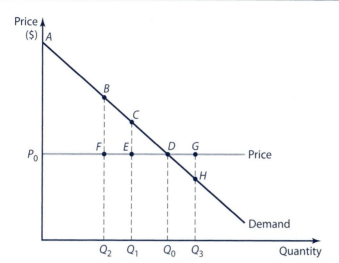

Figure 3.2

Demand and
consumer surplus

happiness will continually decrease the greater the distance from that desired amount. That is, preferences are single-peaked.[6]

When thinking about potential problems with majority voting, one must also consider the nature of the commodity for which preferences must be single-peaked. The commodity must be characterized by a single, quantifiable, and continuous parameter. In the case of government finance, government expenditure (in dollars) appears to be such a measure; however, expenditure is really a measure of input purchases rather than goods and service production. If a government provides several services, a single expenditure amount is consistent with many different service combinations, so that total expenditure may not be an accurate parameter on which to base consumer preferences. The voting system must select the mix of services and the level of total spending. For that reason, the majority voting model of government fiscal choice may be most applicable to single-purpose subnational governments such as school districts or separate utility, park, and transit districts.

Finally, we must consider the possibility of strategic behavior or collusion on the part of voters. Majority voting may be inconsistent if voters do not vote their true preferences in hopes of skewing the result or trading their vote on one issue for others' votes on a different issue. Although vote trading and negotiation may occur in legislative bodies, it should not be as common in general voter elections because of the difficulty of arranging and enforcing collusion among a large number of

---

[6]Of course, individuals still might have extremist positions regarding state–local finance issues, for instance, favoring a high level of education spending so that the public schools provide academic and extracurricular services to all students or, in the alternative, opting for all private education.

Figure 3.3

Illustration of
median-desired
expenditure

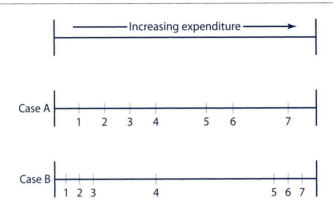

people. Still, legislative bodies make many (if not most) fiscal decisions, which raises many other issues involving vote trading, lobbying, campaign contributions, and other ways of influencing the legislative outcome. The issue is whether state and local fiscal decisions can be represented as if they were made by the participatory majority-voting process, even if a more complex political process was actually involved.

The Median-Voter Theorem

A general rule of majority voting can now be stated:

> *If voters' preferences are single-peaked, if the choice to be made by voting is represented along a single continuum, if all alternatives are voted on, and if voters act on their true preferences, then the choice selected by majority vote is the median of the desired outcomes. For those of you for whom statistics remains a mystery, the* **median** *is the potential outcome in the middle of the continuum—that is, the one with half of the potential choices lower and half of the choices higher.*

Applying this theorem to the choice of government expenditures suggests that if all individuals' demand curves for government services are downward sloping, then the expenditure selected by majority vote will be the median of those individuals' desired expenditure amounts. In the simple example of Figure 3.1, the median is expenditure E_B, which is in the middle between E_A and E_C. Two other cases are shown in Figure 3.3, each with seven voters and seven different desired expenditure amounts. For case A, the median is expenditure amount 4, with three voters preferring a smaller amount and three preferring larger ones. Despite a very different structure of preferences for Case B, the median, and thus the winner of a majority vote, is still the same expenditure amount 4.[7]

---

[7]It is important to think about the economic characteristics of the median voter, particularly whether the median voter is the voter with median income. That issue and the use of the median-voter model for measuring demand are discussed in Chapter 4.

Figure 3.4

Distribution of desired public expenditure

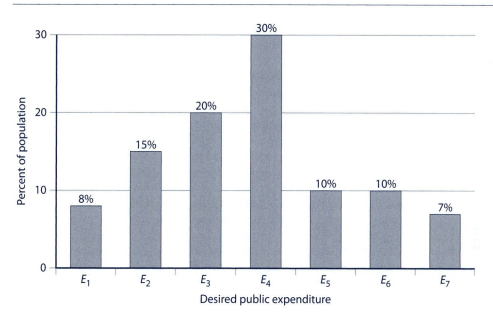

This illustrates an important point about the **median statistic**, and thus the median winner of a majority vote. The median often does not change even if other possible outcomes do change. Although voters 1, 2, and 3 prefer lower amounts in case B compared to case A, and voters 5, 6, and 7 prefer higher amounts, the median is the same in both cases. The government expenditure level selected by majority vote does not depend on the relative *strength* of the voters' preferences but only on their *order*.

All the examples so far have coupled each potential expenditure with only one voter, which may be somewhat unrealistic. A more real-world characterization of preferences is shown in Figure 3.4, with the percentage distribution of voters shown for seven potential expenditure amounts. Thus, 15 percent of this jurisdiction's voters prefer expenditure amount E_2, 20 percent prefer E_3, and so on. The median amount in this distribution is E_4 because if all the voters were counted in order of desired expenditure, the middle (50th percentile) would come among the 30 percent of voters who prefer E_4. This occurs despite the fact that 43 percent of the voters prefer an amount less than E_4 and 27 percent prefer a greater amount. Another way to look at the situation is that 60 percent of the voters prefer expenditures "close to" E_4, 23 percent prefer much lower expenditures, and 17 percent prefer much higher.

This discussion of majority voting to choose a government's expenditure has assumed an actual vote among taxpayers on the issue, usually called *participatory democracy*. In a representative democracy, however, voters elect representatives who then select the expenditure. Will the median-voter theorem still apply? In fact, it may. Suppose that candidates for a representative position campaign on the amount of government expenditure (and thus public service) they propose to implement. One candidate might promise to restrict government spending (perhaps to amount E_2 in Figure 3.4), whereas another might propose new programs that would increase spending to amount E_6. If that happened, a third candidate could defeat those two by proposing spending amount E_4, the median amount. Remember that a majority of voters will always support E_4 over any alternative and thus should support a candidate proposing E_4 over candidates proposing any other amounts. The tendency for political candidates to try to stake out a moderate position in election campaigns is common.

When economists apply the median-voter model to analyze state and local government fiscal decisions, they often assume that those decisions are made as if there had been a direct majority vote of the taxpayers. Although political scientists and economists have examined in detail the conditions under which this is true, the crucial factor for economists seems to be the amount of political competition. If elections are held often and if entry into the political wars is easy, then officials may be pushed toward the median choice to stay in power. This is the parallel of market competition (or potential competition), which pushes firms toward producing and setting prices at minimum average cost (covered in more detail later in this chapter).

Characteristics of the Median-Voter Result

The most fundamental characteristic of the median-voter choice of government expenditure is the inherent dissatisfaction among taxpayers with the outcome. For the example depicted in Figure 3.4, only 30 percent of the voters actually desire the outcome selected by majority vote, whereas 70 percent are dissatisfied to some degree. In fact, it is possible that only *one* voter, the median voter, will be satisfied perfectly with the outcome of a majority vote. This characteristic is inherent in the model because the reason for voting in the first place is to choose among different desired outcomes with the resulting compromise requiring some dissatisfaction.

This characteristic is one reason the median-voter model is attractive to economists. The model predicts what is apparently observed. As part of a series of public-finance surveys taken annually by the U.S. Advisory Commission on Intergovernmental Relations (ACIR), respondents were asked, "Considering all government services on the one hand and all taxes on the other, which of the following comes closest to your view?" Respondents could answer "increase both," "decrease both," or "keep them about where they are." The results for three past years are shown in Table 3.1.

The percentage finding the amount of taxes and spending "about right" varies from 42 to 51 percent, whereas roughly 8 percent would prefer substantially greater amounts of spending (and taxes), and slightly more than one-third would prefer substantially less.

Although the ACIR survey applies to all types of government spending together, similar results are obtained if this type of question is applied to a single service or single state or local government. For instance, the Gallup Poll (Jones 2004)

Table 3.1

ACIR Survey: Desired Changes in Taxes and Spending

Year	Percent Responding*		
	Increase	Decrease	Remain Same
1986	9%	31%	51%
1982	8	36	42
1980	6	38	45

*Totals do not add to 100 percent because a fourth possible response, "no opinion," is not shown.

regularly asks about "the amount of money the government . . . should spend for national defense and military purposes—spending too little, about the right amount, or too much." Since 2002, the fraction responding "about right" has been between 44 and 48 percent, less than a majority. In 2004, 31 percent said "too much," 45 percent "about right," and 22 percent "too little."

Edward Gramlich and Daniel Rubinfeld (1982) used data from a survey of Michigan voters, similar to the ACIR one discussed previously, to estimate individuals' demands for government services. The desired amounts of government service were then compared to the actual service levels in those individuals' jurisdictions. The results showed that two-thirds of the voters in cities in the Detroit metropolitan area and other urban areas in the state want no change in the level of public spending; but about 19 percent of voters favor a large increase or decrease. It is simply true that in almost every community, some voters want a smaller government, some want a bigger one, and a substantial number, sometimes even a majority, are approximately satisfied with the status quo.

A second important characteristic of the median-voter model is that the amount of public expenditure selected is, in general, not the economically efficient amount. Efficiency results really only by accident. Moreover, there is no method for inefficiency to be removed; for example, as shown in Figure 3.1, the median amount chosen by majority vote, E_B, is not equal to the efficient amount E^*. As seen in Chapter 2, the efficient amount requires that the sum of individuals' marginal benefits equal marginal production cost, whereas the median voters' desired amount (which becomes the community's selection) requires only that their marginal benefit equal their marginal tax cost.

Majority voting can lead to government spending greater than the efficient amount, as shown in Figure 3.1, but it is equally possible for majority voting to lead to too little spending. In general, it is not possible to predict which occurs, because the result depends on the relationship of tax price to marginal benefit and on the price elasticity of demand. It is easy to understand, however, *why* majority voting might not be efficient. Suppose that in a community of three voters, one prefers school spending of $3,500 per student, another $7,000, and the third $12,000. If tax shares are the same for all three, these amounts reflect only the relative benefits perceived by the three. The median is obviously $7,000 per student. The choice of the efficient amount, however, recognizes that the third voter has a substantially higher marginal benefit than do the others at every amount, which causes the efficient amount to exceed the median. Majority voting does not take account of strength or magnitude of preference.

To summarize, if the amount of government spending by a state or local government is determined as if a majority vote were taken among the residents, the amount selected is the median of the residents' desired amounts. That median amount is not likely to be economically efficient, and a large number of voters, perhaps even a majority, will be dissatisfied with the choice.

There are at least three ways to reduce dissatisfaction: change prices, change tastes, or adopt a different public choice method. If the government's tax system is altered so that the tax price increases for those voters who now prefer expenditure greater than the median, their preferred amount decreases. If tax price decreases for those who want expenditure less than the median, their preferred amount increases. Because the preferred expenditure amounts move toward the median, the unhappiness with government expenditure decreases. To eliminate the dissatisfaction, tax prices must be proportional to marginal benefits so that each individual prefers the same amount. The difficulties with achieving such a Lindahl benefit tax structure were noted in Chapter 2. Alternatively, tastes could change if the dissatisfied voters left this community for another while new residents with tastes similar to the current median voters moved in. In that case, the differences in demand and the dissatisfaction are eliminated. That possibility is discussed in Chapter 5.

ALTERNATIVE VOTING METHODS

The dissatisfaction that results from voting about fiscal decisions might be lessened by alternative voting methods, but usually at the cost of more difficulty in reaching decisions. Essentially, requiring a *majority* to determine the outcome is nothing magical; in **plurality voting** the winner need only get more voters than any alternative, whereas **super majorities**, such as two-thirds or three-quarters, are sometimes required to win other types of votes (such as amendments to constitutions or other changes deemed especially significant). What, then, are the advantages and disadvantages of other voting methods?

The simplest way to avoid dissatisfaction with the outcome of voting is to require unanimous approval for any choice. Just such a voting method was proposed by the Swedish economist Knut Wicksell (originally published in 1896, reprinted in Musgrave and Peacock, 1967) to eliminate the possibility that a slim majority could adopt government services to benefit themselves at the expense of the minority who contributed to the financing. If everyone approves of the choice, then no one is hurt by that fiscal decision and the outcome achieves Pareto efficiency. Of course, one obvious problem with unanimous voting is that it may be exceptionally costly, or even impossible, to achieve unanimous agreement on many fiscal issues. Because of this, a second major problem is the strategic voting that likely would result. Because any voter could veto a proposal, individuals have an incentive to hold out for an agreement that largely benefits them. Of course, this again makes it harder to reach an agreement. One can imagine the deals that would be considered, or even made, to achieve unanimous agreement on a school tax/expenditure package.[8]

This discussion leads, then, to the obvious possibility of requiring more than a majority of voters to approve a proposal, but less than all voters. James Buchanan and Gordon Tullock (1962) noted a tradeoff in the number of votes required to win. As the percentage of the vote required to win increases, it is less likely that choices will be made that hurt groups of voters (dissatisfaction will decrease) but the costs of decision making rise. Balancing these benefits and costs, the efficient percentage of votes to win might be between a majority and unanimity, for instance, two-thirds. With such a voting rule, it is less likely that choices will be adopted to benefit only very limited groups, but no one voter or group has sufficient power to veto all choices. Although super majorities have been required often in the past for constitutional amendments, in recent years a number of states have required super majorities to override various long-term fiscal controls. At present, 12 of the states with limitations on state spending require a super majority vote of the legislature (usually two-thirds) to exceed the limit.

A major source of the dissatisfaction with the outcome of a majority vote and the primary reason why majority voting does not usually achieve the economically efficient outcome is that majority voting does not account for strength of preference. To alleviate this difficulty, a number of voting methods have been proposed that allow voters to register both their preferred order of outcomes as well as their relative strength of feeling about those outcomes. In **point voting**, for instance, individuals are given a fixed number of points (say 100) that they can assign to the possible outcomes. The outcome with the most points wins.

For instance, suppose three voters are choosing among possible levels of school spending of $3,500 per student, $7,000, or $12,000. If one voter preferred the highest level of spending *very strongly*, that voter could allocate all 100 of the points to that choice. Essentially, such a voter is signaling that he or she strongly prefers $12,000 of spending, and if that level cannot be achieved then either of the others are equally good. An illustration of the possible allocation of point votes in this case is shown here:

	Spending Level		
Voter	**$3,500**	**$7,000**	**$12,000**
1	60	30	10
2	30	50	20
3	0	0	100
Total	90	80	130

Voters 1 and 2 distribute their points over all three options, although voter 1 most prefers $3,500 and voter 2 most prefers $7,000. Voter 3 feels very strongly

---

[8]Some economists have noted the relationship between Wicksell unanimous voting and a Lindahl pricing scheme, where tax shares are proportional to marginal benefits. In that case, all voters demand the same quantity of public service and unanimity can be achieved.

about the preferred level of $12,000 and allocates all 100 points there. As a result, $12,000 gets the most points and is selected. Unlike with majority voting, strength of preference can matter here.

The point of this discussion is not that these alternative voting methods are "better" than majority voting, but that every voting method has different advantages and disadvantages. The disadvantages of majority voting can be offset, but only by creating some other cost.[9]

MONOPOLY MODELS OF FISCAL CHOICE

Although majority voting is the most common public choice method, and the median-voter model predicts some commonly observed conditions, the monopoly model—in which the government has some monopoly power over fiscal decisions—is one of the most interesting alternative models. The majority-voting/ median-voter model implicitly assumes that the government's role is simply to implement voters' desires about government services and in a politically competitive environment. In contrast, monopoly models assume that government officials attempt to implement their own preferences and try to get voters to go along. Officials or bureaucrats may be able to do that if they have more experience or more information than the voters and if they have and can maintain a political monopoly.

William Niskanen (1968) first discussed monopoly models by proposing that bureaucrats attempt to maximize the size of their budgets subject only to a desire to remain in power. Since then, several different variants have arisen. All the variants make several common assumptions, however, so we will examine these types of models by discussing the specific one proposed and used by Thomas Romer and Howard Rosenthal (1979a) to analyze local government spending.[10]

The assumptions of the model are as follows:

1. Government officials have two objectives: maximize the amount of government spending and remain in office.

2. Government officials know the preferences of the residents of their communities.

3. The amount of government spending is selected by majority vote of the residents. Importantly, a limited number of options may be voted on and the government officials select those options.

4. If a majority of voters accepts none of the options proposed by the government, government spending reverts to a predetermined amount.

In essence, there is limited majority voting, but the agenda from which voters may choose is determined by the government officials who want to spend as much as possible.

---

[9]For more discussion of other voting methods, see Johnson (1991) and Mueller (1989).

[10]See Niskanen (1968) and Romer and Rosenthal (1979a).

Figure 3.5

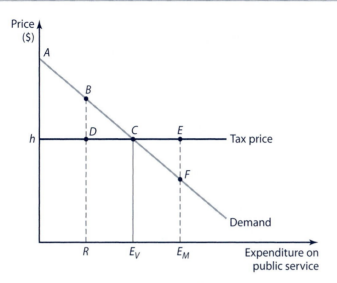

A monopoly
bureaucrat model
of public expendi-
ture choice

The potential outcome of this monopoly, agenda-control model is illustrated in Figure 3.5, which shows both the demand for government services and the tax price of the median voter in the community. This voter prefers expenditure E_V, which is the amount chosen by majority vote of all the options and predicted by the median-voter theorem. If voters do not approve any of the amounts offered by the government in a limited number of votes, expenditure automatically (because of some other law) is set at amount R, which is called the reversion amount. In other words, the reversion amount is the threatened or imposed expenditure if voters do not approve what government officials offer.

Suppose government officials, knowing all of this, propose a spending amount equal to E_M. If this voter understands that this is the only chance to vote, there is a quandary; the choice is effectively R or E_M. Given the conditions in Figure 3.5, this voter is indifferent about R and E_M. That is, this voter would get the same satisfaction from either expenditure amounts R or E_M, which would be less than the satisfaction from the most preferred amount E_V. At amount R, area $ABDh$ represents the consumer's surplus, which equals area ACh minus area BCD. At amount E_M, area ACh minus area CEF represents the consumer's surplus. The latter triangle is subtracted because for all amounts above E_V, the consumer's marginal benefit is less than the price, implying a loss of welfare. Finally, because triangle BCD equals triangle CEF by construction, the consumer's surplus at E_M also equals area $ABDh$. This voter would be equally hurt by less than desired government spending at R or more than desired at E_M.

If the alternative is R, therefore, this voter would *prefer* any amount less than E_M. An expenditure proposal for a small amount less than E_M, even $1 less, would be approved by the voters rather than allow spending to fall to amount R, which would be worse. Because government officials want to spend as much as possible, they would propose spending $\$(E_M - 1)$. As a result, majority voting is used to choose expenditure, and the median voter's demand determines the outcome, but the amount chosen is greater than that most preferred by the median voter and that predicted by the median-voter model.

The crucial features that give this model its characteristics are the nature of the reversion amount and the absence of political competition. Consider each in turn. The simplest reversion is zero—that is, unless the voters approve a proposed expenditure, there will be no government service. Obviously, if voters believe this is a credible threat, it is powerful as well. Most voters would be willing to accept some excess in government spending to prevent the loss of all government services. In reality, however, reversions are usually not zero. In presenting the model, Romer and Rosenthal (1979a) suggest that it represents the situation in many school districts where residents vote on a proposed school budget (or taxes) with the reversion equal to either a state-mandated minimum school expenditure or the previous year's spending amount. As long as the reversion is less than the voter's desired expenditure, the lower the reversion the more monopoly government officials can exploit their positions to increase spending.

Therefore, those government officials also have a great interest in how and at what amount the reversion is set. One of the weaknesses of this model is that the reversion amount is somehow predetermined, although it also must be selected by some type of fiscal-choice mechanism. This method is also risky for government officials. Individuals' preferences can never be known exactly, and officials cannot be sure which residents will be voters. If government officials err in selecting the proposed expenditure and select too high, voters will reject the proposal and effectively accept the reversion. As a result, government officials lose by having a smaller amount of government expenditure than the median voter preferred (remember that officials are assumed to be budget maximizers).

An absence of effective political competition also is crucial for the model's results. If government officials are successful in using a reversion expenditure as a threat to force voters to accept greater amounts of expenditure than they prefer, an opportunity is created for opponents in the next election to campaign on the promise of lower expenditure amounts. In effect, opponents can control the agenda in the election and defeat incumbents by selecting a median position. Of course, nothing is to prevent newly elected officials from playing the same game, except the danger of their potential defeat at the subsequent election.

In other words, this model seems most applicable to governments dominated by a single political party or group, so that effective competition is absent. Notable examples include Democrat Erastus Corning who was mayor of Albany, New York from 1942 until his death in 1983, a period of 42 years; and Democrat Richard Daley who was mayor of Chicago for 22 years. Of course, it could be that these politicians stayed in office so long because they gave voters exactly what they wanted, and the fact that almost everyone recognizes these examples suggests that they are relatively uncommon. Proponents of monopoly fiscal-choice models must identify the institutional factors in each case where the model is to be used, which allow officials to not satisfy the voters' desires continually.

VOTING FOR PUBLIC SCHOOL BUDGETS

The discussion in this chapter shows how majority voting might lead to a political choice of median desired public service levels; however, is there any evidence that this actually happens? After all, the theory as outlined in the chapter requires single-peaked preferences, full participation by residents, nonstrategic voting, and a single operational measure to vote upon. Any of these conditions could be violated in the complicated case of many state–local budget issues. One important research study of the annual budget referenda in school districts in New York, conducted by Robert Inman (1978), supports the conclusion that the majority-voting model, with some adjustments, is "a useful working hypothesis of how single service budgets are determined" (p. 60).

The most important adjustment Inman considers to the model as described in the chapter is recognition that not all residents (or registered voters) usually vote. In the 58 school districts in the study, only about 20 percent of eligible voters participated in the school budget elections. (Such low voter turnout is common for many local or special elections that do not involve major statewide or national candidates or issues.) If the nonvoting group contains a disproportionate number of residents with either relatively high or low demands for public service, then voter participation affects the level of service selected. In fact, Inman finds that lower-income residents both have a relatively low demand for education spending and are less likely to vote. As a result, majority voting on the budget tends to select higher levels of spending than the median for all residents, at least as a result of this effect alone.

Inman also explored how variations in demand among voters influence the budget outcome. The reference voting group in the study was composed of young, non-Catholic homeowners with median family income. This group represented almost two-thirds of the voters in these districts, on average. The concern was that older voters without children would have lower demand for education spending than the reference group, that a number of Catholic families might prefer parochial schools and thus also prefer lower levels of public education spending, and that renters might support higher levels of spending than homeowners if they perceived that property taxes used to finance schools were a burden on landlords rather than on them. Among these three possibilities, Inman found strong statistical evidence only that the elderly exert a significant negative effect on school spending. The preference differences between homeowners and renters or Catholic school users and others was not important.

Even with these adjustments, however, it seems that the idea behind the majority-voting, median-voter model is supported by these results. The effects of poor nonvoters and elderly on the actual outcome were rather small. Inman reported that the level of school spending selected by voting was 0 to 10 percent lower in these districts than that demanded by nonelderly, non-Catholic homeowners with median income. In short, this and other subsequent studies suggest that thinking local fiscal decisions are made "as if" the median voter decided is not a bad approximation of reality.

SUMMARY

State and local governments face three fundamental fiscal choices: the choice of revenue or tax structure, the level of total spending, and how to allocate total spending among the various goods and services demanded by voters. Do not assume that these choices are made separately.

Individuals may have different demands for the same government service either because they have different incomes or because they value the service differently. The price to each individual is his or her share of total taxes. The problem for the government is choosing among the different desired quantities of government service, which result from the combination of demand and tax shares.

The most common voting method used to make government-allocation decisions is majority voting. The victorious position or candidate in a majority vote is supported by at least 50 percent plus one of the voters. If a spending amount is selected by majority vote, it is not necessarily because a majority of the voters preferred it, but because it was the only choice that could receive majority support.

If voters' preferences are single-peaked, if the choice to be made by voting is represented along a continuum, and if voters act on their true preferences, then the choice selected by majority vote is the median of the desired outcomes.

The most fundamental characteristic of the median-voter choice of government expenditure is the inherent dissatisfaction among taxpayers with the outcome. In almost every community, some voters who want a smaller government, some want a bigger one, and a substantial number, although not always a majority, are approximately satisfied with the current state.

A second important characteristic of the median-voter model is that the amount of public expenditure selected is, in general, not the economically efficient amount. The efficient amount requires that the sum of individuals' marginal benefits equals marginal production cost, whereas median voters' desired amount (which becomes the community's selection) requires only that *their* marginal benefit equal *their* marginal tax cost.

Monopoly models assume that government officials attempt to implement their own preferences and try to get voters to go along. Officials or bureaucrats may be able to do that if they have more experience or more information than the voters and if they have and can maintain a political monopoly. Proponents of monopoly fiscal-choice models must identify the institutional factors that allow officials to not satisfy the voters' desires continually.

DISCUSSION QUESTIONS

1. "If school expenditures are selected by majority vote, then most of the voters in the school district will be perfectly happy with the selected amount of spending." Evaluate this statement.

2. "The efficient quantity of a public good is provided if the marginal production cost equals the sum of consumers' marginal benefits. That rule

will be satisfied by majority voting about the level of government services."
True, false, or uncertain? Explain.

3. In one school district, 17,000 voters are choosing among three alternative
proposed levels of spending—$3,000 per student, $6,000 per student, or
$10,000 per student. The preferences of the voters, which are single-peaked,
are shown here:

Spending Level	No. of Voters Who Prefer
$ 3,000	4,000
6,000	6,000
10,000	7,000

If this district chooses among these three levels by majority voting, explain
which level will be selected.

4. Suppose three equal-sized groups of voters in a community are trying to
select the amount of school spending per pupil. The options are to spend
$3,000, $7,500, or $12,000 per pupil. The lowest level would allow only a
bare-bones academic curriculum, the middle level would permit more
varied academic courses and some transportation service, and the highest
level would allow bus transportation for all students and extracurricular
activities in addition to academics. The positions of the three voting groups
are shown here:

Group	Most Preferred	Second Choice	Least Preferred
I	$ 3,000	$ 7,500	$12,000
II	7,500	12,000	3,000
III	12,000	3,000	7,500

Thus, group I represents those trying to minimize government spending,
group II are the middle-of-the-roaders, and group III represents the all-or-
nothing viewpoint.

a. Plot the positions of the three groups on a diagram with level of
preference on the vertical axis and level of expenditure on the horizontal
axis. Connect the plots for each group with lines. Are the preferences of
these groups single-peaked?

b. What level of spending will be selected by majority voting?

c. Can you think of any ways for this community to select a level of school
spending and avoid the problem of majority voting?

SELECTED READINGS

Holcombe, Randall G. "Concepts of Public Sector Equilibrium." *National Tax Journal* 34,
no. 1 (March 1980): 77–80.

Inman, Robert. "Testing Political Economy's 'as if' Proposition: Is the Median Voter Really
Decisive?" *Public Choice* 33 (Winter 1978): 45–65.

Johnson, David. *Public Choice, An Introduction to the New Political Economy.* Mountain View, California: Bristlecome Books, 1991.

Mueller, Dennis C. *Public Choice II.* Cambridge: Cambridge University Press, 1989.

Romer, Ted and Howard Rosenthal. "Bureaucrats Versus Voters: On the Political Economy of Resource Allocation by Direct Democracy." *Quarterly Journal of Economics* 93 (1979): 563–87.

APPENDIX

Indifference Curve Approach to Voting Models

The economic analysis in this chapter used individuals' demand curves and tax prices to determine desired amounts of government service. Welfare comparisons among alternative allocations were made using a simple measure of consumer's surplus. This technique is sufficient for a general understanding of the theory, but to better understand and analyze more complex issues (to come later in the book), we need to examine how consumer's demand is determined. This requires some background in and use of what economists call consumer theory. This appendix does not provide an introduction to that theory; instead, it uses the theory to illustrate some of the conclusions of the chapter. For students having experience with the theory (probably a class in intermediate microeconomics), this and subsequent appendices to other chapters provide another way to view and understand the results.

Demand and Desired Government Service

In the simplest model, consumers choose between two types of commodities: private goods purchased in the market and public goods purchased in the government. Consumers pay for private goods directly through prices charged by the sellers and indirectly for public goods through taxes or fees collected by the government. Individual consumers are assumed to have no influence over prices, which are determined by the market in response to production cost and total consumer demand. Consumers are limited in the amount of both types of commodities they can consume by their available resources or budgets.

It is usually assumed that consumers can always choose among sets of these goods, that consumers' preferences for both types of goods are consistent (if *A* is preferred to *B* and *B* to *C*, then *A* is preferred to *C*), and that consumers can always be made better off by giving them more of at least one of the commodities. Finally, each consumer is assumed to choose the combination of commodities that provides the greatest possible satisfaction or happiness (often called utility by economists). These are standard assumptions used to analyze choice of private goods and are simply extended to public goods as well.

A graphical depiction of such a model is shown in Figure 3A.1. The amount of public goods is represented on the horizontal axis, and total consumption of

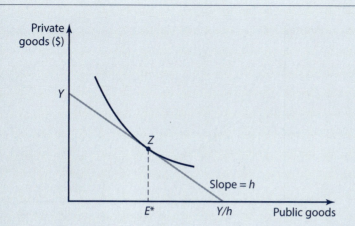

private goods is measured in dollars on the vertical axis. The convention of using dollars as the unit for private consumption is a way of combining all the different types of private goods into one measure. The consumer's resource or budget constraint is the line from point Y to point Y/hP_E, where Y equals the consumer's income, h is the consumer's share of taxes or tax price, and P_E is the cost of producing one unit of public good.[11] In other words, consumers can choose to spend all their income on private goods, all on public goods, or some on each. If this consumer pays h percent of total taxes, then for each dollar of taxes paid, there will be $1/h$ dollars for public expenditure (if $h = 0.33$ this consumer pays one-third of total taxes; a \$1 tax bill means total taxes of \$3). The slope of the budget line in Figure 3A.1, which represents the relative cost of public and private goods to this consumer, is equal to the consumer's tax price h.

The consumer's preferences for private and public goods are represented by a set of indifference curves, one of which is drawn in Figure 3A.1. Indifference curves depict combinations of private and public goods from which the consumer gets equal satisfaction. Each successively higher indifference curve (I_2 compared to I_1) shows combinations that provide greater satisfaction. The convex shape of the indifference curves occurs because of the assumptions about preferences noted previously.

If the consumer tries to get the greatest possible satisfaction given the current conditions, the combination of goods (or bundle) on the highest reachable indifference curve is selected, that is, bundle Z in the figure. Because bundle Z includes public good amount E^*, we say that this consumer will demand E^* given income Y and tax price h. As the consumer's tax price is changed (because the government selects a different tax structure), the budget line changes, and there will be a different bundle similar to Z, which now maximizes the

---

[11]If P_E is assumed to equal 1, then the production of public goods is subsumed and the amount of public good is measured by expenditure in dollars.

Figure 3A.2

Indifference curve
representation of a
monopoly bureau-
crat public-choice
model

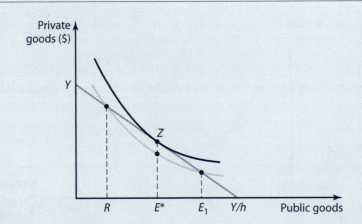

consumer's satisfaction. For each different price (holding income constant), there is a different desired amount of public good, which can then be represented as a demand curve.

Monopoly Models: An All-or-Nothing Choice

This chapter included discussion of how budget-maximizing government officials with political monopoly power could use a predetermined reversion amount to induce consumers to accept a larger amount of government expenditure than desired. That idea also can be understood using the indifference-curve/budget-line analysis outlined previously.

Figure 3A.2 depicts the preferences and budget line for a consumer with desired consumption bundle Z and thus desired amount of public goods equal to E^*. If this individual is the median voter in the community—that is, E^* is the median of individuals' desired amounts—then that amount would be selected by an unrestricted majority vote. However, if government officials allowed only one vote and offered E^1 and if the amount of the public good becomes a revision of R if the officials' proposal were rejected, this voter would be indifferent between E^1 and R. Both lie on the same indifference curve. It follows that any amount of public good just to the left of E^1 would be on a higher indifference curve and thus preferred by the consumer. Government officials could propose spending $E^1 - 1$, which would be accepted by this voter if the alternative is R.

This representation of the monopoly model also makes it clear how the maximum possible amount of public expenditure depends on the level of R. If R is less then the desired amount E^*, the maximum possible spending is greater the smaller is R. If R is greater than the desired amount, then the maximum possible spending equals R.

DEMAND FOR STATE AND LOCAL GOODS AND SERVICES

*Utility . . . maximization has already played a funda-
mental role in the development of such basic economic
concepts as consumer demand functions. . . . It takes
only a few extensions . . . to construct a theory of
state and local behavior. . . .*[1]

—EDWARD M. GRAMLICH

HEADLINES

STATE—LOCAL SPENDING AND PERSONAL INCOME, 2002

| | Dozen Highest Spending States | | | Dozen Lowest Spending States | |
State	Per-capita Spending Rank	Per-capita Income as Percentage of US	State	Per-capita Spending Rank	Per-capita Income as Percentage of US
ALASKA	1	104%	MISSISSIPPI	39	72%
NEW YORK	2	116	INDIANA	40	90
WYOMING	3	100	TEXAS	41	95
CONNECTICUT	4	140	KENTUCKY	42	82
MINNESOTA	5	107	OKLAHOMA	43	85
CALIFORNIA	6	107	IDAHO	44	82
HAWAII	7	94	MISSOURI	45	91
OREGON	8	93	SOUTH DAKOTA	46	88
MASSACHUSETTS	9	127	NEW HAMPSHIRE	47	111
WASHINGTON	10	106	TENNESSEE	48	88
RHODE ISLAND	11	100	ARIZONA	49	86
NEW JERSEY	12	128%	ARKANSAS	50	76%

[1]"Alternative Federal Policies for Stimulating State and Local Expenditures: A Comparison of Their Effects." *National Tax Journal.* 21 (June 1968): 119.

The demand for the goods and services provided by state–local governments is the relationship between the amount of those goods and services desired by consumers and the tax prices, incomes, and social characteristics of those consumers. The task in this chapter is to consider how prices, income, and various characteristics influence demand for state and local goods. After reviewing the basics of price and income elasticity, the sources of data and statistical methods used by economists to measure demand are discussed. The results of those studies are then presented, showing, perhaps surprisingly, that the desired amount of state–local government goods generally *rises* with income.

UNDERSTANDING AND MEASURING DEMAND

The standard measures of how price and income influence demand are the price and income elasticities of demand, which is the percentage change in quantity demanded that results from a given percentage change in those variables. Demand reflects how consumers behave, and the elasticities are simply measurements of that behavior. Although most of you have been introduced to the concept of demand elasticities previously, the appendix to this chapter contains a review, that you should read now if you are not comfortable with these concepts.

To use demand in policy analysis, it is necessary to estimate the price and income elasticities of demand for the specific goods and services provided by state–local governments. Those computations can be made using statistical techniques if data on the amount of services consumed, prices, incomes, and other personal characteristics are available. Those data may come from census measurements of individual governments, such as the amount of government spending, personal income, population, and tax structure for each state; they may come from the observed voting behavior in individual precincts; or they may be collected by surveying individual consumers. Variations in the selected amount of government service in the data can be related to the variations in price and income, which provides estimates of the elasticities.

Suppose, for instance, that the actual selected amounts of expenditures for different categories of services are available for a group of subnational governments (perhaps for all states, cities with populations of more than 100,000, or all school districts in a given state). Many different individuals or voters comprise each of those jurisdictions. Each individual's demand for government service is influenced by that individual's budget. The budget is

$$Y_i = C_i + t_i\,(T)$$

where Y_i = the income of person i
        C_i = private consumption spending by person i
        t_i = the state or local tax share of person i
        T = total tax collected by person i's state or local government.

The budget for the state or local government is

$$E = T + G$$

where E = total spending by the state or local government
       G = lump-sum grants received by the government

Solving for the jurisdiction's taxes T and substituting into the individual's budget yields the following:

$$Y_i = C_i + t_i(E) - t_i(G).$$

The tax share for person i depends on the jurisdiction's tax structure. If the only tax is a property tax, then that person i's tax share is

$$t_i = \frac{V_i(1 - S)}{V}$$

where V_i = taxable property value of person i
       V = total taxable property value in the jurisdiction
       S = the portion of person i's tax that is offset by tax deductions and credits.

If that tax share is substituted into the equation for the individual's budget, the result is

$$Y_i - C_i - \frac{V_i}{V}(1 - S)E + \frac{V_i}{V}(1 - S)G = 0$$

Given income, property values, and tax credits and deductions, the individual desires to consume whatever quantities of C_i and E give the highest happiness or utility from those that can be afforded. The demand for government spending E by this person depends, therefore, on this person's income, tax price (which is determined by the person's property value with a property tax), credits or deductions that reduce this person's tax cost, and the intergovernmental grants to the government.

For each jurisdiction, which individual's tax price and income should be used to characterize that jurisdiction in estimating the price and income elasticities? The answer depends on how the expenditure choice was made in that community. Given the choice or voting system, the issue is which voter in each jurisdiction is decisive in the choice; that is, which voter best "represents" that jurisdiction.

Median-Voter Models of Demand

As shown in Chapter 3, if the choice of the amount of government expenditure is made through majority voting, the selected amount will be the median (middle) of the desired amounts of all the voters. Moreover, the demand by any other voter is irrelevant because only the median position can generate majority support. It is as if the median voter's demand *is* the demand of the entire community. If the individual who desires that median expenditure can be identified, then that individual's characteristics—tax price, income, social characteristics—can be used to "represent" the community to estimate the elasticities of demand. So the issue is finding a way to identify the median, or decisive, voter, assuming that the conditions required by the median-voter model apply in that community.

Figure 4.1

Desired govern-
ment expenditure
is determined by
demand and tax
prices

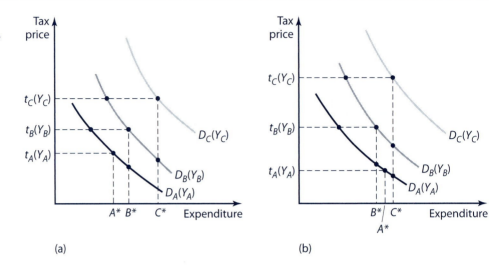

(a)   (b)

Will the median voter have median income? According to the solution to this issue offered by two economists, Theodore Bergstrom and Robert Goodman (1973), under certain conditions, the voter who has the median desired expenditure amount in a community is the voter with median income. Because data for median income and other median social characteristics generally are available for individual subnational governments, this result allows easy computation of demand elasticities, assuming that those conditions exist.[2]

The intuition behind the Bergstrom-Goodman analysis is demonstrated in Figures 4.1 and 4.2. Suppose, for example, that subnational goods are normal (demand rises with income, so the income elasticity is positive) and that tax prices also increase with income. This is different than traditional demand analysis in which different individuals face the same price. The price of a shirt at Your Favorite Store, say $30, is usually the same for both low-income and high-income customers. The prices for government goods are determined by the taxes an individual pays, however, so because taxes are not the same for individuals with

---

[2]Bergstrom and Goodman show that the following conditions are sufficient to ensure that the median voter will be the individual with median income:

1. Individuals' (or family) tax prices, h, are constant elasticity functions of income ($h = wY^c$), where $Y =$ income, and w and c are constants > 0.

2. All individuals (or families) have the same form of demand for public services, which depends only on that individual's tax price and income, and which has constant price and income elasticities ($E = WY^a h^b$). a is the income elasticity and b is the price elasticity.

3. Given the elasticities a, b, and c, ($a + bc$) must not equal zero.

4. All individuals vote in a majority vote based on their actual demand (no strategic voting).

5. The distribution of income for all population subgroups in any one community is proportional to the distribution of income for those subgroups in all other communities.

Figure 4.2

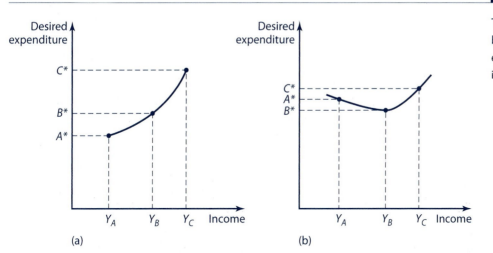

The relationship between desired expenditure and income

(a)

(b)

different incomes, tax prices for subnational government goods and services also will vary by income.[3] Given that $Y_C > Y_B > Y_A$, demand rises as income rises in both cases in Figure 4.1, and tax prices rise with income, although differently, in both cases. Given the demand and tax price for each individual in each case, the desired expenditure amounts for each individual are labeled A^*, B^*, and C^*.

In Figure 4.1a, although prices increase with income, demand increases more, so that desired expenditures rise as income rises. The lowest-income individual wants the least amount of government expenditure, the middle-income individual wants the middle amount of expenditure, and the highest-income individual wants the most expenditure. This is exactly the possibility envisioned by Bergstrom and Goodman. With a majority vote among the three, B^* would win, and individual B has middle or median income. As shown in Figure 4.2a, desired expenditure rises as income rises.

This outcome is not guaranteed, however, as shown by the situation in Figures 4.1b and 4.2b. In that case, the individual with the median desired expenditure is A, the lowest-income individual. In a majority vote among the three desired amounts of expenditure, A^* is selected, so that the median voter is the low-income individual. In this case, Bergstrom and Goodman's conditions are not satisfied. As shown in Figure 4.2b, desired public expenditure is a U-shaped function of income—the high- and low-income voters join to select a higher level of expenditure than desired by the middle-income voter.

The Bergstrom-Goodman result depends on the relationship between desired expenditure and income. If desired expenditure rises with income as depicted in

---

[3]This is true regardless of whether the jurisdiction uses an income tax. For instance, a tax on consumption or on property value also is expected to vary with income because total consumption and the values of houses chosen by different consumers vary by income.

Figure 4.2a or if desired expenditure falls continuously with income, the median desired expenditure is held by the median-income voter. If desired expenditure initially falls with income and then rises with income (the U-shaped relationship) or if desired expenditure initially rises with income and then falls (an inverted U-shaped relationship), the median voter may not be the individual with median income.[4]

Therefore, if assuming that desired expenditure is either a continually increasing *or* decreasing function of income—that is, if one believes that the Bergstrom-Goodman conditions are satisfied for the jurisdictions being considered—then the demand elasticities for the jurisdictions can be found by estimating demand for the median-income individuals. This assumption and method has, in fact, been the most used method in recent years for estimating the price and income elasticities of demand for subnational government goods and services.

But is the method appropriate? Is the relationship between income and desired expenditure always a continuously increasing one? There is some evidence that the answer to both questions is no. Byron Brown and Daniel Saks (1983) examined the spending behavior of Michigan school districts for 1970–1971, partly to test whether a continually increasing or U-shaped relationship existed between desired school spending and income. If the relationship is, in fact, U-shaped, then spending in a school district should depend on the variance, or "spread," of the income distribution as well as on median income because the voters at each end of the income distribution form a coalition to select spending. Brown and Saks reported that school spending in these districts did depend on the variance of the income distribution in each district and concluded that "the correctly specified . . . curve . . . is U-shaped with a minimum at a family income of about $8300" (in 1970 dollars).[5]

Which view of the world is correct? At this point, no one can be completely sure; it remains an unresolved issue in state–local government finance. In fact, it may be possible for *both* views to be correct. For the U-shaped function in Figure 4.2b, desired expenditure decreases with income for incomes less than Y_B and increases with income for incomes above Y_B. Thus, in communities whose residents (mostly) have incomes either below or above Y_B, the relationship in that community is always rising or falling and the Bergstrom-Goodman conditions are satisfied. In communities where residents' incomes substantially fall across Y_B, the function is U-shaped. The minimum may also occur at a different income—that is, at a different Y_B—in different communities. Even in those cases, all is not lost because Brown and Saks and others have developed methods to estimate demand for government goods and services in those instances. The difference is that a single number cannot characterize the entire relationship between income and

---

[4]The result depends on the elasticities a, b, and c from footnote 6. Substituting the equation for tax price into that for demand gives $E = Ww^bY^{a + bc}$. If $(a + bc) > 0$, then E rises as income rises. If $(a + bc) < 0$, E falls with income.

[5]Brown and Saks (1983, 37). Similar results for other cases have been reported by Jorge Martinez-Vazquez (1981) and John Beck (1984).

desired quantity in those cases; you must estimate how income and desired quantity are related at all income levels.

Demand and Voter Participation

Another potential difficulty in using voting models to analyze demand is that typically only a small fraction of eligible voters actually participates in state–local elections. This is particularly true of special fiscal elections or referenda such as those to select government spending or the property tax rate; voter turnout of only 10 to 20 percent is common in those cases. It is actually the characteristics of *voters* that determine local fiscal decisions, not the characteristics of the whole community. Moreover, the choice to vote is not random but influenced by the individual's stake in the outcome. Families with children in public schools, for instance, might be more likely to vote on the local school district budget than others and might also desire higher spending than other residents. Similarly, a larger percentage of higher-income residents as compared to lower-income residents tends to vote in local elections; if desired spending increases with income, then the voter participation patterns lead to a higher level of government spending than desired by the entire community.

The importance of voter participation patterns for measuring demand was illustrated in Chapter 3 by the study of school-spending decisions in 58 Long Island districts undertaken by Robert Inman (1978). On average, about 20 percent of the voters in these districts participated in the school-budget election, and increased voter participation led to lower selected spending levels. Consistent with that result, Inman also reported that income apparently affects both the demand for service and the choice to vote. He concluded that "the poor, who are low demanders but nonvoters, appear to be underrepresented in the public choice process" (p. 56).

Alternative Models of Demand

Of course, not all estimates of the demand for state and local government services have been based on the majority-voting/median-voter theory. One alternative theory assumes that spending decisions are made not by voting but by a government official acting on behalf of residents of a jurisdiction. This so-called dominant party model is intended to represent a situation where no credible political threat exists to the officials or party. The decision-making official is assumed to care about the per-capita (or average) taxes and expenditures in that community. In essence, studies of demand based on this theory statistically relate per-capita spending on government services to per-capita income of the residents, to some measure of per-capita tax burden (as a measure of price), and to other average characteristics of the community. (The study by Gramlich and Galper, 1983, reported on later in this chapter is an example of this type.)

Monopoly bureaucrat theories, previously discussed in Chapter 3, also are used as the foundation for studies of demand. In these theories, spending decisions are made by majority voting, but the bureaucrat controls the choices from which the voters may choose. As a result, one or more voters will be decisive, but the selection is not preferred by those decisive voters, but rather the amount those voters prefer *among those offered* by the bureaucrat. Using this theory, per-capita or median spending is related to per-capita or median-fiscal variables *plus* some political variables representing the limited choices voters face.

EVIDENCE ON DEMAND

Despite these alternative theories on which demand studies are based and very different data sources, two fundamental conclusions have emerged consistently: consumption of most state–local government services is relatively insensitive to price, and demand for state–local services generally rises with income (holding price constant). The typical ranges for estimated income and price elasticities for various categories of state–local government services are listed in Table 4.1. For comparison, the demand elasticities for selected privately provided goods and services also are listed.

Price Elasticity

When all services are aggregated, the price elasticity tends to fall in the range from −.25 to −.50, indicating demand that is very price inelastic. It further appears that

Table 4.1

Representative Estimated Price and Income Elasticities

Good or Service	Price Elasticity	Income Elasticity
For Government Expenditures		
Total Local	−.25 to −.50	.60 to .80
Education	−.15 to −.50	.40 to .65
Police and Fire	−.20 to −.70	.50 to .70
Parks and Recreation	−.20 to −.90	.90 to 1.30
Public Works	−.40 to −.90	.40 to .80
For Selected Private Goods		
Coffee	−.25	0
Electricity (Residential)	−.13 (−1.9LR)[a]	.20
Tobacco	−.51	.64
Alcohol	−.92 (−3.6LR)[a]	1.54
Gambling (Horse Races)	−1.59	.86
Restaurant Meals	−1.63	1.40
Automobiles	−1.35	2.46

[a]Long Run

SOURCES: For government expenditures: Inman (1979, Table 9.1, pp. 286–88). For private goods: Kohler (1982, Tables 4.2–4.4, pp. 101–02); Suits (1979, Table II, p.160).

among local government services, demand for education is relatively more price inelastic than demand for other traditional local government services. The demand for state–local services has similar price elasticities to that for such goods as coffee, tobacco, and (at least in the short run) electricity and alcohol.

Consumers view these services traditionally provided by state and local governments as basic commodities, similar in character to basic foodstuffs and maintenance services. Public safety and quality education are, after all, two of the most sought after characteristics of local communities. Note that it is the *characteristics* of these services that make demand price inelastic and not the fact that they tend to be provided by government. If these estimates are correct, demand for education would be very price inelastic even if education were entirely provided by private schools, just as the demand for coffee would still be price inelastic if suddenly all coffee sales were monopolized by governments.

The fact that demand for state–local government services tends to be price inelastic has many important policy implications. Because consumption is not very sensitive to price, attempts to alter the amount or type of government expenditure by reducing prices—with intergovernmental grants, for example—are only moderately successful. If the prices of state–local services rise, perhaps because of increases in the costs of providing them, consumers are not expected to reduce consumption much, requiring that increasing funds be allocated to those types of consumption. These implications are examined in Chapters 7 and 9.

Income Elasticity

State–local government services are normal goods. That is, increases in income (holding prices constant) tend to cause demand to increase, although for most of these services, demand is income inelastic—demand changes less than proportionally to the income change. Demand appears to be income elastic for parks and recreation services—that is, demand increases more than proportionally to an increase in income. That parks and recreation services are superior goods seems reasonable, given the evidence that the demand for vacations and restaurant meals is also income elastic. These commodities are demanded in greater proportion by higher-income consumers.

Although the income elasticity of demand is a measure of the percentage change in government expenditure due to a percentage change in income, it is sometimes more useful to translate this into a measure of the dollar change in expenditure due to a $1 change in income. Given the actual magnitude of expenditures and incomes, the range of elasticities reported earlier in Table 4.1 is consistent with between a $.01 to $.10 increase in state–local government expenditures for each $1 increase in consumers' incomes.[6]

---

[6] The income elasticity can be written as

$$E_D^Y = (\Delta E / \Delta Y)(Y / E)$$

where E = expenditure, Y = income, and Δ means "change in." Given values for the elasticity, expenditure and income, $\Delta E / \Delta Y$ can be computed.

As with the price elasticity, these income elasticity estimates have important implications for the expected effects of intergovernmental grants on subnational government expenditures (see Chapter 9) and for the prospects of controlling the growth of the state–local government sector through the use of tax and expenditure limits (see Chapter 11).

Introduction to Statistical Analysis

In various sections of this book, the results of specific empirical studies of public finance issues are reported. Some discussion of the statistical concepts underlying these types of studies might be helpful in interpreting the results. Statistical analysis of data to clarify economic issues is called **econometrics.**

The first step in doing econometrics is to postulate some relationship between the variables of interest. This relationship is based upon economic theory or some specific economic model. For instance, one might think of the demand for government services that arises from the median-voter model. Government spending is influenced by median income, the tax price for the median voter, production costs, and the median voter's tastes. A simple mathematical statement of the relationship might be

$$E = a + (b \cdot Y) + (c \cdot P) + (d \cdot N) + (e \cdot D) + u$$

where E = spending
Y = income
P = tax price
N = population
D = population density
u = random error, representing other potential effects on spending not captured by the included variables.

Parameters a, b, c, d, and e are to be estimated and represent the effect of a change in each of the variables on government spending. For instance, if b = .10, then spending increases by \$.10 for each \$1 increase in median income, assuming constant values for all the other variables.

After data are available, various statistical techniques can be used to make these estimates. The most common technique used by economists is multiple regression analysis, which finds the set of estimates for all parameters that "best" characterizes the observed relationship among the variables.[7] Although it is beyond the scope of this book to explain how or why multiple regression analysis works, the basic idea underlying regression analysis can be easily illustrated.

Economic theory suggests that there should be a relationship between the level of spending by a jurisdiction and the incomes of that jurisdiction's residents. Data showing per-capita state–local expenditure and per-capita income for the Northeastern states in 2002 are reported in Table 4.2. Based on economic analysis, one

---

[7]For more information about econometrics, see Jeffrey Wooldridge (2003).

Table 4.2

Spending and Income in the Northeastern States, 2002

	Per-Capita Expenditure	Per-Capita Income
Connecticut	$ 7,105	$42,919
Delaware	6,834	31,955
District of Columbia	10,804	44,731
Maine	6,262	27,324
Maryland	6,004	35,527
Massachusetts	6,698	38,944
New Hampshire	5,132	33,922
New Jersey	6,473	39,122
New York	8,523	35,590
Pennsylvania	5,999	30,240
Rhode Island	6,474	30,434
Vermont	6,264	29,024

might expect the following relationship:

$$E = C + aY + e$$

where E = per-capita expenditure
  C = constant
  Y = per-capita income
  a = marginal effect of a \$1 increase in Y on E
  e = error term.

Using the data for E and Y, regression analysis can be used to derive estimates of the variables C and a. The data points are shown in panel a of Figure 4.3. The regression technique in this case determines what linear function (line) is most consistent with these data points by finding the line for which the sum of squared differences between the actual data points and those on the line is smallest. That is, the computer program calculates the difference between each data point and the point on a line, squares that difference, adds all those squared differences, and finds which line makes that sum smallest. As a result, the line selected has the smallest average error between the estimated data points (those on the line) and the actual points.

It is important to note that this technique provides estimates of the variables in the model but cannot determine those values exactly. In the equation of the model, the error term, e, represents the effects of other factors that influence the relationship between E and Y and are not included in this analysis. Such other factors might include intergovernmental grants received by the state and localities, the state tax structure, and social characteristics of the residents. The technique also yields only estimates because the data usually represent only a sample of all the cases to be described by this model.

The results of the estimation for this example are shown in panel b of Figure 4.3 and here as well:

$$E = 1252.32 + .1609Y$$

Relationships
between income
and per-capita
state–local
expenditure,
Northeastern
states, 2002

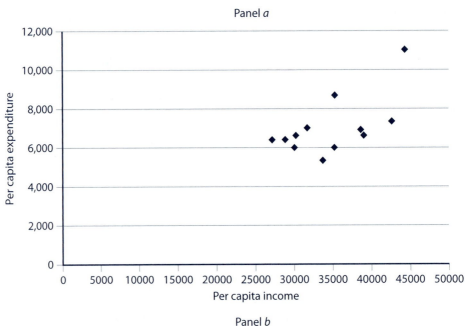

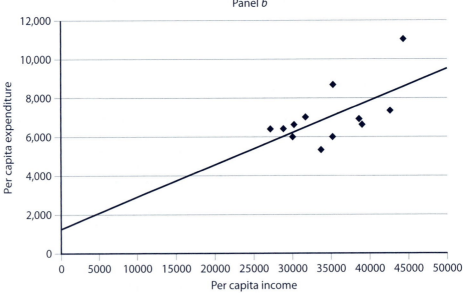

The line described by this equation best "fits" the data and is shown in the figure. Variable "C" is estimated by the Y-intercept of that line (1252.32) and variable "a" is estimated by the slope of that line (.1609). The economic interpretation
of the result is that among the Northeastern states, each $1 change in state per-
capita income is associated with about a $.16 change (in the same direction) in

state–local per-capita spending. Because "a" is positive, state–local services are normal goods.

The fitted regression line in panel b of the figure shows clearly that the model does not fit each state's case equally well. Pennsylvania, with spending of about $6,000, is essentially exactly on the fitted line, and three others, Delaware, Rhode Island, and Vermont, are close. But the model predicts spending relatively poorly for New Hampshire, where actual spending is much lower than estimated, and the District of Columbia, which has actual spending well above that suggested by the model.

These regression results also can be used to predict or forecast values for data points that do not exist currently. For instance, the estimated regression line in panel b implies that a Northeastern state with per-capita income of $33,000 is predicted to have per-capita spending of $6,562 [1252.32 + .1609(33,000)]. Thus, the results can be used to extend the analysis to cases not in the sample or to future periods of time.

The basic idea of regression captured by this example can be extended in many ways. Multiple regression differs from this one-variable case in that the separate, but related, influences of a number of variables are estimated simultaneously. The technique is still to find the relationship (or set of variables) that minimizes the sum of squared errors, but that relationship is not characterized by a single line. Each estimated variable shows the marginal effect of a change in that factor, holding all others constant. The underlying relationship need not be a linear one either. For instance, if the correct model is

$$E = C + aY + bY^2 + e$$

then the variables a, b, and C can be estimated, and the fitted relationship is not a line, but a curve.

Every empirical or econometric study, then, has three main components. One is the relationship expected between the variables based on economic, historical, or political analysis, which is called the model. Second are the data to be used to estimate or test the model. Third is the statistical techniques used to do the estimation. Many statistical issues can arise, so different statistical techniques may be necessary depending on the nature of the data or model.

Two Classic Studies

Although this chapter is intended to explain how economists measure the demand for state–local government services, you may gain a better understanding by examining the actions of specific analysts. The following is a review of two, now classic, studies of the expenditure behavior of state and local governments, one based on a majority-voting model of choice and the other on a theory of decision making by government officials. (If you are not familiar with statistical analysis and estimation, you might want to read the appendix to this chapter before proceeding.)

Bergstrom-Goodman Study. Bergstrom and Goodman (1973) examined the expenditure behavior of 826 municipalities located in 10 states based on 1962 data for three different expenditure categories: total expenditures (excluding education and welfare because not all municipalities in the sample had responsibility for those functions), police expenditures, and parks and recreation expenditures. The analysis was based on the standard median-voter theory, so they assumed that selected expenditures were the desired expenditures of the median-income consumer in each municipality.

Accordingly, actual expenditures for each category in each municipality were related statistically to median income in that municipality, the share of property tax paid by the median voter, the population of the municipality, and a set of social characteristic variables designed to capture differences in costs (density, percentage of population change 1950–1960, employment-resident ratio) or differences in demand not related to income (percentage of population 65 years and over, percentage of nonwhites, percentage of homes that are owner-occupied). Separate estimates were made for each state and combined with the full sample. Their results for that combined sample are reprinted in Table 4.3.

Consistent with other studies, Bergstrom and Goodman reported that price elasticities (with price measured by tax shares) are negative and inelastic. Consumption of these services in these cities in 1962 was not very sensitive to changes in the share of taxes paid by middle-income consumers. The income elasticities are all positive, with the demand for parks and recreation being income elastic ($E_D^Y = 1.32$) whereas the demand for all other services in aggregate is income inelastic ($E_D^Y = .64$). Moreover, by the usual statistical tests, they could conclude that these estimates were significantly different from zero.

Among the other taste/cost variables, population is positively related to expenditures, but the percentage change in population over the previous decade is negatively related, suggesting perhaps that expenditures respond to a growing population only gradually. A larger percentage of the population over the age of 65 seems related to higher expenditures, suggesting that older consumers demand more services than younger consumers with the same income and tax share. In contrast, a larger percentage of consumers who live in their own house seems related to lower expenditures, perhaps because owner-occupiers are more sensitive to property taxes than are renters.

Gramlich-Galper Study. Edward Gramlich and Harvey Galper (1973) actually undertook two analyses based on a budgetary model of behavior. A subnational government official had four objectives: (1) to increase expenditures for current services, (2) to increase private disposable incomes, (3) to increase the stock of government capital, and (4) to increase the amount of financial assets (or saving) held by the government. Obviously, all these objectives are competing, and the official is constrained in achieving them by the available resources, including the resources provided by intergovernmental grants.

Gramlich and Galper used this basic model to analyze both the aggregate annual expenditures for all state–local governments from 1954–1972 and the expenditures of 10 large cities over the period 1962–1970. In the case of the cities,

Table 4.3

Bergstrom-Goodman Results

Determinants of Municipal Expenditures, 1962, All Observations Pooled[a]

	General Expenditures	Police Expenditures	Parks and Recreation
Income elasticity ε	0.64[b]	0.71[b]	1.32[b]
	0.07	0.13	0.22
Tax share elasticity δ	−0.23[b]	−0.25[b]	−0.19[b]
	0.03	0.05	0.08
Population elasticity α	0.84[b]	0.80[b]	1.17[b]
	0.03	0.06	0.11
Crowding parameter $\gamma = [\alpha/(1 + \delta)]$	1.09[c]	1.07	1.44[c]
Percent population change (1950–1960)	−0.04[b]	−0.04[b]	−0.08[b]
	0.01	0.01	0.02
Employment residential ratio	0.12[b]	0.01	0.24[b]
	0.02	0.04	0.06
Percent owner occupied	−0.77[b]	−1.12[b]	−0.78
	0.13	0.25	0.42
Percent nonwhites	0.84[b]	0.90[b]	−0.20
	0.19	0.36	0.60
Density	−0.07[b]	0.01	−0.02
	0.02	0.04	0.06
Percent population 65+	1.75[b]	1.27	4.94[b]
	0.45	0.85	1.43
Percent living in same house (1955–1960)	−0.65[b]	−0.77[b]	−1.99[b]
	0.17	0.32	0.53

[a]Values in italics are the standard errors of the coefficients.

[b]Indicates a coefficient that is significant at the 95 percent confidence level.

[c]Indicates a value of γ that is significantly different from 1 at the 95 percent level.

SOURCE: Bergstrom and Goodman, 1973, Table 4, p. 290, reprinted with permission.

expenditures for education, public safety, social services, urban support, and general government were separated. Gramlich and Galper's analysis differed from Bergstrom and Goodman's both in theory and data. Gramlich and Galper did not have a voting model but assumed that some dictator made all decisions, and Gramlich and Galper used data over a time period—called a time-series—rather than comparing different jurisdictions at a definite time—called a cross-section.

Although the primary focus of Gramlich and Galper's results was on the effects of different types of intergovernmental grants (see Chapter 9), the analysis also provided measures of the price and income elasticities. From the time-series analysis of total state–local expenditures, the price elasticity is −.04, and the income elasticity is 1.08. Here it appears that state–local expenditures *together* increase slightly more than proportionately with income; that is, state–local expenditures are superior. Of course, as previously noted, the state–local sector grew substantially during the period used for this study, 1954–1972. Even so, this elasticity implies that state–local expenditures grow only by $.095 for each $1 increase in income. The results from the analysis of city expenditures are more similar to those of Bergstrom and Goodman. Here the price elasticities vary from −.71 to −.92, and the income elasticity is .86; demand is price and income inelastic.

Subsequent Research

During the past 30 years, there have been many such analyses of the expenditure behavior of state–local governments, a good number using the same theoretical approach as the two studies reviewed. But research involving both alternative theories and improved statistical methods gives the same fundamental results: The demand for state–local government services is, in most cases, price and income inelastic.

Application 4.1

BUSINESS DEMAND FOR GOVERNMENT SERVICE

Although individuals ultimately benefit from and pay for state–local government services, the business sector often plays a role in the public-choice process about taxes and government spending. Taxes are a cost of doing business that may arise from the sale of a product (sales or excise tax) or from the use of a productive input such as labor (unemployment insurance tax) or capital (property taxes). On the other hand, many of the services provided by state–local government become inputs into the production of goods and services by private firms. For instance, businesses use highways and other transportation facilities, are protected from loss by government public-safety services, employ workers who have been educated or trained in public schools and colleges, and use public sanitation and utility services. To the extent that government provides these services or facilities, private firms do not have to provide them separately; in that way,

government services reduce private business costs.

Voting models really do not characterize how business influences these fiscal decisions. *Individuals* vote in elections, not businesses. Businesses try to influence the outcomes of specific elections as well as the decisions of elected representatives, however, by influencing public opinion and by lobbying public officials. As with individuals, businesses are expected to work to achieve fiscal-policy objectives that are in their interest.

The self-interest of business concerning state–local government fiscal policy is not always clear, however, because businesses benefit from services and pay taxes. Certainly, businesses can be expected to and often do argue for lower business taxes, but businesses can also be concerned about the level and quality of government services. The *Wall Street Journal* (1987b) reported about a survey of the factors chief executives said are

Application 4.1—Business Demand for Government Service

"absolutely essential" when considering new office locations. The most often cited factor was "good public schools" (by 23 percent of the CEOs) followed by "a low crime rate" and "an efficient highway system" (both by 20 percent). "Reasonable state and local taxes" was also mentioned (by 17 percent).

The common perception that business groups always oppose taxes may be wrong, therefore. Interest in good state and local services can lead business groups to support higher taxes sometimes. One such case occurred in Colorado. David Shribman (1986) reported that 20 local chambers of commerce in Colorado launched a campaign to *raise* state taxes to maintain and improve public facilities and services. Shribman quoted the chambers' position as the following: "Without additional revenues, Colorado will be left little choice but to woefully underfund areas such as higher education, elementary and secondary education, our state highways, water resources, and vital capital construction and maintenance projects." The chambers took this position because an increase in the number of state residents had reduced the quality of services and because these services were seen as important for attracting and retaining businesses.

Private sector firms also sometimes become partners with the public sector to provide public services. Otis White (2004) reported how the development of the new downtown Millennium Park in Chicago—a project that ultimately cost about $475 million—was nearly half funded by private donations from business firms and real estate developers. Indeed, the private sector component of the costs ended up being more than seven times what the Mayor of Chicago had originally planned. Apparently, these private businesses saw the park as contributing to the attractiveness of Chicago and thus having an indirect benefit for their businesses. Accordingly, the firms were willing to partly fund a public facility.

SUMMARY

The price elasticity of demand is a measure of the responsiveness of consumption to changes in price.

$$\text{Price Elasticity of Demand} = \frac{\text{Percentage Change in Quantity}}{\text{Percentage Change in Price}}$$

If the absolute value of the price elasticity is greater than 1.0, demand is said to be price elastic, and consumption is very responsive to changes in price. If the price elasticity is less than 1.0, demand is said to be price inelastic, and consumption is not very responsive to changes in price.

The income elasticity of demand is a measure of the responsiveness of consumption to changes in income.

$$\text{Income Elasticity of Demand} = \frac{\text{Percentage Change in Quantity}}{\text{Percentage Change in Income}}$$

If the income elasticity of demand is negative, then the quantity demanded falls as income increases, and the good is said to be inferior. If the income elasticity is positive but less than 1.0, reflecting a smaller percentage increase in consumption than income, demand is said to be income inelastic. If the income elasticity is greater than 1.0, then quantity rises by a larger percentage than income rises. In that case, the commodity is said to be superior and demand is income elastic.

Despite the alternative theories on which demand studies are based and very different data sources, two fundamental conclusions have emerged consistently: consumption of most state–local government services is relatively insensitive to price, and demand for state–local services generally rises with income (holding price constant). When all services are aggregated, the price elasticity tends to fall in the range from $-.25$ to $-.50$, indicating relatively price inelastic demand.

Most state–local government services are normal goods. Increases in income (holding prices constant) tend to cause demand to increase, although for most services demand changes less than proportionally to the income change. The range of elasticities reported suggests between a $.01 to $.10 increase in state and local government expenditures for each $1 increase in consumers' incomes.

Some evidence shows that the relationship between income and desired expenditure is not continuously increasing: Brown and Saks (1983) reported that school spending depended on the variance of the income distribution in each district in addition to median income and concluded that "the correctly specified . . . curve . . . is U-shaped with a minimum at a family income of about $8,300" (in 1970 dollars).

DISCUSSION QUESTIONS

1. Suppose you believe that the income elasticity of demand for state government services (measured by expenditures) is 0.80. If state per-capita income is expected to increase by 20 percent over the next three years, what is the expected effect on desired state spending? If the increase in income were the only economic change expected in these years (no inflation, population growth, or change in consumer preferences), what might you expect to happen to state spending as a percentage of state personal income?

2. Suppose in one community there are three groups of voters that differ by income, with P denoting the lowest, M the middle, and R the highest. The demand for local government services by these groups is shown here. Under what conditions would the desired amount of service be the same for all three groups? Is it clear whether the tax structure that generates such a result would be regressive, proportional, or progressive? Is it possible

under other conditions that the low-income group would desire the most service, followed by the M group, and then the R group?

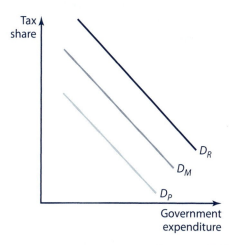

3. There is some evidence that the relationship between desired local government services (spending) and income is U-shaped; that is, lower- and higher-income voters may form a coalition to support higher amounts of local spending than desired by middle-income voters. Using two services for illustration, police protection and education, discuss why this might be the case. Remember that, in general, demand depends on price, income, and tastes.

SELECTED READING

Inman, Robert P. "The Fiscal Performance of Local Governments: An Interpretative Review." In *Current Issues in Urban Economics*, edited by P. Mieszkowski and M. Straszheim, 270–321. Baltimore: Johns Hopkins University Press, 1979.

APPENDIX

Characterizing Demand

Price Elasticity

The price elasticity of demand is a measure of the responsiveness of consumption to changes in price, defined as the percentage change in quantity from a 1 percent change in price, assuming that *only* the price changes—incomes, tastes, and other characteristics are held constant. The definition is

$$\text{Price Elasticity of Demand} = \frac{\text{Percentage Change in Quantity}}{\text{Percentage Change in Price}}$$

Table 4A.1

Price Elasticity Values and Terminology

Elasticity	Name	Effect
$E_D^P > 1$	Price elastic	$P \times Q$ falls as price increases $P \times Q$ rises as price decreases
$E_D^P < 1$	Price inelastic	$P \times Q$ rises as price increases $P \times Q$ falls as price decreases
$E_D^P = 1$	Unit elastic	$P \times Q$ constant as price increases and as price decreases
$E_D^P = 0$	Perfectly inelastic	Demand curve vertical Quantity constant
$E_D^P = u$	Perfectly elastic	Demand curve horizontal Price constant

If demand curves are negatively sloped, as is usually the case, then the price elasticity is negative because price and quantity move in opposite directions; an increase in price causes a decrease in quantity and vice versa. For example, if the price elasticity of demand is −2.0 and price rises by 5 percent (the percentage change in price is +5), then the quantity demanded decreases by 10 percent (the percentage change in quantity is −10).[8]

When evaluating the price elasticity of demand, distinction is made as to whether the (absolute value of the) elasticity is greater or less than one, as outlined in Table 4A.1. If the price elasticity is greater than 1.0, demand is **price elastic** and consumption is relatively responsive to changes in price. For example, a 1 percent decrease in price leads to a more than 1 percent increase in consumption, perhaps 3 percent. If the price elasticity is less than 1.0, demand is **price inelastic.** Consumption is not very responsive to changes in price because a 1 percent decrease in price causes a less than 1 percent increase in quantity, perhaps only 0.5 percent. If the demand curve is vertical, implying that consumers demand the same quantity regardless of price, then the price elasticity of demand equals 0.0 and demand is **perfectly inelastic.** This represents a situation where consumers will pay any price for a product, a commodity that is truly priceless. At the other extreme, if the demand curve is horizontal, implying that any amount will be demanded at a given price, but that none is demanded at a higher price, the price elasticity is undefined and demand is **perfectly elastic.**

---

[8]For convenience, the price elasticity is often presented as the absolute value of the percentage change in quantity divided by the percentage change in price, so the number is positive.

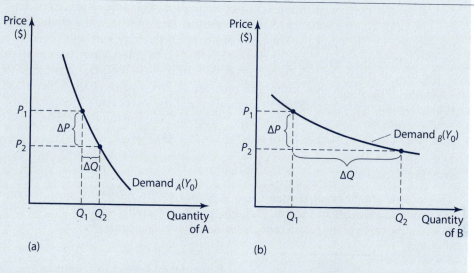

(a) (b)

As shown in Table 4A.1, whether demand is price elastic or inelastic has implications for what happens to total expenditure ($P \times Q$) as price changes. If demand is price elastic, then an increase in price causes a relatively larger decrease in quantity purchased so that total expenditure on the product falls. In contrast, if demand is price inelastic, that same increase in price causes a relatively smaller decrease in quantity so that total expenditure rises. Whether total expenditure rises or falls from a given price change depends on how much consumers react to the price change.

In some cases, the relative magnitude of the price elasticity in different markets is more important than the actual magnitude of those elasticities. For example, the price elasticity might be 0.5 in one market and 0.8 in another. Although demand is price inelastic in both cases, it can be said to be relatively more inelastic in the first market or relatively more elastic in the second. This is represented in Figure 4A.1, with demand curve A being more inelastic than demand curve B, because for the same decrease in price, quantity rises more in market B than in A. For the same reason, it could be said that demand in B is relatively more elastic than demand in A.[9]

Remember that price elasticities are simply measurements of how consumers behave. If demand is price inelastic, then consumers are unwilling or unable to alter their behavior much in response to price changes. Perhaps this is because there are no good substitutes for a commodity or consumers require some time to switch to substitute commodities or to change their behavior. For instance,

[9]To compute an approximation of the price elasticity of demand, use the formula:
$$E_D^P = [\Delta Q/(Q_1 + Q_2)]/[\Delta P/(P_1 + P_2)],$$
where ΔQ equals $Q_1 - Q_2$ and ΔP equals $P_1 - P_2$.

consumers might substitute insulation for heating fuel when heating fuel prices rise, although that substitution will not occur until consumers are convinced that the price change is likely to last for awhile, and even then the change will take some time. In that case, the price elasticity in the long run will be greater than in the short run. Finally, the degree to which consumers alter consumption in the face of price changes depends on how important the price change is to them and how much they value the product. A given price change has more impact the more one spends on a commodity and the lower one's income. Thus, demand may be more price inelastic for higher-income consumers and for products that occupy a small fraction of consumers' budgets.

Income Elasticity

The income elasticity of demand is a measure of the responsiveness of consumption to changes in income, defined as the percentage change in quantity from a 1 percent change in income, assuming that *only* income changes. The definition is

$$\text{Income Elasticity of Demand} = \frac{\text{Percentage Change in Quantity}}{\text{Percentage Change in Income}}$$

For example, if the income elasticity of demand is 2.0 and income rises by 5 percent (the percentage change in income is +5), then the quantity demanded increases by 10 percent (the percentage change in quantity is +10).

Possible values for the income elasticity of demand and some effects of those values are shown in Table 4A.2. If the income elasticity of demand is negative, then quantity demanded falls as income increases, and the good is said to be an inferior good. As consumers become richer, they consume less of this commodity and presumably substitute some others. In contrast, the income elasticity is positive if consumers demand more of a commodity as income increases. These commodities are called normal goods. If the income elasticity is positive but less than 1.0, reflecting a smaller percentage increase in consumption than income, demand is **income inelastic.** Because an increase in income causes a relatively smaller increase in quantity, expenditure rises by a smaller percentage than income, and consumption of the commodity takes a smaller share of the consumer's income than before the income increase. If the income elasticity is greater than 1.0, then the quantity rises by a larger percentage than income rises. In that case, the commodity is said to be superior and demand is **income elastic.**[10] Total expenditure on the product rises by a larger percentage than income so that consumption of this commodity takes a larger share of the consumer's income.

---

[10]Neither of the terms *inferior* or *superior* carry any pejorative connotations about quality. They merely describe consumer behavior.

Table 4A.2

Income Elasticity Values and Terminology

Elasticity	Name	Effects
$E_D^Y < 0$	Inferior good	Q falls as income increases
		Q rises as income decreases
$E_D^Y = 0$	No income effect	Q constant as income changes
$0 < E_D^Y < 0$	Normal good	Q rises as income increases
	Income inelastic	Q falls as income decreases
$E_D^Y = 1$	Normal good	Q rises as income increases
	Unit elastic	Q falls as income decreases
		$(P \times Q)/Y$ falls as income increases
$E_D^Y > 1$	Superior good	Q rises as income increases
	Income elastic	Q falls as income decreases
		$(P \times Q)/Y$ rises as income increases

Figure 4A.2

Demand and
income elasticity

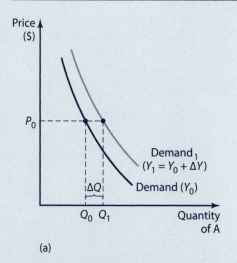

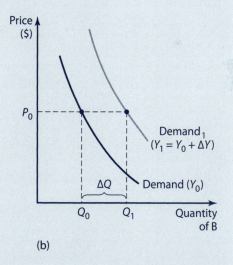

(a)

(b)

Two possibilities are shown in Figure 4A.2. In markets A and B, demand rises as income increases; A and B are normal goods. In both, the increase in income from Y_0 to Y_1 causes an increase in consumption from Q_0 to Q_1, assuming a constant price of P_0. However, the increase in consumption is greater in market B than in market A. Although the income elasticity is positive in both markets, it is larger in B. Demand is relatively more income elastic in market B, or demand is more inelastic in market A. If the income elasticity for A is 0.5 while the income elasticity for B is 1.2, for instance, spending on A becomes a smaller fraction of this consumer's income, whereas spending on B takes a larger share of the consumer's budget.[11]

Again, remember that the income elasticity is a measure of how consumers behave. It is usually argued that demand for basic commodities or necessities such as food is income inelastic because all consumers choose a basic amount of those commodities regardless of income. Of course, even if the demand for food in aggregate is income inelastic, the demand for any one food, say caviar, can be income elastic. Commodities for which demand is income elastic often are referred to as luxuries simply because they tend to be consumed in relatively larger quantities by higher-income consumers.

---

[11]To compute the income elasticity of demand, use the following formula:

$$E_D^Y = [\Delta Q/(Q_0 + Q_1)]/[\Delta Y/(Y_0 + Y_1)]$$

where $\Delta Q = Q_0 - Q_1$ and $\Delta Y = Y_0 - Y_1$

CHAPTER 5

PUBLIC CHOICE THROUGH MOBILITY

Spatial mobility provides the local public-goods counterpart to the private market's shopping trip.[1]
—CHARLES M. TIEBOUT

HEADLINES

ABOUT 14 PERCENT OF AMERICANS (MORE THAN 40 MILLION PEOPLE) CHANGED RESIDENCE BETWEEN MARCH 2002 AND MARCH 2003. RATES OF MIGRATION HAVE BEEN DECLINING BOTH IN THE LONG AND SHORT RUNS. IN THE 1950S AND 1960S, 20 PERCENT OR MORE OF THE POPULATION MOVED ANNUALLY; SINCE 1994, ANNUAL MIGRATION RATES HAVE FALLEN FROM ABOUT 17 PERCENT TO THE CURRENT 14 PERCENT

MOST PEOPLE MAKE LOCAL MOVES. GENERALLY SPEAKING, LOCAL MOVES TEND TO BE FOR HOUSING-RELATED REASONS—THE PURCHASE OF A NEW HOME, A CHANGE OF APARTMENT—OR BECAUSE OF A CHANGE IN FAMILY STATUS (MARRIAGE, CHILDREN, ETC.). OF ALL PEOPLE MOVING (23.5 MILLION PERSONS OR 8.3 PERCENT OF THE TOTAL POPULATION), 59 PERCENT STAYED WITHIN THE SAME COUNTY. MUCH SMALLER PROPORTIONS (7.6 MILLION PERSONS OR 2.7 PERCENT OF THE POPULATION) MOVED TO A DIFFERENT COUNTY IN THE SAME STATE OR TO A DIFFERENT STATE. ONLY ABOUT 1.3 MILLION PEOPLE, ABOUT ONE-HALF OF 1 PERCENT OF THE POPULATION, MOVED FROM ABROAD.

SEVERAL CHARACTERISTICS OF MIGRATION STAND OUT. YOUNG ADULTS HAVE THE HIGHEST MOVING RATES—ABOUT ONE-THIRD OF 20- TO 29-YEAR OLDS MOVED BETWEEN 2002 AND 2003. THE RELATED STATISTIC IS THAT ABOUT ONE-THIRD OF PEOPLE LIVING IN RENTAL HOUSING UNITS IN 2003 MOVED IN THE PREVIOUS YEAR. REGIONALLY, INTERNAL MIGRATION

---

[1]"A Pure Theory of Local Expenditures." *Journal of Political Economy*, 64 (Oct. 1956): 422.

HAS BEEN TO THE SOUTH AND WEST. BETWEEN 2002 AND 2003, BOTH THE MIDWEST AND NORTHEAST EXPERIENCED NET DOMESTIC MIGRATION LOSS OF ABOUT 0.1 MILLION PERSONS, WHEREAS THE SOUTH AND WEST GAINED ABOUT THE SAME NET AMOUNTS. INTERNATIONAL MIGRATION (MOVERS FROM ABROAD) OFFSET THE POPULATION DECLINES IN THE MIDWEST AND NORTH AND AMPLIFIED THE NET GROWTH IN THE SOUTH AND WEST.[2]

[2]U.S. Department of Commerce, Bureau of the Census. *Geographic Mobility: 2002 to 2003*. Washington, D.C., March 2004.

Since the publication in 1956 of "A Pure Theory of Local Expenditures" by Charles Tiebout, economists studying local governments have been fundamentally concerned with the possibility that consumer residential mobility among competing local communities may lead to efficiency in providing local public goods. The conventional wisdom regarding public goods is that because they may be consumed simultaneously by more then one consumer and because it may be difficult to exclude consumers from benefiting once the good is provided, individuals have an incentive to understate their true preference for the public good. They want to be "free riders," people who benefit from public goods provided by others without fully paying for them. This view led Paul Samuelson (1954, p. 388) to conclude that "no decentralized pricing system can serve to determine optimally these levels of collective consumption." However, the work of Tiebout and others who have followed challenges this position by suggesting that a structure of many, small local governments may be a decentralized pricing system, which generates an optimal amount of public goods.

Tiebout's work also provides a contrast to the notion of public choice by voting. In the analysis in Chapter 3, consumers could not move among communities, so any differences in public-good demand had to be resolved by voting. In Tiebout's view, differences in public-good demand may also be resolved by consumers moving to form groups that have the same demand. Consumers, then, may influence fiscal choices either by participating in the local political process (what political scientists call "voice") or by "voting with one's feet" (exit).

Probably no paper in public finance has generated as much subsequent work as that by Tiebout. His model and results have implications not only for the efficiency of the public sector but also for the income-redistribution potential of local governments, the appropriate structure of intergovernmental grants, and the need for policies to correct for fiscal disparities among localities. If stimulus to further inquiry and research is the measure, then perhaps no paper surpasses Tiebout's in importance for subnational government public finance. For that reason, this chapter reports the original Tiebout theory (although it does not substitute for reading the article) and considers some of the criticisms of and subsequent alterations to the concept. The theory and its implications are important for analyzing many issues considered throughout the book.

THE TIEBOUT HYPOTHESIS[3]

Tiebout's objective was to think of a way to achieve efficient public-goods provision and to characterize the specific conditions under which it would work. Tiebout's mechanism is easily stated. One factor individuals consider when choosing where to live is the tax and service package in the community—that is, the tax burden a resident will bear and the benefits from public services a resident will enjoy. If there are many localities, each with a different tax/service package, individuals will select the one that gives them the greatest satisfaction, presumably the one for which taxes and services are closest to their desired amount. In essence, individuals "shop" among localities and "buy" the one best for them. This analogy with private markets is important because it suggests that individuals *can* choose just what they want in the public sector and need not compromise through voting.[4]

The assumptions of the model—outlined next—spell out the conditions under which Tiebout believed this mechanism would work perfectly to bring about the efficient amount of public good in each community:

1. Consumers are mobile and will move their residences to the communities that best satisfy their preferences.

2. Consumers are completely knowledgeable about the differences in tax/service packages among the communities.

3. There are many communities from which to choose.

4. There are no restrictions or limitations on consumer mobility due to employment opportunities.

5. There are no spillovers of public service benefits or taxes among communities.

6. Each community, directed by a manager, attempts to attract the right size population to take advantage of scale economies—that is, to reach the minimum average cost of producing public goods.

Tiebout concludes that under these conditions consumers will locate in the community that best satisfies their preferences. Further, if the production of public goods exhibits constant returns to scale (rather than assumption 6 in the preceding list), and if there are enough communities, then consumers will move to the community that *exactly* satisfies their preferences. With constant returns to scale, communities of even one person can produce services at minimum average cost—community size becomes irrelevant.

---

[3]This section obviously is based on and adapted from Tiebout (1956).

[4]The government fiscal package need not be the only factor individuals consider in selecting where to live. Transportation cost, for example, and other factors also may be important.

Figure 5.1

Public service
demand in
a Tiebout
community

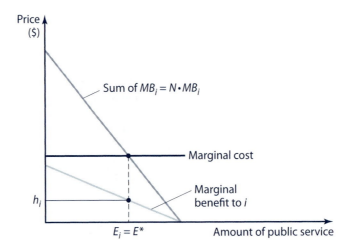

The demand for public service in that case would appear as shown in Figure 5.1. Each individual selecting this community would have the same demand or marginal benefit schedule for public service, denoted as "marginal benefit to i" in the figure. The sum of all individuals' marginal benefits is just the sum of all those identical demand curves. If all consumers pay an equal share of costs, shown as h_i, then the desired amount of public service is E_i, which is the same for all consumers in this community. Moreover, because each individual's share of marginal benefits equals each individual's share of costs (both equal to $1/N$ where N = the number of consumers), the amount of public service desired by each consumer is also the efficient amount of public service. In fact, the result of the Tiebout process in each community can be called a benefit tax equilibrium because everyone's cost reflects the marginal benefit. Unlike the equilibrium of majority voting without mobility, all consumers are perfectly satisfied with the amount of public service provided in their community, and that amount is the efficient quantity.

EVALUATION OF THE MODEL

The Assumptions

Tiebout, in his original article, noted the severity of these assumptions. Concerning the version in which consumer preferences are exactly satisfied, he wrote (1956, p. 421):

> . . . *This model is not even a first approximation of reality. It is presented to show the assumptions needed in a model of local government expenditures, which yields the same optimal allocation that a private market would.*

Although the assumptions characterize an "ideal" world, there is some validity in each.

The first three assumptions should be familiar to students of economics because these assumptions parallel the standard assumptions of a perfectly competitive market. Consumers with complete knowledge of price and quality differences face many sellers of each product and make consumption choices to obtain the greatest possible satisfaction. As Tiebout noted, of these three, the requirement of many communities may be the most troublesome. Because there must be enough jurisdictions to satisfy *every* preference, it is possible that as many communities as individuals may be required. Such one-person governments mean that public goods are consumed as private goods. That effectively eliminates government and collective consumption that would regenerate the efficiency problems for which government was created. Still, the number of different local communities in a given area or region is often large, as reflected by the data in Table 5.1. Thus, desires for many different combinations of public services can be accommodated, at least in larger metropolitan areas. The data in Table 5.1 suggest that choice from 100 to 150 general-purpose local governments and at least 50 different school districts is common even in medium-sized metropolitan areas.

In responding to this set of locational choices, there is little doubt that consumers do consider local government taxes and services in deciding where to live. Often the first question that a new or transferred employee will ask is "How are the schools around here?" Whether individuals have complete or even good knowledge about interjurisdictional tax and service differences is more problematic because collecting information is not without cost. However, one private-market sector, the real estate industry, does specialize in acquiring and providing that information to prospective residents. And other, less formal networks, often through employers, also exist for transmitting the observations of current residents to prospective ones.

Tiebout's assumption concerning scale economies poses a problem because it requires that each community attract just the right population to allow public services to be produced at minimum average cost. If the population is too small, the marginal cost of adding one more person is low, but the average cost per resident is very high. If the population is too large, both the marginal and average costs are high. With the optimal population, the community produces at the minimum of average cost—where average and marginal costs are equal. What happens, however, if the number of people who desire a specific amount of public service is greater than the optimal population for the community? Another community providing the same quantity of service must be created, but there may not be enough people to populate two communities at optimal size. In that case, the community size must change. This difficulty is avoided if the number and geographic size of communities is not fixed or if there are constant returns to scale. In short, not only must there be many communities to choose from, but they must be of efficient size to provide the desired service levels.

The assumption of no employment restrictions on residential mobility removes several potential problems, including any difference in transportation cost between job location and alternative residential locations and the new costs

Table 5.1

Number of Local Governments in Selected Metropolitan Areas, 2002

Metropolitan Area	Population (millions)	Municipalities and Townships	School Districts
New York-Northern New Jersey-Long Island, NY-NJ-PA[2]	18.323	519	492
Los Angeles-Long Beach-Santa Ana, CA	12.366	121	124
Chicago-Naperville-Joliet, IL-IN-WI	9.098	554	370
Philadelphia-Camden-Wilmington, PA-NJ-DE	5.687	375	192
Dallas-Fort Worth-Arlington, TX	5.162	199	116
Miami-Fort Lauderdale-Miami Beach, FL	5.008	97	6
Washington-Arlington-Alexandria, DC-VA-MD	4.796	84	0
Houston-Baytown-Sugar Land, TX	4.715	122	73
Detroit-Warren-Livonia, MI	4.453	209	104
Boston-Cambridge-Quincy, MA-NH	4.391	147	30
Atlanta-Sandy Springs-Marietta, GA	4.248	130	35
San Francisco-Oakland-Fremont, CA	4.124	65	85
Phoenix-Mesa-Scottsdale, AZ	3.252	29	76
Seattle-Tacoma-Bellevue, WA	3.044	78	48
Minneapolis-St. Paul-Bloomington, MN-WI	2.969	326	74
Pittsburgh, PA	2.431	457	110
Denver-Aurora, CO[1]	2.179	25	12
Cleveland-Elyria-Mentor, OH	2.148	126	48
Columbus, OH	1.613	219	57
Providence-New Bedford-Fall River, RI-MA	1.583	138	10
Buffalo-Niagara Falls, NY[2]	1.170	63	37
Louisville, KY-IN	1.162	186	22
Dayton, OH	0.848	97	42
Tucson, AZ	0.844	5	17
Albany-Schenectady-Troy, NY	0.826	101	49
New Haven-Milford, CT	0.824	28	3
Baton Rouge, LA	0.706	35	9
Syracuse, NY	0.650	95	36
Columbia, SC	0.647	29	6
Madison, WI	0.502	108	32
Lansing-East Lansing, MI	0.448	74	28
Ann Arbor, MI	0.323	28	11

Population and number of governments in 2002 for metropolitan statistical areas as defined in 2003.

SOURCE: U.S. Department of Commerce, 2002 Census of Governments.

created by the need to change job location for whatever reason. Tiebout envisioned someone living on capital income so that the amount of income was independent of where one lived. With that exception, and possibly one for certain types of self-employed individuals, this assumption will not be met in reality. Certainly some actual situations come closer to meeting this assumption than do others. For any given job and job location, individuals may have a choice of several or many communities in which to live, with equal transportation cost to that job. This is reflected in traditional urban economics models with a central business district or job center circled by suburbs at different distances. To the extent that a good number of such choices provide different tax/service packages in a given metropolitan area, this assumption may be approximated.

The most important assumption for the efficiency implications of the Tiebout model, and yet the most troublesome, is the absence of externalities or fiscal spillovers. As Tiebout (1956, p. 423) noted, "There are obvious external economies and diseconomies between communities." As noted in Chapter 2 and elaborated on in Chapter 6, the existence of externalities is a primary reason individual consumers *should* group together for collective consumption. If those externalities extend across jurisdiction boundaries and if the amount of public service selected in each community is efficient for that community (as in a Tiebout world), those amounts will not be efficient from the overall society's viewpoint.

There are several ways of correcting for the inefficiency caused by interjurisdictional externalities, two of which are most often discussed. First, externalities can be eliminated if governments are bigger (geographically and with larger population). If all those who benefit or pay for a public service are members of the same government, then there is no externality. But governments large enough to eliminate externalities may be too large to include only individuals with the same preferences for public service. This creates a potential tradeoff of these two factors, which is discussed in detail in Chapter 6. Second, intergovernmental grants can be used to induce local governments to change their amount of public service to that which is socially efficient (discussed in Chapter 17). This can be accomplished without altering the size of those recipient governments.

Recognizing the potential violations of the assumptions in actuality, it is appropriate to note Tiebout's own conclusion (1956, p. 424):

> If consumer-voters are fully mobile, the appropriate local governments . . . are adopted by the consumer-voters. While the solution may not be perfect because of institutional rigidities, this does not invalidate its importance. The solution . . . is the best that can be obtained. . . .

In other words, because there are moving and information costs in reality, consumers may not move from a community because of relatively small differences between their desired public-service amounts and those provided. The Tiebout process may not lead to all consumers in a community having the *same* demand for public service, but they may have *similar* demand. By reducing the variance in public-sector demand, the Tiebout process may reduce the inherent dissatisfaction with a voted public-service amount.

Property Taxes and Stability of the Model

A more fundamental criticism of the model than noting the severity of the assumptions is the possibility that even if the assumptions *are* met, the process may fail to provide an efficient amount of local public goods. This possibility arises if the local public goods are financed by something other than benefit charges or head taxes. For example, property taxes remain the major locally generated source of revenue for local governments. In that case, in choosing to reside in a given community, an individual also selects the amount of public services to receive. The amount of taxes an individual will pay toward those services (the tax price), however, depends on the *value* of the house the individual chooses to consume. In other words, with property tax financing, the choice of where to live and what type of house to consume are made simultaneously and, therefore, must be analyzed together.

The basic elements of the potential difficulty with the Tiebout model created by property tax financing are best shown by an example. Suppose that a metropolitan area is divided into two school districts with the economic characteristics shown in Example 5.1.

Example 5.1

Community A	Community B
Big Houses, $300,000 value	Small houses, $150,000 value
Tax Rate = 4% of value	Tax Rate = 3% of value
Tax per house = $12,000	Tax per house = $4,500
One pupil per house	One pupil per house
Spending per pupil = $12,000	Spending per pupil = $4,500

Suppose also that these two governments were selected through the Tiebout process; that is, each family has selected the district that exactly satisfies their education preferences. In addition, families also have purchased the type of house they demand. Families in community A are *willing* to pay $12,000 for a year of education whereas families in B are willing to pay only $4,500, given the prices for all commodities and their other consumption choices. Given the assumptions of the Tiebout model (no externalities, no moving costs), both communities are providing the efficient amount of education service, and there is no consumer dissatisfaction in either community.[5]

The difficulty with the model is that this Tiebout equilibrium may not be stable because some individuals may be able to make themselves better off by moving. If one of the families in community B was to build a small, $150,000 house in community A, that family would consume the higher amount of education service in that district without paying its full cost. Given the 4-percent tax rate in comunity A, the tax on a $150,000 house would be $6,000 rather than the $12,000 paid by other residents. For that $6,000 in taxes, this new family would enjoy slightly less than $12,000 of per-pupil education spending.[6] Although that family was not willing to pay $12,000 to receive $12,000 of education spending (or else they would

---

[5] Of course, expenditure on education may not measure the amount of education service, particularly if environmental conditions or prices vary between the communities. Here the assumption is that they do not differ. See Chapter 7 for more on this issue.

[6] The per-pupil spending in community A falls because one more pupil is added but only $6000 of new taxes are added. The amount of the anticipated decrease depends on the number of residents of A. For instance, if there were originally 100 families in A, spending falls to $11940.590 ($1,206,000/101). If there are initially "many" families in A, the decrease in spending expected by a mover is insignificant.

Figure 5.2

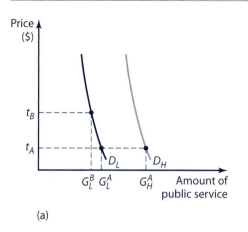

(a)

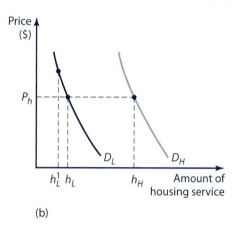

(b)

Demand for
housing and
public services
together

have located in community A to begin with), they might be willing to spend $6,000 to receive, say, $11,950 of education spending. The trick is to own a house with below average value in a community providing a large amount of service.

The important point is that some families might be willing to move to a community with higher-valued property and a different tax rate even if they have to consume more government service and less housing than they demand. The demands for local government service and housing by L-type people (low spending) and H-type people (high spending) are shown in Figure 5.2. If an L-type family builds a small house in Community A, the family's tax price for local services is lower than in Community B and thus the family demands more service (level G_L^A). However, the actual amount provided in Community A is (nearly) G_H^A. If the L-type family moves to A and consumes that level of government service, it will require more taxes and thus less spending on housing h_L^1 versus h_L). But a family might be willing to make that tradeoff, for instance, accepting $11,950 of school spending per pupil (with taxes of $6,000) and buying a somewhat smaller house than demanded. This seems particularly likely if there is a sufficiently lower tax price or if the family values the extra government spending (which it doesn't pay for fully).

In other words, even if a perfect Tiebout equilibrium could be achieved, tax financing generates an inherent instability. The incentive that induced this family to move from B to A exists, of course, for *all* (or at least many of) the families in community B. If any one family makes this move, the Tiebout equilibrium is destroyed. The amount of education spending in community A is no longer equal to the efficient amount; dissatisfaction with the amount of government spending arises as consumers with different public-service demands enter the community.

The homogeneity of demand characteristic of the Tiebout equilibrium can be restored in two ways. Community A could prevent a consumer from having a $150,000 house (discussed in the following section), or the original residents of A could exit to a third community. The residents of A might face the same type of incentive as those of B do in the example, if, for instance, there is a community of $500,000 houses with per-pupil spending of $15,000. It is this possibility that led Bruce Hamilton (1975) to note that the instability of the model could give way to a game of "musical suburbs" with everyone trying to move "up" to a wealthier community.

It is important to note that the potential instability of the model is not unique to property taxes but occurs with any tax other than a pure benefit charge or a head tax. If a proportional local income tax financed the local public good, for example, individuals from a lower-income/lower-spending community would similarly be made better off by moving to a higher-income/higher-spending community. The point is that if *both* the demand for the public service and the demand for the private good that determines taxes (housing for a property tax, leisure for an income tax) are the same (or highly correlated) for all consumers in each Tiebout community, then the difficulty will not arise. This is illustrated in Example 5.2.

Suppose again that two communities comprise a Tiebout equilibrium, providing only education, with economic characteristics as shown in Example 5.2.

Example 5.2

Community A	*Community B*
Big Houses, $300,000 value	Small Houses, $150,000 value
Tax Rate = 4% of value	Tax Rate = 8% of value
Tax per house = $12,000	Tax per house = $12,000
One pupil per house	One pupil per house
Spending per pupil = $12,000	Spending per pupil = $12,000

Unlike Example 5.1, both residents of A and B are willing to pay $12,000 to enjoy $12,000 of per-pupil educational service; that is, they have the same demand for educational service. But the residents of A and B have different demands for housing, which is the commodity that determines their tax payment. Residents of A like big houses whereas those in B prefer small ones. Although this could occur because residents of A have higher incomes than residents of B, it might also occur simply because residents of B prefer to spend their income on something else—vacations to Hawaii, for instance.

As in the first example, this equilibrium is not stable. If a resident of community B builds a small, $150,000 house in A, taxes again would be $6,000 to consume slightly less than $12,000 of educational service. By moving, this consumer suffers a small decrease in government education spending, although the consumer also enjoys a large decrease in tax cost. With the tax savings, the consumer can purchase other goods (including, of course, substitute private education service) to increase happiness.[7]

---

[7]Of course, if the demands for both government service and the good to be taxed locally (such as housing) are highly related to income, then this instability may not arise. In that case, higher-income consumers may demand both more government service and more housing.

EXTENSIONS OF THE TIEBOUT MODEL

Fiscal Zoning

The potential efficiency of the Tiebout mechanism may be blocked if an individual can pay less than the average cost of local public goods. If public goods are to be financed by property taxes, this is accomplished by consuming a less-than-average value home. This difficulty would not arise if there was some method of preventing the consumption of lower-value housing in a community—that is, preventing the migration of consumers desiring small houses into communities of consumers who desire big houses as in the examples. It has been suggested that various forms of land-use restrictions or zoning laws may function, although imperfectly, as such a method.[8]

The simple solution is to merely prohibit consumption of housing with *value* that is less than that of the original houses in each community. Using the conditions of Example 5.1, individuals would not be allowed to move into community A unless they were willing to consume a $300,000 house. In that case, individuals from community B would not move because they would have to pay the full average cost of the education in A, which they revealed as less attractive by originally choosing community B. The *value* of the house is what matters because the value determines the property tax liability in any given community where everyone pays the same tax rate. Thus, individuals could consume small houses in community A if they were willing to have the houses valued as $300,000 houses.[9]

Of course, such explicit value-based zoning rules may not be possible, so the question becomes whether a set of rules defended for a nonexclusionary reason, such as safety, effectively serves the same purpose. For instance, rules on minimum lot size, minimum setback from streets, and required construction methods and materials serve to increase the production cost of housing and to impose a minimum "type" of house allowed in a community. Restrictions also may be imposed privately rather than by government. For example, a new suburban community may be built by one or two developers who effectively zone the community for housing value by building only similar-value houses. These styles can then be preserved through deed restrictions that prevent subsequent owners from altering the character of the community without the consent of all. This practice is common because many builders offer separate developments of "affordable," "family," or "executive" homes.

In fact, there is some difference of opinion among economists and local government experts about whether local jurisdictions can or do actually use zoning to restrict entry to communities or force minimum property tax payments. This issue is important because it is crucial to how one views the property tax, as well as for determining whether local governments provide efficient amounts of service. If local communities use housing zoning and regulations to enforce a minimum required amount or value for housing, and if the number (and size) of communities

---

[8]See, for example, Hamilton (1975), Fischel (1978), and Fischel (1992).

[9]Housing is the target of restrictions only because a property tax is presumed. If public services are financed by a beer tax, then minimum amounts of beer consumption would be required. Similarly, if local governments use an income tax, the residence restriction must be on income.

can vary, then households cannot escape part of the public-service cost by consuming a less-than-average value house. As a result, the local property tax functions as a benefit tax or user charge, with each household paying the full cost of the services in their community. In that case, the property tax on the zoned or regulated minimum house is the price that each household must pay to enjoy that jurisdiction's services, which is also called the "benefit view" of the property tax.

Peter Mieszkowski and George Zodrow (1989) have been prominent in arguing that fiscal zoning usually is not feasible or actually accomplished. Because they believe either that zoning regulations are not sufficient to mandate a minimum house *value* or that legal restrictions prevent the attainment of fiscal zoning even if desired by a community, they argue "that perfect binding zoning is not in fact observed in practice". Further, they take the strong view that "a majority of researchers . . . reject the assumption of perfect . . . zoning and conclude that a national system of property taxes is distortionary [not a benefit tax] . . ." (Mieszkowski and Zodrow, 1989, p. 1140). On the opposite side, William Fischel argues that "Because of the broad statutory authority for zoning and judicial deference to legislative economic decisions, a local government that wants to protect its property tax base can select from a long menu of exclusionary devices" (1992, p. 173). Fischel includes in this menu rules regarding a master plan set by the planning commission, constraints on required street frontage, yard setbacks, off-street parking, minimum house floor area, height restrictions, developer or public service impact fees, as well as the common example of minimum lot size. As Fischel notes, tongue-in-cheek, "The family of eight that wants to rent part of a lot in Scarsdale and park two house trailers on it and send their kids to Scarsdale's fine schools is apt to find a few regulations in the way" (Fischel, 1992, p. 171). This difference of opinion cannot be resolved here, so we will examine the implications if fiscal zoning is used.

If fiscal zoning is used effectively to restrict entry, it means that communities are cross-classified by both the amount of public good or service and housing values. If there are only two levels of desired government spending, High and Low, and two types of houses, Big and Small, fiscal zoning could be used to preserve four different communities, as shown in Example 5.3. Without fiscal zoning, households from the Small:Low community could benefit from moving to Big:High if they could consume a small house. Similarly, households from Small:High (Small:Low) potentially could gain by living in Big:High (Big:Low) if they could consume a small house. That is prevented by house-zoning rules.

Example 5.3

Types of Tiebout Communities

Housing Type	Government Spending	
	High	*Low*
Big	Big:High	Big:Low
Small	Small:High	Small:Low

   The separation of local communities by the demand for housing and public service and the maintenance of the separation by zoning raises an important equity
issue. Because the demands for both housing and public service tend to increase
with income (in economic parlance, both are normal goods), the separation of
communities by those demands may lead to communities classified by income.
Using Example 5.3, households in community Big:High may have the highest
incomes followed in order by communities Big:Low, Small:High, and Small:Low.
In preventing a Small:Low household from occupying a small house in community Big:High by zoning, an explicit decision is made to maintain the satisfaction
of the highest-income households and prevent an increase in the satisfaction of
the lowest-income households to preserve efficiency. Although there may be other
(perhaps even more effective) means of redistributing income, it may still be
objectionable to a free society to legally limit where a person may live based
on income.

   More communities also may be needed to achieve a Tiebout equilibrium as a
consequence of property tax financing and fiscal zoning because each community
must have residents with the same desired amount of public service *and* housing
value. This creates another problem if the number of households with any particular combination of desired amounts is too small to achieve any scale economies
in the production of the public good. It may be, for example, that only one household prefers combination Small:High. The choice then is to have a one-person
community, which would be inefficient, or absorb that household into community
Big:High, which also seems inefficient. There is, however, an economic response
that may allow mixed housing types to coexist efficiently in the same community,
as discussed in the next section.

Fiscal Capitalization and Homogenous Communities

In using zoning to ensure that all residents of a community desire not only the
same amount of public service but also the same value housing, many homogeneous communities are required. But if the tax advantage of a small-house consumer in a big-house community is offset by a higher price for that small house, a
process called tax or fiscal capitalization, then big and small houses might be able
to coexist in the same community as long as consumers still desire the same public service.

   Suppose that one more community (call it Mixed:High) is added to the four in
Example 5.3. This one has a High amount of spending ($12,000 per pupil) but an
equal number of big and small houses (houses that are valued at $300,000 and
$150,000 in the homogeneous communities). If the values are the same in the
mixed community, the average house value is $225,000, necessitating a tax rate of
5.33 percent to generate $12,000 of revenue per household. Big-house owners
would pay almost $16,000 in taxes and small-house owners would pay almost
$8,000, although both would receive $12,000 of educational service. The three communities are characterized in Example 5.4.

Example 5.4

Big:High	*Mixed:High*	*Small:High*
$300,000 Houses	Half $300,000 and half $150,000 Houses	$150,000 Houses
Tax Rate = 4%	Tax Rate = 5.33%	Tax Rate = 8%
Tax = $12,000	Tax, Big = $16,000; Tax, Small = $8,000	Tax = $12,000

The conditions of Example 5.4 will not persist because small-house consumers pay less in the Mixed:High community than for the same amount of service in Small:High whereas big-house consumers pay more in Mixed:High than in Big:High. One expects therefore that small-house consumers would attempt to move to Mixed:High, increasing the demand for small houses in that community and increasing their price. Similarly, big-house consumers are expected to attempt to leave Mixed:High, decreasing the demand for big houses in the Mixed community and reducing their value. The changes in price are expected to continue until the higher price for small houses in the Mixed:High community (compared to the Small:High community) exactly offsets the lower taxes, and until the lower price for big houses in the Mixed:High community (compared to the Big:High community) exactly compensates for the higher taxes.[10]

If this occurs, economists say that capitalization is complete or that the full amount of the tax difference has been capitalized into house values. Please note that capitalization is nothing more than the change in the price of an asset due to a shift in demand. For complete capitalization, the price of a small house in the Mixed:High community must increase by the present value of the tax difference between the homogeneous and mixed communities, while the price of a big house in the Mixed:High community must fall by a similar amount (they will be equal if an equal number of big and small houses exist in the Mixed:High community). Assuming a discount rate of 10 percent, small houses would be valued at $176,087 and big houses at $273,913 in the Mixed:High community.[11]

The total residence cost in any community is the price of the house plus the present value of the future tax payments. The present value of future taxes equals

$$\frac{T_1}{1 + r} + \frac{T_2}{(1 + r)^2} + \frac{T_3}{(1 + r)^3} + \cdots + \frac{T_N}{(1 + r)^N}$$

where

T = Annual tax payment

r = Discount rate

N = Time period

---

[10]Of course, the supply of houses can also adjust, with more small houses and fewer big ones resulting from the change in prices. If this occurs, the tax difference is not capitalized into the value of the house but rather into the value of the land used for a particular type of house.

[11]Hamilton (1976b) derives the equations for full capitalization.

If N is infinite and all tax payments are the same, this equals T/r. The total residence cost is the same for any given type of house regardless of the community. Assuming a 10-percent discount rate and an infinite house life, this is shown in Example 5.5.

***Example* 5.5**

Big Houses in Big:High vs. Big Houses in Mixed:High
$300,000 + $120,000 = $273,913 + $146,087
Small Houses in Small:High vs. Small Houses in Mixed:High
$150,000 + $120,000 = $176,087 + $93,913

This potential for capitalization of interjurisdictional differences in taxes or services has several important implications. First, if capitalization occurs, fewer communities are needed to achieve an efficient equilibrium. (Again, it is necessary to have a separate community only for each desired amount of public service, not for every combination of desired public service and housing amount.) Second, because communities need be homogeneous only in the desired amount of public service and can include households desiring the whole range of housing, the equity concerns about the Tiebout process may be mitigated. A small-house consumer in a high tax-rate community of other small houses is not worse off than another small-house consumer in a lower-rate community because (identical) small houses are less expensive in the high-rate community. Third, complete capitalization means that the local property tax functions as a benefit tax with each household paying the full cost of the services in its community. This may seem strange because small-house consumers pay lower taxes than big-house consumers; however, the true cost of residing in the community and consuming its services is not just the tax but also the difference in price for the type of house desired. The true cost (in present-value terms) of consuming the mixed community's services is $120,000 for *both* types of housing consumers.[12]

Implications and Limits of Capitalization

One important issue is whether this type of capitalization occurs, and if so whether it can be maintained. In the short run, capitalization almost certainly does occur, although it may not be sufficient to offset all fiscal differences. Capitalization results, essentially, from competition for the available land and housing in the fiscally desired community. So first of all, anything that limits that competition will restrict capitalization. Thus, capitalization may be incomplete if there are not enough communities, if individual mobility is limited by jobs or other factors, or if individuals do not have complete information about differences.

---

[12]For big-house consumers, the cost is $146,087 *minus* the $26,087 house price advantage; for small-house consumers, the cost is $93,913 *plus* the $26,087 house price addition.

In the long run, capitalization might not be maintained because either the housing supply or the number of communities might change. If the value of a particular type of housing increases in one community because it is in a fiscally desirable situation, then either more of that type of housing might be constructed, or an entire new community with that type of housing might be created. In either case, the supply of the desired housing increases, and prices fall. Capitalization is eliminated. However, if the new community is farther from work or shopping locations and requires higher transportation cost, then the new houses may not be perfect substitutes for the older ones, and some price differences (capitalization) could remain.

Finally, capitalization may not occur if individuals in one community do not *value* the additional government services offered in another jurisdiction, even if tax rates or housing prices are lower. Suppose that one higher-income community has a higher level of expenditure and lower tax rates than another community. If small house consumers move from the second to the first community, they might pay less than the average cost of the higher level of services in that community but still pay more taxes than currently. For instance, a family might be able to receive $1,000 more per student in educational spending, but have to pay $400 more in taxes. But if the *value or utility* the family receives from the additional educational spending is not worth at least $400, then they would not move between these communities. This possibility, suggested by Yinger (1982), implies that capitalization would not occur (at least fully). If individuals are not willing to move to the high-spending community to take advantage of the lower tax rate, then demand and the price for small houses do not change.

PUBLIC CHOICE: EVIDENCE AND REALITY

What can be said about the comparative role of voting and migration as public-choice mechanisms in reality? No one believes that a perfect Tiebout equilibrium can be obtained because information and moving costs are not zero. Even if it could be obtained, it would likely not be efficient because externalities are always present and because capitalization can remove the incentive for communities to be homogeneous. Casual observation supports this view because community votes on fiscal matters are seldom (if ever) unanimous, which would be expected in a perfect Tiebout world.

Nevertheless, the Tiebout process does seem to apply up to the limits of those transaction costs, so that the greatest differences in desired public service are offset by residential choices. The tendency for individuals with similar demands for public services to group together, particularly in larger urban areas, was demonstrated in research reported by Edward Gramlich and Daniel Rubinfeld (1982). Based on a survey of individuals asking about desired changes in spending and taxes, Gramlich and Rubinfeld estimate individual demand functions for public services. They then test whether demands are similar for people who live in the same community and whether those demands are close to the actual level of services offered in that community. They find that "in these urban communities, there appears to be a high degree of grouping by public spending demands. . . .actual spending does conform to desired levels in these Tiebout-like communities, it does so less in rural communities where a Tiebout mechanism is unlikely to operate. . ." (Gramlich and Rubinfeld, 1982, p. 558). In short, the Tiebout process seems to have reduced the variance in desired government service within the urban communities in their sample.

If individuals with similar public service demands are to group together, then there should be more communities in metropolitan areas where there are greater differences in desired government spending, other factors equal. Research by Nelson (1990) and Fisher and Wassmer (1998) suggests that this is exactly the case in the United States. Based on data from 1982, Fisher and Wassmer show that substantial differences exist in the number and average size of municipalities across major metropolitan areas. The average size municipality in these urban areas had a population of about 34,000; however, in some areas with many more localities, the average municipality was much smaller (average population of 2,300) while in others there were fewer, but larger (average population of more than 700,000) jurisdictions. For instance, the metropolitan areas of Chicago, Philadelphia, Newark, Cleveland, and Louisville all had many, very small localities, whereas in the areas of Baltimore, San Diego, Phoenix, Milwaukee, and New Orleans, there were few relatively large localities. After comparing the number of localities to variation in demand for local government services in the urban area, they concluded that

> "The empirical findings show that after controlling for political, historic and institutional factors, variations in the characteristics that affect demand for local government services do influence the number of local governments. This result is consistent with the hypothesis put forth by Tiebout." (Fisher and Wassmer, 1998, p. 444)

The Tiebout process thus serves to reduce but not eliminate the variance in desired government service within communities, and thus the inherent dissatisfaction with the voted outcome. Because differences are not eliminated, however, voting is required and used to find a compromise position within those remaining differences of opinion. Rather than competing public-choice mechanisms, they are complementary. There is substantial evidence that residential choice is greatly influenced by the type of schools in a community. For instance, families who choose to live in a community are likely to approve generally of the amount of local school spending, but differences may still arise over the allocation of those funds between music and advanced math, for example.

Perhaps the most important legacy of the Tiebout idea is the emphasis on the welfare advantage of a decentralized government structure. That advantage must be balanced against other economic forces that require a more centralized government to bring about economic efficiency. We turn to that issue in Chapter 6.

SUMMARY

If there are many localities, each with a different tax/service package, individuals will select the one that gives them the greatest satisfaction, presumably the one for which taxes and services are closest to their desired amount. This view, offered by Charles Tiebout, suggests that individuals *can* choose just what they want in the public sector and need not compromise through voting.

As a result of the Tiebout process, all consumers can be perfectly satisfied with the amount of public service provided in their community, and that amount can be the efficient quantity.

Because moving and information costs occur in reality, consumers may decide not to move from a community because of relatively small differences between the public-service amounts they desire and the public-service amounts they already have. The Tiebout process, then, may not lead to all consumers in a community having the *same* demand for public service, but they may have *similar* demand.

The Tiebout process may fail to provide an efficient amount of local public goods if public goods are financed by property taxes. By consuming a less-than-average value home, an individual can pay less than the average cost of those goods, thereby preventing the potential efficiency of the Tiebout mechanism.

The inherent instability caused by tax financing would not arise if there were some method of preventing the migration of consumers desiring small houses into communities of consumers who desire big houses. Various forms of land-use restrictions or zoning laws may function as such a method.

If zoning can be used to limit the type of housing in communities and if the number of communities can be changed, the local property tax functions as a benefit tax with each household paying the full cost of the services in its community. A minimum tax is set on each house through zoning that is just sufficient to pay the average cost of the public services.

Because the demand for both housing and public service tends to increase with income (in economic parlance, both are normal goods), the separation of communities by those demands may lead to communities classified by income.

If the tax advantage of a small-house consumer in a big-house community is offset by a higher price for that small house, a process called tax capitalization, then big and small houses can coexist in the same community as long as the consumers desire the same public service.

With capitalization, the price of the house plus the present value of the future tax payments is the same for any given type of house regardless of the community. The true cost of residing in the community and consuming its services is not just the tax but also the difference in price for the type of house desired.

The Tiebout process serves to reduce the variance in desired government service within communities. If the differences are not eliminated, voting can be used to find a compromise position within those remaining differences of opinion.

DISCUSSION QUESTIONS

1. The following data depict the fiscal characteristics of two school districts in a metropolitan area, each composed of identical single-family houses with one pupil per house:

School District A	Characteristic	School District B
$200,000	Per Pupil Property Value	$50,000
25	Property Tax Rate (in dollars per $1,000 of value)	100
5,000	Per Pupil Expenditure	5,000

The voters who have chosen to live in both districts desire and select $5,000 of educational spending per pupil and collect property taxes to finance it. Because B has small (low-value) houses while A has big (high-value) houses, the tax rate in B is much higher than in A.

a. Would a voter in district B prefer to live in a big ($200,000) house in district A? Why?

b. Would a voter in B prefer to live in a small ($50,000) house in district A? Explain.

c. Suppose there is a third school district to choose from with an equal number of big and small houses so that the average per-pupil value is $125,000. What tax rate is required in this district to spend $5,000 per pupil? If small houses also cost $50,000 in this district, are small-house consumers better off here or in B? If big houses also cost $200,000 in this district, are big-house consumers better off here or in A?

d. Given your answers to part c, what do you expect will happen to the demand for big and small houses in this third district? What will happen to the prices of these houses in this mixed district?

e. Characterize the equilibrium that would allow all three districts to exist simultaneously. What does this imply about the equity implications of the Tiebout process? Do you think it is fair if some communities require higher tax rates than others to provide an equal amount of government spending?

2. The Tiebout process in this chapter represents an alternative to the majority voting model described in Chapter 3 as a way of making public fiscal decisions. Compare these two alternative theories in terms of what they predict about the nature of local governments, including political characteristics and whether efficient public-good provision is likely to result.

3. Some people have suggested that political voting and voting with one's feet simultaneously apply in determining the amounts of local public services to provide. Discuss how this might happen. How might the limitations of the assumptions in the Tiebout theory contribute to a role for voting?

SELECTED READING

Fischel, William A., "Property Taxation and the Tiebout Model: Evidence for the Benefit View from Zoning and Voting." *Journal of Economic Literature*, 30 (March 1992): 171–77.

Fischel, Willam A. "Municipal Corporations, Homeowners and the Benefit View of the Property Tax." In Wallace Oates, ed. *Property Taxation and Local Government Finance.* Cambridge, MA: Lincoln Institute of Land Policy, 2001.

Hamilton, Bruce W. "Zoning and Property Taxation in a System of Local Governments." *Urban Studies,* 12 (June 1975): 205–11.

Mieszkowski, Peter and George R. Zodrow, "Taxation and the Tiebout Model." *Journal of Economic Literature*, 27 (September 1989): 1098–1146.

Tiebout, Charles M. "A Pure Theory of Local Expenditures" *Journal of Political Economy,* 64 (Oct. 1956): 416–24.

CHAPTER 6

ORGANIZATION OF SUBNATIONAL GOVERNMENT

. . . It would be extremely desirable to find a mechanism to reduce the inefficiencies that arise from an imperfect correspondence in the provision of public goods.[1]
—WALLACE OATES

HEADLINES

"SINCE THE 1960S, . . . THE HISTORIC ROLE OF LOCAL GOVERNMENTS HAS INCREASINGLY BEEN PRIVATIZED AT THE NEIGHBORHOOD LEVEL. IN 1970, ABOUT 1 PERCENT OF ALL AMERICANS BELONGED TO PRIVATE COMMUNITY ASSOCIATIONS. BY 2004, MORE THAN 17 PERCENT BELONGED TO A HOMEOWNERS OR CONDOMINIUM ASSOCIATION . . . VERY OFTEN THOSE PRIVATE COLLECTIVE OWNERSHIPS WERE OF NEIGHBORHOOD SIZE. SINCE 1970, ABOUT ONE-THIRD OF NEW HOUSING UNITS CONSTRUCTED IN THE UNITED STATES HAVE BEEN INCLUDED WITHIN A PRIVATE COMMUNITY ASSOCIATION.

. . . MOST ASSOCIATIONS PROVIDE COMMON SERVICES OF ONE KIND OR ANOTHER. THE SERVICES MOST FREQUENTLY INCLUDE GARBAGE COLLECTION, LAWN MOWING, STREET MAINTENANCE, SNOW REMOVAL, LANDSCAPING, AND MANAGEMENT OF COMMON RECREATION FACILITIES. ANOTHER IMPORTANT FUNCTION OF MANY NEIGHBORHOOD ASSOCIATIONS IS PROTECTION OF RESIDENTS' PERSONAL SECURITY THROUGH PRIVATE POLICING.[2]"

---

[1]*Fiscal Federalism.* New York: Harcourt Brace Jovanovich, 1972, 53.

[2]Nelson, Robert H. "The Private Neighborhood." *Regulation.* Summer 2004, pp. 40–46.

The work by Tiebout and others emphasizes the advantage of decentralized government for satisfying the diverse public-service desires of consumers in an efficient way. Other economic factors may require that governments be larger than those envisioned by Tiebout to provide services efficiently. Among these are inter-jurisdictional cost or benefit externalities, economies of scale in the production of public goods, and the administration and compliance costs of government itself. The importance of these four factors is not equal for all types of subnational government services. The issue, then, is what structure—size and number—for subnational governments is best to provide each type of service. Alternatively, after a federal system of national and subnational government is in place, the issue is which level of government in the federal system ought to have responsibility for each service.

THE ECONOMIC ISSUES

Variations in Demand

The greater the variations in what individual consumers want from government and the more consumers with similar wants are grouped together, the stronger is the case for decentralized provision—that is, for having many small local governments. If all consumers desire the same amount and type of service, then there is no reason for more than one government, which would be a large one, to provide that uniform service. Conversely, if consumers with different demands for government service are served by a single government, many of those consumers will be dissatisfied because the amount of service provided by the government will be different from the amount desired. That dissatisfaction translates into lower-level happiness or welfare for those consumers than they would obtain in a community of consumers with like demand. It follows that the greater the number of different desired amounts of government service, the more governments required. More governments mean smaller ones or provision at the most decentralized level of a federal system.

The existence of different demands for government service is not sufficient to justify decentralized provision unless consumers with similar demands are, or can be, located geographically together. Two separate government jurisdictions would not help if those with the same demand are not geographically together. If consumers can freely change residential location, then the advantage of decentralized government is strengthened, as Tiebout emphasized.

Spatial Externalities

A **spatial externality** (often called a spillover) occurs when the spatial distribution of the costs or benefits of government services is not confined to the jurisdiction boundaries of the providing government. Nonresidents either pay part of the costs or enjoy part of the benefits of a government's service. Spatial externalities can cause a government's choice about taxes and spending to be inefficient from the viewpoint of the entire society. If there is a spillover of costs, residents underestimate the true social cost and demand too much of the good or service, whereas a spillover of benefits causes residents to underestimate the true social benefit and demand too little. Of course, there can be simultaneous spillovers of costs and benefits, with the effect on the efficiency of provision depending on the relative size of each.[3]

Examples abound of spatial externalities involving subnational government services and taxes. When a nonresident landlord bears part of a city's property tax burden or a city business's property taxes are passed on to buyers of its product, some of whom are nonresidents, there is a spillover of local tax costs. Similarly, when a nonresident drives on the city's streets and finds traffic flowing smoothly and safely, there is a spillover of the city's transportation and public safety benefits. Or when a student is educated at public expense in the city and emigrates to another state or town, there is a spillover of educational service.

The classic economic solution to any externality problem is to internalize the externality—that is, to force the decision maker to consider the true social costs and benefits. A simple way to do this for spatial externalities involving government is to make the government's jurisdiction big enough to include all consumers who bear costs or enjoy benefits. If all consumers who benefit from services and pay taxes are residents, then there is no externality. The possibility of spatial externalities, then, can be a factor requiring a more centralized government structure composed of fewer, bigger subnational governments.

Spatial externalities are the reason a central federal government can best carry out redistribution and stabilization policy. Expansionary fiscal policy by a state government to increase consumption, for instance, would generate benefits in other jurisdictions where the consumer goods are produced. The state's residents would underestimate the benefits of that action and therefore fail to engage in an efficient amount of stabilization policy. Similarly, a state government is unable to internalize all the costs and benefits of an income-redistribution policy. The mobility of consumers and openness of subnational government economies create the spillovers that limit subnational government effectiveness in these areas.

Economies of Scale

Economies of scale, in standard microeconomic usage, refers to a decrease in average cost as the quantity of output rises. In reference to the optimal size for governments, however, the term usually refers to a decrease in cost *per person* for a given amount of service as the population served increases. Economies of scale in that sense exist, for instance, if the per-pupil cost of achieving a given degree of education is smaller for a 5,000-pupil district than a 1,000-pupil district. To put it another way, total cost or expenditure does not have to increase as much as the

---

[3]Reciprocal externalities may also occur—that is, both spillouts of costs and benefits from **and** spillins to a jurisdiction. Wallace Oates (1972) shows that such a condition is also likely to result in an inefficient allocation of resources.

population served to keep the service level constant. This concept of economies of scale is sometimes referred to as the advantage of joint consumption: individual consumers can reduce their costs by sharing the good and its total cost with others.

An example of a good for which joint consumption might reduce per-person cost is a swimming pool. One household could purchase a swimming pool for its own use. That household could also join together with another household to purchase the pool jointly, reducing the per-household cost by half. If sharing the pool does not reduce the benefits by half, then the per-household cost of a unit of swimming service is reduced. As a special case, suppose that both households can swim as much and as easily in the shared pool as in singly owned ones. In that case, the benefit of owning a shared pool is the same as a single one, but the cost is half as great.

The evidence is not conclusive concerning the existence of this type of economies of scale for the goods and services usually provided by state and local governments in the United States. Of course, economies may exist for very small service populations but quickly be exhausted. The size where economies end is different for different services. The reasons most often given for potential economies are the elimination of duplication of inputs, increased coordination, and economies in purchasing. There are cases of services with capital-intensive production, such as water, sewer, electric, and gas utilities, where substantial economies seem to exist. In fact, government- or private-sector consolidation to produce those services is common to avoid duplicating expensive capital structures. Similar gains may be difficult for many subnational government services, which are very labor-intensive. In a review of the literature, Roy Bahl and Walter Vogt (1975, p. 13–14) conclude:

> . . . Most positive findings of scale economies are based on statistical results that show a negative relationship between population size and per-capita expenditures. There are great statistical and theoretical problems with interpreting such results as showing scale economies, and about as many studies that find a negative relationship find a positive one.

In an earlier review, Werner Hirsch (1970) divides government services into those that are horizontally integrated, which results when existing units engaging in one stage of production are under common control, and those that are vertically integrated, which occurs if production and distribution are jointly provided. Hirsch suggests that traditional services such as police and fire protection are examples of horizontally integrated services, with many production "plants" under control of one government; utility services such as water and electricity provision are examples of vertically integrated services. Using this characterization, Hirsch concludes that scale economies appear to be substantial for vertically integrated services but not important for horizontally integrated ones, noting that "the average quasi-long-run cost function of horizontally integrated services tends to be reasonably horizontal over a wide range of operations" (p. 184).

The existence of scale economies may not be relevant to optimal government size anyway if providing the good or service can be separated from producing that good or service. Scale economies arise in the *production* phase. The primary role of the government is to *provide* a given amount of the good or service. Governments too small to achieve all economies of scale on their own can take advantage of those economies by purchasing enough of the good or service for their residents from governments or private firms that are large enough to exhaust all economies.

Suppose, for example, that economies of scale exist for garbage-collection service up to 50,000 households served; that is, the per-household cost of a given quality of garbage collection (once per week, pickup at curb, trash bags required) is greater for a 25,000-household community than for larger ones. This might occur, for instance, if one standard garbage truck combined with one worker can service exactly 50,000 households per week in this area. Communities with less than 50,000 households could find their truck idle for a portion of the week (unless they had some other use for it during those times or wanted to change the quantity of service to more frequent weekly pickups). This difficulty can be resolved without making all governments bigger to include 50,000 households. One possibility is for one 25,000-household community to lease their truck to another 25,000-household community for half of each week. Another is for one 25,000-household community to contract with another 25,000-household community to pick up its garbage, subject to specific quality conditions. Still another is for all communities too small to take advantage of the economies in production to contract with a private firm for garbage pickup in those communities at a quality of service specified by each community.

By contracting with private firms or other governments and through joint purchasing agreements, governments can provide the amount and type of services desired by a small population *and* enjoy the cost advantage of scale economies in production. In contracting, each individual government retains control over the amount of service to be consumed and finances the service by taxes or government fees, although the government does not directly produce the service. When such opportunities exist, scale economies are no longer an economic issue for the optimal size and structure of government.

Joint purchasing agreements among local governments are relatively common. A recent variant of those agreements applies to joint or pooled borrowing of funds by localities to conserve on the fixed (transaction) costs of bond sales. Similarly, governments sometimes enter into joint agreement for allocating or enforcing taxes, such as a state government collecting sales or income taxes for a city. Contracting among governments or between a government and a private firm also has been common for some services (water and sewer services or public transportation, for instance). Contracting has been extended in recent years to police and fire dispatching under the 911 system, for example. In some areas, when residents of all communities dial 911 for emergency help, a central dispatching office operated by one of the communities dispatches the relevant emergency unit from the caller's government.

Administration and Compliance Costs

A final reason for few subnational governments (and thus more centralization) is to conserve the direct costs of administering those governments and the time costs for individuals to participate in the political process. **Administrative costs** include the compensation paid to elected and appointed officials and staff and the overhead (buildings, supplies, utilities) to support those officials. **Compliance costs** include such things as the costs associated with citizens becoming informed on issues and candidate positions and the potential cash and time costs associated with registering an opinion (by participating in hearings or voting, for instance). The existence of fewer subnational governments *may* reduce these costs.

To argue that centralization will reduce administrative costs is to argue that there are economies of scale in administration of government, just as there may be economies in the production of public services. For instance, one might argue that a set of small cities each with a separate manager, finance director, and planning director is duplicative, that a single set of those officers could oversee all the operations of the cities simultaneously with no loss of efficiency. Those costs could therefore be reduced by consolidating those governments into a larger unit. But there is no guarantee that such opportunities will always, or even usually, exist. It could just as easily be argued that administrators become less effective the further removed they are from the people and operations they coordinate. In that case, **diseconomies of scale** result with larger governments requiring proportionally more administrators (perhaps with more layers in the administrative hierarchy) to run as well as smaller ones. Depending on the service (or set of services) provided, administrative scale economies could be a factor in favor of more or less centralization.

A relatively centralized subnational government structure (resulting from the consolidation of small government units perhaps) would reduce compliance costs only if the number of separate governments that each individual must deal with is reduced. For instance, if all city government functions are transferred to existing county governments and each county encompasses several cities, then each resident of the county is a member of one rather than two local governments. This may reduce compliance costs because voters must participate in only one election and become informed about one set of candidates.[4]

In contrast, the consolidation of a set of school districts into one larger but independent district would not reduce compliance costs (although it might reduce or increase administrative costs as discussed previously). Each individual would still be a member of one district. Similarly the transfer of only one or two city government functions to a higher-level government in the federal system, such as a county or state, would not reduce the *number* of separate governments serving each household and thus would not reduce compliance costs.

OPTIMAL GOVERNMENT SIZE[5]

The following is an attempt to develop a structure for applying the economic issues described earlier to actual decisions about government organization and the allocation of service responsibilities among levels of government in that organization. After examining the theory of optimal government size, some applications of that theory to actual policy cases are considered.

---

[4]The gain from this example may be exaggerated. City and county elections may be held at the same time and place, and the ballot for the consolidated county election may be longer.

[5]This section is based on Oates (1972).

The Correspondence Principle

Suppose that governments provide a number of different public goods (nonrival goods), with the benefits of each confined to a fixed and known geographic area. Some of these goods benefit the entire nation (or world) once produced, whereas others benefit only a subset of the nation (perhaps even as small as one household). For example, the defense advantages of a radar system can benefit the entire nation, whereas local fire protection services can be provided feasibly only in a specific square-mile area around its location. (The area is determined largely by response time.) This type of public good, which can be simultaneously consumed in equal quantities by all but only in a limited spatial area, is often referred to as a **local public good**.

Suppose that the population has no mobility, that the average cost of producing these goods is independent of the number of people served (or the size of government), and that there is some variation in the desired amounts of these public goods among the population. Under these conditions, the optimal government structure is a separate government for each area of benefit from a public good. One central government should provide goods that simultaneously benefit all households, such as the defense radar system, and a set of separate subnational governments should provide each good that benefits only a limited number of households—for example, enough governments providing fire protection to supply the good to all households (with each one serving a specific square-mile area). Wallace Oates has called this result the **correspondence principle**, because the size of a government corresponds to the area of benefit from the goods it provides. As a result, each public good is provided in the smallest (that is, lowest-level) government consistent with no externalities.

The correspondence principle generates a federal system of governments along a spectrum from many small local governments to one national government. To justify any subnational governments, there must be variation in the desired amounts of public goods so that each government can provide a different amount of that good and confine the benefits within its boundaries. Otherwise, it would be just as efficient to have one central government provide those goods to all using a number of different production plants. For instance, if all households desired the same amount of fire protection service, then a national government could provide this function through many fire stations located throughout the nation. The only reason to have each station operated by a separate government is to provide different amounts or types of service. This raises another potential problem: The areas that are just consistent with no externalities may encompass households that desire different amounts of a good or service. Although the benefits of the radar system may go to all households in the nation, not all households may want the same amount of radar protection.[6]

---

[6]The correspondence principle applies best to goods and services that provide only direct benefits in a defined spatial area. If individuals benefit by the existence of a service, even if they do not use it directly, then the benefits can be dispersed throughout a wide area, even the nation. For instance, some individuals might want to have the option of using another states' parks, even if they do not do so now.

Figure 6.1

Optimal jurisdiction size for a service

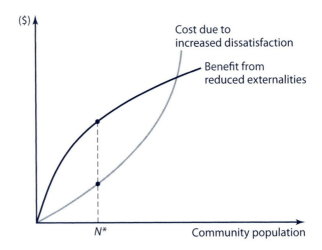

Preferences versus Spillovers

The possibly conflicting objectives of having governments big enough to avoid cost or benefit spillovers but small enough to allow uniform desired amounts of public service suggests a tradeoff between those two factors. For each public good or service, the optimal size government is the one that maximizes social welfare. As government size increases, the welfare gain from a reduced amount of spatial externality can be compared to the welfare loss due to increasing dissatisfaction among government members with the amount of public service selected. The optimal size government for each service is the one where the difference between the welfare gain and loss is greatest.

That choice of the optimal size government for some given service is shown in Figure 6.1. The cost function represents the cost or welfare loss that results as government size increases from combining individuals with different demand for public services. The total cost rises as government size increases, and the marginal cost of increasing government size—represented graphically as the slope of the cost function—also increases as size increases. This occurs if the new residents added first (as government size increases) have demands most similar to the original residents. The benefit function depicts the benefit or welfare gain from reducing spatial externalities as government size increases. Those benefits also rise as size increases, although the marginal benefit of increasing government size—represented by the slope of the benefit function—decreases. That is, the largest gains from reducing externalities occur from the initial actions to form or enlarge local governments. For a public good or service with these characteristics, the optimal population size is N^*.[7]

---

[7]If the population is not mobile, then population size translates directly to a spatial area.

Figure 6.2

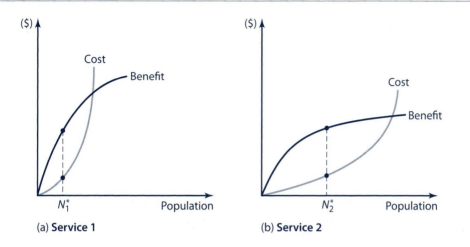

(a) **Service 1**   (b) **Service 2**

Optimal jurisdiction size for different services

For other public goods and services, changes in the benefit and cost functions occur, with a resulting change in the optimal size. For example, if the differences in desired amounts for another service were much greater than the case in Figure 6.1, the cost function would rotate up reducing the optimal N. On the other hand, if the problems of spatial externalities for another good were less severe—that is, a larger fraction of the externality is eliminated at smaller government sizes—the benefit function would rotate down and the optimal N would also decrease.[8]

In this manner, the optimal size government for every public good and service can be determined. Two examples are shown in Figure 6.2, one for a good requiring relatively small governments and one for a good with a larger, optimal-size providing government. This analysis is fully correct only if governments of any size can achieve all economies of scale in production of these goods by outside contracting and joint purchase agreements. If such arrangements are not possible, then the government size determined in this manner is a *minimum* size, with a larger size being optimal if further economies of scale can be achieved by expanding. Similarly, this analysis does not consider potential savings of administration and compliance costs, the issue to which we now turn.

Decision-Making Costs and Clustering

If the optimal government size is determined by this procedure, it is possible, and even likely, that the optimal size will be different for each public good or service. As a result, as many levels of government would be required in a federal system as there are types of public goods and services. Every individual or household would be a member of that number of subnational governments. Such a structure

---

[8]Note that the origin of each function should not change.

Figure 6.3

Clustering of
jurisdictions
by size

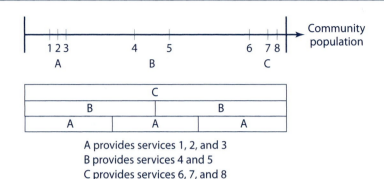

A provides services 1, 2, and 3
B provides services 4 and 5
C provides services 6, 7, and 8

may not be optimal, however, if consideration of the decision-making costs—that is, administration and compliance costs—is added to the externality and preference issues.

Suppose, for example, that the government will provide eight different public goods, which can be denoted 1, 2, 3, . . . , 8. The optimal-size government to provide each is determined by comparing consumer welfare losses from grouping together consumers with different demands for each good against the welfare gains from a reduction of spatial externalities, as described earlier. Those optimal government sizes (measured by optimal population size N) are given in Figure 6.3. Good 1 requires the smallest size government, whereas at the opposite end of the spectrum, good 8 requires the biggest. For instance, goods 1, 2, 3 might represent fire protection, recreation services, and water provision; goods 4 and 5 might represent education and roads; and goods 6, 7, and 8 might correspond to income redistribution, health regulation, and defense. To put it in terms of the required government structure, good 1 (fire protection) would be provided by many, small local governments whereas good 8 (defense) would be provided by the federal government, with the other six provided by intermediate levels.

Oates (1972) has suggested that it is possible to reduce decision-making costs by *clustering* together goods with similar optimal sizes into single government units, reducing both the number of government layers and the number of separate governments in each layer. For the example shown in Figure 6.3, goods 1, 2, and 3 might be clustered together for provision by government level A, goods 4 and 5 by larger governments at level B, and goods 6, 7, and 8 by the federal government at level C. Rather than eight levels of government, there are only three, and rather than, say, five separate localities in the lowest level, there are three.

Of course, this looks suspiciously like the government structure in the United States and other federal nations where the levels are the federal, state, and local governments, although the local government level in reality is more complex than suggested by this example (see Chapter 1). Given that such a structure exists, the common policy question is whether responsibility for providing the goods has been allocated properly.

Table 6.1

Government Structure in Four Federal Nations

Nation	Population (millions)	Area (thousand sq. miles)	States	Territories	Local Governments
United States of America	291.1	3,718	50 (States)	5	87,225
Commonwealth of Australia	19.9	2,978	6 (States)	2	900
Canada	31.6	3,850	10 (Provinces)	2	8,000
Federal Republic of Germany	82.5	138	16 (Länder)	—	16,100

International Comparison

Government Structure in Four Federal Nations

The four major industrialized nations listed in Table 6.1 have federal systems of government; that is, the nations are federations of autonomous states. In all four of these nations, the federal structure is not only important politically but also fiscally. States have some economic and fiscal responsibilities that are independent of the federal government, whereas other fiscal responsibilities are shared. The states establish or oversee local governments with which they share a fiscal relationship similar to that between the states and federal government. Thus the term fiscal federalism reflects the three separate but intertwined levels of government.

Two large regions in both Australia and Canada are called territories rather than states, but in many fiscal respects these areas operate similarly to states. The Australian Capital Territory, where Canberra, the national capital, is located is similar in some ways to the District of Columbia in the United States. The Northern Territory in Australia and the Northwest and Yukon Territories in Canada also are similar; all three are very large, but sparsely populated regions with severe climates and geography. Although called by the same name, all of these are very different than the U.S. territories, such as Puerto Rico or the Virgin Islands.

Although the overall structure in these four nations is similar, the number, and thus average size, of subnational governments differs substantially. Both Australia and Canada are geographically large areas with relatively small populations. Thus, although they have many fewer states than the United States, the average population in those states still is substantially less than in the United States—3.3 million in Australia and 3.2 million in Canada compared to more than 5 million in the United States. States in Germany also average more than 5 million people; although the population in Germany is about one-quarter of that in the United States, so is the number of states.

The number of local governments seems directly related to population, with more localities in those nations with larger populations. The United States has the most fragmented local government structure, however, with the largest number of localities even after adjusting for population differences. About 29 local governments exist for each 100,000 people in the United States compared to 25 in Canada, 20 in Germany, and only 5 in Australia.

POLICY APPLICATIONS

Applying these principles in practice to the issue of proper allocation of service responsibility among levels of government in a federal system usually comes down to a comparison of the importance of "local autonomy" versus concern about externalities, usually expressed as "what's best for all concerned."

For instance, consider a proposal to consolidate all local police departments into one metropolitan-area police authority. Because local governments would continue to provide other services, there would be no savings of political decision-making costs. There appear to be few economies of scale to be achieved, and if they do exist, they may be captured without consolidation by cooperative agreements. Those opposing the consolidation argue that local control would be lost, suggesting that the consolidated authority would not provide the type or amount of police service the local department does. This concern is multiplied if there are varied types of communities and police departments in the area. Those favoring the consolidation argue that public safety is a metropolitan-area problem, that criminals do not recognize local government boundaries, perhaps even that the amount of police protection in some communities is "too low," and that public safety is "too important to be left to localities."

This is a familiar refrain to those with experience in local government. It is repeated again and again in debates over all types of public services. Primary and secondary education ought to be a state government function because the benefits of an educated citizenry accrue to all and because everyone has an interest in ensuring that all students receive some minimum amount and type of education; or primary and secondary education should be a local function because each community knows what type of education is best for its students and because it is dangerous to allow state bureaucrats to determine what students should learn. Even if the issues and principles involved are clear, the best way to measure the importance of these factors in actual cases is often not. One attempt to do that is reported next.

School District Consolidation in New York: Green and Parliament's Study[9]

Kenneth Greene and Thomas Parliament measured the potential welfare losses that could result from consolidation of 12 separate school districts in Broome County, New York, into 1 countywide district. Following the approach in this chapter and Chapter 5, these welfare losses would occur because the single amount of education to be provided by the consolidated district would be different than the amounts provided in many (or perhaps all) of the separate districts. If households were consuming their *desired* amounts of education service in each separate district, then consolidation would force some households to consume other than their desired amounts and thus suffer welfare losses. If consolidation is

---

[9]This example is from Greene and Parliament (1980).

Figure 6.4

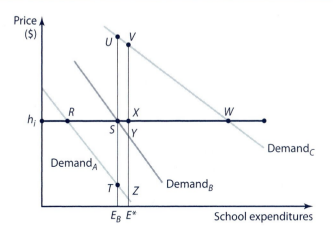

a good idea, these measured welfare losses would have to be offset by gains from fewer externalities or scale economies.

In measuring these welfare losses, Greene and Parliament suggest, however, that every household in each separate district may not be consuming the desired amount of education service. They assume, in other words, that the political choice in each district is represented by the median voter model rather than the Tiebout model. Because of costs and barriers to mobility, homogeneity of demand in each district is not expected. In that case, consolidating education services will make some consumers better off by moving them closer to their desired amount of service. Thus, the potential welfare losses from consolidation are smaller than if one assumes a perfect Tiebout world to start.

Greene and Parliament's approach is represented in Figure 6.4, which shows the demands for education for three types of households in one of the separate school districts. The amount of education expenditure is selected by majority vote, so that the median amount E_B is chosen. Group A prefers less education expenditure whereas group C prefers more. The current welfare loss because A and C are not consuming their desired amounts is represented by areas RST plus SUW, which measures the loss of consumer surplus for these groups.

Now suppose that consolidation occurs and the amount of expenditure chosen is the efficient amount of expenditure—the amount where the sum of marginal benefits equals marginal costs—E^*. Group A is made even worse off because the new expenditure is even farther from its desired amount. Group B is also worse off because it no longer exactly consumes its desired expenditure. Group C, however, is made *better off* because the new expenditure is closer to its desired one. In consumer-surplus terms, the new welfare loss to A is represented by area RXZ, the loss to B by area SXY, and the loss to C by area XVW. The change in welfare due to consolidation is represented by $SUVX - SXTZ - SXY$. This term may be positive or negative. If it is positive, it means that consolidation has *increased* welfare because the gain to group C offsets the losses to groups A and B. In essence, the issue is whether consolidation moves the community toward the efficient level, E^*, because at this level the sum of the consumer-surplus measures is maximized.

Greene and Parliament attempt to measure these welfare changes by first estimating a demand curve for education statistically based on all school districts in New York and then using that demand curve to predict both the amount of education expenditure that would be selected in the consolidated district and the desired amount for different income-class households. The estimated demand curve is

$$ln\ E = -1.21 - .343\ ln\ h + .697\ ln\ Y + .634\ ln\ N - .053\ ln\ P$$

where

$ln\ E$ = natural log of school operating expenditures

$ln\ h$ = natural log of tax price

$ln\ Y$ = natural log of income

$ln\ N$ = natural log of population

$ln\ P$ = natural log of percent of pupils in nonpublic schools

This demand function, in combination with assumptions about the distribution of tax burdens by income, is used to measure the loss of consumer surplus for each of seven income-class households in each separate district. Those losses occur because actual expenditures in each district do not equal those households' desired expenditures. Those results are analogous to the loss to groups A and C in Figure 6.4 when E_B is selected. Similar welfare losses are measured given the predicted expenditure for the consolidated district. These can be compared to show the cost due to the loss of political autonomy from consolidation.

The results are shown in Table 6.2. The average welfare loss for all 12 school districts initially (when they operate independently) is $67 per capita if no tax exporting is assumed or $22 per capita if there is substantial tax exporting. These numbers represent the average per-person cost because everyone in each district does not desire the same education expenditure. If all 12 districts are consolidated, the welfare losses increase to $116 per capita with no tax exporting or $63 with tax exporting. The change in welfare losses caused by consolidation—that is, the political cost of consolidation because households with greater differences in desired expenditures are grouped together—is then $49 per capita if no tax exporting is

Table 6.2

Welfare Costs of School Expenditure Compromise

	Per-Capita Welfare Loss Assuming	
	No Tax Exporting	Substantial Tax Exporting
After consolidation	$116	$63
Before consolidation	67	22
Change	49	41

SOURCE: Green and Parliament (1980).

assumed or $41 with substantial tax exporting. If consolidation is to be economically desirable, there must be cost or welfare savings of that magnitude—perhaps from scale economies or reduced externalities—to be gained by the consolidation.

Greene and Parliament also calculated that the net change in per-capita welfare from consolidation is $64 if one assumed that the initial expenditure in each separate district was efficient. Therefore, the actual welfare losses from consolidation were much smaller than if efficiency in each locality had been assumed.

School District Consolidation in New York: Duncombe and Yinger's Study[10]

All local government consolidations may not lead to welfare losses, however, depending on the differences that exist between localities before consolidation and the effects of the combination itself. Even if there are such welfare costs, those losses may be more than offset by gains in productive efficiency or economies of scale. In fact, those are precisely the results obtained in a study by William Duncombe and John Yinger, who also explore school district consolidation in New York.

Duncombe and Yinger focus on rural school districts, and specifically on 12 consolidations that occurred between 1987 and 1995. They explore the changes in those districts after consolidation and compare those changes to a control group of 190 similar rural districts that did not consolidate. One of their major findings is that the consumer welfare or consumer surplus losses due to changes in school spending from consolidation among these districts were very small. A primary reason is that consolidation may change not only the actual level of education spending or service provided but also the desired levels of spending or service by the residents of the consolidating areas. In the cases examined, the lower spending district before consolidation also had the smaller per-student tax base (and thus a higher tax price for education service). Consolidation lowers the tax price for residents of the lower-spending district, and the lower price induces those individuals to demand a larger quantity of service. Similarly, residents of the higher-spending district before consolidation see their tax prices raised by combining districts, which reduces their desired level of service. Thus, in this case, consolidation moved the desired spending levels closer together and reduced any potential consumer welfare losses from the changes in actual school spending.

In addition, Duncombe and Yinger find substantial evidence of economies of scale for both operating and capital spending among these smaller, rural school districts. They report that ". . . doubling enrollment [which results if two 300-pupil districts combine] cuts total costs per pupil by 28 percent for a 300-pupil district and by 9 percent for a 1,500 pupil district" (Duncombe and Yinger, 2003). They also find economies of scale (per-student costs decline as enrollment increases) for transportation and capital costs, although capital costs initially rise (as adjustment to the consolidation occurs) and then subsequently fall. Indeed, the simple fact that these districts elected to consolidate suggests that the gains from productive

---

[10]This example is from Duncombe and Yinger (2003).

Table 6.3

Use of Contracting by Cities for Service Provision

Category	1982	1988
Percentage of Services with Contracting		
All Cities	30.1%	28.4%
Cities, population > 250,000	36.9	36.3
Percentage of Cities Using Contracting		
Collective Goods and Services[a]	31.2	33.0
Private Goods and Services[b]	50.3	36.9
Percentage of Cities Using Contracting for New Services		
Collective Goods and Services	—	38.7
Private Goods and Services	—	42.9

[a]"Collective goods and services" refers to those from which everyone benefits; what economist call public goods.

[b]"Private goods and services" refers to services provided by government for which individuals can be excluded if they do not pay.

SOURCE: Stein, 1993.

efficiency and lower costs were large enough to offset any potential losses due to different desired levels of spending or capital adjustment costs. Otherwise, voters in these districts would likely not have approved the consolidations.

Service Provision by Contracting[11]

Contracting for service provision with another government or with a private firm is one way for localities to achieve any economies of scale in production of services. In fact, intergovernmental service contracts (under which one government pays another to provide a carefully specified service), private-service contracts (a government pays a firm or nonprofit agency to provide a service), and joint-service agreements (under which two or more governments join in financing and producing a service) are commonly used by local governments in the United States. In the first two types of contracting, provision decisions are retained by the contracting government with production performed by the contractor; in the third case, both provision and production decisions are made jointly.

The International City/County Management Association periodically conducts surveys of cities and counties concerning use of intergovernmental service agreements and other forms of contracting. Regarding intergovernmental contracting, the survey in 1982 showed that slightly more than half of all cities and counties contracted with another government to provide some of their services and that a slightly larger percentage entered into joint service agreements. Moreover, intergovernmental service contracts and joint service agreements tend to be used to an even greater degree by larger cities and counties. As reported by Stein (1993) based on the ICMA data and shown in Table 6.3, about 30 percent of city service

---

[11]This section is based on ACIR (1985b), Stein (1993), and Moulder (2004).

Table 6.4

Percentage of Local Governments Reporting Contracting with Private-Sector Producers for Various Services, 1997 and 2002

Service	1997	2002
Vehicle towing	83%	—
Legal services	53	57%
Residential waste collection	49	40
Tree trimming and planting	37	41
Programs for the elderly	—	38
Vehicle maintenance	—	37
Street repair	35	36
Building and grounds maintenance	—	32
Traffic signal maintenance	24	27
Ambulance service	37	29
Emergency medical service	—	21
Building security	—	20
Street cleaning	—	19
Delinquent tax collection	—	18
Operation of recreation facilities	—	16
Animal control	—	15

SOURCE: Greene (2002); Moulder (2004).

responsibilities involved some form of contractual provision in both 1982 and 1988, with that fraction closer to 37 percent for larger cities (with population above 250,000). There is also evidence that for new service responsibilities taken on by cities, contracting is even more common.

When contracts are used by cities, they most often contract with counties to have services provided; jails, sewage disposal, property tax assessing, animal control, and water supply are the services most commonly contracted out. County governments contract both with other counties and cities for such services as jails, fire protection, and computer- and data-processing services. Joint-service agreements are used to provide police and fire communication, libraries, fire protection, mental health services, and city legal services in addition to the services listed previously.

Based on the 1997 and 2002 ICMA surveys, the services or functions most often contracted to the private sector include vehicle towing, legal services, vehicle maintenance, residential refuse collection and disposal, tree trimming, programs for the elderly, street repair, building and grounds maintenance, traffic signal maintenance, and ambulance service. The survey results for these and other services that are often contracted privately are shown in Table 6.4. (Private-service contracts are also discussed in Chapter 7.)

The dominant reason cited by these local governments for entering into both service contracts and joint agreements was to reduce costs and achieve economies of scale. That reason was cited by 88 percent of those using private contracting in 2002 (Muelder, 2002). Other common cited reasons included "external fiscal pressures, including restrictions placed on raising taxes"; "a change in political climate emphasizing a decreased role for government"; and that it was "more logical to organize services beyond jurisdictional or area limits," which seems to suggest that a larger service area would help reduce benefit spillovers. The most often cited fear about these intergovernmental agreements was a loss of local autonomy, particularly with joint agreements.

Governing magazine (Lemov, 1993) reported about the case of Thorton, Colorado entering into a joint agreement for emergency dispatch services with the county government (Adams County). As a result of contracting with the county to provide the service, the city expected to save some $80,000 annually; however, the city was concerned about giving up "the familiarity and comfort of having its own custom-tailored emergency communications center" (Lemov, 1993, p. 26). To reduce city concerns about the loss of local control and autonomy, the county dispatch center has a control board comprised of members representing the county and all the cities involved in contracting.

Despite these concerns, intergovernmental contracts, government/private-sector contracts, and joint agreements among governments for service provision appear to be used commonly by local governments for many services, primarily as a way of using economies of scale to lower service production costs.

SUMMARY

The greater the variations in what individual consumers want from government and the more consumers with similar wants are grouped together, the stronger the case is for decentralized provision—that is, for having many small local governments.

The correspondence principle requires that the size of a government correspond to the area of benefit from the goods it provides. As a result, each public good is provided in the smallest (that is, lowest-level) government consistent with no externalities.

The possibly conflicting objectives of having governments big enough to avoid cost or benefit spillovers but small enough to allow uniform desired amounts of public service suggest a tradeoff between those two factors. The optimal-size government for each service is the one where the difference between the welfare gain from fewer externalities and the loss from greater demand variety is greatest.

Economies of scale, in reference to the optimal size for governments, usually refers to a decrease in cost per person for a given amount of service as population served increases. Governments too small to achieve all economies of scale on their own can nevertheless take advantage of those economies by purchasing the good or service from governments or private firms that are large enough to exhaust all economies.

A final economic factor that may be a reason for few subnational governments (and thus more centralization) is the desire to conserve on the direct costs of administering those governments and the costs to individuals of participating in the political process.

It may be possible to reduce decision-making costs by clustering goods with similar optimal sizes into single-government units, reducing both the number of layers of government and the number of separate governments in each layer.

Applying these principles to the practical issue of allocating service responsibility among levels of government in a federal system usually comes down to a comparison of the importance of "local autonomy" versus concern about externalities, usually expressed as "what's best for all concerned."

DISCUSSION QUESTIONS

1. "Unless there are economies of scale in the production of government goods and services, they should always be provided by the smallest available government units (that is, the lowest-level government in a federal hierarchy)." Evaluate this position.

2. Suppose that it is proposed to create a single local jurisdiction and government for your entire metropolitan area or region, to be called Metroland. It would replace all cities and/or towns that currently provide basic local services (such as public safety, streets, recreation services).

   a. Make the economic case *for* this consolidation into a metropolitan-area government (there are at least three potentially favorable economic reasons).

   b. Now suppose that you were hired as an economic consultant to advise about this change and your research uncovers four facts: 1) Currently, there is a big difference in per-capita spending among the municipalities to be consolidated, from $2,000 at the top to $500; 2) The variance in per-capita income for people living in the area is relatively large; 3) There is a relatively small variance in per-capita income within each of the municipalities; 4) Currently, many of these municipalities contract with the county (or state) government to have some services (such as jails, emergency dispatch, and parks) provided. Do these facts support or argue against the proposed consolidation? Explain your reasoning for each factor.

3. In the United States, primary and secondary education is usually provided by local government, although partly financed by state government grants. As a result, substantial differences often exist in the quantity and quality of education offered by different schools, even in the same state. Yet in Hawaii, education is a state government function. Similarly, in Australia, which has a federal structure similar to that in the United States, primary and secondary education is provided by the states. And, in some U.S. states, such as Michigan, New Mexico, and Washington, the state government dominates and provides more than 70 percent of the financing for schools, reducing local differences. What reasons might a state government offer to support a proposal to transfer education from a local to a state responsibility?

Why might some individuals oppose such a transfer? Discuss how those reasons might lead one state or nation to select local provision whereas others opt for state provision. Would you favor such a transfer (or the opposite) in your area?

SELECTED READINGS

Bahl, Roy W. and Walter Vogt. *Fiscal Centralization and Tax Burdens: State and Regional Financing of City Services*. Cambridge, Mass.: Ballinger, 1975.

Fisher, Ronald C. and Robert W. Wassmer. "Economic Influences on the Structure of Local Government in U.S. Metropolitan Areas." *Journal of Urban Economics*, 43 (1998): 444–471.

Greene, Kenneth V. and Thomas J. Parliament. "Political Externalities, Efficiency, and the Welfare Losses from Consolidation." *National Tax Journal*, 33, no. 2 (June 1980): 209–17.

Martinez-Vazquez, Jorge, Mark Rider and Mary Beth Walker. "Race and the Structure of Local Government." *Journal of Urban Economics*, 41 (1997): 281–300.

Oates, Wallace E. *Fiscal Federalism*. New York: Harcourt Brace Jovanovich, 1972. See especially Chapter 2.

PROVISION OF STATE AND LOCAL GOODS AND SERVICES

PART

III

THIS SECTION COVERS THE ECONOMIC THEORY AND EVIDENCE ABOUT THE SUPPLY OF GOODS AND SERVICES USUALLY PROVIDED BY STATE AND LOCAL GOVERNMENTS IN THE UNITED STATES. The central issue is how the important economic factors that determine supply—prices of those goods and services, prices of factors of production, and production technology—influence the amount of those goods and services produced and how they are produced. Among the questions to be considered are these: How important are labor costs for subnational governments? How can those governments respond to wage increases? Are there alternative ways of producing government services to hold down costs without sacrificing quality?

The method of financing state and local government goods and services obviously can affect the amount of those goods and services produced, so the effects of user charges, intergovernmental grants, and borrowing also are considered in this section. The characteristics of services for which user-charge financing or borrowing is most appropriate and the ways in which user-charge financing or borrowing can improve the efficiency and fairness of subnational government provision are discussed. Also, the relationship between state–local borrowing costs and federal tax policy is considered. In addition, intergovernmental grants, which serve to affect the prices of goods or services and the resources available to a community, are evaluated as a method of influencing spending and taxing decisions of subnational governments. The potential purposes for grants are presented and matched to the expected effects of grants of different types.

Of course, no discussion about the supply of any commodity can go forward without first specifying the commodity and how it will be measured.

This seemingly straightforward task, however, is fraught with difficulties for many of the services provided by government. What, for instance, is the appropriate measure of service provided by local schools or a city police department? Although amounts of money spent on those functions—expenditures—are the most readily available and commonly used measure of the quantity of service, that measure often is not informative. Additional expenditures that do not translate into more educated students or a safer environment may not represent more "service." Throughout this section of the book, and particularly in Chapter 7, the problems of appropriately measuring service and the limitations of using expenditures as that measure are emphasized.

Finally, governments implement their decisions about providing goods and services through budgets and budget policy. Even before the tax-limit movement, state–local governments had experimented with a variety of budget structures and restrictions. Understanding those constraints and their effects on fiscal decisions may help clarify why some states respond to economic and fiscal changes differently from others and may suggest the advantages and disadvantages of similar budget policies for the federal government.

CHAPTER 7

Costs and Supply of State and Local Goods and Services

... Rising unit costs have been a major (probably the single most important) source of recent increases in local public budgets.[1]
—DAVID BRADFORD, R.A. MALT, AND WALLACE OATES

"Like many states, New Jersey contracts with an outside vendor to handle the back-office side of its welfare and food stamp programs. Part of that operation, run by an Arizona-based company called eFunds, is a small call center that handles telephone inquiries from beneficiaries. State officials caught flack last year when the vendor moved the outfit from Green Bay, Wisconsin to Bombay, where salaries for answering calls are in the range of $2 to $4 an hour. In the welfare-to-work age, critics say, it's unfair—and hugely ironic—to ship entry-level jobs such as these overseas.

So New Jersey negotiated with eFunds to bring the jobs back. In May, a new call center opened in economically depressed Camden, with several new employees hired from the welfare rolls. . . . New Jersey agreed to pay eFunds an additional $888,000 a year as compensation for the higher cost of doing business in Camden.

. . . More and more U.S. corporations are moving call centers, data processing, and other back-office work to nations such as India, Israel, and the Philippines. . .

With their budgets in shambles, state and local governments may be inclined to turn to cheap overseas labor.[2]"

---

[1]"The Rising Cost of Local Public Services: Some Evidence and Reflections." *National Tax Journal*, 22 (June 1969): 201.
[2]"Answering the Call Center's Call." *Governing Magazine*. July, 2003.

In economics, analyzing supply is essentially analyzing production cost. The cost of producing alternative amounts of output, combined with the structure of the market, determines how producers behave. Similarly, the costs of producing services provided by state–local governments and the factors that alter those costs are crucial for understanding and comparing the fiscal behavior of subnational governments.

Before discussing production technology and cost, one needs to define and measure the good or service produced, which is not straightforward for many services, including those provided by state–local governments. For example, education is the dominant subnational government service in the United States; the question is whether education output should be measured by dollars spent per pupil, by the number of graduating students, by student test scores, or by some other measure. The action required to increase each of these alternative measures of education may be different so that the cost of producing "more" of each may vary and even depend on different factors. The first task in this chapter is to consider alternative ways to characterize the output of state and local government services so that "cost" is defined properly and to investigate the factors that affect cost (and thus supply).

MEASUREMENT AND PRODUCTION OF GOVERNMENT SERVICES

Production Functions[3]

To produce services, state–local governments purchase inputs such as labor services, capital goods, materials, and supplies and combine them to provide public facilities, or what can be called **directly produced output**, such as police patrols or classrooms with teachers and books. The ways inputs can be combined to produce this type of output are together referred to as **technology** and can be represented mathematically by a **production function**. For instance, the directly produced education output is a function of the number of teachers and administrators, the number of buildings and classrooms, and the number of books, desks, and other equipment provided. Mathematically

$$Q = q(L, K, X)$$

where

Q = directly produced output

L = labor input

K = capital input

X = the set of other inputs such as materials and supplies

The $q( )$ function represents production technology. Any given amount of directly produced output usually can be produced by different combinations of

---

[3]The discussion in this section follows that in David Bradford, R. A. Malt, and Wallace Oates (1969).

inputs—that is, there is usually more than one way to combine inputs to produce a service. In other words, the production function $q(\ )$ does not specify a unique input combination for each output but rather the possible input combinations to produce each level of output.

The *cost* of producing any amount of directly produced output depends both on this production technology and the prices of the required inputs. In defining production cost, economists usually assume that for each possible level of output, producers select the combination of inputs that will produce the chosen output at lowest cost.[4] For instance, if L_1, K_1, and X_1 are the amounts of inputs that will produce output Q_1 at lowest cost, then the

$$\text{Cost of } Q_1 = wL_1 + rK_1 + pX_1$$

where

$w =$ the price of labor

$r =$ the price of capital

$p =$ the set of prices for the other inputs.

Of course, this cost of the directly produced output is also the **expenditure** of the government on this service.

These public facilities or directly produced outputs provided by state–local governments may not reflect the services consumers desire, however. One can argue that citizens are more concerned about results than production; for instance, the education output of interest is knowledge and skills acquired rather than merely the number of classroom hours per year. The service result, which is what individuals consume or use, depends both on the directly produced output by the government and on the characteristics of the community and the population. For example, an equal number of classroom hours, teachers, and books will not necessarily produce an equal amount of learning in districts with different numbers and types of students. It is useful, therefore, to distinguish **consumer output**, or the final result for consumers, from the directly produced output or facilities. Mathematically,

$$G = g(Q, X, N, E)$$

where

$G =$ consumer output

$X =$ private goods purchased directly by individuals

$N =$ population to be served

$E =$ environment, a set of community and population characteristics

$g(\ ) =$ transformation function from output to results

---

[4]Of course, governments might not always select the minimum cost input mix. For instance, it has been argued that due to patronage consideration or public-employee unionism, state–local governments may choose to use more labor than is cost minimizing.

The "cost" of producing more directly produced output Q is different from the "cost" of producing more consumer output G. The latter depends on private consumption by residents and on community characteristics E and N, which are often outside the direct control of the state or local government. Private consumption may raise G if individuals purchase goods or services that contribute to the public service, such as private education or locks or smoke detectors; private consumption might reduce G if consumption imposes greater burdens on the public service, such as with consumption of alcohol and drunken driving. Changes in population or the environment may require a larger Q, just to keep G constant. For instance, to reduce class size from 25 to 20 students requires 25 percent more teachers and classrooms (assuming teacher workload and school operating hours are to remain the same), but such a change may not provide a 25-percent increase in the desired result of "learning" per student; indeed, it may not increase "learning" at all!

This discussion suggests that the output of state–local governments can be measured in at least three different, broad ways. Output can be measured by the amount of money spent by a government on a service, which is referred to as expenditure; however, expenditure is really a measure of the inputs used by the government in the production process. Alternatively, government service may be measured by the amount of directly produced output provided by the government. Finally, government service may be measured by results, by the level of consumption enjoyed by citizens.

Examples of how these three different measurement concepts can be applied to specific state–local government services are shown in Table 7.1. Fire protection services, for instance, may be measured by the amount of money spent on firefighters, stations, trucks, and other inputs; by the number of hydrants and stations per square mile; or by some mix of the number of fires (prevention) and damage per fire (suppression). Similarly, police protection services may be measured by expenditures on officers, vehicles, jails, and other inputs; by the number of police patrols per square mile; or by the number of arrests made and crimes solved. Similar measures can be devised for every service function or responsibility of state–local governments. But which measure is best? Or perhaps more appropriately, how do the measures differ in the information they provide?

Expenditures Compared to Produced Output

Directly produced output on a service can fall even though expenditures are constant or even increasing. Similarly, two different subnational jurisdictions with equal per-capita expenditures on a particular function can provide different produced outputs for that service.

Expenditures equal costs, and costs depend both on the amount of inputs used *and* the prices of those inputs. If the prices of inputs rise, then it will cost governments more to provide the same produced output. Of course, governments may select a different production technology if relative input prices change—using relatively less of those inputs whose prices increase the most—but even then, total cost for every amount of directly produced output will increase, although perhaps

Table 7.1

Sample Output Measures for Selected State—Local Services

Service	Inputs	Direct Outputs	Consumption
Fire Protection	Firefighters, inspectors, stations, trucks, equipment, water supply	Stations per sq. mile, firefighters per station, trucks per station, hydrants per sq. mile	Fire Prevention and Suppression: No. of fires per household or employer, damage ($) per fire, civilian fire deaths per fire, fire insurance rates
Police Protection	Patrol officers, supervisory officers, stations, radios, vehicles, jails, weapons	Stations per sq. mile, no. of patrols (or patrol officers) per sq. mile, no. of intersections with traffic control, no. of jail cells per capita	Crime Prevention and Punishment: Crimes per capita (perhaps by type), civilian deaths and/or injuries from crime, amount ($) of stolen merchandise, arrests per crime, crimes solved per reported crime
Education	Teachers, books, buildings, desks, classrooms, computers, and other equipment	Teachers per student, books per student, classroom hours per year, class size, no. of subjects taught	Knowledge and Skills: Average &/or variance of test scores, percent graduating "on time," percent attending college, percent employed after x years, added earnings

by less than if the government did not alter production methods. It follows that if input prices differ for different subnational jurisdictions, equal expenditures do not necessarily translate into equal produced output. Simply put, if teachers of the same quality cost more in one state than in another (and all other inputs cost the same), equal per-pupil expenditures in the two states translate into larger class sizes in the higher-cost state or less of some other input (books, for example).

These implications are very important because expenditures are the most commonly used measure of subnational government output, at least for comparisons over time and among different jurisdictions. Over time, however, increases in input prices require increased expenditures unless directly produced output falls or unless new ways (technologies), which require fewer inputs, for producing those services can be found. As with consumer expenditures, one can attempt to allow for changing input prices over time by deflating government-expenditure data with a price index, usually the GNP implicit price deflator, which is separately available for federal and state–local government expenditures. No such general correction is available for comparisons among different jurisdictions, although evidence exists of substantial variation of some input prices among different state–local governments. Particularly, land prices and labor prices appear to vary widely at different locations, and both inputs are purchased in substantial amounts by state–local governments.

Produced Output Compared to Consumed Output

The consumed output or result for a particular service could decline or worsen even though a government provides constant or even increasing direct output. In fact, even if two governments provide equal directly produced output, citizens in those jurisdictions may receive different amounts of consumed output—that is, get different results or benefits as consumers.

The consumer output, which results from a given amount of directly produced output, depends on private consumption and on the environmental characteristics of the community and population. Between two cities with identical fire departments, one might expect more fires and more serious fires in the city with fewer smoke detectors or with older buildings or with more wooden (as opposed to metal or brick) buildings. Equal fire protection in both cities may require more directly produced output in such a city—perhaps fire stations closer together, more pumper trucks per capita, or a more aggressive fire-inspection program. Similarly, as environmental conditions change over time, directly produced outputs must change if consumer results are to remain the same. Of course, the environment can change in a positive way over time as well, requiring less produced output to maintain consumer results. For instance, if building materials and technology mean that newer buildings are at lesser risk from fire or if individuals more commonly keep fire extinguishers at hand, then the amount of directly produced fire-protection output consistent with constant fire protection could decline.

There are four reasons government expenditures may not be very good measures of the ultimate benefits received by consumers from government production. Differences among jurisdictions or changes over time in (1) production technology, (2) input prices, (3) community environmental characteristics, and (4) private consumption patterns all can intervene in that relationship. For instance, rising expenditures may be sufficient to maintain constant produced output, given rising input prices, whereas a deteriorating environment may require increased produced output to maintain results. Thus, rising expenditures may not be inconsistent with falling consumed output or declining service quality. The opposite also may be true. In some cases, decreasing expenditures can be consistent with rising service results or quality if input prices decrease, the production environment improves, and/or individuals substitute private consumption for public service. Therefore, at the very least, these four factors must be considered and evaluated when using government expenditures for comparison purposes.

Among government policy makers, the idea of focusing on results rather than spending is referred to as *benchmarking*. States and localities evaluate their programs by a series of benchmarks or performance measures comparing that jurisdiction to others. For instance, *Governing* reports that "Mississippi plans to shift away from old-style line-item budgeting that merely measures inputs—what the state is spending on specific programs—to one that measures outcomes—what, actually, is the effect of all that government spending" (Walters, 1994, 33). The hope is that the focus on outcomes will allow governments to better allocate resources. Or, as officials in Mississippi contend, "If government begins to measure the effects of its activity rather than merely what it spends on those activities, those effects—'results'—will begin to drive the budget process" (Walters, 1994, 34).

Employment and Labor Costs

When expenditures are used as the measure of the amount of government service supplied, output is actually being measured by the government's costs, and the major component of state and local government costs is for labor. As shown in Table 7.2, about 34 percent of state–local government direct noncapital expenditures in 2002 went to cover compensation of employees. Labor costs represented 45 percent of those expenditures by local governments, on average, but 63 percent of direct expenditures in school districts. In comparison, labor costs were only about 13 percent of federal government noncapital direct expenditures in 2002. The reason for the much greater importance of labor costs to states and localities compared to the federal government is the difference in the nature of services provided by those governments. State and local governments mostly provide goods and services to individuals and businesses, which requires a substantial amount of labor to produce. The federal government mostly transfers money either to people (such as with

Table 7.2

Wages and Salaries as a Percent of Noncapital Direct Expenditure, by Type of Government, Selected Years

					Level of Government				
Year	Federal	State–Local	State	Total Local	County	Municipal	Township	School District	Special District
1967	27.5	54.5	42.7	60.5	48.0	56.2	52.4	74.1	41.7
1972	28.7	51.2	39.7	57.9	44.9	52.3	54.7	73.4	41.6
1977	20.3	45.2	31.5	54.5	47.5	47.5	54.6	68.8	38.4
1982	16.1	42.0	30.1	50.3	45.0	42.9	47.9	66.7	33.0
1987	13.8	40.7	29.3	48.6	42.8	41.6	45.6	65.7	29.1
1992	12.0	37.7	25.1	47.6	40.8	38.4	44.7	65.1	31.4
1997	10.4	36.5	23.8	46.6	39.5	38.7	45.6	64.5	30.3
2002	10.2	33.6	20.4	44.8	40.2[a]	na	na	63.1[a]	27.7[a]

[a]2001

SOURCE: U.S. Department of Commerce, *Compendium of Government Finances*, table entitled Governmental Expenditure by Character and Object, various years. U.S. Department of Commerce, *Governmental Finances*, various years.

social security and Medicare) or to state–local governments (through grants). The federal government produces few services directly, so its labor cost share is lower.

If comparison is limited to expenditures for current operations, labor costs are obviously an even larger share. In 2002, employee compensation was 41 percent of current operation expenditures for state–local governments together, about 27 percent for states, and more than 50 percent for all local governments.[5]

For the 35 years represented in Table 7.2, the labor-cost share of direct expenditures for all levels of government in the United States decreased substantially. From 1967–2002, labor costs decreased from 42.7 to 20.4 percent of direct expenditures for states and from 60.5 percent to 44.8 percent for local governments. Similarly, the labor-cost share of direct expenditures for the federal government fell from 27.5 percent to 10.2 percent. This decline in the labor-cost share partly reflects some external factors (interest-cost shares are greater now), but also reflects changes in what state–local governments do and how they do it. As governments make relatively more transfer payments, for instance, the labor-cost share of spending falls because the government is spending the money on direct payments rather than on labor. Similarly, if government substitutes capital for labor in producing some services—automated trucks for sanitation workers, for example—the labor-cost share also will fall.

In 2002, state and local governments employed more than 14 percent—that is, one in every seven—of all payroll employees in the United States, as shown in Table 7.3. The share of total employees working for state–local governments declined from 1975 to 1997, but has risen a bit since. Similarly, although the number of state–local government employees was about constant from 1980 through 1986, it grew by more than 20 percent from 1990 to 2002. Given the importance of labor costs to state and local governments, it is not surprising that this pattern mirrors the course of state–local government expenditures relative to income noted in Chapter 1—the state–local government sector grew compared to the rest of the economy until the mid-1970s, changed little during the 1980s, but has grown at a faster rate than the economy since.

A substantial number of state and local government employees work part time rather than full time. Although states and localities had more than 18.3 million employees in 2002, only about 13.8 million or 75 percent were full-time employees. Full-time equivalent employment adjusts for part-time workers by computing the number of full-time workers needed to replace part-time workers (so two employees each working half time are equivalent to one full-time employee). Since the mid-1980s, there has been little change in the ratio of full-time equivalent to total employment, suggesting that the use of part-time employees by states and localities has not changed much.

In 2002, state–local governments paid an average salary of about $40,200 to full-time employees. Compared to 1990, this represents about a 45 percent increase in

[5]Direct expenditures are total expenditures excluding intergovernmental transfers. Expenditures for current operations are direct expenditures excluding expenditures for capital, assistance and subsidies, interest, and insurance benefits. Expenditures for current operations represent money spent for current goods and services.

Table 7.3

State and Local Government Employment and Earnings

Year	State–Local Employment (thousands)	Percent of Total Employment[a]	State–Local Full-time Equivalent Employment[b]	Full-time Equivalent State–Local Employment as Percentage of All State–Local Employment	State–Local Ave. Annual Earnings per FTE[c]
1965	7,696	12.7%	6,937	90%	$ 5,616
1970	9,823	13.9	8,528	87	7,818
1975	11,937	15.5	10,111	85	10,900
1980	13,375	14.8	11,047	83	15,142
1982	13,098	14.6	10,829	83	17,826
1986	13,794	13.9	11,852	85	21,631
1990	15,219	13.9	13,080	86	27,732
1992	15,117	13.9	13,182	87	29,529
1997	16,733	13.6	14,214	85	33,273
2002	18,349	14.1	15,602	85	40,235

[a]State–local employment as a % of total nonagricultural payroll employment.

[b]Full-time equivalent employment adjusts for the number of part-time employees.

[c]Average annual compensation per full-time equivalent employee.

SOURCES: Bureau of Labor Statistics Web site; U.S. Department of Commerce, *Public Employment,* various years.

the average state–local salary. During that same period (1990–2002), per capita personal income in the United States increased about 82 percent and consumer prices (measured by the CPI) increased about 38 percent. It is very difficult to compare salaries or wage costs of state–local governments to those of the federal government or private business because of substantial differences in the work activities provided in those different components of the economy. One study by Bradley Braden and Stephanie Hyland (1993) showed that comparing aggregate data, the cost per employee for wages, salaries, and benefits appears to be much higher for state–local governments than for private industry. Much of this difference disappears, however, when accounting for the differences in the mix of work activities. Braden and Hyland note that "Compensation costs were similar for industry activities common to government and the private sector" (1993, 15).

PRODUCTIVITY AND COSTS

Input price increases lead to increased costs of providing state–local government services unless the input price increases are matched by increases in productivity. Further, because of the substantial importance of labor costs for state–local governments, changes in wages and worker productivity should be particularly important. But the market for state and local government workers is not isolated from the rest of the economy. Changes in the demand for and supply of labor throughout the economy can have important implications for the costs of providing state–local government services. This relationship among worker productivity, wages, and production costs between the state–local sector and the rest of the economy is the basis for one well-known theory about state–local government costs. This perspective is valuable in understanding the growth of state–local government spending.

The Baumol Hypothesis

In a now well-known 1967 article, William Baumol argued that productivity increases in some sectors of the economy would force wage increases throughout the economy, increasing the production costs in those sectors where productivity improvements do not occur. Professor Baumol further argued that the nature of some services, including many of those provided by state–local governments, effectively precludes productivity gains because the essence of the service is the labor itself. Higher wages simply cannot be offset by substituting other inputs for labor. For those services, unit production costs would certainly increase, and the choice for consumers is either to reduce consumption of the service substantially or to spend ever-increasing amounts to continue consuming current levels.

The first part of Baumol's argument is represented in Figure 7.1. The economy is divided, somewhat artificially, into two sectors, one where productivity gains occur relatively easily and regularly (Figure 7.1a) and one where productivity gains are difficult to achieve (Figure 7.1b). For this second sector, Baumol has in mind labor-intensive services with little opportunity for capital/labor substitution. In his words (1967, 416),

> "There are a number of services in which the labor is an end in itself, in which quality is judged directly in terms of amount of labor. Teaching is a clear-cut example. . . . Here, despite the invention of teaching machines and the use of closed-circuit

Figure 7.1

Productivity gains cause wage increases

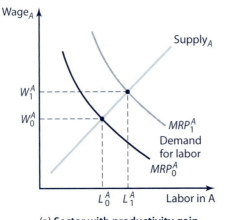

(a) **Sector with productivity gain**

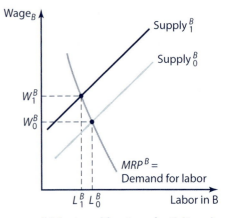

(b) **Sector without productivity gain**

television and a variety of other innovations, there still seem to be fairly firm limits to class size. . . . An even more extreme example is one I have offered in another context: live performance. A half-hour horn quintet calls for the expenditure of 2 1/2 man hours in its performance, and any attempt to increase productivity here is likely to be viewed with concern by critics and audience alike.[6]

Which services and to what degree this characterization applies is debatable. The point here is that productivity gains for some state–local services are more difficult to achieve than in some other industries. Accordingly, the demand for labor in both sectors is shown in Figure 7.1, with demand less elastic in that sector where substitution for labor is more difficult. Note that the demand for labor is labeled the **marginal revenue product of labor** (MRP), which is the extra revenue a firm receives from hiring one additional unit of labor. The marginal revenue product is marginal revenue times the marginal product of labor and thus depends both on labor productivity and the value of the product produced. From microeconomic principles, a profit-maximizing firm will employ additional labor as long as the marginal revenue product is greater than the marginal cost of another worker, which is the wage in a competitive labor market. The demand for labor, then, represents the benefit to a firm from more labor, which must be compared to the cost of hiring another unit of labor.

An increase in labor productivity in sector A is represented by an increase (a shift up) in the demand curve for labor; marginal revenue product is greater for every amount of labor because workers now produce more. The increase in labor productivity brings an increase in wage, at least in a competitive labor market. Presumably, the same occurs in a controlled labor market as unions recognize the increased productivity of their members and bargain accordingly. The increase in wage in labor market A means that workers in sector A are now earning a relatively higher wage compared to those in market B than before the productivity improvement. The relatively higher wages in A attract workers from market B, causing a reduction (a leftward shift) in the supply curve of workers to market B and an increase in the wage of workers in B. In essence, employers in market B must match the wage increase in market A to retain employees.

These wage increases have very different effects in these two sectors. For sector A, workers are earning *and* producing more so that cost per unit of output need not increase. For sector B, the higher wages have been forced by changes in the other market and are not matched by productivity gains; remember that the premise of sector B is that substantial productivity gains are not possible. Therefore, the cost of producing a unit of sector B output rises. If B represents the position of state–local governments (and other industries as well), productivity gains in the industrial sector of the economy *cause* cost increases in the production of state–local government goods and services.

---

[6]Perhaps Baumol did not foresee the advent of computer-based music synthesizers, so that one programmer-performer could produce the horn quintet. But one might suspect that Baumol, and others, would see this option as substantially changing quality. In essence, the performance by the synthesizer is a different good (or bad) completely when compared to the quintet.

Figure 7.2

How increases in costs of government services affect spending on services

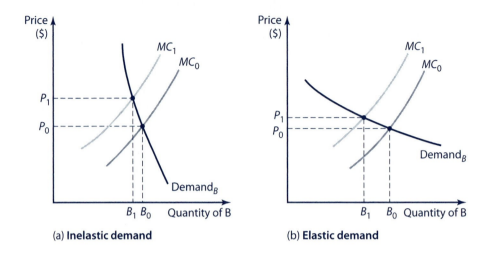

(a) **Inelastic demand**   (b) **Elastic demand**

The effect of these cost increases on consumption of sector B's output is represented by Figure 7.2. If the demand for output B is price inelastic (Figure 7.2a), then the increased cost results in a higher price but only a small decrease in quantity. As a result, total expenditures on service B rise. If demand for output B is price elastic (Figure 7.2b), then the cost increase causes only a small increase in price but a large decrease in consumption. As discussed in Chapter 4, the evidence suggests that the demand for the services provided by state–local governments is very price inelastic. Therefore, the implication of the Baumol hypothesis is that productivity gains in some sectors of the economy will force increasing amounts to be spent on state–local government services. This is consistent with state–local government expenditures representing a larger and larger share of income. This problem will remain as long as private-sector productivity gains continue and public-sector productivity gains are difficult to achieve.

This story, although simplified, seems applicable to many actual circumstances. As wages in manufacturing and the business-service sector rise, fewer students may be attracted to teaching, a phenomenon that can be particularly evident for science, math, or business teachers who may find an attractive private market for their general knowledge and skills. As improved technology becomes a more important factor in manufacturing and demand for engineers and computer specialists rises, it becomes more and more difficult and expensive for universities to staff engineering schools. Of course, as noted by Baumol, the process applies to many other services such as the arts, restaurant meals, fine hand-crafted furniture, and clothes.

Evidence: Government Productivity

It is difficult to measure directly productivity change in the production of government services precisely because it is difficult to measure the output being produced. One study (Hulten, 1984) attempted to measure productivity change in state and local governments indirectly, however, by using the difference between directly produced output and consumed output. Households can be thought of as producing all final services by purchasing and combining different directly produced outputs, some provided by the private sector and some by government. (For instance, a household combines a privately produced recreational vehicle with a publicly provided park to produce a service called camping.) In that case, the share of public-to-private expenditures depends on the relative prices of the products and relative change in productivity and environmental factors for the sectors. The combined change in productivity and environmental factors for the state–local sector can be inferred from observed data on the share of state–local expenditures in GNP and relative prices.

Using quarterly data for the 1959–1979 period, Charles Hulten estimated the annual rate of change of the combined productivity/environmental factor to be −0.50 percent, although the estimate was not significantly different from zero. Hulten reported that one "cannot reject the hypothesis of zero productivity growth for the state–local sector" (p. 261). Perhaps more accurately, if there had been productivity growth over this period, it was not sufficient to offset a deteriorating production environment. After noting that private-sector productivity had increased at an average 1.45-percent annual rate over this period and that the state–local share in GNP had risen substantially in this time, Hulten concluded that "the results of this paper are thus consistent with the Baumol hypothesis on unbalanced growth. . . ." (p. 263).

Evidence: Government Costs

Other studies have directly examined the costs of producing state–local government services and changes in those costs over time. In one such study, the changes in the prices of inputs and workloads from 1962–1972 for different state–local government services were computed and compared to changes in expenditures for those services over the period (Sunley 1976, reporting work by Robert Reischauer). For instance, local school input prices include teacher salaries, book prices, and transportation costs, whereas workload is the number of school-age children. If expenditures increased more than required by increases in input prices and workloads, the remainder is assumed to represent increases in amount or quality of service.

The result of this study was that 52 percent of the increase in total state–local expenditures over this 10-year period was due to increases in input prices and that 13 percent resulted from increased workloads. Thus, only about 35 percent of the increase in state–local government spending in that decade represented increased quality or new service. There were, however, substantial variations for different types of service. Workload and price increases were particularly important for highways and parking, health and hospitals, and police and fire protection. The increase in input prices and workloads alone were sufficient to increase total state–local government expenditures from 11.4 percent of GNP in 1962 to 12.0 percent of GNP by 1972. As shown in Table 7.3, this was a period when state–local government wages were increasing rapidly in an attempt to catch up with private-sector wages. As suggested previously, state–local sector costs are influenced by changes in the rest of the economy, and increases in state–local expenditures do not necessarily represent increases in output or service.

Table 7.4

Percentage Change in Private-Sector Productivity and State—Local Costs

Period	Business		Earnings		Implicit Price Deflator	
	Productivity	Unit Labor Cost	All	State–local	Consumption	State–local Expenditure
1963–1973	27.4	46.7	73.7	81.9	38.6	71.3
1973–1982	4.6	109.1	102.4	89.1	96.1	109.2
1982–1985	6.1	6.5	13.3	17.5	12.6	14.5
1985–1995	16.5	25.7	70.2	86.4	27.8	35.6
1995–2004	32.6	11.7	57.2	46.1	13.0	27.8

SOURCES: *Economic Report of the President*, 1986 and 1993. U.S. Department of Commerce, *Survey of Current Business*, July issues, various years. U.S. Department of Commerce, Bureau of Economic Analysis Web site.

From the latter half of the 1970s through the first half of the 1980s, state–local government expenditures did not rise relative to income, however, suggesting that some aspect of the story changed. Possible explanations are that large productivity gains have, in fact, been made in producing state–local services or that the demand for state–local services has become more price elastic. The evidence reported in Table 7.4, however, suggests that the inverse of the Baumol hypothesis was operating from the mid-1970s through the early 1980s—low productivity growth in private industry helped to hold down relative state–local sector costs.

From 1973–1982, average annual earnings for full-time employees in all industries rose by 102.4 percent, although business productivity, measured as output per unit of labor, rose by only 4.6 percent; consequently, unit labor costs for business rose by 109.1 percent. Over these years, increases in private-sector wages were *not* matched by productivity gains, so business labor costs rose substantially, presumably inducing business to demand *less* labor. Fewer private-sector jobs created some slack in the labor market, allowing state–local governments to hold down wages. Over these years, average annual full-time employee earnings in state–local government rose 89.1 percent, losing ground to private-sector earnings. As measured by the GNP implicit price deflator, the prices of consumer goods rose 96.1 percent over these years while the price of state–local services rose 109.2 percent. Although the price of state–local services rose slightly compared to private consumer goods, the difference was much smaller than in the other two periods, when private productivity gains were large. Therefore, state–local government expenditures decreased from about 11.2 percent of GDP to 10.6 percent over these years.

The short 1982–1985 period is similar to the 1963–1973 period when substantial business productivity gains allowed earnings to rise with only modest increases in labor costs. The increase in state–local earnings during the 1982–1985 period is much greater than the increase in business unit-labor costs, and therefore the price of state–local services is again increasing much faster than the average price of private consumer goods. Thus, as expected, the share of GDP represented by state–local expenditures increased slightly between 1982 and 1985.

Since 1985, the prices of state–local goods have increased relative to those in the private sector. In the 1985–1995 period, productivity growth slowed to about 1.5 percent annually, so the increases in labor earnings (70.2 percent) resulted in increases in business unit-labor costs (25.7 percent). The fact that unit-labor costs in business did not increase even more may be due to increased international labor market competition. Earnings in the state–local sector increased even more, so prices of state–local goods increased more than those of private consumer goods. Beginning around 1995, productivity began to increase substantially at a rate of about 4 percent annually. Earnings continued to grow at about 7 percent annually, but growth of unit-labor costs slowed to only about 1 percent yearly as a result of the productivity change. Although earnings in the state–local sector did not increase as much as in private business, they did grow faster than private unit-labor costs, and thus prices of state–local goods and services rose about twice as much as those of private consumer goods.

The fact that the relative costs of state–local goods continued to increase due to a relative increase in labor costs suggests that states and localities have not discovered ways of increasing labor productivity as much as in the private sector. If governments cannot find these new technologies or production arrangements, then the fundamental assumption of the Baumol hypothesis continues to apply. The resulting fiscal pressure for state–local governments was somewhat hidden in the 1990s, as the state–local tax structure continued to generate substantial revenue as a result of fast national economic growth. As that ended with the national recession in 2001, however, the resulting enormous fiscal pressure for states and localities returned. Two possibilities for government productivity change are considered next: the use of new technology to produce old services in Application 7.1 and the possibility of substituting private production of government goods in the following section.

Application 7.1

TECHNOLOGY AND THE PRODUCTION OF PUBLIC SAFETY

The essence of the Baumol hypothesis is that it is difficult for service providers, including state and local governments, to increase labor productivity by using more capital-intensive production technologies. However, in the case of one traditional state–local service— police protection and public safety—some new technologies involving electronic inputs—computers and information databases, computer analyses of physical and biological evidence, electronic devices for gathering data, new weaponry—are being used by various jurisdictions. These methods hold the promise of producing public safety service more efficiently and perhaps lowering costs, but sometimes also raise difficult questions about the role of government and whether capital technologies change the meaning of "public safety."

The use of cameras always has been common in private security work, including for surveillance in banks, retail stores, apartment building entrances, and in recent years at automated teller machines. However, only

Application 7.1 — Technology and the Production of Public Safety

recently state and local police agencies have adopted and expanded the use of cameras and other electronic equipment. For instance, *The Wall Street Journal* (Patterson, 1988) reported about photo-radar, a high-speed camera attached through a computer to a radar gun, commonly used in Europe and being used in California and some other states. If the radar detects a speeding vehicle, a photograph is taken, the vehicle is identified by the license number, and the registered owner is sent a summons (requiring the owner to pay the fine or appear in court). In Australia, similar types of camera-detectors are used to monitor vehicle stops at traffic lights or signs. Owners of vehicles that run the lights (or signs) are mailed the evidence along with the equivalent of a traffic ticket. The possibilities for this type of enforcement seem limited only by imagination, as reflected by the accompanying *Pepper . . . and Salt* cartoon (Figure 7.3).

Figure 7.3

Pepper . . . and Salt

THE WALL STREET JOURNAL

"This is Officer Halloway. You are exceeding the speed limit by 6 mph. A ticket is being faxed to you."

Source: Reprinted from *The Wall Street Journal*—Permission, Cartoon Features Syndicate. August 27, 1993, p. A9.

Application 7.1 — Technology and the Production of Public Safety

Similarly, computerized information databases hold out the possibility of providing information about individuals, things, or events broadly to public safety officials quickly and at low cost. Information about individuals is perhaps most controversial. In theory, it would be possible for public safety agencies to access extremely detailed personal information about any person that could be used in solving specific crimes or even predicting potential criminal activity. Of course, to be useful this information must be available widely, which increases the danger that it might be misused.

Finally, electronic monitoring now is being used to track or restrict persons who are under investigation or who have been arrested for or convicted of crimes. An "electronic tether" that emits an electronic signal can be attached to an individual's body (usually the ankle), allowing officials to monitor the signal and know the location of the individual. Such a system might be used to prevent flight by someone waiting for trial, as a means of partial confinement (nonwork hours, for instance) for someone who has been convicted, or to monitor the behavior of someone on parole. One can envision other types of electronic aids in enforcing laws, promoting safe behavior, and apprehending violators.

Obviously, some electronic public safety activities might violate various provisions of the U.S. and state constitutions, especially concerning such topics as privacy, unreasonable search and seizure, and the presumption of innocence. Even when these measures are constitutional, however, implementing the measures and gaining public acceptance often cause serious problems. In the case of photo-radar, the camera identifies the vehicle and not the driver, so the penalty must be against the registered owner of the car, who may not be the user. If the owner is required to "prove" that he or she was not driving the vehicle at the time of the infraction to avoid penalty, is the presumption of innocence lost? Technological advances to fight crime also often result in technological advances to defeat the new enforcement technology, as illustrated by the ad in Figure 7.4 for "Photo Blocker" to prevent enforcement cameras from reading license plates. Also, *The Wall Street Journal* reported that manufacturers of radar detectors were working on new devices to detect photo-radar (which is shot across rather than along the road). Finally, thinking about other uses of cameras, one can reasonably ask whether people would feel "better off" or even "safer" if they were being watched *all* the time.

In short, technology can be used to improve efficiency, increase worker productivity, and reduce costs in providing public safety service; however, these technologies also change the nature of the "public safety" service. This issue raises the possibility of an interesting economic choice to be faced by voters. Voters can accept the new technological methods of producing public safety and enjoy lower costs (and taxes) but suffer a loss of privacy, or they can retain privacy by continuing to pay higher and higher costs for producing public safety with less invasive technology. In essence, individuals might be asked to put a value on the privacy that might be lost in adopting these new technologies.

PRIVATE PROVISION OF PUBLIC SERVICES

What Is Privatization?

One idea that has been proposed to increase the productivity of government and thus reduce costs is to transfer production of government services to private firms, which is called **privatization**. The term privatization has been applied, however, to several different ways of increasing the activity of the private sector in providing public services, as outlined in Table 7.5. The traditional public service situation is case 1: public-sector choice, financing, and production of a service. The other cases represent various degrees of privatization: private-sector choice, financing, and production of a service, perhaps involving deregulation of private firms providing services; public-sector choice with private-sector financing and production; and public-sector choice and financing with only private-sector production of the service selected. The first simply means that all responsibility for a service is transferred from the public sector to individual consumers who select the amount of service they desire and purchase that service from private suppliers. As an example, solid-waste collection is provided and produced by some local governments but left to private choice and private collection firms in other communities. This essentially can be characterized as "let the private sector do it alone."

The second and third versions of privatization refer, however, to joint activity of the public and private sectors in providing services. In case 2, the notion is that

Table 7.5

Degrees of Public and Private Involvement in Provision of Services

Case	Choice of Quality/Quantity	Financing	Production
1	Public	Public	Public
2	Public	Public	Private
3	Public	Private	Private
4	Private (Perhaps with Deregulation)	Private	Private

consumers collectively select and pay for the amount and type of service desired through government, which then contracts with private firms to produce the service. The only difference in case 3 is that consumers pay privately for the service selected publicly. As discussed in Chapter 6, some local governments often contract with other governments to produce services in order to take advantage of economies of scale. Contracting with private firms to produce goods and services also may reduce costs. For the example of solid-waste collection, the idea is that the community selects a level of collection service and the government contracts with a private firm to do the collection and disposal. The service might be financed by government taxes and fees or by prices charged by the private producer. The government *provides* for the service, although a private firm *produces* the service. Privatization has been an issue in recent years as some states and localities have experimented with or at least considered privatization for services usually both provided and produced by government in the past. These concepts of privatization are focused on in this chapter.

Private production of publicly selected and financed goods and services can be applied to intermediate goods used by government in producing services (such as cars and trucks, paper, machines, and materials), to services consumed by government in carrying out its responsibilities (such as maintenance and repair, construction, data processing, and management and financial services), and for the final services consumed directly by taxpayers (such as education, police and fire protection, and transportation). In the first instance, privatization is nearly universal. Few, if any, governments or government agencies produce their own furniture, forms, buses, or computers—all are purchased by the government from private producers. Concerning the other possibilities, in a review of privatization experience, Robert Poole and Philip Fixler (1987, 617) noted that "most privatization at state and local levels of government has been applied to either routine housekeeping services in which government itself is the customer (maintenance of public buildings, vehicles, and infrastructure) or public services with well-defined tangible outputs (garbage collection or recreation, for example)." Increasingly, however, government is considering or experimenting with private production of traditional public goods, including public safety services and education.

How Might Privatization Reduce Costs?

In its simplest form, the argument is that government producers have no incentive to hold down production costs, whereas private producers who contract with the government to provide service do. Suppose, for example, that a private firm contracts with a local government to pick up six bags of garbage per house per week in the community for a fee of $100 per house per year. Obviously, the lower the cost incurred by the firm in satisfying the contract, the greater profit it makes. Competition among potential private suppliers for this contract (for a limited period, after which government can change contractors) is expected to bring government the lowest possible cost for the specified level of service. As summarized by Janet Rothenberg Pack (1987, 527), "... *competitive* bidding by profit-maximizing firms for a well-specified output guarantees that the product will be produced at the lowest cost. The absence of competition and profit incentives in the public sector is not likely to result in cost minimization."

The simple notion that government has no incentive to hold production costs down may be too strong, at least in the local government context, because local officials face competition from potential candidates and communities face competition from other communities for residents and businesses. If government production costs for a service in one community are higher than they need to be, then taxes in that community also are higher than they need to be. As a result, households or businesses might move, as in the Tiebout process (see Chapter 5), to those communities with lower production costs for a given level of service. Similarly, candidates for public office could make the production inefficiency an issue in the local election. Therefore, it may be more accurate to argue that the incentive to hold cost down is *greater* for a profit-maximizing firm than it is for a government but not completely lacking in the latter. Essentially, the contention is that economic competition is more effective than political competition.

The three potential sources of lower production costs for private firms most often cited are lower labor costs, better management, and more research/development and faster innovation of the results. Lower labor costs may arise either from lower wages (which means that the government was paying wages higher than necessary for a given skill) or from less labor input (which means that government was hiring unnecessary workers or that fewer workers are needed with an alternative production method). A private firm may more readily try out different production approaches, whereas government may tend to stick with the current approach, given that change often creates substantial political difficulties for local officials. Better management or experimentation and innovation with different production methods may be the reason a given level of service can be produced with fewer workers. In addition, private firms may use retained earnings to finance research or to purchase new capital equipment, which lowers unit production costs, whereas government may not be able to allocate tax revenues to those purposes as easily, given the many competing demands for a share of the government's budget.

When Might Privatization Not Work Well?

The three most often cited potential problems with private provision of government services arise from the bidding process, the precise specification of the contract, and monitoring and enforcing the contract. First, competitive bidding may not provide the service at lowest cost to the contracting government if there are only a few (or even one) potential suppliers and the government has a limited idea about the level of costs. This might be the case especially in rural areas or when the production technology is relatively new. In addition, potential suppliers initially might offer a price to the government that is less than actual production costs to induce the government to adopt privatization or to win the contract. Subsequently, the contractor then would demand a higher price after the government has eliminated or dismantled its own production system. The chance of such "low-balling" in the bidding process may be reduced if the local government requires relatively long-term contracts.

The second potential difficulty with privatization concerns specifying the service to be provided in the contract. Earlier in this chapter, you learned that the output of a government service can be characterized by the inputs used or by alternative measures of the produced output or final result, none of which are unique for a particular service. Characterizing output for some services is particularly difficult when the government has multiple objectives. If society and the government are not certain what "good" education is and how to measure it, for instance, how can government contract for it? In the discussion about producing education in Chapter 19, the distinction between the average student test score and the variance of scores is emphasized. Getting the highest average test score may require applying more educational resources to the better students with the effect of reducing the scores for the students at the bottom. As a result, the variation in test scores increases, which might contradict the distributional objective of government provided education. It is difficult to think about how one would begin to specify the contracted output for police protection (a specified percentage of different types of crimes must be "solved"?) or fire protection (fires must be responded to in X minutes with average damages limited to Y?).

The third potential problem with private provision concerns monitoring the service quality provided by the private supplier and enforcing the contract when problems arise. Monitoring the performance of the private contractor itself creates costs, which may be substantial, for the government. In some cases, new data may have to be collected and analyzed. As one example, consider the costs of the U.S. Department of Defense in testing and evaluating weapons produced by private contractors to ensure they meet the contract standards. In addition, there must be a reasonable remedy if the supplier does not provide or stops the expected service. Suppose that the contractor underestimates the cost of production so that the price charged the government is not sufficient to cover all production costs, resulting in losses for the firm. If the firm simply stops providing the service, the implications could be serious in the case of many services such as police and fire protection.

David Sappington and Joseph Stiglitz (1987) have termed these contractual issues "the need for and costs of intervention in the private production process."

They suggest that government should consider both the probability that intervention will be necessary and the costs of intervening if necessary. They conclude that "two important elements of this calculation include the complexity of the task under consideration and the need for rapid adaptation to unforeseen contingencies. When the task is particularly novel and complex, unforeseen contingencies are likely to arise. If rapid adaptation to these events is crucial, . . . public provision is more likely to be the preferred mode of organization" (p. 581).

Experience with and Prospects for Privatization

The available evidence shows that nearly all state–local governments contract with private firms to provide *some* final services to consumers or intermediate services to the government, but which services are contracted for varies greatly among governments. Donald Kettl (1993) reports that only two services (vehicle towing and legal services) were contracted out by at least half the local governments surveyed by the International City/County Management Association, and only 15 of the 75 service categories were contracted for by at least one-third of localities. According to this survey and others, the other most common examples of government contracting with private firms include legal services; hazardous waste disposal and solid waste collection; vehicle leasing and maintenance; vehicle towing; street light operation; street repair; landscaping and grounds maintenance; management of public facilities such as stadiums/arenas and convention centers; architectural, engineering, and management consulting; ambulance and EMT services; and some public-health services, especially for mental health and drug treatment. (The detailed list is in Table 6.4.) In addition, government continues to purchase most intermediate goods from private producers.

Kettl notes that government contracting is more likely, as with the preceding examples, when that service already is commonly provided in the private market. In such cases, government provision of these services may not be necessary when private provision is already readily available. Conversely, only a very small fraction of state and local governments contract for traditional programs central to those governments, such as prisons, police service, fire protection, traffic enforcement, libraries, or water and sewage treatment. As a result, privatization attempts in these areas are among the most dramatic and controversial.

One area where privatization has been tried but remains very controversial is public safety. For many years, fire-protection service in Scottsdale, Arizona, has been provided by a private contract service. Although this case has received substantial attention and at least one study shows it to be less costly than public protection, private fire-protection service is mostly restricted to specialized cases such as airports. A 1997 survey of local governments by the International City/County Management Association (Werntz, 1999) showed that only about 2.5 percent of localities reported providing fire prevention or suppression service through contracts with private firms. Public safety areas in which contracting with private firms was used substantially included ambulance and emergency medical services (a quarter to a third of localities) and vehicle towing and storage (80 percent of local governments).

Even more attention has been focused on the private ownership or operation of prisons, of which there are currently about 50 in operation spanning 14 states

Figure 7.5

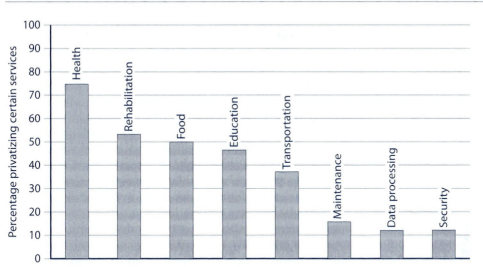

Privatization of services to public prisons

Note: Data based on survey respondents from 25 corrections agencies in 22 states.
SOURCE: Reprinted with permission, *Governing* magazine, copyright 1993, 1994, and 1995.
May 1993, p. 47.

(Lemov, May 1993). So far, most of these contracts have been for detention centers and minimum-security facilities, although there is some movement toward expanding the trend to higher-security facilities. Short of actually operating prisons, it is even more common for states to contract for private provision of some services in prisons, particularly health care, food service, and rehabilitation and education, as shown in Figure 7.5.

Many of the potential advantages and problems about privatization discussed previously are illustrated by the case of public safety. So far, any lower costs from private operation seem to have come mostly from lower wages or benefits paid to workers, but some firms are developing new educational or work programs for inmates. In establishing contracts, governments often try to specify both cost limits (often as a percentage of the cost at a state prison or a limited rate of growth) as well as performance measures to ensure that lower costs do not arise simply by providing worse conditions for prisoners. Governments that have privatized prisons believe that monitoring the actions of the contractor is crucial and thus often maintain a monitoring state inspector at the prison. Yet, serious worries about liability remain. If an employee was seriously negligent, it seems possible that both the private contractor and the state could be sued. As a result of the damages, the private contractor could go bankrupt, leaving the state to pay damages and to absorb the costs of running the prison.

Poole and Fixler (1987, 619) argue that "four other functions generally carried out by government today are likely candidates for privatization in the next decade: transit, highways and freeways, water supply, and education." Private provision already is used in all four of these areas to some degree. For instance, a number of private bridge firms have been employed, including the firm operating the tunnel under and the bridge over the Detroit River between Detroit and Windsor, Ontario, and the company operating the private toll bridge between Fargo, North Dakota and Moorhead, Minnesota. Both California and Virginia are experimenting with private toll roads that will compete with "free" public roads. Chicago, New York, and other cities have contracted out the collection of parking fees and some traffic fines.

Privatization of education may turn out to be most controversial, however. Education already involves a mixture of public and private provision in not only private elementary and secondary schools but also private day care, nursery schools, tutorial services, and extracurricular activities (for example, music and sports). But the notion of additional privatization in education as usually envisioned by its proponents involves either private provision entirely or direct competition between private and public schools. Individuals could receive education vouchers from the government that could be "spent" for any school desired. Thus, government would continue to finance a substantial portion of education through taxes, but the education service would be produced by private schools. Proponents argue that the resulting competition would reduce education costs and/or improve education results, partly because students would select schools most appropriate for them. Opponents of more privatization in education usually cite concerns about the distributional effects if students become more sorted by ability or other characteristics than they are with the current system. Indeed, some have argued that a diverse student mix is essential to the socialization objective of education and are concerned that there would be less diversity with private education than with the current public schools' structure. If education involves such important externalities, then public provision may be called for. These issues are considered in further detail in Chapter 19.

Substantial and increasing evidence also supports that the use of private firms to produce services has resulted in lower costs, especially for the more typical types of privatization. Kettl (1993) reports that 80 percent of localities that tried contracting out had cost savings of at least 10 percent (suggesting that localities are selecting the correct services to contract for in aggregate). For instance, studies by E. S. Savas and Barbara Stevens (1977) and by James McDavid (1985) have found that public solid waste-collection services are 50 to 70 percent more expensive than equivalent private collection services. (This may not be too surprising because waste collection is entirely a private-sector activity in many communities, suggesting that there may be specific reasons why collection remains a public service in certain areas). These cost savings almost all are labor savings arising from more flexible methods of organizing and using workers or from paying lower wages than government or, most importantly, from providing fewer or lower-level benefits.

From a different perspective, John Donahue (1989) argues that any cost savings and other benefits from privatization arise not so much from contracting out per se, but rather from competition. Greene (2002) stresses this point as well. He notes that the research about costs of residential solid waste collection shows that government contracting with private firms is least costly, but that an entirely open or private system is most costly. This may suggest that substantial monopoly power may arise in an entirely private system. Having government compete with private producers—as well as the private producers competing with each other—may help maintain competition and keep costs lower.

Governments may be able to enjoy the benefits of economic competition without contracting out by encouraging public agencies or divisions to bid for projects against private firms or other public entities. In Rochester, New York for example, city refuse collection workers changed their methods to keep costs below those of a private firm the city considered, contracting with. On the other hand, contracting may not generate lower costs or better quality if there are few private suppliers who therefore have monopoly power (especially if competition from public provision is eliminated). For instance, Kettl reports that only two main firms are involved in hazardous waste disposal, and that requests for mental health contracting in Massachusetts drew only 1.7 proposals from private producers, on average. With few private suppliers and little competition in bidding, the government has few options if the contractor does not carry out the contract satisfactorily. From this perspective, the main focus of government officials should be on developing and maintaining competition among producers of government-provided services.

Application 7.2

PRODUCING CITY FIRE PROTECTION SERVICES[7]

In a classic example of detailed examination of a single service, Malcolm Getz (1975) surveyed 371 central-city fire departments about inputs and production methods, costs, city characteristics, and results. The survey resulted in usable data from 187 different cities covering 44 states plus the District of Columbia. Many other state–local government services have been studied also (transportation and education are discussed in subsequent chapters), but this detailed examination of fire protection provides an especially interesting example of many issues discussed in this chapter.

Getz discovered great diversity among these city fire departments in the amount and types of inputs used to produce fire protection. On average, each fire station served an area covering three and one-half square miles, although the range was from one station for one square mile to one for nine square miles. Similarly, there were 6.8 firefighters per station on average, with a range from 3.3 to 11.6. Perhaps even more interesting, given their low

cost, is the large variation in the number of fire hydrants; on average, there were 85.6 hydrants per square mile, although the standard deviation was 50 and the range from 14 to 302! Input prices also varied substantially. Compensation cost per full-time employee (a weighted average of salaries and fringes for a first-class firefighter and a department captain) varied from $27,000 in Springdale, Arkansas, to $119,000 in Washington, D.C. An index of the cost of building and operating a fire station in these cities varied from 76 to 114, with an average of all the city values equal to 96.

Economists would suspect that the amount and type of inputs selected by these departments would be influenced by input prices. Getz reported that the elasticity of labor per square mile with respect to the wage was −.36; cities with higher wages used fewer firefighters per square mile, although demand is relatively inelastic. Interestingly, cities with higher wages also used *fewer* stations and trucks per square mile. Apparently, these fire

---

[7]See Getz (1979).

Application 7.2 — Producing City Fire Protection Services

departments attempted to keep the amount of firefighters and trucks per station constant and responded to higher wages by decreasing use of all three. Getz also found that the amount and mix of inputs depended on city characteristics. Cities with older housing tended to use more of all inputs, cities with more manufacturing used relatively more aerial trucks compared to pumpers, whereas cities that had more business than residential activity also used more of all inputs.

Getz attempted to measure how variations in inputs influenced the effectiveness of the fire department but found very little statistical relationship between additional inputs and improved output. Fire-department output was measured by number of fires per 1,000 houses and per 1,000 commercial and residential employees, by the dollars of damage per fire, and by the number of civilian fire deaths per million population. Two results that did appear were that more fire-code inspectors decreased the number of multi-family house fires and that more stations per square mile decreased the amount of damage per industrial fire. In the statistical work, both the number of and damage from fires were mostly related to the age of structures in the city—cities with older structures had more fires and more serious fires.

The premise of the Baumol hypothesis is that productivity improvement is difficult to achieve for some services, state–local government services included. But Getz did find some major technological changes in the methods and equipment used in fire fighting. Among methods, upon arriving at a fire, a department must choose whether to first run water-supply hoses from the nearest water supply or to immedi-

ately attack the fire using a relatively small amount of water carried in a pumper truck. The latter method, called a "booster attack," was introduced around 1922 and is now routinely used by more than half of the departments. Technological changes involving equipment include use of breathing apparatus (first used in 1940); power saws for quick access (1958); chemicals added to water for fighting flammable-liquid fires, called "light water" (1956); and a quick-connect hose coupling (1964).

One other major attempt to increase productivity and lower costs of fire (and police) protection has been the creation of consolidated public safety departments to provide both fire and police functions.[8] Some departments are fully consolidated with all duties performed by public safety officers, others perform dual duty only for some services or in limited geographic areas, and still others are consolidated only at the administrative level. Crank (1990) reported that only 1 to 2 percent of local police and fire services are provided through consolidated departments, with the middle 1970s the most common period for initial consolidation. Not surprisingly, consolidated service tends to be more common among smaller localities where there are potential cost savings from economies of scale. Because of quality concerns about training of dual-service personnel and economic concerns about appropriate wages and benefits, some states and localities have forbidden such a production arrangement. Therefore, it appears that some productivity improvement has occurred in producing fire protection, but it is not clear that the gain has been sufficient to prevent cost increases nor that all such possibilities will be embraced.

[8]See Crank (1990).

Application 7.3

PRIVATIZING ENTIRE STATE DEPARTMENTS[9]

Governing Magazine reported about an attempt in Texas to take privatization in a new and much more expansive direction than has been used in the past. As previous discussion in this chapter suggests, most privatization by the state–local sector is applied to purchases of specific inputs used by the government (such as motor vehicles) or to very specific, direct services (such as health care in prisons or computer systems programming). But Texas is now exploring the option of consolidating state departments and contracting as much of the operation of those departments as possible.

A recent law directs the Texas Health and Human Services Commission to consolidate 12 health and human service agencies into 4 and then to seek private sector operation of as much of the work of those agencies as possible. If implemented, the Commission would serve the continuing political or traditional role of state government, contracting with private firms to undertake the day-to-day work of the agencies. The initial intent is to contract with a private firm to establish a call center staffed by private employees who would evaluate the circumstances of individuals and determine whether and what benefits they might be eligible for. So, rather than visiting the local office of the state human services department to apply for specific benefits, the individuals would telephone the center and have those decisions made by the contractor. As this approach is expanded, the state is on the verge of transferring substantial operational decisions—and perhaps even policy decisions—to individuals who are not state employees but contractors. The goal, it seems, is to be more efficient— to deliver more service at constant cost or constant service at lower cost.

Expanding privatization in this manner clearly is controversial and will be watched closely. It may or may not turn out to be a mechanism to reduce costs. Imagine, if you will, not going to your local school for class taught by a teacher employed by the school district. Instead, students go to Language, Inc. for Spanish class, Math R Us for math class, and so on—each provided by a private contractor hired by the school system. That is the nature of the issue.

SUMMARY

The output of state–local governments can be measured in at least three different, broad ways. Output can be measured (1) by the amount of money spent by a government on a service, referred to as expenditures; (2) by the amount of directly produced output provided by the government; and (3) by results—the level of consumption enjoyed by citizens.

State–local governments purchase inputs such as labor services, capital goods, and materials and supplies and combine then in some way to provide public facilities or what is called directly produced output. The cost of the directly produced

---

[9]See Walters, Jonathan. "Going Outside." *Governing Magazine*, May 2004, pp. 23–29.

output, which depends on the production technology and the prices of the inputs, is the expenditure of the government on this service.

The service result, called the consumer output, depends on the directly produced output provided by the government, on the private consumption decisions of individuals, and on the characteristics of the community and the population.

If the prices of inputs rise, then it will cost governments more to provide the same produced output. And if input prices differ for different subnational jurisdictions, equal expenditures by different jurisdictions do not necessarily translate into equal produced output.

Expenditures for direct-labor services represent about half of the expenditures by state–local governments on average. State–local governments are also one of the largest employers in the economy, employing about one of every seven employees.

Baumol argued that productivity increases in some sectors of the economy would force wage increases throughout the economy, increasing the production costs in those sectors where productivity improvements do not occur. The nature of some state–local government services precludes productivity gains because the essence of the service is the labor itself. For those services, unit production costs would certainly increase, and the choice for consumers is either to substantially reduce consumption of the service or to spend ever-increasing amounts to continue consuming current levels.

DISCUSSION QUESTIONS

1. "If one city spends more on police-protection services per capita than does another, one expects less crime in the first city than in the second." True, false, or uncertain? Explain.

2. At a public-budget hearing, a citizen once argued, "Education expenditures have increased 5 percent in each of the past three years even though student enrollment has been declining. Where is the extra money going? It seems to me that if the number of students declines, expenditures should also decline." Is the citizen right or wrong?

3. "If the Baumol hypothesis is correct concerning local government finances and if the price elasticity of demand for local services is inelastic, then we are in trouble—eventually, spending for education, police and fire protection, and sanitation will require half of our incomes." Evaluate this concern. What changes could occur to prevent this from happening?

4. Competing with private-sector salaries is a common problem for some academic departments in universities, particularly in engineering, accounting, other business fields, and biological science. If universities do not match the salaries, they may be unable to hire professors, or at least the better candidates; if they do match the salaries, then the cost of operating those programs (and eventually tuition) will increase. How might universities change the production of engineering or business education to

avoid this problem—that is, how could professors be substituted for or made more productive? Do you think those changes would affect the "quality" or nature of education in these fields? Does this problem apply to private as well as public universities?

SELECTED READINGS

Baumol, William. "Macroeconomics of Unbalanced Growth: The Anatomy of the Urban Crisis." *American Economic Review*, 62 (June 1967): 415–26.

Bradford, David F., R. A. Malt, and Wallace E. Oates. "The Rising Cost of Local Public Services: Some Evidence and Reflections." *National Tax Journal*, 22 (June 1969): 185–202.

Greene, Jeffrey D. *Cities and Privatization*. Upper Saddle River, N.J.: Pearson Education, 2002.

Hirsch, Werner. "State and Local Government Production." In *The Economics of State and Local Government*. New York: McGraw-Hill, 1970, 147–65.

Kettl, Donald F. *Sharing Power: Public Governance and Private Markets*. Washington: The Brookings Institution, 1993.

Pack, Janet Rothenberg. "Privatization of Public-Sector Services in Theory and Practice." *Journal of Policy Analysis and Management*, 6 (Summer 1987): 523–40.

PRICING OF GOVERNMENT GOODS—USER CHARGES

The economic case for the expansion and rationalization of pricing in the urban public sector rests essentially on the contribution it can make to allocative efficiency. Prices will provide correct signals to indicate the quantity and quality of things citizens desire. . . .[1]
—SELMA J. MUSHKIN AND RICHARD M. BIRD

HEADLINES

"GOLF AND SWIMMING ARE ACTIVITIES THAT ARE GOOD CANDIDATES FOR USER FEES. BOTH REQUIRE PHYSICAL STRUCTURES THAT ARE EXPENSIVE TO MAINTAIN, BUT NOT ALL RESIDENTS OF A COMMUNITY WILL USE THESE FACILITIES. THE LOCAL GOVERNMENT CAN OFFSET SOME OF THE MAINTENANCE COSTS BY ASSESSING A FEE FOR USE OF THE FACILITIES. OFTEN RESIDENTS OF A COMMUNITY DO NOT WANT TO PAY FOR SERVICES THAT THEY DO NOT USE. ALTHOUGH GOLF AND SWIMMING POOL FACILITIES ARGUABLY ENHANCE THE QUALITY OF LIFE IN A COMMUNITY, A LOCAL GOVERNMENT THAT CHARGES USER FEES MORE FAIRLY DISTRIBUTES THE RESPONSIBILITY FOR PAYMENT." (MOULDER, 2002, P. 4)

A SURVEY OF LOCAL GOVERNMENTS IN 2001 BY THE INTERNATIONAL CITY/COUNTY MANAGEMENT ASSOCIATION SHOWED THAT NEARLY 34 PERCENT OF LOCALITIES PROVIDE GOLF FACILITIES AND NEARLY 67 PERCENT REPORTED OWNING A SWIMMING POOL OR LEASING A PRIVATE POOL FOR PUBLIC USE. OF THOSE LOCALITIES PROVIDING GOLF COURSES, 99 PERCENT CHARGE USER FEES AND 78 PERCENT CHARGE RENT FOR PRIVATE USE OF THE FACILITIES. AMONG THOSE LOCALITIES WITH SWIMMING POOLS, 93 PERCENT CHARGE USER FEES AND 79 PERCENT COLLECT RENTAL FEES FOR PRIVATE USE.[2]

---

[1]"Public Prices: An Overview." In *Public Prices for Public Products*, edited by Selma Mushkin, 11. Washington, D.C.: The Urban Institute, 1972.

[2]Moulder, Evelina. *Financing Parks and Recreation: User Fees and Fund-Raising as Revenue Sources.* Washington, D.C.: International City/County Management Association, 2002.

Farcus

by David Waisglass
Gordon Coulthart

www.farcus.com

© 1993 Farcus Cartoons

WAISGLASS/COULTHART

"You know, of course, there's a toll."

User charges, which are prices governments charge for specific services or privileges to pay for all or part of the cost of providing those services, have always been important (although perhaps not as much as the *Farcus* cartoon suggests) but have become increasingly so in the past decade. User charge financing is different from financing through general taxes, because with tax financing no direct relationship exists between tax payment and service received. Common examples of user-charge financing in the state–local government arena include water charges, tuition at public colleges and universities, public hospital charges, parking fees, highway tolls, subway or bus charges, and park entrance fees.

TYPES AND USE OF CHARGES

The types of financing methods considered as user charges include direct charges for using a public facility or consuming a good or service, license taxes or fees paid for undertaking some activity (such as fishing license and driver license fees), and special assessments, a type of property tax levied for a specific service and based on some physical characteristic of the property, such as front

Table 8.1

Amounts of Charges and Fees, State and Local Governments, 2002[a]

Type	Amount (billions of dollars)	Percent of General Revenue	Total
User Charges	$253.19	15.0%	77.0%
License Taxes and Fees	36.72	2.2	11.2
Special Assessments	4.78	0.3	1.5
Other Unallocable Taxes	34.08	2.0	10.4
Total	328.77	19.5	100.0

[a]This measure of charges excludes revenue from public utilities (electric, gas, water) and liquor stores. In most cases, these services are sold directly, so that user charges represent the bulk (more than 80 percent) of financing. See Netzer, 1992.

SOURCE: U.S. Department of Commerce, *Governmental Finances: 2001–02* (2005).

Table 8.2

State–Local User Charges and Expenditures, by Category, 2002

Category	Category User Charge as Percentage of All User Charges	Category User Charge as Percentage of Direct Expenditures in Category
Education	28.6%	12.2%
Hospitals	25.9	75.2
Sewers and Sanitation	15.1	76.1
Air Transportation	4.9	76.1
Highways	3.3	7.2
Parks and Recreation	2.8	23.3
Other	14.9	—

[a]For comparison, Netzer (1992) reports similar ratios in 1989 for water supply (81.8), electric power supply (93.7), and gas supply (103.1).

SOURCE: U.S. Department of Commerce, *Governmental Finances: 2001–02* (2005).

footage (for example, assessments for sidewalk construction). State–local governments collected nearly $329 billion in these types of charges in 2002, with traditional user charges accounting for about 77 percent of the total, as shown in Table 8.1.

The magnitude of state–local traditional user charges, either in nominal or real dollars, clearly has risen substantially since the early 1960s and particularly fast since the mid-1980s (Figures 8.1a and 8.1b). Current charges increased faster than the general level of prices over this entire period, except for 1978–1980, and much faster than the general inflation rate since then. All charges and fees together represented 19.5 percent of the general revenue of state–local governments in 2002 with traditional user charges alone representing 15 percent of revenue.

Most state–local user charges arise in the budget categories for education and hospitals.[3] As shown in Table 8.2, on average nearly 55 percent of all subnational government direct user charges are attributable to those categories. Of all other

[3]When state or local government owns and operates public utilities (electric or natural gas) and liquor stores, the prices for those services also represent user charges. See Netzer, 1992.

Figure 8.1a

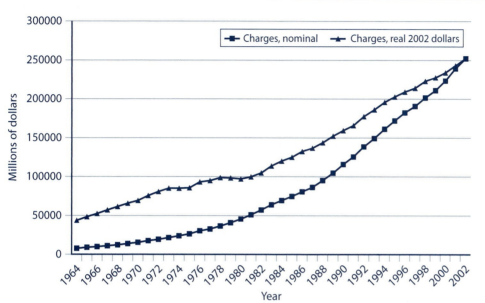

State–local current charges (nominal and real dollars)

Figure 8.1b

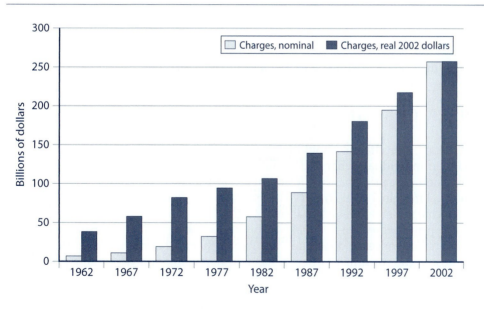

State–local current charges, selected years

individual categories, sewers and sanitation account for 15 percent of charges, the only one that is more than 10 percent. For that reason, extreme caution must be used when comparing user-charge use among different states (or localities). Without large public higher-education and hospital systems, user charges may appear as a small fraction of revenue simply because those services are not provided. Interjurisdictional comparisons should be made by budget category.[4]

More than half of state–local expenditures on airports, hospitals, and sewer and sanitation systems are financed by user charges, whereas only about 12 percent of education expenditures are financed that way. Although tuition and other charges by public colleges and universities are a large fraction of total user charges, they represent a small fraction of total state–local education expenditures when the mostly tax-financed primary and secondary school expenditures are included. The opposite is true for airports, sewer and sanitation systems, and parks and recreation services, for which user charges are a small fraction of all charges but represent a large fraction of spending in those categories.

By 2002, user charges (broadly defined) accounted for more than 14 cents for every dollar of state revenue and 18 cents per dollar for local governments (including nearly 23 cents per dollar for cities). Changes in the pattern of user-charge reliance since 1962 for different types of subnational governments are depicted in Table 8.3. Reliance on user charges, license fees, and special assessments together has increased for both state and local governments since the 1970s, compared to decreases in reliance on those charges in the 1962–1977 period. Among local governments, county governments have continually increased reliance on user charges although municipalities and townships followed the general pattern of decreasing reliance until the late 1970s and then subsequently increasing. Charges provide a small (and decreasing) fraction of revenue for school districts and a relatively large fraction (more than 40 percent) for special districts. Focusing on direct user charges alone, reliance by states and localities changed little from 1962 to the late 1970s and increased substantially since. Clearly, total user charges of state–local governments, whether broadly or narrowly defined, have increased faster than other revenues since the late 1970s.

THEORY OF USER CHARGES

In theory, user charges should operate as benefit taxes (discussed in Chapter 2), with an individual's charge depending both on the benefit (use) and cost of the provision. The principal rule for economic efficiency requires that marginal benefit equal marginal cost. For services that primarily benefit the direct consumer, the price charged should equal marginal cost.

The principal reason this makes economic sense is simple. If consumers believe that public services and facilities are "free"—that is, that more can be produced at no cost to the consumer (when in fact additional amounts do entail a production

---

[4]In fact, user charges as a percentage of general revenue are largest for states with relatively lower per-capita revenue and smallest for high-revenue states. The five states with the largest fraction of revenue from user charges are Alabama (25.2 percent), South Carolina (21.56 percent), Mississippi (20.1 percent), Utah (20.0 percent), and Idaho (19.7 percent), whereas the five with the smallest user-charge ratios are Connecticut (7.7 percent), Rhode Island (8.4 percent), Alaska (9.6 percent), Massachusetts (9.8 percent), and Maine (9.9 percent). Similarly, Netzer (1992) reports that increases in state per-capita incomes are associated with decreased reliance on user charges.

Table 8.3

User Charges and User-Associated Taxes as a Percent of General Revenue, by Level of Government, Various Years

| Year | States | All | Local Governments | | | | |
			Counties	Municipalities	Townships	School Districts	Special Districts
1962							
Charges	7.1%	10.6%					
All[a]	16.3	13.7	11.9	17.8	7.8	6.6	48.2
1972							
Charges	7.9	10.5					
All	14.0	12.7	13.4	15.3	7.7	5.7	44.3
1982							
Charges	6.4	11.4					
All	11.7	14.7	16.6	17.3	9.3	4.9	38.1
1987							
Charges	7.6	13.2					
All	11.9	15.6	17.2	19.2	10.9	4.5	38.4
1992							
Charges	8.7	14.6					
All	12.6	16.8	18.5	20.9	12.1	4.6	42.8
1997							
Charges	8.9	15.9					
All	12.7	18.1	21.0	23.1	12.5	4.4	42.9
2002							
Charges	9.4	15.4					
All	14.3	17.7	20.7	22.8	13.2	4.3	41.6

[a]Charges plus license taxes and fees plus special assessments plus other unallocable taxes.

SOURCE: Census of Governments, *Compendium of Government Finances,* various years.

cost)—consumers will be induced to demand more than the efficient amount of those services or facilities. One function of user charges is to make consumers face the true costs of their consumption decisions and create an incentive for efficient choice.[5]

The basic idea of that choice is illustrated by Figure 8.2, which depicts the marginal benefit schedules for both direct users (MB_U) of a service or facility and all of society (MB_S), who also benefit generally. Those marginal benefits are added together to determine the aggregate marginal benefit to the entire society or community from an additional unit of the service ($\sum MB_i$). Given a cost of producing one more unit equal to MC, the efficient amount of the service or facility is Q^*. The private marginal benefits to users and general marginal benefits to all at that quantity determine how the production costs should be divided among users (a user charge) and all of society (general taxes). In this case, user charges should account for MB_U^*/MC of the facility's cost. Because direct users face a marginal cost of MB_U^*, they demand quantity Q^*, which is the efficient quantity.

---

[5]You may want to review the section on public goods and benefit taxation in Chapter 2.

Figure 8.2

Allocation of costs
to direct users and
society in general

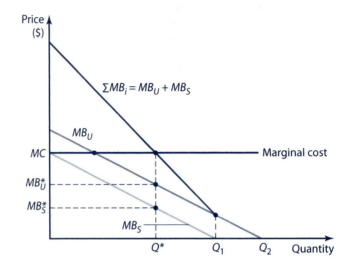

In contrast, if users perceive the marginal cost to be zero, they demand amount Q_2. This is not efficient because the marginal benefits to everyone—the sum of the marginal benefits to direct users and to society generally—are less than the cost of producing all the units of output between Q^* and Q_2. That difference between marginal cost and aggregate marginal benefit represents the potential efficiency cost of not charging appropriate prices for this service.

Several general principles of efficient user charges follow from this analysis:

1. The greater the share of marginal benefits that accrues to direct users, the more attractive user-charge financing becomes.

2. User-charge financing requires that direct users can be easily identified and excluded (at reasonable cost) from consuming the service unless the charge is paid, assuming that most of the benefits of a service or facility go to direct users.

3. The efficiency case for user-charge financing is stronger, the more price elastic is demand. In the special case of a perfectly inelastic (vertical) demand, price does not matter. No inefficiency results if consumers underestimate cost. Obviously, the more price elastic demand is, the greater the potential for inefficiency if consumers do not face true costs.

4. Marginal benefits, not total benefits, matter for determining user charges. For instance, in Figure 8.2, quantities of the facility beyond Q_1 provide benefits only to direct users. Thus, despite the fact that all of society benefits some from this facility, direct users should finance *entirely* the production of amounts greater than Q_1.

This last principle deserves additional explanation. The general rule is that costs should be allocated in proportion to benefits, but the question is which costs? Here it is helpful to distinguish between the capital costs for the *amount* of a service or facility to provide—the long-run production decision—and the operating costs associated with the *use* of a given facility—a short-run decision. For instance, a local community faces a decision about the appropriate number and size of parks to provide, whereas a state government selects the number and size of public colleges. After a given amount of those facilities is provided, however, each government also faces a choice about how much and by whom those facilities are to be used. Should park use be free or should there be an entrance charge? Should the charge be different for residents and nonresidents? Should the charge be different at different times? Similar questions apply to college tuition. User charges can have a role to play in the decisions both about amount and use.[6]

Allocating Access (Capital) Costs

The costs for constructing or acquiring a public facility should be paid by those groups in society who will benefit from the *existence* of the facility, which may be different from those who benefit from using the facility directly. For instance, an individual who may never drive a car still benefits from roads as a result of transportation of goods and other people. Individuals may benefit from a facility, even if they do not use it directly, in three main ways. First, the facility's existence provides individuals the *option* of using it in the future, should their demands change. An individual may not use a particular bridge currently, but may move in the future to an area that would require using the bridge to commute. Such *option value* is particularly significant when it would be very costly, or even impossible, to provide the public facility in the future. Such might be the case with public parks that preserve land in a relatively undeveloped state (as it might be impossible to reverse development after it has occurred).

Second, individuals who are not direct users also might benefit if the facility generates spillovers in the form of additional economic activity. Such monetary benefits to nonusers associated with public facilities or services might include spending on private services that complement public services (a private bait shop near a public park), attracting funds from other jurisdictions (tourism), or improving the environment and attracting workers (which increases the supply of labor and holds labor costs down).

Third, nonusers might benefit from pure altruism, receiving personal benefits from providing service to others. If all residents of a jurisdiction benefit from the existence of or access to a public service or facility, then all residents should contribute toward acquiring that facility based on those general benefits, which are independent of use.

---

[6]It may not be practical to separate long-run and short-run pricing decisions, however, because that might require prices to change substantially over time. If price is set equal to short-run marginal cost, higher prices are called for as demand rises. Because those prices will be greater than long-run average cost, funds will be provided to finance the desired capital expansion. But after the facility is enlarged, marginal costs, and thus prices, will fall again. Some type of average cost pricing would maintain more price stability but would be inefficient. Price stability in itself might be desirable, however.

If all residents as well as users should pay all or part of the long-run production costs of public facilities, these charges should be independent of the amount
of actual use of the facility. These charges therefore might be flat per-capita or
per-household charges, or perhaps charges based on property size if long-run
capital costs vary by size. Examples include a fixed-service charge common in
public water systems to cover the capital costs (pipes, pumps, storage) and special
assessments for sidewalks, street lights, and neighborhood parks. Of course, these
access costs might also be covered from general tax revenues if everyone benefits
equally from the existence of the facility.

Allocating Use (Operating) Costs

After a public facility—whether a park, road, water system, or college—has been
provided, attention must turn to covering the variable or operating costs. How this
is accomplished determines how much and by whom the facility is to be used. The
general principle of efficiency, again, is that marginal benefit should equal marginal cost, but now the relevant marginal cost is short-run marginal cost, the cost
of accommodating an additional consumer or providing another unit given the
capital input selected. At issue here is the appropriate charge for each gallon of
water consumed or for each admittance to the park.

Operating costs should be allocated based on marginal benefit from *use*. In many
and perhaps most cases, the benefit from additional use (as opposed to existence)
goes only to users. If so, then it may be appropriate to charge fees to users to cover
all the marginal operating costs. In some cases, however, external (nonuser) benefits may be associated with the additional use of a facility or service, such as the
benefit to society from having an additional person educated. In those cases, only
that portion corresponding to their share of marginal benefits from use should be
charged to direct users.

Assuming that users are to pay all the operating costs, some possibilities are
illustrated in Figure 8.3. In Figure 8.3a, the short-run marginal cost is positive and
constant; each additional unit of service imposes a constant additional variable
cost of a_0. Demand for this service is represented by $Demand_w$. The appropriate use
charge (if users can be identified and excluded) is a_0 dollars *per unit* consumed—
for example, $.01 per gallon of water or $2 per car for admittance to a park. In Figure 8.3b, marginal cost is zero up to quantity Q_C. If demand is $Demand_Y$, then the
correct user charge is zero; there are no operating costs at the margin to cover.

Allocating Congestion Costs

For some services, an additional consumer may impose extra costs on other users,
called **congestion costs**. As roads and bridges become more crowded, traffic slows
and the (time) costs to all users increase; as parks become more crowded, there is
less space for those in the park to enjoy activities; and when all the parking spaces
and tennis courts are occupied, other potential users incur a waiting cost (or must
forego the activity). Because the government incurs no additional cost by providing a service to an additional consumer (if one additional car parks in a space or

Figure 8.3

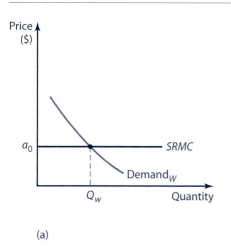

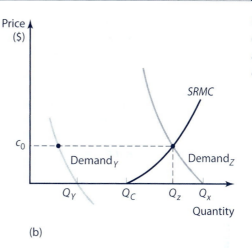

(a)

(b)

Efficient user charges with and without congestion

an additional couple uses a tennis court), the government does not need to collect more revenue for operating expenses. Yet, governments should and sometimes do charge user fees for all these services. The purpose of use fees in those situations is to allocate a scarce resource among competing demands.

This economic notion of congestion is shown in Figure 8.3b. For quantities of use or service less than Q_C, additional consumers can be accommodated without imposing any costs on other users. In essence, the facility is not yet "crowded." Because marginal cost (operating and congestion) is zero, the efficient price is also zero; no use fee is required. If demand for the service is $Demand_Y$, no use fee should be charged, with capital costs covered either out of general taxes or by some fixed charge as discussed earlier. For quantities of use or service above Q_C, the facility starts to become crowded; additional consumers impose congestion costs on other users (at an increasing rate in Figure 8.3b). Therefore, if demand for this service is $Demand_Z$, the appropriate use fee is c_0, with a resulting amount of use equal to Q_Z. If no use fee is charged, the amount of use is Q_X, and the facility is overused, that is, "too crowded."[7]

Correcting for congestion costs may require charging different fees at different times. For the service represented in Figure 8.3, demand might sometimes be $Demand_Y$, requiring an efficient use charge of zero, and sometimes $Demand_Z$, when the efficient use charge is c_0. For instance, parks may be crowded on weekends and not during the week, demand for bridge crossings may be great at the commuting hours and low at other times, or public-transit facilities may be used extensively at rush hour and little at other times. In other words, demand may be different at *peak times* (when higher use fees are appropriate) than at *off-peak times* (when lower or even zero use fees may be appropriate).[8]

---

[7]At Q_Z, the marginal benefit to the last user is c_0, equal to the marginal cost that user imposes on all other users.

[8]Examples of congestion pricing for roads and highways are discussed in Chapter 20.

Obviously, efficiently applying use charges could generate revenue, which is not necessary to cover extra operating expenses. In Figure 8.4b, a congestion charge at price c_0 during peak demand time generates net revenue because the marginal operating cost is zero. This is one of the advantages of user charges, that they measure the real demand for new facilities and provide the resources to create those new facilities. If current users are paying the appropriate costs of their consumption (including congestion costs) and excess demand still exists (evidence of serious congestion), then the facility is too small and consumers would pay, and are paying, to expand the facility. The revenue above operating costs, which was paid by the peak-time users, can be used to expand the facility or create another one.

Potentially, therefore, user charges can be composed of three separate parts: (1) an access charge to cover all or part of capital costs, (2) a use fee to cover all or part of the operating costs to the government associated with use, and (3) a congestion charge to cover the costs imposed by an additional user on other users. An alternative but equivalent way to think of determining user charges is to consider how a single producer should set its price based on its costs, including both its fixed and variable costs. That is the approach that follows for a natural monopoly.

User Charges with Natural Monopoly

A natural monopoly exists if the production of a good or service exhibits increasing returns to scale, so that the long-run average cost continually decreases as output increases, as depicted in Figure 8.4. This situation often arises when capital or fixed costs are large relative to variable costs. As the fixed cost is spread over a

Figure 8.4

Two-part pricing by a natural monopoly

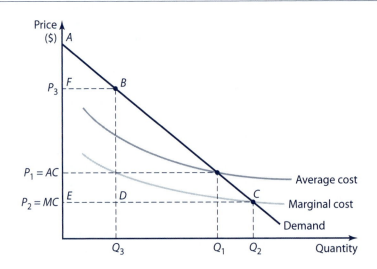

larger and larger output, the decreasing average fixed cost (combined with relatively small marginal costs) causes average total cost to decrease as well. Average
total cost always decreases as output rises and marginal cost is always less than
average cost. This leads naturally to monopoly because any given output can be
produced at lower average cost by one large firm than by several smaller firms.

This cost situation is believed to characterize most utilities, including electricity, natural gas, and perhaps water and sewer and public-transit services, but also
may apply to many other facilities provided by state and local governments,
including parks and beaches, roads, bridges, airports, and others. In all these cases,
fixed (capital) costs are large relative to variable (operating) costs, and the facility
has some unique aspect that generates monopoly power. Therefore, the usual
approaches are either for the government to grant a private firm monopoly rights
to a given market and then regulate the prices the firm may charge or for the
government to become the producer directly.

Setting an efficient price or use charge when there are increasing returns to scale
faces an inherent conflict. If price is set equal to marginal cost (for instance, at P_2),
then price is less than average cost, and the firm or operating authority cannot
cover all its costs. If price is set equal to average cost, at P_1, so that the firm or public authority can cover both operating and fixed costs, then price is greater than
marginal cost, causing the capital facility to be used less than efficiently. It is sometimes suggested that the government should set or enforce a price equal to marginal cost, with the government using general tax revenues to cover the resulting
financial losses. That could be an appropriate user charge strategy if everyone
were to contribute toward the capital costs, with users covering only operating
costs. But that, too, leads to inefficiency because of the inherent inefficiencies created by the taxes necessary to offset the entity's operating losses. In practice, utility
regulation often settles on solutions that effectively set charges equal to average
cost—for example, at P_1—allowing the regulated utility just to cover costs and earn
average profits.

One possible and often practical solution to this difficulty is to set a **two-part
price,** charging different prices for different quantities of the service. For example,
in Figure 8.4, one could set a price of P_3 for quantities up to Q_3 and a price of P_2 for
amounts greater than Q_3. Because the charge for marginal units of output is equal
to marginal cost, total consumption equals the efficient amount of Q_2. But the
producer may be able to avoid operating losses because the price discrimination
generates larger revenue than if a single price is charged. With the two-part price,
revenue is $P_3Q_3 + P_2(Q_2 - Q_3)$ or $(P_3 - P_2)Q_3 + P_2Q_2$, which is greater than the
revenue from a single price, equal to P_2Q_2.

Two-part pricing takes advantage of the fact that some consumers are willing
to pay prices higher than marginal cost for so-called inframarginal units (units
other than the last one purchased). The two-part price captures some of that consumers' surplus for the producer, allowing the producer to charge a marginal cost
price for marginal units and still cover all costs. With a single price of P_2, consumers enjoy a surplus represented by the area of triangle ACE. With the two-part
price involving P_2 and P_3, consumers' surplus is smaller, represented by the areas

of triangles *ABF* plus *BCD*. Rectangle *BDEF* represents the added revenue to the producer.

Of course, there is no reason why the inframarginal price needs to be set at P_3; that price must be selected to generate enough extra revenue to cover the producer's operating losses, if possible. In fact, the inframarginal price could apply only to the first unit consumed, effectively serving as a type of cover or access charge. In the case of Figure 8.4, that could entail charging a price of $A for the first unit and a price of P_2 for all subsequent units. This is equivalent to charging a set access fee to cover capital costs and then a use fee to cover operating costs.

Two-part prices of this type already are common, but this technique probably could be expanded with other user charges. Many public water systems charge a fixed monthly access charge as well as a per-gallon use fee. The access charge is a second price effectively imposed on the first gallon of water consumed and covers the fixed costs. Some public-transportation systems sell passes that allow riders to pay a lower fee for each ride than paid by consumers without the pass. Those who purchase the pass effectively pay a high price for the first ride in each period (the inframarginal ride) and a low price (usually zero) for all subsequent rides (the marginal ones). It is not hard to think of other potential user charge applications of this type. A public refuse system might levy a fixed monthly access charge in addition to a small fee per unit or bag collected, or a public parking facility could offer lower hourly parking charges to individuals who have purchased a monthly pass.

Two-part prices also can make sense even if the marginal cost of an additional user is zero. In that case, the first price covers the fixed costs, and the second price (the marginal use fee) is zero. Some private amusement parks (including the Disney parks) price this way, charging a single admission fee and no extra charge for each ride. Similarly, the Michigan Department of Natural Resources allows users to purchase an annual vehicle pass for Michigan state parks for $24, which entitles that vehicle to unlimited admittances without further charge to all state parks for that year. Those who purchase the pass therefore pay $24 for the first admittance in a year and a zero price for all others. Without such a pass, each vehicle admittance costs $6.[9]

It is relatively easy to add a congestion charge to the two-part price when appropriate. For instance, for those who purchase a monthly pass for $20, a public-transit system might charge $.50 per ride during off-peak times (compared to $1 for others) and $1 during peak periods (compared to $1.50). Or a park system might offer an annual pass for $20 that permits free use of the park on weekdays, although weekend use entails an additional $4 fee. In both cases, the additional marginal price during high-demand periods represents the marginal congestion cost.

---

[9]Even with the pass, there is a daily charge for camping in the park, rather than just a visit.

PRICING AT CONGESTED TENNIS COURTS

At one university, the school's policy was to not charge students and faculty members any fee for using the tennis courts, the argument being that using the university's facilities should be "free" to those who already paid tuition or worked for the school. Because this university is in a northern city and the tennis courts are outside, this policy posed no problem for half of the academic year. In the fall and especially in the spring, however, there was substantial excess demand for the tennis courts; waits of 30–60 minutes for a court were common. The courts were therefore not "free" but were allocated by having people wait. Presumably, those who had the lowest-valued time ended up using the tennis courts more. This university had no summer session and so made their tennis courts available to the general public during the summer months. The difference was that a use fee was charged in the summer to everyone—students who remained in the town, faculty, and the public. Not surprisingly, there were many vacant courts during the summer.

This situation is represented in Figure 8.5. The supply of tennis courts is fixed at Q_C, so marginal cost is zero for quantities less than Q_C (vacant courts mean there is no cost to accommodate another player); however, marginal cost becomes very high after all the courts are in use (the cost of accommodating another user is the cost of building another court). When demand is *Demand$_Y$*, as during the summer in the preceding story, there is excess capacity, and no fee should be charged. When demand is at the peak level of *Demand$_Z$*, a use fee equal to C_Z would generate efficient use—only those who are willing

Figure 8.5

Efficient pricing when supply is fixed

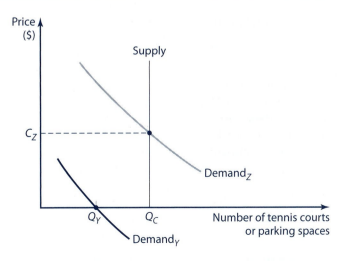

Application 8.1 — Pricing at Congested Tennis Courts

to pay C_z, that is, those who get C_z dollars worth of benefit from using the tennis court would play. With the fee, no excess demand exists for the facility. By charging a fee during the summer when demand was low (when the university was not in session) in an attempt to generate revenue from the public, the university's facilities were wasted from society's viewpoint. By not charging a fee during the spring when demand was high, the university made an implicit decision to allocate the scarce tennis courts by having people wait—what is often called "first come, first served." Although allocation either by fees or waiting gives some consumers an advantage over others, under the first come-first served system, potential tennis players do not know the charge (the required amount of time to wait) until they arrive at the courts.

One might believe that the proper policy for the university in this case is to build more tennis courts because the excess demand during the spring and fall suggests that more are "needed." That analysis is faulty, however, because the excess demand occurs only because tennis court use appears to be "free." Although the extra courts would be used during the peak times, they would enlarge the excess capacity that exists during the off-peak time. As the discussion about the efficient *amount* of public facilities showed, more tennis courts should be built only if those who demand the courts are willing to pay the full cost of constructing them (assuming that extra tennis courts benefit only direct users). Interestingly, use fees provide a test of that hypothesis. The efficient use fee C_z in Figure 8.5 equals the marginal benefit of a tennis court to users. If the fee that equates supply and demand turns out to be large enough to finance another court—that is, if marginal benefit is greater than marginal cost—then another court should (and can) be built.

Application 8.2

PARKING FEES AND PARKING METERS

Here is a do-it-yourself application that you can use to see how well you understand user charges and congestion. The analysis and diagram of Application 8.1 can be applied to the question of parking meters. Consider the following argument:

> *The streets have been paid for and belong to the people. Therefore, parking meters should be abolished.*

Analyze that position and prescription in light of the preceding discussion. If there were no parking meters or fees, how do you think the available parking spaces would be allocated? Would that allocation system be better? For whom? Without parking fees, do you think people would perceive that there is more or less of a "parking problem"? If parking fees are to be used, should they vary by location? Time of day? Time of year?

Other User-Charge Issues

The theoretical discussion suggests that user charges are most appropriate when most of the benefits of a government service go to identifiable direct consumers whose demand shows some price elasticity. Two other potential advantages of user charges should be noted as well. Many public services provide benefits to individuals who are not residents of the providing jurisdiction, and user charges are one way for those nonresidents to pay for the benefits they enjoy. Having users directly finance (at least partly) the services and facilities from which they benefit may portray a type of fairness in public policy that results in more public acceptance of state and local government provision of certain services.

Several potential problems with user charges should be addressed as well. Sometimes objection is raised to user fees on the grounds that they are a disadvantage for consumers with lower incomes. That notion is often coupled with the statement that general taxes, in contrast, are based on "ability to pay." The presumption of such an argument is that it is not fair to base consumption of the government service in question on income or "willingness to pay," as is done when following the "benefit principle" of public finance.

It is certainly true that allocating any good or service by money prices gives an advantage to those consumers with more money. But because that point is general, the relevant issue is why a particular government service that mostly benefits direct users should be treated differently than privately provided goods and services such as medical care or Mercedes automobiles. One possible explanation is that the service is a means of redistributing income, which is one of the fundamental economic roles of government. This is undoubtedly part of the reason primary and secondary education is financed almost entirely from taxes. Education provides external benefits to all of society; one of these benefits is a means of improving the economic conditions of the poor. One needs to be careful not to carry this argument too far, however. It is not clear that free use of public golf courses, for instance, is a very effective way of assisting the poor.

Avoiding user charges also may be an inefficient way of helping the poor. Some state–local government services are consumed much more by higher-income consumers than lower-income ones. Avoiding user-charge financing in those cases to assist lower-income consumers may actually benefit higher-income consumers to a greater degree. It could be more efficient for the government to charge everyone the user charge and give direct assistance of some type or a specific subsidy to the lower-income consumers affected by the charge.

A second potential problem with user charges is that the administration costs (to the government) and compliance costs (to the consumers) of collecting the charge are, in some cases, large enough to offset any expected efficiency gains from user-charge, as opposed to tax, financing. Typically, administration costs include the costs of measuring use, billing users, and collecting the fee, whereas compliance costs include delay at road or bridge toll booths and the time and postage costs of making the required payments. Besides the other necessary conditions, therefore, user-charge financing is attractive only if the charge can be collected at a reasonable cost. (For instance, the advantages and disadvantages of alternative ways of administering highway user charges are discussed in Chapter 20.)

APPLICATION OF USER CHARGES

The application of user charges to five specific state–local government services— public higher education, K-12 education, water and sewer service, refuse collection, and parks—is discussed in this section. Discussion of transportation-related user charges is presented in Chapter 20, and charges to offset the infrastructure costs associated with economic growth and development are covered in Chapter 22.

Financing Public Higher Education[10]

For most readers of this book, and especially for those attending public colleges and universities, tuition is the best known of all subnational government user charges and the one with the most immediate personal as well as academic impli-cations. In the United States, tuition historically covered between 30 and 50 per-cent of the expenditures of public colleges and universities, with the remainder financed mostly from state (and for community colleges, sometimes local) taxes. In recent years, the share financed by tuition has grown and is now commonly more than 50 percent. There is substantial variation among states in the reliance on tuition, however; for many years, in fact, some states provided "free" college edu-cation to qualified residents. This naturally leads to a question of whether public college students should pay a larger (or smaller) fraction of the cost of their college education and how those charges should be structured.

Those who argue that tuition (or other user charges) should be more important in financing public higher education usually suggest that most of the benefits of that education are captured directly by the students in the form of higher incomes, jobs with more prestige, and information that assists those individuals in all aspects of their lives. Moreover, those beneficiaries are directly identified, the charge can be collected at low cost (indeed at zero extra cost after any tuition is levied), and students easily can be prevented from consuming the service unless they pay the charge. With that viewpoint, higher education seems to meet all the tests for substantial user-charge financing. However, at least four issues suggest that this view is incomplete.

First, public institutions of higher education usually produce research and pub-lic service in addition to education of students, although those three outputs are clearly not independent. Even if one believes that all the benefits of the *education* component of output are captured by students, the research and public service components of output benefit all of society and are thus appropriately financed by the government. Pure scientific research is usually identified as a classic public good; discoveries, once made, can be used by anyone at zero marginal cost to

---

[10]For discussion and evidence concerning these issues for specific states, see Lee Hansen and Burton Weisbrod (1969) and John Goddeeris (1982).

society. Research and public service *should* therefore be financed by the general society and not directly by students.[11]

It remains to be determined what fraction of public higher-education output is research and public service compared to education, a fraction that undoubtedly differs by type of institution. In major state universities, research and public service usually represent at least half of a faculty member's job and similarly at least half of the university's output. The output of community colleges, in contrast, is usually almost entirely education. It follows therefore that the appropriate degree of user-charge (tuition) reliance might be greater for institutions primarily producing education as opposed to those producing education and research. Indeed, public subsidies to four-year colleges generally are greater than to two-year colleges.

Second, students already bear a larger fraction of the social cost of public higher education than it appears from comparing tuition and state appropriations. A hypothetical but illustrative computation of both the social and private cost of public higher education for one student is shown in Example 8.1.

Example 8.1

Per-Student Economic Costs of Higher Education

Category	Social Cost ($)	Student Cost ($)	Percentage
Instruction	$ 16,000	$ 8,000	50%
Books, supplies, transportation	1,500	1,500	100
Foregone income	15,000	15,000	100
Total	32,500	24,500	75.4

The cost of instruction, which is essentially the college or university expenditures per student, is assumed to be $16,000, of which one-half is covered by student tuition. The cost of books, supplies, and transportation represents expenditures on these items that are greater than if the student did not attend college. These costs are therefore true opportunity costs of choosing to attend college. Similarly, foregone income represents the difference between the income the student could have earned if not attending college and actual income earned. In the example, $15,000 is the approximate annual earnings for a full-time employee paid $7 per hour, slightly above the minimum wage. This foregone income is a true social cost, in addition to a cost to the student, because society gives up the goods and services that this individual's work would have produced, the value of which can be estimated by the factor payment.[12] In the example, then, students bear more than

---

[11]For that reason, it is often argued that research should be largely financed by the federal government. And the federal government, through such entities as the National Science Foundation, the National Institute for Education, and the National Institutes for Health, does substantially support university research.

[12]This computation is different than the out-of-pocket budget students usually consider; for instance, costs of room and board are not included. Because some room and board costs are incurred regardless of whether the individual attends college, those costs would be included in the economic cost computation only to the extent that they are larger because of college attendance.

75 percent of the social cost of their public college education, not the 50 percent that appears from comparing tuition to college operating expenses.[13]

Third, even if, after considering these two issues, a state desires greater reliance on tuition for financing public higher education, it may be difficult for that individual state to act unilaterally. Potential college students can change their states of residence toward those states that rely on tuition less and away from those states that rely on tuition more. Moreover, with an increasingly mobile society, the social benefits from higher education are not likely to be confined to any given state.

Fourth, the cost to the university of adding another student or having a student take more classes—the marginal cost—might be close to zero, at least for some limited number of additional students. If the university is not crowded—that is, if another student can be accommodated without reducing the education provided to other students—then it is inefficient to charge a positive price at the margin. Of course, the solution to this problem might be a two-part price, charging a fixed tuition per year or semester and a lower or zero charge for each class or credit taken. The fixed tuition could cover the fixed costs of the university without creating a disincentive for students to take additional academic work.

The argument usually raised against increased reliance on tuition—that it would prevent many lower-income students from attending college—also may be faulty. The evidence shows that college students, including public college students, tend to be mostly from higher-income (above the median) families; at least, the fraction of students attending college increases with family income. To maintain low reliance on tuition for all students, then, provides substantial benefits to many students who clearly are not poor.

If equity is the concern, an alternative to low reliance on tuition, and an alternative to low reliance on user charges generally, is targeted assistance to lower-income consumers. Of course, this is already done in higher education. The state or university can set tuition at a level that seems efficient given the perceived social benefits and costs, and lower-income students can then be assisted with some type of income-based financial aid. This method has the potential to be a more efficient way of improving equity because society decides which consumers require and deserve assistance and provides aid based on those criteria.[14]

Financing K-12 Education[15]

Among all state and local governments, local school districts rely on user charges least. As shown previously in Table 8.3, user charges account for only about 4 percent of school district general revenue currently, a share that has actually declined in the past 40 years at the same time that user charge reliance has grown for all

---

[13]The results in the example are very similar to the results reported by Hansen and Weisbrod (1969) for the California state college and university system.

[14]It is also sometimes argued that lower-income students face a problem in financing higher education because the capital markets do not work properly; if these students will indeed earn higher incomes due to education, then financial institutions should be willing to make loans against those future earnings. If financial institutions will not, then an appropriate solution is government-sponsored education loans.

[15]See Robert Wassmer and Ronald Fisher, 2002.

other governments. Nearly two-thirds of school user charges arise from prices or fees for school lunches. Activity fees, which represent about 20 percent of the total, are the other major category of school charges.

This relatively minor reliance on user fees by school districts raises the question of whether K-12 schools might be able to increase use of charges either to supplement revenue or to permit tax reduction. Work by Robert Wassmer and the author suggests that the strongest case for increased use of user fees by public schools is for providing auxiliary services—such things as meals, transportation, after-school care, medical care, adult education, and perhaps certain clubs or special activities—that are not necessarily part of the standard curriculum. These types of services tend to provide substantial private benefits, may be consumed by only a fraction of students in a school, have close private substitutes, and have relatively low-cost collection mechanisms available. By one measure, schools spent more than $30 billion on these types of services in 1992, amounting to about 13 percent of expenditure.

So, why don't public schools use charges and fees more? Or equivalently, what factors have affected the choice of fees by schools in the past? One factor is obvious, as school user fees are prohibited or limited by state law in some states (although that fact just raises the parallel question of why some states have adopted these limits). User fees tend to be used more by schools in large districts where there may be greater variation in the types of services that are used by different students. User fees also are used to a greater degree by districts that are constrained by property tax limits, as those limits effectively force districts to find alternative revenue sources. User fees also seem to be relied upon less in states that exhibit a liberal or left-leaning political bias. This last point may arise because individuals with those political beliefs may be more concerned about the equity implications of charging all students, regardless of family income, prices for some school-related services.

Financing Water and Sewer Services[16]

Water use fees are common, whether water service is provided by a local government or by a privately operated water utility company. These fees actually comprise, either explicitly or implicitly, three separate charges: a connection charge, a capital and distribution charge, and a water-supply charge. The water-supply charge is intended to cover the marginal cost of additional gallons of water and therefore ideally should be based on the amount of water used. Use is sometimes approximated by the number of water outlets per structure or by the number of persons per structure, but it is far more common for the actual number of gallons of water consumed to be measured by a water meter. Assuming that marginal cost per gallon of water is constant, which appears reasonable for all but some special industrial users, a use fee can be computed from the measured usage and the appropriate constant per gallon charge.

The capital and distribution charge is usually a fixed charge, which may depend on the location or size (front footage) of the structure served. A charge based on front footage is intended to represent the extra cost of the water-supply pipe, as

---

[16]For a more comprehensive discussion of these issues, see Paul Downing and Thomas DiLorenzo (1981).

distribution costs depend on user density. It is sometimes argued that these distribution charges also should depend on distance from the supply source, although applying that concept is problematic. The location of the supply source, the water-treatment plant, is not fixed but is selected by the government. In fact, that location may be changed after many consumers have selected their locations. In addition, although a new and isolated development far from the supply source entails large extra costs of service for running new supply lines, a new development next to an existing one requires only extension of the water line (unless an entirely new and larger supply line was required). In practice, this charge is most often a fixed, front-footage charge.

Water users also are often charged for the direct costs of hook-up to the water system. This one-time connection charge may depend on the length of pipe required or it may be a flat charge reflecting the large fixed costs to the utility.

Analysis of potential user charges for sewer services is essentially similar to that for water (sewer disposal is a result of indoor water consumption); costs depend on the amount and type of sewage disposed and on the size and location of the structure. However, actual metering of sewer discharge is not common, except for certain industrial users. Apparently, sewage flow meters are relatively expensive compared to water meters. The usual approach, particularly for residential users, is to assume that sewage flow is some percentage of water consumption and to compute a sewer-use fee from that number of gallons and a per-gallon charge. Of course, there is no reason for the sewer per-gallon charge to be the same as the water per-gallon charge. This method does not allow for variation among users concerning the purpose for water consumption, but it may still be the best option given the measuring costs.

These charges usually are collected from consumers through monthly or quarterly billings, much the same as electricity, natural gas, or telephone bills. The water and sewer charges are usually on one bill, and the capital/distribution charges may be combined into a single amount per front foot, paid through a monthly service charge, or included in the gallonage charge.

Randolf Martin and Ronald Wilder (1992) estimated the potential effects on residential water use from user charge pricing. Using monthly household data from Columbia, South Carolina in the 1980s, they estimated the price elasticity of water demand to be between $-.3$ and $-.6$ when price was measured by the per gallon charge. If price was measured by the average total water bill per unit of water, the estimated elasticity was between $-.5$ and $-.7$. Therefore, demand for water is price inelastic, so that residential consumers do reduce use when user charges are applied. Noting the relative magnitudes of the estimated elasticities, the authors conclude the results are "consistent with the notion that households tend to respond to the total water and sewer service bill, rather than to the marginal price alone" (Martin and Wilder, 1992, p. 100).

Financing Refuse-Collection Services

The costs of collecting refuse arise from both collection and disposal. Disposal costs depend on the amount and type of refuse and should include the cost of any environmental damage resulting from the disposal. A user charge to cover these disposal costs should therefore be a unit charge that varies by type of unit (the disposal cost of a pound of household garbage is different from that of a pound of used nuclear fuel). One difficulty in applying such a use fee is in measuring the amount of refuse. Possible measures include the number of specific-size cans collected or the weight of refuse collected. The first measure suffers because different amounts of garbage may be packed into a fixed-size container, and both entail substantial administrative costs to make and record the measurement. Even if those problems could be overcome, individuals would have an incentive to deposit their refuse at a neighbor's location, which gives rise to all sorts of silly notions about enforcement and neighborhood wars.

One innovative solution to this measurement problem, used in many localities, is to require that all refuse be deposited in specific bags sold only by the local government. Typically, the bags are delineated by unusual colors and insignia. The fee per bag charged by the government includes not only the cost of producing the bag (what would be charged in a store) but also the disposal cost per bag. This method avoids both the administrative costs of measuring use and the incentive for individuals to shift their costs to neighbors. There is a compliance cost to users, however, because they must arrange to purchase the special bags. To facilitate this and reduce those compliance costs, the local government may arrange to have the bags sold by private retailers rather than just at the government offices, although counterfeiting is a potential problem. An alternative is to permit residents to use any disposal bag, but afix a sticker sold by the city. This method could also be extended to provide different charges for different types of refuse (bottles and cans versus paper, for example) by having different color bags or stickers sold for different fees. As noted previously, it also might be appropriate to charge a fixed disposal fee per month or year to be eligible to use the bag system.

Any use fee based on the actual amount of refuse generates an incentive for consumers to avoid the charge by littering and creates a corresponding cost to the government for enforcement. For instance, illegal dumping might occur on vacant land, in business dumpsters, or into surface-water sewer systems. The costs from those externalities might outweigh any gains from requiring a refuse-collection fee. On the other hand, a use fee based on quantity also generates an incentive for consumers to avoid refuse through recycling, using returnable containers, and substituting reusable for disposable materials (such as cloth towels rather than paper towels). One alternative is to impose a fee on manufacturers or sellers to induce them to change the packaging or nature of products, such as a disposable-diaper tax considered in Arizona. Another option is a recycling fee that is returned to the consumer if the product is recycled, such as bottle and can deposits.

Refuse collection costs depend on the type of refuse and the density and location of the users. Obviously, collections requiring a special vehicle or extra trip (for example, collection of household durables, such as refrigerators) should ideally entail a specific charge. In practice, however, it is not clear that the absence of such a charge generates much inefficiency—replacing those durables is probably insensitive to disposal costs. The argument for these special collection charges, then, must be fairness. Routine collection costs, on the other hand, depend mostly on time and the density of consumers. It takes longer to collect from widely spaced single-family residences, for example, than from multifamily residences with all refuse in one location, perhaps deposited in specially designed large containers. It may be appropriate therefore, as some localities do, to charge a lower fee per unit of refuse for apartments and commercial establishments than for residences.

In practice, both local governments and private firms provide refuse-collection services. In the first case, financing out of general taxes still is most common, although fixed charges per structure per month are sometimes used. Among private firms, fixed monthly charges are most common, although the charge often applies to a fixed, maximum amount of service; extra service brings extra charges. In many rural areas, refuse disposal is still the responsibility of individual consumers who make the weekly trip to a disposal site or recycling facility, which may be operated by the government or a private firm and is financed either from taxes or dumping charges.

Financing Public Parks and Recreation Areas

Paying for admission to private recreational facilities (such as beach clubs, pools, tennis courts, and camping facilities) is expected. Similar use fees are used for some types of public parks, beaches, and recreation facilities, such as the Narragansett (R.I.) Town Beach, but three issues seem to be important in limiting the broader application of state–local user fees in this area.

First, taxpayers often question the fairness of charging for the use of public facilities that have been acquired with general tax revenues, arguing that such facilities already have been paid for and thus should be "free" to all taxpayers. Partly this viewpoint reflects a misunderstanding about the difference between fixed capital or access costs and variable operating costs. Both types of costs must be paid somehow, and it might make sense to charge everyone for the first cost and only users for the latter cost. Indeed, one can ask whether it is "fair" not to charge users for operating costs, if those services primarily benefit those users.

This distinction and resulting policy was explained as follows in an unusually candid letter to the editor by the director of a state natural resources department:

> Proposal D [allowing the state to borrow funds by selling bonds to be repaid from future taxes] provided $60 million for badly needed repair of existing facilities . . . includ[ing] updating sewage systems, replacing electrical services, repairing bathhouses, picnic shelters and rustic cabins, and repaving roads. The bond money will not pay operational costs.
>
> Operation is primarily financed by the users. Approximately 80 percent is from the motor vehicle entrance fee and fees collected for camping and other services. The remaining 20 percent is from general tax revenues. Fees pay wages, provide maintenance, and pay operational expenses such as electricity. . . . (Hales, 1989)

It seems important, as is done in the preceding, to explain to taxpayers the types of costs to be paid by all taxpayers and those specifically by users.

Second, in some cases, there is just not a sufficient level of use of these facilities to warrant user fees. Two forces often work together here. At low use levels, there may be no marginal operating costs, which calls for a zero price. Even if an efficiency reason exists for use fees, collection costs may be prohibitive when use is low. It usually doesn't make sense to pay a toll collector $5 an hour, if toll collections aren't greater than that (and perhaps substantially so).[17]

Third, combining the first two issues, even if sufficient use or crowding calls for charges, congestion seems to be the least understood and often most opposed reason for fees. A probable reason is that the government or public authority incurs no identifiable direct costs to justify the charge. Rather, the reason for the congestion charge is to ration use of a public facility, with some preferring a different rationing mechanism (first-come, first-served; a lottery; or whatever) and others denying that rationing is called for. Of course, one possibility is to dedicate the congestion charge to a fund for expansion or improvement of the facility, thereby creating a direct reason for the extra use fee. Even though congestion charges are exceedingly common in the private sector (higher prices at recreational resorts or parks during peak demand periods such as holidays and weekends), their use by state and local governments remains problematical.

INTERNATIONAL COMPARISON

Whether to utilize user charges to finance publicly provided goods with private-good characteristics is a classic issue in many nations, not just the United States. For instance, there has been increased attention paid to how water service should be financed in Australia. In 1992, the federal Industry Commission recommended that the state and local water authorities move toward a complete user charge system, under which consumers would be billed for water by the liter. The Commission based its position on a concern about efficient use of resources, arguing that if consumers see water as "free," they are more likely to waste it. The Commission noted that user charge financing ". . . will reduce water consumption and thereby waste water discharges and bring financial savings by deferring investments to expand water and sewage networks" (Tideman, 1992, p. 9).

In the past, water service had been financed mostly through a property tax. Most consumers paid a separate water property tax (a water rate), allowing consumption of water with no additional charge up to an annual limit. Water charges apply over the limit. Because the limits often are high, however, in most cases, a household's water payment depended on the value of the house or property rather than the amount of water actually used. Not surprisingly, therefore, many consumers living in high-valued houses support a move to water charges, because they believe that their water property tax is more than what direct water charges based on use would be.

Some changes in financing have occurred. The Melbourne Water Corporation increased use of charges, which now account for 31 percent of its revenues. Officials in Melbourne believe an opportunity exists for consumers to conserve, especially because they estimate that 40 percent of water consumption goes for gardens and 20 percent for toilets. One local government official in Adelaide noted that the discussion of charges "has made people aware of the value of the

---

[17]An alternative here is a voluntary "honor system" for collection of fees. But even such a system is likely to require enforcement (and costs) some of the time to encourage participation.

resource. . . . If people waste water they have to pay for it." But the great bulk of water consumption in Australia nationally is for agricultural uses. Some agricultural industries have opposed water use charges over concern both that consumer prices for some agricultural commodities might increase and that the higher production costs that result might hurt the ability of agricultural producers to export their goods, which is an important part of the Australian economy. For instance, reacting to the Industry Commission recommendation, an official of the sugar cane industry argued that many sugar cane growers would go out of business if the Queensland state government adopted the recommendations. *(Daily Mercury,* 1992, p. 9). The absence of water fees, then, may not only encourage and subsidize excessive consumption by households, but also represent a subsidy to specific industries.

SUMMARY

User charges, prices charged by governments for specific services or privileges and used to pay for all or part of the cost of providing those services, have always been important but have become increasingly so in the past decade. They are to be distinguished from financing services through general taxes, with no direct relationship between tax payment and service received. User charges create an incentive for efficient choice because consumers face the true costs of their consumption decisions.

Financing methods, which can be considered as user charges, include direct charges for use of a public facility or consumption of a service, license taxes or fees paid for the privilege of undertaking some activity (such as fishing license and driver license fees), and special property tax assessments levied for a specific service.

Charges and fees represented about 19.5 percent of the general revenue of state–local governments in 2002, with traditional user charges alone representing 15 percent of revenue. Education and hospitals are the two budget categories from which most state–local user charges arise; on average about 55 percent of all subnational government direct user charges are attributable to those categories. Total user charges of state–local governments, whether broadly or narrowly defined, have increased faster than other revenues and faster than the general price level since 1980.

User-charge financing is more attractive, the greater is the share of marginal benefits that accrues to direct users, the greater the percentage of benefits of a service or facility that go to direct users, the more easily users can be identified and excluded (at reasonable cost) from consuming the service unless the charge is paid, and the more price elastic is demand. Two other potential advantages of user charges are that they are one way to have nonresidents pay for the benefits they enjoy, and the perception of fairness from users paying may result in more public acceptance of state and local government provision of certain services.

Objection is raised to user fees on the grounds that they are a disadvantage for consumers with lower incomes and that the administration costs (to the government) and compliance costs (to the consumers) of collecting the charge may offset any expected efficiency gains.

Even if there is no additional cost to the government of providing a service to an additional consumer, that consumer may impose congestion costs on other users. The purpose of use fees in those situations is to allocate a scarce resource among competing demands and provide a measure of the demand for new capital investment.

Potentially, user charges can be composed of three separate parts: (1) an access charge to cover all or part of capital costs, (2) a use fee to cover all or part of the operating costs to the government associated with use, and (3) a congestion charge to cover the costs imposed by an additional user on other users. Two-part prices can be one way to accomplish this; the first price covers the fixed costs and the second price (the marginal use fee) covers marginal operating and congestion costs.

DISCUSSION QUESTIONS

1. In many large cities, the government operates a museum, library, and zoo that are visited by substantial numbers of people who are not residents of the city. They may come from the metropolitan area or from around the state. What economic reasons would justify the city financing these services through user charges? What problems would user-charge finance present in these cases? Consider how the charges might be structured for each service.

2. Suppose that your state provides a number of parks with majestic mountains, beautiful beaches, and unspoiled wilderness areas. These parks were acquired and operated in the past using the state's general tax revenue. Now the state proposes to charge a daily entrance fee of $5 per vehicle, with the revenue earmarked for the "state park fund" (to be used for operating expenses, capital improvements, and acquisition of new parks). At a public hearing on the proposal, one citizen complained "It is unfair to require taxpayers who have paid for these parks with their tax dollars to now also pay a fee to use them." As director of the state parks department, how would you respond to this citizen?

3. Suppose that partly as a result of this type of complaint, the state park user-fee proposal is revised so that no fee will be charged for park use Monday through Friday, a $5 fee will be charged on weekends, and a $10 fee will be charged on holidays and holiday weekends (Memorial Day, Fourth of July, Labor Day, and so on). Is there any economic rationale for such a structure? Do you think it is fairer than charging the same fee at all times? More efficient?

4. Suppose that the apartment building you live in at college has only one water meter for the entire building. The landlord receives a water bill from the city each quarter based on the gallons of water used, but each apartment or tenant is not charged separately—the cost of water is

effectively included in the rent. Now the water department decides to install separate meters for each apartment and to bill each separately rather than the landlord (so the rent is reduced by $X per person for all tenants). The city justifies the cost of the extra meters and billings on the grounds that the city's scarce water resources will be used more efficiently. What is the price to a tenant or apartment per gallon of water before and after the new meters are installed? Do you think the new procedure will reduce water use? If so, how might the student tenants of these apartments act to conserve water? Will there be a gain in economic efficiency?

SELECTED READING

"Costing and Pricing Local Government Services." *Governmental Finance*, 11 (March 1982): 3–27.

Gramlich, Edward, "Let's Hear It for User Fees." *Governing* (January 1993): 54–5.

Muskin, Selma, ed. *Public Prices for Public Products*. Washington, D.C.: The Urban Institute, 1972.

Netzer, Dick, "Differences in Reliance on User Charges by American State and Local Governments." *Public Finance Quarterly*, 20 (October 1992): 499–511.

CHAPTER 9

INTERGOVERNMENTAL GRANTS

*The basic economic justification for federal functional
grants-in-aid is provided by the widespread, and ever-
increasing, spillover of benefits from some of the most
important state and local expenditure programs.[1]*

—GEORGE F. BREAK

HEADLINES

"THE FEDERAL GOVERNMENT SPENT $1.9 TRILLION IN THE STATES, THE DISTRICT OF COLUMBIA, PUERTO RICO, AND OUTLYING AREAS DURING 2002, ACCORDING TO TWO REPORTS RELEASED TODAY BY THE COMMERCE DEPARTMENT'S CENSUS BUREAU. THIS WAS AN 8 PERCENT INCREASE OVER 2001.

CALIFORNIANS BENEFITTED THE MOST, RECEIVING $206 BILLION, FOLLOWED BY THE PEOPLE OF NEW YORK ($129 BILLION), TEXAS ($123 BILLION), FLORIDA ($105 BILLION), AND PENNSYLVANIA ($86 BILLION). ONE-THIRD OF ALL FEDERAL EXPENDITURES WENT TO PEOPLE LIVING IN THESE FIVE STATES, WHICH ACCOUNT FOR 36 PERCENT OF THE TOTAL U.S. POPULATION.

ALTOGETHER, SOCIAL SECURITY, MEDICARE AND MEDICAID ACCOUNTED FOR $890 BILLION (47 PERCENT) OF THE U.S. GOVERNMENT'S 2002 DOMESTIC SPENDING.

GRANT AWARDS CLIMBED TO $412 BILLION, AN 11.6 PERCENT INCREASE OVER 2001, WITH MEDICAID, THE LARGEST, AMOUNTING TO $148 BILLION, UP 11.1 PERCENT.[2]"

---

[1] *Intergovernmental Fiscal Relations in the United States.* Washington, D.C.: The Brookings Institution, 1967, 105.

[2] U.S. Department of Commerce. Press release entitled "Federal Domestic Spending Up 8 Percent in 2002, Census Bureau Reports," June 4, 2003.

Intergovernmental grants, sometimes called **grants-in-aid,** are transfers of funds from one government to another, most often from a higher-level government in the federal system to a set of lower-level governments. These grants are of many different types and are intended to improve the operation of a federal system of government finance. In this chapter, the purposes for grants, the economic effects of the different types of grants, and then an appropriate policy of grant use are considered.

GRANTS IN THE U.S. FISCAL SYSTEM

In 2002, the federal government transferred more than $360 billion of aid to state–local governments, which represented about $.27 for every $1 raised by state–local governments from their own sources. By 2003, federal grants had increased to nearly $386 billion. The Census Bureau report for 2002 shows 663 different federal grant programs applying to state or local governments. Similarly, state governments transferred more than $355 billion to local governments, or about $.60 for every $1 collected by local governments from their own sources. As reflected by the data in Figures 9.1 and 9.2, intergovernmental grants, both from the federal government to states and localities and from the states to localities, have been a dominant feature of the federal fiscal system in the United States for more than 30 years.

Although the absolute magnitude of these grants generally has increased annually over these years (1982 and 1987 being exceptions for federal aid), the purchasing power of grants has not. After adjusting for price increases (measured

Figure 9.1

Federal grants to state–local governments

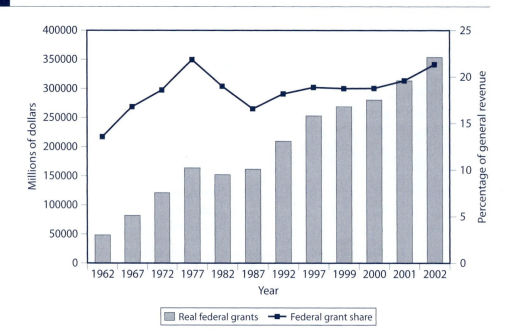

Year

Real federal grants ■—■ Federal grant share

Figure 9.2

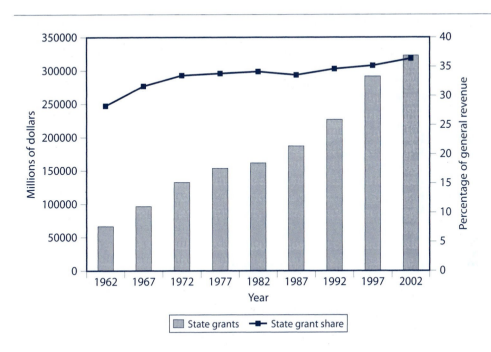

by the implicit GDP deflator), the real value of federal grants (measured in 2002 dollars) declined in 1973 and substantially from 1978 to 1982, despite increases in the nominal amounts, as shown in Figure 9.1. Essentially, grants increased during these periods at a slower rate than prices rose. The real value of federal grants essentially then remained the same until 1990 and has increased substantially since. In contrast, the real value of state grants to local governments never really declined, although it was nearly constant from 1979 to 1984 and from 1989 to 1991, and has increased in the past decade.

The relative importance of intergovernmental grants increased in the 1960s and early 1970s, peaked in the late 1970s, and has increased gradually since 1987. As shown in Figure 9.1, federal aid increased from about 13 percent of state–local general revenue in 1962 to about 22 percent by 1977. After a decline, it had risen back to about 22 percent of general revenue for 2002. Over that same period, federal aid increased from less than 9 percent of total federal government outlays to 17 percent by 1978. Federal aid's share of the federal government budget then decreased to less than it was in 1969, only to begin rising again since 1990. Although state and local governments, on average, received $.32 of federal aid for every local dollar collected in 1978, and that amount fell to $.18 in 1989, it rose to $.27 by 2002. Similar decreases in the relative importance of state aid for local governments also occurred in the 1980s, at least partly because states were receiving less federal aid to pass along to localities, as shown in Figure 9.2.

Intergovernmental grants are an important source of revenue for nearly all state–local governments, as confirmed by the data in Table 9.1. In 2002, state

Table 9.1

Intergovernmental Grants as a Percent of General Revenue, by Type of Government, Various Years, 1962–2002

		Local Governments					
Year	**States**	**Total**	**Counties**	**Municipalities**	**Townships**	**School Districts**	**Special Districts**
1962							
Federal	22.8%	2.0%	0.7%	2.5%	0.8%	1.4%	8.9%
State	—	28.4	36.3	16.3	20.6	37.3	3.2
Total[a]	24.0	30.4	38.6	20.4	22.5	40.8	21.1
1972							
Federal	27.2	4.3	1.7	7.3	1.3	1.9	15.5
State	—	33.4	39.1	24.1	19.6	42.0	3.9
Total[a]	28.4	37.7	42.1	32.9	22.0	45.0	29.6
1977							
Federal	27.1	9.2	9.0	14.7	7.5	1.5	21.7
State	—	33.7	34.5	23.2	20.4	47.3	7.4
Total[a]	28.8	42.9	45.3	39.7	29.7	50.2	38.2
1982							
Federal	24.0	7.6	6.5	12.0	5.8	1.0	18.5
State	—	33.9	34.1	20.8	22.6	51.7	7.6
Total[a]	25.1	41.5	42.0	34.6	30.1	54.3	34.7
1987							
Federal	22.8	4.8	3.6	6.5	3.4	0.9	16.0
State	—	33.3	31.7	20.3	22.5	52.8	5.3
Total[a]	24.4	38.1	36.8	29.0	28.1	55.3	29.4
1992							
Federal	26.1	3.5	2.2	4.6	1.2	0.7	14.2
State	—	34.2	33.5	21.3	21.0	52.0	6.8
Total[a]	27.9	37.6	37.3	28.3	24.3	54.0	29.4
1997							
Federal	26.5	3.9	2.6	5.3	1.3	0.7	14.9
State	—	34.6	33.5	20.7	19.7	53.3	8.7
Total[a]	28.3	38.4	37.5	28.3	23.3	55.2	32.3
2002							
Federal	29.9	2.9	2.9	5.3	1.2	1.0	17.3
State	—	35.7	33.8	21.9	19.7	54.5	9.2
Total[a]	31.6	38.6	38.4	29.8	23.3	57.4	31.7

[a]Includes grants from local governments.

SOURCE: U.S. Department of Commerce. *Governmental Finances*, 1962, 1972, 1977, 1982, 1987, 1992, 1997, 2002.

governments received essentially 30 percent of their revenue through intergovernmental grants, and local governments received more than 38 percent, with counties and school districts being the types of local governments most reliant on grants, at least on average. Although state aid is substantially more important than direct federal aid for all types of local governments except special districts, some of that state aid arises from federal grants to the states, which effectively are "passed on" to localities. The particularly high reliance on state aid by school districts reflects a

Table 9.2

Federal and State Aid by Budget Category, 1997

	Federal Aid		State Aid	
	Category Aid as Percentage of Total Aid	**Category Federal Aid as Percentage of State–Local Category Expenditure**[a]	**Category Aid as Percentage of Total Aid**	**Category State Aid as Percentage of Local Category Expenditure**[a]
Education	14.7%	8.6%	63.7%	53.4%
Highways	8.1	24.2	4.1	32.0
Public Welfare	50.8	61.0	10.9	74.2
Health and Hospitals	5.2	11.3	8.5	52.4
Other	14.3	8.1	12.8	10.9
Total	100.0	19.6	100.0	35.7

[a]Expenditure measured as direct general expenditure in category.

SOURCE: U.S. Department of Commerce, Bureau of the Census, *Compendium of Government Finances*, 1997.

growing role for state governments in financing local education, a topic discussed more comprehensively in Chapter 19. In fact, the reliance on aid by local governments has not changed dramatically in the past 25 years, except for school districts, whose grants increased from about 45 percent to 57 percent of revenue.

About 75 percent of federal aid to states and localities is directed nominally toward the three budget categories of education, transportation, and public welfare, the last category alone represents more than 57 percent, as shown in Table 9.2 and Figure 9.3. In contrast, education is the dominant category of state aid to localities, accounting for about 64 percent of state aid. As a result of this aid, the federal government finances more than half of public welfare expenditures (61 percent), although state governments finance more than half of expenditures on education (54 percent), even though welfare service is provided directly by states and education by localities.

PURPOSES OF GRANTS

Traditionally, four potential roles for intergovernmental grants in a federal fiscal system are identified. Grants may be used to correct for externalities—service benefits or tax costs that cross jurisdiction boundaries—and thus can improve the efficiency of fiscal decisions. Grants can be used for explicit redistribution of resources among regions or localities. Grants may be used to substitute one tax structure for another, for instance to take advantage of scale economies in tax collection. Finally, grants have been considered as a macroeconomic stabilizing mechanism for the subnational government sector.

Recall from Chapter 2 that interjurisdictional externalities, or spillovers, can cause service decisions by individual subnational governments to be inefficient from society's viewpoint. If nonresidents benefit from a state or local service, but those nonresident benefits are not considered in the decision about the amount of

Figure 9.3

Distribution of federal grants by program area

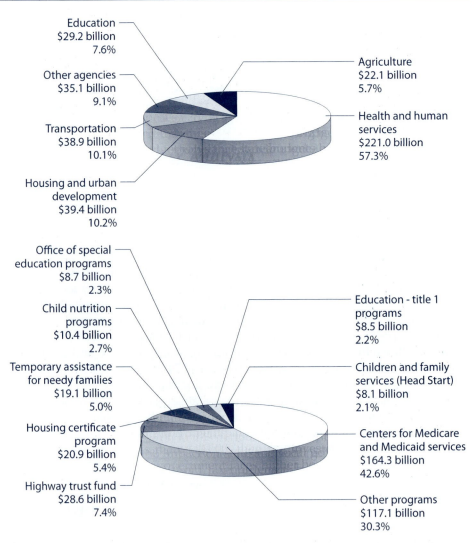

Education
$29.2 billion
7.6%

Other agencies
$35.1 billion
9.1%

Transportation
$38.9 billion
10.1%

Housing and urban
development
$39.4 billion
10.2%

Agriculture
$22.1 billion
5.7%

Health and human
services
$221.0 billion
57.3%

Office of special
education programs
$8.7 billion
2.3%

Child nutrition
programs
$10.4 billion
2.7%

Temporary assistance
for needy families
$19.1 billion
5.0%

Housing certificate
program
$20.9 billion
5.4%

Highway trust fund
$28.6 billion
7.4%

Education - title 1
programs
$8.5 billion
2.2%

Children and family
services (Head Start)
$8.1 billion
2.1%

Centers for Medicare
and Medicaid services
$164.3 billion
42.6%

Other programs
$117.1 billion
30.3%

Note: Total federal aid to states and local governments in fiscal year 2003 was $385.7 billion (100.0%).

SOURCE: U.S. Census Bureau, Federal aid to states for fiscal year 2003.

the service to provide, social marginal benefits will be underestimated and too little of the service will be provided. In such a case, an intergovernmental grant can be used to induce the subnational government to provide more of that specific service, as efficiency requires. Moreover, because the grant funds are generated from taxes collected by the granting government, those nonresidents who benefit from the service end up paying for part of the service through their state or federal taxes.

Recall from Chapter 5 that individual migration among local communities also may involve a type of externality, if that migration imposes costs on the other residents. Individuals may move to avoid subnational taxes or to gain services. If the new residents pay less than the average cost of services they consume, however, existing residents face either receiving less service with the same amount of taxes or paying higher taxes to maintain the services. The potential migrants have no incentive to include those costs imposed on other residents in their decision about whether to relocate, so the distribution of population among localities may become inefficient. Again, intergovernmental grants may be used to resolve this difficulty. Grants to high-tax or low-service localities may forestall some of the migration in search of lower taxes or more services and contribute to a more efficient structure of local government.

Intergovernmental grants effectively substitute the granting government's tax revenue for that of the recipient government. If the taxes used by the granting government are more efficient than the ones they replace, this tax substitution is another way that grants may improve the efficiency of the federal system. Because mobility is so much greater among subnational jurisdictions than among nations, a tax levied nationally may generate fewer inefficiencies than a set of similar subnational taxes. The revenue can be generated nationally but spent locally, with a system of intergovernmental grants. This is at least part of the rationale for revenue-sharing programs.

Also, intergovernmental grants sometimes are suggested as a method of explicit income redistribution for equity reasons. Taxes collected by the federal government or a state may be used to fund grants to lower-level governments that are allocated inversely proportional to income or property value, resulting in an implicit transfer from governments in higher-income jurisdictions to governments in lower-income jurisdictions. The effects of this type of income redistribution are not always clear, however, because jurisdictions seldom are completely homogeneous in income and because the local government determines how the grant funds are to be spent. Even jurisdictions that are low-income on average may have high-income residents, in some cases, a substantial number. If the objective is to assist low-income individuals and families, it seems preferable in most cases to give grants directly to those individuals, rather than the state or local government where they reside.

TYPES OF GRANTS

As depicted in Figure 9.4, intergovernmental grants usually are characterized by four factors: (1) whether use of the grant is intended for a specific service or may be used generally, (2) whether grants automatically are allocated by a formula or require an application associated with a specific project, (3) whether the grant funds must be matched by recipient government funds, and (4) whether the potential size of the grant is limited.

Specific, or **categorical, grants** are the dominant type, both by number and amount of funds, offered by the federal and state governments. As shown in

Figure 9.4

Types of
intergovernmental
grants

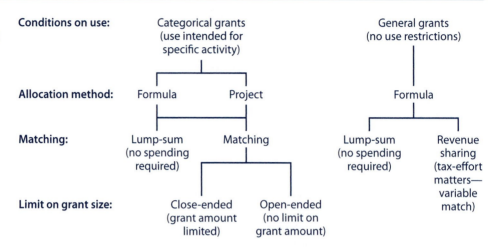

Table 9.3, in 1993, the federal government had 578 different categorical grant programs, representing more than 97 percent of the number of federal grant programs and more than 88 percent of federal aid dollars. The dominant state program provides specific grants for local education.

If the amount of these specific grants does not change as a recipient government changes its taxes or expenditures, then they are called **lump-sum, or nonmatching grants.** The amount of the grant cannot be altered by fiscal decisions of the recipient government. In 1993, 280, or about 48 percent, of federal categorical grants were nonmatching (see Table 9.3). **Matching grants,** on the other hand, require recipient government taxes or spending, with the size of the grant depending on the amount of those taxes or that spending. Typically, a specific matching aid program offers to match each dollar of recipient tax or expenditure on that specific service with R grant dollars, intended to be spent on that service. R is called the matching rate. If $R = 1$, then each local dollar generates $1.00 in grant money, so that the grant finances half of the expenditure. If $R = .5$, then each local dollar generates $.50 in grant funds, and the grant finances one-third of the expenditure ($.50/$1.50). Generally, then, the share financed by the grant (denoted by M), is

$$M = R/(1 + R)$$

For predicting the effects of matching grants, note that through this matching rate, the grant reduces the price of additional amounts of the aided service to the recipient government. If $R = 1$, the grant finances one-half of expenditures, so the cost in local taxes of increasing spending by $1 is only $.50. In general, the local tax price (denoted by P) of an additional dollar of service (the local marginal cost) is

$$P = 1 - M$$
$$= 1 - [R/(1 + R)]$$
$$= 1/(1 + R)$$

Table 9.3

Federal Grants, by Type, 1993 (Billions of Dollars)

Type	Amount	Percentage of Amount	Number	Percentage of Number
General purpose[a]	$ 2.4	1.1	—	—
Block grants (for health [5], community development [2], ground transportation [2], social services [2], income security [2], and one each for education and employment and training)	21.8	10.6	15	2.5
Categorical grants	182.2	88.3	578	97.5
Matching			298	51.6[b]
Formula			87	
Open-Ended			12	
Project			211	
Nonmatching			280	48.4[b]
Formula			72	
Open-Ended			5	
Project			208	
Total	206.4	100.0	593	100.0

[a]"General-purpose" grants include a few small payments by federal departments and payments to Puerto Rico and the District of Columbia.

[b]Percentage of categorical grants only.

SOURCE: ACIR, (January 1994).

If $R = 1$, each additional dollar of service costs local residents $.50 in local taxes. If $R = .5$, the local tax price of $1's worth of additional service is $.67. If $R = .25$, the local tax price is $.80; local residents pay $.80 for each additional dollar of expenditure on the specific aided service.

Both matching and nonmatching categorical grants may be allocated either by formula or a project-by-project basis and may be either open-ended (no limit on the grant amount) or closed-ended (the grant amount is somewhat limited because the funds appropriated for the grant program are fixed). Project categorical grants have outnumbered formula grants by more than two to one, while less than 3 percent of federal categorical grants have been open-ended. The class of open-ended, formula, nonmatching, categorical grants (of which there are very few) should be clarified. In these cases, the formula allocating subnational government grants implies a fixed payment for factors outside of the recipient government's control, such as population or population characteristics, but there is no limit on the amount of aid. Programs in this class include unemployment compensation and some child nutrition grants.

General grants, those without use restrictions (or with very loose restrictions), are rare among federal government grants, although somewhat more common among state grants. These grants, which are sometimes said to provide general fiscal assistance, almost always are allocated by formula. If the formula includes factors outside of the government's direct control, such as population or per-capita income, the grant is a pure lump sum to the government. On the other hand, if the formula includes factors controlled by the recipient government, such as tax collections or tax effort, then the amount of the grant can be altered by recipient government decisions. This method, used for the federal and some state revenue-sharing grants, creates a type of matching grant, although the total amount of grant dollars is fixed and the matching rate varies, as discussed later in this chapter. Note that matching, open-ended, general-purpose grants are not a good idea because by redefining all consumption as part of government, all of consumption could be matched. For instance, if residents of a city agreed to buy all food and clothing through the city government, all those expenditures would be matched. It obviously is impossible for this to happen generally.

The best-known general-purpose grant was the U.S. General Revenue Sharing Program, begun in 1972, which initially provided grants totaling about $6 billion annually to state–local governments. The funds first were divided among the states by a formula that included population, per-capita income, and tax effort, with one-third of a state's funds allocated to the state government and the remaining two-thirds distributed to local governments in that state, again by formula. The size of the grant fund was increased slightly in 1976, although states were removed from receiving revenue-sharing grants and the fund decreased proportionately in 1984. The federal revenue sharing program for local governments expired in 1987.

There is also a class identified as **block grants.** Block grants are specific grants in categories that are broadly or loosely defined. For instance, two separate block grants are available for community development. Correspondingly, there is a long list of approved activities that can be financed with these funds in that general category. The number and size of block grants has been growing in recent years as individual categorical grants have been combined into new block grants. The idea is that these fall in some intermediate area between narrowly defined categorical grants and grants with no use restrictions at all. As you will see later in this chapter, in most cases, these block grants effectively are general grants because the categories are broad enough to allow most recipient governments leeway for reallocating other funds.

ECONOMIC EFFECTS: THEORY

Intergovernmental grants may affect recipient government fiscal decisions either by increasing the resources available to provide government services, called an **income effect,** or by increasing resources and reducing the marginal costs of additional services, called a **price effect.** Either effect may influence the amount of government service demanded, although in different ways. In taking this approach to analyzing intergovernmental grants, economists retain the notion of individual demands for government services, as discussed in Chapter 4, which must be coordinated by a political choice system. If political decisions are made by voting, then the effect of the grant on a government's decisions is determined by the effect of the grant on the decisive voter.

Accordingly, most economic analyses of the expected effects of intergovernmental grants start with the effects of the grants on individual demands, as shown in Figure 9.5. An increase in available resources, which arises from a lump-sum grant,

Figure 9.5

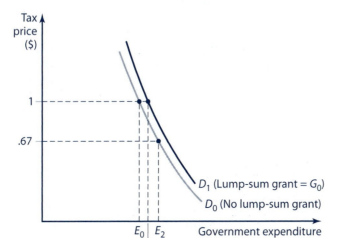

Income and price
effects of a grant

causes the demand curve for government services to shift out (assuming that government services are normal goods, as supported by empirical evidence). With the marginal cost of an additional dollar of expenditure remaining at $1, desired expenditure increases from E_0 to E_1. On the other hand, a matching grant reduces the marginal cost (or price) of additional expenditure, which causes an increase in the amount of government service demanded, for instance from E_0 to E_2. In economic parlance, lump-sum (nonmatching) grants increase demand via an income effect, whereas matching grants increase the desired amount of service due to a price effect. Given the characteristics of the grant program and the local political choice system, the economic effects of the grant can be predicted. Several general results follow.

Matching Grants Are More Stimulative Than Lump-Sum Grants

Perhaps the most fundamental result of microeconomics is that a decrease in price has a greater effect on consumption than an increase in income, even if that increase is large enough to give a consumer the same choices as the price decrease. When the price of a product decreases, whether for hamburgers or education, consumers are influenced by two separate factors. The product whose price has fallen now is relatively less expensive compared to other goods than before the price change, *and* the consumer's purchasing power has increased—even with constant income, more of all goods can be afforded. The first is called the substitution, or price, effect because it is an incentive for consumers to substitute more of the now relatively less expensive commodity. The second is the income effect. For normal goods, both of these influences are an incentive for consumers to consume more of the product whose price has decreased.

When consumers receive an increase in income, purchasing power rises, but the relative price or cost of different products does not change. Therefore, if the income effect that arises from a price decrease is the same magnitude as the income effect from an increase in income, the price decrease should affect consumption more. The income effects are the same, but the price decrease has an additional substitution effect. In essence, price changes are expected to stimulate greater changes in consumption than equivalent changes in income because price changes alter purchasing power *and* relative costs, whereas income changes alter only purchasing power (and the two changes in purchasing power are the same size).

The implication of this microeconomic principle is that an open-ended matching grant is expected to increase government expenditure on the aided service by a greater amount than an "equal size" lump-sum grant, where "equal-size" is defined to mean a lump-sum grant large enough to allow the government the same expenditure as selected with the matching grant. Although the government could select the same expenditure in both cases, it does not because of the price incentive. The change depicted earlier in Figure 9.5 represents this principle. A matching grant that provides $.50 for each $1 of locally financed expenditure reduces the local tax price per dollar of expenditure to $.67, thus inducing an increase in government expenditure on the specific service from E_0 to E_2. If a lump-sum grant equal to G_0 were offered instead, which would be large enough to allow the recipient government to select expenditure E_2, the theory argues that the actual expenditure selected would be smaller, for instance, equal to E_1.

The same principle is shown by the numerical illustration in Table 9.4. Assuming initial spending and taxes of $1,000 per capita and a price elasticity of demand for government expenditure equal to $-.5$, a matching grant providing $.50 for each $1 of local tax reduces the tax price to $.67, a 33 percent decrease, and induces a 16.5 percent increase in spending to $1,165.00. As a result, the jurisdiction receives a matching grant of $388.33 (one-third of total spending). If this jurisdiction received a lump-sum grant equal to $388.33 per capita and assuming per-capita income of $5,000 and an income elasticity of 0.5, income rises by 7.76 percent and spending rises by 3.88 percent to $1,038.80. The matching grant has stimulated a greater increase and level of spending than the equal-size lump-sum grant.

This analysis applies directly to open-ended matching grants but must be modified for closed-ended matching grants. Suppose, for example, that a matching grant is offered of $.50 for each $1 of locally financed expenditure up to a maximum local expenditure of $1,000 per capita. The maximum grant is $500 per capita. The local tax price is $.67 as long as local per-capita expenditure is less than $1,000; above $1,000, the local tax price is $1. In other words, this is initially a matching grant for recipient governments that spend less than $1,000 per capita before the grant program begins, but it is a lump-sum grant for governments that spend $1,000 per capita or more. Equivalently, this is a matching grant for governments that spend less than $1,500 per capita, *including the grant*. For instance, a government spending $1,350 per capita on the specific aided function (composed of $900 in local money and $450 of grant) can increase per-capita expenditure by $1 with an extra $.67 of local money. When total per-capita expenditure reaches $1,500, the grant is at its maximum and is, therefore, a lump-sum grant.

Table 9.4

Expenditure Effects of Matching and Lump-Sum Grants

Initial Fiscal Circumstances

Per-capita expenditure	$1,000
Per-capita local tax	$1,000
Price elasticity of demand	−0.5
Income elasticity of demand	0.5
Per-capita income	$5,000

Grant Conditions and Effects

Matching Grants		Lump-Sum Grants	
Matching rate	0.50 ($.50 for each $1.00 of each tax)	Per-capita grant amount	$388.33
Tax price with grant	$0.67 ($1.00/$1.00 + $.50)	Percentage increase in per-capita income	7.76% ($388.33/$5000)
Percentage decrease in price	33%		

16.5%	Percentage increase in per-capita expenditure	3.88%
$1165.00	Per-capita expenditure with grant	$1038.80
388.33	Per-capita grant	388.33
776.67	Per-capita local tax	650.47
165.00	Increase in per-capita expenditure	38.80
223.33	Decrease in local tax	349.53
388.33	Sum = grant amount	388.33

The closed-ended nature of the grant complicates the analysis because (1) it is not possible to determine whether the grant is effectively matching or lump sum without knowing the recipient government's position, and (2) a recipient government's reaction to the grant can move its per-capita expenditure across the boundary, transforming an apparent matching grant into a lump-sum grant, or vice versa. For governments "near" the expenditure cap on the grant, the full price effect of the grant may never apply. One expects, therefore, that closed-ended matching grants are more stimulative, in aggregate, than pure lump-sum grants (because some governments feel some price effect), but less stimulative than open-ended matching grants (because some governments reach the maximum).

Matching Grants Provide Tax Relief

The preceding analysis argues that matching grants induce an increase in spending on the aided category, but the increase is not as large as the grant. As a result, the matching grant also can increase government spending in other budget categories or allow for local tax relief. As long as the demand for government service is price inelastic, a matching grant increases expenditure by less than the amount of the grant, thus freeing local funds to be spent in other ways. Because the evidence, reported in Chapter 4, shows that demand for most state–local services is price inelastic, matching grants are expected to be used for tax relief in part. The expenditure and tax effects of matching grants are demonstrated numerically in Table 9.4.

Focusing again on the illustration in Table 9.4, the local tax price falls from $1 to $.67, a decrease of 33 percent. If the price elasticity of demand for the aided service is less than one (inelastic), then expenditures will increase by less than 33 percent and local taxes can decline. In the illustration, spending rises by 16.5 percent to $1,165.00, to be financed by $776.67 of local money and $388.33 of grant money. The matching grant increases total expenditure but decreases the amount of local funds spent on the category by $223.33. This $223.33 can be spent by the government on other services or on local tax relief.

If demand is price inelastic, matching grants do stimulate increases in total expenditure but do not stimulate increases in locally raised money spent on the service. This led to some confusion as to whether matching grants are stimulative, the confusion resulting from just what "stimulative" means.

Specific Lump-Sum Grants May Be No Different Than General Grants

A lump-sum grant of $G that is restricted for use in a specific category may be no different, from the viewpoint of the recipient government, than a grant of $G with no use restrictions. That is, the two grants may have the same effect on a recipient government's fiscal behavior. This issue depends on whether the government can and does reallocate locally raised funds from the specific budget category to others because of the grant.

The possibilities are depicted in Figure 9.6, which shows the budget options for a community (or individual) between government expenditures on the aided

---

Figure 9.6

Comparison of alternative lump-sum grants

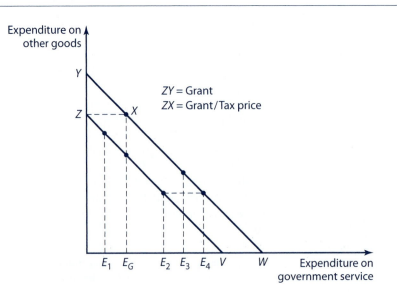

ZY = Grant
ZX = Grant/Tax price

category and expenditures on all other (government and private) goods. With no grant, this community can spend a maximum of $Z on other goods *or* a maximum $V on the specific service *or* any combination on the budget line between those two points. A lump-sum grant expands the set of affordable options, that is, it shifts the budget line out. A general lump-sum grant equal to ZY shifts the budget line to YW; the government receives ZY dollars that can be spent on anything, including entirely on "Other Goods." A lump-sum grant of the same size that *must* be spent on the aided category shifts the budget line to ZXW; the recipient government *must* buy ZX units of the aided service, the amount that can be purchased using all the grant funds. Thus, all the grant funds are spent on the intended service.

Two implications follow. First, the restriction on use of the grant "matters" to the recipient only if intended expenditures on the aided category are less than what the grant will buy, that is, less than E_G. If the recipient government would have spent more than E_G anyway, local funds equal to the amount of the grant can be shifted to other uses. Local funds are **fungible** within the entire budget. Put another way, beyond E_G, the budget choices from the two grant programs are identical. Second, a lump-sum categorical grant does not guarantee that expenditures on the aided category will increase by the full amount of the grant. A government initially spending E_2 on the specific service already spends an amount equal to the grant. Rather than increasing to E_4, the change from increasing expenditures by the full amount of the grant, the government more likely would increase expenditures to some intermediate level like E_3, freeing funds for increased spending in other areas as well.

In the illustration reported in Table 9.4, a lump-sum grant equal to $388.33 per capita is provided. Suppose that per-capita income is $5,000 and the income elasticity of demand is .5. The per-capita grant of $388.33 increases income by about 7.76 percent, causing an expenditure increase of 3.88 percent. As a result of the grant, per-capita expenditure increases by $38.80 to $1,038.80, which is financed with $650.47 of locally raised money and the $388.33 grant.[3] Accordingly, the amount of local funds spent on the category decreases by $349.53, which can be spent on other services or tax relief.

Students often are experts on fungibility. Suppose your parents visit you at school and as they are leaving give you a gift of $20, which they insist *must* be spent on pizza. Even if you always obey your parents, does this mean you will spend $20 *more* on pizza this week than you usually do? Not necessarily. If you normally spend $25 per week on pizza, you might increase your pizza consumption to $30, including the $20 gift, and shift your own $15 you would have spent on pizza to some other necessity, perhaps books. You satisfied the restriction without having to increase consumption by the amount of the gift. In effect, you behaved in the same way as you would have if the gift came with no use limitation.

The potential for specific-purpose, lump-sum grant funds to be shifted to other uses in this manner has led some to consider other types of use restrictions,

---

[3]Another way to think of the result that arises from this income level and the income elasticity of demand is that $.10 of each additional grant dollar is used to increase government expenditure, so the lump-sum grant of $388.33 increases spending by about $38.83.

particularly requiring maintenance of local effort. This restriction requires not only that the grant funds be spent on the aided category, but also that local funds spent on the category not be reduced. Even this restriction may not be as severe as it seems, however, because expenditure normally would increase annually without the grant. If a government spends $100 on a specific service in one year and plans to spend $110 in the following year, a $10 lump-sum grant with an effort maintenance restriction is the same as a $10 grant with no restriction. The grant can be spent on the specified service, and the additional $10 the government would have spent on that service can be reallocated to other uses. In general, the effort maintenance restriction is binding only if the grant is larger than the increase in expenditure that would be selected without the grant (which is not observed).

Tax Effort Grants Are Matching

One common factor in the allocation formula for revenue-sharing grants, once used for the U.S. Federal Revenue Sharing Program and still for about one-quarter of state revenue-sharing funds, is tax effort. **Tax effort** is usually measured either by tax revenue as a fraction of income or, for many local governments, property tax as a fraction of taxable value. In these revenue-sharing programs, a higher tax effort generates a larger grant, given no change in any other allocation factor. A high tax effort can reflect either a great demand for government service in a jurisdiction, a relatively low tax base, or a high production cost for government service. Because a subnational government chooses its tax effort, those recipient governments can affect the size of the revenue-sharing grant (similar to matching grants).

The operation of a representative state revenue-sharing program is demonstrated in Table 9.5, simplified with two equal-size recipient local governments. The state revenue-sharing program divides a fixed amount of state tax collections ($100) between the two localities based on population (POP_i) and tax effort, here defined as the effective property tax rate (T_i/V_i). Both jurisdictions initially collect equal property taxes, but because jurisdiction A's property value is lower, its tax effort is twice as great as jurisdiction B's. Because they have equal populations, A receives 66.7 percent ($66.70) of the revenue-sharing funds, and B receives the remaining 33.3 percent ($33.30).

What happens if one of these governments (B) increases property taxes by 20 percent to $600 while A holds taxes constant? Jurisdiction B's relative tax effort rises, and therefore its share of the revenue-sharing funds also rises. In this example, because B gains $4.20 in revenue-sharing funds from the $100 increase in taxes, the new local tax price is $.96. Jurisdiction A loses the $4.20 of revenue-sharing funds, a 6.3-percent decrease, even though it made no fiscal changes.

Several implications follow. A recipient jurisdiction can increase its revenue-sharing grant by increasing taxes at a greater rate than its competitor jurisdictions. Even if a jurisdiction does not seek a larger revenue sharing-grant, it must increase taxes just to avoid losing grant funds if any other recipient jurisdiction raises its taxes. Each jurisdiction is in competition with all others for the limited revenue-sharing funds. Because all jurisdictions face these same opportunities and each is

Table 9.5

Sample Revenue Sharing Program

Feature	Jurisdiction A	Jurisdiction B
Population	50	50
Property tax	$500	$500
Taxable value	$5,000	$10,000
Effective tax rate—tax effort	10%	5%
Relative tax effort	1.50	0.75
$\dfrac{T_i/V_i}{T_i/V_i}$		
Grant share	66.7%	33.3%
$\dfrac{RTE_i \times POP_i}{(RTE_i \times POP_i)}$		
Grant (fund = $100)	$66.70	$33.30
Effect of Property Tax Change		
New property tax	$500	$600
New relative tax effort	1.36	0.82
New grant share	62.5%	37.5%
New grant amount	$62.50	$37.50
Change in grant	−$ 4.20	+$ 4.20
Percentage change in grant	−6.3%	+12.6%
Price of tax increase	na	$0.96

uncertain about the behavior of its competitors, a general incentive exists for an increase in government expenditures. This program is different from a standard open-ended matching grant because the total amount of grant funds is fixed and because the rate at which local taxes are matched by increased grants changes as all the recipient jurisdictions react to the grant. As one special case, if all the recipient jurisdictions increase taxes at the same rate, no one's revenue-sharing grant changes, although all increase government spending.

HEALTH CARE AND THE CHANGING COMPOSITION OF GRANTS

Federal grants to state–local governments increased at relatively high rates since the early 1990s. Federal grants in the years 1992–2002 increased annually on average of more than 10 percent and thus went from representing about 2.8 percent of GDP and about 14 percent of federal government outlays to 3.4 percent of GDP and nearly 18 percent of federal spending. State–local governments went from receiving about $.22 in grants for each dollar of own-source revenue to about $.27 per dollar of revenue by 2002.

One might think that the relatively rapid growth of federal aid might ease the fiscal problems of states and localities, but instead, much of the growth in grants seems to have

Application 9.1 — Health Care and the Changing Composition of Grants

been caused by rapid increases in costs faced by states, particularly for health care. About half (actually 46 percent) of the increased federal grant amount since 1992 was an increase in grants to finance Medicaid, which pays health care expenses for low-income individuals and families. Grants for state Medicaid expenditures rose by about 123 percent from 1992 to 2002, whereas the amounts for all other federal grants rose about 88 percent. As a consequence of the relatively larger growth of Medicaid grants compared to others, federal grants for health care (almost all of which is for Medicaid) represented nearly 41 percent of total grant dollars in 1992, but 56 percent in 2002.

The relatively rapid growth of grants for health services (and especially Medicaid) is

Figure 9.7

Federal aid to state and local governments, annual amounts by major agency: fiscal years 1981–2003

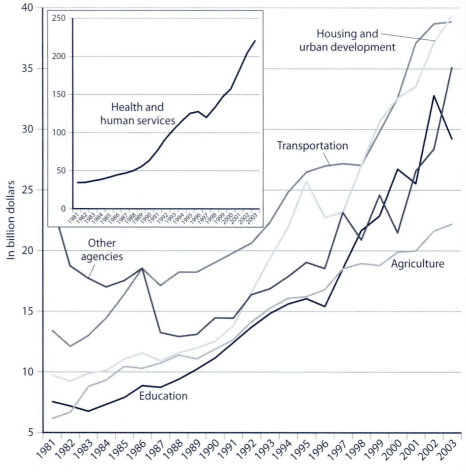

SOURCE: U.S. Census Bureau, Federal aid to states for fiscal year 2003.

Application 9.1 — Health Care and the Changing Composition of Grants

reflected in Figures 9.7 and 9.8. Figure 9.7 shows the dramatic growth in grants from the Department of Health and Human Services since 1997 from about $125 billion to almost $220 billion. When the analysis is by program (rather than granting agency), as shown in Figure 9.8, the story is the same. Grants for medical assistance programs grew from about $70 billion in 1992 to nearly $180 billion

by 2002. In contrast, grants for road building and maintenance from the Highway Trust Fund grew by only about $15 billion, although grants for cash assistance payments for the poor (TANF) actually declined.

Because federal grants to states for Medicaid are open-ended matching grants, the substantial increases in the amount of those grants resulted from increases in state

Figure 9.8

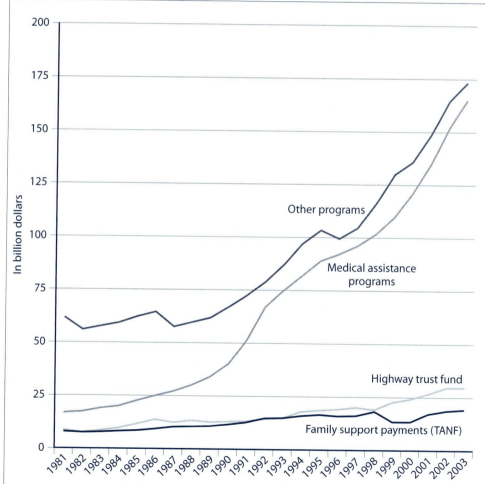

Federal aid to state and local governments, annual amounts by major program area: fiscal years 1981–2003

SOURCE: U.S. Census Bureau, Federal aid to states for fiscal year 2003.

Application 9.1 — Health Care and the Changing Composition of Grants

spending on Medicaid. State spending on Medicaid can increase either because states expanded their programs by easing eligibility or raising benefits, or because the costs of providing a given set of health-care services to the eligible population increased substantially. Not surprisingly, the correct explanation is mostly the latter one. The substantial increase in the demand for and costs of providing health care greatly increased state expenditures for Medicaid. Only a portion of the increased state expenditures are paid by additional federal grant amounts. As a result, rather than easing state budget problems, these increased federal grants arose from the increased demand for state services, which caused additional budget pressures for both states and the federal government. For more on the issues concerning financing of Medicaid, see Chapter 21.

ECONOMIC EFFECTS: EVIDENCE

It is difficult and somewhat dangerous to make generalizations about the estimated effects of intergovernmental grants because there seems to be substantial variation in how different governments respond to different grants and because the results of different economic studies often vary greatly even for the same grant program. Nevertheless, some conclusions are broadly supported about the general direction and relative magnitude of effects caused by different grants.

First, open-ended, categorical matching grants seem to increase expenditures on the aided category by a larger amount than equal-size specific lump-sum grants, as predicted by theory. Because the estimated price elasticities for most subnational government services are less than one (in absolute value), the expenditure increase from a matching grant is smaller than the grant, allowing funds to be diverted to other expenditure categories or to tax relief. The numerical example in Table 9.4 generally is representative, therefore, of the statistical evidence.

Although open-ended matching grants are not the most common type of federal grant, as previously noted, they have been used for two well-known programs: Aid to Families with Dependent Children (AFDC) until 1996 and Medicaid. Robert Moffitt's (1984) analysis of state government responses to federal AFDC grants supports the general conclusions noted previously. Through grants to states, the federal government paid a percentage of state AFDC benefits (the exact percentage differs by state). Using 1970 data, Moffitt estimated that the elasticity of a state's per-capita AFDC benefit with respect to the national subsidy rate is .15; a 10 percent increase in the subsidy rate increases per-capita benefits by 1.5 percent. At that time, the average per-capita AFDC benefit was $45, with the federal government paying about 60 percent of the marginal cost (an additional $1 of benefit costs the state $.40). If the subsidy rate were increased to 70 percent, about a 16 percent increase, the per-capita benefit would increase by about 2.4 percent ($16 \times .15$), or about $1. The average state would have received approximately $1.20 more in per-capita grant, with about $1 going for increased AFDC benefits. More discussion of these types of welfare grants is presented in Chapter 21.

Second, there is some evidence that closed-ended categorical matching grants sometimes have greater expenditure effects than open-ended matching grants, which seems contrary to theory. Closed- and open-ended grants are not used for the same services, however, so the different expenditure effects most likely result from differences in demand for the services. For instance, the closed-ended categoricals, which are the most common type of federal grant, may be used for services that state–local governments were not substantially providing or may include effort maintenance provisions. In either case, the opportunity to use grant funds to shift resources to other budget categories is limited, forcing a larger increase in spending on the aided category. Also, the demands for the services aided by closed-ended grants might be more price elastic than those for which open-ended grants are used.[4]

Third, lump-sum grants also cause an increase in government expenditures, which seems in most cases to be smaller than the grant. The estimated expenditure effects of lump-sum grants vary widely, however, from an expenditure increase of $.20 up to $1 per dollar of grant received. Again, two reasons for this difference are differences in initial spending on the category by subnational governments and different use restrictions among the grants. The majority of the estimates fall in the range of a $.25 to $.50 increase in expenditure per dollar of grant. If those results are representative, then $1 of lump-sum grant provides between $.50 and $.75 for expenditures in other budget areas or for local tax relief.

The evidence that a substantial portion of both matching grants and lump-sum grants effectively is diverted to uses other than those nominally intended raises the issue of which other budget categories benefit. This "leakage" of grant funds may occur both among different services and different local governments, which overlap in tax authority. As an example of the latter, aid to municipalities is expected to increase municipal expenditures and decrease local municipal taxes. The lower municipal taxes may, therefore, allow local school districts to also increase expenditures (by reducing opposition to increased local school taxes). In fact, there is evidence of just this sort of cross-government general-equilibrium effect; aid to either municipalities or independent school districts appears to cause increased spending by both.

The possibility of grant substitution among different budget categories for a single government was examined in detail by Steven Craig and Robert Inman (1985), who studied state government expenditure responses to federal welfare and education grants. Craig and Inman concluded that although federal welfare and education grants to states do increase state expenditures in those categories, both influence expenditures in other areas by a larger amount. For instance, they estimate that an additional $1.21 from open-ended federal welfare grants to states would generate $.34 more in welfare spending, $.54 less in state education expenditures, $.63 less in state taxes, and thus $.78 more on other state services ($1.21 - .34 + .54 - .63 = .78$). Similarly, they found that $1 of additional lump-sum federal

---

[4] It does appear that demand for state–local welfare expenditures is less price elastic than the demand for state–local services generally.

education aid to states increases state education expenditure by $.43, increases state welfare expenditures by $.23 (only $.09 of which is state money due to matching federal welfare aid), decreases state taxes by $.39, and thus allows $.09 to be spent on other state services. Although the specific magnitude of these estimates surely is not precise, it seems clear that intergovernmental grants do have some substantial unintended or unexpected effects on recipient government budgets.

Finally, evidence suggests that an additional $1 of lump-sum grant money has a greater government expenditure effect than a $1 increase in residents' incomes. The results of a number of studies show that although $1 of increased income is expected to increase subnational government expenditure by about $.05 to $.10, $1 in lump-sum grant money appears to increase expenditure by $.25 to $.50. This result has become known as the **flypaper effect,** reflecting the notion that money paid to a government tends to "stick" in the public sector. If true, this means that a $1 grant has very different allocation effects than a $1 tax decrease by the granting government (which increases income by $1). These results have generated some controversy about whether they reflect important characteristics of political behavior or are illusory and caused by incorrect or imprecise economic analysis. That debate is presented next.

Is Grant Money Different Than Tax Money?

Do increases in lump-sum grants and increases in private personal incomes affect subnational government expenditures equally? If not, why not? These two issues have received increasing amounts of attention as a result of the empirical results mentioned previously. The answers seem to fall into two categories. One position is that no flypaper effect really exists—that the empirical results arise from incorrect statistical work or misinterpretation of those results. The other position, that the flypaper effect is real, is then divided on the cause—whether it reflects political power and control by government officials or behavior actually desired by voters, who may be misinformed.

First, why would economists think that grants and income *should* influence expenditures equally, anyway? That view arises from the belief that the public-choice process (voting) works to reflect perfectly the desires of various voters, or at least the decisive voter. The majority-voting/median-voter model so favored by economists is in this class; government selects the expenditures desired by the median voter, and if government does not select the desired expenditures, political competition will arise to move the government in that direction. For an individual voter, increases in income or grants to the voter's government are the same because both increase the resources available for consumption. An individual can convert grant funds into personal income through decreased local taxes.

The idea can be demonstrated through an individual's budget, which leads to that individual's demand for government services, as presented in Chapter 4. The budget is

$$Y_i = C_i + t_i(T)$$

Because local taxes must make up the difference between expenditures and grant funds,

$$Y_i = C_i + t_i(E - G)$$

$$Y_i = C_i + t_iE - t_iG$$

$$Y_i + t_iG = C_i + t_iE$$

where

Y_i = income for person i

C_i = private consumption by person i

t_i = the local tax share for person i

T = total tax collected by person i's local government

E = expenditures by person i's government

G = the lump-sum grant to person i's local government

The left-hand side of the budget equation represents the resources available to be spent on either private consumption or government services. The individual's price for government services is the tax share, t_i. An individual voter's implicit share of lump-sum grants received by the government is the voter's tax share multiplied by the amount of the grant; this is the amount of local taxes the individual would have to pay to generate the same amount of revenue as the grant. Equivalently, if all the grant were used to lower local taxes, this represents the tax savings to that voter. With this view, it should not matter whether resources arise from an increase in Y_i or an increase in G; because both expand the individual's budget and should increase demand for normal goods.[5] The same idea is illustrated by Figure 9.6. An increase of ZY in private income shifts the budget line in exactly the same way as a lump-sum grant equal to ZX.

The key to the argument, of course, is whether individuals have the option or desire to convert lump-sum grants received by the government into private income through tax reductions. If individuals suffer from some type of fiscal illusion or if budget-maximizing, monopoly government officials create such an illusion, then the grant funds may be treated differently than income. One possible type of illusion occurs because lump-sum grants reduce the *average cost* to residents of recipient government spending. A jurisdiction that spends $100 per capita and receives a $30 per-capita grant pays only 70 percent of the cost, on average. If individuals believe that this average cost is the price, then it appears that the lump-sum grant has reduced the price of government service similar to a matching grant. As a result, the expenditure effect would be greater than from the income effect alone. This is an illusion because the grant is a lump sum (constant). An increase in spending of $1 would cost the local jurisdiction $1; the marginal cost has not been reduced.

---

[5]From the budget equation, a $1 increase in Y_i should be precisely equivalent to an increase of $1/t_i$ in G.

The flypaper effect also could result from the nature of the political process rather than incorrect perceptions by voters. By controlling the set of options from which voters choose, budget-maximizing officials may be able to get voters to approve taxes to finance desired expenditures and then also spend the grant funds. The grant funds therefore would cause increased spending rather than tax relief. This will work only if voters do not give grant funds the same careful consideration they do taxes, and political competitors do not arise to give voters a different set of choices.

The competing position holds that the flypaper effect really does not occur, with the apparent evidence caused by statistical and analytical error. One possibility is that in studying grants, analysts may make mistakes in classifying grants as lump sum or matching. Howard Chernick (1979) has argued, for example, that in choosing among competing projects applying for closed-ended lump-sum funds, officials of the granting government may favor those projects where the recipient government agrees to spend the largest amount of local funds. This converts a nominally lump-sum grant effectively into a matching one. If an analyst considers the grant a lump sum when it is in fact a matching grant, it is not surprising to find an unexpectedly large expenditure effect. With some 600 different federal grant programs plus state grants to consider, many of these types of errors are possible.

Another possibility, suggested by Bruce Hamilton (1983), is that residents' income may affect the cost of providing government services as well as demand. For instance, it may require less government spending to bring students up to a given test-score level in a higher-income community than a lower-income one, due perhaps to nursery school or other educational services purchased privately by the families. If income does affect cost, then increases in income cannot be compared directly to increases in grants. In Figure 9.9, an increase in income increases the demand for service and reduces the cost of providing that service. The increase in

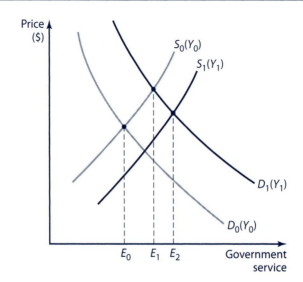

Figure 9.9

Increases in income can affect both demand and cost for government service expenditure from E_0 to E_1 is due to the income effect on demand, although the increase from E_1 to E_2 reflects the cost reduction. Studies that ignore this possibility underestimate the expenditure effect of income increases, which can be part of the reason for the flypaper effect results.

Whether the flypaper effect is a political fact or a figment of imprecise analysis is, as yet, unresolved. In general, those who believe that substantial political competition between potential officials and economic competition among jurisdictions are prevalent, tend to believe that the flypaper effect must be small or weak. Those who believe government officials can maintain monopoly power and manipulate public opinion tend to believe that the flypaper effect is real and strong.

INTERGOVERNMENTAL GRANT POLICY

Economic theory and evidence about the effects of alternative types of intergovernmental grants lead to three major conclusions about grant policy. First, open-ended categorical matching grants are best if the objective is to increase recipient government expenditures on a specific function. A matching grant with a matching rate equal to the nonresident share of benefits offsets the effects of interjurisdictional externalities by reducing the local tax price. The lower price induces the increase in expenditures necessary for efficiency. For instance, if the marginal social benefit of additional highway spending is half of the total, a matching grant to states that pays $1 for each $1 of state money reduces the state's cost by half and restores efficiency. Although other grants also could be used to increase expenditures, an open-ended matching grant induces the desired expenditure response with the smallest possible grant; matching grants provide the largest expenditure effect per dollar of grant.

Second, general lump-sum grants are a better mechanism than matching grants to redistribute resources among subnational jurisdictions. No economic reason exists for such grants to go to all jurisdictions; of course, they should be targeted to low-income or high-cost jurisdictions. These grants should be lump sums so as not to alter the relative price of government compared to private consumption. Although substantial tax relief is expected to result from such a program, these grants are not equivalent to federal tax reductions if the flypaper effect results are correct.

Third, categorical lump-sum and closed-ended matching grants should generally be avoided. Closed-ended matching grants become lump-sum grants after the maximum grant is reached, and categorical restrictions do not alter grant effects unless the grant is large compared to recipient government expenditures in the category. Open-ended matching grants are preferred, however, if the objective is to increase expenditures or to induce recipient governments to begin spending on a specific function.

As we have seen already, the actual intergovernmental grant system in the United States departs substantially from these rules. Categorical closed-ended grants are the most common form of federal grant (both in number and dollars). When matching grants are used, the matching rates often do not seem to correspond to the share of benefits that go to nonresidents. Revenue-sharing grants, the basic general-purpose grants, were given to all general-purpose local governments and included matching-grant effects due to tax effort allocation. The specified categories for block grants are so broad that they effectively are general grants. Consequently, "reforming" the federal grant system is continually discussed.

One reform option advanced by a number of economists is to substitute open-ended grants for closed-ended or lump-sum grants and to set matching rates to correspond to nonresident benefits. Gramlich (1985b) has suggested that in many cases this would require *reducing* matching rates for current open-ended matching grants. The reduction in many matching rates for those programs would then free up resources that could be used to fund larger grants for those programs where no matching exists currently or where there are low caps on matching provisions. As a result of such a policy change, federal grant programs would become more stimulative across a broader set of functional areas. As noted, this policy makes sense if the primary objective of grants is to offset spillovers and establish economic efficiency.

However, research by Robert Inman (1988) suggests that offsetting spillovers may not be an important objective of federal grant policy in practice, even if economists argue it should be. Inman compares the interstate distribution of federal grants to variables that might capture the potential for spillovers—these variables include a measure of out migration by residents, the number of new housing starts (reflecting immigration), and the number of local governments per square mile—and finds either no relationship between grants and these measures or the wrong relationship. He concludes that ". . . the spillover rationale for aid does little to help us understand the actual distribution of federal assistance" (Inman, 1988, p. 49).

In contrast, Inman does find support for the idea that a main purpose of federal grants is to further economic equity, that is to bring about a more equitable distribution of resources and thus, perhaps, a more equitable distribution of public goods. After correcting for other factors, he reports that "federal aid is almost always inversely related to the level of state income," and that "almost all federal aid is equalizing" (1988, p. 51). The state-by-state distribution of per-capita federal grants for 2003 is shown in Figure 9.10. Even without holding constant other factors that influence the interstate distribution of grants, a negative correlation remains between per-capita grants and per-capita income, although perhaps a bit weaker than that found by Inman. For instance, the state with the smallest amount of per-capita grants, Virginia, has a per-capita income that was 7 percent above the national average in 2002, while the state with the largest per-capita grant (excluding Alaska) is Wyoming, with a per-capita income about equal to the national average.[6] If federal grants are intended to redistribute resources among states, then it is not surprising that they do not seem related to spillovers. If the intention is to redistribute resources only, then general block grants may make more sense than matching grants.

---

[6]The lowest-income state, Mississippi, receives per-capita federal grants of about $1700 (in 2003), whereas the highest-income state, Connecticut, received about $1,300. A regression of the log of per-capita grants (G) on the log of per-capita income (Y) is

$$lnG = 9.06 - 0.26 \, lnY,$$

$$(4.06) \ (-1.13)$$

suggesting that each 1 percent increase in per-capita income is associated with about a quarter of 1 percent decline in per-capita grants.

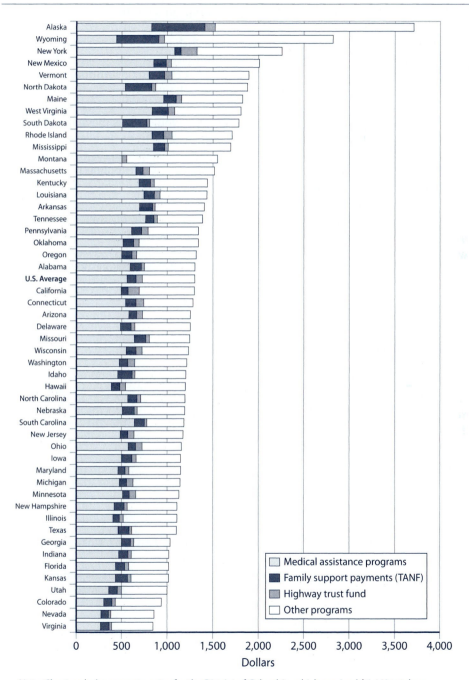

Figure 9.10

Federal aid to state and local governments, per-capita amounts by state, by major program area: fiscal year 2003

Note: Chart excludes separate entry for the District of Columbia, which received $6,449 total per capita federal aid.

SOURCE: U.S. Census Bureau, Federal aid to states for fiscal year 2003.

Another often-suggested reform is for the federal government to reduce grants to states and localities and simultaneously reduce or eliminate some federal tax. The theory of such "revenue turnbacks," as they are often called, is that states would be free to raise a state tax to replace the federal tax and the federal grants. Of course, states would have the option not to do that as well, essentially providing residents fewer public services but more private consumption. President Reagan offered just such a proposal in 1982 (see Chapter 21 for details).

If the objective of federal grants is to redistribute resources to poorer states, then a simultaneous reduction in federal grants and taxes would not achieve the objective, unless the federal tax was collected disproportionately from poorer states, which seems unlikely. We have seen previously that federal grants go disproportionately to poorer states. Similarly, to the extent that states have responded to the price-incentives of matching grants, state–local spending on the aided categories would fall if the grants are removed, even if the states received the same resources in the form of lower federal taxes. Finally, the cost of collecting taxes might be lower at the federal than state level, and such economies of scale alone might justify a federal grant structure. In short, the idea of "revenue turnbacks" makes sense only if no economic reasons exist for the federal grants in the first place or if these reasons no longer apply.

INTERNATIONAL COMPARISON

Grants in Major Federal Nations

Intergovernmental grants are a common feature of almost all nations regardless of their intergovernmental structure, but they are particularly important and potentially more complicated in federal nations, where at least three separate levels of government exist. Despite the widespread use of grants, the magnitude, main purpose, and structure of intergovernmental grants vary substantially, even among federal nations.

As shown in Table 9.6, among these four nations the magnitude of intergovernmental grants is much greater in Australia and Canada when compared to Germany

Table 9.6

Use of Grants in Federal Nations, 2002

Nation	Level	Grants Received as a Percentage of GDP	Grants Received as a Percentage of Revenue
Australia	State	7.1	49.5
	Local	0.4	17.2
Canada	State	3.3	16.0
	Local	2.8	38.8
Germany	State	2.1	17.0
	Local	2.5	35.1
United States	State	2.8	26.0
	Local	3.7	40.1

and the United States. Total spending for grants is a larger share of the economy in those nations, and grants provide a larger share of revenue for state and local governments there, on average. Grants are especially important for state governments in Australia (more than 49 percent of revenue) and local governments in the United States (40 percent), Canada (nearly 39 percent), and Germany (35 percent). In Australia, states are the main providers of direct services but have limited tax authority; thus, they depend on federal government grants for a large portion of their revenue. In Canada, local governments provide a number of social services that are selected and mandated by the provinces (states), which are then funded by provincial grants to localities. In the United States, the dominant grants received by local governments are to school districts for K-12 education.

What these data do not show is the difference in the main purposes and structure of grants in these countries. As you have already seen, grants in the United States are mainly narrow categorical grants intended to affect spending in particular service categories. The main purpose of grants in the other three countries, however, is for regional redistribution and equalization, accomplished by broad-purpose, revenue sharing type grants. In Australia, the Australian Grants Commission—an independent authority established by the federal government—recommends a distribution of grants among the states and territories to equalize the states' capability to provide a standard set of services, given their costs and local revenue base. In Canada, the federal government provides general equalization grants to the states based on the states' capability to generate revenue; a state receives an equalization grant if its per-capita revenue from a fixed average set of tax rates is less than the national average revenue yield.

Despite substantial regional economic differences in the United States, general grants with an explicit equalizing objective have been relatively unimportant. The federal government did operate General Revenue Sharing for a few years in the mid-1970s and early 1980s, but its magnitude was always very small. Thus, ACIR (1981, p. 97) noted that "Fiscal equalization is less accepted as a goal and consequently is pursued to a lesser extent in the United States than in any of the other three federal nations. . . ." However, even if regional redistribution or equalization has not been an explicit objective of U.S. grant policy, it is certainly true that redistribution has occurred and perhaps was implicitly intended.

SUMMARY

Intergovernmental grants, sometimes called grants-in-aid, are transfers of funds from one government to another, most often from a higher-level government in the federal system to a set of lower-level governments.

In 2003, the federal government transferred nearly $386 billion of aid to state–local governments, about $.27 for every $1 raised by state–local governments from their own sources. Similarly, state governments transferred about $355 billion to local governments, or about $.60 cents for every $1 collected by local governments from their own sources. The importance of intergovernmental grants relative to the revenue of recipient governments peaked in the late 1970s; after declining, it has been increasing since.

Seventy-four percent of federal aid to states and localities nominally is directed toward the three budget categories of education, highways, and public welfare, the last representing more than 50 percent. In contrast, education is the dominant category of state aid to localities, accounting for about two-thirds of state aid.

Grants may be used to correct for externalities that arise from the structure of subnational governments and thus can improve the efficiency of fiscal decisions. Grants also can be used for explicit redistribution of resources among regions or localities. Grants also have been considered as a macroeconomic stabilizing mechanism for the subnational government sector.

An open-ended matching grant is expected to increase government expenditure on the aided service by a greater amount than an equal size lump-sum grant, where "equal size" is defined to mean a lump-sum grant large enough to allow the government the same expenditure as selected with the matching grant. If the demand for government service is price inelastic, a matching grant increases expenditure by less than the amount of the grant, thus freeing local funds to be spent in other ways.

A restriction on the use of a lump-sum grant "matters" to the recipient only if intended expenditures on the aided category are less than what the grant will buy. Effort maintenance restrictions are binding only if the grant is larger than the increase in expenditure that would be selected without the grant (which is not observed).

Lump-sum grants cause an increase in government expenditures, usually in the range of $.25 to $.50 increase in expenditure per dollar of grant. A lump-sum grant of $1 thus provides between $.50 and $.75 for expenditures in other budget areas or for local tax relief.

Economic theory and evidence about the effects of alternative types of intergovernmental grants led to three major conclusions about grant policy. A matching grant with a matching rate equal to the nonresident share of benefits is best if the objective is to offset the effects of interjurisdictional externalities. General lump-sum grants are a better mechanism than matching grants to redistribute resources among subnational jurisdictions. Categorical lump-sum and closed-ended matching grants generally should be avoided in favor of the other two.

DISCUSSION QUESTIONS

1. Because nonresidents benefit from local government public-safety services, suppose that the federal government offers localities a public-safety grant equal to $1 for $1 of local tax money spent on that service.

   a. What is the effect of this grant on the price of public-safety spending to these localities? How might the grant correct for the spillover problem?

   b. Suppose that Central City currently levies a property tax for public safety at a rate of $10 per $1,000 of taxable value on a base of $10 million of taxable property. If the price elasticity of demand for public safety in Central City is 0.2, calculate and explain the expected effect of the grant on public-safety spending, public-safety taxes, and tax rates in Central City.

2. Instead of the matching grant in the first problem, suppose Central City received a lump-sum grant of $55,000 that must be spent on public safety. If the total income of Central City residents is $22 million and the income elasticity of demand for public safety is 0.8, what is the expected effect of this grant on public-safety spending and taxes? Why does the matching grant increase spending more than the lump-sum grant?

3. Suppose that Central City received a lump-sum grant of $55,000 with no restrictions as to how that money must be spent. Do you think the effect on public-safety spending would be different from the specific lump-sum grant in problem 2? Why or why not?

4. Periodically, it is proposed that the federal government should reduce its role in intergovernmental fiscal relations by eliminating a number of smaller matching intergovernmental grants and simultaneously reducing federal taxes by an equal amount, particularly any that directly finance these grants. This concept is sometimes referred to as "revenue turnbacks," which is the idea that individuals will retain the resources and the option to tax those resources to continue the programs now financed by the grants. If such a change were made, how do you expect states would respond? Do you expect that state spending on the aided categories could rise or fall if states had to finance that spending from the additional private resources?

SELECTED READING

Break, George. *Financing Government Expenditures in a Federal System*. Washington, D.C.: The Brookings Institution, 1980. See Chapter 3, "The Economics of Intergovernmental Grants," and Chapter 4, "The U.S. Grant System."

Fisher, Ronald and Leslie Papke. "Local Government Responses to Education Grants." *National Tax Journal*, March 2000, 153–168.

Gramlich, Edward M. "Intergovernmental Grants: A Review of the Empirical Literature." In *The Political Economy of Fiscal Federalism*, edited by Wallace Oates, 219–39. Lexington, Mass.: Lexington Books, 1977.

APPENDIX

Indifference-Curve Analysis of Grants

One also can demonstrate the effects of different types of grants using the traditional consumer-theory tools of indifference curves and budget lines, continuing the presentation in the appendix to Chapter 3. In Figure 9A.1, an individual faces budget constraint AF in choosing between governmentally provided good G and a composite good X, representing consumption on all other goods. The slope of the budget line represents this individual's tax price. At the utility maximizing bundle, this individual consumes G_0 units of good G and spends X_0 dollars on all other goods.

A comparison of
matching and
lump-sum grants

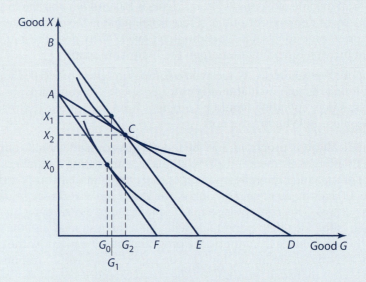

If this individual's jurisdiction receives an open-ended matching grant, the tax price is reduced because of the match so that this individual's budget line shifts to *AD*. Each unit of good *G* now costs less in local taxes because of the grant so that this individual can afford more *G*; as more *G* is consumed, the grant increases. At allocation *D*, all this individual's income is being spent on *G*, which is matched with grant funds at the matching rate. The individual's utility maximizing bundle with the matching grant is bundle *C*, involving G_2 units of *G* and X_2 dollars spent on *X*. In this case, the grant has induced an increase in consumption of the aided good *G* and an increase in spending on other goods as well.

Now suppose a lump-sum grant is offered instead of a matching grant, with the lump-sum grant just large enough to allow consumption of the same bundle as selected with the matching grant, that is, bundle *C*. A lump-sum grant equal to *AB* dollars shifts the budget constraint to *BE*, which goes through bundle *C*. A grant equal to *AB* is just large enough to allow this consumer to select bundle *C*. Because the lump-sum grant does not alter the prices of goods, this new budget line is parallel to the original. Faced with this lump-sum grant and budget line *BE*, this individual's utility maximizing bundle is G_1 and X_1.

The lump-sum grant increases consumption of the government good compared to that with no grant, but the increase in consumption of *G* is smaller with the lump-sum grant than under the matching grant. This is required, given the usual convex shape of indifference curves, because the bundles on budget line *BE* to the left of bundle *C* provide the consumer higher utility with lower consumption of *G* (but more spending on *X*). The absence of the price reduction on G means that fewer resources are allocated to consuming G. Therefore, the open-ended matching grant is more effective at increasing consumption of G than an equal-size lump-sum grant. The lump-sum grant, however, increases the recipient's utility more because the choice of consumption mix is not distorted by a price change.

Now consider a close-ended matching grant offered at the same matching rate as before but only applying to the first G_2 units of good G purchased with local funds. The budget line facing the consumer is now ACE. The matching grant lowers the price up to bundle C, which provides the maximum grant. Beyond consumption level G_2, the price of additional units of G returns to the original price with no grant. The budget line is thus parallel to the original but shifted out, due to receipt of the maximum grant. If the utility maximizing bundle is less than G_2, the closed-ended grant is matching; if it is greater than G_2, the grant is a lump sum. As Figure 9A.1 is drawn, the utility maximizing bundle is at C; the consumer takes advantage of the full matching potential of the close-ended grant.

10 CHAPTER

BORROWING AND DEBT

A subsidy geared to the volume of borrowing by a governmental unit is objectionably stimulative of borrowing.[1]
—JAMES A. MAXWELL

HEADLINES

"LAST YEAR [2003] WAS MARKED BY AN UNUSUAL PHENOMENON IN PUBLIC FINANCE: A LOT OF STATES, NOTES CLAIR COHEN, VICE CHAIRMAN AT THE RATING AGENCY FITCH, WERE 'TRYING TO BORROW TO COVER THEIR DEFICIT' AND DOING MORE OF IT THAN COHEN, A LONG-TIME OBSERVER OF THE MUNICIPAL BOND MARKET, HAS EVER SEEN. LOOKING BACK ON 2003, SHE NOTES THAT 'EVERYTHING HAS BEEN BONDED THAT COULD BE.' (KITTOWER, 2004)"

"CONTINUING LAST YEAR'S [2004] TREND, ECONOMISTS PREDICT AN INCREASE IN NEW-MONEY MUNICIPAL BOND ISSUANCE, WHICH WILL BE OFFSET SOMEWHAT BY A DECLINE IN REFUNDINGS. . . . TOTAL LONG-TERM MUNICIPAL BOND VOLUME IN 2005 WILL LIKELY BE SOME-WHERE BETWEEN $325 BILLION AND $350 BILLION, ACCORDING TO LYNN REASER, MANAGING DIRECTOR AND CHIEF ECONOMIST AT BANC OF AMERICA CAPITAL MANAGEMENT. . . . OF THE $358.6 BILLION SOLD IN 2004 AS OF DEC. 30, $232.1 BILLION WERE LONG-TERM, NEW-MONEY BONDS . . . THE FIGURES ALSO COMPARE WITH $383.7 BILLION OF LONG-TERM BONDS . . . THAT ISSUERS SOLD IN 2003, SURPASSING THE PREVIOUS RECORD OF $358.8 BILLION IN ALL OF 2002." (NEWMAN, 2005)[2]

---

[1]*Financing State and Local Governments.* Washington, D.C.: The Brookings Institution, 1965, 236.

[2]Kittower, Diane. "Deal of the Year." *Governing.* April, 2004, p. 55. Newman, Emily. "Reading the Numbers: Economists See Rising Rates, Fewer Bonds. *The Bond Buyer.* January 3, 2005.

THE ROLE OF DEBT FINANCE

How Large Is State and Local Government Debt?

In 2002, state–local governments in aggregate had total outstanding debt of nearly $1.7 billion, which amounts to more than $5,850 per person in the United States. And, as shown in Table 10.1, the magnitude of that debt has grown substantially in the past 40 years, as states and localities increased their borrowing for a variety of purposes. The magnitude of state–local government debt has, however, remained relatively stable compared to the size of the economy (13 to 16 percent of GDP) and compared to the annual total revenue of subnational governments (90 to 120 percent). Still, the relative size of the debt fluctuates as states and localities pay off old debt and add new borrowing. Most all the outstanding state–local debt has been used to finance capital expenditures and so is balanced by state–local assets. Since the 1960s, there has been some centralization of subnational government borrowing, with the state government debt now representing about 38 percent of the total subnational government debt, up from about 27 percent in 1964.

Why Do State and Local Governments Borrow?

State–local governments borrow money for three primary purposes: (1) to finance public capital projects such as schools, roads, water and sewer systems, or public facilities; (2) to support and subsidize private activities such as private home mortgages, student loans, and industrial or commercial development; and (3) to provide cash flow for short-term spending or for special projects. In addition, state–local governments may borrow new funds to pay off old debt sooner, if interest rates fall (called refinancing or refunding). In that case, the government is merely replacing one debt with another lower-cost one. In contrast to the federal government, state constitutions or laws often prohibit state–local governments

Table 10.1

State and Local Government Debt Outstanding

Year	Total Debt (Billions)	Per-Capita Debt	Debt as Percentage of GDP	Debt as Percentage of Annual Receipts[a]	State Share of Debt	Local Share of Debt
2002	$1686.1	$5855	16.1%	119.4%	38.1%	61.9%
1997	1221.5	4562	14.7	111.3	37.4	62.6
1992	975.6	3923	15.4	115.4	38.2	61.8
1987	718.7	2953	15.9	109.6	37.0	63.0
1982	399.3	1719	13.0	90	36.9	63.1
1977	257.5	1190	12.9	86	35.0	65.0
1972	174.5	838	14.4	97	31.2	68.8
1967	114.6	579	14.0	122	28.3	71.7
1964	92.2	480	14.5	133	27.1	72.9

[a]Total receipts as defined in the national income and product accounts.

SOURCE: U.S. Bureau of the Census, *Governmental Finances,* various years; U.S. Department of Commerce, Bureau of Economic Analysis, National Income Accounts data, various years.

Table 10.2

Table 10.2

State and Local Government Capital Expenditure

| Year | Total Expenditure (Billions) | Per-Capita Expenditure ($) | Percentage for | | | |
			Education	Highways	Water & Sewerage	Other Utilities
2002	$257.2	$894	27.8%	25.7%	9.2%	7.7%
1997	173.0	646	25.8	26.0	11.6	6.6
1992	136.5	549	22.7	27.2	13.5	7.5
1987	98.3	404	18.1	28.8	13.6	9.5
1982	66.4	285	16.5	27.4	14.5	13.1
1977	44.9	208	20.6	27.8	14.5	8.5
1972	34.2	164	23.5	36.0	10.0	4.7
1967	24.5	124	27.3	38.9	8.8	4.0

SOURCE: U.S. Bureau of the Census, *Governmental Finances,* various years.

from borrowing to finance deficits in operating budgets. Each of the three major reasons for borrowing is considered separately next.

Capital spending traditionally has represented one major reason for state–local government borrowing. In 2002, state–local governments spent more than $257 billion on capital goods, or about $894 per person, as shown in Table 10.2. The largest share of that amount, nearly 28 percent, went for educational facilities, with another 25.7 percent for highway expenditures, a little more than 9 percent for water and sewer systems, and 7.7 percent for other state–local utilities including electric, natural gas, and public transit. Thus, these four categories account for more than 70 percent of state–local capital outlays. From the late 1960s until the mid-1980s, the share of capital spending for education facilities and highways declined, as schools and highways were in place and demand for additional facilities lessened. Beginning in the later 1980s, however, this trend reversed as the education share of capital spending began rising and the share of capital spending for highways stabilized. This new capital spending in these areas represents both maintenance and replacement of the original facilities created in the past 30 to 40 years, which are now wearing out, and building of new facilities to accommodate a growing school-age and general population.

The key economic characteristic of capital goods is that a relatively large initial expenditure is required to purchase facilities that then generate benefits over a number of years. State–local governments can finance such capital purchases in two alternative ways: either by building up a reserve of funds from taxes over several years (pay-as-you-go) or by borrowing the funds to be repaid with interest from taxes in future years (pay-as-you-use). Pay-as-you-use finance recognizes both the irregular nature of capital expenditures and the fact that those who will benefit from the capital facility are the future residents of the jurisdiction. By borrowing the cash for the facility now but effectively paying for the facility with future taxes, those who receive the services from the facility will be paying for them. But pay-as-you-use finance also is criticized sometimes as creating an incentive for overcapitalization by subnational governments if the individual voters who approve projects do not perceive their future costs. Such an incentive may be larger in jurisdictions where a greater fraction of the voters are temporary residents.

State–local governments traditionally have financed capital expenditures with three types of funds: federal grants, borrowed funds, and current revenues (taxes). Although expenditures for individual capital projects clearly are "lumpy," many governments do tend to make some capital expenditures annually, if only for maintaining the existing capital stock. Therefore, spending on capital goods is smoother from year-to-year than one might expect, and some fraction of annual revenues can be spent on capital goods each year. In 2002, state–local governments issued about $130 billion in new long-term, general-obligation debt, but made capital expenditures of almost $260 billion, which suggests that borrowed funds account for only about half of capital expenditures. The remainder is financed from federal grants and current taxes.

There are substantial differences among states, however, in both the amount of capital investment and the share of capital expenditure financed with general obligation borrowing. Temple (1994) reports that higher income states engage in larger amounts of general obligation borrowing per person for two reasons: (1) residents of higher income states demand more capital spending than those in lower income states and (2) higher income states finance a larger share of capital expenditures by borrowing compared to other means. One possible reason is that higher income states may be perceived as better credit risks and thus face lower borrowing costs. Another possibility is that higher income states have more mobile residents who prefer borrowing, as the costs are deferred to the future.

In recent years, state–local government borrowing to subsidize investment by private individuals and firms has become the second major component of state–local borrowing, and in some cases the leading component. State–local governments face lower interest rates on borrowed funds than do private individuals and businesses (because the interest income to investors in state–local bonds is not taxed by the federal government, as discussed in the next section). Therefore, state–local governments can borrow at relatively low interest rates and then reloan those funds to businesses and individuals at the same or slightly higher interest rates, but still lower rates than those private investors face alone. Examples include borrowing for subsidized mortgage and student loan programs, for waste treatment facilities, for industrial or commercial development loans, or for financing sports facilities. This type of borrowing has been facilitated by the proliferation of various state government financing authorities and local economic development corporations, agencies that often carry out this state–local borrowing for private purposes. In essence, state–local governments themselves or through their agencies transfer their authority to borrow at tax-exempt interest rates to private investors who would otherwise face higher borrowing costs.

The third primary reason for state–local government borrowing is to even out cash flow between the periods when these governments receive revenue or to correct a short-term budget shortfall as a result of an error in revenue forecasting. Typically, state–local governments do not receive revenue uniformly over the fiscal year; rather, receipts tend to be concentrated at particular times of the year. Local governments usually collect property taxes only once or twice a year, and those times may not correspond to the start of the localities' fiscal year when spending begins. Although most state government taxes are collected monthly or quarterly (through income withholding, for instance), that pattern of receipts may not match the pattern of state spending. Some states, for instance, make intergovernmental aid payments to localities at the beginning of the state's fiscal year.

Therefore, if a state or local government wants to spend revenue in a fiscal year before that revenue is received, it may borrow for a short period against that revenue to be received later. Similarly, a government might borrow in one fiscal year to cover a revenue shortfall, with the funds made up in the next year. Borrowing for cash-flow purposes is typically for only a three- or six-month period. It is important to understand that this type of borrowing is *not* to finance deficits on a permanent basis. The budget is balanced, over a one- or two-year cycle, and it is just that the revenue and spending do not occur at the same times in that period. A parallel in personal finance may be the use of bank credit cards to make purchases that are then fully paid at the end of the month when the individual receives a salary payment. The individual is not spending more than is earned but is borrowing to spend before the income is received.

How Do State and Local Governments Borrow?

State–local governments borrow money by selling bonds. A **bond** is a financial agreement or promise between a borrower and a lender (sometimes called an investor). The lender buys the bond from the borrower now, providing funds to the borrower. In exchange, the lender receives a promise from the borrower to pay a fixed amount of money (or interest rate) per year for a fixed period and to repay the original amount at a future date. For instance, a state or local government might sell a bond with a face value of $10,000 that carries with it annual payments of $500 for 20 years, at which time the loan is repaid. If a lender (investor) pays $10,000 for such a bond, then the lender earns a five percent return ($500/$10,000 = .05), and the state or local government pays a 5 percent interest cost on borrowing. If the bond sells for less than $10,000, then the investor earns a higher rate of return, and the borrowing government faces higher borrowing costs. For instance, if the bond sells for $9090.91, the effective interest rate is approximately 5.5 percent ($500/$9090.91 = .055).[3]

Different types of state–local government bonds correspond to the different reasons state–local governments borrow. The great majority of bonds issued, and thus the great bulk of state–local government debt, is **long-term debt,** which carries a repayment period of more than 1 year, typically 10, 20, or even 30 years. Long-term debt historically has accounted for more than 90 percent of state–local debt; in 2002 about 97 percent of the total outstanding state–local debt was for long-term bonds, as shown in Figure 10.1. Long-term debt is used for nearly every purpose except cash flow borrowing, which by nature is short-term debt. Long-term borrowing is particularly appropriate in financing capital projects on a pay-as-you-use plan because the term of the loan can be set to correspond to the expected life of the asset.

---

[3]The effective interest cost is slightly higher because the borrower must repay the lender $10,000 at maturity.

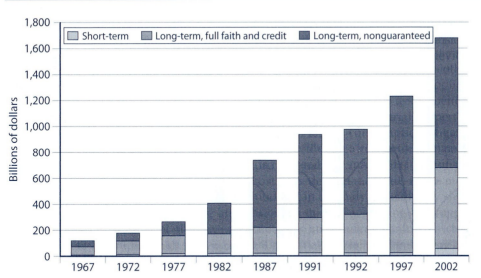

Figure 10.1

State–local government debt outstanding (by type of debt)

Long-term state–local government bonds are of two types: general obligation bonds and revenue bonds. **General obligation (GO) bonds** pledge the **full-faith and credit** of the issuing government as security. This means that the issuing government must use funds from any available source to pay the interest and repay the principal to the investors. The government may use revenue from any tax or charges to repay the debt, and if existing revenue sources are not sufficient for that purpose, then the government pledges to raise taxes or charges to generate the necessary funds. If for some reason a state or local government is unable or unwilling to generate sufficient funds to repay the bondholders, then the government is said to **default** on the bonds. In that case, the government is effectively in bankruptcy and the bondholders may go to court to seize the assets of the government or agency. GO bonds accounted for about 38 percent of the outstanding state–local long-term debt in 2002 (see Figure 10.1). Similarly, about 36 percent of the total long-term bonds sold in 2004 were GO bonds (see Figure 10.2).

The second type of long-term bond is called a **revenue,** or **nonguaranteed, bond.** With revenue bonds, only the revenues from a particular source are pledged to pay the interest and repay the principal to the investors. If the revenues from that particular source are not sufficient to pay the interest or principal fully, then the bondholders suffer the loss. In general, therefore, revenue bonds are more risky investments than GO bonds from the point of view of investors. As an example, a state transportation agency might issue revenue bonds to finance the building of a bridge, pledging the revenues from bridge tolls to repay the investors. If the actual amount of bridge use is less than forecast and if the difference cannot be made up with higher tolls, the bondholders may suffer a loss. Or, as another example, a state university might issue revenue bonds to build residence halls, pledging the room charges of the students to repay the loan. The security or risk of those bonds

Figure 10.2

Amount of
state–local bonds
issued (short-
and long-term,
1980–2004)

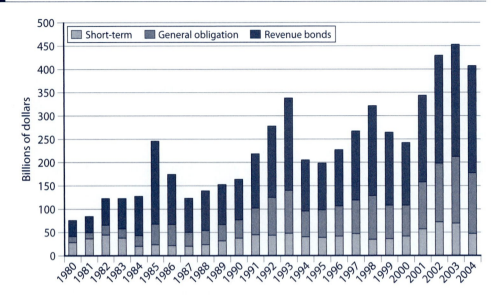

depends on the success of the university in filling those residences. (Note that this may be one reason why some colleges and universities require students of particular ages or classes to live on campus.)

State–local governments also use revenue bonds when the borrowed funds are slated to support allowed private investment, which is called **private-activity bonds.** For example, a state government authority may sell revenue bonds and use the proceeds to make home mortgage loans to lower-income families. In that case, the bondholders will be repaid from the mortgage payments made by the individual homeowners or perhaps from the sale of properties that are mortgaged. Obviously, the security of these bonds depends on the economic conditions of the homeowners and the housing market. If too many individuals do not make their mortgage payments or the value of housing falls, then there may be insufficient revenue to repay the bondholders. The security of these private-activity revenue bonds depends on the economic success of the private individuals or firms that are subsidized. By 2002, about 62 percent of outstanding state–local long-term debt was for revenue bonds, although about 64 percent of new long-term bond issues in 2004 were revenue bonds (Figures 10.1 and 10.2).

It also is useful to understand a bit about the procedural details involved in selling state–local government bonds. First, the issuing government employs the services of several intermediaries in the actual process of selling bonds. These include **bond counsel** (attorneys), who examine the legality of the issue, assure the prospective investors that the government has taken all required and appropriate legal steps to sell the bonds, and work to ensure that the interest will be exempt from federal income tax; and a **financial advisor and underwriter** (which may be the same or different firms), who advises on the structure of the bonds, prepares the necessary financial documents, and markets the bonds to investors. Second, state–local government bonds are usually given a **credit rating** by at least one of the two private rating firms, Moody's Investor Service or Standard and Poor's. The credit rating (denoted AAA, AA, A, BBB, and so forth) provides information to potential investors about the perceived risk of the bonds and thus depends both on the economic and fiscal health of the issuing government and the specific purpose or project for the borrowed funds.[4]

Finally, generally there is an active market for existing state–local tax-exempt bonds, through mutual funds if no other way. This means that some investors may sell state–local government bonds to other investors, thereby receiving return of the principal before the term of the bond is up. Of course, the price for which owners may sell the bonds depends on the annual interest payment, current market interest rates, and the remaining term of the bond. In some cases, the bonds may be repurchased by the issuing government before the planned term. In that instance, the bonds have a **call provision,** or have been called, which means the seller may repurchase the bonds at a predetermined maximum price. An issuing government may want to repurchase the bonds to pay off the debt ahead of time to avoid future interest costs or so that the debt may be refinanced if interest rates have declined.

Trends in the Sale of State–Local Bonds

Beginning around 1970, the most obvious trend in state–local bond activity was the dramatic rise in use of nonguaranteed or revenue bonds, as states expanded the purposes for which they borrowed into traditionally private purposes or private activities. As shown in Figure 10.2, in each year since 1980, the sale of long-term revenue bonds has greatly outpaced the sale of general obligation bonds. By 2002, therefore, about 62 percent of outstanding long-term debt of states and localities was for nonguaranteed bonds, as shown in Figure 10.3. This is a dramatic change in the nature of state–local debt. In the 1950s, 1960s, and 1970s, more than half of state–local debt was for general obligation or full-faith and credit-bonds; 56 percent of debt was of that form as late as 1977. In addition to financing more private activities, this shift toward revenue bonds also may have arisen because state–local governments typically face more restrictions in issuing GO than revenue debt, including state debt limits and often a requirement of voter approval to issue new GO bonds.

A second dramatic change in the state–local bond market has been the tremendous growth in the use of tax-exempt state–local bonds for nontraditional private purposes. These **private-activity tax-exempt bonds** effectively allow state–local governments to transfer their tax-exempt borrowing authority to private individuals and firms for activities that would otherwise be financed through taxable debt. These private entities are able to borrow at the generally lower tax-exempt interest rates rather than taxable interest rates. The largest categories of these bonds are for small-issue industrial development bonds, which are bonds sold by subnational governments or their development authorities, such as EDCs, with the funds to support private investment in the subnational jurisdiction; mortgage

---

[4]For more detail on the practice of state and local government borrowing see Kaufman, (1987, p. 287–317).

Figure 10.3

State–local
government
long-term debt,
by type

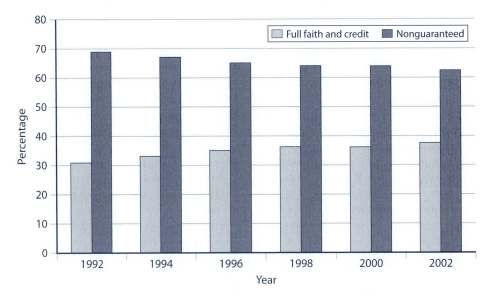

revenue bonds to provide mortgage loans to individuals for owner-occupied housing; bonds for investment by nonprofit organizations, such as hospitals and
educational institutions; and bonds for higher-education student loans, construction of rental housing (particularly for lower-income individuals), and solid waste
disposal (Kenyon, 1991, 83).

Private-purpose tax-exempt bonds are revenue bonds; the bondholders are repaid
from proceeds of the underlying private activity. In the case of industrial development bonds, for instance, the funds from the bond sale may be used to finance partially construction of a new shopping center or expansion by a manufacturer. The
interest and principal on those bonds effectively is paid by the shopping center developer and the manufacturing firm, although the funds may be paid through a development authority. Similarly, a state or locality may sell bonds and use the funds to
make mortgage loans through private financial institutions. Those loans would carry
interest charges below private mortgages and typically are restricted to households
with income less than some percentage, perhaps 125 percent, of the area's median
income. The security for the bondholders in this case comes from the mortgage payments by the borrowers and the market value of the mortgaged properties.

The change in the purposes for which states and localities use long-term debt is
reflected by the data in Figures 10.3 and 10.4. In 2002, 20 percent of state–local
long-term debt was used for educational facilities. In 1967, in contrast, education
accounted for more than 30 percent of state–local long-term debt. By 2002, public
debt for private purposes accounted for about 25 percent of state–local debt, more
than for education or such other traditional functions as highways, although down
from the 30 percent share in 1992. Similar changes, although a bit less dramatic, are
evident for local government debt. At the local level, the share of borrowing going
for educational facilities has been rising in the past decade, although the share of
borrowing for utilities and private purposes has been declining. Still, borrowing

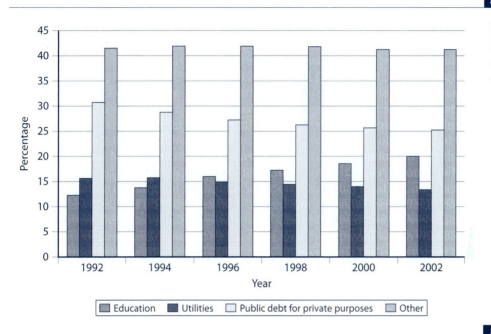

Figure 10.4a

Long-term debt, by purpose— state and local government

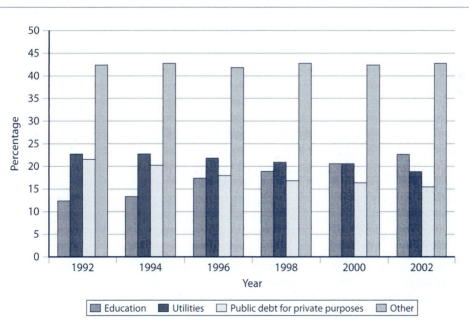

Figure 10.4b

Long-term debt, by purpose— local government

for "private purposes" represented about 15 percent of outstanding local government debt. Again, these changes reflect both the substantial completion of an educational, highway, and water and sewer infrastructure, as well as the increasing use of private-activity bonds.

A third obvious trend is the increasing magnitude of state–local borrowing and debt. From around 13 percent of GDP in the late 1970s and early 1980s, outstanding state–local debt rose to more than 16 percent of GDP by 2002. Similarly, outstanding debt went from less than 90 percent of annual revenue to nearly 120 percent of revenue over the same period. For one thing, the increase in use of revenue bonds for private activities did not so much replace general obligation debt, but rather increased the aggregate amount of borrowing and debt. The annual volume of GO debt issues has continued to grow, as shown in Figure 10.2. Debt levels seemed especially high in 2002 as state–local governments turned more toward borrowing to offset fiscal difficulties caused partly by the national economic slowdown.

The final important factor to note is the sensitivity of state–local borrowing to interest costs and federal tax policy. Part of the substantial increases in the volume of bonds issued in 1991–1993 is attributable to the fact that interest rates fell to their lowest nominal levels in more than a decade. But the annual sales of state–local bonds also are sensitive to federal tax changes. The unusually high sales in 1985 largely reflected anticipated changes in taxes in 1986 that would both make bonds less attractive to investors and restrict the uses of bonds by governments. Accordingly, many states and localities rushed to sell bonds before those changes, sales that might otherwise be delayed for a year or two. Anticipated tax changes in 1992 and 1993 induced more investors to desire state–local bonds, which held down interest costs and contributed to the expanded sales in those years. In fact, bond sales were very low in the two following years, reflecting how borrowing activity had been moved up. Finally, low interest rates in 1998 sparked another surge of borrowing. The link between the state–local bond market and federal income taxes is exceedingly important and thus the issue to which we turn next.

TAX EXEMPTION FOR STATE AND LOCAL BOND INTEREST

The fundamental economic characteristic about state–local government bonds and some private-activity bonds issued by states and localities is that the interest income received by investors is not taxed by the federal government, either by the individual or corporate income taxes. States may tax that interest income, however. Typically, states exempt the interest income paid to residents from bonds issued by that state or its localities but not from bonds issued by other states. Similarly, state income taxes exempt interest income on federal government bonds. Accordingly, state–local government bonds are a type of tax shelter or tax-favored investment for lenders.

The federal tax exemption of state–local bond interest dates from the first federal Income Tax Act of 1913. For many years, some argued that the federal government did not have the constitutional authority to impose a tax on the income from state–local government securities. Beginning with the case of *McCulloch v. Maryland* in 1819, the U.S. Supreme Court established the doctrine of "reciprocal

Table 10.3

Effect of the Tax Exemption for State–Local Bonds on Different Investors

$10,000 Face Value Bond

Marginal Tax Rate	Tax Exempt State–Local Bond 6% Interest Rate			Taxable Corporate Bond 8% Interest Rate		
	Annual Interest	Tax	Net Return	Annual Interest	Tax	Net Return
.15	$600	0	6%	$800	$120	6.8%
.25	600	0	6	800	200	6.0
.28	600	0	6	800	224	5.76
.32	600	0	6	800	256	5.44
.36	600	0	6	800	288	5.12
.50	600	0	6	800	400	4.0

immunity," holding that both the states and the federal government are immune from tax interference with the other. However, the Sixteenth Amendment to the Constitution established the right of the federal government to collect direct taxes on income "from whatever source derived." The constitutional issue was whether the Sixteenth Amendment gives the federal government authority to tax state–local bond interest. In a 1988 case (*South Carolina v. Baker*), the Supreme Court ruled that the federal government does have the authority to tax state–local bond interest. The federal government's decision to exempt certain state–local bond interest from income taxation, then, is an explicit decision to subsidize those investments.

The primary economic effect of the tax exemption is to allow lower interest rates for state–local bonds than for similar taxable bonds. As a result, the tax exemption subsidizes both state–local governments through lower borrowing costs and investors in state–local bonds through higher net (after-tax) returns. These effects of the tax exemption are demonstrated in Table 10.3. In this example, a state–local bond with a face value of $10,000 that carries an interest rate (also called a coupon rate) of 6 percent is compared to a corporate bond of the same risk and maturity but paying an 8-percent interest rate. An investor in the nontaxable state–local bond would receive a $600 interest payment annually on which no federal income tax would be owed and no state income tax if the bond were issued in that state. Therefore, the net or after-tax return to any investor who pays $10,000 for the bond is 6 percent ($600/$10,000).

Continuing the illustration, an investor who buys the taxable corporate bond, in contrast, receives an annual interest payment of $800 and must pay federal and state income tax on that amount. The amount of tax to be paid depends on the investor's **marginal income tax rate,** that is, the investor's tax bracket. A tax-payer with a 15-percent marginal tax rate therefore would owe $120 of tax on the $800 of interest income. That taxpayer's net or after-tax return is thus $680, or 6.8 percent ($680/$10,000). With a 25-percent marginal tax rate, the net return is

$600, or 6 percent. A taxpayer with a 28-percent tax rate, however, receives only a 5.76-percent net return from the taxable bond (tax equals $224, so the net return is $576). If t = the marginal tax rate and r = the nominal interest rate on the taxable bond, then the net return to an investor in a taxable bond is equal to $(1 - t)r$. Thus, the investor with a 50-percent marginal tax rate earns a net after-tax return of 4 percent by investing in an 8-percent taxable bond.

As shown in Table 10.3, taxpayers with marginal tax rates above 25 percent earn higher net returns by investing in the 6-percent tax-exempt state–local bond than in the 8-percent taxable corporate bond. On the other hand, taxpayers with a marginal tax rate of 25 percent get exactly the same net return—6 percent—from either investment, while those with marginal tax rates of less than 25 percent earn higher net returns by investing in the taxable bonds and paying the required income tax. *The marginal income tax rate at which an investor gets the same return from both a taxable and nontaxable bond is equal to the percentage difference between the interest rates on the taxable and tax-exempt bonds.* Mathematically, this relationship is

$$t^* = (r - s)/r$$

where

t^* = tax rate at which an investor is indifferent between a taxable and tax-exempt bond

r = taxable-bond interest rate

s = tax-exempt bond interest rate.

It follows therefore that state–local government bonds can carry lower interest rates than comparable private sector or U.S. government bonds because of the tax exemption. The annual yields on long-term state–local government bonds, 30-year U.S. Treasury bonds, and AAA-rated corporate bonds from 1974 to 2003 are shown in Table 10.4. The yields on the tax-exempt bonds are lower than the yields on taxable bonds, although the yield differential varies over time with supply-and-demand conditions for the specific securities. During the 1970s, the yield differential between state–local and corporate bonds generally was between 20 and 30 percent. Similar yield differentials also held in the 1960s, although differences of 30 to 40 percent prevailed in some previous periods. The yield differential between taxable and tax-exempt bonds has been substantially smaller in recent years, however, averaging less than 20 percent between state–local and corporate bonds in the 1980s and in the mid 20s in the 1990s. This change resulted partly from the reduction in federal marginal income tax rates in the 1980s. The interest rate differential was low in 2003 as a result of large sales of bonds by state–local governments in 2002 and 2003.

The yield differential between tax-exempt state–local bonds and taxable U.S. Treasury bonds generally is smaller than that between state–local and corporate bonds, reflecting the perceived lower risk of the U.S. government bonds compared to corporate securities. The yield differential between state–local and Treasury bonds is substantially more variable than that between the state–local and

Table 10.4

Comparative Bond Yields, 1970—1993

Year	Annual Yield Tax Exempt State–Local Bonds[a]	Annual Yield 30-Year Treasury Bonds	Difference from St.–Loc. Rate as % of T-Bond Rate	Annual Yield AAA Corporate Bonds	Difference from St.–Loc. Rate as % of Corp. Rate
2003	4.73	4.01[b]	−17.96%[b]	5.67	16.58%
2002	5.05	4.61[b]	−9.54[b]	6.49	22.19
2001	5.19	5.49	5.46	7.08	26.69
2000	5.77	5.94	2.86	7.62	24.28
1999	5.43	5.87	7.50	7.04	22.87
1998	5.12	5.58	8.24	6.53	21.59
1997	5.55	6.61	16.04	7.26	23.55
1996	5.75	6.71	14.31	7.37	21.98
1995	5.95	6.88	13.52	7.59	21.61
1994	6.19	7.37	16.01	7.96	22.24
1993	5.63	6.59	14.57	7.22	22.02
1992	6.41	7.67	16.43	8.14	21.25
1991	6.89	8.14	15.36	8.77	21.44
1990	7.25	8.61	15.80	9.32	22.21
1989	7.24	8.45	14.32	9.26	21.81
1988	7.76	8.96	13.39	9.71	20.08
1987	7.75	8.59	10.01	9.38	17.59
1986	7.38	7.80	5.38	9.02	18.18
1985	9.18	10.79	14.92	11.37	19.26
1984	10.15	12.41	18.31	12.71	20.14
1983	9.47	11.18	15.30	12.04	21.35
1982	11.57	12.76	9.33	13.79	16.10
1981	11.23	13.45	16.51	14.17	20.75
1980	8.51	11.27	24.49	11.94	28.73
1979	6.39	9.29	31.22	9.63	33.64
1978	5.90	8.49	30.51	8.73	32.42
1977	5.56	7.75	25.07	8.02	30.67
1976	6.49	7.86[c]	17.43	8.43	23.01
1975	6.89	8.19[c]	15.87	8.83	21.97
1974	6.09	8.05[c]	24.35	8.57	28.94

[a]Standard and Poor's index, high-grade municipals.

[b]10-year Treasury Bonds.

[c]20-year Treasury Bonds.

SOURCE: *Economic Report of the President*, various years.

corporate bonds, reflecting the related operation of supply-and-demand factors in the markets for those two types of bonds. In recent years, there has been about a 5 to 7 percent difference between the yields on U.S. Treasury bonds and tax-exempt state–local bonds, although the yield on state–local bonds was actually greater than that on U.S. Treasury's in 2002 and 2003.

The perceived default risk of these various bonds also influences their relative yields. Treasury bonds are believed to be the least risky in this regard, but the relative risk of state–local as compared to corporate bonds as a group is not clear. The state or local government's credit rating, which depends in large measure on the economic and fiscal conditions in that jurisdiction, determines the actual rate paid by that government, and defaults occasionally do occur with state–local bonds, as happened in the case of the Washington (state) Public Power System in the mid-1990s. Of course, corporate bonds are similarly rated based on the economic health of the firm, and corporate defaults and bankruptcies also occur. Perhaps the most accurate characterization is that among both state–local and corporate bonds, the degree of default risk varies greatly and is reflected by yield differentials within each category of bond.

Costs of Private-Purpose Bonds

Because of the interest cost differential, the use of state–local governments' tax-exempt borrowing authority for otherwise private purposes creates several economic problems. Substitution of tax-exempt bonds for taxable debt by individuals and firms reduces the revenue yield of the federal income taxes, necessitating higher federal income tax rates, lower federal government expenditures, or larger federal budget deficits. An estimate prepared for the 2004 federal government budget showed that the income tax exemption for interest on private-purpose state–local bonds was expected to reduce federal revenue by more than $6 billion in 2005.[5] Moreover, this revenue cost to the federal government is greater than the interest-cost savings by the borrowers. Research by the Office of Tax Analysis of the U.S. Department of the Treasury showed that the substitution of $10 billion of tax-exempt debt for the same amount of taxable corporate debt increased the federal government budget deficit by $1.31 for each $1 of borrowing costs saved by the corporations.[6] The difference between the revenue cost to the federal government and the cost savings to the borrowers goes to the buyers of the tax-exempt bonds. Extension of tax-exempt borrowing rights to private individuals and firms also exacerbates the inefficiency resulting from the exemption, which was described previously. Investment funds are transferred to those projects that are selected by state and local governments to receive the borrowing subsidy.

Limits on Private-Purpose Bonds

Beginning around 1968, the federal government, reacting both to the perceived reductions in federal income tax revenue and to investment distortions caused by the borrowing subsidy, began to restrict the uses of tax-exempt debt by subnational governments. The first restrictions applied to so-called industrial development bonds (IDBs), defined as bonds in which more than 25 percent of the funds were used by a private firm or for which more than 25 percent of the debt service was to be paid from private business activity. If both conditions were true, the

---

[5]See *Analytical Perspectives, Budget of the U.S. Government, Fiscal Year 2004* (Table 6-2).

[6]Toder and Neubig (1985, p. 410).

bonds could not be tax exempt. However, many exceptions were allowed, including for (1) residential property; (2) sports or convention facilities; (3) airports, parking, mass transit, and other transportation facilities; (4) waste disposal and local utility facilities; (5) pollution control facilities; (6) development of land for industrial parks; and (6) so-called "small-issue" IDBs, those involving less than $5 million. This long and broad list of exceptions left many opportunities for states and localities to continue to use tax-exempt borrowing for nontraditional, private purposes.

Between 1968 and 1984, Congress made a number of changes to the rules defining allowed types and amounts of tax-exempt state–local bonds. Congress extended the tax exemption to student loan bonds in 1976, increased the limit on small-issue IDBs to $10 million in 1978, imposed restrictions on mortgage revenue bonds in 1980 to target the mortgage loans to lower-income individuals and placed limits on the amount of mortgage bonds a state could issue, eliminated the use of small-issue IDBs for certain functions (including retail food and beverage service) in 1982, and the set a maximum amount per state for issues of IDBs and student loan bonds by way of the 1984 Deficit Reduction Act.

The Tax Reform Act of 1986 made the most substantial changes to the tax-exempt bond market, including imposing tighter restrictions on the use of tax-exempt bonds for what were now then to be called "private activities." First, state–local bonds are classified as **private-activity bonds** if more than 10 percent of the bond funds is used by a private business or individual (the business or use test) *and* if more than 10 percent of the principal or interest is secured by payments from a private business or individual (the security interest test). Bonds that do not meet both conditions are called **governmental bonds** and are tax-exempt. All other state–local bonds are private-activity bonds, and only those private-activity bonds issued for purposes expressly specified in tax law can be tax-exempt. Tax exempt private-activity bonds are allowed for such purposes as mortgage loans, student loans, small-issue IDBs, nonprofit organizations, and a variety of other purposes. Private-activity bonds for all other purposes are taxable.

Second, the Act tightened the annual maximum limits by state for these allowed tax-exempt private-activity bonds. These "volume caps" were reduced to the larger of $50 per capita or $150 million in 1988 and are now increased annually. Finally, the use of tax-exempt bonds for some types of projects—airports, convention centers, sports stadiums, parking or private mass-transit facilities, and industrial parks—was explicitly prohibited or severely limited. The rules and process determining whether state–local bonds are tax exempt are outlined in Table 10.5. The intent of all these tax-law changes was to decrease the amount of tax-exempt borrowing by state and local governments for these types of private purposes.

The tax exemption for state–local government bonds and the resulting differential in interest rates between these and other types of securities is the fundamental factor underlying most economic issues about state–local government borrowing. Therefore, we turn now to these economic implications and analysis of the tax exemption.

Table 10.5

Defining Tax-Exempt State—Local Bonds

Governmental Bonds

No more than 10 percent of funds used by a private business or individual *or* no more than 10 percent of the interest payments secured by payments from a private business or individual.

Private-Activity Bonds

More than 10 percent of funds used by a private business or individual *and* more than 10 percent of the interest payments secured by payments from a private business or individual.

Tax Exempt

Taxable (not tax exempt) [Including funds for sports and convention facilities, parking, private air, water, mass transit, pollution control, industrial parks, and all other private activities without a specific exception.]

Exceptions for Specified Uses

Limited

$50 per person or $150 million per state per year (whichever is greater).

[Funds for mortgage loans, student loans, small-issue IDBs, multi-family rental housing, sewerage and private solid waste facilities, water and other utilities, hazardous waste disposal, government mass transit facilities, redevelopment of distressed areas.]

No Limit

[Funds for nonprofit organizations; governmentally owned airports, docks, wharves, and solid waste disposal facilities; and veterans' mortgages.]

IMPLICATIONS AND ANALYSIS OF THE TAX EXEMPTION

Nature and Behavior of Investors

Fundamentally, investors in stocks, bonds, and other instruments seek the highest after-tax return for any given amount of risk. Thus, investors find tax-exempt state–local government bonds attractive financially if the investors' marginal income tax rate is high enough to make the tax exemption sufficiently valuable. This occurs if the person's income tax rate is greater than the percentage difference

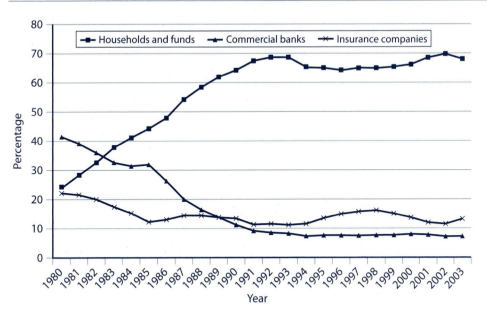

Figure 10.5

Ownership of outstanding state–local bonds (1980–1993)

in the interest rate on tax-exempt bonds compared to that on alternative taxable securities. This general rule also applies to different types of investors, both individuals and firms. In the illustration in Table 10.3 with a tax-exempt interest rate of 6 percent and a taxable interest rate of 8 percent, investors with marginal tax rates greater than 25 percent get a higher net return from the tax-exempt bond. Such individuals and firms are, therefore, expected to be the suppliers of funds (buyers of bonds) to state–local governments.

Historically, state–local government bonds have been purchased almost entirely by three distinct groups—individuals (both directly and through mutual funds), commercial banks, and property and casualty insurance companies—as demonstrated in Figure 10.5. These three groups have owned 80 to 90 percent of the outstanding state–local government bonds since the 1980s. Banks and insurance companies (but commonly not other types of corporations) can be substantial holders because their business essentially is investment of cash. Substantial changes have occurred in the distribution of ownership among these three groups over the years, however. Although individuals owned more than 40 percent of state–local debt in the 1950s, their share gradually declined to about 25 percent in 1980 but increased dramatically to about 68 percent by 2003. In contrast, the share owned by commercial banks rose substantially throughout the 1960s and early 1970s but declined subsequently starting in the 1980s, to only about 8 percent of outstanding debt today. The share owned by insurance companies also declined in the 1980s (also to about 12 percent), but less dramatically than for banks.

These ownership data reflect the aggregate or average ownership of state–local bonds, not the demand for new issues of bonds. There is no presumption that new issues of bonds will be purchased by these groups in these ratios. In many cases, it is more useful for economic analysis to consider which of the groups represent the **marginal investors,** that is, those whose tax rates make tax-exempt bonds just marginally attractive financially. Suppose, for example, that a 25-percent difference exists between the yields on taxable and tax-exempt bonds. If the corporate tax rate were 36 percent, then presumably profitable banks and insurance companies would find tax-exempts attractive and would have increased their holdings of them. A similar argument applies to individuals with (state and federal marginal) tax rates well above 25 percent. If more bonds are to be sold, which requires more investors, the likely source of those investors is individuals with tax rates around or slightly below 25 percent. If the percentage difference in interest rates is narrowed (as has happened in recent years), those individuals would then find tax-exempt bonds attractive. In that case, the marginal investment group is middle-income individuals with lower federal marginal income tax rates, even though the bulk of outstanding bonds may be owned by banks, insurance companies, and high-income individuals.

Individuals

Historically, individual investors in state–local bonds had come mostly from higher-income households for two reasons. First, when yield differentials were in the range of 30 percent, investors must have had relatively high marginal federal income tax rates, generally in the 30 to 40 percent range, for yields on tax-exempt bonds to be attractive. Given the graduated rate structure of the federal individual income tax at that time, marginal tax rates of that magnitude required relatively high gross incomes.

Second, state–local bonds are sold in relatively large denominations (usually at least $10,000), which historically restricted the set of purchasers to individuals willing to invest at least those amounts. In recent years, this constraint has been eased by the proliferation of tax-exempt bond mutual funds in which a financial intermediary buys the bonds and sells shares in a fund comprised of many different bonds for relatively small amounts. In addition to opening up the tax-exempt bond market to more individual investors, this method also reduces the risk to individuals by effectively allowing them to own fractional shares of different bonds from many different issuing governments. Individuals can also more easily convert bonds into cash before maturity, because they can cash their shares in the fund.

In recent years, however, the yield differential between tax-exempt and taxable bonds has been only about 15 to 20 percent, making tax-exempt bonds potentially attractive to a broader set of individuals. This change in interest rates coupled with the easy availability and liquidity of tax-exempt mutual and money-market funds has fueled the increase in individual ownership, either direct or indirect through funds, of tax-exempt bonds.

Corporations and Banks

Analysis of the behavior of corporate investors in state–local bonds, particularly banks and insurance companies, is somewhat more uncertain than that of individuals for several institutional reasons. Commercial banks borrow funds at taxable interest rates, for instance by taking deposits from individuals and selling certificates of deposit (CDs). Until 1987, commercial banks were allowed to deduct these interest costs paid on deposits against their federal corporate income tax, even if the funds were used to buy tax-exempt state–local bonds. Accordingly, the borrowing cost for the banks was the nominal interest rate paid on deposits minus the benefit of the corporate tax deduction. If that borrowing cost were less than the yield on tax-exempt bonds, banks could make profits by taking more deposits and buying more tax-exempts.

For example, suppose that the interest rate on bank deposits is 10 percent and the corporate tax rate is 34 percent. If a bank sells a $10,000 CD to an individual, the bank pays the depositor annual interest of $1,000; however, because that interest cost is tax deductible for the bank, the net cost to the bank is $660 (interest × (1 − tax rate) = $1000 × .66). Now if the $10,000 deposit is used to buy a tax-exempt state–local bond with a 7-percent yield, the bank receives annual interest payments of $700. The bank is engaging in **arbitrage,** effectively incurring a $660 cost to earn $700 and is therefore expected to continue these transactions as long as those gains are possible. But the process of selling additional CDs and buying more state–local bonds by all banks is expected to increase the nominal interest rate on CDs and reduce the rate on state–local bonds until all arbitrage opportunities are eliminated. For instance, if the CD rate is 10.25 percent but the tax-exempt bond yield is 6.75 percent, the bank's net borrowing cost of $676 is just about matched by the potential tax-exempt bond earnings of $675—all arbitrage opportunities are eliminated.

As part of the 1986 Tax Reform Act, banks were no longer allowed to deduct interest cost on deposits when the funds were used to purchase tax-exempt bonds. This was expected to reduce banks' interest in holding tax-exempt bonds, which is exactly what transpired. In the example in the previous paragraph, a bank would not want to purchase a tax-exempt bond paying 7-percent interest with deposits on which the bank pays depositors 10-percent interest. Commercial banks continue to purchase and hold some tax-exempt bonds due to the banks' own tax liability (which can be reduced by earning tax-exempt interest) and as investments matched to some savings deposits that earn very low interest rates for depositors.

Similar types of arbitrage opportunities also may be available to other corporations, such as insurance companies, to the extent that those firms can adjust their taxable income in different ways. One well-known theory (Miller 1977) is that firms adjust their mix of debt to equity so that the net cost of corporate debt (which is a deductible cost for the firm) equals the net cost of equity income to shareholders (which is taxed). The marginal investor in the corporation then has a federal marginal income tax rate equal to the corporate tax rate. If investors view corporate equity income and tax-exempt bond income as substitutes, then the corporate tax rate also determines the yield differential between corporate and tax-exempt bonds.

The common result of all these arbitrage models is that the percentage differential between taxable and tax-exempt bonds equals the corporate tax rate. This occurs because these models make the corporations the marginal investors, and thus the yield differential should make nontaxable bonds just as attractive to corporations. As the data in Table 10.4 illustrate, the yield differential generally has been less than the corporate tax rate (which was between 48 and 46 percent until 1987 and 34 to 39 percent since). Two alternative institutional explanations have been offered as to why bank and insurance company arbitrage has been less than complete. One possibility is that state–local government bonds are perceived as more risky than comparable U.S. Treasury and corporate bonds. Although that notion of relative risk may be true regarding Treasury bonds, it does not seem likely that state–local bonds as a group are any more risky than corporate bonds in aggregate. A second possible explanation concerns the preferred maturity of bonds by different investors. If banks prefer short-term obligations (to maintain liquidity) and insurance companies prefer long-term obligations, then individuals may be the marginal investors in long-term state–local bonds. In that case, arbitrage may be incomplete because the buyers of each type of tax-exempt bond are limited by the amount of bonds of a given type and maturity.

Efficiency of the Tax Exemption

If the objective of the tax exemption for interest on state–local government bonds is to subsidize subnational government borrowing costs, then the tax exemption is an inefficient subsidy because the federal government loses more than $1 of tax revenue for each $1 of interest cost saved by state–local governments. This inefficiency is demonstrated in Table 10.6, in which the interest-cost saving to the state or local government from tax-exempt—as opposed to taxable bonds—is compared to the federal income tax saving of investors. The latter is, of course, also the tax revenue loss to the federal government.

Table 10.6

Efficiency of the Tax Exemption for State—Local Bonds

$10,000 Face Value Bond
6% Interest Rate on Tax Exempt Bonds
8% Interest Rate on Taxable Bonds

Marginal Tax Rate	Interest Cost Saving to State–Local Government Due to Tax Exemption	Federal Income Tax Saving to Investor in State–Local Bond Compared to Taxable Bond
.15	Not a Tax Exempt Investor	
.20	Not a Tax Exempt Investor	
.25	$200	$200
.28	200	224
.32	200	256
.36	200	288
.40	200	320
.50	200	400

The example in Table 10.6 again concerns a $10,000 bond with a 6-percent interest rate for tax-exempt securities and an 8-percent rate for taxable ones. For each bond sold, the issuing state or local government saves $200 of interest cost per year. The federal tax saving to an investor from the tax-exempt bond as compared to the taxable bond depends on the investor's federal marginal income tax rate. The tax savings is $800 (the interest payment) multiplied by the tax rate, or $224 for taxpayers in the 28-percent tax rate bracket, $256 for taxpayers with a 32-percent marginal tax rate, $288 for taxpayers with a 36-percent marginal tax rate, and $400 if there was a 50-percent tax rate bracket. All investors in tax-exempt state–local government bonds with marginal tax rates greater than t^*— the tax rate at which the after-tax return on both type of bonds is equal (25 percent in the example)—save more in federal income taxes from buying the tax-exempt bond than the state or local government saves in interest cost. To put it another way, all tax-exempt bond investors with tax rates above t^* are receiving greater returns than necessary to induce them to buy the state or local bond. The difference between the amount of interest saving to subnational governments and the tax loss of the federal government is a net gain to these investors with high tax rates.

As the demand and supply of bonds changes, thereby affecting the yield between taxable and tax-exempt bonds, the tax rate at which an investor is indifferent between taxable and tax-exempt bonds also changes. In essence, that tax rate (and the relative yields) adjusts so that just enough investors are willing to buy the supplied bonds. Whatever the identity of these marginal investors, however, those investors with higher tax rates earn economic benefits from the tax exemption.

In some cases, the state or local government (and implicitly, their taxpayers) can benefit from the differential in yields on taxable and tax-exempt bonds. If a state or local government sells bonds at the tax-exempt rate and invests those funds at the higher taxable rates, the government earns profits because it is not liable for any tax on the income from the taxable bonds. This is a type of arbitrage by the subnational governments—effectively playing on the difference in rates. Internal Revenue Service (IRS) rules restrict the opportunity for subnational governments to earn arbitrage profits in this manner but do not eliminate them. Capital projects are expected to require some time to get started, so a government may sell bonds to finance a capital construction project but not face any bills for some subsequent period. If the funds are invested over that period, the government can earn arbitrage profits. The Tax Reform Act of 1986 limits the period for such activity to six months, however. In other cases, subnational governments may sell bonds for a specific purpose (for example, student loans or cash flow) even though they have surplus funds on hand. Using the borrowed funds rather than the reserve funds for the projects allows the reserve funds to be invested at the higher taxable interest rates. This, too, is a type of arbitrage permitted by the IRS.

Besides being an inefficient way for the federal government to subsidize state–local government borrowing, tax exemption also increases the amount of state–local government borrowing by lowering the borrowing cost. Similarly, tax exemption induces some investors who otherwise might not do so to buy state and local government bonds. If some of the investors in state–local bonds bought corporate bonds instead, that could lower the borrowing costs of private firms. Therefore, in the absence of some imperfection in the capital markets that works against state–local bonds or some externality among subnational governments that leads to an inefficiently low amount of investment by those governments, any subsidy of state–local borrowing costs can lead to an inefficient use of society's resources.

Growth of Private Purpose Bonds

Clearly, state–local governments find tax-exempt bonds an attractive way to attempt to subsidize investment and stimulate economic development. This tool appears to impose no cost on the state–local governments themselves (or their taxpayers) in contrast to direct expenditures or direct state–local tax breaks given to firms or individuals. In fact, if individual state–local governments believe that the cost of private-purpose bonds is imposed on all federal income taxpayers nationwide, then each government implicitly believes that it is exporting part of its economic development costs to residents of other states or localities by selling private-activity bonds. Indeed, because a state's taxpayers bear costs from all states' private-purpose bonds in proportion to their federal taxable income, a state can "win" in the game only by issuing more and more tax-exempt bonds. Those states whose share of tax-exempt bond volume is greater than their share of federal taxable income are presumably the "winners" from the interest tax exemption.

The perception by state–local governments that private-purpose tax-exempt bonds are costless to them may be faulty, however. The increase in funds to borrow required by state–local governments for these purposes is expected to increase the interest rate on all long-term state–local tax-exempt bonds. The relatively higher return on tax-exempt bonds is required to induce additional investors to supply the funds, that is, buy the bonds. One report suggested that each $1 billion of additional tax-exempt bonds in the entire market increased the tax-exempt interest rate between 1 and 7 basis points (a basis point is one one-hundredth of a percentage point).[7] Another report shows that an additional $6 million of bonds issued by one state increased that state's borrowing costs by 22 basis points.[8] In these cases, use of tax-exempt bonds for private activities increases the cost to state–local governments for borrowing for traditional public purposes (such as construction of roads, schools, and water and sewer systems).

This possibility is demonstrated in Figure 10.6, which shows a positively sloping supply curve for funds supplied by investors to state–local governments (a higher yield is required to induce more individuals and firms to loan money to

---

[7]Clark (1986, p. 59).

[8]Capeci (1990).

Figure 10.6

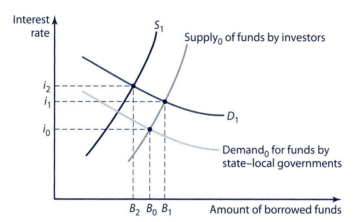

The market for state–local borrowing

subnational governments) and a negatively sloping demand curve for funds by the state–local governments (subnational governments are willing to borrow more when tax-exempt interest rates are lower). Given the initial market conditions, the interest rate on long-term tax-exempt bonds is i_0. If state–local governments want to undertake additional borrowing for these private purposes, then the demand for borrowed funds by state–local governments increases to D_1. If the underlying behavior of investors does not change (supply remains the same), then the interest rate rises to i_1. Consistent with this viewpoint, Temple (1993) reports that an increase in the use of GO debt for capital expenditures and an increase in the over-all level of outstanding debt induces states to sell *fewer* tax-exempt private-activity bonds. Apparently, greater use of debt for capital purposes increases borrowing costs and makes tax-exempt borrowing for private purposes less attractive.

States and localities showed no sign of curtailing the use of tax-exempt borrowing for private activities, so in 1986, the federal government limited the use of those bonds, as previously explained. Although tax-exempt bonding for some functions was prohibited entirely, most other types of private-activity bonds are constrained by state-by-state annual limitations, initially equal to the greater of $50 per person or $150 million total.[9] For 2005, the limit for any state is the greater of $80 per person or $239.2 million total. Such a constraint does not treat all states equally. Thus, states with fewer than 3 million people have an aggregate limit of $240 million and a per-capita limit that is greater than $80 ($240 million ÷ state population). States with a population greater than 3 million have an aggregate limit that equals $80 times population.

For these limits actually to constrain the use of tax-exempt debt, the limit must be less than the amount of debt a state wants to or would issue in the absence of

---

[9]If a state does not use all of its allowed private-activity bond amount in one year, the state may carry the unused amount forward for three subsequent years with approval of the IRS.

the limit. A state could be constrained by the volume cap, however, even if it does not use all of its allowed amount, due to the magnitude of investment projects and typical bond issues. For instance, a state like Wisconsin with a population of about 5.5 million would have a limit of about $440 million per year. If Wisconsin had agreed to sell $350 million worth of private-activity bonds for various purposes, which uses 80 percent of its cap, it would be unable to use bonds for a new proposed $90 million project. Thus, that project might not get funded at all or it might be delayed to a future year. Although Wisconsin did not use all of its bond cap that year, the cap constrained the state from issuing all the bonds it might have otherwise. On the other hand, states are allowed to carry forward unused limits to future years. In the example of Wisconsin, the state could apply the unused $90 million to the next year, creating a limit of $530 ($440 plus $90) million.

Research by Daphne Kenyon (1991, 1993) and others suggests that the caps on private-activity bond amounts have limited the use of these bonds in a number of states, although the effects are uneven. According to Kenyon (1993), 12 states— Arkansas, California, Connecticut, Florida, Kansas, Minnesota, Oklahoma, South Carolina, Texas, Utah, and Wisconsin—used at least 80 percent of their allowed amounts in each year from 1989 to 1991 and thus likely were constrained by the limit. In contrast, 10 states used 50 percent or less of their allowed amounts in each of those years, including Alaska, Delaware, Hawaii, Idaho, Montana, Nebraska, New Mexico, South Dakota, Vermont, and Wyoming. These states certainly seem unconstrained by the limits. In general, the per-person limit that applies to larger-population states is more limiting than the aggregate amount that applies to less-populous states. Wyoming, with about 500,000 people, can issue nearly $480 of private-activity bonds per person per year, compared to only $80 per person in a state such as Minnesota.

Using statistical analysis of state bond use, Kenyon (1990) reports that the tax-exempt volume caps reduced the amount of private-activity bonds nationally by $30 to $36 per person in 1989 and 1990. If the volume caps are effective in aggregate, then the lower demand for borrowed funds by states and localities should hold down the interest costs that states face for all types of borrowing. However, the existing volume caps are expected to continue to have a greater constraining effect in larger states, perhaps inducing more interest in taxable debt in those states or lowering the relative interest costs in those states even more.

Effect of Federal Income Tax Changes

Federal income tax changes have substantial effects on both the supply of funds to the tax-exempt bond market—that is, on the behavior of buyers of bonds—and on the demand for funds by state–local governments—that is, on the sellers of bonds. By affecting both the supply and demand for funds, federal tax policy greatly affects the interest rate paid on state–local bonds.

First among the influences on the supply of funds (buyers of bonds) are changes in marginal tax rates. Recall that the investor's marginal tax rate compared to the percentage difference in yields on taxable and tax-exempt bonds determines the attractiveness of tax-exempt bonds as an investment. For any given difference in yields, therefore, a decrease in marginal tax rates will make tax-exempt bonds unattractive to some investors for whom they were previously a good deal. To retain or reattract those investors to tax-exempts requires relatively higher yields—that is, a smaller difference in yields between taxable bonds and tax-exempts. In Figure 10.6, a reduction in federal marginal income tax rates is expected to reduce the supply of funds to the tax-exempt market to S_1. This change alone is expected to cause an increase in interest rates for tax-exempts from i_1 to i_2 (and a narrowing of the differential).

Federal income tax-rate reductions were the main tax story of the 1980s. The Tax Reduction Act of 1981 reduced federal marginal income tax rates across the board over a three-year period. Even more important, given the fact that tax-exempts were purchased by higher-income individuals, the maximum personal income tax rate was reduced from 70 to 50 percent.

The Tax Reform Act of 1986, which involved several changes that make tax-exempt bonds less attractive investments, reduced marginal income tax rates further—only two personal income tax-rate brackets of 15 and 28 percent remained at that time (33 percent if the phase out of the personal exemption for very high-income taxpayers is included), and the top corporate tax rate was reduced to 34 percent from the previous 46 percent. These reductions in marginal federal tax rates made tax-exempt investments less attractive and reduced the supply of funds to the market. In 1993, however, the highest federal marginal income tax rate was increased to 39.6 percent. This rise in tax rates had the opposite effect, making tax-exempt bonds somewhat more attractive; however, marginal tax rates were still well below the levels before the 1980s. Since 2000, the direction has been in favor of further reductions in federal marginal income tax rates, which will make tax-exempt state–local bonds attractive to fewer individuals.

A second category of tax changes influencing buyers of tax-exempt bonds concerns alternative tax-favored investments. The 1981 tax act expanded the opportunity for individual *tax-deferred* investment through Individual Retirement Accounts (IRAs), Keogh plans, and other tax-deferred savings options primarily intended for retirement saving. With respect to IRAs, individuals were allowed to invest up to $2,000 annually without paying income tax on that amount or on the interest that accrued until the funds subsequently were withdrawn to be spent (presumably at retirement). Although the tax simply is deferred and not eliminated, such savings opportunities are expected to have reduced the relative attractiveness of tax-exempt bonds for some individual investors. This further curtailed the supply of funds to the tax-exempt market, creating additional pressure for an increase in tax-exempt interest rates.

However, the expanded opportunity for tax-deferred saving through retirement accounts introduced in 1981 was cut back by the 1986 Tax Reform Act. Families with incomes above $50,000 with a member covered by a pension plan are no longer allowed a tax deduction for the amount of IRA saving, although the interest can still accrue on a tax-deferred basis. Other types of tax-deferred savings also were restricted. Second, the opportunity for individuals to shelter income with depreciation deductions or credits from passive investments (investments in businesses in which they do not work) was cut back greatly. These two changes together were expected to make tax-exempt bonds more attractive to some investors—in essence, tax-exempt bonds are one of the remaining allowed tax shelters. Both the individual and corporate income taxes include a minimum tax computed on a base that includes some types of tax-exempt income, especially interest earned on private-purpose tax-exempt bonds. This may induce investors to prefer public-purpose tax-exempt bonds and cause higher interest rates for private-activity revenue bonds.

The combined effect of the 1981 tax changes may go a long way in explaining why the difference in yields on long-term taxable and tax-exempt bonds narrowed substantially in the early 1980s. The expected effect of both the tax-rate reductions and the liberalized rules for individual tax-deferred saving is a decrease in the supply of funds to the tax-exempt bond market. On the other hand, the 1979 increase in the maximum size of IDBs and state–local expansion of borrowing for private purposes increased the demand for funds by the tax-exempt market. As shown in Figure 10.6, the combined effect of an increased demand for and reduced supply of funds is an increase in the tax-exempt interest rate from i_0 to i_2 (or a narrowing of the differential between taxables and tax-exempts). This increase in the interest rate could be accompanied by an increase, decrease, or no change in the total value of bonds issued. (In the figure, the quantity actually falls from B_0 to B_2, but any change in quantity is possible depending on the relative size of changes in demand and supply.)

Empirical support for the idea that changes in tax characteristics affect the interest rates on tax-exempt bonds is reported by James Poterba (1986), who statistically related the interest-rate differential between taxable and tax-exempt bonds to various tax-policy events from 1955 to 1984. Poterba (p. 6) concluded that

> By examining data from four events that substantially altered tax rates—the 1964 Kennedy-Johnson tax cut, the Vietnam War tax surcharge, 1969 Tax Reform Act, and the 1981 tax cut—this study provides new evidence that both personal and corporate tax changes affect the relative yields on taxable and tax-free bonds.

Poterba's results suggest that the 1981 tax changes explain one-quarter to one-half of the changes in interest-rate spread from 1980 to 1982. The evidence that personal tax rates matter suggests that corporations do not solely comprise the set of marginal investors.

The expected overall effect of the Tax Reform Act of 1986 on the market for tax exempt bonds was uncertain. The demand for tax-exempt funds was expected to be reduced due to restrictions on the use of private-activity tax-exempt bonds, which should allow for lower interest rates. But the overall effect on the supply of funds was unknown—lower tax rates, end of the bank deduction, and the minimum taxes implied a decrease in the supply of funds, but the curtailment of tax shelters and tax-deferral opportunities suggested an increase in the supply of funds. Even if the overall effect was a decrease in the supply of funds to the tax-exempt market, if the decrease in demand for funds was bigger, tax-exempt interest rates could decline (or, more correctly, the difference in taxable and tax-exempt yields could widen, so that the relative borrowing cost for state–local governments declines).

In fact, the differential in interest rates between taxable and tax-exempt bonds widened from 1987 to 1992. The difference in yields between Treasury bonds and tax-exempt bonds rose from about 10 percent in 1987 to about 16.4 percent in 1992, although the difference between corporate bonds and tax exempts rose from 17.6 to 21.2 percent, as shown in Table 10.4. Apparently, then, the dominant effect of the 1986 Tax Act was a decrease in demand for funds, allowing a reduction in relative borrowing costs for states and localities.

Another important change occurred in 1993. Although interest rates declined generally in 1993, Treasury-bond rates fell more than tax-exempt bond rates. Again, federal income tax effects are thought to be part of the reason. Two new income rate brackets for higher income taxpayers—at 36 percent and 39.6 percent—were enacted. Such a tax rate increase makes tax-exempt bonds more attractive to investors and should increase the supply of funds to states and localities. In response to the very low interest rates available in 1993, many states and localities sought to sell bonds; a record at the time of nearly $338 million of bonds were sold that year. The combined effect of increased supply of funds by investors but substantially increased demand for funds by the governments actually reduced the yield difference between Treasury and tax-exempt bonds in 1993. As a consequence of the new higher income tax rates, the yield differential between tax-exempt bonds and taxable corporate bonds rose again to a range of 22 to 26 percent from 1994 through 2002.

Taxable Municipal Bonds

Because of the problems created by the tax exemption of interest from state–local bonds, economists have long suggested that state–local governments issue taxable bonds with the federal government using a direct subsidy if it wanted to reduce state–local borrowing costs. For instance, if a subnational government issued taxable bonds at an 8-percent rate when tax-exempt bonds had been yielding 6 percent, a federal subsidy equal to 25 percent of the state or local government's interest cost would reduce borrowing costs equally to the tax exemption. The prime advantage of this method is that it would cost the federal government $1 for each $1 saved by the subnational governments rather than more than $1, as is the case with the tax exemption. In other words, this direct payment would be a more efficient way for the federal government to subsidize state–local borrowing costs.

Historically, state–local governments had not been very interested in taxable debt with or without a direct federal subsidy. Subnational governments seem to have been wary about substituting a subsidy payment for the tax exemption in part because a direct federal subsidy could be changed by the federal government in the future. If state–local governments no longer had a tax-exempt bond option, there is no guarantee that the federal government always would offer a subsidy rate equal to that obtainable from the tax exemption.

The restrictions on the use of tax-exempt state and local government debt for private purposes included in the Tax Reform Act of 1986, however, induced states and localities to begin using taxable debt to a greater degree than in the past. Johnson (2004) reports that issuance of taxable state–local bonds has grown substantially in the past eight years—from less than $10 billion in 1997 to a record $40 billion in 2003 and more than $21 billion in 2004.[10] Still the record amount of taxable state–local debt issued in 2003 represented only about 9 percent of all long-term state and local issues.

Now that the new restrictions have taken effect, some states and localities are using taxable debt at least for those private purposes that are no longer eligible for tax exempt financing. As Peers (1986) noted, "Taxable debt is more expensive for municipalities and other issuers, but it can be put to uses that Congress doesn't approve for tax-exempt bonds, such as aid to farmers, pollution control projects, and loans to local businesses." States are also using taxable bonds to fund some public-purpose projects, however, especially now that the yield spread between taxable and tax-exempt government bonds is so small. Johnson (2004) reports that taxable bonds were used for education, student loans, public utilities, public transportation, housing, and funding of public pensions in 2003 and 2004.

Kenyon (1991) notes also that the shift from tax-exempt to taxable debt may be greater than it appears. In the past, states and localities were issuing tax-exempt debt on behalf of private individuals and businesses. Now that this type of tax-exempt debt is prohibited, those private entities may be issuing taxable debt for themselves.

Some local governments already have been innovative in using taxable debt. As part of a plan to refinance some tax-exempt debt at lower interest rates in 1986, Los Angeles County issued both new tax-exempt and taxable bonds. The taxable bonds carried an interest rate about 4 percentage points higher than the new tax-exempt bonds, but the county was not bound by the IRS rules against arbitrage and thus could invest those funds at the highest interest rate they could find. It turned out that Los Angeles County was able to earn a higher return from investing those funds than the taxable bonds cost (Carlson 1986a). In 2005, the city government of Detroit is planning to issue $1.2 billion of taxable bonds to cover future pension liabilities (Carvlin, 2005). In doing so, the city government believes that these bonds will have lower interest cost than past debt to cover pension costs and will free up current revenue for other expenditure responsibilities. As state and local governments expand their use of taxable debt, their financial experience will become similar to that of private firms who have always relied heavily on taxable bonds.

---

[10]Johnson, Matthew. "Despite Lower Volume, Taxables Continue Expansionary Trend." *The Bond Buyer,* December 2, 2004.

FINANCING FOR SPORTS FACILITIES: NEW OPTIONS

As a result of changes in the rules regarding tax-exempt borrowing by states and localities included in the 1986 Tax Reform Act, many activities once favored by tax-exempt debt now had to find other options, not the least of which is professional sports facilities. A number of local governments engaged in tax-exempt borrowing to finance renovation of old facilities or construction of new ones. The various ways that cities often subsidize stadium development and the economics of the entire issue are explored by Zimmerman (1998, 1), who notes that in addition to loans for construction, "billions of state–local taxpayer funds are likely to be expended to finance operating deficits over the life of the stadiums." In some cases, these sports arenas and stadiums were owned by the local government and leased to the professional team (sometimes at an unusually low rate), although in other cases, the facility was owned by the team but partly financed by the locality. In either case, these professional sports facilities were subsidized through the tax-exempt borrowing power of state–local government and/or through taxation. This activity was so popular at one time that it even spawned a conference for local government officials on how to get approval for these ventures.

But state–local tax-exempt debt for sports facilities seemed to be expressly prohibited by the 1986 Tax Act, although state–local governments still could use tax-exempt financing for infrastructure associated with or required because of the facility, such as new or reconstructed roads, expanded utility access, and some auxiliary development. The question, then, was how localities and professional teams would react. Would this end the often cozy relationship between local government and professional sports franchises? Would professional teams increasingly finance and operate the facilities themselves? Would local government pursue taxable bond options to continue to fund sports facilities? Or would localities find ways to continue to finance stadiums consistent with the new federal rules?

In at least one instance, the experience in Portland, Oregon, the actual response was a combination of several of these possibilities.[11] The Portland Trail Blazers sold $155 million worth of private taxable bonds without governmental support to finance the construction of a new arena. The bondholders will be paid solely from revenue generated by the arena. Because tax-exempt bonds might have been used for this activity before the federal restrictions, this may represent a substitution of taxable for tax-exempt debt, even though the city did not issue the bonds. The city government in Portland also played an important role in this project. The city sold bonds to improve infrastructure around the new arena, to construct two new parking garages, and to renovate the older arena, the Portland Coliseum, to be used for other events. Part of the funds borrowed by the city will be repaid from a tax on tickets at the new arena and from a share of parking and arena

---

[11]This discussion is based on "Good Sports." *Governing*, June 1994, 64.

Application 10.1 — Financing for Sports Facilities: New Options

leasing fees. A part of the bonds sold by the city are taxable bonds, and only a small amount of the debt is of a limited general obligation variety.[12]

The Portland experience has some economic, if not political, rationale. Because tax-exempt financing for the arena is not allowed and because the bonds were to be backed by arena revenue anyway, there was no advantage to using government revenue bonds—the risk and rates would be the same essentially. Of the auxiliary projects being undertaken by the city, most of the work (streets, sidewalks, parking) was necessitated because of the new arena and would mostly benefit users of the arena. Applying standard user charge principles (Chapter 8), it makes sense for the users of the arena to finance much of these capital costs, which is precisely what happened. Those attending basketball games at the new arena will pay a surtax, although other users of the arena will contribute toward the public capital costs through their rent or parking fees. Of course, some of the city project may provide general benefits to city residents (from events at the older Coliseum, for instance), and thus some general city revenue contribution to the project may be warranted.

A more recent experience in the District of Columbia was more contentious.[13] The District was competing with a number of other localities to attract a Major League Baseball franchise that had been located in Montreal. The city reached an agreement with Major League Baseball for the team to play in a renovated Robert F. Kennedy Stadium for three years beginning in 2005 and then to move in to a new stadium in 2008 that the city would finance and build. Under the original plan, the city would have financed most of the $450 to $550 million project with bonds backed by local taxes (including a tax on concessions) and rent paid by the team. However, the City Council refused to approve that arrangement, with business opposition to new local business taxes and general concern about using public funds for such a purpose. When the original proposal was not approved, Major League Baseball threatened to cancel the entire arrangement and move the team elsewhere.

Eventually, an agreement between all parts of city government and Major League Baseball was reached for the city to provide part of the funding, but to seek private funding for at least half of the cost of the project. At the time of this writing, the city is taking proposals from a number of private firms to share in the financing of the new stadium in exchange for some other development rights. With this arrangement, again state–local borrowing authority is being used to finance a sports facility. A tax on local businesses backs these bonds, so essentially the entire local community contributes toward the project on the basis of believing that there are general local benefits from the team. A substantial part of the financing also comes from identified private firms that would receive specific private benefits.

[12]Personal communication, Bryant Enge, City of Portland.

[13]This discussion is based on Nakamura, David and Thomas Heath. "Amended Deal on Stadium Approved." *The Washington Post*, December 22, 2004.

SUMMARY

State–local governments borrow money for three primary purposes: (1) to finance capital projects such as schools, roads, water and sewer systems, and power plants; (2) to support and subsidize capital investment by private individuals and businesses; and (3) to provide cash flow for short-term spending or for special projects. In 2002, state–local governments in aggregate had total outstanding debt of nearly $1.7 trillion, which amounts to about $5,850 per person in the United States.

In 2002, state–local governments spent about $257 billion on capital goods, traditionally the major reason for borrowing. Capital purchases may be financed by building up a reserve of funds to be repaid with interest from taxes in future years. In practice, state–local governments finance capital expenditures from intergovernmental grants, with borrowed funds, and the remainder with current funds.

State–local governments borrow money by selling bonds. A bond is a financial agreement or promise between a borrower and a lender (sometimes called an investor). The lender buys the bond from the borrower now and receives a promise from the borrower to pay a fixed amount of money (or interest rate) per year for a fixed period and to repay the original amount at a future date.

Long-term state–local government bonds are either GO, which pledge the full faith and credit of the issuing government as security, or revenue bonds, with only the revenues from a particular source pledged to repay the investors. In 2002, about 38 percent of state–local government debt was of the GO or full-faith and credit variety, whereas 62 percent was from revenue bonds of various types. This relative importance of revenue bonds reflects a substantial change in the borrowing behavior of state and local governments since the 1960s.

The interest income received by investors in state–local government bonds is not taxed by the federal government, either by the individual or corporate income taxes. The primary economic effect of the exemption is to allow lower interest rates for state–local bonds than for similar taxable bonds.

The marginal income tax rate at which an investor gets the same return from both a taxable and nontaxable bond is equal to the percentage difference between the interest rates on the taxable and tax-exempt bonds. Consequently, individual investors in state–local bonds are expected to have relatively high marginal income tax rates, at least greater than the percentage difference in bond yields. Due to reductions in tax-exempt bond purchases by banks, changes in interest rates, and the growing availability of tax-exempt bond mutual funds, individuals are now the primary buyers and holders of state–local bonds.

The tax exemption for interest on state–local government bonds is an inefficient way to subsidize subnational government borrowing costs because the federal government loses more than $1 of tax revenue for each $1 of interest cost saved by state–local governments.

The most dramatic change in the state–local bond market over the past 25 years has been the tremendous growth in private-purpose tax-exempt bonds, effectively allowing state–local governments to transfer their tax-exempt borrowing authority to private individuals and firms. As a result, this option was limited substantially by the 1986 Tax Reform Act, forcing states and localities to seek new ways of financing some of these activities.

DISCUSSION QUESTIONS

1. Suppose that a city must replace aging water pipes in the city system, which is expected to cost $50 million. The new pipes are expected to last for about 30 years. The city has an annual budget of about $250 million and is trying to decide whether to finance the pipe replacement out of current revenues, through a one-year, temporary tax increase, or by borrowing the money by selling 30-year bonds at an interest cost of 5 percent. Outline the advantages and disadvantages of each financing method. Which would you recommend? Might there be any reason to combine the methods?

2. "Exempting the interest on state–local government bonds from federal income taxation is the lowest cost way for the federal government to subsidize state–local borrowing costs." Evaluate this statement.

3. Describe and explain the expected effect on state–local bond interest rates of each of the following federal changes:

   a. Lowering the maximum federal personal income tax rate from 50 to 28 percent.

   b. Enacting a federal law that restricts the use of private-activity tax-exempt bonds by state–local governments.

   c. Eliminating IRAs, a form of tax-deferred personal savings.

   d. Increasing the use of tax-exempt bonds by cities to provide home mortgages.

   e. Raising the maximum federal personal income tax rate from 31 to 36 percent.

4. State–local governments often use their borrowing authority to provide low-cost loans to the private sector through the sale of tax-exempt revenue bonds. Taking mortgage-revenue bonds as an example, what are the costs of this activity to a state that issues such bonds? To the nation? What are the benefits to the state? Do you believe that it would be in an individual state's interest to cut back on the use of these revenue bonds? Explain.

SELECTED READING

Kenyon, Daphne. "Private-Activity Bond Cap: Effects Among the States." *Intergovernmental Perspective* 19, No. 1 (Winter 1993): 25–33.

Leonard, Paul A. "Debt Management." In *Management Policies in Local Government Finance*, edited by J. Aronson and E. Schwartz. Washington, D.C.: International City/County Management Association, 2004.

Poterba, James J. "Explaining the Yield Spread Between Taxable and Tax-Exempt Bonds: The Role of Expected Tax Policy." In *Studies in State and Local Public Finance*, edited by H. Rosen, 5–49. Chicago: University of Chicago Press, 1986.

Zimmerman, Dennis. *The Private Use of Tax-Exempt Bonds*. Washington, D.C.: Urban Institute Press, 1991.

Zimmerman, Dennis. "Tax-exempt Bonds." *The Encyclopedia of Taxation and Tax Policy,* Cordes, Joseph, J., Robert D. Ebel, and Jane G. Gravelle, eds. Washington, D.C., Urban Institute Press, 1999, 99. 443–445.

THE BUDGET PROCESS

Unbalanced budgets are almost always possible in real-world fiscal systems.[1]
—JAMES M. BUCHANAN

HEADLINES

AMID A SLOWLY RECOVERING ECONOMY, MANY STATES REALIZED SLIGHT REVENUE GAINS IN FISCAL 2004. AS A RESULT, MANY STATES HAVE BEEN ABLE TO INCREASE SPENDING AND FEWER HAVE BEEN FORCED TO CUT THEIR ALREADY ENACTED BUDGETS, AND THE CUTS THAT DID OCCUR WERE SMALLER THAN IN PREVIOUS YEARS . . . IN FISCAL 2004, 15 STATES MADE CUTS TO ENACTED BUDGETS, TOTALING NEARLY $2.2 BILLION . . . BY COMPARISON, 38 STATES CUT THEIR BUDGETS BY NEARLY $13.7 BILLION IN FISCAL 2002, AND 40 STATES CUT THEIR ENACTED BUDGETS BY $11.8 BILLION IN FISCAL 2003 . . .

IN ADDITION TO CUTTING ENACTED BUDGETS, STATES USE AN ASSORTMENT OF STRATEGIES TO KEEP THEIR BUDGETS BALANCED THROUGHOUT THE FISCAL YEAR. IN FISCAL 2004, SIX STATES ENACTED ACROSS-THE-BOARD SPENDING CUTS, FOUR STATES DREW FROM RAINY DAY FUNDS, THREE STATES LAID OFF EMPLOYEES, AND SEVERAL STATES REDUCED AID TO LOCAL GOVERNMENTS, REORGANIZED PROGRAMS, INCREASED FEES, AND FURLOUGHED EMPLOYEES.[2]

---

[1]*Public Finance in Democratic Process: Fiscal Institutions and Individual Choice.* Chapel Hill: University of North Carolina Press, 1967, 98.

[2]National Governor's Association and National Association of State Budget Officers. *The Fiscal Survey of States.* Washington, D.C., December 2004.

A budget is the blueprint for how government intends to achieve its objectives of influencing and altering society. The process by which that budget is formulated is important because it may impose restrictions on the outcome and it reflects the inherent economic difficulties of government budgeting. In this chapter, therefore, we consider the budget process of state–local governments, including typical budget timetables; problems of revenue and expenditure forecasting; types and effects of budgeting rules, including balanced budget requirements and tax or expenditure limits; budget treatment of different types of expenditures; and the degree of and reasons for earmarking revenues for specific expenditure categories. As you will see, the diversity that is so characteristic of state–local government finance extends to budget practices as well.

STATE BUDGET RESULTS

Before discussing the budget process, it is important to review the macroeconomic results of state–local budgeting and fiscal policy. The aggregate budget surplus or deficit for state–local governments as a fraction of GDP, as defined in the National Income and Product Accounts, is shown in Figure 11.1. There is an aggregate budget surplus in most years, although the magnitude varies according to national economic conditions. Since 1960, the state–local surplus has been as high as 1.3 percent of GDP (in 1972) and has fallen to a low of negative .25 percent (in 2002); it averaged about .5 percent of GDP over this period.

It is apparent from Figure 11.1 that the state–local surplus is quite sensitive to the national economy. The surplus fell substantially during the recessions in 1974–1975, 1980–1982, 1990–1991, and 2001, reflecting both a reduced growth of

Figure 11.1

State–local government surplus or deficit

state–local revenues and increased spending, partly for recession-related services. This pattern partly explains why the state–local sector traditionally has provided a counter-cyclical element to national macroeconomic policy. During national recessions, states and localities have tended to maintain or even increase spending, which works against the decline in national economic activity. To accomplish this, states and localities draw down any surpluses or balances they have accumulated (including those in a budget-stabilization fund) and sometimes raise tax rates. Similarly, surpluses tend to rise during economic expansions.

This historical pattern of change in both state budgets and state revenue is shown in Figure 11.2. Panel a shows that state budgets have grown in most years, even during national economic recessions, although that growth sometimes slows (as especially happened in the 1980–1982 and 2001–2002 periods). Similarly, national economic conditions also affect state legislative changes to revenues, as illustrated in panel b. States commonly enact revenue increases (through taxes or fees) during recessionary periods (as happened especially in 1980–1981 and 2001–2002). In contrast, states took advantage of the sustained economic growth in the 1990s to enact tax cuts in many years.

As shown in Figure 11.3, the fiscal position of state and local government deteriorated dramatically between 2000 and 2001, a situation that continued through 2003. The surplus of current revenue over current expenditure was essentially eliminated in one year's time, with current deficits resulting in the next two years. As a consequence, the net state–local fiscal position involved substantial and increasing amounts of borrowing. In fact, the current deficit of state–local governments in 2002 was the largest it has been relative to GDP—essentially two or three times as great as in the past two major national recessions. The very high level of the state–local deficit in 2002 and the continuing fiscal difficulties of state and local governments since 2000 have been the subject of substantial inquiry, especially because the national recession in this period was both shorter and less serious than in past cases. Why was the impact on state and local governments disproportionately serious this time?

A combination of factors seems to have contributed. According to McGuire and Steuerle (2003) reporting on the results of a conference about this issue, important factors included the reductions in taxes and increases in expenditures made by state–local governments during the extended period of strong economic growth in the 1990s. McGuire and Steuerle (2003, p. 360) conclude that as a consequence "... when the downturn in the economy hit and revenues fell, expenditures exceeded revenues by a fair amount." Other important factors included especially large declines in personal income tax revenue (partly because of changes in capital gains), less substantial enacted tax increases than in past recessions, and new state revenue systems that were more cyclical then in the past. Of course, traditional factors such as increases in Medicaid spending also contributed but perhaps no more than in past instances.

State–local governments generally do not have operating budget deficits over the long run, at least by the definitions states use. Some states and local governments may have an operating deficit in one year that is carried forward and corrected in the

Figure 11.2

Changes in state
budgets and
revenues

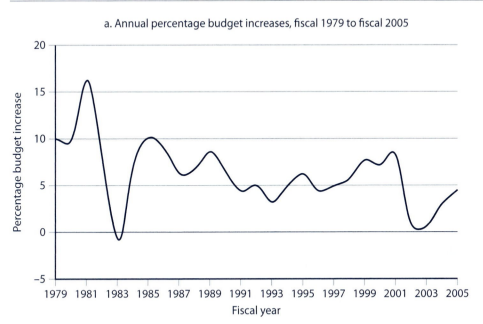

a. Annual percentage budget increases, fiscal 1979 to fiscal 2005

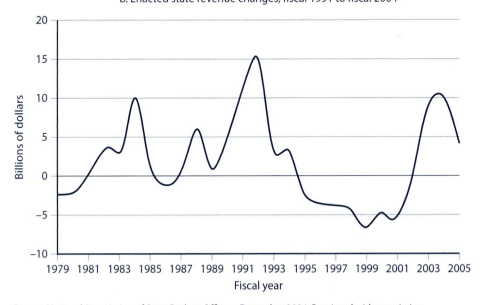

b. Enacted state revenue changes, fiscal 1991 to fiscal 2004

Source: National Association of State Budget Officers; December 2004. Reprinted with permission.

cases, the ultimate economic and financial restrictions (the unwillingness of investors to lend these governments additional amounts) did more to force balanced budgets than did the legal restrictions.

THE STATE BUDGET SCHEDULE

State governments budget on either a one- or two-year cycle, with 29 states adopting annual budgets and the other 21 adopting biennial (that is, two-year) budgets, as shown in Figure 11.4. Of the 21 states with a biennial budget cycle, 9 also have biennial legislative sessions, so that the legislature theoretically meets once in two years and adopts a budget for the following two years. In some of these biennial budget-cycle states, the budget may be reviewed and revised annually, whereas in others, no opportunity exists for revision during the period. Finally, 12 states budget over a biennial cycle, but have annual legislative sessions so that annual review and revision of the budget is possible and in some cases expected.

All states but four begin their fiscal years on July 1: Alabama and Michigan follow the practice of the federal government in beginning the fiscal year on October 1, New York begins April 1, and Texas begins September 1. In most cases, local government fiscal years follow the schedule of the state in which they are located.[5] With the exception of Kentucky, Virginia, and Wyoming, biennial budget states begin the budget cycle in odd-numbered years. Thus, for instance, a budget would be adopted for the July 2005 through June 2007 biennium, which is consistent with the political cycle if legislators are elected in November of even years and serve a two-year term from January of the following year, for instance, January 2005 through December 2006.

A representative budget cycle and process for a state government on an annual budget cycle is shown by Table 11.1, which centers on a budget for fiscal year (FY) 2005–2006. The governor's formal budget proposal for that year would be formulated by the executive departments in the fall of 2004, although individual departments of state government would have begun the process of developing and honing their budget requests well before that. After the governor's priorities for the following fiscal period are decided, the budget will be developed based on revenue and expenditure forecasts for that coming fiscal period, which in turn depend on an economic forecast for that period. An economic and budget forecast must be made in the fall of 2004, therefore, for a period of 18 to 21 months in the future (through June 2006). It is not surprising that those forecasts often are not very accurate. The magnitude of this difficulty is substantially greater if the state adopts a biennial budget.

After the governor presents the budget proposal for FY 2005–2006, usually in the form of a budget or state-of-the-state message to the state legislature in January 2005, the relevant legislative committees review that proposal and almost always revise it. The revision may reflect differences between the executive and legislative

---

[5]There are exceptions. For instance, local governments in Michigan and New York begin the fiscal year on July 1, rather than with the state government; New Jersey municipalities operate on calendar years.

Figure 11.4

State legislative and budget schedules

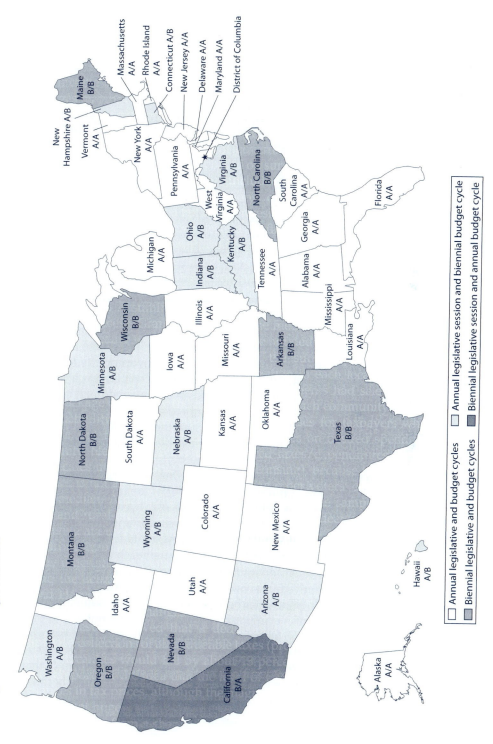

Legend:
- ☐ Annual legislative and budget cycles
- ☒ Biennial legislative and budget cycles
- ☐ Annual legislative session and biennial budget cycle
- ☒ Biennial legislative session and annual budget cycle

Washington A/B
Oregon B/B
California B/A
Nevada B/B
Idaho A/A
Montana B/B
Wyoming A/B
Utah A/A
Arizona A/B
North Dakota B/B
South Dakota A/A
Nebraska A/B
Colorado A/A
New Mexico A/A
Minnesota A/B
Iowa A/A
Kansas A/A
Oklahoma A/A
Texas B/B
Wisconsin B/B
Illinois A/A
Missouri A/A
Arkansas B/B
Louisiana A/A
Michigan A/A
Indiana A/B
Ohio A/B
Kentucky A/B
Tennessee A/A
Mississippi A/A
Alabama A/A
Georgia A/A
Florida A/A
Pennsylvania A/A
West Virginia A/A
Virginia A/B
North Carolina B/B
South Carolina A/A
New York A/A
Vermont A/A
New Hampshire A/B
Maine B/B
Massachusetts A/A
Rhode Island A/A
Connecticut A/B
New Jersey A/A
Delaware A/A
Maryland A/A
District of Columbia
Hawaii A/B
Alaska A/A

Table 11.1	
	Representative State Budget Cycle, Fiscal Year 2005–2006
October–December 2004	Formulate budget for fiscal year 2005–2006; prepare economic and budget forecasts through June 2006.
January 2005	Governor presents FY 2005–2006 budget proposal.
January–June 2005	Legislature reviews and reworks budget proposal; forecasts redone as new information becomes available; legislature adopts FY 2005–2006 budget; governor signs FY 2005–2006 budget.
July 1, 2005	Fiscal year 2005–2006 begins.
July 2005–June 2006	Expenditures and revenues monitored, with differences from budget estimates noted, corrective action taken if deficits appear.
October–December 2005	Formulate fiscal year 2006–2007 budget; prepare forecasts through June 2007.
January 2006	Governor presents FY 2006–2007 budget proposal.
June 30, 2006	Fiscal year 2005–2006 ends.
July 1, 2006	Fiscal year 2006–2007 begins.
July–September 2006 or later	Expenditures and revenues for FY 2005–2006 audited; final FY 2005–2006 accounting prepared and presented.

branches in priorities for state action and/or differences in economic and budget forecasts. If, for instance, the legislators believe there will be greater economic growth and thus more revenue than does the governor, the legislature may propose different amounts or types of expenditures or perhaps a tax cut. Eventually the legislature adopts a budget and sends it to the governor.

The governor may sign (signifying approval), veto (requiring the legislature to try again), or, in 43 states, veto only part of the budget. In the last instance, most commonly the governor has *line-item veto authority*, the option of vetoing individual "lines" or specific expenditures in the budget. When the governor has authority to veto the entire budget or individual lines, the legislature may override that veto, usually by vote of more than a majority of the legislators.[6] As a result of this process, a final budget is agreed on, and the fiscal year begins on July 1, 2005.

A line-item veto may give the executive level substantially different influence over the final budget than an overall veto does. At the federal level, the president may veto any individual appropriations bill, although each bill may contain the budget for an entire department or several departments' activities in a specific program area. Thus, the executive must choose or reject the appropriation as a package. If legislators are willing to trade votes because the bill includes something that each wants (even though it may also contain some things each does not want), then the legislature may be able to override an executive veto. If the executive has a line-item veto, individual parts of the appropriation or budget may be rejected—say a new dam for one state or a new building at one particular state college campus. In that case, it may be harder for legislators to build coalitions to override the veto because those legislators whose favorite projects are not vetoed are unlikely to support the override.

[6]The Governor has no veto authority in North Carolina.

As the fiscal year unfolds, both expenditures and revenues are monitored, the budget forecast is reestimated as actual data become available, and adjustments to the budget may, and often are, made. One common type of adjustment is a "supplemental appropriation," in which the governor and legislature agree to add expenditures in some area to the initially approved budget. On the other hand, if the revised forecast suggests that the fiscal year is likely to end with a budget deficit, the governor and/or legislature may act to increase revenue, decrease expenditures, or do both in an attempt to avoid the deficit. In fact, in many states, this type of action is required, as discussed later in this chapter. Before the fiscal year ends, the process starts again with planning for the next year's budget. Finally, the ultimate revenue and expenditure statement for FY 2005–2006 will not be completed until well after the start of the FY 2006–2007. This final accounting is delayed partly because some taxpayers have not settled accounts due to filing extensions or compliance reviews, partly because some bills that are incurred during the year may not be settled until after, and partly because of the time required to collect, review, and tabulate all the material.

Budget and Revenue Forecasting

The length and inherent overlap of the budget process—usually at least two years from the start of budget formulation to the final accounting for a single fiscal year—creates several economic problems, the most significant of which are forecasting problems. A budget forecast requires both a revenue and expenditure forecast, which in turn depend on expected economic conditions—that is, an economic forecast. State (and local) taxes (on income, sales, profits) obviously are sensitive to changes in economic conditions, although to different degrees. Because states generally rely on a much broader mix of taxes than does the federal government, the revenue forecasting problem for states may be greater than at the federal level. State expenditures—for instance, Medicaid, unemployment compensation, public assistance, or even public safety—also may change with economic conditions. Accordingly, it is often suggested that a forecasting error of 1 to 2 percent is excellent for states; but a 2-percent overestimate of revenues combined with a 2-percent underestimate of expenditures generates a 4-percent budget deficit.

Revenue forecasting is more common and probably more significant than expenditure forecasting at the state–local level. The following sample revenue forecasting model, involving just two state taxes, suggests some common features of forecasting models as well as two sources of forecasting error. Suppose the forecasting equations for the two taxes are

$T_1 = f$(State Income, State Employment)

$T_2 = g$(National Income, State Employment, Price of Gasoline)

Revenue $= T_1 + T_2$.

Based upon the past experience of the state, the first tax, perhaps an income or sales tax, is found to depend on state income and employment. Similarly, the second tax, perhaps a fuel or tourism tax, is thought to depend on national income, state employment, and the price of gasoline. This model, or specific set of fore-casting equations, has been determined and estimated using past tax collection and economic data for the state. To use this model to forecast tax collections in the future, a forecast must be made of what the economic variables (state and national income, state employment, and the price of gasoline) will be in the future. The forecast or expected economic conditions, coupled with a model based on past state experience, produces an estimate of future revenue.

This illustration also shows two common technical reasons for errors in a tax forecast. In essence, the revenue forecast is only as good as the underlying model and the economic forecast on which it depends. If an important change has occurred in the state's economy or in the behavior of residents, consumers, or investors in the state, then the model based on past experience may not be appro-priate any longer. Forecasters continually must evaluate their underlying models and be willing to make adjustment as economic behavior changes. Even if the model is correct, however, the revenue forecast depends on the accuracy of the rel-evant economic variables forecast. If the forecasting agency underestimates (over-estimates) the level of state income and employment, then it may underestimate (overestimate) revenue even if it has the right model. Similarly, differences in the basic forecasting model or differences in expected economic conditions often explain why different agencies or forecasters may not have the same forecast.

Intergovernmental aid also creates difficulties in forecasting because a state may not know the amount or type of federal aid it will receive during a fiscal year. This difficulty often is even worse for local governments who may be uncertain about both federal and state aid, which together often account for more than a third of a local government's general revenue. A school district or a city may be planning a budget for the fiscal year beginning July 1 at the same time that the state is plan-ning and debating its own budget for the same time period. The final state budget may not be approved until just before the fiscal year starts (or in some cases even after). The locality may have to delay the adoption of the final budget or a have to adopt a budget based on an expected amount of state aid. If the expectation turns out to be wrong, a midyear budget correction may be required. This difficulty can be exacerbated by differences in fiscal years, for instance, if the local government fiscal year starts before the state's fiscal year.

Another problem is that the deficit or surplus from one fiscal year is not known exactly before the next fiscal year begins. In most cases, states are prevented from ending a year with an operating deficit or must eliminate the deficit in the next year. Similarly, a budget surplus from one year in most cases becomes a starting balance, which can be applied to the next year. A budget surplus from one year, then, provides a cushion against forecasting error for the subsequent year.

Finally, revenue forecasting often is as much a political activity as an economic one. By using overly optimistic or pessimistic assumptions about future economic conditions, forecasters can make it appear as if surpluses or deficits are likely. For instance, an official who wants to generate political support for a tax cut might use an optimistic economic forecast to produce a forecast of substantial revenue growth, allowing for the tax reduction. In most states (31 of the 50 according to the National Association of State Budget Officers, 2002), revenue forecasting is the responsibility of the executive branch, either the budget department (18 states), the revenue department (3), or both (10). In 16 states, however, a separate forecasting board (alone or jointly with the executive office) conducts revenue estimating. Obviously, having more than one group prepare forecasts is advantageous in that it both minimizes the technical errors and reduces the possibility of political adjustments to the forecast.

STATE BUDGETING RULES

As mentioned, most state governments face some type of legal (as opposed to economic) restrictions regarding budget deficits, as shown in Table 11.2. The governor must *submit* a balanced budget in 44 states and the legislature must *pass* a balanced budget in 40. Although this may require the parties to think in balanced budget terms, this alone imposes little restraint because a budget balanced when adopted can quickly become a budget in deficit in practice. Therefore, in some cases, the requirement for an initially balanced budget is combined with a requirement that expenditures be reduced if a deficit arises, as described in greater detail next.

Thirty-seven states are prohibited, either constitutionally or statutorily, from carrying over a budget deficit into the next fiscal year or budget biennium. This is somewhat more restrictive than merely requiring an initially balanced budget because it requires that states do *something* to offset an actual budget deficit before the next fiscal period. Theoretically, however, that something could be borrowing, that is, selling bonds to raise funds to cover the operating deficit or borrowing internally from state trust accounts. In that case, the debt service and repayment schedule on those bonds or loans appears in subsequent budgets, but there is no deficit to carry over. Consequently, tight constitutional debt limitations are imposed in many of these states. Because many of these limitations are small (for instance, $250,000 in Iowa), the option of converting operating deficits into bonded debt is effectively limited. Of course, such action also may be blocked economically if the credit markets are unwilling to accept such bonds.

Only one state, Vermont, has no type of balanced budget restriction. The governor is required to recommend in the proposed budget methods to correct deficits that occurred in past years, but the proposed budget need not be balanced.

Procedures When a Deficit Arises

For those states that cannot carry forward a budget deficit into the next year, in most cases, the governor has the responsibility for dealing with the impending deficit. For example, the operative sections of the current Michigan Constitution, adopted in 1963, read, in part:

> *Art. 5, Sec 18. The governor shall submit to the legislature . . . a budget for the ensuing fiscal period setting forth in detail, for all operating funds, the proposed*

Table 11.2

Balanced Budget Requirements

State	Governor Must Submit Balanced Budget	Nature of Requirement	Legislature Must Pass Balanced Budget	Nature of Requirement	Governor Must Sign Balanced Budget	Nature of Requirement	May Carry over Deficit
Alabama	X	C,S	X	S	—	—	
Alaska	X	S	X	S	X	S	
Arizona	X	C,S	X	C,S	X	C,S	
Arkansas	X	S	X	S	X	S	
California	X	C	—	—	X	S	Yes*
Colorado	X	C	X	C	X	C	
Connecticut	X	S	X	C,S	X	C	
Delaware	X	C,S	X	C,S	X	C,S	
Florida	X	C,S	X	C,S	X	C,S	
Georgia	X	C	X	C	X	C	
Hawaii	X	C,S	—	—	X	C,S	*
Idaho	*	—	X*	C	—	—	—
Illinois	X	C,S	X	C	X	S	
Indiana	—	—	—	—	—	—	
Iowa	X	C,S	X	S	—	—	
Kansas	X	S	X	C,S	—	—	
Kentucky	X	C,S	X	C,S	X	C,S	
Louisiana	X	C,S	X	C,S	X	C,S	
Maine	X	C,S	X	C	X	C,S	
Maryland	X	C	X	C	*	C*	
Massachusetts	X	C,S	X	C,S	X	C,S	
Michigan	X	C,S	X	C	X	C,S	*
Minnesota	X*	C,S	X*	C,S	X*	C,S	
Mississippi	X	S	X	S	—	—	
Missouri	X	C	—	—	X	C	
Montana	X	S	X	C	—	—	
Nebraska	X	C	X	S	—	—	No
Nevada	X	S	X	C	X	C	
New Hampshire	X	S	—	—	—	—	
New Jersey	X	C	X	C	X	C	
New Mexico	X	C	X	C	X	C	
New York	X	C	—	—	*	—	
North Carolina	X	C,S	X	S	—	—	
North Dakota	X	C	X	C	X	C	
Ohio	X	C	X	C	X	C	No
Oklahoma	X	S	X*	C	X*	C	
Oregon	X	C	X	C	X	C	
Pennsylvania	X	C,S	—	—	X	C,S	X*
Rhode Island	X	C	X	C	X	S	
South Carolina	X	C	X	C	X	C	
South Dakota	X	C	X	C	X	C	
Tennessee	X	C	X	C	X	C	No
Texas	—	—	X	C,S	X	C	
Utah	X	C	X	C,S	X*	—	
Vermont	—	—	—	—	—	—	
Virginia	*	—	*	—	*	C	No
Washington	X	S	—	—	—	—	S*
West Virginia	—	—	X	C	X	C	—
Wisconsin	X	C	X	C	X	C,S	
Wyoming	X	C	X	C	—	—	
Puerto Rico	X	C	X	C	X	C	
TOTAL	45		41		35		

Codes: C = Constitutional; S = Statutory.

Reprinted with permission from National Association of State Budget Officers (NASBO). *Budget Processes in the States.* January 2002.

expenditures and estimated revenues of the state. Proposed expenditures from any fund shall not exceed the estimated revenue thereof.

Art. 5, Sec. 20 . . . The governor, with the approval of the appropriating committees of the house and senate, shall reduce expenditures authorized by appropriations whenever it appears that actual revenues for a fiscal period will fall below the revenue estimates on which appropriations for that period were based.

Note that section 20 states that "the governor . . . *shall* reduce expenditures. . . ." In Michigan, therefore, the governor is required to submit a balanced budget *and* to reduce expenditures if an actual deficit arises. Procedures for dealing with impending deficits vary widely among the other states.

According to NASBO (2002), in 36 states the governor has authority to adjust expenditures when deficits appear likely by reducing expenditures selectively or across the board without consulting the legislature, usually with some relatively small exceptions. In some of those states, the governor's authority to reduce the budget is limited to some maximum amount, specified either as a percentage of the total budget or as a maximum percentage for each category of the budget. In Virginia, for instance, the governor's reductions are limited to no more than 25 percent of an agency's appropriation and 15 percent of employee salaries with appropriations for interest payments, certain pensioners, some employee benefits, and some capital construction projects protected. Another 8 states require that the governor consult with or obtain the approval of the legislature before budget reductions can be made. In those cases, the governor usually proposes changes to the legislature. Michigan's procedure, noted earlier, is representative of this group, although some states require approval of the full legislature rather than just the budget committees.

Planning for Deficits: State Budget Stabilization Funds

One possible way for state governments to deal with unanticipated deficits is for the state to maintain a contingency or budget stabilization fund, which can be used to augment revenue as needed. Following the old adage that "the time to fix your roof is when the sun is shining," such a fund can be added to in good economic years for use in years with slow or nonexistent economic growth, thus serving as a type of "state savings account." In fact, these contingency funds are sometimes referred to as "Rainy Day Funds." These funds mitigate against states having to increase and decrease tax rates with economic contractions and expansions and provide a way for states to maintain spending during recessions. Historically, it has been considered good budgeting practice to maintain a reserve balance equal to 5 percent of a state's general spending, and some states have used this as an objective. Although these contingency funds may be good budgeting practice, they often create political difficulties. Some groups always want to spend all the government's available funds on favorite programs now, although others object to the government holding surplus funds rather than returning them to taxpayers through a tax cut.

According to NASBO (2002), 46 states now have authorized formal budget stabilization funds by creating separate accounts in the state budget by statute, although not all of them actually may have a balance at any given time. The statute typically specifies when and from what source money is to be added to the account, the maximum size of the account, and when and for what purposes account funds may be withdrawn and spent. The expectation is that by formalizing the contingency fund procedures and placing the money in a special account, there will be less of an incentive to raid the funds for additional spending or tax cuts in good times.

Money is added to these stabilization funds either by specific appropriation of the legislature or according to a specified rule or formula, most commonly by depositing into the fund a fraction of a state's surplus in any year, although a few states relate payments to the fund to economic conditions. Almost half of the states with funds base deposits on a formula or required amount, often based on the level of spending or growth in revenue. In 13 states, the deposit is based on the year-end surplus (essentially using the funds as a politically acceptable way of retaining surpluses), while 5 states rely on explicit appropriations, as shown in Table 11.3. For example, in New Jersey, 50 percent of the difference between actual and forecast revenue is transferred to the Surplus Revenue Fund, up to a maximum of 5 percent of the anticipated revenue, although in Indiana, a transfer is made to the Counter-Cyclical Revenue and Economic Stabilization Fund if the growth of personal

Table 11.3

State Budget Stabilization Funds, 2002

Characteristic	Numbers of States
States With Funds	46
Deposit Methods	
Year-End Surplus	13
Formula or Requirement	22
Specific Appropriation	5
Other or not applicable	6
Maximum Size Specified	29
Limit Distribution (percentage of revenue or expenditure)	
3%	3
4%	1
5%	14
6%	2
7%	2
10%	6
15%	1
Fixed amount	1
Withdrawal Methods	
Revenue Shortfall	7
Deficit (only)	6
Revenue Shortfall or Deficit	2
Formula (income or unemployment)	4
Specific Appropriation (only)	20

Source: National Association of State Budget Officers. *Budget Processes in the States.* January 2002.

income is greater than 2 percent. The amount transferred is the growth rate minus 2 percent times the total general fund revenue.

Stabilization funds may be withdrawn and spent either by appropriation of the legislature or automatically when certain conditions are met; 20 states use the appropriation method for spending, and the other 26 have some spending formula or condition. Seven states use the fund when revenue is less than forecast, 6 states use the fund when a deficit is looming, with the other states following a variety of special rules. For example, in Vermont, the Budget Stabilization Trust Fund is spent automatically to cover a state operating deficit; in North Dakota, the actual revenue must be 2.5 percent below forecast revenue for the Budget Stabilization Fund to be applied; and in Michigan, the Countercyclical Budget and Economic Stabilization Fund is applied based on a formula related to economic conditions.

Whether or not stabilization funds successfully protect state governments from unanticipated economic difficulties and thus smooth the pattern of state expenditures across economic expansions and recessions depends on the magnitude of the fund compared to the magnitude of the economic difficulty. Only 29 states with funds impose a limit on the size of the fund, and some of those limits (usually expressed as a percentage of annual revenue or expenditure) are large (5 percent is most common). There is danger in tying the fund size too closely to *annual* budgets if they are to be large enough to offset the effects of a downturn lasting several years. On the other hand, very large funds may become appealing political targets for raiding for other purposes. If states are unwilling to maintain balances, either because of the absence of appropriations or raids on funds that are automatically built up, then obviously the funds will not avoid the political pressures and cannot solve the budget uncertainty problems.

State Budget Flexibility

In most states and localities, the budget is separated into different funds representing expenditures for various purposes, in many cases with specific revenue sources earmarked for specific expenditures or funds. The general fund receives state revenues not earmarked for specific purposes and is the fund from which expenditures can be made on any service. Earmarking serves as a way of codifying, either constitutionally or by statute, how state revenues are to be spent and thus generally reduces the flexibility of state officials in changing the nature of the budget. As always in state–local finance, the states vary substantially, this time in the degree of earmarking.

According to NASBO (2004), state general funds represented only about 44 percent of total state government expenditures in aggregate in 1986. Massachusetts and Wyoming represented the opposite budget approaches. Nearly 75 percent of Massachusetts' budget was part of the general fund and thus not earmarked for specific uses. In contrast, the general fund represented only 30 percent of Wyoming's total budget. Most of state revenues in Wyoming were therefore earmarked for specific purposes. More earmarking tends to occur in states with biennial budgets than in those with annual budget review, perhaps because the earmarking limits administrative discretion in spending in the relatively long time between legislative or budget sessions.[7] In addition, on average about a quarter of state tax collections was earmarked for specific functions in 1988, a fraction that had been declining over the past 40 years. Of course, the share of *revenues* that is earmarked is expected to be greater than for taxes alone as a large portion of fees and grants are earmarked by definition.

Some types of tax and revenue earmarking are the most common. In almost every state, motor fuel tax revenue is earmarked for roads and highways and allocated to a separate transportation fund. State aid payments to local governments are usually specified in statute and connected to specific revenue sources. Snell (1990) reports that the state taxes most often earmarked for local government grants are alcoholic beverage taxes and general sales taxes. In contrast, extensive earmarking of income taxes is rare. Other than taxes, hunting and fishing license revenue often is earmarked for wildlife management or recreation. In recent years, most of the state governments operating lotteries have earmarked lottery revenue for a specific purpose, most commonly education. As we have seen, federal grants to states often carry categorical use restrictions. Among local governments, all the revenue to independent school districts is earmarked implicitly to primary and secondary education because that is the only function provided by those jurisdictions.

The practice of a specific state, Michigan, with a restricted budget suggests how earmarking works. In fiscal year 2004, the state government received total revenues of about $37.2 billion. Of this total, $21.8 billion was deposited in the state's **general fund** and $15.4 billion in a variety of **special revenue funds**. The latter, which includes some taxes, grants, and fees, represents part of the earmarked funds. However, only part of the general fund, amounting to about $8.7 billion or 40 percent, is completely unrestricted, which is called general fund-general purpose revenue. General fund-special purpose revenues account for the other 60 percent of the general fund and represent restricted revenue for which there is no separate state budget account. In total then, $28.5 billion of the total $37.2 billion of revenue is restricted in some way.

What Are the Advantages and Disadvantages of Earmarking?

Earmarking revenues for a specific purpose can have economic advantages by establishing a benefit tax system and providing some revenue certainty to assist in long-run planning. If the revenue is generated in relation to the benefits of the service provided, then the revenue source is a benefit tax, and tying revenues and expenditures together may be reasonable. This is usually the argument regarding gasoline taxes and transportation expenditures, as described in Chapter 20. If earmarking makes it more difficult, either procedurally or politically, to reduce

---

[7]The general fund was a smaller fraction of state expenditures than the national average in 14 of the 21 biennial budget states, and in 6 of the 8 states that also have a biennial legislative session.

expenditures in an area, then providers and recipients can be more certain of services in that area. When gasoline taxes are earmarked for transportation, expenditures are affected during an economic downturn proportional to the decrease in gasoline consumption, but it is difficult to reduce transportation expenditures more and transfer those taxes to other purposes.

Earmarking often is said to provide political benefits, as well. There is ample evidence that taxpayers often do not have a good understanding of government budgets, both the magnitude of different revenue sources and the types of services provided by expenditures. When a particular revenue source is tied to specific expenditures, that aspect of the budget is often better understood. Government officials sometimes use this procedure in an attempt to increase the attractiveness of some revenue sources by earmarking that revenue source to a service with easily identified and highly valued benefits, as has been the case with many state lotteries.

The main problem caused by earmarking is a reduction in budget flexibility for the government, which, of course, is the other side of the revenue certainty point noted as an advantage. Earmarking may make it more difficult to change the priorities in the state budget over time and to respond, in the short run, to economic fluctuations. This may be particularly true if the earmarking is constitutionally specified because amending the state constitution usually requires a supermajority vote of the legislature, a vote of the electorate, or both. Earmarking also may make it politically difficult to alter the budget simply because the revenue-expenditure tie becomes well known and accepted. State governments commonly have surpluses in one or more earmarked funds while facing an operating deficit in the general fund.

These advantages and disadvantages of earmarking are illustrated in the following example. Suppose that the efficient amount of spending in a state is $6,000 per person, with residents desiring the following (unrestricted) allocation of that spending among four functions:

E1	E2	E3	E4
$3,000	$1,500	$1,000	$500

Now suppose that a particular revenue source is earmarked for service *E3*, and that the revenue source provides $800. If the government was providing exactly the levels of spending desired by residents, then this type of earmarking may have no effect. Although the state's general fund is now $5,200 (rather than $6,000), the state can allocate only $200 from the general fund to service *E3*, keeping total spending in that category at $1,000 and the same spending in each other category as before.

Thus, earmarking does not necessarily guarantee that a state will spend more on the earmarked service than if it was financed with general revenues. In some cases, states augment the earmarked revenues for a service with general fund revenue as well, thus choosing to spend more than the earmarked source provides. The state government is responding to the demand for that particular service, so the earmarking is effectively not a constraint. The fungibility of general revenue allows the government to substitute earmarked funds for general funds that would have been allocated to that service.[8]

On the other hand, suppose that the earmarked revenue source provides $1,200. This creates a problem because now the state's general fund is only $4,800, which is not sufficient to continue funding at the prior desired level in all the other service categories. The government must either increase spending on service E3 above what is desired by residents or continue spending $1,000 per person on E3 and put the remaining $200 into a special revenue fund for future spending on service E3. In either case, funding on some other service must fall. If government was providing the spending levels desired by residents and that are economically efficient, then earmarking in this instance has lowered economic efficiency by restricting government flexibility. In effect, the earmarking constrains the government from achieving the choice residents prefer.

But what if the government is not providing the levels of service and spending desired by residents? In that instance, earmarking can improve the economic performance of government and increase economic efficiency, as suggested by Buchanan (1963). Continuing the example, suppose that the state spends $0 on service E3 (even though residents prefer $1,000) and $1,500 on service E4 (when residents want $500). Now if a revenue source is earmarked for service E3 and that source provides $800, earmarking forces the state to spend at least that much on this service, moving spending closer to what residents desire. In this example, the partial earmarking raises spending on E3 to $800. As a result, the government must spend less on some other service, although this may not be service E4. If the government spends $800 more on E3 and $800 less on E4, then residents clearly are better off as actual spending is closer to what they desire. However, if the $800 increase in spending on E3 results in an $800 decrease in spending on E1 or E2, then residents may not be better off; spending is closer to the desired level for E3 but further away for E1 or E2.

In practice, the evidence seems to suggest that earmarking state budgets and taxes has little effect on either the level or mix of spending. Research by Richard Dye and Therese McGuire (1992) found that earmarking had no effect on the level of total state spending, with the exception of earmarking for highways, which seemed to reduce the overall level of spending. Nor did earmarking seem to change the mix of spending substantially. They report that earmarking an additional dollar of revenue had no effect on spending for education or aid to local governments. Earmarking seemed to make a difference only for highway spending, and even there each additional dollar of revenue earmarked for highways increased total highway spending by only $.65.

Local Government Budgeting

Although most of the discussion in this chapter has concentrated on state government budgeting rules and procedures, that material is directly applicable to local

---

[8]For more on this point, see Oakland, 1985.

governments as well; however, some important differences also exist in state and local budgeting. One important difference between states and localities already has been noted—local governments are typically more reliant on intergovernmental aid than are states. The other important factor is that local governments are, in most cases, created and regulated by states as a legal matter. Therefore, the budget options that localities have—types of revenue sources, some required or mandated expenditures, restrictions on tax rates, tax levels, or tax and expenditure growth—all are specified by the state government.

TAX AND EXPENDITURE LIMITS

Nearly all local governments and almost half of the state governments are constrained in their budgeting by statutory or constitutional limits on taxes, spending, or both. Local government tax limits (imposed by state governments) date at least since the late 1800s. Prior to 1970, the most common form of state-imposed local tax limit was a maximum property tax rate either for specific services, for specific types of local governments, or for overall local government taxes. Beginning around 1970, a number of state governments acted to add new or different tax and expenditure limits on local governments under their authority. In the late 1970s and early 1980s, taxpayer-initiated tax and expenditure limits affecting both local and state governments were adopted in a number of states, with California's Proposition 13 in 1978 often identified as the start. These limits—and the tax revolt they were said to represent—have altered the way in which state and local tax and expenditure decisions are made in many cases. Still, the effectiveness of these limits in reducing the level or growth of spending is unsettled and their desirability is still questioned.

Types and Use of Limits

Local Tax Rate Limits

In general, limits may be directed at tax rates, tax revenue, amount of expenditure, or the growth rate of revenue or expenditure. Indeed, all these types are applied to local governments by states. The oldest and most common form of local limit is a **maximum property tax rate,** either for overall property taxes or only those for specific purposes. According to the tabulation of the ACIR (1993a), 33 states imposed an overall property tax rate limit, a specific property tax rate limit, or both on local governments in 1992. Such a maximum rate obviously has no restricting effect when tax rates are well below the maximum. If tax rates are at the maximum, property tax revenue can increase only to the extent that the property tax base increases (because revenue equals the rate multiplied times the base). Thus, rate limits do not prevent increases in revenue but may restrict increases in revenue to the growth rate of the tax base. This is the type of limit adopted when California voters approved Proposition 13—the local property tax rate is limited to no more than 1 percent of assessed value, and assessed value is defined to be the market value in 1975–1976 plus a maximum annual 2-percent increase for inflation.[9] Similarly, the limit adopted in Massachusetts was called Proposition 2½ and limited the property tax rate to no more than 2.5 percent of value. In addition to limits on property tax rates, local governments with the authority to levy local income or sales taxes also are restricted by state-imposed maximum rates.

Local Revenue Limits

A second relatively common form of local tax limit is a **limit on tax revenue,** either for a specific tax or overall—often called a **levy limit** in the case of local property taxes. Revenue, or levy, limits usually are specified as a maximum allowed percentage increase from the prior year or by a maximum percentage of income that tax revenue can take. For instance, some local governments are restricted to property tax increases of no more than 5 percent (for instance) per year or to percentage increases no greater than the percentage growth in the Consumer Price Index (the inflation rate) and the percentage growth in population. Property tax levy limits were used in 23 states in 1992 (ACIR 1993a). In 3 states, local governments face overall limits on own-source revenue, specified either as an allowed percentage increase or a maximum share of income. In the case of overall revenue limits, individual revenue sources may increase more than the limit allows if that increase is balanced by some other revenue source increasing less than is allowed.

Local Expenditure Limits

The third type of state-imposed local limit is a restriction on the **maximum allowed level of expenditure,** usually set as a maximum allowed annual percentage increase. General local expenditure limits applying broadly to general-purpose local governments persist today in only three states: Arizona, California, and New Jersey (municipalities only). School expenditure limits are sometimes used as well in conjunction with state education aid programs in an attempt to equalize per-pupil school spending among different districts in a state.

State Revenue and Expenditure Limits

In contrast to many local government tax and expenditure limits, all the 27 current state government tax or expenditure limits were adopted since 1976, when New Jersey adopted a general limit on the growth of state government expenditures. The state governments currently with general tax or expenditure limits are Alaska, Arizona, California, Colorado, Connecticut, Delaware, Florida, Hawaii, Idaho, Iowa, Louisiana, Massachusetts, Michigan, Mississippi, Missouri, Montana, Nevada, New Jersey, North Carolina, Oklahoma, Oregon, Rhode Island, South Carolina, Tennessee, Texas, Utah, and Washington (NASBO 2002).

These limits generally restrict the annual growth in own-source revenue or expenditures to the percentage growth rate of state personal income (17 states), to the percentage growth in population and the general price level (4 states), or to

---

[9]However, properties can be reassessed at their full market value when sold. See Chapter 7.

fixed percentage limit (6 states). For instance, in Washington, the growth in spending cannot exceed the average rate of inflation and population growth over the past three years; in California, the annual growth rate of appropriations is linked to the percentage increase in population and personal income; and in Rhode Island, annual appropriations are limited to 98 percent of projected revenue.

In several cases, taxpayers initially proposed the limits by using the initiative and referendum process, although in most cases the state legislature—perhaps prodded by an actual or threatened citizen-initiative proposal—proposed the limit. Regardless of how proposed, about half of these state limits eventually were directly approved by the voters with the others adopted by vote of the state legislature. In describing these state government limits, Daphne Kenyon and Karen Benker (1984) note that none of these limits applies to all state expenditures or revenues, that several of the limits are not very restrictive in that they apply only to *proposed* expenditures (that is, appropriations), and that some provision for exceeding the limit exists in each case. As with local government limits, in 12 states, supermajority votes are required to exceed the limit.

Objectives of Tax and Expenditure Limits

In general, fiscal limits can be designed to set a maximum level for taxes or expenditures, to reduce the level or alter the growth of taxes or expenditures, or to require some specific action to alter taxes or expenditures. The ultimate intent of these types of limits can be to reduce the level of government taxes and spending, to impose more political control over changes in taxes and spending, to alter the mix of government revenue sources, or to alter the relative fiscal roles of state compared to local governments. These ultimate objectives are not mutually exclusive— some limit proposals are intended to accomplish more than one objective, although voters perceive others as having multiple objectives or results. In one analysis of state limits on local governments adopted in the 1970s, Helen Ladd (1978) reported that states with higher per-capita property taxes and those with higher rates of growth of per-capita expenditures were more likely to have adopted limits, suggesting that lower expenditures and property taxes were likely objectives.

Consistent with Ladd's results, of all the potential objectives of tax limits, the attempt to reduce the level of taxes and spending has received the most attention. But why would individual voters attempt to use the political process to reduce government taxes and spending when the level of taxes and spending was originally chosen through that same political process? The answer must be that voters perceive that the political system is imperfect, so government is not providing the magnitude of taxes and spending that the public desires. Of course, as you learned in Chapter 3, this conclusion can be consistent with several economic models of voting on government fiscal issues. In one of those cases, the monopoly bureaucrat model, the government acts as a monopolist in offering voters the choice between two alternative expenditure levels—one at a level higher than that most desired by the median voters and the other at a very low level. Given that and only that choice (because political competition has been eliminated by the government officials), voters select the higher expenditure level. From this viewpoint, tax and

Figure 11.5

A spending limit
may increase
economic
efficiency.

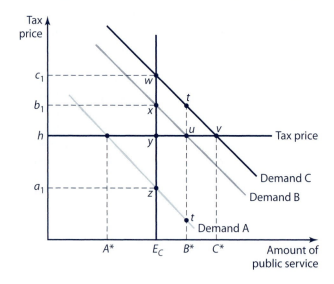

expenditure limits can be seen as an attempt to create political competition—to lower spending levels by reducing the monopoly government's capability to control the choices proposed to voters.

Suppose that political competition does exist (either from viable alternative political candidates or from interjurisdictional competition for residents and businesses), and that fiscal choices are made by majority voting. Recall that in this case, voters select the median-desired level of taxes and spending—indeed, this is called the median-voter model. Might fiscal limits make sense even when fiscal decisions are made by majority voting with political competition? The answer is yes because there is no guarantee that majority voting will result in the economically efficient level of expenditure being selected. This possibility is illustrated in Figure 11.5. If the voting groups with the three different demands shown all face the same tax price, then their desired levels of spending are A^*, B^*, and C^*. With majority-voting expenditure, level B^*—the median level—is selected.

Now suppose that a fiscal limit is imposed that reduces expenditures to E_C. Groups B and C are made worse off because the new spending level is farther from their desired levels than B^* is, but group A is made better off because E_C is closer to A's desired spending level than B^* is. The welfare gain by group A would be greater than the sum of losses by B and C if the original spending level B^* was inefficiently too high. In Figure 11.5, the loss of consumer surplus by B is represented by triangle yxu, which is the difference between the value of government service to B and the cost to B for the quantity eliminated by the limit. For each $1 of spending between E_C and B^*, the value to B is greater than B's tax cost. Similarly, the welfare loss to group C is represented by area $ywtv$. On the other hand, group A gains because each $1 spent beyond A^* is worth less to A than the tax cost. The gain to A is represented by area $zyut$. Depending on the nature of demand, the tax price, and the level of the limit, the gain to A may be greater than, equal to, or less than the sum of welfare losses by B and C.

This also can be seen by comparing the value of the marginal unit of public expenditure at the controlled level, E_C, for each group to the tax cost for each group. The marginal value of additional public expenditure is c_1, b_1, and a_1, respectively, with $(c_1 - h) + (b_1 - h) \gtreqless (a_1 - h)$ depending on the nature of the demands at E_C. As explained by Michael Bell and Ronald Fisher (1978, p. 391–92), the possibility that a fiscal limit can improve economic efficiency and increase welfare "occurs because majority voting takes account only of each group's rank-order of expenditures and does not compensate for different magnitudes of preference. Thus a net welfare gain would be possible if the difference in provided and desired service levels was much greater for the group desiring less than the median amount than the group desiring more. . . ." In any case, tax and expenditure limits may be intended to correct inefficiencies that result from the political choice process.

A similar argument can be made concerning limits intended to alter the relative use of different revenue sources or the roles of the state government compared to local governments. Voters who desire a very different fiscal environment than the one in place may seek such limits, and those voters would be made better off if the limit is adopted and is effective. Other voters would be made worse off. For instance, homeowners and other capital owners might seek a limit on local property tax revenues with the expectation that the state government would substitute state aid collected through the state sales tax. Such a change might reduce the relative tax share of substantial capital owners. Whether an overall gain in economic efficiency occurs depends on the choice selected by voting or some other political system and on the differences in the desired nature of fiscal policy among the different voting groups.

In some cases, fiscal limits are supported because of voters' perceptions about the expected effects, even if some of those perceptions are contradictory. Suppose, for instance, that a limit to reduce local property taxes is proposed with no provision for substituting a different source of revenue. A logically correct and economically defensible position (for some voters, at least) is that a reduction in local government or state government services would result, which would be desirable if the voter preferred private choice and private provision of those services. But research about voters' perception of tax limits shows that three other, often faulty, perceptions are common:

1. **Free Lunch Perception:** Voters believe that the effect of the limit will be to reduce taxes but have no effect on government-provided services. The notion is that the limit will induce government officials to "reduce waste." This perception usually is faulty either because "waste" in the sense of unnecessary expenditures may not exist or because if it does, government officials have no reason to reduce it. If government officials are budget maximizers, as is often claimed by proponents of limits, then reducing services in response to the limit may be the most effective way to eliminate the limit.

2. **Head-in-the-Sand Perception:** Voters believe that the effect of the limit will be to reduce taxes and government services, which is fine, because those voters do not believe they get any benefits from government services. These voters have their heads in the sand because such a perception is nonsense—everyone benefits from some services provided by state–local governments.

3. **Optimist Perception:** Voters believe that the effect of the limit will be to reduce taxes and government services, but these voters are confident that the services to be cut will not be those that give them benefits—only other voters' favorite services will be cut, as reflected in the accompanying *Pepper . . . and Salt* cartoon. Again, this perception seems contrary to the political notion that makes limits attractive in the first place. If government officials are trying to maintain expenditures higher than the voters desire, then the politically strategic response of such officials to the limit is to reduce services enjoyed by most voters—so that the limit might be rejected or overturned.

Several surveys of voter attitudes about government taxes and spending and about proposed fiscal limits support the existence of these faulty perceptions. Jack Citrin (1979) analyzed survey data that included California voters' positions on Proposition 13, their socioeconomic characteristics, and their preferred change in

Pepper . . . and Salt

THE WALL STREET JOURNAL

"Not ours, dammit! We meant for you to cut back on someone else's government benefits!"

Printed with permission.

taxes and spending on a variety of different services. Citrin reported that, in most cases, a majority preferred the status quo level of taxes and spending despite the approval of the proposition. He argued (p. 127) that his findings "confirm that the main intention of California voters in passing Proposition 13 was to cut taxes rather than eliminate a wide range of government services." Paul Courant, Edward Gramlich, and Daniel Rubinfeld (1980) analyzed a survey of Michigan voters from 1978 taken at a time three different constitutional tax-limitation proposals were on the ballot. In the survey, voters were asked about how they voted on each proposal, about their desired changes in state–local taxes and services, and about their perceptions of the likely effects of each proposal. Voters who perceived that the limit would reduce taxes were more likely to vote for the amendments, *even if they did not desire a reduction in spending*. Courant and his colleagues concluded (p. 19) that "it appears that voters are perceiving that their own taxes will be cut without expenditures being cut, either because of supposed efficiency gains, greater uncertainty about the spending side of the budget, or the unending search for a free lunch."

Effectiveness of Tax and Expenditure Limits

Although evaluating the effectiveness of tax and expenditure limits is difficult because the objective is not always clear, several studies have examined the changes in taxes and spending that occur after limits are imposed and compared those changes to states without limits. The results are somewhat ambiguous. Regarding local government limits, the ACIR (1977) analyzed local government expenditures and local property tax reliance for all states in 1974, with the states divided into those with rate limits, those with levy limits, and those with no limits. Those results showed that local per-capita own-source expenditures tended to be lower in states with limits than those without, but no general difference in property tax reliance was evident. These results are consistent with two possible hypotheses—either (1) the existence of limits held down spending but did not induce a shift away from property taxes, or (2) those states whose citizens preferred a lower level of spending adopted fiscal limits to reflect their viewpoint.

Kenyon and Benker (1984) examined the change in state spending relative to state personal income for all states between 1978 and 1983 to see whether a difference existed between those states with state government tax or expenditure limits and those with no state limits. They concluded that tax or expenditure limits have not restricted growth in taxes and spending in most cases, a conclusion borne out both by the opinions of state budget officers and actual expenditure data. As previously noted, most state limits restrict some components of state taxes or spending to a fixed maximum percentage of state personal income. Kenyon and Benker report that expenditures increase faster than income in some years and slower than income in others for states with and without limits. Over the entire period, state expenditures in aggregate remained at a nearly constant share of personal income.

The fact that limits restricting the growth of own-source expenditures or revenue to the growth rate of personal income are not effective is consistent with the

common finding of an income inelastic demand for state–local government services. In that case, expenditures did not increase faster than income if that was the
only factor changing. A growing economy, then, is consistent with a constant or
declining share of income going to own-source state–local spending if the relative
costs of providing government services is not also rising.

The Kenyon-Benker results about the general ineffectiveness of state government tax and expenditure limits are confirmed by an AICR study (1987a) focusing
on state spending, taxes, deficits, and overall debt for 1984. Those statistical results
showed that the existence of state tax or expenditure limits did *not* result in lower
per-capita own-source expenditures, lower per-capita state taxes, a lower level of
per-capita state debt, or fewer state deficits.

SUMMARY

An aggregate state–local budget surplus exists most years, although the magnitude varies according to national economic conditions. The state–local sector traditionally has provided a counter-cyclical element to national macroeconomic
policy. During national recessions, states and localities have tended to maintain or
even increase spending, which works against the decline in national economic
activity as states and localities draw down any surpluses or balances they have
accumulated (including those in a budget-stabilization fund) and often raise
tax rates.

State governments budget on either a one- or two-year cycle, with 29 states
adopting annual budgets and the other 21 adopting biennial (that is, two-year)
budgets.

The length and inherent overlap of the budget process creates difficult forecasting problems. A revenue forecast is only as good as the underlying model and the
economic forecast on which it depends. Intergovernmental aid also creates difficulties in forecasting because a state may not know the amount or type of federal
aid it will receive during a fiscal year. The deficit or surplus from one fiscal year is
often not known exactly before the next fiscal year begins.

States' budgets usually are separated into different funds representing expenditures for various purposes; in many cases, specific revenue sources are earmarked for specific expenditures or funds. The general fund receives state
revenues not earmarked for specific purposes and is the fund from which expenditures can be made on any service. State general funds represent only about
44 percent of total state government expenditures, with about a quarter of tax
revenues earmarked for specific functions as well as substantial amounts of fees
and grants.

Earmarking revenues for a specific purpose can be used to establish a benefit tax
system and provide some revenue certainty to assist in long-run planning. A
potential problem caused by earmarking is a reduction in budget flexibility for the
government, making it more difficult to change the priorities in the state budget
over time and to respond, in the short run, to economic fluctuations.

Most state governments face some type of legal (as opposed to economic) restrictions regarding budget deficits. The governor must *submit* a balanced budget in 44 states and the legislature must *pass* a balanced budget in 40. Thirty-seven states prohibit, either constitutionally or statutorily, carrying a budget deficit over into the next fiscal year or budget biennium, with tight constitutional debt limitations imposed in many of these states.

The authority to adjust expenditures when deficits appear usually rests with the executive branch, sometimes only up to some maximum amount. State governments also may prepare for unanticipated deficits by maintaining a budget stabilization fund to augment revenue as needed. Forty-six states now have authorized formal budget stabilization funds by creating separate accounts in the state budget by statute, although not all of them actually may have a balance at any given time.

Nearly all local governments and more than half of state governments are constrained by statutory or constitutional limits on taxes or spending or both. Property tax rates are limited in 33 states, property tax amounts in 23, local general revenues or expenditures in 6, and state own-source revenue or expenditures in 27.

DISCUSSION QUESTIONS

1. Using news reports or official reports from your state government, examine the fiscal position of your state and your locality over the past three years. Have budgets been growing or declining in real terms? Have the budgets tended to result in deficits or surpluses? If deficits were likely, how did those governments adjust to avoid the shortfall? If surpluses were the likely outcome, what did those governments elect to do with the surplus funds (more spending, tax cuts, rebates)?

2. From your library or state budget office, get a summary of a recent state government budget and examine the degree to which state revenues are earmarked for specific budget categories or funds. How restricted is your state's budget as to how revenues must be spent? If all earmarking of revenues were ended today, how do you think your state's spending mix would change, if at all?

3. Unlike the federal government, most state governments are limited in their capability to engage in deficit finance either by an explicit requirement that the state budget be balanced each fiscal period or by a tight limit on the issuance of state debt. How might a budget be balanced at the start of a fiscal year and not at the end? What options does a state have to balance a budget during a fiscal period without reducing spending? How might a state "borrow" to finance a deficit without actually issuing bonds or other financial instruments—that is, how can a state borrow internally?

4. A number of states have now established stabilization funds that are paid into in years when the state's economy is strong and drawn from

when the state's economy is in recession. This means that state taxes are greater than spending in good economic years and less than spending in bad years. How can these contingency funds actually stabilize a state's economy? An alternative would be for states to have lower tax rates in good economic years and to increase rates to maintain spending during recessions. What are the economic and political advantages and disadvantages to saving as opposed to periodic adjustment of tax rates?

5. Suppose a state is considering three different types of fiscal limits for local governments in the state—a maximum property tax rate, a limit that property tax revenue may not increase more than population and inflation together, or a limit that spending may not increase more than 5 percent. In each case, the limit may be exceeded by majority vote. Which limit is most restrictive and why? Contrast the three in terms of the sources of allowed increases in taxes or spending and the potential effect on local services.

SELECTED READING

Brennan, Geoffrey and James Buchanan. "The Logic of Tax Limits: Alternative Constitutional Constraints on the Power to Tax." *National Tax Journal Supplement*, 32 (June 1979): 11–22.

Friedman, Lewis. "Budgeting." In *Management Policies in Local Government Finance*, edited by J. Aronson and E. Schwartz, 91–119. Washington, D.C.: International City Management Association, 1981.

Kmitch, Janet H. and Bruce E. Baker. "State and Local Government Fiscal Position in 1999." *Survey of Current Business*, 80 (May 2000): 6–13.

McGuire, Therese J. and C. Eugene Steuerle. "A Summary of What We Know—and Don't—About State Fiscal Crises." *State Tax Notes*. August 4, 2003, 357–361.

National Association of State Budget Officers. *Budget Processes in the States*. Washington, D.C., January 2002.

National Governor's Association and National Association of State Budget Officers. *The Fiscal Survey of States*. Washington, D.C., December 2004.

Snell, Ronald K. "State Balanced Budget Requirements: Provisions and Practice." National Conference of State Legislatures, Denver, March 2004.

Suits, Daniel B. and Ronald C. Fisher. "A Balanced Budget Constitutional Amendment: Economic Complexities and Uncertainties." *National Tax Journal*, 38 (Dec. 1985): 467–77.

REVENUE FOR STATE–LOCAL GOVERNMENTS

S TATE AND LOCAL GOVERNMENTS RECEIVE REVENUE FROM A VARI-
ETY OF TAXES, FROM GOVERNMENT PRODUCTION OR SALE OF
GOODS AND SERVICES (SUCH AS ELECTRICITY, LIQUOR, AND
GAMBLING), CHARGES AND FEES, BORROWING, AND INTERGOVERN-
MENTAL GRANTS. The latter three of these already have been discussed
in the previous section of the book. The remaining two revenues from a
government's own sources are discussed in detail in Chapters 12
through 18, which focus particularly on analyzing taxation by state–local
governments.

In this part, we consider the traditional economic revenue issues of efficiency, equity, and administration, both by examining the institutional
arrangements for these revenue sources and by presenting the economic
analysis of their effects. The key features of state and local government
analysis—mobility and diversity—will be very much in evidence here. The
relative ease of moving economic activity among subnational governments
creates an additional avenue of escape from taxation that can substantially
influence the expected economic effects of taxes. The great diversity of state
and local government revenue systems both magnifies the influence of
mobility and raises a question of just how state and local governments
select their revenue structures.

This part begins in Chapter 12 with an overview of the basic tools of economic tax analysis, with an emphasis on those issues that are most important for the state–local government situation. Although this overview is
not intended to substitute for a more intensive study of the economic
effects of taxes, it should provide a sufficient framework around which to

organize the discussion of each specific revenue source. Thereafter, each revenue source is discussed in turn beginning with the "big three taxes"—property, income, and sales—and finishing with business taxes and government enterprises, such as utilities, lotteries and gambling, and sale of alcoholic beverages.

CHAPTER 12

PRINCIPLES OF TAX ANALYSIS

> *. . . No local, state, or federal government conducts its finances in an economy closed to the outside. . . . So there is little reason to believe either that all taxes are borne by residents of taxing regions or that the ultimate interregional distribution of these tax loads is very simple.*[1]
> —CHARLES E. MCLURE, JR.

THE FACES OF STATE AND LOCAL TAXES

Income & Business	Consumption	Wealth
PERSONAL INCOME TAX	SALES TAX	PROPERTY TAX
CORPORATE INCOME TAX	USE TAX	ESTATE TAX
VALUE-ADDED TAX	MOTOR FUEL TAXES	INHERITANCE TAX
LICENSE TAXES	ALCOHOLIC BEVERAGE TAXES	TRANSFER TAXES
	TOBACCO PRODUCTS TAXES	
	HOTEL/MOTEL TAX	
	RESTAURANT MEALS TAX	
	TELEPHONE CALL TAXES	
	GAMBLING TAXES	

---

[1]"Commodity Tax Incidence in Open Economies." *National Tax Journal,* 17 (June 1964): 187.

The basic economic issues and tools of tax analysis are introduced in this chapter. You should know and understand the methods and results discussed in this chapter because they will be directly applied to specific taxes in the following chapters. If you have never studied economic analysis of taxation, this should be sufficient introduction to allow a general analysis of the effects of different subnational government taxes. For others, this chapter may be a review.

THE ECONOMIC ISSUES: INCIDENCE AND EFFICIENCY

Tax Incidence

Tax incidence is the analysis of which individuals bear the ultimate burden of taxes, that is, the burden after the economy has adjusted to any changes caused by the taxes. **Incidence** is usually defined as the change in private real incomes and wealth because of an adoption or change of a tax. Because individuals and firms may react to taxes by changing behavior, the taxpayers who bear the ultimate burden of a tax—that is, the economic incidence—may be different from the taxpayers from whom the tax is initially collected or levied upon, the statutory incidence of a tax. Incidence analysis usually considers the distribution of the amount of revenue generated by a tax, the revenue burden. That burden must be compared to something, however, so incidence is usually a relative concept. One possibility is to compare the incidence of one tax to the incidence of another tax that generates an equal amount of revenue, the **differential incidence**. A second possibility is to compare the incidence of the revenue of a tax to the incidence of the benefits of the goods and services financed by the tax, the **balanced-budget incidence**.[2]

The first step in doing incidence analysis is to determine which prices change and by how much they change as a result of the tax (or the tax and spending package). Of course, the prices of consumer goods and services as well as factors of production can change, so a tax may affect individuals both from their uses of income (consumer purchases) and their sources of income (factor prices such as wages, rents, and interest). Suppose such an analysis shows that the price of consumer good X rises and the price of factor of production Y falls because of a tax change. Thus, consumers of good X and suppliers of factor Y bear the burden of this tax. With this information, how can one determine the burden on a specific individual or a group of individuals, say those with incomes between $20,000 and $30,000? You must know the amounts of good X consumed and factor Y supplied by this individual or group of individuals. Those quantities, multiplied by the change in prices caused by the tax, show the magnitude of the tax burden imposed on each class. For instance, a person may bear none of the tax burden (if that person neither consumes X nor supplies Y),

---

[2]A third possibility is absolute incidence, which is the incidence of a tax change when neither other taxes nor government spending are changed. The tax change would alter the government surplus or deficit and have macroeconomic effects.

some of the tax burden (if that person consumes X but does not supply Y, or vice versa), or the full effect of the tax burden (if the person both consumes X and supplies Y).[3]

After the burden of a tax change—because of the changes in prices of goods and services—is determined, that burden is usually characterized by its effect on income distribution. The terms progressive, proportional, and regressive are used to describe the effect of a tax on private-income distribution. Unfortunately, these terms can have more than one definition and meaning in tax analysis. In this book, we adopt the most common usage of these terms, describing tax burden as a percentage of income (unless a different specific definition is given). Those definitions are as follows:

- **Progressive tax:** Tax burden/income rises as income rises.
- **Proportional tax:** Tax burden/income constant as income rises.
- **Regressive tax:** Tax burden/income falls as income rises.

A **progressive** tax change therefore imposes a burden that is a greater fraction of income for higher-income persons than lower-income individuals. In contrast, a **regressive** tax change imposes a greater percentage burden on lower incomes as opposed to higher incomes. Continuing the previous example, suppose that the amount spent on good X as a fraction of income is greater for higher-income than lower-income taxpayers, although suppliers of input Y are distributed equally throughout the income distribution. A tax change that increases the price of X and decreases the price of Y would be progressive. This definition is still somewhat uncertain, however, because income could be annual income or some longer-term measure such as lifetime income. The importance of these different measures of income will be considered in Chapter 14.

Efficiency

As discussed in Chapter 2, an economy is efficient if marginal social cost equals marginal social benefit for all goods. The efficiency cost of a tax change refers to the changes in production and consumption of goods caused by the tax change that causes marginal social cost and marginal social benefit to no longer be equal. The tax revenue generated by the tax change does not represent an efficiency cost because that money is simply transferred from one part of the economy to another; the tax revenue is used to provide government goods and services that have corresponding benefits. The efficiency cost of a tax arises, rather, because individuals and businesses change their behavior due to the tax. By consuming different goods, which are less desirable than those that would be consumed in the absence of the tax, and by supplying different amounts of factors of production, the economy is moved to a less efficient or lower welfare position by the tax change.

---

[3]If input Y is also used to produce other products, then the analysis is still more complicated. Consumers of those
    other products could be affected.

The **efficiency cost of a tax change** refers to the lost private welfare beyond that caused by the transfer of private income to tax revenue for the government. This is called the **excess burden** of taxation, that is, the burden over and above the revenue generated. The implicit assumption in this definition is that it may be possible to use some tax structure to collect a given amount of revenue at zero efficiency cost. Any other potential tax structure that can be used to generate the same revenue can be evaluated against this standard in terms of the efficiency cost, which is the welfare burden in addition to the revenue (the same for both tax structures).

A General Rule for Tax Analysis

If there is one general rule for economic analysis of taxes, it is this: *The only way to avoid a tax (legally) is to change your behavior.* For instance, if a tax is imposed on the consumption of cigarettes, consumers can reduce their tax burden only by reducing the amount of cigarettes consumed or by purchasing cigarettes in a different (lower-tax) location. Similarly, a tax on the sale of gasoline can be avoided or shifted by firms only if producers sell less gasoline or sell it in a lower-tax jurisdiction. The rule also applies to broader-based taxes, in addition to specific excise taxes. An individual can reduce income tax liability only by earning less income or earning income in a lower-tax jurisdiction.[4]

This rule makes clear that tax incidence and tax efficiency are inherently connected. If individuals and businesses do not change their behavior in response to a tax change, then no efficiency cost is created and determining tax incidence is simple—the tax change is a burden only for those directly taxed. If, on the other hand, individuals and businesses do change their behavior because of the tax-induced price changes, then the tax change will have an efficiency cost. Determining tax incidence will be more complicated as individuals and businesses act to shift the tax burden to others.

There is an important corollary to this general rule. If the only way individuals and businesses can avoid tax burdens is by changing their behavior, it stands to reason that the more an economic agent is willing to change behavior, the more the tax burden can be avoided. For instance, an individual who drives a car but stops driving entirely because of the imposition of a gasoline tax and switches to a bicycle obviously pays less of the gasoline tax than someone who continues to drive exactly the same amount as before the tax. But an efficiency cost may have been created if the bicycle transportation that this individual substitutes for driving is less preferred by that person (such as when it is cold or wet). A person who does not drive a car at all still may bear part of the gasoline tax if that tax is included in the prices of other goods this person consumes.

---

[4]It is sometimes argued that businesses also can avoid a tax by raising prices. But higher prices are expected to reduce the amount demanded by consumers, requiring lower output. Thus the businesses would change production.

SINGLE-MARKET TAX ANALYSIS

It is useful to consider how to apply the general principles outlined previously to specific tax situations. The easiest way to illustrate those principles is to consider the effect of a tax on only one market, the market in which the tax is directly levied, called **partial-equilibrium analysis.**

A Unit Excise Tax

Suppose that a tax of $\$t$ per gallon is to be imposed on the consumption of gasoline. Suppose also that gasoline is a commodity provided in a competitive market, as represented in Figure 12.1. Before the tax is imposed, the market is in equilibrium at price P_0 and quantity of gasoline G_0.

The imposition of a specific tax on a commodity can be analyzed either by shifting the demand curve down by the amount of the tax or by shifting the supply curve up by the amount of the tax—the methods are equivalent. In this case, because the tax is imposed on the consumers, we analyze the tax by shifting the demand curve down to $Demand_1$. If consumers are to consume the same amount of gasoline after the tax is imposed, the price the seller charges must fall by the amount of the tax so that consumers would still pay P_0. That is exactly what demand curve $Demand_1$ represents. In essence, $Demand_1$ shows the amount of gasoline demanded for different prices *received by the seller after tax*, whereas demand curve D shows the amount demanded for different prices *paid by the buyer*. The two prices differ by the amount of the tax, so *Demand* and $Demand_1$ also differ by t.[5]

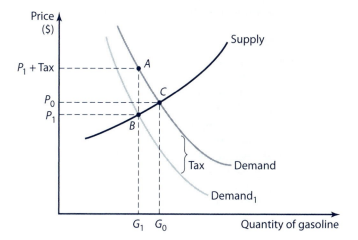

Figure 12.1

Incidence of a unit excise tax by shifting demand

---

[5]It is said that demand is shifted *down* (rather than to the left) because the change is of $\$t$ and dollars are measured vertically on this graph.

Incidence of a unit
excise tax by
shifting supply

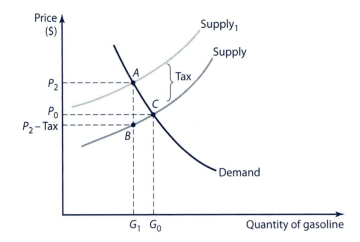

After the tax is imposed, the new market equilibrium is shown by the intersection of supply and $Demand_1$, which is the demand defined by the seller's price. As
a result of the tax, the amount of gasoline sold falls to G_1, and the price charged by
sellers falls to P_1. Remember, consumers must pay the seller's price plus pay the
tax in this case, so the full price to a consumer is $P_1 + t$, which is shown on the
graph as the price from demand curve D at quantity G_1. In sum, the tax causes consumers to pay a higher price for gasoline and thus to buy less, while sellers also
receive a lower price for gasoline than they did before the tax.

As noted, the same results are obtained if the tax is analyzed by shifting supply.
Suppose, instead of the preceding example, that a tax of $\$t$ per gallon of gasoline
is levied on the sale of gasoline and collected from sellers. Such a tax increases the
marginal cost of selling gasoline by exactly $\$t$ and thus can be represented as shift-
ing the supply curve up to $Supply_1$, as shown in Figure 12.2. Because the sale of
gasoline is more costly to sellers than it was previously, less is offered for sale or
supplied at every price. The original supply curve shows the quantity supplied
for different prices received by the seller excluding the tax, whereas the new
supply curve shows the amount of gasoline supplied for different prices including the tax.

The new market equilibrium is shown by the intersection of *Demand* and *Sup-
ply$_1$*. As before, the amount of gasoline sold falls to G_1, the price paid by consumers
rises to P_2 (equivalent to $P_1 + Tax$ in Figure 12.1), and the price received by the
seller after paying the tax falls to $P_2 - Tax$ (equivalent to P_1 in Figure 12.1). These
are the same results that were obtained by analyzing this tax with a demand shift.
This illustrates a more important point, however, than just the equivalence of these
two analytical methods. Concerning incidence and economic effects in a competitive market, it does not matter whether a given unit tax nominally is levied on or
collected from sellers or buyers—a unit tax levied on consumers produces exactly
the same market effects as the same tax collected from sellers.

Incidence

Who bears the revenue burden of this tax? In this case, consumers *and* sellers of gasoline bear the revenue burden. Referring to Figure 12.1, due to the tax, the price consumers pay has risen from P_0 to $P_1 + t$, which is less than the amount of the tax. The price sellers receive has fallen from P_0 to P_1. The total tax revenue collected is tG_1, with the consumers' share being $(P_1 + t - P_0)G_1$ and the sellers' share equal to $(P_0 - P_1)G_1$. In this particular case, consumers bear a larger portion of the burden than sellers. You should understand, however, that the burden on sellers is a burden on *people*, not some business entity. The sellers' burden may result in lower profits to the owners, lower wages to employees, or lower prices for other factors of production. How the sellers' burden is divided among factors cannot be determined in single-market analysis.

What determines the division of revenue burden between consumers and sellers? Following the general rule noted earlier, the agents (consumers or sellers) who are less willing to change their behavior bear the larger share of the burden. Willingness to change behavior as a tax alters prices is characterized by the price elasticity. If consumers are more willing to change behavior than sellers, then demand will be relatively more price elastic than supply, and sellers will bear the greater burden of any tax. In contrast, if sellers are more willing to change behavior, then supply will be more price elastic than demand, and consumers will bear the greater share of the revenue burden.

Following this rule, two special cases are presented in Figure 12.3. In Figure 12.3a, *supply is perfectly inelastic*, reflecting the fact that the same quantity is supplied regardless of price; in essence, there is a fixed amount of this product. The imposition of a tax is shown by shifting the demand curve down by the amount of the tax, so price falls from P_0 to P_0 minus tax. Because sellers will not change their behavior—that is, alter production—as the tax changes the price, sellers bear the full burden of this tax. In Figure 12.3b, just the opposite situation is depicted. If *demand is perfectly inelastic*, then consumers will not change their behavior as a tax alters price, so the consumers' price rises by the full amount of the tax, and thus consumers bear the full burden of the tax.

Efficiency

This unit excise tax on gasoline also creates an efficiency cost. When the tax is imposed and the consumers' price rises, consumers move up along their demand curve and purchase less gasoline. Presumably, consumers are instead purchasing substitute fuels such as gasohol, substituting more fuel-efficient vehicles, traveling less, or purchasing gasoline in a different market, perhaps from stations in a neighboring locality. In any case, consumers have been induced to switch to less desirable alternatives, creating an efficiency cost. Similarly, as the tax causes the sellers' price to fall, sellers move down along their supply curve and produce less gasoline. Instead, those resources previously used for gasoline production are switched to the production of something else. If those resources cannot be used as efficiently in the production of those other commodities, an additional efficiency cost is created.

Figure 12.3

Incidence with
perfectly inelastic
supply and
demand

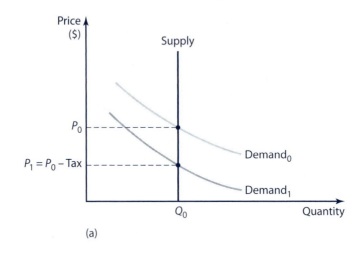

(a)

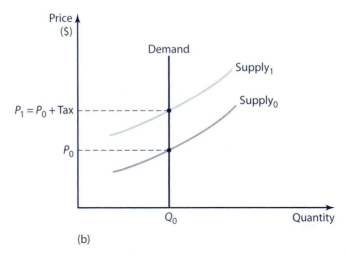

(b)

Measurement of the efficiency cost due to changes in consumers' behavior is depicted, for a simplified case, in Figure 12.4. In this case, the market-supply curve, which you may recall arises from the firm's marginal cost of production, is perfectly elastic (horizontal). The assumption of perfectly elastic supply means that any amount of the product can be supplied at the market price, but that none will be supplied if the price falls below that market equilibrium. One example of such a situation is a product that is sold in many locations but whose price is set in a national or world market according to costs. For instance, after the world price of oil is determined, sellers need not sell oil in any market where the price is below that world price, because they can sell in other markets at the world price. This exact situation is common in the world of state–local government finance, with

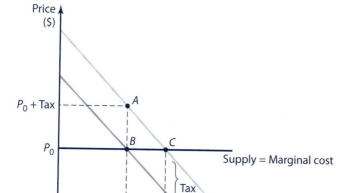

Figure 12.4

Efficiency cost of
a unit tax

individual states or localities being small enough that they are price takers for goods sold in national (or world) markets.[6]

The imposition of a tax is analyzed by shifting the demand curve down by the amount of the tax. As a result, the quantity falls from Q_0 to Q_1, the sellers' price remains constant at P_0, and the consumers' price rises by the full amount of the tax to $(P_0 + tax)$.[7]

The efficiency cost is the difference between the benefit to consumers and the opportunity cost to the society of each unit of the product not produced—that is, the difference between marginal social benefit and marginal social cost. Assuming that one can approximate marginal social benefit by demand, the efficiency cost of the tax is the difference between *Demand* and marginal cost (*MC*) for those units no longer produced due to the tax $(Q_0 - Q_1)$. Thus, the efficiency cost is represented graphically by triangle *ABC* in Figure 12.4. The tax generates revenue of tQ_1. The resources no longer needed to produce as much of this product, equal to $(Q_0 - Q_1)MC$, are shifted to the production of other products at no efficiency loss because marginal cost is constant.

The efficiency cost, which is represented by triangle *ABC*, can be computed with a simple formula. The area of any triangle is equal to ½ × the length × the height. Applying that formula to triangle *ABC*, the area is ½(*AB*)(*BC*), which

[6]Even for commodities sold in national markets, it is possible that prices may differ by location because of transportation costs, for instance. But for some pricing strategies, firms will bear transportation-cost differences and charge equal prices in all locations, such as the single "destination charges" used by automobile manufacturers. For a discussion of the theoretical issues, see Martin Beckmann (1968).

[7]Because supply is perfectly elastic, all the tax burden is borne by the consumers. If the sellers' price fell below P_0, none of the product would be offered for sale, as the price would be less than marginal cost.

equals $\frac{1}{2}t(Q_0 - Q_1)$. One half the tax times the change in quantity can be rewritten to produce the result that

$$\text{Efficiency Cost} = \frac{1}{2}t^2 EQ/P$$

where E = price elasticity of (compensated) demand.[8] In other words, the efficiency cost depends on the price elasticity of demand, the amount purchased, and the tax rate squared. This last factor is very important because as a tax rate is increased, the efficiency cost rises at a faster, quadratic rate.

One should note three important warnings about using this formula to approximate efficiency costs. First, the formula applies exactly only if the demand curve is linear so that the efficiency cost is represented exactly by a triangle. Second, the formula applies only if the supply function is perfectly elastic (horizontal). If supply is somewhat elastic (the function is upward sloping), then the formula is more complicated and includes the price elasticity of supply. Third, the formula suggests that if the price elasticity of demand is zero (the demand curve is perfectly inelastic or vertical), then the efficiency cost is also zero. This is generally not correct. The problem arises because this is single-market analysis and ignores the behavior of consumers in other markets. Because the price of the taxed product has changed, consumers may alter their behavior in other markets (by purchasing less of some other product or by working less, for example), which would create an efficiency cost. This possibility is examined in the appendix to this chapter.[9]

One other case exists in which a tax may not have an excess burden or efficiency cost. You learned in Chapter 2 that efficiency requires that marginal social cost equal marginal social benefit. The production or consumption of some commodities produces external costs, however, so the social cost of the activity is greater than the private cost and private benefit. Air pollution resulting from gasoline combustion and use of automobiles is one example. In such a case, a tax actually can improve economic efficiency by forcing consumers or producers to perceive the full costs of their activity. If automobile use imposes costs on everyone that are not taken into account by drivers, there will be too much auto use and too much air pollution from society's viewpoint. A tax on auto emissions or a tax on gasoline use would make drivers see the full cost of their activity and lead to less use and less pollution. An excise tax used to offset such an externality is often called a **Pigouvian tax**, named after the British economist A.C. Pigou.

How Is a Percentage Tax Different?

The preceding analysis is for a unit tax—that is, a tax of so many dollars per unit of product, such as $.18 per gallon of gasoline. The analysis of the more common percentage or *ad valorem* tax, such as a sales tax of 5 percent of the price, is only

---

[8]The price elasticity of demand, E, is the percentage change in quantity/the percentage change in price. That is,
$E = [(Q_0 - Q_1)/Q_0]/[t/P_0]$. Solving for $(Q_0 - Q_1)$ and substituting into the equation for area gives the result.

[9]For a good discussion, see Harvey Rosen (1999, p. 285–294).

Figure 12.5

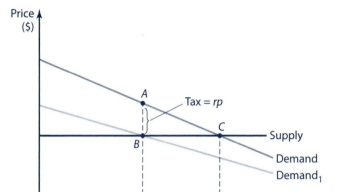

Analysis of a
percentage tax

slightly different. As before, the tax can be analyzed by shifting the demand curve down by the amount of the tax per unit or by shifting the supply curve up. The difference is that the tax per unit depends on the price. If the tax rate is r percent, then

$$\text{Tax Revenue} = r(\text{Price})(\text{Quantity})$$

The tax per unit is then

$$\text{Tax Revenue}/\text{Quantity} = r(\text{Price})$$

Obviously, the higher the price, the larger the tax per unit in dollars, and the more the demand or supply curve must be shifted to reflect the tax. In Figure 12.5, the demand curve is shifted down by the amount of the tax with the distance being larger, the higher the price is.

Although the analysis of the efficiency cost of this tax is exactly the same as for the unit tax, the formula to compute the approximate efficiency cost is different, as shown here:

$$\text{Efficiency Cost} = \tfrac{1}{2}r^2 EPQ$$

As before, the efficiency cost depends on the price elasticity of demand, the amount of the commodity purchased (now measured in dollars), and on the tax rate squared.[10]

Incidence and Efficiency of a Subsidy

Single-market analysis also can be applied to examine the incidence and efficiency of a subsidy offered in that market. A **subsidy** is a payment from the government

---

[10]Again, the area of the efficiency cost triangle is $\tfrac{1}{2}(AB)(BC)$, which equals $\tfrac{1}{2}rP(Q_0 - Q_1)$. Because $Q_0 - Q_1$ equals rEQ, the efficiency cost area equals $\tfrac{1}{2}r^2 EPQ$.

Figure 12.6

Incidence and
efficiency effects
of a subsidy

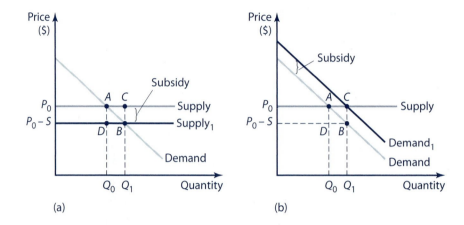

(a)

(b)

that lowers the price or cost of some economic activity to individuals or business-es. Examples among state–local government programs include food stamps, which reduce the price of purchasing food for eligible households; mortgage revenue bonds sold by states to make low-interest housing loans to eligible families, which reduce the price of homeownership; state or local support of higher education, which allows the private price of higher education to fall short of total cost; and perhaps Medicaid, which pays all or part of the cost of health care for certain low-income persons (although some argue that health care is not sold in a competitive market).

Suppose the government offers a subsidy of $\$S$ per unit consumed or sold for some commodity sold in a competitive market. For clarity, assume that the supply of this product is perfectly elastic, reflecting the idea that the price is determined in some broader market. Just as with taxes, the subsidy can be analyzed by either adjusting supply or demand. In Figure 12.6a, the subsidy on units sold reduces the marginal cost of producers and is analyzed by shifting supply down by the amount of the subsidy, S. As a result of the subsidy, the price to consumers falls by the amount of the subsidy (from P_0 to $P_0 - S$), and quantity bought and sold rises from Q_0 to Q_1. Because we have assumed that supply is perfectly elastic, the price received by sellers, including the subsidy, remains at P_0. Thinking about the inci-dence of the subsidy, then, all the benefits go to consumers, who see the price fall by the full $\$S$.

If the subsidy were offered directly to consumers, an equivalent analysis res-ults from shifting the demand curve up by the amount of the subsidy, as in Figure 12.6b. Again, for the same market conditions, the price to consumers falls to $P_0 - S$ and consumption rises to Q_1.[11]

---

[11]Subsidies can be thought of as negative taxes, and thus the analysis is exactly reversed. A tax increases producers' costs and sifts supply up vertically, although a subsidy reduces costs and shifts supply down. A tax reduces demand (shifting it down), whereas a subsidy increases demand (shifting it up).

Continuing the parallel to tax analysis, the benefits of a subsidy are divided between consumers and sellers based on the relative elasticities of demand and supply. If supply is perfectly elastic, as in Figure 12.6, then price is set at a given level and consumers benefit from the full subsidy. Sellers can lower the price to $P_0 - S$ and still receive the world price of P_0 when the subsidy is added. If the quantity supplied is fixed (perfectly inelastic supply), then suppliers get all the benefits from the subsidy. Consumers continue to pay the original price for the fixed amount of the product and sellers pocket the subsidy.

In addition to costing the government a direct amount, the subsidy also has an efficiency cost. In Figure 12.6a, the subsidy lowers the price and provides benefits to all those who would have purchased this good without the subsidy (Q_0), and the subsidy provides benefits to those consumers who are induced to consume more of the good (from Q_0 to Q_1) due to its lower price. The magnitude of the benefit to original purchasers is shown graphically by the area $S\,Q_0$ or $P_0ADP_0 - S$, and the benefit to new purchasers is represented by the area ADB, which is the difference between the marginal benefit (demand) to those consumers for each unit from Q_0 to Q_1 and the marginal cost (supply). The sum of these two benefits, represented by area $P_0ABP_0 - S$, is less than the amount of the subsidy paid, represented by area $P_0CBP_0 - S$. The difference between the two, triangle ABC, represents the efficiency cost or excess burden of the subsidy.

This efficiency cost also can be explained or understood from a different perspective. For each unit from Q_0 to Q_1, the marginal social cost (Supply) is greater than the marginal social benefit (Demand). The subsidy makes it seem that this commodity is cheaper then it really is and thus induces society to allocate too many resources to its production or consumption. For instance, if a state subsidizes the consumption of housing, then consumers ignore the source of the subsidy, believe that housing is now less expensive, and increase consumption of housing. That increase in housing consumption may require that consumers change their behavior elsewhere as well, however, perhaps consuming less of something else (clothing) or working more. Because consumers made this change *due to the subsidy*, they really prefer more clothing or leisure. The subsidy has induced consumers to make an inefficient choice.

Just as with taxes, however, this efficiency analysis has one important qualification. As noted in Chapter 2, if a product provides benefits to other than the direct consumers, which occurs if there are externalities, then a subsidy is called for to offset the external benefits. For instance, if education provides benefits to everyone in society in general, then each person would underestimate the benefits and choose too little education from society's viewpoint. In that case, a subsidy for education corrects an inefficiency rather than creates one.

Limitations of Single-Market Analysis

Although single-market analysis is helpful in illustrating the general principles of tax analysis, it is often not very precise for two reasons. First, the effects in other markets, whether for other goods or for the same good in a different location, are not considered. Second, the manner in which any sellers' burden gets distributed among the various factors of production is not analyzed explicitly. Although this may not be much of a problem in some cases where intermarket effects are small, often intermarket effects can be substantial, particularly in the world of state–local governments with relatively easy mobility among jurisdictions. Therefore, we turn now to multimarket analysis, effectively applying the same type of supply-and-demand analysis not only for the market in which the tax is directly imposed but also for other, closely connected markets.

MULTIMARKET ANALYSIS

Effects in Parallel Markets

Here we consider the effects of a tax, including the effects of the tax in the markets for complementary or substitute goods. As an example, we can expand consideration of the effects of a unit tax of $\$t$ on gasoline to include those in the market for motor scooters, assuming that cars and motor scooters are substitutes. That situation is shown in Figure 12.7, with the simplifying assumptions of perfectly elastic supply of both gasoline and motor scooters. Given the national price for Best Unleaded Gasoline and Your Favorite Motor Scooter, sellers will require that price in all markets in the long run. As before, the imposition of the unit tax on gasoline is represented by a downward shift in the demand for gasoline (to $Demand_{G1}$). As a result, the quantity of gasoline consumed decreases and the consumers' price rises, in this case by the full amount of the tax because of the perfectly elastic supply. Consumers now purchase G_1 units of gasoline at a price of $P_0 + t$.

Figure 12.7

Multimarket analysis of a unit excise tax with constant costs

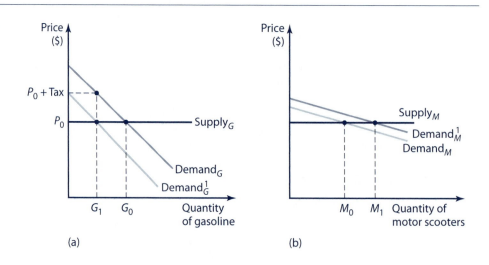

(a)   (b)

Figure 12.8

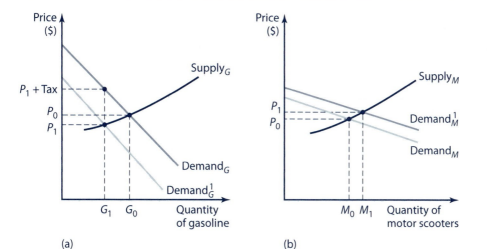

Multimarket analysis of a unit excise tax with increasing costs

(a)   (b)

Because the price of gasoline has increased, consumers will act to reduce consumption, perhaps by substituting 80-mile per-gallon motor scooters for 20-mile per-gallon cars. Thus, the demand for motor scooters is expected to increase, shown by the rightward shift of demand from $Demand_M$ to $Demand_{M1}$ in the motor scooter market. Assuming perfectly elastic supply, the amount of motor scooters purchased and produced rises, but the price remains the same in the long run. By consuming less gasoline, consumers have reduced the amount of gasoline tax they pay. (Consumers pay tG_1 rather than tG_0.)

The situation is only slightly more complex if constant costs do not prevail so that the supply curves in both markets are not perfectly elastic but are positively sloped, as depicted in Figure 12.8. In this instance, as previously discussed, the unit tax on gasoline causes both an increase in the consumers' price (but by less than the amount of the tax) and a decrease in the sellers' price. The increase in the consumers' price of gasoline causes an increase in the demand for motor scooters, which now causes an increase in the price of motor scooters due to the upward sloping supply. Because additional numbers of scooters cost more to produce than the previous ones, the price must rise to make that extra production worthwhile.

Because of this price increase, the original motor scooter consumers (those who purchased quantity M_0) also are hurt by the gasoline tax; the higher motor scooter price is charged to all consumers, not just those who switch from cars due to the gasoline price increase. Motor scooter consumers pay an increased amount equal to $(P_1 - P_0)M_0$; however, this amount is not transferred revenue to the government, nor is it an efficiency cost lost to the economy. This extra amount consumers pay is transferred to the sellers through the higher price of motor scooters. To complete this multimarket analysis, then, it is also necessary to expand the analysis to the factor markets behind these consumer-goods markets.

Figure 12.9

Effects of an excise
tax on gasoline in
factor markets

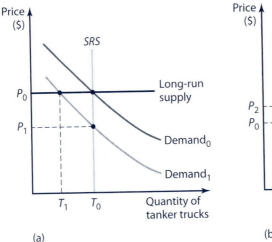

(a)

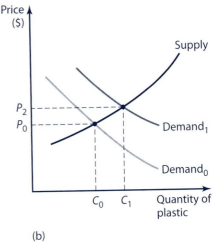

(b)

Effects in Factor Markets

Changes in consumption away from gasoline and cars and toward motor scooters
as a result of an excise tax on gasoline also may have implications for the factors
of production used in producing those goods. Some of those potential implications
are shown in Figure 12.9. The decrease in the consumption of gasoline could lead
to a decrease in the demand for the services of tanker trucks to carry gasoline to
wholesale distributors and retail outlets. The immediate effect, given the number
of trucks T_0, is a decrease in their value to P_1. If the long-run supply of tanker
trucks is perfectly elastic, as depicted earlier in Figure 12.7a, then the effect will be
a reduction in the number of tanker trucks over time, so that the value of the
trucks, or the rental rate for tanker-truck services, returns to the previous level. Of
course, the reduction in the number of tanker trucks or in the amount of tanker-
truck service used may have implications for the drivers or producers of trucks.

Similarly, the increase in demand for motor scooters due to the tax on gasoline
may increase the demand for plastic, assuming that motor scooters primarily are
constructed from plastic (and little plastic is used in producing cars). In this instance,
we assume that the long-run supply of plastic is positively sloped, thus requiring a
price increase to induce more production. The tax on gasoline therefore has the
effect of increasing the revenue to producers of plastic, who *benefit* in effect from the
gasoline tax. Recall that in Figure 12.8 you saw that motor scooter consumers pay an
increased amount to motor scooter producers as a result of the gasoline tax. In the
example, at least part of that gain to motor scooter producers becomes a gain to plastic producers. The excise tax on gasoline imposed a burden on gasoline consumers,
but also caused a transfer of resources from consumers to plastic producers.

Obviously, this story can continue, for instance, by asking whether the gain
to plastic producers ultimately benefits workers in the industry or suppliers of

chemicals used in plastic production. One important aspect of multimarket tax analysis is determining into how many different markets or how many different stages of production to carry the analysis. The appropriate answer depends on the case, including both the economic conditions in a market, which determine how large a price change is expected, and the importance of that market for the equity or efficiency result.

Application to State and Local Government Issues

Multimarket analysis is essential when dealing with state–local government taxes because the focus is often on the effect of a tax levied by one state or locality when there is mobility among states or local jurisdictions. Examples abound. A consumer may go over a boundary to a store in a different location or order through a catalog or Web site to avoid sales tax. An individual may move his residence and work location to avoid an income tax, or an individual may change residence (but not job) location to reduce the residential property tax. Finally, a business may change its operating location to avoid a state business tax or local property tax. In all these cases, there might very well be economic effects in more than one market or location, both the one that imposes the tax and the one to which the economic activity moves. Multimarket tax analysis is required.

A simple relabeling of Figure 12.7 shows how the models in this chapter can be applied to these types of issues. Rather than thinking of one market for gasoline and one for motor scooters, it is just as correct to let Figure 12.7a represent the market for gasoline in jurisdiction G and Figure 12.7b represent the market for gasoline in jurisdiction M. Before taxes, gasoline sells for the same price in both locations. Now G imposes a t unit tax on gasoline, so that consumers in jurisdiction G pay a price equal to $P_0 + t$, which is greater than the price in M. Consumers in G now not only have the choice of switching to motor scooters from cars but also of purchasing gasoline at a station in jurisdiction M. Obviously, some consumers from jurisdiction G decide to buy their gasoline from a station in M where the price is lower because there is no tax.[12]

Why don't *all* consumers switch their gasoline purchases to a station in M? They will unless switching is costly or unless they are not aware of the price difference. It might be costly to buy gasoline at a gas station in M rather than a station in G if an individual had to drive, say 10 miles, from his house to the nearest gasoline station in M. In that case, the cost (both in money and time) of the drive could outweigh the tax savings on gasoline. In contrast, someone who works in jurisdiction M but lives in jurisdiction G could switch gasoline purchases to M at little extra cost.

What is the gain to jurisdiction M from more gasoline sales? Possibly, there are now more retailers in M and fewer in G or at least more employment in M and less in G. The increased retail sales activity in jurisdiction M could also mean that

---

[12]It is just as correct to think that both G and M tax gasoline, but the tax in G is higher by t.

property values in *M* increase. These changes would benefit workers in *M* (regardless of where they live) and property owners in *M*. The increased retail activity could (although it is not guaranteed) also increase the tax revenue to jurisdiction *M* from property taxes or from a local sales or income tax, if one exists.

If the price of gasoline is not determined in a national market (which is shown by the perfectly elastic supply) but rather determined in each local market, then the supply curves in each jurisdiction are positively sloped, as in Figure 12.8. In that case, as consumers switch their gasoline purchases from jurisdiction *G* to *M*, the price paid by consumers for gasoline in jurisdiction *G* falls, and the price in *M* rises. The market now creates a natural constraint on the movement of purchases from *G* to *M*; in the absence of costs of changing purchase location, consumers will reallocate their purchases until the consumers' prices in *G* and *M* are again equal.

This analysis of the interjurisdictional effects of taxes using a standard multi-market model is not limited to taxes on consumer goods but can be applied just as easily to taxes on factors of production, such as labor, land, and capital. Of course, firms' payments for these factors become the wages, rent, and profits received by individuals, so these factor taxes are sometimes referred to as taxes on the sources (as opposed to uses) of income. One common application of this type is for subnational government taxes on capital. The rate of return on capital investment is determined in a national (or world) market, so any one jurisdiction is a price taker; that is, the supply of capital to that jurisdiction is perfectly elastic (Figure 12.7). The suppliers of capital are individual investors, however, whereas the demanders are business firms. If one jurisdiction imposes a tax on capital, then the effect (just as with the gasoline tax in Figure 12.7) is expected to be a decrease in the amount of capital in the taxing jurisdiction and an increase in the other jurisdiction. These changes in the amount of capital are expected to have implications (considered in detail in Chapter 14) for consumers, workers, and landowners in both jurisdictions.

According to *The Wall Street Journal* (Carlson, 1988), there were two primary reasons for this elasticity to diesel-fuel demand. Some drivers on transcontinental trips were taking routes that avoided Colorado, traveling across Wyoming or New Mexico instead. In addition, some drivers who traveled in Colorado arranged for fuel stops to occur in neighboring states. For instance, at the time, the diesel fuel tax in Wyoming was 8 cents per gallon.

In addition to reducing diesel fuel sales in Colorado, it is easy to trace at least two other effects in other markets due to the relatively high tax rate in Colorado. First, as a result of the changes in behavior of some drivers, demand for and sales of diesel fuel in neighboring states, particularly Wyoming and New Mexico, are expected to increase. Thus, both of these states receive increased tax revenue without increasing tax rates (indeed, their increased revenue came from Colorado's higher tax rate). Second, if fewer truck drivers were stopping in Colorado, then decreases in sales of other goods in Colorado, such as food and incidentals, are also expected. Indeed, the *Journal* reported that one truck stop owner in Colorado believed the typical driver spent an average of $28 in purchases other than fuel for

STATE DIESEL FUEL TAXES: MULTIMARKET ANALYSIS IN PRACTICE

All states levy taxes on diesel fuel, which is used mostly by trucks, including long-haul trucks making interstate trips. Because diesel fuel is transported easily and the market is worldwide, the supply to any one state is expected to be very elastic (perhaps essentially perfectly elastic). As a result, prices will differ by state due to the state tax differences. Because interstate truckers have some leeway in deciding what route to take or where to fuel their trucks, demand is expected to be somewhat elastic. Thus, fuel price differences due to tax differences can affect fuel sales in multiple states.

The experience of Colorado in 1986–1987 is an example. In July 1986, Colorado increased its diesel fuel tax by 7.5 cents per gallon to a then national high of 20.5 cents per gallon, a 57-percent increase in the unit tax. In the following 12 months, diesel fuel sales in Colorado fell by 11 percent from about 204 million gallons to about 182 million. Despite the decrease in the amount of fuel sold, state revenue from the tax increased from about $26.5 million to about $37 million, a revenue increase of about 40 percent. Tax revenue did not increase as much as the increase in tax rate because of the fall in gallons sold.

The Colorado case is illustrated in Figure 12.10. The tax increase is analyzed by shifting the supply up by the amount of the tax change. Because a perfectly elastic supply is assumed, the price of diesel fuel rises by the full amount of the tax increase, 7.5 cents. Because of that tax and price increase, quantity sold falls from 204.5 to 182 million gallons. If the initial price of diesel fuel was about $1.00 per gallon, a 7.5 percent increase in price resulted in about an 11 percent decrease in quantity, implying that the price elasticity of demand for diesel fuel in Colorado was about 1.46 (11 percent/7.5 percent).

Figure 12.10

Colorado diesel fuel tax increase

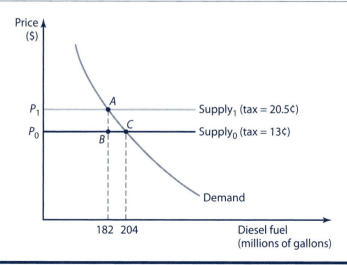

each stop. Thus, the decrease in sales for the fuel tax could spill over to markets for other commodities as well.

If supply is very elastic, as hypothesized and as seems likely, then the revenue burden of the tax increase falls on consumers of diesel fuel, which are the truckers and the consumers of trucking services. It is important to emphasize that even though the tax increase caused sales of fuel in Colorado to fall, it brought about an increase in revenue. The 57 percent increase in the tax rate generated about a 40 percent increase in revenue due to the fall in sales. The tax increase also created a larger excess burden or efficiency cost of the tax, represented by area *ABC* in Figure 12.10. In practical terms, this increased efficiency cost arose from the changes in trucker behavior—taking less efficient routes or longer driving times without stopping—that were used to avoid the tax increase.

Interestingly, in the period since this experience in Colorado, both the level and variation in state excise taxes on diesel fuel have increased. Average diesel fuel tax rates have risen from about $.15 per gallon at that time to about $.21 today; however, Colorado's tax rate has not changed so the relative tax rate between Colorado and other states has decreased.

SUMMARY

Tax incidence is the analysis of which individuals bear the ultimate burden of taxes, that is, the burden after the economy has adjusted to any changes caused by the taxes. Incidence is defined as the change in private real incomes and wealth because of an adoption or change of a tax. This is different than statutory incidence, which refers to the actual payments made by taxpayers from whom the tax is collected.

The general rule of tax analysis is the only way to avoid a tax (legally) is to change your behavior. Consumers or sellers who are less willing to change their behavior will bear the larger share of the burden.

The efficiency cost of a tax change arises because consumers or producers change their production or consumption so that marginal social cost no longer equals marginal social benefit.

Tax incidence and tax efficiency are inherently connected. If individuals and businesses do not change their behavior in response to a tax change, then no efficiency cost is created and the tax change is a burden only for those directly taxed. If individuals and businesses do change their behavior, then the tax change will have an efficiency cost, and determining tax incidence is more complicated.

Multimarket analysis is essential when dealing with state and local government taxes because the focus is often on the effect of a tax levied by one state or locality when there is mobility among states or local jurisdictions.

Perfectly elastic supply means that any amount of the product can be supplied at the market price, but that none will be supplied if the price falls below that market equilibrium. This situation is common in state–local government finance, with individual states or localities being small enough that they are price takers for goods sold in national (or world) markets.

DISCUSSION QUESTIONS

1. Suppose that the local legislative body in Your College Town (YCT) decides to levy a tax of $.50 for each 12 ounces of beer sold in the city (both by-the-drink and packages). The city sees the tax as a way to have students pay more for the city services they receive. Suppose that the beer market in YCT is competitive, the long-run industry supply in YCT is perfectly elastic, and the demand for beer in YCT is very price-elastic.

   a. What will the effects of the tax be on the price of beer in YCT, the amount of beer sold, and the number of liquor stores and bars in YCT?

   b. Why might the demand for beer in YCT be so price elastic, given that it is known that overall demand for beer is rather inelastic? In view of that, what do you expect the effect of the tax will be on beer sales and the number of stores and bars in surrounding cities?

2. "If supply of a good is perfectly inelastic, then the sellers of that good are expected to bear the full revenue burden of an excise tax on the sale or consumption of that good." Evaluate this statement. Can you think of any examples of goods whose supply is (at least almost) perfectly inelastic?

3. If a unit tax is increased from $1 per unit sold to $2, the efficiency cost of the tax more than doubles. Explain.

4. Under what conditions would it be possible for an excise tax to have no efficiency cost and, in fact, increase economic efficiency? Give an example or two.

SELECTED READINGS

Oates, Wallace E. *Fiscal Federalism*. New York: Harcourt Brace Jovanovich, 1972. See Chapter 4.

Rosen, Harvey S. *Public Finance*, 5th ed. Boston: Irwin/McGraw-Hill, 1999. See Chapters 13 and 14.

APPENDIX

Indifference-Curve Analysis of Tax Efficiency

An exposition of the consumer-demand model using indifference curves and budget lines was presented in the appendix to Chapter 3. Those tools can be used to more carefully describe the consumption changes and resulting efficiency cost from taxation than is possible with basic supply-and-demand analysis. Therefore, the consumer-theory model is used in this appendix to compare excise taxes on specific commodities with a general lump-sum tax.

Indifference-curve
analysis of a unit
excise tax

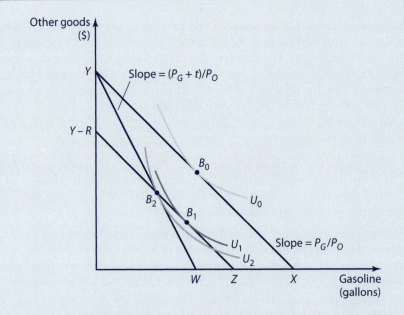

Suppose that consumers, who are price takers and have fixed amounts of resources (income), choose between gasoline and other goods. The consumer's budget before any taxes is shown by line YX in Figure 12A.1. This consumer can consume \$$Y$ of other goods by purchasing no gasoline or can consume a maximum of X gallons of gasoline by consuming no other goods. For this consumer, the consumption choice that gives highest utility is bundle B_0, implying that both gasoline and other goods are consumed.

If an excise tax is levied on the consumption or sale of gasoline and thus the price of gasoline rises, the maximum amount of gasoline this consumer could afford, given a fixed income, decreases to W gallons. Now the consumer's budget limits choices to those on line YW. Because the slope of the budget line represents the ratio of the price of gasoline to the price of other goods, and the tax causes an increase in the price of gasoline, the budget line becomes steeper, reflecting the fact that gasoline is now relatively more expensive compared to other goods than before the tax. Given the new budget, the consumption bundle that gives this consumer highest utility is B_2; in this case, the consumer purchases less gasoline and spends less on other goods due to the tax. The amount of tax paid by the consumer is shown as the vertical distance between the two budget lines $[y - (y - R)]$, which is the difference between income that would be available to be spent on other goods if there were no tax and the amount actually spent on other goods.

The same amount of tax revenue could have been collected by a lump-sum tax equal to amount R, which would create budget line $(Y - R)Z$. Given those consumption choices, this consumer would receive highest utility at bundle B_1. The lump-sum tax also induces this consumer to reduce consumption of gasoline and

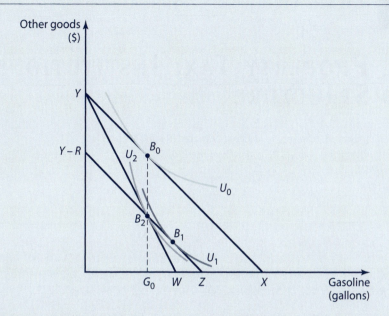

other goods, but the decrease in gasoline consumption is less than occurs with the gasoline tax because the price of gasoline has not increased. With a lump-sum tax, the change in consumption occurs solely from the reduced available income.

Both taxes reduce this consumer's utility from private consumption (ignoring the utility received from the public services financed by the tax revenue), but the excise tax on gasoline reduces utility more than the lump-sum tax, even though both taxes raise the same amount of revenue. Although both taxes have the same revenue burden, the excise tax has an **efficiency cost** or **excess burden**. That efficiency cost can be measured by the difference between utility level U_1 and utility level U_2. The efficiency cost of the excise tax arises because the tax alters relative prices and thus causes an extra change in the consumption pattern beyond that caused by the tax revenue.[13]

This efficiency cost exists regardless of which bundle on budget line YW is selected, because budget line YW is always steeper than line $(Y - R)Z$. In particular, even if the consumption of gasoline is unchanged with the excise tax, an equal-yield lump-sum tax would provide this consumer higher utility than a gasoline tax. This is shown in Figure 12A.2. When the tax is levied and the budget line shifts to YZ, a consumer with preferences represented by these indifference curves keeps consuming the same quantity of gasoline, G_0, and reduces consumption of other goods. Utility and gasoline consumption would be higher with a lump-sum tax, however. Thus, to find the source of an excess burden, it is necessary to look not just at changes in behavior in the taxed market but also at changes in economic behavior in all other markets.

---

[13]The revenue burden of the tax is the difference between U^0 and U^1.

THE PROPERTY TAX: INSTITUTIONS AND STRUCTURE

. . . No major fiscal institution . . . has been criticized at such length and with such vigor; yet no major fiscal institution has changed so little. . . .[1]

—DICK NETZER

HEADLINES

WHICH DO YOU THINK IS THE WORST TAX—THAT IS, THE LEAST FAIR?

FROM 1972 TO 1994, THE ADVISORY COMMISSION ON INTERGOVERNMENTAL RELATIONS POLLED AMERICANS ON THE QUESTION, "WHICH DO YOU THINK IS THE WORST TAX—THAT IS, THE LEAST FAIR: FEDERAL INCOME TAX, STATE INCOME TAX, STATE SALES TAX, OR LOCAL PROPERTY TAX?" RICHARD COLE AND JOHN KINCAID RECENTLY UPDATED THE ACIR SURVEY FOR 1999. IN THAT YEAR, 35 PERCENT CHOSE THE FEDERAL INCOME TAX AS THE LEAST FAIR, EDGING OUT THE LOCAL PROPERTY TAX, WHICH WAS SELECTED BY 29 PERCENT OF THE RESPONDENTS. ONLY 16 PERCENT PICKED THE STATE SALES TAX, AND 11 PERCENT CHOSE THE STATE INCOME TAX. SINCE THE POLL BEGAN, THE FEDERAL INCOME TAX AND LOCAL PROPERTY TAX HAVE ALWAYS BEEN RANKED FIRST OR SECOND AS "LEAST FAIR," WITH THE LOCAL PROPERTY TAX USUALLY FINISHING FIRST IN THE 1970S AND THE FEDERAL INCOME TAX FIRST IN THE 1980S. THE TWO ALTERNATED POSITIONS IN THE 1990S.[2]

---

[1]*Economics of the Property Tax.* Washington, D.C.: The Brookings Institution, 1966, 1.

[2]Cole, Richard L. and John Kincaid. "Public Opinion and American Federalism: Perspectives on Taxes, Spending and Trust." *Spectrum: The Journal of State Government,* Summer 2001.

Despite its fiscal importance, the property tax is perhaps the most confusing and least understood of local fiscal institutions. Accordingly, this chapter focuses exclusively on the mechanics of property taxation: how the base of the tax is defined and measured, what political groups are responsible for setting tax rates and how those rates are measured, and what policies are used to reduce property taxes overall or to alter the distribution of taxes among different types of properties and taxpayers. The economic effects of property taxes are then discussed in Chapter 14.

PROPERTY TAX RELIANCE AND TRENDS

In 2002, state–local government property taxes generated nearly $280 billion of revenue, representing about 31 percent of total state and local government taxes and about 16.5 percent of the total general revenue of state–local governments. This is slightly more than the percentage provided by federal aid. Property taxes amounted to about $969 per person and 3.1 percent of personal income in the United States.

The property tax has been and remains, however, primarily a source of revenue to local governments, with 96.5 percent of all property tax revenue going to local governments. Independent school districts collect the largest share of property taxes, nearly 43 percent. Not only do most property taxes go to local governments, but local governments also are very reliant on that tax. In 2002, property taxes provided about 27 percent of the general revenue of local governments, second only to state aid in importance (Table 13.1). Despite the adoption of local sales and income taxes by some local governments, property taxes still provide almost three-fourths of total local government taxes, as shown in Table 13.2. For all practical purposes, property taxes are just about the only tax used by school districts (96 percent of tax revenue) and townships (92 percent).

Table 13.1

Property Taxes as a Percentage of General Revenue, by Level of Government, Various Years

		Local Governments					
Year	States	All	Counties	Municipalities	Townships	School Districts	Special Districts
1962	2.1%	48.0%	45.7%	44.2%	65.3%	51.0%	25.0%
1967	1.7	43.2	42.1	38.1	61.8	46.9	21.5
1972	1.3	39.5	36.5	31.3	64.9	47.3	17.3
1977	1.3	33.7	31.0	25.8	56.8	42.1	14.0
1982	1.1	28.1	26.6	21.4	52.1	35.8	9.5
1987	1.1	28.3	27.1	20.9	52.7	36.4	10.4
1992	1.2	29.9	27.8	23.1	56.0	37.5	10.7
1997	1.3	27.9	24.7	20.7	55.9	36.0	11.9
2002	0.9	27.1	24.2	20.4	55.8	34.2	11.0

SOURCE: U.S. Department of Commerce, Census of Governments (1962, 1967, 1972, 1977, 1982, 1987, 1992, 1997, 2002).

Table 13.2

Property Taxes as a Percentage of Taxes, by Level of Government, Various Years

| | | | | **Local Governments** | | | |
Year	States	All	Counties	Municipalities	Townships	School Districts	Special Districts
1962	3.1%	87.7%	93.5%	93.5%	93.3%	98.6%	100.0%
1967	2.7	88.6	92.1	70.0	92.8	98.4	100.0
1972	2.1	83.7	85.6	64.3	93.5	98.1	94.9
1977	2.2	80.5	81.2	60.0	91.7	97.5	91.2
1982	1.9	76.1	77.2	52.6	93.7	96.8	79.6
1987	1.9	73.6	73.5	49.1	92.3	97.5	70.3
1992	2.2	75.6	74.4	52.9	93.0	97.4	66.8
1997	2.3	73.3	69.4	48.7	92.4	96.9	76.5
2002	1.8	72.9	69.1	48.6	91.6	96.2	69.8

SOURCE: See sources to Table 13.1.

The clear long-run trend is that local government reliance on property tax declined steadily, except for a period in the late 1980s and early 1990s. Property taxes provided 48 percent of aggregate local government general revenue in 1962, 28 percent in 1982, and 27 percent in 2002. The decrease in relative property tax reliance resulted from relative increases in state and federal aid compared to property taxes over the period and from increased use of local government sales and income taxes and user charges. However, property taxes are still larger than any other single source of local government revenue, except for state grants.

THE PROPERTY TAX PROCESS

The property tax is different from other state–local government taxes in at least two important ways. First, the government determines both the tax rate and the tax base. Unlike an income or sales tax, for which the value of the base (income or sales) is usually identified by private economic activity, the property tax base—which is property value—often must be estimated when market transactions are unavailable. This arises because the property tax is based on wealth, a stock variable, rather than an annual economic flow. Therefore, methods and procedures for assessing the value of property for tax purposes must be part of the property tax structure. Second, different government agencies, and sometimes even different levels of subnational government, are responsible for different aspects of the property tax process. Both of these factors have contributed to a general confusion about property taxes, which in turn has contributed to taxpayers disliking property taxes, even compared to other taxes.

The typical procedure for assessing, levying, and collecting property taxes is outlined in Figure 13.1. First, an assessor computes the **assessed value** (taxable value) of each piece of property from an estimate of the property's market value

Figure 13.1

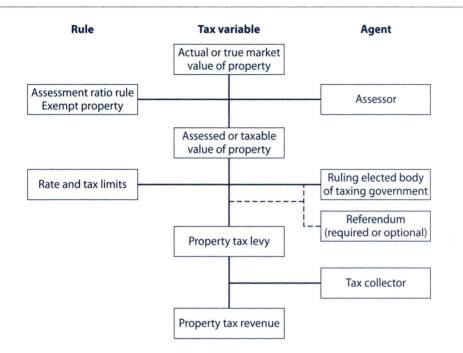

Property tax process

according to a specific set of procedures, usually established by state law. Given that estimate of market value, the assessed value is specified by law or common practice as some specific percentage of market value, called the **assessment ratio rule**, or at least must be within some specified range of percentage of market value. Tax assessors are now most often professional employees of general-purpose local governments such as cities and townships, although in some areas assessors are elected local government officials. In most states, local assessors are constrained by state laws and procedures, and county and/or state officials review assessments. Assessment practices and procedures are discussed in greater detail later in this chapter.

If different types or classes of property are assessed according to different assessment ratio rules so that the effective rate varies for different types of properties, the tax is called a **classified property tax**. Classified taxes exist in 18 states, usually with residential property assessed at a lower ratio than commercial and industrial property. For instance, in Tennessee, residential property is assessed at 25 percent of market value, commercial and industrial property at 40 percent of market value, and utilities at 55 percent of value. Classification provides a way to alter the distribution of property tax burden among different types of property. In addition, some types of property may be exempt from property tax. The assessed value of these properties is implicitly set equal to zero, although in practice assessors usually do not consider or evaluate exempt properties.

The revenue from any tax is computed by multiplying the tax base by a tax rate. Given the total assessed value of all properties in a taxing jurisdiction, therefore, the governing body of each local government—such as the city council, town commission, or school district board—sets a tax rate sufficient to generate the desired property tax revenue. In every state, state laws constrain the local governments in setting the property tax rate by limiting the tax rate, property tax revenue, or both. States vary greatly in both the types and magnitudes of these limits, as described in Chapter 11. In some cases, a referendum (popular vote) is required to approve or select the property tax rate or revenue.

Property tax rates have been specified in **mills** historically, with the property tax rate referred to as the **millage**. One mill is one-tenth of 1 percent, or $1 of tax for each $1,000 of taxable value. Recently, the term mills has been used less in favor of characterizing the property tax rate as a percentage (similar to other tax rates) or by dollars per unit of taxable value. Both reduce misunderstanding of, and confusion about, the property tax.

The property **tax levy**, or **bill**, for each property is determined from the tax rate and the assessed value for each property. A tax collector, often the municipal or county treasurer, then collects the property taxes. A single local government commonly collects the total property tax bill on a given piece of property, even though that tax liability reflects rates imposed by several overlapping local governments. The property tax collections are then divided among the taxing jurisdictions proportional to their rates. In most states, property taxes are collected annually or semiannually. Many individual homeowners with mortgages pay a monthly amount to the mortgage lender (with their mortgage interest and principal payment) to cover property taxes; the government then collects the property tax from the financial institution according to the property tax collection schedule.

The following sample property tax computations illustrate the process. Suppose that state law requires that all properties be assessed at 50 percent of market value and that the tax rate (the sum of tax rates for all the taxing local governments) in the jurisdiction where the single-family house is located is $50 per $1,000 of assessed value, whereas the tax rate in the jurisdiction where the commercial office building is located is $40 per $1,000 of assessed value. After the market values of these properties are estimated, the tax can be computed:

Tax Variable	Single Family House	Commercial Office Building
Market Value	$200,000	$5,000,000
Assessed Value	$100,000	$2,500,000
Tax Rate	$50 per $1,000 of AV	$40 per $1,000 of AV
Tax	$ 5,000	$ 100,000
	($50 × $100)	($40 × $2,500)
Effective Rate	2.5%	2.0%
(tax as a % of	($5,000/$200,000)	($100,000/$5,000,000)
market value)		

The **effective rate** of tax, the ratio of tax to market value, is a useful way to characterize property tax levels on different properties or in different jurisdictions. Because tax is compared to market value, the effective rate corrects for any difference in assessment ratio. Stating that the property tax is 2.5 percent of value, as with the single-family house in the example, is much clearer than explaining the tax rate in mills and with the assessment ratio.

Although property taxes primarily are local government taxes, the state government also plays a role in the property tax process to a varying degree in different states. The state government plays a leading role in two states, Maryland and Montana, where a state agency handles all property assessment. The more common model is for initial property assessment to be done locally, although subject to procedures specified by the state, with the state government performing subsequent reviews of assessments. In most cases, the essence of the review is to ensure that each local government applies the assessment ratio rule in aggregate for all property in the jurisdiction, if not for each property. The approach is to equalize the aggregate assessment ratio for all local governments at the state standard. To accomplish this, the state specifies a proportion by which all property values in a community are multiplied, which increases the assessment ratio to the standard. For instance, if a local government assesses at a ratio of 40 percent of market value when the state standard is 50 percent, the state could impose an equalization factor of 1.25; a 25-percent increase in assessments brings the locality up to the state standard.

State governments have adopted uniform assessment ratio standards primarily for two reasons. First, taxable property value per capita or per student may be used to allocate state aid, with more aid going to less wealthy communities, that is, those with lower per-capita assessed values. This creates an obvious incentive for local governments to underassess so they can be eligible for more state aid. Assessment equalization is an attempt to avoid this problem by ensuring that assessed values are consistent measures across different localities. Second, uniform assessment ratio rules also may improve the equity of assessment within localities, moving toward the objective that all taxpayers in a given community with property of equal market value pay the same tax. For these purposes, it does not matter what assessment ratio is selected, just that it is consistent across properties and communities. Of course, differences in assessments may not lead to differences in taxes if property values adjust in response to the different assessments. Such a possibility is considered in the next chapter.

Who Is Responsible for Property Tax Increases?

Separating responsibility for assessing property and setting tax rates can contribute to taxpayer confusion about who is responsible for property tax increases. If property is required to be assessed at a given percentage of market value, then increases in the market value of property (even increases consistent with a general rise in prices) *should* lead to increases in assessed values. If assessed values increase and tax rates remain constant, however, property tax revenues will increase. In other words, a general rise in property values allows local governments to increase property tax collections without increasing tax rates. Not surprisingly, some individuals are led to conclude that the assessment increase *caused* the tax increase.[3]

---

[3]The same process happens with any other tax; for instance, income tax revenues increase as incomes increase. However, with property taxes, unlike the others, the base is set by a government official.

This view is not correct because each local government with property tax authority controls and selects, either explicitly or implicitly, the amount of property tax revenue to levy. Typically, the assessed values for a community are determined and known before the local governments adopt their budgets for the coming fiscal year. Given those tax bases, the governing bodies can adjust the amount of property tax revenue by adjusting tax rates. A decision to keep tax rates constant, knowing that assessed values have increased, is a decision to increase property tax revenue. The announcement by a local government that "taxes will not be increased this year" must be scrutinized to determine whether the tax rate or the tax revenue is being held constant. It may be easier politically to increase tax collections by keeping rates constant (with increased assessed values) rather than by increasing rates (when assessed values do not increase), but there is no fiscal difference.

The possibility for assessors (rather than elected government officials) to bear the political responsibility for property tax increases has induced a number of states to adopt truth-in-taxation procedures. Typically, these procedures require local governments to establish the property tax rate that will generate the same amount of *revenue* in the next fiscal year as was collected in the previous year, given the known change in assessed values. If the local government wants to set a tax rate greater than this "equal revenue" rate, special procedures are required, usually including advertising the proposed tax increase, public hearings, and a specific vote of the local governing body on the property tax rate. A sample newspaper advertisement of the proposed increase and hearings required by the Michigan law is shown in Figure 13.2. The purpose of these truth-in-taxation laws is to ensure the appropriate political accountability for property tax decisions.

PROPERTY ASSESSMENT

Taxable Property: Types, Numbers, Values

Beginning in 1957 and continuing to 1987, the US Census Bureau collected and reported detailed data for the number of parcels and assessed values of real property in six property use categories as part of the Census of Governments, which is completed every five years for the years ending in "2" and "7." This Census survey, called *Taxable Property Values*, also included estimates of assessed values compared to market values for selected categories of taxable property. These data not only provided consistent, national estimates of taxable properties in various classes, but also permitted assessors and other officials in individual states to compare their assessment practices to the standard in those states and to the practices of other states.

For the 1992 Census of Governments, the Census Bureau collected and reported a much less comprehensive set of data regarding taxable property values. Only assessed values for real property (buildings and equipment), personal property, and land are listed. There is no information about the number of properties and, importantly, no comparisons of assessed value and market value. Since 1992

Figure 13.2

INSTRUCTIONS TO NEWSPAPERS

The following notice is required by Act 5, P.A. 1982, which provides:
1. The body of the notice must be set in 12 point type or larger.
2. The headline "Notice of Public Hearing on Increasing Property Taxes" must be set in 18 point type or larger.
3. The notice cannot be smaller than 8 vertical column inches by 4 horizontal inches.
5. The notice cannot be placed in the portion of the newspaper reserved for legal notices or classified advertising.

Truth in taxation notice

Notice of Public Hearing on Increasing Property Taxes

The _____
name of governing today

of the _____
name of taxing unit

will hold a public hearing on a proposed

increase of _____ mills in the operating tax
rate

millage rate to be levied in _____.
year

The hearing will be held on _____,
day

_____ at _____
date   time

o'clock in the ☐ a.m. ☐ p.m. at

_____
place—address

If adopted, the proposed additional millage will increase operating revenues from ad valorem property taxes   % over such revenues generated by levies permitted without holding a hearing.

The taxing unit publishing this notice, and identified below, has complete authority to establish the number of mills to be levied from within its authorized millage rate.

This notice is published by:

name of taxing unit

address

address

telephone no.

SOURCE: Michigan Department of Treasury

Table 13.3

Assessed Property Values by Type, 1991

Type of Property	Amount (billions of dollars)	Percent of Gross or Net Assessed Value
Gross Assessed Value	$6924.2	100%
Tax exempt portion	242.6	3.5
Net Assessed Value	6681.6	100%
State Assessed Property	285.8	4.3
Locally Assessed Property	6395.8	95.7
Real Property	5806.7	86.9
Personal Property	589.0	8.8

SOURCE: U.S. Department of Commerce, 1992 Census of Governments, *Taxable Property Values.*

(for the 1997 and 2002 Census of Governments), the Census Bureau no longer collects and reports even these data. As a consequence, current information about the nature of taxable property values nationally is lacking. Instead, each state usually publishes data about taxable property values in that state However, major differences in definitions and calculation methods often mean that these various state reports are not comparable. Most professional analysts of state and local government finance, therefore, find the decision by the Census Bureau to discontinue the *Taxable Property Values* report unfortunate.

The most recent report from the 1992 Census of Government reports assessed value data for 1991, as shown in Table 13.3. Total taxable assessed value was more than $6.9 trillion.[4] The Census Bureau first characterizes property by whether it is initially assessed by local governments, which includes nearly 96 percent of total assessed value, or by state governments, which is the other 4 percent of value and mostly is composed of railroads, telephone companies, and other utility property. The locally assessed property is then divided into **real property** (land and buildings), which represents 87 percent of total assessed value and **personal property** (equipment, inventories, motor vehicles, and household property), which represents about 9 percent of total assessed value (state-assessed represents the other 4 percent).

In most states, all real property is subject to property taxation with the exception of real property owned by governments and religious and charitable organizations, although as noted the degree of taxation may vary by type of real property. Much less uniformity exists in the property tax treatment of tangible personal property. Commercial and industrial personal property, which generally means business equipment and fixtures that are not permanently attached to buildings, is taxed in most states. Business inventories, on the other hand, are included in personal property and taxed in only about one-third of the states. Motor vehicles

---

[4]If the value of taxable property increased at the average rate of prices for all consumer goods since 1991 and assessment ratios remained constant, total assessed value would be about $10 trillion in 2005.

Figure 13.3

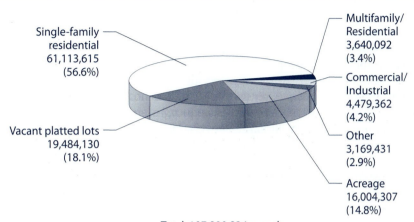

Single-family
residential
61,113,615
(56.6%)

Vacant platted lots
19,484,130
(18.1%)

Multifamily/
Residential
3,640,092
(3.4%)

Commercial/
Industrial
4,479,362
(4.2%)

Other
3,169,431
(2.9%)

Acreage
16,004,307
(14.8%)

Total: 107,890,834 parcels

Number of locally
assessed taxable
real property
parcels by use
category: 1986

SOURCE: U.S. Department of Commerce, 1987 Census of Governments, *Taxable Property Value*

Table 13.4

Michigan Taxable Property Values, 2002

Type of Property	Total Taxable Value (millions of dollars)	Real Property	Personal Property	Percentage of Total by Property Type
Agriculture	$7,911.1	$7,910.6	$0.5	2.9%
Commercial	48,666.6	37,625.0	11,041.6	17.7
Industrial	29,501.7	18,082.5	11,419.2	10.7
Residential	180,842.8	180,641.2	201.7	65.8
Utility	7,625.6	0.0	7,625.6	2.8
Other	493.0	493.0	0.0	0.1
Total	$275,040.9	$244,752.3	$30,288.6	100
Percentage of Total	100	89	11	

SOURCE: Michigan Department of Treasury. *The Michigan Property Tax, Real and Personal, 2002*. Lansing, Michigan, June 2003.

are taxed as personal property in many states, but household personal property such as furniture, appliances, clothes, and the like are broadly taxed in only a few states. When personal property is broadly taxed, it is usually not specifically and separately assessed, but rather a value is imputed as a percentage of the house value.

As always, these averages obscure substantial differences among the states. As noted previously, the absence of comparable state-by-state Census data, however, makes it very difficult to identify those differences. To help illustrate the categories of assessed value better, taxable property value data for Michigan are shown in Table 13.4. In Michigan, property is identified as one of seven different types, although just five categories account for essentially all the value. Those main categories are residential (single- and multifamily dwellings—nearly 66 percent of assessed value), commercial (office buildings, stores, warehouses, and equipment—nearly 18 percent), industrial (manufacturing plants and equipment—nearly 11 percent), agricultural property (farms and land—about 3 percent), and utility property (electricity, natural gas, and communications facilities—about 3 percent). Aggregating all categories, real property (land and buildings) accounts for 89 percent of taxable value, and personal property (mostly business equipment and fixtures) represents only about 11 percent of the total.

The data for Michigan illustrate several factors that also generally apply nationally. Residential property, and especially single-family homes, constitute in value and number the largest single class of property subject to property taxes. In 1986, for instance, single-family homes represented about 45 percent of the total assessed value nationally and 57 percent of the parcels of assessed property. Of course, a large residential property share does not automatically translate into a large single-family value share, as rental property is more important in some parts of the nation than others.

Commercial property provides the second largest share of taxable property value. In general, the share of value from commercial and industrial property is somewhat less varied from state-to-state than for residential property, although the range is still large. Not surprisingly, the average value of a typical commercial or industrial property is substantially greater than the average value of residential property. Therefore, the share of commercial and industrial properties is much less than the share of commercial and industrial property *value*.

It is important to remember that any interstate differences reflect both differences in the state economies and differences in state rules regarding what types of property are subject to tax and how they are assessed. For instance, two states may have the same amount of all types of property, but one state chooses to assess commercial and industrial property at a smaller fraction of value than residential property and the other assesses both at the same ratio. As a result, the commercial and industrial share of assessed value is greater in the second state than in the first, and the residential share is correspondingly greater in the first.

Assessment Methods

Property assessors use three basic methods to estimate market values of properties from which assessed values can be determined. The three approaches, which differ in the data used to estimate value, are (1) the comparative sales approach, which uses data from actual sales and property characteristics to estimate the values for properties that are not sold; (2) the cost approach, which bases the value on historic cost adjusted for depreciation and construction cost changes; and (3) the income approach, which measures value by the present value (sometimes called capitalized value) of the future net income expected to be generated by the property. In most instances, the comparative sales approach is used to assess single-family homes and land for which there are often numerous sales, while the cost and income approaches are usually used for commercial and industrial properties, which may be unique and for which comparative sales data are not available.

To implement the comparative sales approach, the assessor first prepares a listing of all properties, including their location and physical characteristics—often called a *tax roll*. Sale prices for some of those properties can be used to estimate statistically implicit values (sometimes called *shadow prices*) for property characteristics. Using standard appraisal techniques, the assessor combines the value of each characteristic with the quantity of those characteristics in a property to estimate the total value of the whole property. As an illustration, suppose that a statistical analysis of sales prices and property characteristics of single-family homes yields the following regression:

$$V = 10{,}000 + 75 \; FT + 18{,}000 \; BATH + 4{,}000 \; BR + 4{,}500 \; GAR$$

where

V = value of the house (observed for sales)

FT = square footage of the house

$BATH$ = number of bathrooms

BR = number of bedrooms

GAR = number of stalls in the garage

These results are simply estimates of the average effect of these characteristics on value. The interpretation is that an additional square foot of space adds $75 to the value, an additional bathroom $18,000, an additional bedroom $4,000, and so on. These results for houses that actually sold can be used to estimate value for those that do not sell in a particular period if the characteristics of all houses are known. A 2,000-square-foot house with two baths, three bedrooms, and a two-car garage would have an estimated market value of $217,000, whereas a 1,600-square-foot house with one bath, three bedrooms, and a one-car garage would be expected to have a value of $169,000.[5]

Although it is theoretically possible to reassess properties each year, in most cases properties are assessed based on their specific characteristics only at selected intervals, for instance, every 10 years. This may be because the characteristics of properties are not updated each year or because the statistical analysis is not done each year. If specific reassessment is infrequent, some method for estimating changes in values in the intervening period is required. One common method is to subdivide an assessing jurisdiction into areas or neighborhoods, measure the percentage change in values each year in that neighborhood based on sales data, and apply that percentage to all properties in the neighborhood. This method is more accurate the greater the homogeneity of the properties and the less the characteristics of the properties are altered. Some states do reassess annually, however, with

---

[5]For the 2000-square-foot house, the computation is $10,000 + $75 · 2000 + $18000 · 2 + $4000 · 3 + $4500 · 2. The computation for the smaller house is similar.

the help of computers. If the assessment roll is computerized, changes in characteristics can be entered as they occur (using data from building permits, for instance) and used with annual estimates of shadow prices to estimate annual values.

The cost approach to assessment is based on the principle that the market value of a property cannot be greater than the cost of constructing that property. If an identical duplicate of an existing structure can be constructed for $100,000, then no informed buyer would pay more than that $100,000 for the existing structure. (This refers to the value of the structure only; the land on which the structure sits has a value of its own.) On the other hand, the market value of an existing structure, which depends on the demand for structures of that type, can be less than the construction cost. Of course, people usually do not consider constructing an identical duplicate of an existing structure, but rather they build a replacement for that structure (it is impossible to construct a 15-year-old factory, for instance). Accordingly, the historic cost of a structure must be adjusted for economic depreciation and any change in construction costs to get an estimate of the maximum potential market value of the existing property. To make these adjustments, assessors use factors specific to location and property type that are provided by state governments or appraisal firms to adjust historic cost. For instance, a factor of .5 for retail stores after 10 years implies a 50-percent reduction from cost for that type of property with that age. To implement the cost approach, assessors require up-to-date adjustment factors and detailed data on historic cost for different components of all properties to be assessed.

The income approach to assessment is based on the notion that the value of an asset depends on the demand for that asset, and that demand depends on the net income or profit that asset will generate. The following example illustrates the principle.

Suppose an apartment building has 20 apartments, each renting for $500 per month, thus generating revenue of $120,000 per year ($500 × 12 × 20). The annual cost of owning and operating the apartment building, including all opportunity costs, is $100,000, so that the annual net income or profit is $20,000. This building is expected to continue to operate in exactly the same way for the next 20 years (although this is unrealistic because costs may rise or rents fall as the building becomes older), and the building will be worth $0 at the end of that period. A potential buyer can therefore expect to receive net income of $20,000 per year for the next 20 years from the building.

What is the maximum amount a buyer would be willing to pay now for that stream of future profits? The answer is the present value of the stream, which depends on the buyer's discount rate—that is, the rate that could be earned on alternative investments. If that rate is 8 percent, the present value of $20,000 per year for 20 years is $212,072. That is, $212,072 invested now at 8 percent will generate the same income as receiving $20,000 a year for 20 years. Therefore, the value of the apartment building is the value of the net income the building will generate, or $212,072. (In addition, the land on which the building sits must be valued.)[6]

Implementing the income method requires data on current profits of the business or operation, an assumption about future conditions in the market of this business, the expected future life of the asset, and an appropriate discount rate. Firms may be unwilling to divulge detailed profit information, and the other required factors are likely to be very uncertain. Not surprisingly, different applications of the income method can lead to substantially different value assessments.

Perhaps the preferred method of assessing commercial and industrial properties is to use both the cost and income approaches when feasible and to use a weighted average of the two estimates to determine assessed value. In many cases, however, the absence of solid current and future income data prevents use of the income approach, so assessment based on cost plus depreciation still is the most common approach for business properties.

This basic discussion of property assessment methods does not do service to the many difficult economic, procedural, and legal problems that can occur when applying these basic ideas and approaches. Problems can arise in defining types of property, in interpreting tax implications of various contractual conditions, in acquiring and interpreting economic data, in defining the relevant market for a property, and in many others areas. One of these problems, which shows the interaction of legal and economic principles, is discussed in Application 13.1. Partly for these reasons, property assessment has become a specific profession, regulated by many state governments and with its own professional association, the International Association of Assessing Officers (IAAO).

Considering the complexity of assessing, assessors could became frustrated in trying to measure the true market value of taxable properties. Assessors do seem to maintain a sense of humor regarding their many challenges, however, as reflected in the well known "assessor's poem":

> *To find a value good and true*
> *Here are three things for you to do:*
> *Consider your replacement cost,*
> *Determine value that is lost,*
> *Analyze your sales to see*
> *What market value really should be.*
> *Now if these suggestions are not clear,*
> *Copy the figures you used last year!*[7]

---

[6]The formula for the present value of $1 to be received or paid t years in the future is

$$PV = 1/(1 + i)^t,$$

where i = discount rate, usually the interest rate available on alternative investments or projects. The present value of the 20-year stream of profits is

$$\sum_{t=0}^{19} 20,000/(1.08)^t.$$

[7]I thank Professor William Bogart for suggesting this "real world" insight.

OPPORTUNITY COST AND THE VALUE OF LEASED COMMERCIAL PROPERTIES

Suppose that a business signs a long-term (say, 10-year) lease for commercial office or retail space at a monthly rent of $10 per square foot. Five years after this lease is signed, however, rents on similar properties have risen to $12 per square foot, per month. This tenant continues to pay $10 because the owner is prevented from raising the rent by the contract. Has the value of this property increased, should the assessed value rise, and if so, who should be liable for any increased tax, the tenant or the owner?

Several institutional details are relevant. In most states, both the real and personal property involved are taxed. In some commercial rentals, the building owner commonly provides a shell, with the tenant adding and *owning* the interior, including walls, floors, fixtures, and display materials. Therefore, some of the real property (that is permanently attached to the building) may be owned by the building owner and some by the tenant, although the tenant generally owns the personal property. Moreover, many commercial lease contracts specify that the tenant pays all property taxes, not just the personal property component.

Economically, this tenant has enjoyed a gain due to the rise in market rents for similar properties. The opportunity cost of the asset—the leased property—has increased, but the actual cost to the tenant remains constant. This business enjoys lower costs for the remaining length of the contract than for competitors who must pay the current market rent of $12. This tenant could even sublease the property for the $12 market rent and realize the gain. Economic principles imply therefore that the assessed value of the leased property based on the income approach to assessing should increase (to keep the assessed value at a percentage of market value), and that the tenant should be liable for the tax increase (because the gain is to the tenant).

Several legal complications are involved, however. Suppose the tenant's contract specifically prohibits subleasing. A basic legal principle holds that one cannot sell what one does not own; this suggests that because the tenant's gain is not marketable, there is no gain in market value. Suppose that subleasing is not prohibited, but the tenant still does not engage in subleasing. The tenant has a property right but no explicit gain, so some argue that this property is intangible and thus not taxed under most property taxes (which usually apply only to tangible property). Finally, suppose the lease contract requires the building owner to pay real property taxes and the tenant to pay the tax on any personal property. The increase in market rents has increased the value of the rental space—the building—but the implicit gain goes to the tenant, not the building owner. In fact, the building owner is prevented from capturing the gain by the contractually specified rent, which makes it inappropriate to increase the assessed value of the building and increase the owner's tax. An

Application 13.1 — Opportunity Cost and the Value of Leased Commercial Properties

alternative is to define a new type of personal property, called *leasehold interests,* which is equal to the difference between market and contracted rent, and to assess that interest to the personal property of the tenant.

Although this specific issue is interesting and important, the purpose of this application is to illustrate the nature of problems that can arise in determining market and assessed values in actual, complicated situations. Even when market prices or values are observable, applying the assessment approaches to determine an accepted value is not always a straightforward process.

Evaluating Assessment Results

Given that property assessment is a difficult task, how can assessment quality be measured, how good of a job are assessors actually doing, and what accounts for less–than-perfect assessment (leaving to Chapter 14 the issue of the economic effects of nonuniform assessment)? Assessment quality has traditionally been measured by the variation in assessment ratios for different properties within the same assessing jurisdiction. This measure presumes that good assessment involves uniform assessment ratios for different properties, rather than achieving any specific assessment ratio. That is, assessing all properties at 40 percent of value when the legal target is 50 percent is better than assessing some at 40 percent and some at 60 percent. The statistic commonly used to measure the variation in assessment ratios within a community is the **coefficient of dispersion**, which is the *average percentage deviation from the median assessment ratio.* A sample coefficient of dispersion is shown in Table 13.5.

Table 13.5

Sample Coefficient of Dispersion for Assessment Ratios, Single-Family Houses, One City

Amount or Calculation	Property		
	A	B	C
Market Value	$ 40,000	$ 60,000	$100,000
Assessed Value	$ 25,000	$ 30,000	$ 40,000
Assessment Ratio	.625	.50	.40
Median Assessment Ratio		.50	
Difference from Median Ratio	.125	0	.10
Average Difference		.075	
		(.125 + .10)/3	
Average Percentage Difference or Coefficient of Dispersion		.15	
		(.075/.50)	

In the table, the actual sales prices of three properties are compared to their assessed values at the time of sale (so the assessor did not have the sales information when making the assessment). Property B is assessed at 50 percent of its actual sales value, which is assumed to be the statutory assessment ratio; property A is overassessed at 62.5 percent of value; and property C is underassessed at 40 percent of the market price. Therefore, the median (middle) assessment ratio is .50, and the coefficient of dispersion (the average percentage difference from the median) is .15, which means that, on average, assessment ratios vary 15 percent from the median.

Actual coefficients of dispersion of assessment ratios within jurisdictions for single-family houses have been computed in the past by the Census Bureau for individual assessing districts based on sales data and prior assessed values, with the distribution and median reported for each state. For all states in 1981, the median coefficient of dispersion was .213, or 21.3 percent variation of assessment ratios within assessing jurisdictions. The information in Table 13.5 represents a more uniform assessment result than was typical in 1981. State coefficients of dispersion for 1981 varied from a low of 11.4 percent to a high of 52.0 percent, with only eight states showing a median coefficient of 15 or lower. At that time, at least, the information shown in Table 13.5 represented very good assessment compared to actual practice.

A potential economic reason for the lack of assessment uniformity is that property assessment is costly and competes with all other government services for a share of the available budget resources. For instance, assessment results can be improved by reducing the time between complete reexamination and reevaluation of all properties, which requires more assessing and appraisal personnel, or by increasing the use of computers to store characteristics data about properties and analyzing and applying sales data, which requires not only more computers but also appropriately trained assessing officials. The nature of the community also influences the cost of assessing. Assessing is likely to be more costly in communities with a very heterogeneous property mix than in those with a homogeneous one because assessing some types of large commercial and industrial properties is more difficult than houses or land, and maintaining uniform assessments is more difficult in communities with rapid growth and changes than in more stable communities. Because of its costs, "good" assessment should be less in demand in lower-income states and states that make relatively low use of property taxes. In fact, of the nine states with the highest coefficients of dispersion of assessment ratios within communities in 1981—all at 33 percent or greater—eight had per-capita incomes below the national average, eight had property taxes as a lower percentage of personal income than the national average, and seven had property taxes that were a smaller fraction of total taxes than nationally.

PROPERTY TAX-RELIEF OR REDUCTION MEASURES

States use a variety of measures to reduce property taxes for specific classes of property or specific types of taxpayers. Often, these measures are advocated as a way of making the property tax and the overall state–local tax structure more progressive by reducing relative tax burdens for lower-income taxpayers. Five such methods of tax relief are considered here, including limits on assessed values, exemptions of assessed value for homesteads, state government credits or rebates for local residential property taxes, state and federal individual income tax deductions for property taxes, and special assessment methods for farmland. Broad property tax relief also may be provided by intergovernmental grants (discussed in Chapter 9) and property tax limits (discussed in Chapter 11), while targeted property tax relief for businesses may be used as an economic development tool (discussed in Chapter 22). The discussion here focuses on those methods that are intended to reduce residential and agricultural property tax burdens specifically, as shown in Table 13.6.[8]

Limits on Assessed Values

In an effort to restrain property tax growth or to limit assessment of some property types, some states have imposed limits on the changes in the assessed value of properties, effectively limiting the growth of property tax bases. Typically, the annual growth in the assessed value of each property of a particular type (houses) must be less than a fixed amount, for instance 5 percent; however, the properties can be fully assessed according to their full market value when they are sold. At that time, the market value is obviously known, and assessed value can be set using the appropriate assessment ratio rule. Selectively reassessing properties at the time of sale may, in fact, lead to less uniform assessment, however, because different properties sell at different rates. A single-family house that sells three times in 10 years would have an assessed value closer to the nominal assessment ratio than one that is owned and occupied by one family for a longer period, say 30 years.

The experience of California since the adoption of Proposition 13 in 1978 illustrates that problem. That state constitutional amendment was primarily intended to reduce and limit the growth of property taxes. To achieve these objectives, the amendment set assessed values of each property equal to market value in 1976 and limited the annual growth from that value to no more than 2 percent, except when a property is sold or added to by new construction. When sold, a property is reassessed at the current market value, and any newly constructed portions of a property are similarly assessed at current value. Because the assessed value of any property that is not sold or altered by new construction cannot increase by more than 2 percent per year regardless of the actual rate of increase in market values, the assessment ratio for these properties will continually decline as long as market prices are rising more then 2 percent. For properties that turn over in the market, the assessed value will reflect the actual market value. As a result, identical properties may be assessed at different amounts and therefore have different effective tax rates even if located in the same jurisdiction.

A study by Michael Wiseman (1986) of effective property tax rates in San Francisco confirms this expectation. Wiseman reports a coefficient of dispersion in 1984 for

---

[8]It is impossible in one table or in the text to capture fully the details of state differences in property tax features. For more information, see information published by the Federation of Tax Administrators, the National Conference of State Legislatures, and the individual states.

Table 13.6

State Property Tax Relief Methods, 2002

Legend		
	X	has feature
	A	all homeowners and/or renters
	L	limited, specific groups
	S	seniors
	D	deferred taxation or recapture
	U	use value assessment

State & Region	Residential Circuit Breaker	Homestead Exemption or Credit	Tax Deferral	Deduction from State Income Tax	Special Farmland Assessment
New England					
Connecticut	S	L		X	U
Maine	A	A	S	X	D
Massachusetts	S	L	S[a]		D
New Hampshire		S[a]	S	Limited tax	D, Contracts
Rhode Island	S			X	D
Vermont	A	L		X	D, U, Contracts
Middle Atlantic					
Delaware				X[b]	D
District of Columbia				X	Contracts
Maryland	A	A	S	X	D
New Jersey	A	A			D
New York	A	A		X[b]	D, U
Pennsylvania	S	L	S[a]		D, Contracts
Great Lakes					
Illinois	S	A	S		U, D
Indiana	S	A			U, D
Michigan	A		S[a]		U, Contracts
Ohio	S	A[b]			D, U
Wisconsin	A	A	S[a]		Tax credits
Plains					
Iowa	S	A	A	X	U
Kansas	A	L		X	D
Minnesota	A	A	S	X	D
Missouri	S				U, D
Nebraska		S		X	D
North Dakota	S		S[a]	X	U
South Dakota	S		S[a]	No tax	U
Southeast					
Alabama		A		X	D
Arkansas		A		X	U
Florida		A	A	No tax	U, D
Georgia		A	S[a]	X	Contracts
Kentucky		S		X	D
Louisiana		A		X	U
Mississippi		A		X	U
North Carolina		S[a]		X	D
South Carolina		A		X	D
Tennessee		S[a]	S[a]	Limited tax	D

Table 13.6

(continued)

State & Region	Residential Circuit Breaker	Homestead Exemption or Credit	Tax Deferral	Deduction from State Income Tax	Special Farmland Assessment
Virginia		S	S[a]	X	D
West Virginia	S	S			U
Southwest					
Arizona	S	A	S[a]	X	U
New Mexico	S	A		X	U
Oklahoma	S	A		X	U
Texas		A		No tax	D, Contracts
Rocky Mountain					
Colorado	S	S	S	X	U
Idaho	S	A		X	U
Montana	A	A		X	U
Utah	S	A	S	X	D
Wyoming	A[b]		S[a]	No tax	U
Far West					
Alaska	S[c]	S		No tax	D
California	S[c]	A	S	X	U, Contracts
Hawaii	Local	A		X	D, Contracts
Nevada	S[c]			No tax	D
Oregon	S[c]		S	X	D
Washington	S	S[a]	S	No tax	Contracts

[a]Low income only

[b]Real property only

[c]Renters only

SOURCES: NCSL. *A Guide to Property Taxes: Property Tax Relief.* November 2002.

Russell, Faith. *Individual Income Tax Provisions in the States.* Madison: Wisconsin Legislative Fiscal Bureau, 1999.

US Census Bureau. *Taxable Property Values.* 1992 Census of Governments, 1994.

single-family houses of 0.58, consistent with the 0.53 coefficient reported by the Census Bureau for San Francisco for 1982. In contrast, four different studies for the years between 1971 and 1978, the last year before Proposition 13 took effect, found coefficients of dispersion in the city of between 0.09 and 0.16. Substantially less uniformity of assessment ratios exists for single-family houses since Proposition 13 than before. Wiseman concludes that "in 1978, a majority of California voters chose to sacrifice equity in property taxation for certainty regarding year-to-year changes in tax liability" (1986, p. 31).

An illustration of the California case is given in Table 13.7. Market values are assumed to increase 5 percent per year, but assessed values can increase only 2 percent per year until the property is sold. At sale, the property can be assessed at its market value. House A rises in value from $100,000 to $121,554 over five years, but because it is never sold, assessed value rises only from $100,000 to $108,243. By the fifth year, House A is assessed well below its true market value. Assuming a constant tax rate of $20 per $1,000 of assessed value, tax on House A increases from

Table 13.7

Assessment and Property Tax with Assessment Limits

Market values increase 5 percent annually; assessed values are limited to maximum 2 percent annual growth until home is sold; at sale, reassessment to market value.

Year	House A	House B	House C
1	V = 100,000 AV = 100,000 T = 2000[a]	V = 100,000 AV = 100,000 T = 2000	V = 90,000 AV = 90,000 T = 1800
2	V = 105,000 AV = 102,000 T = 2040	V = 105,000 AV = 102,000 T = 2040 Sale	V = 94,500 AV = 91,800 T = 1836
3	V = 110,250 AV = 104,040 T = 2081	V = 110,250 AV = 110,250 T = 2205	V = 99,225 AV = 93,636 T = 1873
4	V = 115,763 AV = 106,121 T = 2122	V = 115,763 AV = 112,455 T = 2249	V = 104,186 AV = 95,509 T = 1910
5	V = 121,551 AV = 108,243 T = 2165	Sale V = 121,551 AV = 121,551 T = 2431	Sale V = 109,395 AV = 109,395 T = 2188

[a]Tax Rate = $20 per $1,000 of assessed value. Tax equals Rate × Assessed Value or $20/$1,000; $100,000 = $2000 in this case.

$2,000 to $2,165. House B is identical to House A, except that House B sells twice in this five-year period. When House B is sold and reassessed in the third year, the assessed value and tax become greater than for the identical House A. By the fifth year and second sale of House B, the difference is even greater. Even though Houses A and B remain identical, B's assessed value and taxes are much greater.

Similarly, full reassessment at sale also can cause the taxes on a lower-value house to be greater than those for a higher-value house. House C begins with a value of $90,000, which rises to $109,395 after five years. However, because House C is sold in the fifth year, its assessed value ($109,395) and tax ($2,188) then actually is greater than House A, assessed at $108,443 but with a market value of more than $121,500.

These types of inequities led some taxpayers to challenge the California law as unconstitutional, arguing that tax differences for similar properties violated the contributional guarantee of "equal protection under the law." In a 1992 decision (*Nordlinger v. Hahn*), however, the U.S. Supreme Court ruled that the California assessment is contributional. In an 8-1 vote (Justice Stevens dissenting), the court argued that this assessment procedure is allowed if it "further[s] a legitimate state interest" (Barrett, 1992). The Court believed that the desire of property owners to moderate property tax increases and the fact that the procedure encourages continuing homeownership were such legitimate interests. The Court also noted that potential homebuyers can calculate what the new property taxes will be after the house is sold, so the tax is not hidden or capricious.

In 1994, Michigan voters adopted a package of tax changes that included a limit on the growth of taxable property values similar to that in California. Annual growth of the taxable value of individual properties is limited to the lesser of 5 percent or the annual rate of inflation, until the property is sold or changes owners. At a change of ownership, properties can be reassessed at 50 percent of market value, which is the formal state standard.

By 2002, this limit had the substantial effect of reducing taxable values (Feldman, Courant, and Drake, 2003). Taxable value ($275 billion) was only about 80 percent of equalized value at the official state standard of a 50-perecnt assessment ratio ($343 billion). The difference is a measure of the amount that taxable value was reduced by the assessment limit. The limit on the growth of taxable values affected different types of properties differentially. Agricultural properties benefited the most, with taxable values less than 60 percent of what they would be without the limit. Taxable values of residential properties, on the other hand, were nearly 80 percent of what they would be otherwise. The limit likely had a greater effect for agricultural than residential property because ownership changes less often for agricultural property. So, as in California, the limit on assessed values until a property is sold led to greater variation in taxable values than previously.

Even if the procedure is constitutional, the question remains of whether it is good policy. Full assessment at sale inevitably leads to substantially different taxes for similar properties, which creates a strong incentive *not* to sell a house. Thus, individuals might not want to take a new (and better) job if it requires changing residential location, that is selling the current home and buying another, both of which are then reassessed. Or individuals might not change the nature of their housing as their life circumstances change. Often individuals buy a small house to start, switch to a larger house as the family gets bigger, and then change to a smaller or more convenient house (single floor, less land) at retirement. With reassessment at sale, each transaction leads to a higher assessed value and higher taxes. So the concern about reassessment at sale is partly an equity concern and partly an efficiency issue, as this tax policy may change people's behavior.

Homestead Exemptions and Credits

The simplest and most widely used tax-relief method for houses is exemption from taxation of a specific amount of homestead value, similar to personal exemptions that are commonly used with income taxes. In some states, a fixed amount or percent of residential property taxes are credited or rebated. These credits are similar to exemptions in that a fraction of property tax is relieved, but the value of an exemption depends on the tax rate, which is not true for a credit. Homestead exemptions or credits of some type are used in 46 states plus the District of Columbia, although only 27 allow the exemption broadly for taxpayers of all ages. Of these states, 10 limit the exemption to senior citizens and other specialized groups, and another 10 states limit homestead exemptions to specific limited groups of taxpayers only, such as veterans or disabled homeowners. As shown in Table 13.6, broadly applied homestead exemptions tend to be most common in the South and West. In some cases, the exemption/credit is a fixed amount for all eligible taxpayers; in others, the exemption/credit varies by income or some other taxpayer characteristic.

These types of homestead exemptions are illustrated by those used in Louisiana, Idaho, and Kentucky in 2002. In Louisiana, an exemption of $7,500 of assessed value applies for all homeowners. In Idaho, the exemption similarly applies to all homeowners, but the exemption is 50 percent of assessed value, up to a maximum exemption of $50,000. In Kentucky, an exemption of $26,800 of assessed value is available only for all elderly and disabled homeowners, with the value of the exemption adjusted for inflation every two years.

The operation of a simple exemption equal to $10,000 of assessed value is shown by Example 13.1.

Example 13.1

Simple Exemption Equal to $10,000 of Assessed Value

	Without Exemption	With Exemption[9]
Market Value	$100,000	$100,000
Assessed Value	$ 50,000	$ 50,000
Exemption	0	$ 10,000
Taxable Value	$ 50,000	$ 40,000
Tax Rate	$40 per $1,000 of Taxable Value	
Tax	$ 2,000	$ 1,600
New Tax Rate	$60 per $1,000 of Taxable Value	
New Tax	$ 3,000	$ 2,400
Increase in Tax	$ 1,000	$ 800
Percentage Change in Tax	50%	50%

The exemption reduces the tax by the amount of the exemption times the tax rate ($10,000 × $40/$1,000 = $400). It follows, therefore, that a given exemption is more valuable the greater the property tax rate. Also, an important point of this example is that if assessed value is greater than the exemption, the exemption does not affect tax increases. Both with and without the exemption, a 50-percent increase in the tax rate causes a 50-percent increase in tax (although from a smaller base). Tax increases from $2,000 to $3,000 if no exemption exists, but from $1,600 to $2,400 with the $10,000 assessed value exemption.

Homestead "Circuit Breaker" Tax Credits or Rebates

A third major property tax-relief mechanism, used in some form in 33 states plus the District of Columbia, is a state government-financed credit or rebate for property taxes paid to local governments. Property tax relief of this type applies to property taxes that exceed some specified percentage of a taxpayer's income (thus

---

[9]This assumes that the exemption does not affect market values, correct at least in the very short run.

the name "circuit breaker"), usually takes the form of a rebate paid to the taxpayer or a (refundable) credit against the state income tax, and generally is targeted to specific groups of taxpayers. These credits have come to be called circuit breakers because the relief applies only when a taxpayer's income is "overloaded" by property taxes. In fact, property tax credits, or circuit breakers, were devised as a way of preventing senior citizens with high-valued houses relative to their retirement income from having to sell houses because of the property tax.

Of the 34 circuit breaker property tax credit/rebate programs, 23 are limited to elderly taxpayers (or sometimes elderly and disabled taxpayers) with 19 of the 23 applying to renters as well as homeowners. Taxpayers of all ages are eligible for the credits or rebates in another 11 states, all of which allow both renters and homeowners to benefit. All but one of the states with these programs impose an income ceiling on eligibility, although that ceiling varies widely (from $3,750 in Arizona to $82,650 in Michigan for single taxpayers in 2002). The state with no income limit is Maryland, although Maryland does impose a limit of $200,000 in net worth. The 5 states with the seemingly broadest and therefore largest programs are Maryland, Michigan, Minnesota, Wisconsin, and Vermont. The credit programs in Michigan and Vermont illustrate how the general circuit-breaker idea can be applied.

Michigan

The state government program in Michigan, begun in 1974, provides property tax relief to homeowners, renters, and farmers in the form of a refundable credit against the state income tax. For most taxpayers, the credit equals 60 percent of homestead property taxes that are greater than 3.5 percent of the household's income, up to a maximum credit of $1,200. Senior citizens are eligible for credits equal to 100 percent of property taxes greater than a specified percentage of income, which varies from 0 percent to 3.5 percent by income. Renters use 20 percent of rent paid as a proxy for property tax in computing the credit. Beginning in 1992, the credit was reduced by 10 percent for each $1,000 of income above $70,950 (indexed to the Detroit CPI). Thus, households with 2002 income of $82,650 or more receive no credit. Taxpayers must have been a Michigan resident for at least six months in the tax year and may claim the credit for tax on one principal residence only. In many cases, farmers are eligible to claim the credit for taxes on their homestead and all farmland. The credit formula is

General Taxpayers	Senior Taxpayers
Credit = 60%(Tax − 3.5% Income)	Credit = (Tax − 3.5%[10] Income)
up to a maximum credit of $1,200	

In 2002, about 1.4 million Michigan taxpayers received credits from this program totaling about $682.6 million, an amount equal to about 7 percent of the residential and agricultural property taxes collected by local governments in the state.

---

[10]Or less.

The average credit among recipients was about $500. Senior citizen credits equaled about $284 million or about 42 percent of the total.

Vermont

The Vermont program, adopted in 1969, provides property tax refunds equal to all property taxes greater than a specified percentage of income, varying from 3.5 percent for incomes less than $5,000 to 5 percent for incomes of $25,000 or more. Homeowners and renters must be full-year residents to receive the refund. Taxpayers with incomes of $47,000 or greater are not eligible. The maximum rebate is $1,500, and renters use 20 percent of rent as the proxy for property tax paid. The formula is

$$\text{Rebate} = (\text{Tax} - 3.5\%[11] \text{ Income}), \text{ up to a maximum rebate of } \$1,500$$

In 2003, the Vermont program provided total property tax rebates of $25.3 million to 37,843 taxpayers, for an average rebate of about $670.

Differences and Characteristics of Tax Credit Plans

These two programs illustrate two important differences and three common characteristics of the various state property tax-credit plans. First, some of the state plans, such as the Michigan plan for senior taxpayers and the Vermont program, provide relief for *all* property taxes above the income threshold, whereas others, such as the Michigan credit for general taxpayers, provide relief for only a portion of taxes above the threshold. Second, some states follow the Michigan example by setting the eligibility threshold and ceiling so that a substantial fraction of taxpayers will receive some benefit, whereas other states limit eligibility to smaller groups, either explicitly or by the threshold and ceiling amounts. Something of a tradeoff may exist here between providing some relief to many taxpayers as opposed to providing a larger amount of relief to smaller targeted groups of taxpayers.

One common characteristic of these credits is that they reduce the **marginal cost of property taxes** for eligible taxpayers who receive less than the maximum credit or rebate. For the Vermont program and Michigan senior-citizen program, the marginal cost to a relief recipient of a property tax increase is $0 because the credit covers all property taxes over the income threshold. With the Michigan general property tax-credit program, the marginal cost of a $1 increase in property tax is $.40 because the credit covers 60 percent of the tax over the threshold. This reduction of marginal property tax cost raises the question of whether these credits induce taxpayers to support higher property taxes, an issue considered in Chapter 14.

The second common characteristic of these state programs is that they introduce some progressivity into state tax structures because their structure favors lower-income taxpayers. This is done either explicitly by limiting the program to

---

[11]For income less than $5,000; larger percentages for higher incomes.

lower-income residents or implicitly by applying a higher-income threshold in the relief formula for higher-income taxpayers.

The third common characteristic is that because these plans provide state government rebates for local property taxes, they are equivalent to a set of state grants to localities.

Income Tax Deductions for Property Taxes

Another tax feature that can reduce property taxes is the income tax deduction for residential property taxes available to federal income taxpayers who itemize deductions and to taxpayers who itemize on state income taxes (in 32 states). A deduction reduces taxes paid by the amount of the deduction multiplied by the taxpayer's marginal tax rate (the income tax rate applying to the last dollar of income). For instance, if the income tax rate is 30 percent, the taxpayer bears only 70 percent of the cost of the deductible item. If the taxpayer's property tax bill rises by $1, the deduction offsets $.30 of that increase so that the taxpayer bears only $.70.[12]

Analyzing the deductibility of property taxes is even more complicated because the deduction may be available for both federal and state income taxes. Itemizers can also deduct state income taxes against federal income taxes and can deduct federal income taxes against state taxes in eight states. If a property taxpayer deducts property taxes only on the federal income tax, the net cost per dollar of property tax is $(1 - f)$, where f represents the taxpayer's federal marginal income tax rate. If a taxpayer deducts property taxes against the state income tax and both property and state income taxes against the federal income tax, the net cost is $(1 - f)(1 - s)$, where s represents the taxpayer's marginal state income tax rate.[13] The expression for the net property tax price when there is reciprocal deductibility of state and federal income taxes is still more complicated.[14]

Regardless of the institutional structure, the federal and state income tax deductions for residential property taxes do reduce the net property tax burden for taxpayers who itemize deductions. Of course, the degree to which taxpayers with the option of itemizing deductions actually do so (rather than taking a standard deduction if available) depends on the unique characteristics of each state's situation and thus is expected to vary substantially among the states. Because the income tax reduction that occurs from a deduction equals the amount deducted times the income tax rate, the value of an income tax deduction of local property taxes depends directly on the magnitude of the income tax rate. If the income tax

---

[12]This assumes that none of the foregone income tax revenue is made up by higher income tax rates, which is a reasonable assumption for any single taxpayer to make because the increase to offset only that taxpayer's deduction would be insignificant.

[13]f percent of the property tax is offset by the federal deduction and s percent by the state deduction. However, the reduction of state income taxes equal to s reduces the federal deduction also by s, which **increases** federal tax by fs. The net cost is therefore $1 - f - s + fs$, which equals $(1 - f)(1 - s)$.

[14]See Fisher (1978, 399).

has a progressive rate structure, the value of the deduction is greater for higher-income taxpayers.

From the numbers of states with homestead exemptions or credits, state property tax circuit breakers, and state income tax deductions for property taxes, it is apparent that many states use more than one of these programs, either for the same taxpayers or for different groups of taxpayers. In fact, every state uses at least one of these methods, and 18 states plus DC use all three of these residential property tax-relief mechanisms to some degree. Most of the rest of the states use two of these programs. This is part of the reason why computing property taxes is confusing, and why comparing effective property tax burdens among different states is so difficult.

Special Assessment of Farmland

Every state uses some method of limiting property taxes on agricultural land, usually by using a different procedure for assessing farmland than other properties. The traditional approach, used by 27 states, is to assess the value of farmland in its current use, which may be less than the full market value of the land. For instance, the income approach can be used to estimate the value of farmland by capitalizing the profits generated by farming activity on the land. However, there may be alternative uses for the land that would generate a greater stream of profits and thus a higher value; these alternative uses are referred to as the highest and best use of the property.

For instance, farmland on the edge of an urban area might be more valuable if used for residential property, and rural farmland might be converted into recreational use. **Use-value assessment** of farmland prevents increases in property taxes on farmland as these alternative uses become more attractive. The traditional reason for adopting use-value assessment is to reduce the conversion of farmland into these other uses, particularly where urban areas are expanding.

Another variation of use-value assessment, now used by 31 states, allows farmland to be assessed according to current use but imposes a deferred tax on the full value for some fixed number of past years if the property is converted to a non-farm use. In this way, the tax advantage conferred by use-value assessment, at least for some number of years, is recaptured by the taxing governments if the tax advantage does not succeed in preventing conversion.[15]

Several states require a contract between the government and farmland owners for the farmland to receive preferential assessment. The contract specifies that the owner will not convert the farmland into other uses for a specific period of years, usually 10, in exchange for use-value assessment or some other tax reduction. If the owner wishes to convert the land to other uses before the contract expires, back taxes at the full value of the property are levied, and sometimes a penalty is also added.

---

[15]Some states have options for both use value assessment and deferred taxation that apply for differing circumstances. Therefore, the sum of states with each policy is greater than 50.

SUMMARY

The property tax is different from most other taxes, partly because methods and procedures for assessing the value of property for tax purposes must be part of the property tax structure.

In the typical procedure for assessing, levying, and collecting property taxes, an assessor first computes the assessed value (taxable value) of each piece of property from an estimate of the market value of the property. The assessed value is specified by law as some specific percentage of market value, called the assessment ratio rule. The governing body of each local government sets a tax rate sufficient to generate the desired property tax revenue. Property tax rates have historically been specified in mills, equal to $1 of tax per each $1,000 of taxable value. The property tax levy, or bill, for each property is determined from the tax rate and the assessed value for each property.

Real property—that is, land and buildings—represents 87 percent of total assessed value, and is further subdivided into residential, commercial (office buildings, stores, warehouses, equipment), industrial (manufacturing plants, equipment), agricultural, and utility property. Single-family homes constitute, both in value and number, the largest single class of property subject to property taxes.

Property assessors use three basic methods to estimate market and assessed values of properties: (1) the comparative sales approach, which uses data from actual sales and property characteristics to estimate the values for properties that are not sold; (2) the cost approach, which bases the value on historic cost adjusted for depreciation; and (3) the income approach, which measures value by the present value (sometimes called capitalized value) of the future net income the property is expected to generate.

Several states limit annual increases in assessed values but allow properties to be fully reassessed to market value when they are sold. Such a procedure leads to property tax inequities and creates an incentive for owners to retain their properties.

The simplest and most widely used tax-relief method for houses is a homestead exemption from taxation of a specific amount. A second major property tax-relief mechanism is a state government-financed credit or rebate for property taxes. Of the 41 states with a broad-based individual income tax, 32 also provide for deductions for local government residential property taxes.

Every state uses some method of limiting property taxes on agricultural land, usually by using a different procedure for assessing farmland than other properties.

A classified property tax is one in which the effective tax rate varies for different classes of property, usually by assessing these different property classes using different assessment ratios. Classified property taxes exist in 18 states, usually applying a lower assessment ratio to residential property than to commercial and industrial property.

DISCUSSION QUESTIONS

1. In an annual budget message, one city's mayor remarked "I am particularly pleased that due to our sound financial planning and careful budgeting, no property tax increase is needed this year." Yet a careful examination of the detailed budget submitted by the mayor showed expected property tax revenue in the coming year to be 10 percent greater than in the previous year. How can you explain the apparent contradiction in the mayor's statement and proposed budget?

2. Suppose that you live in a house with a market and taxable value of $100,000 in a community with a property tax rate of $40 per $1,000 of taxable value.

   a. What is your property tax amount?

   b. What happens to your property tax bill if the market value of your property increases by 10 percent and the assessment ratio is kept constant? What if the tax rate increases by 10 percent along with the value?

   c. Now suppose your community allows an exemption of the first $20,000 of taxable value. How much would the exemption reduce your property tax bill? What happens to your tax savings from the exemption as value increases? As the tax rate increases?

   d. Suppose instead of the exemption that you are allowed a credit equal to one-half the amount of property tax that is greater than 5 percent of your income. If your annual income is $40,000, how much does the credit reduce your property tax? What happens to your tax savings from the credit as value increases? As the tax rate increases?

3. a. Recalculate parts c and d of question 2 for a house with a market and taxable value of $200,000 now owned by someone with an income of $60,000.

   b. What is the effect of the value exemption and the credit on the progressivity of the property tax? Compare the $100,000 and $200,000 houses.

4. Suppose you are assigned to assess a 50,000-square-foot office building that currently is fully leased at $10 per square foot. The owner's annual costs of operation for the building (interest, maintenance, insurance) are $400,000. The building is 10 years old and is expected to have an additional 20 years of useful life. Assuming these market conditions continue, estimate the current market value of the building under the income approach if the discount rate is 10 percent. How does the estimate differ if the discount rate is 5 percent?

5. The magnitude of property tax and the distribution of types of property varies from state to state. Using reports (usually available online) from the

relevant state government agency, try to find the amount of property taxes collected, the importance of property taxes to local and state government budgets, how property taxes have been changing over time, and the distribution of taxable property values in your state among the three main types of property—residential, commercial and industrial.

6. One thing that makes the property tax different from other taxes is that the government must estimate each taxpayer's tax base, that is, the value of the property. This assessment process is handled differently in various states. Find out how property assessment is handled in your jurisdiction. Consider which level of government does assessing, how assessors are selected, what assessment ratio(s) is used, how often assessments are redone or how annual adjustments are made, whether local assessment is subject to state review or correction, and the procedure for taxpayers to appeal a property assessment.

SELECTED READINGS

Duncombe, William and John Yinger. "Alternative Paths to Property Tax Relief." In *Property Taxation and Local Government Finance*, edited by W. Oates. Cambridge, Massachusetts: Lincoln Institute of Land Policy, 2001, Chapter 9.

Mikesell, John L. "Patterns of Exclusion of Personal Property From American Property Tax Systems." *Public Finance Quarterly*, 20 (October 1992): 528–542.

Preston, Anne E. and Casey Ichniowski. "A National Perspective on the Nature and Effects of the Local Property Tax Revolt, 1976–1986." *National Tax Journal*, 44 (June 1991): 123–146.

Raphaelson, Arnold H. "The Property Tax." In *Management Policies in Local Government Finance*, edited by J. R. Aronson and E. Schwartz. Washington, D.C.: International City/County Management Association, Washington, 2004, Chapter 10.

Wallis, John J. "A History of the Property Tax in America." In *Property Taxation and Local Government Finance*, edited by W. Oates. Cambridge, Massachusetts: Lincoln Institute of Land Policy, 2001, Chapter 5.

Zelio, Judy. *A Guide to Property Taxes: the Role of Property Taxes in State and Local Finances*. Denver, CO: National Conference of State Legislatures, 2004.

PROPERTY TAX: ECONOMIC ANALYSIS AND EFFECTS

. . . The property tax system for the nation as a whole depresses the return on capital and changes the cost of capital to higher-tax communities and decreases the cost of capital to low-tax communities.[1]

—PETER MIESZKOWSKI

HEADLINES

"ONLY ONE-FIFTH OF PENNSYLVANIA'S 501 SCHOOL DISTRICTS DECIDED TO PARTICIPATE IN A PROGRAM THAT WOULD USE REVENUE FROM SLOT MACHINES TO REDUCE HOMEOWNER'S PROPERTY TAXES.

THE PLAN INVOLVED LEGALIZING SLOT MACHINES AND USING THE REVENUE TO PROVIDE $330 IN TAX RELIEF PER HOUSEHOLD, OR $1 BILLION IN ALL, AND TO REDUCE SCHOOL DEPENDENCE ON PROPERTY TAXES.

BUT TO QUALIFY FOR A SHARE OF THE GAMBLING REVENUE, HOWEVER, SCHOOL BOARDS WOULD HAVE TO RAISE LOCAL INCOME TAXES BY A SMALL AMOUNT AND AGREE THAT ANY FUTURE PROPERTY-TAX INCREASES EXCEEDING INFLATION WOULD NEED APPROVAL BY VOTERS.[2]"

---

[1]"The Property Tax: An Excise Tax or Profits Tax?" *Journal of Public Economics,* 1 (1972): 94.

[2]The Associated Press. "Pa. Governor Laments Rejection of Tax Plan," *http://www.nytimes.com,* June 1, 2005.

Now that you have an understanding of microeconomic analysis of taxes and the specific property tax institutions used by state–local governments, attention turns to analyzing the economic effects of property taxes. As always, those effects include equity issues—that is, the effect on the distribution of the tax burden—and efficiency questions such as the effects of the tax on the amount, type, and location of property selected. The analysis has a number of important policy implications, particularly regarding proposals to provide property tax relief either to specific types of taxpayers or specific types of communities.

PROPERTY TAXES AS CAPITAL TAXES

Modern economic analysis most often considers property taxes as one of several taxes levied on the income from or value of capital, which is one of the major inputs (with labor and materials) into the production of goods and services. Other capital taxes include the federal corporate income tax and state–local government corporate income or general business taxes. This characterization is important because it suggests thinking about property taxes as taxes on production, or specifically on a factor of production, rather than as a tax on consumption or consumer goods.

The characterization seems straightforward enough when thinking about commercial and industrial property—the tax is on the plant, land, and equipment, not the value of the product—but sometimes seems unusual when applied to housing, as people tend to think of a house as a consumer good. However, the physical residential housing unit is only one input into the production of the consumer good "housing services," a fact most clearly demonstrated in rental housing. The producer (the owner and landlord) combines land, labor, and a housing unit to provide housing service to the tenant or consumer. The only difference in the case of owner-occupied housing is that the producer and consumer are the same person. Therefore, the approach followed in this chapter is to first consider the effect of various property tax structures on the price and amount of capital and then to consider the effect of changes in the price and amount of capital on the prices and quantities of other inputs (such as labor) and consumer goods (particularly, housing services).

A Uniform National Property Tax

The first implication of this approach is that a uniform national tax on all property at a single rate would impose an unshiftable burden on all property owners, at least in the short run. Remember the simple rule of tax analysis from Chapter 12: the only way to avoid or shift a tax is to change behavior. If all property is taxed at the same rate in all jurisdictions, however, changes in the type of property owned by an investor or the location of the property will not reduce the tax liability. The only way to avoid the tax is to reduce the amount of property owned, that is, to reduce investment. Note that a property owner cannot avoid the tax by selling the property to another investor. After the tax is imposed and known, any

Figure 14.1

Incidence with
perfectly inelastic
supply

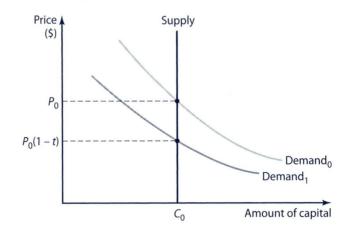

potential buyer would be willing to offer less for the property because the future after-tax return is lower than it would be if there were no tax.

This situation is depicted in Figure 14.1, which shows a perfectly inelastic supply of capital at quantity C_0; this would occur if the amount of capital investment were fixed in the long run. The property tax is represented by a shift down in the demand curve, and the net or after-tax return on capital falls from P_0 to $P_0(1 - t)$, where t is the property tax rate. The rate of return earned by property owners falls by the full amount of the tax because those owners at the time the tax is levied have no options to change behavior in an effort to avoid the tax.

Differential Taxation of Different Types of Property

Obviously, the example of a uniform national property tax is not realistic, so adjustments to that case are necessary. Suppose, instead, that some types of property are exempt from taxation (or taxed at a zero rate) with all other property taxed everywhere at a uniform rate. Investors then can avoid the tax by decreasing their investment in taxable property and increasing their investment in exempt property; however, that investor reaction itself will cause additional changes to the prices (and rate of return) of property. As investors reduce the amount (supply) of taxable property, the price of, and investor return from, that which remains increases, offsetting the tax burden. At the same time, increases in the supply of exempt property reduce the price and rate of return for those investments, mitigating the incentive to switch to nontaxable property. Equilibrium is reached when the rates of return—net of taxes—that are available from both types of property are equal.

This case is represented in Figure 14.2, which shows an initial equilibrium at rate of return R_0 for two types of property (A and B) when there are no taxes (or both are taxed equally). Investors presumably are indifferent between the two types of investments because the (risk-adjusted) returns available from each are equal. If a property tax is imposed on type A only, the immediate effect is a reduction in the

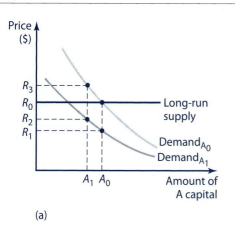

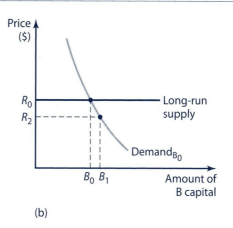

(a)   (b)

Figure 14.2

Effect of a
property tax
differential in
the allocation
of capital

rate of return from type A property to R_1, as reflected by $Demand_{A1}$, which includes the tax. An investor in type A property earns a return of R_0, pays tax of $(R_0 - R_1)$, and retains a return of R^1. Because the tax has reduced the rate of return from type A property compared to that available from investing in type B property, investors are expected to switch from A to B, as noted earlier.

As the amount of type A property falls below A_0, the rates of return from type A property rise, and as the supply of type B property rises, the price of, or rate of return from, that property falls. From another perspective, potential investors in type B property need not be offered as high a return when there was no tax on A, because the property tax on type A has made investment in B relatively more attractive. In Figure 14.2, equilibrium is reached at quantities A_1 and B_1, with a net-of-tax rate of return in both markets equal to R_2. Of course, owners of type A property still have to pay the tax; so to earn a net (after-tax) rate of return equal to R_2, they must receive a gross (before-tax) return of R_3. For instance, the income from investing in type A property might provide a 10-percent return before taxes are considered but only, say, 7 percent after taxes are paid. In that case, an investor in type B property would receive a 7-percent return and pay no tax. In contrast, when there were no taxes, all investors received return R_0, perhaps 9 percent, to continue the numerical example.

Another way to view this case is to consider the prices for each property type as those charged to rent those properties. After the tax is imposed, the price to the consumer to rent property A is higher than the price to rent property B (R_3 compared to R_2), so that the owners of both properties earn equal net-of-tax rent of R_2, which is, however, less than the rent received by the owners before taxes were imposed (R_0).

An important implication of this analysis is that *owners of both taxable and exempt property will bear an ultimate tax burden,* even though taxes are nominally collected only from owners of type A (taxable) property. Part of the tax levied on type A property is shifted to type B property through the market effects caused by the behavioral change of investors. Remember, the reason to change behavior (in this case, switch from investing in type A to type B property) is to avoid or shift the tax, in this instance to owners of exempt property.

The analysis in Figure 14.2 shows that the differential taxation of types of property creates economic inefficiency. The inefficiency arises because the tax differential creates an incentive for the economy to have more of the untaxed property, even though the productivity of type B capital has not risen. If the initial long-run supply R_0 represents the marginal social cost for both types of capital and initial demand the marginal social benefit, the tax differential induces an increase in the amount of type B capital so that marginal cost is greater than benefit. Similarly, the reduction in the amount of type A capital causes its marginal benefit to be greater than marginal cost. Because marginal social cost no longer equals marginal social benefit in each market, the change has reduced economic welfare or created an efficiency cost. The economy is supplying too much type B capital and too little type A.

Implicit in this discussion is an assumption that capital is perfectly mobile, whereas consumers of these capital services are immobile. This implies that profit-maximizing investors will always attempt to earn the highest possible return or profit, but consumers are unable to shift between the two types of properties. What happens if these assumptions are incorrect? If investors do not or are prevented from altering their investment types in response to the tax, then all the tax burden falls on owners of taxed property. Essentially, the situation is again that represented earlier in Figure 14.1.

If users of these types of capital can switch from one to the other, then the equilibrium we have identified is temporary. Because the consumer's price for type A property is now greater than that for type B property, the demand for type A property is expected to decrease and the demand for type B property is expected to increase. As a result, the price charged for type A property declines and the price charged for type B property increases until the prices are equal again, meaning that investors in type A property earn lower net returns than investors in type B property. Because of the differential tax on type A property, it is impossible for investors in both types of property to earn equal net returns *and* for users of both types to be charged the same price. Economists usually assume that it is easier for investors to move investments among different types of capital than for users of capital to change demand. For instance, if capital owned by profit-making businesses is taxed while capital used by nonprofit entities is exempt, the tax treatment of the property depends on its use, not any inherent characteristic of the property. To avoid the higher prices, profit-making firms would have to become nonprofit entities to consume type B property.

Differential Tax Rates by Location

In the preceding example, all taxed property was taxed at a uniform rate, which is also unrealistic. The next step, then, is to extend the analysis by considering taxation of identical property at different tax rates by different jurisdictions. This extension is easy, however, because it is analytically identical to the case just considered and represented in Figure 14.2, with type A capital now representing property in jurisdiction A, and type B capital representing property in lower-tax jurisdiction B. Although the example reflects some tax in A and no tax in B, it is just as applicable to a situation where some tax is in B, say $30 per $1,000 of assessed value, and a higher tax is in A, perhaps $35 per $1,000. Only the *differential in tax rates* influences movement between the localities.

The initial effect of the higher tax in A is to lower the rate of return received by owners/investors in A compared to that available in B. If capital is mobile, investors are expected to shift their investments from jurisdiction A to jurisdiction B. The resulting reduction in the supply of property in A raises the value of, or return from, that which remains; the increase in supply of property in B reduces the return from that property. Again, equilibrium is reached when the net-of-tax returns available to investors in both jurisdictions are equal. For that to happen, the user's cost of capital must be greater in jurisdiction A than in B; users of capital face higher costs in A, the higher-tax jurisdiction. The differential in tax rates between the jurisdictions reduces the amount of property and increases the user's price for property in the higher-tax jurisdiction, with just the opposite effects in lower-tax jurisdiction B.

As before, *some of the tax burden from the higher-tax jurisdiction is shifted to property owners in the lower-tax jurisdiction* through the decrease in the rate of return, which is caused by the increased supply. If users of capital also are mobile, the story continues. Because the price (rental charge) for capital is greater in A than in B, some users of capital might move their operations to B to take advantage of those lower prices. That shift of demand reduces prices in A—the higher-tax jurisdiction—and raises them in B. The outcome of this chase depends on the relative mobility of suppliers compared to demanders. Remember that capital or property in this discussion is considered an input to production, so the users of capital are firms that produce goods and services and households who own their residences and are thus "producers" of their housing services. Therefore, to determine the effect of the differential capital (property) tax on prices of other goods and services, one must consider what happens to the return to supplies of other factors of production and to the prices of consumer goods.

Labor

If capital is mobile, the higher tax rate in jurisdiction A causes less capital to be invested in that jurisdiction, which is expected to affect the demand for labor in jurisdiction A as well. If labor and capital are complementary, then the reduced amount of capital investment also reduces the demand for labor, causing wages in jurisdiction A to fall. Just the opposite happens in jurisdiction B, where increased capital investment causes an increase in demand for labor and an increase in wages. If workers do not or cannot change jobs in response to these wage changes, the story stops; part of the differential property tax burden in A has been shifted to workers in A. However, if workers are mobile and respond to the change in relative wages, the supply of labor falls in A (driving wages back up), and the supply in B rises (driving wages down). In that case, the effect of the

Figure 14.3

Effect of a capital
tax on housing
prices

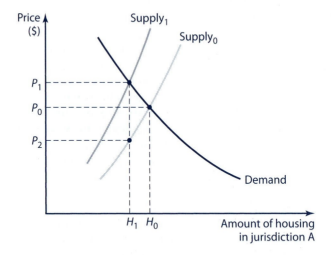

property tax differential in A is a reduction in employment rather than a change
in wages.[3]

Local Consumer Goods (Housing)

Changes in the user prices of capital in jurisdictions A and B, caused by the difference in property taxes, also are expected to affect the prices of goods produced and
consumed locally that use capital in the production process. Because the user's
price of capital (the rental rate) has increased in jurisdiction A, the prices of local
goods that are capital intensive are also expected to rise. Chief among these goods
is housing. The price of housing service in A—that is, the consumer's cost of living
in a house or apartment—is expected to rise. In contrast, the decrease in the consumer's price of capital in jurisdiction B is expected to reduce the price of housing
services in B.[4]

The changes in jurisdiction A are depicted in Figure 14.3, with the shift of the
supply curve resulting from the increased cost of producing housing services due
to the higher property tax. The tax differential causes the cost of living in a housing unit in jurisdiction A to rise from P_0 to P_1. Note also that if demand has some
elasticity, the net return to the owner of the housing unit also falls, from P_0 to P_2,
implying that this unit now commands a lower selling price. How can the cost of
living in a house go up at the same time that its market price falls? Market price
falls by less than the amount of the tax, so the total cost of the house plus tax rises.

---

[3] If labor and capital are substitutes, then the story is reversed: The decreased capital investment increases the demand
for labor.

[4] This analysis applies to locally produced and consumed goods. Goods that are sold on a national market presumably
trade at a uniform price everywhere, except for differences caused by transportation cost and the consumer's
cost of discovering any arbitrage opportunities. Even for local goods, the analysis is somewhat more complicated.
For instance, the price of some labor-intensive local goods could even fall if the price of labor falls.

Of course, if this is an owner-occupied house, the distinction is irrelevant because the owner and consumer are the same person.

Just as with labor, whether the story stops or continues depends on whether housing consumers respond to the change in the relative price of housing services between the two jurisdictions. If consumers are aware of the differences and are mobile, then more consumers are expected to seek housing in B, where the price has decreased, and fewer consumers are expected to seek housing in A. However, the increase in housing demand in B will increase housing prices again, while the decrease in housing demand in jurisdiction A will bring housing prices down. If consumers are perfectly mobile, the resulting effect of the property tax differential, then, is a decrease in the amount of housing in A and an increase in the amount of housing in B, but the relative prices do not change.

Land

Because of the positive property tax rate differential in jurisdiction A, the amount of capital investment in A is expected to fall, which decreases the demand for the complementary input land. Further, if housing consumers react to the increased housing service price by leaving for other jurisdictions, the demand for land will decline further. These decreases in the demand for land reduce the price (value) of land in A. However, landowners do not have the option available to owners of other types of capital of moving their investment (land) to a lower-tax jurisdiction; the supply of land in jurisdiction A is fixed, as represented earlier in Figure 14.1. If all other capital, inputs, and consumers are mobile, then the burden of the tax differential that remains is reflected in a decreased value of land. If land is the only immobile commodity or agent, then all the burden of the tax differential is capitalized into land values in the higher-tax jurisdiction, A in the example. Those hurt by the tax differential are the landowners in jurisdiction A at the time the tax was increased (although landowners in B benefit).

Putting the Analysis Together

The actual property tax environment, with effective tax rates differing by location and sometimes by type of property, can be analyzed by combining the three different theoretical scenarios presented previously. For instance, suppose that a third of all jurisdictions tax property at an effective rate of 2 percent, another third at 3 percent, and the final third at 4 percent (and all have equal amounts of property), so that the average effective rate is 3 percent. This is equivalent to a national tax at that 3-percent rate coupled with an additional 1-percent tax levied by one-third of the subnational jurisdictions and a 1-percent subsidy (a negative tax) provided by another third. This situation can be examined by first analyzing a national 3-percent tax and then coupling that with an analysis of the effects of the 1 percentage point differential from the average existing in some of the jurisdictions.

The effect of the average property tax rate, which can be thought of as a national tax at that rate, is a reduction in the return (income) from capital ownership and a burden imposed on all capital or property owners, as discussed previously and depicted in Figure 14.1. Recall that this burden falls on owners of all types of property if capital is mobile, regardless of whether a particular type of property is taxed directly, and if taxed, whether at a high or low rate. This conclusion changes somewhat if the overall amount of capital in the society (that is, from savings and investment) is reduced by the fall in the rate of return from capital, which could raise goods prices or lower labor prices in the future. In that case, the average property tax rate imposes a burden on consumers and workers as well as capital owners in the long run.

The 1 percentage point property tax rate differential may cause changes in the prices of some consumer goods, of labor, and of land in the different jurisdictions. The nature and magnitude of these *excise effects* depend on the relative mobility of capital, labor, and consumers, as described earlier.

Consider one extreme set of assumptions first: capital is perfectly mobile, whereas workers and consumers are perfectly immobile (workers and consumers do not move their economic activity across jurisdiction boundaries because of tax-induced price differences). Under these assumptions, the tax rate differential causes lower wages and land values and higher prices for locally produced consumer goods (housing) in the higher-tax jurisdictions as compared to the lower-tax ones. This set of assumptions, although precisely unrealistic, may in fact be an adequate approximation (or at least a good starting point) for analyzing *interstate* tax differentials. It is costly for individuals to become aware of prices available in other states, and individuals sometimes face substantial costs to take advantage of those price differences. In many, although not all, cases, individuals have to change both their work and consumer location if they want to change either.

In one study, Robert Wassmer (1993) analyzes the effect of differences in effective property tax rates compared to the national average rate on property values and the quantity of property for 62 large U.S. cities from 1966 to 1981. Wassmer reports that a 1-percent change in the difference between the city and national average tax rate is associated with a .13-percent decline in the value of property units in the city. Similarly, evidence exists of a decline in the number of property units in the above-average rate cities. Thus, as suggested by the theory, the excise effects from property tax rate differences impose burdens on immobile factors in the higher-tax jurisdictions.

Many analyses and discussions of property tax effects often refer to the "traditional view" of property tax incidence. This "traditional view" held that local factors of production and consumers, and specifically local housing consumers in the form of higher housing prices, bore the burden of local property taxes. (This perspective is explained further in the upcoming "Is the Property Tax Regressive?" section.) But here it is relatively clear that this result is one possibility—a special case—of the general view of the property tax as a tax on capital. If, as explained previously, capital is perfectly mobile while labor and consumption are perfectly immobile, then essentially all the burden of a local property tax increase falls on local consumers and suppliers of factors of production. That is, housing prices and prices of other locally produced consumer goods rise, and prices of local factors of production, such as labor, fall. Although additional conditions are needed so that the *only* effect is a rise in housing prices, which is precisely the traditional view, clearly the excise effects in the capital tax approach capture the essence of the traditional view.

The opposite set of extreme assumptions—that workers, consumers, and capital are perfectly mobile—leads to very different results. Because price differences cause and are ultimately removed by economic mobility, the remaining effect of the tax rate differential is to lower the value of land in the higher-tax jurisdictions compared to that in the lower-tax jurisdictions. This set of assumptions, although also unrealistic, is often applied to analyzing tax differentials *within* states or metropolitan areas. Because individuals often are aware of price differences within their area and because they can change their jobs or residential locations without changing both, the costs of mobility are less than for interstate differences. In this case, the burden of any tax differential is likely to fall on landowners of the higher-tax jurisdictions (who may or may not be residents of those jurisdictions).

A study by Robert Carroll and John Yinger (1994) of rental housing in the Boston metropolitan area illustrates that exact point. The authors estimate the incidence on both landlords and tenants of a $1.00 increase in city property taxes used to provide an additional dollar of city services that benefit tenants. On average, landlords bear $.91 of the $1.00 tax increase, with a range among the cities from $.98 to $.70. Thus, because tenants (consumers) are relatively more mobile than landlords (suppliers), the landlords are prevented from shifting a large share of the property tax burden to renters.

One important policy implication of this view is that how the property tax reduction is carried out determines who will benefit from it. For example, if a national program reduced property taxes in all states and localities, the average rate of tax decreases, with little or no change in the tax differential between jurisdictions. A reduction in the national average rate of tax increases the return to all capital owners and provides a benefit proportional to the amount of capital owned. On the other hand, if one (relatively small) state reduced property taxes uniformly within that state, the effect on the national average rate of tax is insignificant, and no change occurs in the tax differentials among localities within the state. However, the relative position of that state compared to all the others is altered, with the expected theoretical effect of raising wages and land values and lowering housing prices in that state.

Similarly, suppose that only one city lowered property taxes (holding services constant). Now the changes to both the national and state average rates of tax are insignificant, with only the differential between this city and others in its area altered. If the extreme set of assumptions is applied as stated previously, the expected result is an increase in land values in the city that lowered taxes. The new, more advantageous tax differential of this city is capitalized into higher land values, benefiting those who own land in the city at the time the tax is reduced.

Accordingly, it is impossible to state with certainty *the single* effect from lowering (or raising) property taxes. As the preceding discussion illustrates, the expected result of any property tax change depends both on what all jurisdictions are doing simultaneously and on how individuals respond.

IS THE PROPERTY TAX REGRESSIVE?

In his classic analysis of the property tax published in 1966, Dick Netzer (1966, p. 23, 40) wrote:

> *In the past forty years, there has been little theoretical controversy over the incidence of the American property tax. By and large, the "conventional wisdom" is accepted. . . . In general, the results [of Netzer's analysis with 1957 data] conform with the conventional wisdom: the property tax is on balance somewhat regressive when compared to current money income.*

Writing just nine years later, Henry Aaron (1975, p. 19) offered a very different view:

> *Economic analysis of differential tax incidence has undergone massive revision in the last decade. As a result, opinions among economists engaged in the study of tax incidence bear little resemblance to views generally held even a few years ago. The main contribution of recent research has been to show that the patterns of gains and losses generated when a single state or locality changes property taxes will differ markedly from that appearing after a change in the nationwide use of property taxes, and that none of these patterns resembles the profile of burdens from property taxes that economists formerly described.*

The analysis to which Aaron refers is what you have read in the previous part of this chapter. The analysis that underlies Netzer's comment was the "traditional view" of property tax effects noted previously. Although the viewpoint articulated by Netzer was held by economists and policymakers for more than 50 years, the analysis in this chapter—the "capital tax view"—is now the predominant new conventional wisdom about the property tax among many economists and increasingly among policymakers as well.

The long-standing notion that property taxes are regressive (that is, impose a more than proportionate burden on lower-income families and individuals) arose from a simple theoretical proposition and two statistical observations. It was assumed, following the traditional view, that property taxes operated as excise taxes on commodities and increased the price of the taxed goods. Residential property taxes were therefore assumed to increase the price of housing services and thus impose a burden in proportion to the amount spent on housing consumption. Nonresidential property taxes were assumed to increase the prices of goods produced with that property, thereby imposing a burden in proportion to the amount spent on the consumption of goods, excluding housing. Because both annual consumption and housing expenditures are a greater proportion of annual income for lower- as opposed to higher-income individuals, the conclusion clearly followed that property tax burdens were a greater proportion of income for lower-income taxpayers than for higher-income ones. The property tax was perceived to be regressive.

By thinking of the property tax as a tax on capital rather than on consumer goods, it became clearer that property tax burdens could be imposed on profits, wages, or land rents in addition to consumption, making the conclusions more ambiguous. One conclusion was that the burden that arises from the average rate of property tax in the nation is imposed on owners of capital in proportion to the amount owned, at least in the short run. Because capital is more than proportionally owned by higher-income families and individuals, the burden of this part of the property tax is expected to be progressive (more than proportionally borne by higher-income taxpayers).

What of the tax burden that arises from the differences in property tax rates around that national average? The theory suggests that these burdens will fall on workers, landowners, and consumers in the higher-tax rate jurisdictions; how the burden is divided among these groups depends on relative mobility. One must know something about which jurisdictions have above-average tax rates to evaluate these burdens. If the high-tax rate jurisdictions are high-income jurisdictions, on average, then mostly those high-income taxpayers will feel the decreased wages and land values and increased housing prices that result from the tax differential. The relationship between effective property tax rates and income is crucial to this evaluation.

Aaron (1975) reports that among the states a positive correlation exists between per-capita income and effective property tax rates; the high-tax-rate states tend also to be the high-income states. Because the property tax rate differentials among the states hurt those with the higher rates, these burdens seem to be progressive. Aaron also reports a positive relationship between income and property tax rates among counties within states, although that relationship is not as strong as that among the states. In contrast, Aaron found a negative relationship between property tax rates and income among localities within counties in New Jersey, suggesting that the tax burdens that arise from property tax rate differentials within counties or metropolitan areas may, in fact, be regressive. Of course, this conclusion can vary by state or even for different areas within a state, so the facts must be examined for specific cases. Aaron suggests that when these factors are combined, they do not support a conclusion of general property tax regressivity. In fact, increases in the average use of property taxes nationwide, at least, seem to introduce more progressivity into the state and local government tax structure.

A recent analysis by Plummer (2003) of residential property tax burdens in Dallas County, Texas also illustrates the importance of the relationship between property tax rates and community income for the incidence results. Plummer (2003, p. 752) reports the following: "After allowing for the federal income tax deduction of property taxes, total [residential] property taxes combined are approximately proportional." But this aggregate result arises because she finds that county and school taxes are proportional or slightly progressive, although city property taxes are regressive. Plummer explains: "Tax rates contribute to the regressivity of city taxes because lower-income cities tend to have relatively high tax rates."

The range of possible incidence conclusions about property taxes is reflected by the results reported by Joseph Pechman (1985), who calculates effective rates by annual income class for various taxes under alternative theoretical assumptions about the economic effects of those taxes. For property taxes, the assumption at one end of the spectrum is that all property tax burdens fall on owners of capital, which would result from a national uniform property tax. The opposite possibility is that

Table 14.1

Pechman's Analysis of Effective Property Tax Rates, 1980

Family Income (thousands of dollars)	Property Tax Burdens on Capital Ownership (%)	Property Tax Burdens on Consumption (%)
0–5	1.0%	7.9%
5–10	0.6	3.0
10–15	0.9	2.4
15–20	0.9	2.1
20–25	1.0	2.1
25–30	1.2	2.1
30–50	1.4	2.2
50–100	2.2	2.3
100–500	3.9	2.2
500–1000	5.2	2.2
1000 and up	5.8	2.3

SOURCE: Pechman (1985, p. 56).

property tax burdens fall on consumption due to higher prices of goods. This could occur if property tax rate differentials are large, and consumers do not change their behavior to avoid the resulting price differentials. Pechman's results for 1980, reported in Table 14.1, are not surprising. If all property tax burdens fall on owners of capital in proportion to the amount of capital, the property tax is roughly proportional for families with annual incomes below $25,000 (in 1980) and very progressive among families with higher annual incomes. If the property tax is assumed to increase consumer good prices, the property tax burden is regressive among families with annual incomes below $15,000 and proportional or slightly progressive among families with incomes above $15,000.

One potential problem with this measure of property tax incidence, regardless of the theoretical assumption adopted, is that property tax burdens are compared to *annual incomes*. Family or individual choices about the value of residence to purchase or own are long-run decisions, however, depending not just on current income but also on expected future income. Most individuals do not buy more valuable houses annually as their income rises but buy a residence for a number of years based on their expected lifetime income or at least income over some period. Current incomes are often poorly correlated with average lifetime incomes, particularly at the bottom and top of the income distribution. For instance, the typical low income of someone in medical school or just beginning a medical residency program greatly understates that individual's expected economic welfare. If housing choices are based on average long-run incomes, then comparing property tax burdens to that same long-run income gives a more accurate picture of the true income distribution of the burden. If property tax burdens are compared to average lifetime income rather than annual or current income, the distribution is less regressive or more progressive.

An Alternative Perspective: The Benefit View

Finally, recall from Chapter 5 that property taxes may serve as benefit taxes. If consumers choose residential locations based on the property tax and service package offered by the local government, and if some mechanism arises to maintain the equilibrium (such as zoning rules), consumers who desire the same fiscal package are grouped together. The property tax is the "price" for consuming local services, with all consumers paying the costs that their consumption imposes on the government. In that case, discussing the incidence of the tax separate from the provision of public services doesn't make sense, because the tax simply reflects the demand for the services. For instance, a high-income community may have high taxes because residents demand a relatively large quantity of public service. The correlation between income and tax rates does not reflect any redistribution from higher-income taxpayers. Such individuals are simply paying for the services they demand.

If property taxes do serve as benefit taxes or fees, then the taxes do not distort allocation decisions. That is, if property taxes are fees for public services, there is no incentive to reallocate capital between jurisdictions or between uses, and thus rates of return to capital would not change. Therefore, whether to think of property taxes as taxes on mobile capital or as fees for residing in a particular jurisdiction and benefiting from the services provided in that jurisdiction remains a controversial issue among some public finance analysts.[5]

One approach to resolving the controversy, advanced by Zodrow (2001), is that under certain conditions, the outcome of the capital tax approach may be similar to that from the benefit tax approach. If local consumers and workers are not mobile (while capital is), then a local property tax imposes burdens on local residents. However, they are the same people who presumably benefit from the services financed by the higher property tax. This is a similar situation, but not exactly the same, as envisioned by those thinking of property taxes as benefit taxes. Advocates of the benefit tax approach, such as Fischel (2001), generally do not accept, however, that the concept of benefit taxation can be seen as a special result of the capital tax approach. Rather, these advocates envision an entirely different structure of local fiscal decision-making. One way to think of or better understand the controversy is to focus on the mobility of capital. The mobility of capital in response to different tax rates drives the results in the capital tax approach; however, from a benefit tax or Tiebout perspective, property taxes may create little or no incentive for capital mobility if the tax burdens are precisely matched by service benefits.

In the end, which view or perspective comes closer to describing the actual process that results from property tax changes is largely an empirical question. So far, there are no definitive empirical studies. Supporters of the benefit tax view point to studies showing the predominance of Tiebout-type sorting among localities—that

---

[5]For a recent debate on this question, see the "Forum on the Incidence of the Property Tax" in the March 2001 issue of the *National Tax Journal*. George Zodrow, a leading proponent of the capital tax view, and William Fischel, perhaps the leading proponent of the benefit tax view, each outline their positions in separate papers.

is, having many varied and relatively homogeneous localities in a metropolitan area—and to the popularity of complicated zoning rules that may serve to maintain community homogeneity. Supporters of the capital tax view point to the need for a very large number of separate, homogeneous communities in any metropolitan area to make the benefit tax view work and to the concern that many zoning rules are not binding or not sufficiently tied to housing. Therefore, this issue remains an important one for continuing additional research, perhaps even by some readers of this book!

LAND VALUE TAXATION

Most property tax rates are applied to the aggregate value of a property, effectively applying the rate equally to both the land and structure components of that property value. At least in concept, however, the value of the land can be separated from the value of the structure (building) on that land and different property tax rates can be applied to those two values.[6] Such a tax is called a **two-rate**, **split-rate**, or **graded property tax**. In fact, in 1879, Henry George advocated a special version of two-rate tax, arguing for zero tax on structures and high tax rates on land (high enough to generate the necessary revenue). Recent attention has focused on a less extreme option of levying a tax rate on land that is perhaps twice as great as that on structures.

The potential advantage of a two-rate tax is that it encourages more intensive use of land, essentially encouraging greater investment in property and housing and discouraging the holding of vacant land (especially for speculative purposes). In addition, because the supply of land is fixed (perfectly inelastic), some argue that higher land taxes do not affect the behavior of landowners and thus create no efficiency cost or excess burden.

These effects are illustrated graphically in Figure 14.4. Suppose that the tax rate on land is increased, which is analyzed by shifting the demand curve down by the amount of the tax increase. As a result, the quantity of land remains constant and the user's cost (rental price) of land remains at R_0, but the owner's after-tax return (rent) falls to R_1. Because the owner cannot reduce the amount of land, all the burden of the tax is on the landowner. The additional revenue from the higher tax on land allows lower tax rates on structures (holding government spending constant), which is shown by a shift down in the supply of structures (reflecting lower cost of structures due to the tax decrease). As a result, the quantity of structures rises. In total, then, there is more physical structure on the same amount of land—land is used more intensively—which Oates and Schwab (1995) call the capital-intensity effect.[7]

---

[6]In some cases, the owner of the structure is different from the owner of the land. In the case of commercial property, and sometimes even with housing, the owner of a structure leases the land on which the structure is located.

[7]When this analysis is put in a spatial model, sometimes the effect is a smaller urban area. Essentially, the quantity of structures is squeezed into a smaller geographic area.

Figure 14.4

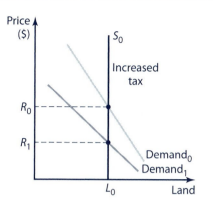

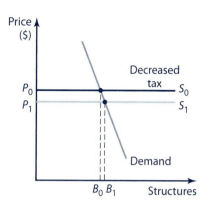

Effects of increased land taxes and decreased taxes on structures

This capital-intensity effect also can be illustrated with a numerical example. Suppose a landowner purchased a parcel of land for $10,000, which is leased out for an annual rent of $1,000. This landowner thus earns a 10-percent rate of return annually. Now suppose a tax of 2 percent of the *value* of the land is levied *each year*, which amounts to an annual tax of $200 (.02 × $10,000). This landowner now earns a net, after-tax return of $800 per year (the $1,000 rent minus the $200 tax), which provides an annual 8-percent rate of return. How could the landowner reclaim the lost rent or return? One option is to lease the land to a developer who will put a larger, more valuable structure on the land. With a larger structure, the rent also can be greater. If the rent rises to $1,250 per year, the value of the property rises to $12,500, the annual tax is $250, and the net return to the landowner returns to $1,000.

Two potential difficulties arise with such two-rate property taxes. The first is simply the mechanics of separately assessing the land and the structures on that land, as both together produce the income from that property. Part of the problem concerns valuing land based on how it is being used currently as opposed to determining its value if the land were in its "highest and best" use. The other potential problem is that depending on how land is assessed, the higher tax on land may induce development of land sooner or at a faster pace than is efficient. Because of the high tax on vacant (or underused) land, the owner may be induced to develop the land now, even if waiting awhile would allow a socially preferred different use later. (For instance, land may be used initially for an industrial use, even though it has greater value subsequently for residential use.) In this case, the land tax is inefficient and creates an excess burden.

How have two-part property taxes worked in practice? A few municipalities in Pennsylvania and elsewhere have used two-part taxes with higher rates on land, but the experience in Pittsburgh has received the most careful analysis. Before 1979, Pittsburgh taxed land at twice the rate of structures; beginning in 1979, the city changed to taxing land at about five times the rate of structures. At the same time, however, the city began a program of granting generous property tax abatements for new construction of commercial and residential property, effectively reducing the tax on structures. Finally, apparently a serious shortage of commercial office space in the city in 1980 (occupancy rates were about 99 percent) resulted from increased demand.

In a careful analysis, Wallace Oates and Robert Schwab (1995) examined building activity in Pittsburgh in the 10 years after the property tax change and compared Pittsburgh's experience to that of other cities in that region that did not use this tax system. Pittsburgh did enjoy a construction boom in that decade, which was different from most other cities in the sample. Oates and Schwab conclude that the most important factors in stimulating construction in the city were the increased demand for commercial office space and the reduced taxes on structures. They note, however, that these two factors together do not explain all the increased construction. Thus, the higher tax on land alone also must have had an effect. They argue as follows: "What the Pittsburgh experience suggests to us is that the movement to a graded tax system can, in the right setting, provide some stimulus to local building activity" (Oates and Schwab, 1995, 10).[8] Because two-rate property taxes have been used in only a few locations and there is limited analysis of those cases, at present there still is great uncertainty about whether and to what degree two-rate taxes can stimulate property investment.

VOTING ON PROPERTY TAXES

One relatively unique aspect of property taxes compared to other taxes is that taxpayers often have the opportunity to select, or at least influence, the tax rate through a referendum. In some cases, such a referendum is mandatory; in others, a referendum is optional or required only under certain circumstances. These fiscal referenda are most common among independent school districts but sometimes are used by general-purpose local governments. The vote may be on the property tax rate directly or on the budget, which implicitly determines the tax rate.

Data from these local fiscal elections often are used to estimate the demand for local government services, especially education, as described in greater detail in Chapter 4. These demand studies show how various economic and social factors influence the amount of services selected and thus the amount of property tax levied. Not surprisingly, the two principal economic variables influencing demand are the tax price for additional services as perceived by the voters and the resources available to the voters, including income and intergovernmental grants. Three important features of the property tax environment—the amount of nonresidential property in a jurisdiction, federal and state income tax deductibility of property taxes, and state property tax credits—can affect the choice of the amount of property taxes or expenditures by altering voters' perceived tax prices for additional services.

---

[8]For other significant discussions of land value taxation, see Brueckner (1986), DiMasi (1987), and Anderson (1993).

Property Tax Prices

The property tax price for additional services facing any taxpayer is the net share of property taxes paid by that taxpayer. This price depends on that taxpayer's property value compared to the total taxable value in the jurisdiction and on any deductions or credits available to that taxpayer. This property tax price (h_i) for any individual (i) can be represented as follows:

$$h_i = \frac{N \cdot V_i(1 - S)}{V}$$

where

N = jurisdiction population

V_i = property value owned by taxpayer i

V = total property value in the jurisdiction

S = portion of taxpayer i's tax that is shifted through deductions or credits

The total property value in the jurisdiction is composed of both residential and nonresidential property—that is, $V = R + NR$, with R representing the value of residential property and NR the nonresidential value. Assuming that individuals do not perceive or bear any burden from property taxes on nonresidential property in their jurisdiction, increases in nonresidential value reduce an individual's property tax price. Given this assumption, the expression for the property tax price can be written:

$$h_i = \left[\frac{N \cdot V_i(1 - S)}{R} \right] \frac{R}{V}.$$

An individual's property tax price or share depends on three things: (1) that individual's residential property value relative to the average residential value in the jurisdiction, (2) the portion of that individual's tax that can be eliminated by deductions or credits, and (3) the share of total property value in the jurisdiction that is residential (because the nonresidential property tax is assumed to impose no burden on resident individuals). We now consider research about those factors that influence $(1 - S)$ and R/V and how those reductions in tax price affect property tax votes.

Composition of the Property Tax Base

If individual voters believe there is no burden from imposing property taxes on "business" property in the jurisdiction—that is, industrial, commercial, and agricultural property—then increasing per-capita government spending and taxes by $1 costs individuals less the more business property that exists. Voters should select higher property tax rates in jurisdictions for which residential property is a smaller fraction of total property value, all other factors equal. When the residential share of property value is included as a variable in statistical studies explaining per-capita taxes or spending among local governments, it commonly does have a significant, negative effect.

The idea that higher and higher property tax rates can be imposed on industrial and commercial property with no cost to local residents is naive because capital is mobile at least to some degree. As tax rates increase, at some point some of the industrial and commercial tax base will be lost due to competition from other juris-dictions with lower tax rates. Such a loss would increase the tax prices for gov-ernment spending faced by individuals in that jurisdiction. If voters perceive this effect, then the existence of nonresidential property should have less of an effect on the choice of property tax rates. Moreover, if individuals believe that the potential for mobility of industrial property is different than for commercial property, then jurisdictions with substantial amounts of industrial property are expected to behave differently than those with substantial commercial property.

Helen Ladd (1975) examined the possibility that the composition of the local property tax base will influence the choice of local per-capita taxes and spending in a study of school expenditures in the Boston metropolitan area for 1970. Ladd's adjusted measure of the perceived residential share of the tax base is $1 - aC - bI$, where C represents commercial value, I is industrial value, and a and b are para-meters representing the shares of the commercial and industrial bases that are perceived not to burden local residents. If a and b equal 1, none of the business prop-erty tax burden falls on residents (as in the previous formulation). If a and b equal 0, voters treat business property the same as residential property, believing that all the property tax is a local burden.

In Ladd's analysis, a was estimated to be 0.79 while b was estimated to be 0.45. This means that the voters did not act as if commercial and industrial property taxes had no local burden. Rather, it appears these voters believed that about 20 percent of commercial property taxes and a little more than half of industrial taxes did create local tax burdens. The voters apparently believed that the indus-trial tax base was substantially more sensitive to tax rates than was the commercial base, so that communities with relatively larger amounts of commercial property were more likely to select higher tax rates than were communities with relatively larger amounts of industrial property, all other factors equal, because of a fear of driving out that industrial property. These results are in accordance with the general notion that commercial location decisions are tied to the local market, whereas industrial property is more footloose and thus more sensitive to local fiscal conditions. The conclusion is that the existence of commercial and industrial property reduces individuals' perceived tax prices and contributes to higher selected tax rates and expenditures, however, voters do not perceive commercial and industrial property taxes as completely "free."

Income Tax Deductions for Property Taxes

Consideration of federal income tax reform almost always includes a discussion of the federal itemized deduction for property and income taxes, including whether changes to the deduction might affect property or income tax use and spending by state and local governments. That certainly was the case with the major federal income tax reform bill adopted in 1986. Although some proposals would have ended the federal income tax deductibility of property taxes altogether, deductibil-ity for property taxes was retained, although increases in the standard deduction and changes in other deductions reduced the number of taxpayers who itemize deductions and thus who deduct property taxes in practice. Moreover, the value of the property tax deduction is reduced for those who continue to itemize because of the decrease in marginal income tax rates. (Initially, there were only two nominal rates, 15 and 28 percent for joint filers, compared to a maximum rate of 50 percent in the previous structure. Subsequently, rates of 36 and 39.5 percent were added for high-income taxpayers.) By altering property tax prices, these federal income tax changes may have several effects on local government fiscal policy.

A primary concern among local government officials was that by increasing property tax prices for some taxpayers, federal tax reform might induce voters to select lower property tax rates or amounts of government expenditure. Edward Gramlich (1985a) examined this possibility, based on survey data of individual taxpayers in several Michigan cities. The survey included information on whether a taxpayer itemized federal income tax deductions, on taxpayer income (which allows calculation of marginal federal tax rate), on residential location, on whether the taxpayer votes, and on the taxpayer's desired simultaneous percentage change in local government taxes and expenditures. Gramlich used the survey data to compute the desired tax/expenditure change for each taxpayer, which was based on the tax price with property tax deductibility and what the tax price would be if deductibility were ended and tax rates lowered. Gramlich assumed that the price elasticity of demand is .5. Assuming that the median voter model can represent the local fiscal choice process, Gramlich identifies the median desired tax/expenditure change in each locality when taxes are and are not deductible.

Under the tax structure existing at the time of the survey (property taxes deductible), Gramlich reported that the median position in each locality is "no change in taxes/expenditures." That is, the local governments had selected the tax/expenditure package desired by the median voters in each community. When property tax deductibility ends, the property tax price rises for taxpayers who itemize deductions, but the effect of those price increases on desired spending varies by community. No change occurred in desired taxes/expenditures in the two large central cities in the sample (Detroit and Lansing), because the median voter in those cities is not an itemizer, and changes in other voters' desired taxes do not alter the median. Among the other communities in the sample (including city suburbs and rural areas), desired taxes/expenditures decrease from 1 to 10 percent, averaging about a 5-percent decrease.

These results from Gramlich's simulations with an assumed price elasticity of .5 are supported by other studies (notably, Inman 1985 and Holtz-Eakin and Rosen 1988) examining the actual taxing behavior of localities. For instance, Douglas Holtz-Eakin and Harvey Rosen related changes in taxes and expenditures from 1978 to 1980 for 172 localities to changes in tax prices caused by federal income tax deductibility. Their results showed that if deductibility of all local taxes were removed completely, collections of all deductible taxes (property, income, and sales taxes together) by localities would fall by about 13 percent on average. So these studies provide support for the idea that the level of taxes adopted by taxpayers responds to changes in tax prices, although the magnitude of the effect due to federal deductibility is not huge.

A second concern arises from a change in the distribution of desired taxes. Not surprisingly, desired taxes and expenditures decrease more for higher-income taxpayers (and communities) because many of those taxpayers itemize, and their relatively high income tax rates make the property tax deduction more valuable. If higher-income taxpayers are not the median voters in their communities, their decreases in desired taxes/expenditures will not occur. This may be of particular concern in the large central cities in which there is a large distribution of incomes. Gramlich (1985a, p. 458) notes that "this is likely to lead to a subtle form of intra-community fiscal tension, to changes in the character of public spending (increasing the bribe for the rich to stay put), or to emigration of the rich."

State Property Tax Credits

State property tax credits are an additional intergovernmental tax incentive that reduce property tax prices and thus may affect the choice of property tax rates and local government expenditures. These credits operate similarly to tax deductions, except that the net cost of a $1 increase in property taxes is reduced by the credit rate rather than the taxpayer's marginal income tax rate. The Michigan property tax credit is illustrative. The formulas for the Michigan property tax credit are as follows:

General Taxpayers	Senior Citizens
$C = .60[PT - .035Y]$, up to $1,200	$C = PT - aY$, up to $1,200 with $0 \leq a \leq .035$, by income

where

C = property tax credit

PT = homestead property tax

Y = household income

The credit is reduced 10 percent for each $1,000 of income above $73,650, so no credit is available to households with income above $82,650.

As a result of this program, Michigan taxpayers fall into one of four main categories with respect to the net cost of property tax increases. General taxpayers who received a property tax credit less than the maximum $1,200 and with household income less than $73,650 had a net cost of $.40 for each $1 increase in property tax (because the credit increases by $.60 if property tax rises by $1). Similarly, senior citizen taxpayers who received a credit less than the maximum with household income less than $73,650 faced a net cost per dollar of property tax increase equal to zero (the credit increases $1 for each $1 increase in tax). Credit recipients with income between $73,650 and $82,650 in 1992 faced marginal property tax prices between $.40 (zero for seniors) and $1. Taxpayers who received no property tax credit or who were at the $1,200 maximum faced a $1 net property tax price for each $1 increase in property tax. Therefore, most Michigan taxpayers paid either 0 percent, 40 percent, or 100 percent of marginal property tax increases.

Data from 2001 show that about one-third of taxpayers filing Michigan state individual income tax returns had their property tax price reduced by the state property tax credit. Relatively more homeowners than renters receive credits, and if homeowners are more likely than renters to vote in local property tax rate elections, then the potential for the property tax credit to affect those votes is greater than that reflected by the overall distribution of prices. Some analysts have suggested, however, that individual voters may not be aware of how the property tax credit reduces property tax prices, and thus the credit will not influence property tax votes. R. Hamilton Lankford (1985) reports the results of a survey of taxpayers in Marshall, Michigan, showing that the differences between *perceived* and *actual* property tax costs, net of federal and state tax incentives, "are consistent with the expectation that such individuals do not consider the potential credit when formulating perceptions of net property tax costs. Even many of those who claim the credit apparently do not understand the effect of the credit on costs" (Lankford 1985, p. 84–85). Yet Lankford's results also show that *voters* are much more likely to perceive property tax costs correctly than are nonvoters.

The issue of whether the Michigan state property tax credit program affected property tax amounts has been examined (Fisher 1986) by comparing local government property tax changes from 1974 to 1976, the two years immediately after credits were introduced, to property tax changes in the 1972–1974 period, when no property tax credit existed. The results show that, after adjusting for other factors affecting property tax changes, property taxes increased more from 1974 to 1976 in those counties for which the credit reduced property tax prices the most. No similar effect of the property tax credit parameters was found for the 1972–1974 period. Fisher (1988, p. 17) concluded that "the level of property tax in 1976 was between 5 and 12 percent greater than it would have been without the property tax credit. Given the mean price decrease of about 22 percent due to the credit, these results suggest that the elasticity of the level of taxes with respect to the price is between $-.2$ and $-.5$."

More recently, Alan Brokaw and colleagues (1990) have shown that voters in a specific Michigan school district continue to perceive the effect of the credit in reducing tax prices and respond to that price reduction in property tax votes. Brokaw *et al.* reported that taxpayers were more likely to vote for a property tax rate proposal, the lower was the marginal property tax price (for instance, due to the credit) or the lower the percentage increase in property tax for that individual.

Michael Bell and John Bowman (1987) have examined the effect of a similar state property tax credit in Minnesota on local government property taxes. They reported that the state credit, which provides a 54-percent marginal subsidy of property taxes up to a maximum credit of $650, induces statistically significant increases in local property taxes net of credits. They concluded that because "local officials can increase local services by $1 without having to raise local taxes by $1,... a bloating of the public sector results from divorcing the pain of taxing from the pleasure of spending" (Bell and Bowman 1987, p. 293).

SUMMARY

Modern economic analysis considers property taxes as one of several taxes levied on the income from, or value of, capital, which is one of the major inputs (with labor and materials) to the production of goods and services.

The first implication of this approach is that a uniform national tax on all property at a single rate would impose an unshiftable burden on all property owners at least in the short run. A second implication is that owners of both taxable and exempt property will bear an ultimate tax burden. The effect of the average national property tax rate is a reduction in the return (income) from capital ownership and is thus a burden imposed on all owners of capital or property.

Any differential in tax rates between jurisdictions reduces the amount of property and increases the user's price for property in the higher-tax jurisdictions, with just the opposite effects in the lower-tax jurisdictions. Thus, property tax burdens can be imposed on profits, wages, or land rents in addition to consumption. If capital is perfectly mobile, while workers and consumers are perfectly immobile, the tax-rate differential causes lower wages and land values and higher prices for locally produced consumer goods (housing) in the higher-tax jurisdictions as compared to the lower-tax ones. If workers, consumers, and capital are perfectly mobile, any tax-rate differential lowers the value of land in the higher-tax jurisdictions as compared to that in the lower-tax rate jurisdictions.

These factors combined do not support a conclusion of general property tax regressivity. Increases in the average use of property taxes nationwide particularly will introduce more progressivity into the state–local government tax structure.

Taxpayers often can select, or at least influence, the property tax rate through a referendum. Three important features of the property tax environment—the amount of nonresidential property in a jurisdiction, federal and state income tax deductibility of property taxes, and state property tax credits—have the potential to affect the choice of the amount of property taxes or expenditures by altering voters' perceived tax prices for additional services.

DISCUSSION QUESTIONS

1. "If one city lowers property taxes, then most of the benefits go to landowners in that city when taxes are reduced." Evaluate this statement in terms of economics by analyzing first the effects of the tax decrease on the amount of capital in the city and then the effects on the markets for land, labor, and housing in the city.

2. Suppose the national government creates a grant program to provide funds to all local governments and, as a result, all local governments nationally reduce property taxes proportionally. Discuss the economic effects of this property tax change. Which types of individuals are expected to benefit? Will the property tax change lead to a more progressive or less progressive tax structure?

3. Suppose that all types of property are assessed equally in a given state with taxable value equal to market value. Now suppose that a change is made to assess industrial property at 0 percent of market value, so that effectively no property tax is levied on industrial properties in the state.

   a. If the other types of property are commercial and residential, analyze the expected effect of this change on the amount, prices, and rate of return of industrial and other property in the state. Does it make any difference whether this tax change attracts any new investment from outside the state?

b. How would the analysis and results be different if the state reduced industrial property taxes but required that total property tax revenue remain the same?

4. Suppose one state introduces a new property tax relief program that provides state-financed property tax credits equal to 20 percent of taxes up to a maximum of $1,000 for all homeowners with incomes no greater than $30,000. In one school district, homeowners pay $4,000 in property taxes to finance per-pupil expenditures of $4,000. You believe that the elasticity of property taxes with respect to the taxpayer's property tax price is 1.5.

a. What is the effect of the credit on the marginal property tax price for taxpayers in this district with income less than $30,000? For taxpayers with income above $30,000?

b. The school district proposes to increase homeowner property taxes by $500 to $4,500 to provide education services of $4,500 worth per pupil. Would district taxpayers with income less than $30,000 support such a change? Explain. (Hint: Compare the gain in benefits to the gain in taxes net of the credit.)

SELECTED READINGS

Aaron, Henry J. *Who Pays the Property Tax*. Washington, D.C.: The Brookings Institution, 1975.

Fischel, William A. "Homevoters, Municipal Corporate Governance, and the Benefit View of the Property Tax." *National Tax Journal* 54, No. 1 (March 2001): 157–173.

Hamilton, Bruce W. "A Review: Is the Property Tax a Benefit Tax?" In *Local Provision of Public Services: The Tiebout Model after Twenty-five Years*, ed. George R. Zodrow. New York: Academic Press, 1983.

Ladd, Helen F., editor. *Local Government Tax and Land Use Policies in the United States*. Cheltenham, UK: Edward Elgar, 1998.

McLure, Charles E. Jr. "The 'New View' of the Property Tax: A Caveat." *National Tax Journal* 30 (March 1977): 69–75.

Mieszkowski, Peter. "The Property Tax: An Excise Tax or a Profits Tax?" *Journal of Public Economics* 1, No. 1 (April 1972): 73–96.

Property Taxation and Local Government Finance. Wallace Oates, ed. Cambridge, MA: Lincoln Institute of Land Policy, 2001.

Zodrow, George R. "The Property Tax as a Capital Tax: A Room with Three Views." *National Tax Journal* 54, No. 1 (March 2001): 139–156.

SALES AND EXCISE TAXES

The most extensive use of retail sales taxation in any country is to be found in the states of the United States.[1]
—JOHN F. DUE

HEADLINES

". . . THE ANNOUNCEMENT BY SEARS THAT IT PLANS TO BUY LANDS' END SET THE RETAIL INDUSTRY ABUZZ.

WHATEVER IT MAY MEAN TO THE BUSINESS SECTOR, THE SEARS-LANDS' END DEAL SUGGESTS SOMETHING ENTIRELY DIFFERENT TO THE 45 STATES AND 7,500 LOCALITIES THAT LEVY SALES TAXES: THE POSSIBILITY OF SPLITTING A POT OF $90 MILLION A YEAR. . . .

THE $90 MILLION REPRESENTS ROUGHLY THE AMOUNT OF ANNUAL SALES-TAX REVENUE THAT WISCONSIN-BASED LANDS' END CURRENTLY DOES NOT COLLECT ON ITS $1.6 BILLION IN SALES . . .

THAT'S BECAUSE . . . THE U.S. SUPREME COURT RULED THAT STATES CANNOT COMPEL A COMPANY TO COLLECT TAXES FOR THEM IF THAT COMPANY HAS NO PHYSICAL PRESENCE IN A STATE. LANDS' END HAS NO PHYSICAL PRESENCE—NO NEXUS—IN 46 STATES.

SEARS, ON THE OTHER HAND, OPERATES RETAIL STORES IN ALL 50 STATES. . . ."[2]

---

[1] *Sales Taxation*. Urbana: University of Illinois Press, 1957, 290.
[2] Lemov, Penelope. "The Untaxables." *Governing Magazine*, July 2002.

State–local governments use three major types of taxes to tax consumption by residents: so-called general sales taxes levied on retail sales, companion use taxes on resident purchases made in other jurisdictions, and excise taxes on specific goods or services. Examples of the latter are taxes on tobacco products, motor fuels, alcoholic beverages, transient accommodations, some utility services, and others. After reviewing recent trends in the use of these taxes and some important institutional details about their structure, we will consider the principal economic issues about the incidence and efficiency implications of these taxes.

RELIANCE ON CONSUMPTION TAXES

Just as property taxes are the major source of tax revenue for local governments, sales or consumption taxes remain the largest single source of revenue for state governments, providing about 28 percent of aggregate state government general revenue in 2002. State general sales, use, and gross receipts taxes alone accounted for about 19 percent of state general revenue, second in magnitude only to federal aid, as shown in Table 15.1. State government reliance on general sales taxes has increased slightly since 1962, rising from 16.4 percent of revenue in that year, largely because of rate increases. State and local general sales taxes generated more than $229 billion of revenue in 2003, representing 2.5 percent of personal income and a per-capita payment of about $798. General sales taxes are (and have been since 1969) used by 45 states, with current rates varying from a low of 2.9 percent in Colorado to a high of 7 percent in Mississippi, Rhode Island, and Tennessee, with 8 states at 5 percent and 13 states at 6 percent (see Figure 15.1).[3] The interstate variation in tax rates can be somewhat misleading, however, because substantial interstate variation also exists in sales tax bases (described in the next section).

Although about 81 percent of total general sales tax revenue went to state governments in 2002, about 7,500 local jurisdictions spread among 34 states also used local government general sales taxes. As reflected by the data in Table 15.1 and Figure 15.2, these local sales taxes were used mostly by counties, where they accounted for 5.8 percent of revenue in aggregate, and by municipalities, where they provided 7.1 percent of general revenue. In one special case, many boroughs (counties) and municipalities in Alaska use sales taxes even though the state government does not use a general sales tax. The combined state and local sales tax rate can become high in some locations—for instance, 9.25 percent in Memphis and Knoxville (Tennessee); 9 percent in Chicago and New Orleans; 8.5 percent in San Francisco; and 8.25 percent in Dallas, Houston, Los Angeles, and New York. The importance of local government sales taxes generally has risen in the past 30 years as more localities were given authority to, and then adopted, local sales taxes.

State–local governments also impose a number of "selective" sales taxes, which accounted for about 4.9 percent of state government general revenue and

---

[3]The states without a general sales tax are Alaska, Delaware, Montana, New Hampshire, and Oregon. The most recent sales tax adoption was by Vermont in 1969.

Table 15.1

General and Selective Sales Taxes as a Percent of General Revenue, by Level of Government, Various Years

Year	States	All	Counties	Municipalities	Townships	School Districts	Special Districts
		Local Governments					
1962							
General[b]	16.4%	2.5%	1.1%	6.6%	a	a	a
All[c]	38.6	3.8	1.5	9.9	1.5	a	a
1972							
General	17.9	2.6	3.2	5.4	a	0.2	0.8
All	33.7	4.1	3.8	9.1	1.6	0.2	0.9
1977							
General	18.3	3.1	3.9	5.8	a	0.3	1.2
All	31.0	4.6	4.7	9.6	2.1	0.3	1.2
1982							
General	18.3	3.6	4.4	6.9	a	0.4	2.2
All	28.6	5.3	5.5	11.1	0.1	0.4	2.2
1987							
General	19.0	4.2	5.7	7.3	a	0.3	3.8
All	28.6	6.0	6.9	12.0	0.1	0.3	3.8
1992							
General	17.9	4.2	5.9	7.4	a	0.3	4.1
All	27.0	6.0	7.2	12.1	0.2	0.3	4.1
1997							
General	18.7	4.1	5.8	7.1	a	0.3	4.4
All	27.8	6.0	7.1	11.9	a	0.3	4.4
2002							
General	18.7	4.1	5.8	7.1	a	0.3	4.4
All	27.8	6.0	7.1	11.9	a	0.3	4.4

SOURCES: U.S. Department of Commerce, Bureau of the Census. State and Local *Government Finances,* various years.

[a]Less than 0.1 percent.

[b]*General* includes state and local government general sales and gross receipts taxes.

[c]*All* includes state and local government selective excise taxes as well as general sales and gross receipts taxes.

1.8 percent of aggregate local government general revenue in 2002, on various goods and services. Unlike general sales taxes, the share of state and local government revenue provided by these selective excise taxes has declined over the past 25 years. Selective sales taxes amounted to slightly more than $108 billion in 2003, or about $378 per capita. These selective sales taxes may be unit taxes, as with gasoline and cigarettes, or *ad valorem* (percentage) taxes, as are commonly used for hotel accommodations or telephone services. In many cases, these selective sales taxes are imposed in addition to the general sales tax on the sale of these goods or services.

Figure 15.1

State general sales taxes, 2005

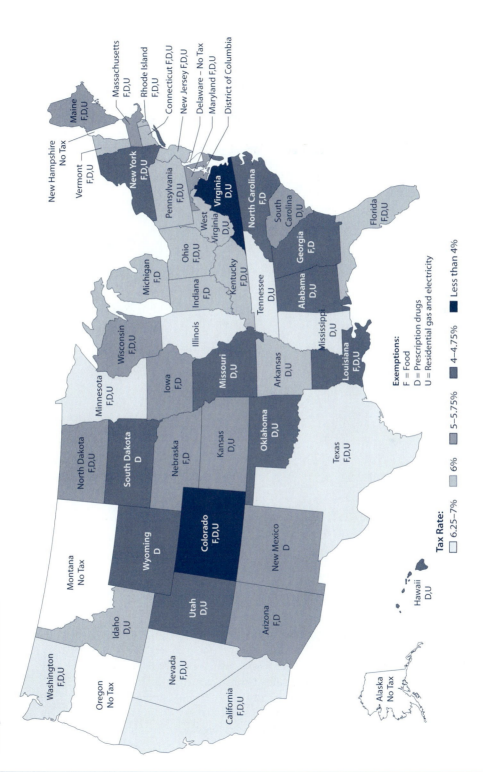

Exemptions:
F = Food
D = Prescription drugs
U = Residential gas and electricity

Tax Rate:

- 6.25–7%
- 6%
- 5–5.75%
- 4–4.75%
- Less than 4%

Figure 15.2

Local sales taxes, 2005

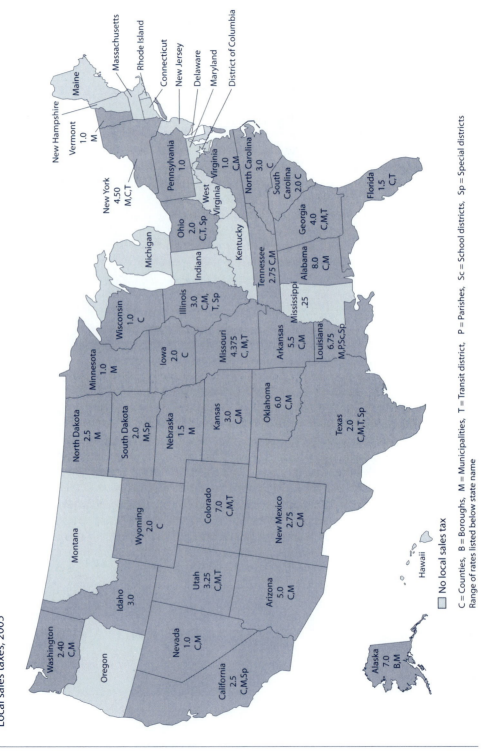

Washington
2.40
C,M

Oregon

Idaho
3.0

Montana

Nevada
1.0
C,M

California
2.5
C,M,Sp

Utah
3.25
C,M,T

Wyoming
2.0
C

Colorado
7.0
C,M,T

North Dakota
2.5
M

Minnesota
1.0
M

Wisconsin
1.0
C

Michigan

Maine

New Hampshire

Vermont
1.0
M

Massachusetts

Rhode Island

Connecticut

New York
4.50
M,C,T

Pennsylvania
1.0

New Jersey

Delaware

Maryland

District of Columbia

West Virginia
1.0
C,M

Virginia
1.0
C,M

Ohio
2.0
C,T, Sp

Indiana

Illinois
3.0
C,M,
T, Sp

Iowa
2.0
C

South Dakota
2.0
M,Sp

Nebraska
1.5
M

Kansas
3.0
C,M

Missouri
4.375
C, M,T

Kentucky

Tennessee
2.75 C,M

North Carolina
3.0
C

South Carolina
2.0 C

Georgia
4.0
C,M,T

Alabama
8.0
C,M

Mississippi
.25

Arkansas
5.5
C,M

Louisiana
6.75
M,P,Sc,Sp

Florida
1.5
C,T

Oklahoma
6.0
C,M

New Mexico
2.75
C,M

Arizona
5.0
C,M

Texas
2.0
C,M,T, Sp

Alaska
7.0
B,M

Hawaii

☐ No local sales tax

C = Counties,   B = Boroughs,   M = Municipalities,   T = Transit district,   P = Parishes,   Sc = School districts,   Sp = Special districts
Range of rates listed below state name

CONSUMPTION TAX STRUCTURE ISSUES

General Sales and Use Taxes

In principle, general sales taxes are intended to tax the total final personal consumption of the residents in the jurisdictions levying the tax. In practice, state general sales taxes fall short of this principle because (1) a substantial amount of personal consumption is statutorily exempt from taxation (such as food for home consumption), making these taxes somewhat less than "general"; (2) final (retail) as opposed to intermediate consumption is difficult to define, so the taxes end up applying to sales of some intermediate goods (goods used to produce final consumer goods) in addition to consumer goods; and (3) states face inherent administrative difficulties in collecting taxes on purchases of final consumer goods made by residents in other jurisdictions. These deviations from the principle correspond to the three traditional features that characterize a sales tax structure: the *base* on which the tax is to be applied, the *stage(s) of production* at which the tax is to be collected, and the *location* at which the activity is to be taxed.

Tax Base

For sales taxes to be truly general consumption taxes, they would apply to total personal consumption—that is, all uses of income except for investment (saving by individuals) and purchase of government services.[4] In fact, no state's sales tax base approaches total personal consumption; all states exempt major categories of consumption from sales taxation, although the use of these exemptions also varies greatly among the 45 sales tax states, as shown previously in Figure 15.1. First, state sales taxes typically apply more commonly to consumer goods than services. Sales of housing services, for instance—whether from owner-occupied houses or rental housing—are exempt from direct sales taxation in all states. Generally, sales of professional services (medical, legal, financial) are not taxed, although sales of personal services (laundry, grooming) and repair services are partially taxed only in some states. The states that include many services in their sales tax base are Hawaii, New Mexico, South Dakota, and West Virginia; however, medical services are included in the general sales tax base only in Hawaii. In addition, sales of food for home consumption (groceries) are exempt in 28 states and D.C., sales of prescription drugs are exempt in 44 states and D.C., and sales of electricity and natural gas to residential consumers are exempt in 32 states.

The net effect of these exemptions is that state general sales taxes apply to perhaps only 40 to 60 percent of personal consumption in aggregate with obvious substantial variation among the states, depending on the degree of exemptions used.[5]

---

[4]In simple macroeconomic models, national income comprises personal consumption, investment, and purchases of government goods and services, that is,

$$Y = C + I + G.$$

[5]In 2002, state government general sales tax revenue was about $180 billion, while total personal consumption was $7385 billion. At the median state sales tax rate of 5.5 percent, this implies a sales tax base equal to about 44 percent of personal consumption.

Table 15.2

Potential Sales Tax Bases, 2004

Category	Amount (Billions of Dollars)	Percentage of Personal Consumption
Personal Income	$9673.0	117.5%
Disposable Personal Income	8634.0	104.9
Personal Consumption	8229.9	100.0
Consumption Expenditures on		
Food	1150.3	14.0
Clothing	326.5	4.0
All Services	4859.0	59.0
Housing	1239.0	15.1
Medical Care	1391.7	16.9
Household Gas and Electric	177.9	2.2
Consumption Less Expenditures on Food and All Services	2220.6	27.0
Consumption Less Expenditures on Food, Housing, Medical Care and Household Gas and Electric	4271.0	51.9
Consumption Less Expenditure on Housing and Medical Care	5599.2	68.0

SOURCE: *Consumer Expenditure Survey, 2000.*

Cline and Neubig (1999) estimate that only about 34 percent of consumption spending is subject to state and use taxation. Mazerov (2003) shows that purchases of durable goods plus purchases of nondurable goods, excluding food, account for only about 33 percent of household expenditures. The data in Table 15.2 illustrate how much the sales tax base can be eroded by even a few exemptions. In 2002, food purchases accounted for 14 percent of personal consumption, expenditures for housing services for 15 percent, and medical care services for another 17 percent. For illustration, if purchases of all services and food are excluded from the sales tax, the remaining base is only about 27 percent of the total personal consumption. If only purchases of food, electricity/natural gas, and housing/medical care services are exempt, the remaining base represents about 52 percent of personal consumption. Even if only housing and medical care services are exempt from the sales tax, the sales tax base would represent only about 68 percent of personal consumption.

This suggests that in some ways distinguishing between "general" and "selective" sales taxes is an illusion; both apply only to some consumer purchases of goods and services, although the general sales tax base is still broader than the sum of the purchases to which selective sales taxes are applied. One interesting economic implication of the general sales tax exemptions is that they provide consumers a way to avoid sales taxes by shifting consumption toward goods and services that are not directly taxed. Of course, such a change in behavior entails efficiency costs for the economy due to the changes in goods consumed and produced only due to the sales tax effects. In that sense, the analysis of general and selective sales taxes is similar.

Stages of Production

Sales taxes can be levied at any and all stages of production of goods and services, although three options are generally considered. At one end of the spectrum, the tax is levied only on the final sale of goods and services for private consumption, at the so-called retail level. In this case, the sale of intermediate goods—that is, goods to be subsequently used to produce other consumer goods and services—is not subject to the tax. Because the tax is levied only at the last or final stage of production, the total or effective tax rate faced by consumers is the nominal rate.

At the opposite end of the spectrum, a sales tax is levied on *all* sales or transactions, that is, at all stages of production. Such a tax is often called a **multistage gross receipts tax,** because it applies to the gross receipts or sales of all firms. For instance, if a 1-percent gross receipts tax is applied to the production of bread, 1 percent is levied on the sale of wheat by farmers to millers, 1 percent is levied on the sale of flour by millers to bakers, 1 percent is levied on the sale of equipment by manufacturers to bakers, 1 percent is levied on the sale of bread by bakers to retailers, and, finally, 1 percent is imposed on the sale of bread by retailers to consumers. The taxes levied at the stages of production before final retail sale become part of the costs of production and are therefore imbedded in the retail price charged to the consumer. The gross receipts tax is said to **cascade** or **pyramid** through the various stages of production, and therefore the total or effective rate of tax paid by the consumer is greater than the nominal rate levied on the retail sale.

Multistage taxes of this type generate a number of equity and efficiency problems. Part of the tax burden is implicit or hidden, and because that implicit tax burden varies for different types of goods, the effective tax rate also varies among different goods. Because intrafirm transactions are not taxed, firms have an incentive to integrate vertically (produce intermediate goods internally) to reduce taxes. If only some producer inputs are subject to sales tax, the change in the relative cost of inputs creates an incentive for firms to alter production techniques. These issues are discussed in detail in Chapter 17 (because gross receipts taxes have been used by some states as general business taxes).

A sales tax also can be levied at one stage of production but before final retail sale. For instance, the tax might be levied on the sale of goods from wholesalers to retailers, with no additional tax then collected on the sale from the retailer to the consumer. Or a sales tax might be imposed only on the sale of a product by the manufacturer to a distributor, wholesaler, or retailer, a so-called manufacturer's sales tax. This tax structure avoids some but not all the problems created by multistage sales taxes. No cascading of the tax occurs—that is, no tax is imposed upon prior tax—because the tax is levied only at one stage of production; however, the effective tax rate paid by consumers varies by product and producer, depending on the relative importance of the taxed stage in the final cost of the product. For instance, a wholesale sales tax would apply only to the cost of goods purchased by retailers to resell. But the retailer's business costs also include the labor and capital costs of the retail business. The wholesale sales tax would be a larger fraction of total retailer cost for retailers with *lower* labor and capital costs. Similarly, the larger the manufacturing costs of a good (compared to distribution, marketing, and sales costs), the greater the effective rate to the consumer of a sales tax imposed only at the manufacturing stage.

If state sales taxes are intended to be retail taxes on the final sale of consumer goods and services, then sales of all goods used in production would have to be exempt, but no state goes that far. Nearly all states provide sales tax exemptions for the sales of goods that are to be resold and then taxed and for sales of materials used in production that become a *physical ingredient of the final product*. States diverge in their sales tax treatment of equipment and machinery, of materials that are used in production but that do not become an ingredient of the product (fuels, for example), and of materials and supplies used in business but not in production (computers, for example). Regarding equipment and machinery, John Due and John Mikesell (1994) reported that 25 of the 45 sales tax states fully exempt capital assets used in production, with a common requirement that the machinery and equipment must be *directly used in production*. Another 15 states provide a partial exemption or tax machinery and equipment purchases at a lower rate. Regarding materials that do not become an ingredient of the final product, Due and Mikesell (1994) report that 24 states have general exemptions and a few other states provide limited exemptions. Accordingly, state sales taxes are not exclusively retail taxes but apply to at least some purchases of intermediate goods (including capital goods) by businesses.

State sales tax treatment of business purchases often also varies depending on whether the sale of the product is taxed. It is fairly common sales tax practice for firms that produce or sell nontaxable goods or services to be treated as the final consumers of taxable goods or services used in the business. Thus, these firms must pay sales tax on those purchases. For instance, if the sale of a house is not taxed, the builder may have to pay sales tax on materials and supplies used to construct the house. (Sale of material to contractors is taxable in 42 states.) The economic effect of this treatment is equivalent to that from a direct sales tax on the goods or services produced by such firms, although at a lower rate than the general rate. If a firm providing a tax-exempt service spends 20 percent of its total costs on taxable materials and supplies (the other 80 percent being spent on labor, real property, and utilities that are not taxed) at a sales tax rate of 5 percent, the tax raises the firm's costs by 1 percent. If fully passed on to consumers, this is equivalent economically to a 1 percent tax on the sale of the firm's service. Consumers of goods or services that are not taxed at the retail sale may still bear a sales tax burden, therefore, if sales tax is paid by the businesses producing those goods or services.

States often exempt business purchases by issuing exemption certificates or exemption numbers to businesses that regularly purchase otherwise taxable goods or services that are to be used for production rather than for consumption. It is sometimes difficult to distinguish at the time of sale whether the good will be consumed or used in the production of other goods, which depends on the nature of the buyer rather than on the nature of the good. For instance, a truck purchased by an individual for private use is private consumption, and the sale should be taxed under a retail sales tax; but a truck purchased by a manufacturer and used in production (to transport parts, perhaps) is an intermediate good, with that sale ideally not to be taxed under a retail sales tax. With the presentation of the certificate or number, a seller does not collect sales tax on sales of otherwise taxable goods or services to these businesses. The use of exemption certificates and numbers creates some administrative problems and the potential for fraud, however; a business owner may purchase items for personal use but represent them as business purchases, or counterfeit exemption certificates may be used.

Tax Location and Use Taxes

Consumption taxes may be based either on the **origin principle,** with tax based on the location of the sale, or on the **destination principle,** with tax based on the location of consumption or of the consumer. Again, in theory, state sales taxes are intended to be destination-based taxes, taxing consumption where it occurs. Accordingly, state sales taxes are not collected on purchases of otherwise taxable goods if those goods are to be delivered to a consumer in another state. For this reason, consumers usually are not charged sales tax on mail-order or Internet purchases if the selling company is located in a different state from the purchaser. On the other hand, sales tax is charged on purchases by a nonresident if the buyer takes possession of the good in the state where the purchase occurred. The presumption is that consumption occurs where the buyer receives the good.

To implement the destination principle, however, a state's residents must be taxed on *all* taxable consumption, regardless of where the good was purchased. But buyers pay *no* sales tax on purchases that are delivered to the state of residence from other states. The resident's state cannot impose a sales tax because no sale occurred in that state. To correct this difficulty, all states with general sales taxes also impose a companion **use tax** on the use of taxable goods and services at the same rate as the sales tax; the use tax is collected only if the sales tax is not. An individual who avoids sales tax by purchasing a good in another state, therefore, owes **use tax** to his state of residence instead, equal to what the sales tax would have been. The collection of use taxes is administratively difficult, which limits the degree to which the destination principle is achieved. Simply put, collecting use taxes is often prohibitively expensive. In practice, retail businesses can be required to collect use tax for other states on sales to residents of those other states if that firm also has establishments (nexus is the legal term) in those other states. Otherwise, the collection of use taxes generally is limited to large purchases (such as taxable business equipment) and those that can be tracked through a state government's regulatory authority (such as automobiles, boats, airplanes).

Application 15.1

SALES TAXES ON SERVICES

Including broad sets of services in state sales tax bases has become an important and controversial state–local tax issue. When most state general sales taxes first were adopted in the 1930s and 1940s, the idea was to tax the sale or exchange of a tangible item, essentially broadening the concept of excise taxes on specific commodities. In addition, services were less important economically than goods, with expenditures on services accounting for less than one-third of purchases in the 1940s and that for goods about two-thirds. By 2002, however, the situation had nearly reversed, with expenditures on services representing almost 60 percent of consumption and that on goods only a little more than 40 percent.

As the nature of personal consumption and the national economy evolved over these years, many states added some specific services to sales tax bases, as shown in Table 15A.1. Services that commonly are taxed by state sales taxes include telephone use, rental of hotel rooms and other lodging as well as rentals of other tangible property, admission to amusements and some recreational activities, some personal services such as laundry and dry cleaning or shoe and garment repairs, and some services that often are consumed by businesses as much as individuals, such as photo finishing, photocopying, and packaged software. However, when measured by dollars of spending, the bulk of services remain untaxed, including professional activities such as medical, legal, and engineering services and personal activities such as barber and beauty services, and some repairs, installation, or fabrication. In addition,

housing service is not taxed directly (as noted previously, construction usually is not taxed, but the sale of materials that go into a house's construction are).

These state service-tax decisions reflect some pattern and economic logic. Most states tax personal property rentals because most of the service involves the exchange of that property (much as would occur if someone bought the item and then resold it later). When the sale of property and service can be separated, as with some repairs, many states tax the good but not the service. Many services that involve tangible property substantially, such as photofinishing or photocopying, are also taxed. On the other hand, services that do not involve substantial exchange of tangible property, such as beauty, financial, legal, or medical services, are not taxed generally. Recognizing the concept that the general sales tax is intended as a tax on final sales to consumers, states usually avoid taxes on services that are purchased mostly as intermediate goods by businesses.

Still, strange results often arise even if this general pattern is followed. Almost all the sales-tax states place a tax on the sale of packaged software, but only 16 states tax the sale of custom-made software. Apparently the idea is that packaged software is a good while the custom-designed software is a service. Similarly, videotape or DVD rentals are taxed in 45 of the 46 sales tax jurisdictions (because rentals are taxed generally), but cable television service is taxed in only 24 jurisdictions and admission to theaters in 31. Apparently, having a tape or DVD of a movie in your possession (temporarily or permanently) involves

Application 15.1 — Sales Taxes on Services

Number of States (and the District of Columbia) Including Specific Services in the General Sales Tax, 2004

Service	Number of States
Residential intrastate telephone	42
Cellular telephone service	40
Residential electricity and gas	24
Photofinishing	44
Photocopying	42
Packaged software	45
Custom software	16
Mainframe computer use (service)	11
Videotape rentals	45
Cable television service	24
Admission to professional sporting events and amusements parks	36
Admission to school/college sporting events	25
Admission to cultural events	31
Health clubs and gyms	20
Parking	20
Taxi service	8
Legal services	5[*]
Medical services	4[*]
Repair, materials	46
Repair, labor	23
Rental of personal property	44
Insurance services	6
Banking services	3
Barber and beauty services	6
Laundry and dry cleaning	21
Carpet cleaning	15

SOURCE: Federation of Tax Administrators, *Sales Taxation of Services*, http://www.taxadmin.org/, 2004.

[*]Includes businesses gross receipts taxes in Delaware and Washington.

transfer of a good and creates a tax liability while just viewing the movie at a theater or on television does not. Laundry and dry cleaning (for clothes) is taxed in 21 instances, but carpet cleaning in only 15. Barber and beauty services (what one might think of as personal cleaning) are taxed in only 6 states. Car parking in lots and garages is taxed in 20 states, but taxi service in only 8. Other anomalies result from specific public policy decisions. For instance, 42 states include local residential telephone services in the sales tax base, but only 24 include residential electricity or natural gas service, and 36 states tax admissions to professional sporting events while only 25 tax admissions to college/school sports events.

State taxation of one particular service—Internet access—has been restricted by federal law. The Internet Tax Freedom Act of 1998 effectively prohibited the adoption of any *new* taxes on Internet access services for a

Application 15.1 — Sales Taxes on Services

three-year period. That moratorium was subsequently extended until November, 2003. After expiring, the moratorium on Internet access taxation was then extended by Congress until 2007. So, as this is being written, federal law prevents states and localities from adding Internet access service to the sales tax base.

What alternative policy might states follow regarding sales taxation of services and what would the resulting economic effects be? Although it has been suggested that states tax all services, such a policy would not be in keeping with the traditional sales tax idea of taxing final sales to consumers. Sales of services to businesses—for example legal, accounting, engineering, computer, or advertising services—should remain tax exempt if the final sale of goods or services produced using those inputs is taxed.[6] In some instances, this principle requires that sales of particular services (such as legal) to final consumers be taxed while sales of that same service to businesses is exempt (as is done currently with the sale of some goods). Of course, if sales taxation of services is limited to final sales to consumers of currently untaxed services, the revenue potential is much smaller than if all services were taxed.

Fox and Murray (1988) report that if all services were taxed, sales tax revenue could increase by more than 46 percent. Almost half of that increase comes from taxing construction, however, much of which represents an intermediate purchase by businesses. More recently, Mazerov (2003) estimates that full sales taxation of services purchased by households—excluding medical, legal, housing, education, banking, insurance, and public transit services—has the potential to increase state sales tax revenue by 25 to 35 percent, depending on the state.

At least three other major factors should be noted. First, consumption expenditures on some services vary substantially as economic conditions change. For instance, Dye and McGuire (1991) report that expenditures on residential utilities and personal services are highly variable, which could increase the business-cycle variability of state sales taxes. Second, it seems unlikely that state sales taxation of consumer services could cause much relocation of economic activity among states. The local nature of most services implies that locational effects on sales should be small. (It seems unlikely that people would go to other states to purchase utility services, repairs, personal services, or medical care to avoid state sales taxes.) Finally, the evidence suggests that the effect of taxing services on the distribution of overall tax burden depends on which services are taxed. Siegfield and Smith (1991) report that sales taxes on electric and gas utilities and hospital services are highly regressive, but that taxes on services by banks, hotels, and educational institutions are progressive. The broad Florida sales tax on services adopted and then repealed during 1986–1987 (which affected most all services, including intermediate goods, but excluding health and educational services) was reported to be regressive for the bottom 20 percent of the income distribution but nearly proportional after that.

---

[6]Exempting the sale of steel to an automobile manufacturer and then taxing the sale of the car to the consumer is equivalent to not taxing the sale of advertising service to the manufacturer but taxing the sale of the car. The sales price of the car includes all the manufacturer's costs, including for the steel and the advertising.

Application 15.1 — Sales Taxes on Services

Broader taxation of consumer services seems almost necessary if state general sales taxes are to be thought of as state taxes on final consumption. Such taxes need not apply to intermediate purchases of services by business, but exempting business purchases complicates the tax (as it does with goods). Extending state sales taxes to consumer services will require many more sellers to participate in sales tax collection (increasing compliance and administration costs) and may alter the variability and progressivity of state tax structures. By applying broadly to consumer purchases, however, the tax will not create an incentive to purchase services over goods and will continue to reflect consumer expenditures as consumer decisions continue to change in the future. Some argue that given the changes in the nature of consumption by households, which are expected to continue, the issue is having a sales tax for the 21st Century economy.

Selective Sales Taxes

State–local governments also impose sales taxes on the sales of many specific commodities, usually including tobacco products, motor fuels, alcoholic beverages (in the bottle and/or by the glass), hotel and motel accommodations, restaurant meals, and some utility services (often telephone service). Unlike general sales taxes, for which often both the tax rate and tax base differ among the states, excise tax bases vary little among the states, although tax rates vary substantially. The 2005 rates for two common state excise taxes on cigarettes and gasoline are shown in Table 15.3. Cigarette excise taxes vary from $.05 per pack of 20 (in North Carolina) to a median of $.695 per pack to a high of $2.46 per pack (in Rhode Island). State gasoline excise taxes vary from $.075 per gallon (in Georgia) to a median of $.21 per gallon to a high of $.31 per gallon (in Rhode Island).[7] Perhaps surprisingly, interstate tax rates vary more on cigarettes than on gasoline, an issue we turn to later when considering the incentive created by sales taxes to change where purchases are made.

As with general sales taxes, excise taxes also may be levied at the manufacturing, wholesale, or retail stages of production. Commonly, state gasoline and local hotel taxes are levied at the retail stage, whereas state cigarette taxes are levied at the wholesale or distributor stage, for instance. These excise taxes are not necessarily substitutes for state sales taxes. As shown previously in Table 15.3, cigarette sales are subject to the general state sales tax in 37 states, while gasoline also is subject to the sales tax in 9 states.

Besides generating revenue, excise taxes can serve two other purposes. One is to change consumer behavior, reducing consumption of goods that create

---

[7]The federal government also imposed excise taxes of $.39 per pack of cigarettes and $.184 per gallon of gasoline (in 2005).

Table 15.3

Selected State Excise Taxes, 2005

Jurisdiction	Cigarettes		Gasoline	
	Excise Tax (Dollars/Pack)	State Sales Tax Applied	Excise Tax (Dollars/Gal.)	State Sales Tax Applied
New England				
Connecticut	1.51	X	.25	
Maine	1.00	X	.252	
Massachusetts	1.51		.21	
New Hampshire	.52		.18	
Rhode Island	2.46		.31	X
Vermont	1.19	X	.19	
Mideast				
Delaware	.55		.23	
Maryland	1.00		.235	
New Jersey	2.40		.105	
New York	1.50	X	.232	X
Pennsylvania	1.35	X	.18	
Great Lakes				
Illinois	.98	X	.201	X
Indiana	.555	X	.18	X
Michigan	2.00	X	.19	
Ohio	.55	X	.26	
Wisconsin	.77	X	.291	
Plains				
Iowa	.36	X	.205	
Kansas	.79	X	.24	
Minnesota	.48	X	.20	
Missouri	.17	X	.17	
Nebraska	.64	X	.263	
North Dakota	.44	X	.17	
South Dakota	.53		.22	
Southeast				
Alabama	.475	X	.18	
Arkansas	.59		.215	
Florida	.339	X	.145	
Georgia	.37	X	.075	X
Kentucky	.30	X	.174	
Louisiana	.36	X	.20	X
Mississippi	.18	X	.184	
North Carolina	.05	X	.2685	
South Carolina	.07	X	.16	
Tennessee	.20	X	.214	
Virginia	.30	X	.175	X
West Virginia	.55	X	.27	
Southwest				
Arizona	1.18	X	.18	
New Mexico	.91	X	.189	
Oklahoma	1.03	X	.17	
Texas	.41	X	.20	

Table 15.3

(continued)

	Cigarettes		Gasoline	
Jurisdiction	Excise Tax (Dollars/Pack)	State Sales Tax Applied	Excise Tax (Dollars/Gal.)	State Sales Tax Applied
Rocky Mountain				
Colorado	.87		.22	
Idaho	.57	X	.25	
Montana	1.70		.27	
Utah	.695	X	.245	
Wyoming	.60		.14	
Far West				
Alaska	1.60		.08	
California	.87	X	.18	X
Hawaii	1.40	X	.16	X
Nevada	.80	X	.23	
Oregon	1.18		.24	
Washington	1.425	X	.28	
Median	.695		.21	

SOURCE: National Conference of State Legislatures, http://www.ncsl.org/; Federation of Tax Administrators, http://www.taxadmin.org/fta.

consumption externalities or goods that are otherwise determined to be socially undesirable. Excise taxes with this purpose are sometimes called **sumptuary taxes** and are intended to increase economic efficiency by offsetting negative externalities. Excise taxes also can be used for equity reasons, to alter the distribution of tax burden. For instance, excise taxes on goods consumed relatively more by higher-income individuals will increase the progressivity or reduce the regressivity of the state and local tax structure.

ECONOMIC ANALYSIS: EFFICIENCY

Sales taxes can influence economic decisions in three major ways. First, the tax reduces consumers' disposable incomes and thus induces changes in consumption of all goods. This **income effect** arises because the tax transfers resources from private consumption to government (which would occur with any revenue source used to generate equal collections). Second, if the sales tax is at least partly paid by consumers, it raises the relative price of taxed compared to untaxed goods, which may induce some consumers to substitute exempt commodities for taxable ones. Third, if some states or localities do not tax a commodity as heavily as other jurisdictions, and if use taxes cannot be collected effectively, consumers may be induced to substitute purchases in other jurisdictions for purchases in their own. These latter results, called **substitution or price effects,** arise because sales taxes affect prices. These price effects are the sources of the potential efficiency costs of sales and excise taxes. Each is considered separately.

Optimal Sales Tax Structure

Because sales and excise taxes alter the relative prices of some goods, creating incentives for consumers and producers (to the extent sales of intermediate goods are taxed) to change their behavior, the tax can result in a loss of economic efficiency or the creation of an excess burden. It is natural therefore to consider what sales tax structure will minimize this efficiency loss for any given revenue yield—that is, what sales tax structure is optimal, where structure refers to the effective tax rate levied on consumption of various goods and services. As a policy matter, the question is usually phrased in terms of whether it is preferable to apply the sales tax to the broadest possible base of consumer goods and services all taxed at one rate or to allow numerous exemptions, effectively taxing some goods at lower or even zero rates.

The general theoretical rule for optimal commodity taxation, usually attributed to Frank Ramsey (1927), is deceptively simple: *The optimal set of sales taxes should cause an equal proportionate decrease in the compensated quantity demanded of all commodities* (the compensated demand is the demand after the consumer is compensated for the income effect of the tax).[8] If all consumer goods, including leisure, can be taxed, then the rule implies that an equal proportionate tax is best. With an equal percentage tax on all commodities, the *relative* prices of all goods are not changed, and consequently no substitution effects are created. The tax has only an income effect and is equivalent to a lump-sum tax. But what if, in practice, it is impossible to impose a sales tax on all commodities, especially leisure (inherently, time)? In that case, the rule becomes more complicated, and a uniform proportionate tax is no longer most efficient.

The intuition behind this notion is illustrated in Figure 15.3. $Demand_A$ and $Demand_B$ are the compensated demand curves for the only two taxable commodities, A and B (assume leisure is the other good). Before any taxes, the prices of both are equal to P_0, which reflects the social marginal cost of each, with consumption equal to A_0 and B_0. Suppose a tax rate of t_A is levied on consumption of A and a lower rate of t_B is levied on B. These rates were selected so that the consumption of both goods decreases by 20 percent, to A_1 and B_1. The efficiency cost of these taxes is represented by the loss of consumer surplus in both markets, equal to the sum of areas ZYX and WVU in Figure 15.3. If, instead, an equal tax rate sufficient to generate the same revenue, shown as t_C in the figure, was levied on the consumption of both goods, the resulting efficiency loss would be greater. In essence, the somewhat smaller efficiency cost in consuming A (because of the lower tax rate) is more than offset by the much larger efficiency cost in consuming B (from tax rate t_C compared to t_B). Given the conditions of the illustration, the differential rates t_A and t_B generate a given amount of revenue with less excess burden than the single rate t_C.[9]

On pure economic efficiency grounds, then, this result contradicts what has often been the conventional policy wisdom favoring broad coverage. For instance,

---

[8]The compensated demand curve represents how consumers change quantity purchased when price changes if consumers' real income is held constant. The reason for looking at compensated demand curves is that the issue is the structure of the tax, not the level; presumably, the same revenue is to be collected from consumers whatever tax structure is used.

[9]In this illustration, the demand for these two goods is independent; changes in the price of one do not affect the demand for the other. The price changes caused by the taxes may, however, affect the demand for the other commodity, leisure. The Ramsey rule applies as well if commodities are substitutes or complements.

Figure 15.3

Efficiency cost of
alternative sales
tax rates

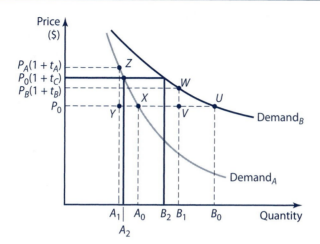

in their treatise on sales taxes, Due and Mikesell (1994, p. 15) state that "[the tax] should apply to all consumption expenditures, and thus to all sales for consumption purposes, at a uniform rate." However, the preceding illustration shows that differential rates may be more efficient than a single rate. Moreover, the optimal rate on some commodities could be zero—that is, having sales tax exemptions could be optimal. Of course, economic efficiency is not the only criterion by which a tax structure should be evaluated. As Due and Mikesell also argue, consideration of equity objectives and cost of administration need to be taken into account.

In general, the optimal sales tax rule depends on whether it is feasible to set tax rates based on the price elasticity of demand and supply for those goods and on the cross-price effects among commodities. Unfortunately, this economic research often has been more successful at characterizing nonoptimal tax structures than in identifying feasible rules to guide policy decisions. David Bradford and Harvey Rosen (1976, p. 96) have stated that "the extensive . . . work [on optimal taxation] has shown how difficult it is to sustain *any* simple rules for commodity taxation. . . ." Nevertheless, the optimal tax rules for some conditions can be a guide to policy.

First, if the demands for different commodities are not related—that is, if they are neither substitutes nor complements—then the Ramsey optimal tax rule implies that commodities should be taxed inversely proportional to their price elasticity of demand; higher tax rates should apply to commodities with relatively less elastic demand. The intuition behind such a rule is simple. Because inefficiency results from consumers' changing behavior in response to the tax-induced price increase, inefficiency is minimized by imposing relatively higher taxes on consumers who will change behavior relatively little. In fact, this is exactly the case shown earlier in Figure 15.3 because the demand for both A and B is not affected by changes in the price of the other good. The efficient tax structure required a higher tax rate on commodity A, the one with the less price-elastic demand.

Second, if taxing leisure directly with sales taxes is not feasible, efficiency may be increased by imposing relatively high tax rates on commodities that are complementary to or jointly consumed with leisure. Certainly, these commodities should not be exempt from tax. By imposing taxes on those commodities consumed with leisure, an indirect tax is imposed on the consumption of leisure. This argument can be used to support sales taxation of admissions to sporting events and other types of entertainment and of club dues, as well as selective excise taxes on goods used for leisure-time activities, such as boats or other recreational equipment.

Although no researcher has attempted to measure the efficiency consequences of state sales tax exemptions in the United States directly, Charles Ballard and John Shoven (1985) estimated efficiency effects of a uniform value-added tax (VAT) imposed by the national government in the United States compared to a VAT with exemptions and differential rates. A VAT of the type they considered is a type of national sales tax (although collected through businesses at each stage of production). They compare a tax at a flat rate on all personal consumption to one that exempts housing and services and imposes a lower rate on food, which, of course, is very similar to the typical state sales tax base. Ballard and Shoven (p. 17) base their estimates on a simulation model of the U.S. economy and conclude that "the rate differentiation reduces the efficiency gain offered by a consumption-type VAT [compared to the U.S. income tax] by an enormous amount. . . . The welfare sacrifice caused by rate differentiation is 17 percent of GNP [in 1973 dollars], and about .46 percent of the present value of future welfare (including leisure)."

If these results are accurate, they suggest that the current exemptions from state sales taxes do reduce economic efficiency when compared to more complete coverage, but that does not mean that some other sales tax structure of exemptions and differential rates might not be more efficient than a uniform tax. In many cases, however, policy evaluation of sales tax exemptions and the use of differential tax rates depend on more easily quantifiable factors such as the border effects from sales taxes and administrative cost considerations. Each of those issues is now considered.

Border Effects

Individuals also may be able to avoid or reduce sales taxes by changing the location of their purchases, generally by making purchases in jurisdictions that are different from the one in which they reside. Two different opportunities for avoiding the tax are available. First, an individual may purchase goods in one state or locality for delivery to a different location, presumably the state or locality where the individual lives. The individual is not subject to sales tax in the jurisdiction of the purchase, but is subject to any use tax levied by the jurisdiction of residence. If that use tax is not or cannot be collected, no state or local consumption tax is levied on the purchase. Second, if purchases of goods or services are taxed at a lower rate in one jurisdiction than in another, an individual may make purchases and take possession in the lower-tax jurisdiction, thus paying the lower sales tax rate. Again, this individual may be liable for a use tax equal to the difference between the tax rates, but that tax may not be feasible to collect.

Both of these opportunities are concerns particularly along borders between states or between localities where local sales taxes are used, although they are not limited to border areas as the illustration about Internet and mail order sales in Application 15.3 makes clear. The option to buy and take possession of goods in a lower-tax jurisdiction arises from a difference in tax rates or sales tax bases. The option of buying goods in one jurisdiction and having them delivered to another arises solely because of the difficulty in collecting use taxes. The magnitude of both effects depends on the size of transportation costs (of goods and/or consumers) compared to the potential tax savings, the variety of different goods or shops available in different locations, consumer awareness of tax differences and goods availability, and the effectiveness of administrative arrangements to collect use taxes.

Assuming that the net-of-tax prices of commodities sold in national markets are equal at all locations (implying horizontal supply curves at each location equal to the national price), then the economic effects of a sales tax rate differential between jurisdictions are straightforward. The consumer's price for any given commodity will vary between high- and low-tax jurisdictions by the full amount of the tax-rate difference. For example, Levi brand jeans are sold in a national market and are thus expected to carry the same net-of-tax price everywhere. Differences in tax rates would then lead to differences in consumer prices for Levis including the tax. This difference in prices, which is assumed to persist, induces consumers to buy in the lower-rate jurisdiction instead of in the higher-rate jurisdiction. Accordingly, retail sales increase in the lower-tax jurisdiction while decreasing in the higher-tax jurisdiction. With these assumptions, the tax-rate differential can never be eliminated by changes in demand until *all* purchases occur in the lower-tax jurisdiction.

For many practical tax-rate differential cases, it may be more reasonable to assume that the retail sector is characterized by increasing costs (upward-sloping, long-run supply curves), as shown in Figure 15.4. The positively sloped supply curves would result, for instance, if expansion of the retail sector in any area or state caused an increase in factor prices, perhaps an increase in land values or higher wages required to attract additional employees. In the figure, good X is sold at price P_0 in both locations without any tax differential (either no tax or equal taxes in both

Figure 15.4

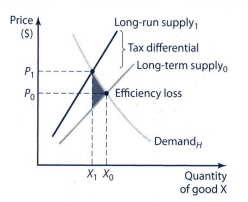

(a) **Higher-tax jurisdiction**

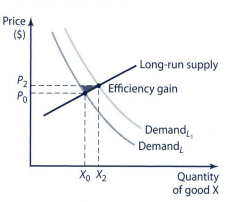

(b) **Lower-tax jurisdiction**

Effect of a sales tax rate differential

locations). Any tax-rate differential that arises (either because one taxes while the other does not or because one taxes at a higher rate) can be reflected by an upward shift in the supply curve to equal the amount of tax differential. As a result of that tax differential, the quantity of good X sold in the higher-tax jurisdiction falls because the price rises, while the demand for good X in the lower-tax jurisdiction also rises. As a result of that increase in demand, the amount and price of good X sold in the lower-tax jurisdiction rises. A price differential between the two juris-dictions may remain due to transportation or information costs (for instance, P^1 compared to P^2), although that price differential is less than the tax rate differential. Although the lower-tax jurisdiction has gained additional sales of good X, con-sumers who always made purchases in that jurisdiction now face higher prices.

The efficiency cost of the additional tax in the one jurisdiction is also shown in Figure 15.4. The efficiency loss from reduced consumption of X in the higher-tax jurisdiction is the difference between the marginal value of the good to consumers and the marginal social cost of production, shown as the shaded triangular area in Figure 15.4a. This loss is partially but not completely offset by an efficiency gain (shown in Figure 15.4b) due to the increased sale of X in the lower-tax jurisdiction (the price paid by consumers, which reflects their value, is greater than marginal cost). The tax-rate differential results in a net efficiency cost even if total consump-tion of X remains the same because consumers incur extra costs or inconvenience to purchase the commodity in the different location.

The effects of a tax-rate differential on consumption are not expected to be the same for all commodities. Tax savings per purchase is directly related to the price of the product and the quantity to be purchased, that is, proposed expenditure per trip. However, any transportation cost incurred in making a purchase in a differ-ent location is usually related to distance and travel time rather than the amount spent. One expects therefore that the tax differential effect is more important for commodities purchased with a relatively large expenditure at one time. One excep-tion to this generalization is if use tax can be collected on purchases such as auto-mobiles or commodities sold by firms with establishments in both locations. Another exception is if consumers can change the location of purchases without incurring any extra transportation cost. In addition to Internet and mail-order pur-chases, that may be easy for individuals who work and reside in different locations with different sales tax rates. Those individuals can often transfer purchases from their residential to their work location without additional cost.

Many studies have been conducted to examine the degree to which sales tax rate differentials actually do induce consumers to change the location of purchases, most of which examine the experience in specific geographic areas, although one is a general cross-section analysis of all large metropolitan areas in the United States.[10] These studies are consistent in finding that a disadvantageous sales tax rate differential leads to a statistically significant but relatively small reduction in sales in the higher-tax jurisdictions.

---

[10]For a general review, see Fisher (1980b). More recent analyses are Mikesell and Zorn (1985), Fox (1986), and Walsh (1986).

For instance, this author examined the effect of sales tax differentials between the District of Columbia and the surrounding Maryland and Virginia suburbs on retail sales in the District over the period from 1962 to 1976 (Fisher, 1980b). Generally, the District had a higher general tax rate than the suburbs, including a higher tax rate on food than in Maryland but a lower rate on food than in Virginia. The study found no significant effect of the tax-rate differential on aggregate sales in the District but a significant negative effect on food sales. With respect to food, the analysis showed that 1 percentage point rise in the tax-rate differential (holding the District's rate constant) led to a 7-percent decrease in District sales tax revenue from food. The effect on food sales but not on sales of other commodities apparently arose because the food tax rate differences were greater than the differences in the general rates, and the District had effective agreements with many retail firms with both suburban and District locations to collect District use taxes, at least for purchases of durable goods delivered to a District location.

John Mikesell and Kurt Zorn (1985) examined the effect of a temporary (three and one-half years) one-half percentage point sales tax differential in the small (population 7,891) city of Bay St. Louis, Mississippi. Over the period 1979–1982, the sales tax rate was 5.5 percent in Bay St. Louis and 5.0 percent in surrounding areas. Their analysis showed that the rate difference did reduce retail sales in the city (a 1-percentage point rate differential lowers sales by about 2.3 percent) primarily from lower sales per seller on average rather than a decrease in the number of sellers. This rate difference was planned and announced to be temporary, so city retail sales returned to the prior level after the rate difference ended.

Results of this magnitude imply that increases in sales tax rates in individual cities are expected to increase revenue even with the small reduction in city sales. The increase in the tax rate more than offsets the small reduction in the sales tax base. In the District of Columbia case, an increase in the District's food rate from 2 to 3 percent (a 50-percent increase in tax rate) was estimated to increase sales tax revenue from food purchases by about 35 percent. In the Bay St. Louis case, an increase in the tax rate from 5.0 percent to 5.5 percent (a 10-percent increase) was estimated to increase sales tax revenue by about 8.8 percent.

These economic effects of sales tax rate differentials and the resulting attempts by state tax administrators to enforce use taxes raise several difficult issues inherent to a fiscal federalism. States (and the local governments they create) have autonomy in the selection of tax structures, including sales tax bases and rates. But because state and local governments encompass substantially open economies, tax decisions by individual states can influence interstate economic activity, regulation of which is reserved for the federal government by the Constitution. For states to levy taxes indirectly on that interstate activity requires either the cooperation of other states or intervention by the federal government, which may impinge on the autonomy of the states. The following two policy illustrations, concerning state cigarette taxes and Internet (mail-order) sales, show some of the options available for resolving this issue, and how the federal government decided to take opposite positions in the two cases. The federal government adopted a law and increased enforcement in the 1970s to assist states in collecting cigarette taxes but so far has not intervened to assist states in collecting use taxes on Internet or mail-order sales.

Application 15.2

CIGARETTE TAXES AND CIGARETTE SMUGGLING[11]

States levy widely differing excise taxes on the sale of cigarettes, as shown earlier in Table 15.3. Because cigarettes are easily transportable, these tax differences create a possibility for individuals to purchase cigarettes in low-tax states for use or resale in higher-tax states, avoiding the state tax in the latter. This problem became particularly acute in the mid-1970s, leading to the adoption of a federal law restricting this possibility. In addition, federal law prohibits state governments from levying cigarette excise taxes on sales of cigarettes on military bases, and various federal agreements and treaties similarly prevent state taxation of cigarette sales on Indian reservations. These two exemptions not only mean that cigarette consumption by military personnel and residents of Indian reservations escape state taxation but also create another opportunity for evading tax on sales to other state residents. Presumably, the higher the state cigarette tax, the greater the incentive for illegal sales from these sources to avoid the tax.

While some variation has always existed in state cigarette taxes, those differences have increased greatly over time. State cigarette excise taxes varied from $0 to $.08 in 1960, from $.02 to $.18 by 1970, and from $.02 to $.21 in 1980. As noted in Table 15.3, cigarette excise taxes currently vary from $.05 to $2.46! The U.S. Advisory Commission on Intergovernmental Relations (ACIR) estimated that states were losing about 10 percent of potential cigarette excise tax revenue in 1975 due

to cigarette smuggling across state boundaries and from sales on military bases and reservations, with the losses being particularly large in 14 states. Although state laws made such transport and sale of cigarettes illegal, states were not very effective in enforcing those laws alone, at least partly due to the inherent interstate nature of the activity. As a result of requests by the states and a recommendation by ACIR, the federal government adopted the Contraband Cigarette Act in 1978, which made it a federal crime to transport, receive, ship, possess, distribute, or purchase more than 60,000 cigarettes (3,000 packs or 300 cartons) without paying the state tax of the state in which the cigarettes are located.

The Bureau of Alcohol, Tobacco, and Firearms, a branch of the U.S. Department of the Treasury, enforces this law. By some accounts, this federal intervention, coupled with expanded state enforcement activity, curtailed interstate cigarette sales to avoid state taxes, at least initially. A subsequent study by ACIR showed that state revenue losses from illegal and exempt sales of cigarettes had declined to about 5 percent of cigarette excise tax revenue by 1983 and remained a serious problem in only two states (Connecticut and West Virginia). More recently, Alamar, *et al.* (2003) estimated that in 2003, about 1–4 percent of cigarettes smoked in California had been smuggled into the state.

Recently there is some evidence that organized crime, including in some instances

[11]See ACIR (1985a), Bartlett (2002), and Horowitz (2004).

Application 15.2 — Cigarette Taxes and Cigarette Smuggling

individuals with potential terrorist links, may now be involved with interstate cigarette smuggling. Horowitz (2004) reports about two such cases—one involving North Carolina (tax is $.05 per pack) and Michigan (tax is $2.00) and another involving Virginia (tax is $.30) and New York (tax is $1.50). The allegation in these and other cases is that the profits from interstate cigarette smuggling are being used to purchase weapons or explosives or otherwise support terrorist activity. Horowitz reports that as a consequence, ATF was acting to enhance enforcement of the federal Contraband Cigarette Act.

In essence, states have been able to maintain and even increase the differences in state excise taxes on cigarettes in large part because the federal government has helped to prevent evasion of those state tax laws. The experience since the 1970s suggests that it is unlikely that states could or would have maintained as large a difference in cigarette tax rates as currently exists without that assistance. If tax-rate differences of the current magnitude were attempted without such enforcement, the likelihood is that high-tax rate states would have collected substantially less revenue than they currently do with the federal law and enforcement.

Cigarette bootlegging to avoid state taxes has not been confined to the United States, but also occurs internationally among nations. It also occurs in Australia, where all the continental state governments—except Queensland, which has no such tax—levy a "license fee" on tobacco products of between 25 and 35 percent. In 1986, an Australian High Court reinterpretation of a constitutional provision allowed states to levy the fees on interstate trade as long as trade within the state was treated equally. As a result, the government of New South Wales began collecting its 30-percent fee on shipments from other states. The *Financial Review* (Jay 1987) reported that the New South Wales government had seized three shipments of cigarettes worth a total of $1 million (Aus.) from Queensland where the fee was evaded. As further evidence of the potential effects of smuggling, the state of Tasmania, which is an island and thus more likely to be able to control smuggling, was able to collect a fee of 50 percent.

E-COMMERCE AND STATE TAXATION

Interstate sales over the Internet or by mail order, although creating somewhat different administrative problems than state cigarette taxes, involve a similar issue of federalism. Because of the destination principle, states do not levy sales tax on purchases for delivery to other states. The buyers owe use tax on those purchases in their state of residence (if the state has a sales/use tax that taxes the commodity); however, as a result of a series of court decisions, states cannot force the firms selling over the Internet (or by mail) to collect those use taxes if the firm has no business presence in the

Application 15.3 — E-Commerce and State Taxation

state.[12] One question, as with cigarette taxes, is whether the federal government should intervene in some way to assist states in collecting use taxes on those sales.[13]

In a 1967 decision (*National Bellas Hess v. Illinois Department of Revenue*), the U.S. Supreme Court held, largely on the basis of the Interstate Commerce Clause of the Constitution, that states could not require out-of-state firms to collect state use taxes if the firm's business in the state is limited to the sending of catalogs and similar advertising. However, if an Internet or mail-order firm also has a "business presence" in a state, such as retail outlets, then that state can require that firm to collect sales or use tax on ordered purchases for delivery in that state. For instance, most states (except Maine, Maryland, New Hampshire, New Jersey, and Virginia where L.L. Bean has retail stores) cannot require L.L. Bean, Inc., to collect use taxes on Internet, telephone, or mail-order sales. In contrast, most if not all states can require J.C. Penney to collect use taxes on orders, given that Penney's has retail outlets in most states.

In the latter 1980s, a number of states changed state use-tax laws in an attempt to avoid the limitations of *Bellas Hess*. States attempted to define a business presence in a state (nexus) as including "regular or systematic solicitation in a state that is substantial and recurring" in addition to the traditional idea of property or employees. States argued both that technology (involving computers, the Internet, cable video transmission, and telephone) had changed the concept of business presence, and that the sales firms benefited from state–local services (refuse collection and disposal of catalogs, security protection of goods in transit, and so on). But in a 1992 decision *(Quill Corp. vs. North Dakota)*, the U.S. Supreme Court found again that such state rules interfere with interstate commerce, so that only companies with a physical presence (employees or property) in a state are subject to use-tax rules. However, the Court also found that because the Constitution gives Congress the authority to regulate interstate commerce, Congress can require or authorize states to require such firms to collect state use taxes. Such requirements authorized by Congress would be Constitutional and would not violate the firm's rights to "due process."

ACIR (1991) estimated that state and local government sales and use taxes would have generated an additional $3.3 to $3.9 billion in 1992 if sales and use taxes had been collected on mail-order sales of taxable commodities. More recently, Bruce and Fox (2004) estimate that the loss to state and local sales tax revenue from e-commerce activity that would otherwise be taxed was about $15.5 billion— or about 6–7 percent of sales tax collections— in 2003. Because these transactions are not all recorded and remain untaxed, such estimates remain controversial. But not surprisingly, the magnitude of this tax enforcement issue seems substantially larger than that for cigarette taxes.

---

[12]If you order a computer from Big Byte, Inc. in New York, which is Big Byte's only store, the computer is shipped to you in your state (other than New York), and your state taxes computer purchases, then you owe use tax to your state based on the purchase price.

[13]For historical background about these issues, see ACIR, *State and Local Taxation Of Out-Of-State Mail Order Sales,* 1986, and Coleman, 1992.

Application 15.3 — E-Commerce and State Taxation

Requiring Internet or mail-order firms to collect state–local government use taxes on sales could create substantial administrative costs for those firms. In addition to the 45 states that have sales and use taxes, 7,500 local governments also levy such taxes. Moreover, wide differences exist in the tax bases and rates of those governments—a commodity sent to one city in state X might be taxed at a different rate than the same commodity sent to a different city in the same state, or a commodity might be taxed in one state but be exempt in another. States sometimes also define taxable products differently; for instance, what does a "food" exemption mean? It could be difficult and expensive for an e-commerce or mail-order firm to determine the appropriate tax on all sales.

In view of all these considerations, several options have been suggested. The federal government could require Internet or mail-order firms to collect a federal sales tax at a single rate on all sales with the revenue distributed to states based on sales tax collections, income, or population. Or the federal government might adopt a law allowing states to require such firms to collect state (but not local) taxes, to reduce the compliance costs for firms. Or local taxes might be collected at a uniform national rate. Or the federal government might give the states authority to enter into cooperative agreements among themselves to have states collect the tax for each other from Internet or mail-order firms in their jurisdiction. In the meantime, states have tried various ways to get taxpayers to pay use taxes voluntarily, either through increased information and enforcement or by including use-tax forms or calculation along with or as part of income tax forms.

THE STREAMLINED SALES TAX PROJECT[14]

To help resolve the problems created by the *Quill* decision, in 2000 a group of state and local governments along with some private sector entities (under the umbrella of the Federation of Tax Administrators and the Multistate Tax Commission) instituted an effort first to simplify state and local sales taxes and then to encourage the federal government to adopt legislation requiring e-commerce and mail-order firms to collect the simplified state–local sales and use taxes. Now including 42 states and the District of Columbia, this effort is called the Streamlined Sales Tax Project. The goals of the project include simplifying sales tax laws, adopting more efficient administrative procedures, and using emerging technologies to reduce the burden of sales and use tax collection substantially.

[14]See http://www.streamlinedsalestax.org/.

Application 15.4 — The Streamlined Sales Tax Project

Model state legislation, the Streamlined Sales and Use Tax Agreement, was adopted in 2002 by a coalition of states. Under this agreement, states would (1) agree to uniform tax base definitions, (2) have only one state tax rate per state, with the possibility of a second rate for certain exemptions (food and drugs), (3) have a single local government sales tax rate per state, (4) use a common tax base for both the state and local sales tax in a single state, (5) use state government administration of both state and local sales taxes (so that firms would not need to file sales tax returns with both the state and local governments), (6) agree that all sales taxes will be destination based (so that the rate that applies is the rate in the jurisdiction where the product is delivered or used), and (7) provide state funding for the technology needed to implement tax collection of such a streamlined system. The states drafting this agreement also agreed that it would take effect when at least 10 states with at least 20 percent of the population formally adopted enabling legislation. In theory, this threshold was reached in 2004; however, problems have arisen.

Within the states, the greatest problem has arisen in states that have substantial local sales taxes. Under the Agreement, local sales taxes are based on the location of the buyer—the product's destination. In most states with local sales taxes, however, taxes have been based on the location (local jurisdiction) of sale. The change creates two potential difficulties. First, this can cause a major reallocation of sales tax revenue. Local jurisdictions where there is a concentration of retailers will lose revenue if sales taxes are

based on the location of consumers compared to taxation based on the location of sale. According to a report in *State Tax Notes* (Humphrey, 2005), this problem recently caused Tennessee to delay the effective date for the legislation. The issue also has been controversial in Washington (Swope, 2004). Second, if multiple local tax rates still apply in a state, then sellers need to calculate the sales tax based on the location of the buyer, which further complicates tax administration. Although the Agreement envisions a single local tax rate in each state, destination taxation creates this problem until that single rate is accepted. Swope (2004) reports that this has been a major controversy in Kansas.

Even if a sufficient number of states adopt this voluntary Agreement for more uniform and simplified sales and use taxes, two practical issues remain. First, business firms will need appropriate software linked to state–local tax databases to calculate and collect the appropriate sales or use tax. For states with local sales taxes in some locations, the database needs to identify the appropriate tax rate for each address. This software and the necessary databases are in development. Second, even if the states adopt and implement the Agreement to simplify their taxes, firms cannot be required to collect the sales or use taxes until the federal government adopts legislation mandating this change, as identified in the *Quill* decision. Substantial opposition remains among many retailers who believe that the Streamlined Project still does not simplify state–local sales and use taxes sufficiently to reduce collection costs to reasonable levels.

ECONOMIC ANALYSIS: EQUITY

Tax Incidence

A truly general sales tax on all personal consumption would impose burdens on consumers in proportion to their amount of consumption. Consumers would be very limited in their ability to shift the tax because the tax would apply to nearly all consumer goods and services, although one remaining option for consumers would be to increase consumption of leisure, which is presumably untaxed. An increase in leisure consumption is equivalent to a decrease in the supply of labor; individuals may be able to shift a general consumption tax, then, by working less, earning less income, and consuming fewer taxable goods and services in aggregate. These possible long-run effects may be minor, however, if the aggregate supply of labor is relatively price inelastic, as is usually assumed.

The typical incidence assumption about a general sales tax, then, is that it imposes tax burdens in proportion to the amount of consumption. Because the share of income represented by personal consumption tends to be smaller for higher-income as opposed to lower-income individuals (higher-income individuals do more saving), the conclusion is drawn that general sales taxes are regressive; that is, sales tax burdens as a proportion of income decline as one moves up the income distribution. For instance, if a family with a $50,000 income spends $40,000 on consumption, a 1-percent tax equals $400, or .8 percent of income; but if a family with a $10,000 income spends $9500 on consumption, the tax is $95, which represents .95 percent of income.

Exemptions

This perception of sales tax regressivity is the primary reason for most sales tax exemptions of consumer goods and services. Exemptions of goods and services that are relatively more important in the budgets of lower-income individuals, — sometimes thought of as "necessities," are used to alter this distributional pattern. This is the rationale usually used to support such exemptions as food consumed at home, prescription drugs, housing, residential electric and gas utilities, clothing, and medical services.

Consumer spending on various categories of personal consumption as a fraction of income is reported in Table 15.4. As suggested, expenditures on food at home, residential electric and gas services, housing, and medical care decline as a fraction of income as income rises. Note, also, that total consumption decreases as a fraction of income as income rises, with consumption being greater than income at the lower-income classes. Following the preceding reasoning, then, exempting food and residential electric and gas sales from the sales tax should reduce any regressivity of the tax.[15]

---

[15]Of course, not all exemptions are made purely for these distributional reasons; other political factors often come into play. For instance, most states exempt sales of newspaper and magazines from the sales tax. While often defended on the grounds of not interfering with public information and free speech, these exemptions also might be related to the old axiom "don't pick a fight with someone who buys ink by the barrel."

Table 15.4

Personal Consumption Expenditures as a Percent of Income, 2002

Income Class[a]	Total Personal Consumption	Food at Home	Utilities and Fuel	Housing	Medical Care
5–9.99[b]	213.4%	23.8%	20.2%	78.6%	14.7%
10–14.999	168.3	18.6	15.2	57.1	14.9
15–19.999	144.4	14.3	11.9	49.3	12.2
20–29.999	117.7	11.3	9.5	39.2	9.3
30–39.999	101.9	8.7	7.3	32.7	6.9
40–49.999	94.0	7.3	6.2	29.6	5.8
50–69.999	85.5	6.0	5.3	25.9	4.8
70 and over	66.3	3.9	3.3	20.5	2.8
All consumers	86.1	6.5	5.4	27.3	4.9

SOURCE: U.S. Department of Labor. *Consumer Expenditure Survey*, 2002.

[a]In thousands of dollars.

[b]Data for consumer units with income less than $5,000 are not meaningful.

The results of many empirical studies of sales tax incidence confirm these effects. For instance, Donald Phares (1980) estimated the distribution of tax burden for each tax in each state and concluded that "there is little question about [the general sales tax's] regressive incidence," although "state-by-state data on general sales effective rates do suggest a less regressive pattern in states that exempt food" (p. 96). Although this analysis shows the sales tax to be regressive over the entire income distribution, it also shows that the tax is nearly proportional in the middle-income range between $6,000 and $25,000 (measured in 1976 dollars). Pechman (1985) has estimated effective rates for federal, state, and local taxes for selected years between 1966 and 1985 arranged both by income class and population decile. Assuming that sales and excise taxes impose burdens proportional to consumption, the results for federal, state, and local sales and excise taxes together for 1980, shown in Table 15.5, confirm the expected regressive pattern. However, for the upper-middle half of the population in the fourth through eighth deciles, the burden is nearly proportional, falling between 4.5 to 5.5 percent of income.

This conventional wisdom about sales tax incidence can be reconsidered in at least three ways. First, as previously noted, the general sales taxes used by states are really not very general, typically exempting at least half of private consumption. As a result, consumers may be induced to shift consumption from taxed to untaxed goods as depicted earlier in Figure 15.4. As a result of those consumption shifts, the sales tax may impose burdens on suppliers of factors of production; in essence, demand for factors used to produce taxable goods and services may decrease and, correspondingly, demand for factors used to produce nontaxable commodities may increase. Although these burdens could theoretically alter the overall distribution of sales tax burdens by income, they typically are ignored on the grounds that there is no reason to expect that taxable goods are *produced by* any higher- or lower-income individuals than are nontaxable goods. That is, there is no

Table 15.5

Pechman's Estimates of Sales and Excise Tax Incidence, 1980

(Effective Rates: Tax Burden as Percent of Family Income)

Family Income[a]	Effective Rate	Population Decile[b]	Effective Rate
0–5	17.9%	First	8.4%
5–10	7.7	Second	7.0
10–15	6.2	Third	5.9
15–20	5.6	Fourth	5.5
20–25	5.2	Fifth	5.1
25–30	4.9	Sixth	4.9
30–50	4.5	Seventh	4.6
50–100	3.3	Eighth	4.5
100–500	1.6	Ninth	3.9
500–1,000	0.7	Tenth	2.1
1,000 and over	0.6		
All Classes	4.0	All Deciles	4.0

SOURCE: Pechman (1985, Tables 4.9 and 4.10).

[a]Thousands of dollars.

[b]Percentages of the population grouped by income from lowest to highest. The income classes and population deciles do not correspond.

reason, *a priori*, to expect that workers producing services that are not taxed have, on average, different incomes than workers producing tangible goods, which are taxed.

Second, even if consumers do not shift consumption between taxed and untaxed commodities, assuming that the effective tax rate on untaxed commodities is zero is generally not correct. In many cases, those who purchase exempt commodities bear an indirect sales tax burden because those who produce exempt commodities may have paid sales taxes on materials, supplies, or services used in their business. As previously noted, no state exempts all purchases of intermediate goods from sales tax. For example, although seven states exempt the retail sale of food from sales tax, many of those states levy sales tax on purchases of display equipment by food retailers, on the purchase of trucks and gasoline used to transport food, or sometimes on the equipment and supplies used in agriculture. These sales tax burdens are part of the cost of producing food commodities and are embedded in the retail price of those food commodities. Similarly, all states (except Hawaii) exempt medical care services from the retail sales tax, but many levy sales tax on the purchase of medical equipment and supplies by medical care providers. It is more correct to state therefore that those who purchase exempt commodities bear a sales tax burden, but at a rate less than the nominal general sales tax on taxed commodities.[16]

---

[16]Siegfield and Smith (1991, p. 41) report that "The main effect of . . . taxes levied on intermediate products is to move the overall distributional effect of a sales tax more toward proportionality, because the wide variety of uses for most intermediate products spreads the impact of a tax on them throughout the economy. . . ."

These indirect sales tax burdens that arise from taxing intermediate goods purchases also have an important implication for interstate comparison of sales tax burdens. Among states with the same nominal rate and identical sets of exempt consumer goods, the effective rate is expected to be greater in the states that levy the tax on a broader set of intermediate goods purchases. Similarly, it is entirely possible that the effective rate could be lower in a state with a 5-percent nominal rate and little taxation of intermediate goods (such as West Virginia) than in another state with a 4-percent rate but broad taxation of intermediate goods.

Finally, annual income may not be the best measure of a taxpayer's ability to pay taxes and may lead to inaccurate perceptions about tax incidence. In any given year, many individuals' annual incomes are not reflective of their average lifetime circumstances. This is particularly true for persons in temporary or short-run situations, such as retired folks, the unemployed, or college students. Therefore, some measure of lifetime or permanent income may give a more accurate, or at least different, picture of tax incidence. Over an individual's lifetime, all income is either consumed or transferred to subsequent generations for consumption. Assuming that sales tax burdens are proportional to total consumption and taking the view that all income is eventually consumed, sales taxes can be thought of as proportional taxes.

An intermediate approach between these two views is to measure sales tax incidence by consumption of taxed commodities only relative to some estimate of permanent or lifetime income. Such an analysis by Daniel Davies (1969) shows that sales taxes are indeed less regressive with respect to lifetime income than annual income and confirms that exempting food for home consumption and utility services from the sales tax base makes the sales tax burden even less regressive. An analysis by Metcalf (1994) goes even further in showing that under certain restrictive assumptions about consumption and lifetime income, state sales taxes might even be progressive or proportional.

Sales Tax Credits Compared to Exemptions

The major alternative to exemptions to reduce the expected regressivity of sales tax burdens is a tax credit, usually taken against the state income tax, to offset sales tax liability on some commodities for at least some taxpayers. In practice, these credits are most often used as an alternative to an exemption for sales of food. According to ACIR, seven states used income tax credits to offset sales tax liability in 1993, six of which do not provide a food exemption (the exception is Vermont, which exempts food and provides a credit). In many cases, these credits apply only to lower-income taxpayers or to senior citizens. If the tax credits apply only to a subset of taxpayers, they can achieve the desired increase in progressivity at lower revenue cost than through general exemptions applying to all taxpayers.

Although both sales tax exemptions and income tax credits can alter the distribution of tax burden, they are not expected to influence consumer behavior in the same way. An exemption eliminates the tax on all purchases of an exempt commodity (such as for food for home consumption) and thus effectively reduces the price of that commodity relative to those that are taxed. Therefore, besides reducing the regressivity of the sales tax, exemptions also create an incentive for consumers to buy more of the exempt commodities. When income tax credits are used to offset sales tax liability on some commodities, however, the credit is usually set as a flat amount per person or per household (such as $200 per household), sometimes declining as income increases. The amount of the credit for any individual is usually not related to the actual amount spent on the taxed item. Therefore, the credit does not reduce the price of the taxed commodity but changes the overall tax burden and distribution. The effect of a credit program is to make the state's overall tax structure more progressive (or less regressive).

Contrary to what some analysts have suggested, it is not necessarily poor policy for a state to use both sales tax exemptions and an income tax credit. If a state has two policy objectives, both to make food less expensive and to increase the overall progressivity of the state's tax structure, both tools may be used simultaneously (although why a state would want to decrease food prices may be problematical). In other words, tax credits may be used to offset any regressive elements of the tax structure, not just those that arise from the sales tax. Note that income tax credits typically are restricted to state residents, whereas sales tax exemptions apply to all purchasers regardless of residence. Of course, those exemptions may induce nonresidents to make additional purchases in the state or may induce residents not to make purchases in other states.

Sales tax exemptions and income tax credits also may differ in their administration and compliance costs. Exemptions increase collection costs for sellers—particularly those who sell both taxable and exempt commodities—and audit costs for the state. On the other hand, tax credits require that taxpayers be informed about the credit and take the effort to file the required forms. State experience with these credits suggests that these compliance costs prevent some taxpayers, often those with lowest incomes or those who do not have a state income tax liability, from receiving the intended benefit.

SUMMARY

State–local governments use general sales taxes levied on retail sales, companion use taxes to tax resident purchases made in other jurisdictions, and excise taxes on specific goods or services. Sales or consumption taxes remain the largest single source of revenue for state governments. Although about 81 percent of total general sales tax revenue went to state governments in 2002, local government general sales taxes were also used by about 7,500 local jurisdictions spread among 34 states.

General sales taxes are intended to be taxes on the total final personal consumption of the residents of the jurisdictions levying the tax. In practice, state general sales taxes fall short of this principle because (1) a substantial amount of personal consumption is statutorily exempt from taxation, (2) the taxes end up applying to sales of some intermediate goods in addition to consumer goods, and (3) states face inherent administrative difficulties in collecting use taxes.

The net effect of exemptions is that state general sales taxes apply to perhaps only 40–60 percent of personal consumption in aggregate, with obvious substantial variation among the states.

Because sales and excise taxes alter the relative prices of some goods, creating incentives for consumers and producers (to the extent sales of intermediate goods are taxed) to change their behavior, the tax can result in a loss of economic efficiency. The general theoretical rule for optimal commodity taxation is deceptively simple: The optimal set of sales taxes should cause an equal proportionate decrease in the compensated quantity demanded of all commodities.

Individuals also may be able to avoid or reduce sales taxes by making purchases in jurisdictions different from the one in which they reside. Individuals may purchase goods in one state or locality for delivery to a different location, or individuals may make purchases, take possession in a lower-tax jurisdiction, and pay the lower sales tax rate. A number of studies are consistent in finding that a disadvantageous sales tax rate differential leads to a statistically significant but relatively small reduction in sales in the higher-tax jurisdictions.

The typical incidence assumption about a general sales tax is that it is regressive. Exemptions of goods and services that are relatively more important in the budgets of lower-income individuals are commonly used to alter this distributional pattern. The major alternative to exemptions to reduce the expected regressivity of sales tax burdens is a tax credit. Exemptions effectively reduce the price of that commodity relative to those that are taxed and create an incentive for consumers to increase purchases of exempt commodities. Credits do not reduce prices but make the state's overall tax structure more progressive (or less regressive).

DISCUSSION QUESTIONS

1. Suppose that a state government levies an *ad valorem* sales tax on the purchase of all goods at retail but not on the purchase of services. The tax is levied only on final sales of goods and not on sales of any intermediate goods. The state has a companion use tax but makes little effort to collect that tax for consumer purchases except for automobiles. Discuss the various ways (there are at least four) an individual consumer could change behavior to avoid or reduce liability for the state sales tax. What economic costs could arise from each type of action?

2. "It would be unfair to tax the sale of medical or legal services because effectively that would be taxing peoples' misfortune." Discuss this viewpoint. Would the same principle apply to the sale of car repairs? What about the purchase of a fire extinguisher or a child's car seat?

3. "Sales taxes are fairer than income taxes because sales taxes cannot be avoided by the rich." Evaluate this idea. Describe the evidence about the distribution of sales tax burdens among different income taxpayers. Would it be possible to design a sales tax that is more progressive than an income tax?

4. The sales tax treatment of Internet and mail-order purchases is controversial, as discussed in the chapter. Think about the products you have
purchased using the Internet or by mail order in the recent past and
roughly how much you spent. Does your state have a use tax? Did you
pay the use tax on taxable items? Why or why not? How much did the
opportunity to avoid sales tax influence your decision to purchase over
the Internet or by mail order? Do you think that companies that sell
through the Internet or by mail order should be required to collect state
sales or use taxes on purchases? If not, then what other methods might
states use to collect these taxes?

SELECTED READINGS

Due, John F. and John L. Mikesell. *Sales Taxation, State and Local Structure and
Administration*. Washington, D.C.: The Urban Institute Press, 1994.

Fox, William F., ed. *Sales Taxation: Critical Issues in Policy and Administration*. Westport,
CT: Praeger, 1992.

Fox, William F. "Can the Sales Tax Survive a Future Like Its Past?" In D. Brunori, ed.,
The Future of State Taxation. Washington, D.C.: The Urban Institute Press, 1998.

Mikesell, John L. "The Future of American Sales and Use Taxation." In D. Brunori, ed.,
The Future of State Taxation. Washington, D.C.: The Urban Institute Press, 1998.

16 CHAPTER

INCOME TAXES

A Federal Fiscal System faces two kinds of tax coordination problems. The first arises when two or more different levels of government use the same tax base, as when the federal goverment and a state government tax the same income; . . . the second appears when . . . mobile individuals carry out economic activities in many different taxing jurisdictions at the same level of government. . . .[1]
—GEORGE F. BREAK

HEADLINES

STATE INCOME TAXES ARE, IN PRINCIPLE, TAXES LEVIED AT THE ORIGIN OF INCOME—WHERE THE INCOME IS EARNED—RATHER THAN THE DESTINATION OF THAT INCOME—WHERE THE WORKER RESIDES. FOR MOST PEOPLE WHO EARN INCOME ONLY IN THE STATE WHERE THEY RESIDE, THIS IS OF NO CONSEQUENCE, OF COURSE. BUT THE CASE OF WORKERS WHO EARN SUBSTANTIAL AMOUNTS OF INCOME IN MULTIPLE STATES RAISES A NUMBER OF ISSUES. SUCH TAXPAYERS MAY BE REQUIRED TO FILE TAX RETURNS AND PAY TAXES IN EVERY STATE (AND PERHAPS CITY) WHERE THEY WORK OR LIVE—AN INCOME ALLOCATION THAT BURDENS THEM AND THEIR EMPLOYERS. IN ADDITION, TAX AUTHORITIES FACE QUESTIONS OF HOW TO MONITOR AND COLLECT THESE TAXES.

ALTHOUGH THIS SITUATION MAY AFFECT A VARIETY OF INDIVIDUALS (ENTERTAINERS, SPEAKERS, AND SO ON), THE CASE OF PROFESSIONAL ATHLETES HAS RECEIVED SPECIAL ATTENTION. IN PART, THIS ATTENTION FOLLOWS FROM THE VERY APPARENT NATURE OF PROFESSIONAL ATHLETICS AS WELL AS THE EXCEPTIONALLY HIGH LEVEL OF SALARIES NOW COMMON IN MANY PROFESSIONAL SPORTS LEAGUES. HAWKINS, *ET AL.* (2002, P. 551) REPORT THAT THIS

---

[1] *Intergovernmental Fiscal Relations in the United States.* Washington, D.C.: The Brookings Institution, 1967, 28.

ATTENTION BEGAN IN 1991 WHEN ". . . CALIFORNIA BEGAN AGGRESSIVELY PURSUING TAXATION OF VISITING ATHLETES (INCLUDING PLAYERS FOR THE CHICAGO BULLS). IN RETURN, THE ILLINOIS LEGISLATURE APPROVED LEGISLATION THAT WOULD IN TURN TAX VISITING ATHLETES IN THAT STATE. THE LAW WAS DUBBED 'MICHAEL JORDAN'S REVENGE . . .'" HOFFMAN (P. 187) REPORTED THAT "TODAY, 20 STATES HAVE SOME FORM OF THE JOCK TAX, LEAVING ONLY FOUR AND THE DISTRICT OF COLUMBIA THAT HAVE A PROFESSIONAL SPORTS TEAM BUT NO JOCK TAX. . . ." THUS, ONE MAJOR QUESTION IS WHETHER PROFESSIONAL ATHLETES (AND PERHAPS ENTERTAINERS, AS WELL) ARE BEING SINGLED OUT FOR SPECIAL ATTENTION AMONG ALL NONRESIDENT INCOME EARNERS.

SEVERAL POSSIBLE SOLUTIONS TO THESE ISSUES HAVE BEEN CONSIDERED. CURRENTLY, MOST STATES ALLOCATE PROFESSIONAL ATHLETE INCOME BASED ON "DUTY DAYS," THE NUMBER OF DAYS IN THE VISITING STATE COMPARED TO THE TOTAL NUMBER OF DAYS FROM THE START OF PRESEASON TRAINING THROUGH THE LAST GAME. ONE OPTION TO SIMPLIFY THE SITUATION IS TO PERMIT CONSOLIDATED FILING, THROUGH WHICH ALL PLAYERS ON A TEAM COULD FILE A SINGLE RETURN WITH STATES THEY VISIT. IN THE PAST, THE MAJOR PROFESSIONAL SPORTS LEAGUES AND RELATED PLAYER ASSOCIATIONS JOINTLY PROPOSED THAT ALL OF A PLAYER'S INCOME BE ALLOCATED TO HIS HOME TEAM'S STATE. THE PLAYER WOULD FILE JUST ONE STATE RETURN, UNLESS HE LIVED IN ANOTHER TAXING STATE. THE PLAN MAY BE PARTICULARLY APPROPRIATE FOR TEAM SPORTS BECAUSE OF THE ALMOST PERFECT RECIPROCITY INVOLVED—EVERY GAME IS AT HOME FOR ONE TEAM AND AWAY FOR THE OTHER. SO FAR, NEITHER OF THESE ALTERNATIVES HAS BEEN ADOPTED.[2]

---

[2]For background and detail, see the following articles: Hoffman, David. "State Income Taxation of Nonresident Professional Athletes." *State Tax* Notes, October 21, 2002. Hawkins, Richard, Terri Slay, and Sally Wallace. "Play Here, Pay Here: An Analysis of the State Income Tax on Athletes." *State Tax* Notes, November 25, 2002. Duncan, Harley. "'Jock Tax' Analysis Way Off." *State Tax Notes,* July 28, 2003.

Issues surrounding the use of personal income taxes by states and local governments are considered in this chapter. After examining the history of reliance on income taxes by states and localities, the alternative bases for these income taxes, and the patterns of tax rates, attention turns to coordinating income taxes both among subnational governments and between the federal government and the states. The relationship between the federal and state income taxes is particularly important, including both the effect of one on the other and how together they effect economic decisions by individuals and firms.

Table 16.1

Individual Income Taxes as a Percent of General Revenue, by Level of Government, Various Years

		Local Governments					
Year	States	All	Counties	Municipalities	Townships	School Districts	Special Districts
1962	8.8%	0.8%	0.1%	2.0%	0.2%	0.3%	—
1972	13.2	2.1	0.8	5.4	0.7	0.3	—
1977	15.1	2.1	0.9	5.1	1.1	0.3	—
1982	16.6	1.8	1.0	4.3	1.4	0.3	—
1987	18.1	1.9	1.0	4.7	1.3	0.3	—
1992	17.2	1.8	1.0	4.7	1.5	0.3	—
1997	17.8	1.9	1.2	4.8	1.6	0.3	—
2002	17.5	1.7	1.3	4.2	1.7	0.3	—

SOURCES: U.S. Department of Commerce, Census of Governments, *Compendium of Government Finances.*

RELIANCE ON INCOME TAXES

Individual income taxes have become an increasingly important source of revenue for state–local governments in the past 40 years. In 2002, income taxes provided 17.5 percent of state government revenue on average, double the share provided by that tax in 1962, as shown in Table 16.1. Local reliance on income taxes increased more, with county governments in aggregate receiving more than 1 percent of their revenue from income taxes in 2002 compared to only .1 percent in 1962, while the income tax share of revenue for municipalities rose from 2.0 to 4.2 percent over that period. In 2002, state individual income taxes generated $185.7 billion, with local income taxes providing an additional $17.2 billion. Together these represent a payment of about $704 per person, or 2.3 percent of personal income on average.

Currently, 41 state governments and the District of Columbia collect broad-based individual income taxes, and two states (New Hampshire and Tennessee) collect income tax on a narrow base of capital income only (see Table 16.2). Individual income taxes are also used by about 4,000 local governments spread over 11 states, although more than 2,800 of these local governments are in the state of Pennsylvania alone.[3]

In 1962, only 32 states used broad-based income taxes but a number of new adoptions occurred in the late 1960s and 1970s; Michigan and Nebraska in 1967; Illinois and Maine in 1969; Ohio, Pennsylvania, and Rhode Island in 1971; and New Jersey in 1976. Most recently, in 1991, Connecticut expanded the limited tax on capital income only that had existed since 1969 to a broad-based tax on all income including wages and salaries, whereas Alaska repealed its state income tax in 1979.

---

[3]Local income taxes are also authorized but not currently used in two other states: Arkansas and Georgia.

Table 16.2

Income Tax Characteristics by State, 2004

State	Tax Base Relationship to Federal	Tax Rates (Percent)		Taxable Income Brackets		Federal Tax Deductible	Local Income Tax
		Low	High	Low	High		
New England							
Connecticut	AGI	3	5	10,000	10,000		
Maine	AGI	2	8.5	4,350	17,350		
Massachusetts	AGI	5.3		-----Flat rate-----			
New Hampshire		State income tax is limited to dividends and interest income only.					
Rhode Island	AGI	25.0% of federal tax liability		-----			
Vermont	TI	3.6	9.5	29,900	326,450		
Mideast							
Delaware	AGI	2.2	5.95	5,000	60,000		X
Maryland	AGI	2	4.75	1,000	3,000		X
New Jersey	None	1.4	8.97	20,000	500,000		X
New York	AGI	4	7.7	8,000	500,000		X
Pennsylvania	None	3.07		-----Flat rate-----			
Great Lakes							
Illinois	AGI	3		-----Flat rate-----			
Indiana	AGI	3.4		-----Flat rate-----			X
Michigan	AGI	3.9		-----Flat rate-----			X
Ohio	AGI	0.743	7.5	5,000	200,000		X
Wisconsin	AGI	4.6	6.75	8,840	132,580		
Plains							
Iowa	AGI	0.36	8.98	1,242	55,890	Y	X
Kansas	AGI	3.5	6.45	15,000	30,000		
Minnesota	TI	5.35	7.85	19,890	65,350		
Missouri	AGI	1.5	6	1,000	9,000	Y (limited)	X
Nebraska	AGI	2.56	6.84	2,400	26,500		
North Dakota	TI	2.1	5.54	29,050	319,100		
South Dakota		No state income tax					
Southeast							
Alabama	None	2	5	500	3,000	Y	X
Arkansas	None	1	7	3,999	28,500		
Florida		No state income tax					
Georgia	AGI	1	6	750	7,000		
Kentucky	AGI	2	6	3,000	8,000		X
Louisiana	AGI	2	6	12,500	25,000	Y	
Mississippi	None	3	5	5,000	10,000		
North Carolina	TI	6	8.25	12,750	120,000		
South Carolina	TI	2.5	7	2,460	12,300		
Tennessee		State income tax is limited to dividends and interest income only.					
Virginia	AGI	2	5.75	3,000	17,000		
West Virginia	AGI	3	6.5	10,000	60,000		
Southwest							
Arizona	AGI	2.87	5.04	10,000	150,000		
New Mexico	AGI	1.7	6	5,500	16,000		
Oklahoma	AGI	0.5	6.65	1,000	10,000	Y	
Texas		No state income tax					

Table 16.2

(continued)

State	Tax Base Relationship to Federal	Tax Rates (Percent) Low	High	Taxable Income Brackets Low	High	Federal Tax Deductible	Local Income Tax
Rocky Mountain							
Colorado	TI	4.63		-----Flat rate-----			
Idaho	TI	1.6	7.8	1,129	22,577		
Montana	AGI	2	6.9	2,300	13,900	Y	
Utah	TI	2.3	7	863	4,313	Y (limited)	
Wyoming	No state income tax						
Far West							
Alaska	No state income tax						
California	AGI	1	9.3	6,147	40,346		
Hawaii	TI	1.4	8.25	2,000	40,000		
Nevada	No state income tax						
Oregon	TI	5	9	2,650	6,550	Y (limited)	
Washington	No state income tax						
DC							
Dist. of Columbia	AGI	5	9	10,000	30,000		

[a]The state income tax base may be determined by starting from federal adjusted gross income (AGI) or federal taxable income (TI). In one case, the state tax is a percentage of the federal tax.

SOURCE: Federation of Tax Administrators, see http://www.taxadmin.org/fta/rate/.

INCOME TAX STRUCTURE

Before focusing on the specific income tax issues that arise from applying the tax at the state and local levels, it is useful to have some understanding of the fundamental concepts underlying income taxation as well as the overall structure of income taxes in general. Income taxes are intended to be based on *ability to pay* rather than any measure of benefit from or use of government services, so it is crucial to begin by attempting to define what *ability to pay* means.

Generally, it has been argued that if income is to be the measure of ability to pay taxes, then income should be defined as broadly as possible to include all resources that contribute to a taxpayer's welfare, and thus the taxpayer's ability to pay taxes. One definition of total income proposed by two economists, which has been widely used to evaluate income taxes, is **Haig-Simons income,** defined as *consumption plus change in net wealth.* (The term is named after Robert Haig and Henry Simons, who did much of their research in the 1930s.) By this definition, anything that provides consumption benefits to taxpayers or contributes to an increase in wealth (net of costs) is considered to raise welfare and ability to pay.

The use of the Haig-Simons concept of total income has a number of implications. Consumption may result from money used to purchase goods or services or from the receipt of goods or services directly. Thus, both money received and payments to individuals in kind rather than money, such as an employer-provided automobile or health insurance, can represent consumption and should then be included in such a broadly defined tax base. Essentially, the argument is that in-kind benefits substitute for money receipts and allow taxpayers to spend more on other things. Thus, ability to pay is greater and tax payments should be too. Similarly, anything that increases net wealth, such as income that is saved rather than spent or increases in the value of assets owned by a taxpayer, represent potential spending and thus are part of ability to pay. Again, these should be included in the broad tax base.

The Haig-Simons concept of income has been advanced as a way of achieving **horizontal equity** in taxation, that is, treating taxpayers with an equal ability to pay (income) in equal ways. Taxpayers may receive their Haig-Simons income in different ways, but if that total income is the same, then the concept of horizontal equity creates the argument that the tax system also should treat them equally. If the Haig-Simons concept of income taxation is implemented, however, a number of adjustments to the tax base often are made to account for different taxpayer circumstances in recognition of other equity objectives or the efficiency implications of the tax. The common structure of those income tax features is considered next.

A general structure for income taxes and common income tax terms is shown in Table 16.3. The starting point is defining **adjusted gross income (AGI)**, those types and amounts of income that are deemed to represent ability to pay and that are to be taxed. From taxable income, taxpayers may be allowed to subtract **personal exemptions** and various types of **deductions**. Exemptions are per-person amounts, perhaps to account for necessary subsistence spending, which are subtracted from income before tax is calculated. Deductions may be fixed amounts per household (called a **standard deduction**), or they may be amounts of expenditures on specific goods and services (called **itemized deductions**). Adjusted gross income minus exemptions and deductions is called **taxable income,** which is the tax base to which rates are applied to calculate the tax.

Tax rates, the percentage of the tax base that will be charged as tax, are multiplied by the tax base (or segments of the tax base) to calculate tax. A **flat rate** or **proportional rate tax** applies one rate to the entire base, whereas a **progressive rate tax** applies greater tax rates as the tax base increases. In a progressive rate tax, the **marginal tax rate** is the tax rate that is collected from the last dollar of the tax base. For instance, if the tax rates are 5 percent for AGI up to $10,000 and 10 percent for amounts of AGI greater than $10,000, the tax is calculated as follows:

AGI	Tax Amount	Marginal Tax Rate
$ 8,000	$400 = $8,000 × .05	.05 or 5 percent
$18,000	$1,300 = ($10,000 × .05) + ($8,000 × .1)	.1 or 10 percent

Finally, **tax credits** are amounts that are subtracted from the amount of tax. Credits may be fixed amounts per person or per household, or they may be related to specific taxpayer circumstances, such as particular expenditures (as with a

Table 16.3

Income Tax Terminology and Structure

The general form of an income tax is
Tax = [(Income − Exclusions − Personal Exemptions − Deductions) × Rates] − Credits

Definitions of terms:
Exclusions are types of income that are not taxed, that is, excluded from tax.
Adjusted Gross Income = (Income − Exclusions), which represents income that can be taxed.
Personal Exemptions are per person amounts that can be subtracted from income before tax is calculated; amounts
  that are exempt from tax.
Deductions are personal expenditures that can be subtracted from income before tax is calculated; expenditures that
  are deducted.
Taxable Income = (Adjusted Gross Income − Exemptions − Deductions), which is the tax base that is multiplied by
  the tax rates.
Tax Rates are the percentage of the tax base that will be owed as tax. A *flat rate tax* applies one rate to the entire tax
  base, whereas in a *progressive rate tax* greater tax rates are applied as the tax base increases. In a progressive rate
  tax, the *marginal tax rate* is the tax rate that is collected from the last dollar of tax base.
Credits are amounts that are subtracted from tax owed. Credits may be per-person amounts, may be related to
  specific expenditures, or may relate to other taxpayer circumstances.
Average Effective Tax Rate = Tax/Income

Example:
Income = $50,000
Exclusions = $100 of tax exempt bond interest
Personal Exemption = $3,000 per person, with three people in the household
Deductions = $9,700 per household
Adjusted Gross Income = $49,900 [$40,000 − $100]
Taxable Income = $31,200 [$49,900 − ($3,000 × 3) − $9,700]
Tax Rate = 10 percent
Tax = $3,120 [$31,200 × .1]
Credit = $120 for child care expenses
Tax Payment = $3,000 [$3,120 − $120]
Average Effective Tax Rate = .06 (6 percent) [$3,000/$50,000]

child care credit or credits for contributions) or even income (as with the earned income credit). Because credits are subtracted from the tax amount (after rates have been applied) rather than from taxable income, a given credit reduces tax equally for all taxpayers eligible for the credit.

A numerical example using all these concepts and terms to illustrate how income tax is determined is shown at the bottom of Table 16.3 With this general understanding of income tax structure, we turn now to the specific issues of defining the tax base and tax rates for state and local income taxes.

Tax Base

Although states consider many factors when selecting an appropriate income tax base, the two principal issues are the degree of coordination between the federal and state income tax definitions and the treatment of income that crosses jurisdiction boundaries. In the first case, states can parallel the federal government to varying degrees to determine what income base is to be taxed, or they can adopt an entirely different definition of taxable income. In the second, states must determine how to treat both income earned in other states by residents and income earned in this state by nonresidents (including the treatment of taxes paid to other states). This latter issue is central to the case described in the *Headlines* section at the start of the chapter.

Federal-State Tax Base Coordination

Similar state-federal definitions of the individual income tax base provide advantages both to taxpayers, by reducing recordkeeping and making it easier to compute the tax, and to state tax administrators, by making it easier to check for income tax compliance. If states substantially adopt the same income tax rules as the federal government, however, changes in those rules and definitions by the federal government may generate automatic changes in the states' taxes, unless the state governments explicitly act to offset the federal action.

State income taxes can be grouped into four general categories of tax base conformance with the federal individual income tax, as shown in Table 16.4. In Rhode Island, a taxpayer's state income tax liability is a percentage of the federal income tax, with only minor adjustments for any itemized deduction of the state income tax (included in the base), for interest earned on federal government securities (excluded from tax) or interest from other states' securities (included in the base).

Table 16.4

Alternative State Income Tax Base Conformance with the Federal Income Tax

Federal Base $= I - X - N \times E - D$
Where
I = Income
X = Income excluded from tax
N = Number of personal exemptions
E = Value per exemption
D = Deductions, standard or itemized
Federal Tax = Federal Base (Federal Rate Structure) − Federal Credits

Group 1: *State Tax Is a Percentage of Federal Tax*

State Tax = State Rate (Federal Tax)

Group 2: *State Tax Base Equals Federal Taxable Income*

State Tax = Federal Base (State Rate Structure) − State Credits
State Tax $= (I - X - N \times E - D)$(State Rate Structure) − State Credits

Group 3: *State Tax Base Equals Federal Adjusted Gross Income*

State Tax $= (I - X -$ State Exemptions and Deductions)(State Rate Structure) − State Credits

Group 4: *State Tax Base Is Unrelated to the Federal Tax*

State Tax = (State Defined Base)(State Rate Structure) − State Credits

In essence, Rhode Island adopts the income exclusions, deductions, exemptions, credits, and overall tax rate progressivity used by the federal government. This is illustrated by the Group 1 category in Table 16.4. Of course, additional state income tax credits can be applied as well if desired. Discretionary changes in state income tax revenue are accomplished by adjusting the state percentage rate that is applied to federal liability.

The next closest conformance to the federal tax occurs if the state tax base equals federal taxable income, again with some minor adjustments. The 10 states taking this approach effectively accept federal income exclusions, personal exemptions, and deductions but apply their own tax-rate structure and tax credits, as illustrated by Group 2 in Table 16.4. In this case, state income taxes are sensitive to changes in the definition of the federal tax base but not to changes in federal tax rates. Moreover, taxpayers and tax officials enjoy essentially the same compliance and administrative advantages with this system as when the state tax is a percentage of federal tax.

The most common way to determine the state income tax base—used by 26 states and the District of Columbia—is to start with the federal adjusted gross income, that is, gross income less exclusions, and then apply state-defined personal exemptions and deductions. The state tax is then computed from this base using a state rate structure and any state income tax credits. This approach is particularly common in the Great Lakes, Plains, and Southwest states, where it is used by 12 of the 14 states with income taxes. States using this method then may allow tax-payers the same number of exemptions as the federal tax but apply a different value to the exemptions or follow both different exemption number and value rules. These states also may allow deductions, either choosing which of the vari-ous federal deductions they want to allow, adopting specific state deduction defi-nitions, or both (see Group 3 in Table 16.4). States taking this approach still will enjoy substantial compliance and administrative advantages if they follow federal rules that determine the *number* of exemptions and the federal definitions for deductions the states want to have. Computing the state tax then requires similar recordkeeping and follows the same pattern as the federal, with different values for the exemption and tax-rate parameters.

Five states make no specific attempt to relate the state income tax to the federal tax, opting instead for specific state definitions and rules regarding income exclu-sions, personal exemptions, deductions, credits, and rate structure. Three of the five states using this approach are in the Southeast (Alabama, Arkansas, and Mississippi) and the other two in the Mideast (New Jersey and Pennsylvania). This dual income tax system potentially complicates matters for both taxpayers and tax administrators, although it leaves state government fully insulated from any direct effects of changes to the federal income tax (see Group 4 in Table 16.4).

Deductions for State or Federal Income Taxes

Besides some commonality in the definition of income for tax purposes, state-federal income taxes also are related by deductions for income taxes paid to the other type of government. In computing itemized deductions for the federal individual income tax, taxpayers are allowed to include deductions for state and local government income taxes.[4] If the total value of all itemized deductions for a taxpayer exceeds the standard deduction for that filing class ($9,700 for married taxpayers filing jointly and $4,850 for single taxpayers in 2004), the itemized deductions are claimed. In that case, the federal individual income tax base is income minus state and local taxes (and other itemized deductions), so that a lower federal income tax liability offsets part of the taxpayer's state and local government income taxes. In 2002, about 35 percent of federal income taxpayers itemized deductions, although that percentage rises to about 88 percent for taxpayers with AGIs above $70,000 (a group that includes about 15 percent of returns but slightly more than half of total income).

In addition to these federal deductions for state and local taxes, eight states allow a deduction for federal individual income taxes when computing the state tax. This **reciprocal deductibility** means not only that the federal tax base is income minus state and local income taxes, but also that the state income tax base is income net of federal tax. This substantial narrowing of the state tax base may therefore necessitate higher tax rates.

Typically, the rationale for providing income tax deductions for income taxes levied by another level of government is to prevent tax rates from becoming too high through their cumulative effect. Theoretically, at least, the sum of federal, state, and local income tax rates can approach or even exceed 100 percent if those various governments set rates independently and without regard for the others. However, such confiscatory rates would be counterproductive for all those taxing governments. Deductibility softens this effect of combining income tax rates.[5]

It is also sometimes suggested that income net of other governments' taxes is theoretically a better measure of "ability-to-pay," on the assumption that those other government's taxes are not direct charges for service, but rather mandatory fees that reduce resources available for other spending. This argument seems tenuous, at best, because individuals select their state and local government tax/service package by voting or choosing where they live. The economic effects of income tax deductibility are considered in the next section of this chapter.

Coordination Among Different States

The final intergovernmental tax-base issue, which applies to local as well as state taxes, concerns the treatment of income that crosses jurisdiction boundaries, including income earned by the residents of a taxing jurisdiction for services performed in another jurisdiction (residents' income earned in other states) and

---

[4]Other allowed itemized deductions include home-mortgage interest, property taxes, some charitable contributions, work-related costs, and medical expenses.

[5]Prior to 1981, the top federal marginal income tax rate was 70 percent. This, combined with a 10–15 percent state rate and any additional local income tax, could have approached this situation. With the current top nominal federal tax rate at 35 percent, this concern seems less important.

income earned in a given taxing jurisdiction by residents of another jurisdiction (nonresidents' income earned in the state). Four possibilities exist:

- Income could be taxed only in the jurisdiction where it is earned.
- Income could be taxed only by the jurisdiction where the earner resides.
- Income could be taxed in both places.
- Income could be taxed in neither place.

In practice, most states tax all the income of residents, regardless of where it is earned, and all income earned in that state by nonresidents. Residents are allowed a credit, however, for taxes paid to other states. If all states followed this practice, the effect would be basically to tax income where it is earned, with two exceptions. Income earned in a state that does not have an income tax would be taxed in the earner's state of residence. Second, if the income tax rate is greater in an individual's state of residence than in the state where the income is earned, the state of residence would collect tax on that income proportional to the difference in rates. These rules typically apply among states that enter into agreements with each other to ensure consistent treatment of each others' residents. In the absence of these agreements, individuals may be subject to tax on such income by more than one state or by neither state.

The practice regarding local government income taxes is somewhat more confusing, if only because there is more variability as to which rules are applied. First, many local "income" taxes exclude property income and apply only to so-called earned income. These are often referred to as wage taxes. James Rodgers (1981) reports that local income taxes are generally residence-based in Maryland (where the tax applies only to residents), Michigan, and Pennsylvania (except Philadelphia where taxpayers receive a credit for tax paid to the jurisdiction where they live against any tax due the jurisdiction where they earned the income). In contrast, the tax of the jurisdiction where the income is earned has preference in Alabama, California, Kentucky (where the base is income earned in the jurisdiction only), Ohio, and Philadelphia (where taxpayers receive a credit for tax paid to the jurisdiction where they earned the income against any tax levied by the jurisdiction where the taxpayer lives).

The practice in Pennsylvania is particularly confusing because different rules apply to Philadelphia as opposed to other jurisdictions in the state. Philadelphia has first claim compared to other Pennsylvania municipalities to tax the income earned by nonresidents in the city. Because the tax rate in Philadelphia is greater than that allowed in the surrounding jurisdictions, these jurisdictions can effectively collect no tax on income earned by their residents in Philadelphia. Therefore, as Rodgers notes, many of those surrounding jurisdictions have not adopted income taxes. In other parts of the state, the jurisdiction of residence has first claim to residents' income earned in other jurisdictions. Consequently, Rodgers reports that after Pittsburgh adopted a local income tax, most of the surrounding jurisdictions followed immediately to retain that income tax base for themselves.

George Break (1980) has suggested that the sensible treatment of nonresident income by local government income taxes depends on the nature of the service to be financed with the revenue. If the benefits of a service primarily accrue to residents of a jurisdiction, then a residence base rule seems most appropriate. Break argues that this situation applies if the income tax is used to finance local schools (given that state government revenue is also provided to schools to account for the external or social benefits of education). On the other hand, if the tax is to finance general city or county services, then Break argues that at least part of the tax should be origin-based to offset the service benefits received by nonresidents who work in the jurisdiction (such as local police protection, traffic control, or local parks). In the absence of user charges for such services, the local income tax may be the most effective way to reach those nonresident commuters.

Tax Rates

Not only do state income taxes differ widely in the definition of the tax base and somewhat in the treatment of nonresident income, but they also involve a wide variety of rate structures, as shown previously in Table 16.2. Only 6 of the 41 states with broad-based taxes (Colorado, Illinois, Indiana, Massachusetts, Michigan, and Pennsylvania) used flat rates in 2004. In the other states, the rate structure is progressive, although again to widely differing degrees. For example, in Utah, the tax rates vary from 2.3 to 7.0 percent, but the highest rate applies to all taxable income above $4,313 ($8,626 for taxpayers married filing jointly); consequently, this is nearly a flat rate tax for many, if not most, taxpayers.[6] In contrast, 1993 tax rates in California varied from 1.0 to 9.3 percent, with joint filing taxpayers having taxable income of about $78,000 reaching the maximum rate of 9.3 percent. Thus, the progression in the rate structure affected a substantial number of taxpayers in California. As stated previously, comparing states based on tax rates is often very misleading because of the differences in tax bases. For income taxes, this includes differences in the starting point for computing the base and in the allowed exemptions, deductions, and credits.

ECONOMIC ANALYSIS

Incentive Effects of State and Federal Income Taxes Combined

A crucial element of any income tax is that it creates incentives for individuals to change their behavior. Individuals may react to income taxes by changing the amount that they work (and thus the amount of income earned), by changing the amount of income they save, or by changing how they spend their income in response to various tax deductions. The income tax characteristic that determines

---

[6]Given personal exemptions and the standard deduction in Utah, the highest rate would apply at an income of about $27,600 for a family of four persons.

Application 16.1

FEDERAL COLLECTION OF STATE TAXES

The Federal-State Tax Collection Act of 1972 authorized the U.S. Department of the Treasury to enter into agreements with states to administer and collect state income taxes along with the federal tax at no cost to the state governments. To be eligible, the state tax on residents had to take one of two possible forms:

1. The state tax applying to residents has a base that equals federal taxable income (federal AGI less federal exemptions and deductions) minus interest on federal securities plus federal deductions for state and local income taxes and interest on bonds issued by other states or localities (thus states would not tax the interest income from federal bonds but would tax the interest from other states' bonds). A state rate structure would be applied to this base, with the possibility of a credit for income taxes paid to other states.

2. The state tax on residents equals a percentage of federal tax liability, after adjustment to remove any interest income from federal government bonds. States may also make other adjustments or use credits as noted previously.

The state tax on nonresidents had to be as follows: States can add a supplement to the federal tax of any nonresident who earns at least 25 percent of labor income in that taxing state, with nonresidents to be taxed no more heavily than residents. This allows states to tax nonresident income earned in that state based on the federal definition of taxable income and federal rates, but only if 25 percent of the taxpayer's labor income arises in that state.

No state ever accepted this offer and entered into a tax collection agreement with the federal government, so this provision of the Internal Revenue Code was eliminated in 1990. Such agreements would have imposed substantial conformance between state and federal income taxes and would have subjected the states to automatic revenue changes from nearly any and all revisions to the federal tax code. With the first possible structure in the preceding list, states would have effectively adopted the federal exclusions, exemptions, and deductions; whereas with the second possibility, states effectively would have adopted the entire federal structure. Although states could offset those revenue effects through rate changes, they were apparently unwilling to give up their autonomy to design their own income tax structures. The rule for taxing nonresidents would have restricted states' capabilities to tax nonresidents compared to current practice. In addition, states would have given up their independent tax-auditing and tax-collection operations. The advantages of this federal collection of state income taxes would have been easier tax compliance for taxpayers, lower administrative costs for states, and perhaps lower administrative costs overall, if economies of scale exist in tax collection.

A less ambitious form of federal collection of state taxes might be possible by allowing federal *processing* of state returns without restrictions on structure. Obviously, however, such a system would work best for those state taxes that currently conform most closely to the federal tax, although states would not be required to automatically adopt all future federal tax changes. In fact, in Indiana, Maryland, and New York, local income taxes can be collected by the state along with the state tax, and in Canada 9 of the 10 provincial income taxes are collected along with the national government tax.

the magnitude of these incentives is the **marginal tax rate**, that is, the *tax rate that applies to the last dollar earned*. This marginal tax rate determines how much the tax can be reduced by working one less hour or by making a charitable contribution and taking that amount as a deduction. For instance, if a taxpayer faces a marginal tax rate of 50 percent, then an extra hour's work at $10 per hour would increase after-tax or take-home pay by only $5, while an extra $20 charitable contribution would reduce taxes by $10.

The marginal tax rate facing any taxpayer depends on the combined effect of all income taxes—federal, state, and local—paid by that taxpayer. Therefore, the relevant item is the aggregate marginal tax rate from all income taxes that applies to a given income or deductible expenditure amount. However, the marginal tax rate that results from a set of income taxes depends not only on the separate tax rates but also on any deductibility of one tax against the other, as noted previously.

The effect of income tax deductibility on marginal tax rates is demonstrated in Table 16.5. The illustration assumes that a taxpayer faces a federal marginal tax rate of 28 percent and a state tax with a marginal tax rate of either 5 or 10 percent. With no deductibility of one tax against the other, the combined marginal tax rate is simply the sum of the two individual rates, either 33 percent or 38 percent depending on the state tax. Deducting the state tax from the federal tax reduces the combined marginal tax rate. If f represents the federal rate and s represents the state rate, the combined rate is $f + s - sf$ because the increase in state tax of s per dollar of income becomes a federal deduction equal to s, which reduces federal tax by sf. In the numerical example, the combined marginal rate is 32 percent if the state rate is 5 percent (compared to 33 percent with no deductibility) and 35 percent if the state rate is 10 percent (compared to 38 percent without deductibility). Thus, federal deductibility of the state tax not only reduces marginal tax rates but also narrows the difference in marginal rates between low-rate and high-rate state taxes.

Reciprocal deductibility—that is, simultaneous federal deductibility of the state tax and state deductibility of the federal tax—has much the same effect on

Table 16.5

Combined Marginal Tax Rates from Federal and State Income Taxation

Tax Structure Characteristic	General Case	Example One	Example Two
Federal Marginal Tax Rate	f	.28	.28
State Marginal Tax Rate	s	.05	.10
Combined Marginal Tax Rate If No Deductibility	$f + s$	.33	.38
Combined Marginal Tax Rate If State Tax Deducted Against Federal Only	$f + s(1 - f)$	.32	.35
Combined Marginal Tax Rate With Reciprocal Deductibility	$\dfrac{[f + s(1 - 2f)]}{1 - fs}$	.31	.33

marginal rates, although to a greater magnitude. In this case, the combined rate of $f + s$ is reduced by sf due to the federal deduction for the state tax and by fs due to the state deduction for the federal tax. However, the rate is then *increased* by f^2s due to a smaller state tax deduction against the federal and by s^2f due to a smaller federal deduction against the state tax, and so on. In Table 16.5, a taxpayer with a 28 percent federal tax rate faces a combined marginal rate of 31 percent when the state tax rate is 5 percent and 33 percent when the state tax rate is 10 percent. Again, the marginal tax rate is lowered and the difference between the states is narrowed by reciprocal deductibility, both compared to no deductibility and federal deductibility of the state tax alone.

This table is a bit misleading because although it shows the effect of deductibility on a given rate structure, it ignores changes in the rates that may be required if deductibility is allowed. Because state deductibility of the federal tax reduces the state tax base, higher average state tax rates are required to generate the same revenue as would be collected without that deductibility. Thus, those states that now allow taxpayers to deduct the federal tax may have adopted higher income tax rates than otherwise; however, given those rates, the difference in rates between that state and others is less than nominally appears. In terms of this example, the choice for a state may be between a 5-percent rate with no deduction for the federal tax and the 10-percent rate with the deduction. The difference in combined marginal rates is 33 percent compared to 35 percent, less than the difference in the state rates alone.

An example of the effect of a charitable contribution on taxes based on Table 16.5 shows the importance and usefulness of these combined marginal tax rates. Suppose an individual who itemizes deductions for federal taxes and whose state income tax has a 10-percent rate and also allows a deduction for a charitable contribution makes a new $100 contribution to an eligible charity. The after-tax "price" or "cost" of the contribution to the taxpayer per dollar is $1 -$ marginal tax rate. If there is no reciprocal deductibility (only the state tax is deductible against the federal and not the converse), then the contribution reduces total taxes by $35 and "costs" the taxpayer $65 [$100 \cdot (1 - f - s + fs)$]. With reciprocal deductibility, the contribution costs the taxpayer $67 (the marginal rate is 33 percent). In both cases, the contribution costs more than the $62, which appears to be the cost from analyzing the state-federal taxes separately and ignoring intergovernmental tax deductibility.

State Tax Amounts and Progressivity

Intergovernmental income tax deductibility also reduces the progressivity of the tax structure, with implications both for choosing a tax structure within a subnational government and for intergovernmental tax competition. The general effect of income tax deductibility on tax liabilities is shown in Table 16.6. For the example, the federal tax has a 25-percent tax rate, a $3,000 personal exemption, and no deductions except the state tax; the state tax has a $1,500 personal exemption, no deductions except the federal tax (for the reciprocal deductibility case), and either a 5- or 10-percent rate. Taxes are computed for a family with four exemptions and income equal to $60,000.

Table 16.6

The Effects of Income Tax Deductibility on Tax Liability

Assumptions: Family with $60,000 Income and 4 Exemptions
Federal Personal Exemption Is $3,000
State Personal Exemption Is $1,500

Tax Structure	Federal Tax	State Tax	Total Tax	Effective Rate
Case A: Federal Tax Rate = .25, State Tax Rate = .05				
No Deductibility	$12,000	$2,700	$14,700	.245
State Tax Deducted				
from Federal	11,325	2,700	14,025	.234
Reciprocal Deductibility	11,468	2,127	13,595	.227
Case B: Federal Tax Rate = .25, State Tax Rate = .10				
No Deductibility	12,000	5,400	17,400	.290
State Tax Deducted				
from Federal	10,650	5,400	16,050	.268
Reciprocal Deductibility	10,923	4,308	15,231	.254
Implications				

	Total Tax in Case B / Total Tax in Case A
No Deductibility	1.18
State Tax Deducted from Federal	1.14
Reciprocal Deductibility	1.12

As expected, deductibility with either state tax rate decreases total tax liability and thus the effective tax rate. More importantly, however, deductibility also reduces the *difference* in tax liability between the 5- and 10-percent tax rates. Taxes are 18 percent higher with the 10-percent rate rather than the 5-percent rate given no deductibility, but only 14 percent higher when the state tax is deducted against the federal tax and 12 percent higher with reciprocal deductibility. Put another way, although the state income tax is $2,700 greater with the 10-percent than 5-percent tax rate, the deduction of that additional state tax against the federal reduces the federal tax by $675 (.25 times $2,700). As a result, the total tax liability is greater only by $2,025. With reciprocal deductibility, the difference in total tax liability between a 5- and 10-percent state tax rate is only $1,636. Thus, intergovernmental income tax deductibility mitigates the effect of a higher state–local income tax rate, effectively reducing the progressivity of state income taxes compared to the statutory rates.

One implication of this effect is that states may choose more progressive income tax-rate structures due to federal deductibility of their tax than they would without those deductions. Higher-income taxpayers who could be affected by a more progressive state income tax structure are likely to itemize deductions for their federal tax and thus deduct the state tax. Therefore, a lower federal liability offsets part of those taxpayers' state income tax liability; in essence, part of those taxpayers' state tax is paid by all taxpayers in the United States, perhaps in the form of higher federal rates necessitated by the lower federal tax collections. In a report prepared for the Minnesota Tax Study Commission, Joel Slemrod (1986, p. 130–31) argues the following:

> *Because the proportion of itemizing households increases with income, in general the more progressive is the state income tax, the greater will be the degree of tax exporting. In a sense, by loading the tax burden onto those high-income taxpayers who tend to be itemizers and also have high marginal federal income tax rates, the total net tax burden borne by Minnesotans declines.*

Similarly, in a study of state–local tax incidence for 1976, 1985, and 1991, Howard Chernick (2005) reports that intergovernmental tax deductibility induces states and localities to adopt more progressive tax structures than otherwise, so much so that federal deductibility *increases* the overall progressivity of state–local tax systems. Chernick (p. 105) notes that

> *". . . a 1 percentage point increase in the percentage itemizing [and thus deducting state–local taxes from the federal tax base] would increase net progressivity by about 1 percentage point. . . . This strong result suggests that eliminating the deductibility of state and local taxes . . . would substantially reduce the progressivity of state and local tax systems."*

A second implication of deductibility is that states may be able to collect more revenue (that is, have higher average tax rates) and thus spend more than without deductibility. Again from Table 16.6, if a state increases its tax rate from 5 to 10 percent, the state government's revenue from this $60,000 income family rises by $2,700 (from $2,700 to $5,400), but the family's *total tax bill* (federal plus state) rises by only $2,025. In essence this family can "buy" another $2,700 worth of state government services by paying only $2,025. Deductibility may therefore induce some voters to support higher state taxes and expenditures than they would otherwise. For taxpayers who itemize deductions, the incentive is of greater importance the greater the federal marginal tax rate; so the incentive is expected to be more significant for higher-income taxpayers. Whether the change in the voters' positions translates into a change in state behavior depends on the political system. In the median-voter framework, for instance, the issue is whether deductibility influences the median voter or changes the median voter's identity.

A third implication of the effect of deductibility is that interstate differences in taxes are less than is suggested by differences in income tax rates. Returning to the example in Table 16.6, if one state has a 5-percent tax rate and another a 10-percent tax rate, the difference in tax for a $60,000 family is $2,025 rather than $2,700, if the state tax is deducted against the federal income tax. Deductibility therefore reduces the incentive for taxpayers who itemize federal deductions to move to lower-tax states or localities. Moreover, the effect of deductibility is proportional to the federal income tax rate. Therefore, this mitigating effect of deductibility on state taxes becomes stronger as the taxpayer's income increases because higher-income taxpayers face higher tax rates in the progressive federal income tax.

The combined result of these implications is likely to be higher state–local expenditures and more progressive state–local tax structures in at least some states due to the federal deductibility of state income taxes. Again, this result should be most prevalent in those states where a relatively large fraction of taxpayers itemize federal deductions and have higher incomes (thus facing the higher marginal federal tax rates). Prior to the federal income tax changes in 1987, 30–40 percent of federal taxpayers itemized deductions in a structure with federal marginal tax rates as high as 70 percent before 1981 and up to 50 percent in 1986. With such a federal tax structure, state income tax deductibility was particularly valuable. For a taxpayer with a 50-percent federal marginal tax rate, half of the individual's state income tax was offset by the deduction. With the maximum federal income tax rate now at 35 percent, the value and incentive effects of federal income tax deductibility of state–local income taxes has been lessened compared to the past.

Application 16.2

STATE INCOME TAXATION AND AN AGING POPULATION

It is no secret that the population in the United States is aging in aggregate, but the fact that the changing age distribution of the population has important implications for state (and federal) income taxes is not as well known. As the population ages and the fraction of the population not working or retired increases, the sources of income for spending change dramatically. The income and source of spending for retired senior citizens (who are not working currently) comes from private pensions; interest, dividends, rent, and other forms of capital income; and social security benefits. How state income taxes apply to these forms of income differs widely, although all are taxed less heavily than wages and salaries, in aggregate.

In 1960, about 38 percent of the population in the United States was 18 years of age or younger, and about 9 percent was 65 or older. By 2004, only about 25 percent was 18 or younger and 12.5 percent 65 or older. As the "baby boomers" (those born between 1945 and 1960) age, this trend will continue.

This trend is shown dramatically by the population pyramids for the United States for 1960 and an estimate for 2025, shown in Figure 16.1. Partly because of this aging and partly because of enhanced pensions and social security, people have been retiring at younger ages than in the past. Thus, the fraction of the population who is retired is also rising.

Related to these changes in the age distribution and retirement, the relative importance of various sources of income has also changed, as shown in Table 16.7. Wages and salaries accounted for 66 percent of personal income in 1960, but only 60 percent in 1980 and 55.5 percent in 2004. In contrast, social security benefits increased from 2.7 percent of personal income in 1960 to 8 percent in 2004, whereas other personal transfers (mostly private pensions) from 1.1 to 5.2 percent. Similarly, interest income rose from 6 to 9.8 percent and dividend income from 3.3 to 4.6 percent. This relative increase in the importance of social security, pension, and capital income has arisen from several factors—policy

Application 16.2 — State Income Taxation and an Aging Population

Figure 16.1

Population
Pyramids for the
United States,
1960 and 2025

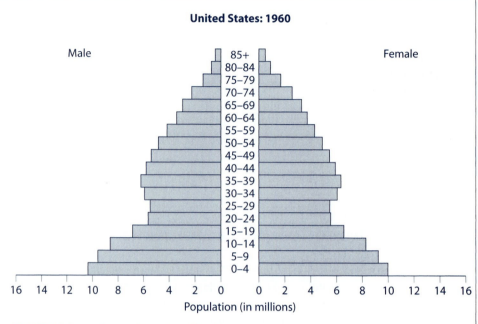

SOURCE: U.S. Census Bureau, International Data Base.

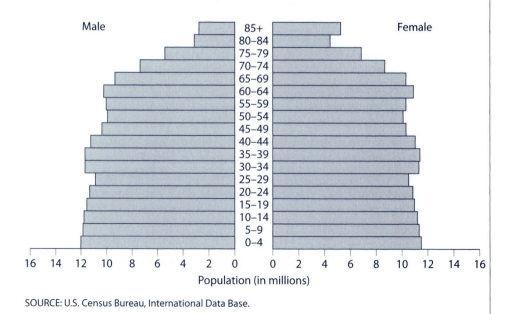

SOURCE: U.S. Census Bureau, International Data Base.

Application 16.2 — State Income Taxation and an Aging Population

Table 16.7

Sources of Personal Income

	1960	1980	2000	2004
Wage and salary disbursements	66.3%	59.7%	57.3%	55.5%
Employer contributions for employee pension and insurance funds	3.5	8.0	7.2	9.0
Employer contributions for government social insurance	2.3	3.9	4.1	4.1
Personal interest income	6.0	11.9	12.0	9.8
Personal dividend income	3.3	2.8	4.5	4.6
Old-age, survivors, disability, and health insurance benefits	2.7	6.7	7.4	8.0
Family assistance	0.2	0.5	0.2	0.2
Other personal transfer receipts	1.1	3.2	4.2	5.2

SOURCE: U.S. Department of Commerce, Bureau of Economic Analysis, http://www.bea.doc.gov/.

decisions to increase social security benefits, growth of private pensions, higher interest rates, personal saving, and others. The enhancement of nonwage income options has, in turn, influenced retirement decisions.

For a variety of reasons, states have often provided special income tax treatment for senior citizens and retirement income. Special tax treatment is provided through additional personal exemptions or credits for senior citizens that are part of state income taxes in at least 20 states. For instance, Arizona taxpayers receive a personal exemption of $2,100; senior citizens get an additional $2,100 exemption. Similarly, California taxpayers receive a personal tax credit of $80 (in 2004); senior citizens receive an additional $80 credit. Income that is important for senior citizens also often receives special treatment. According to the Federation of Tax Administrators, social security benefits were exempt from state income taxation in 26 states in 2000, and pension or retirement income was fully taxed in only 5 states (California, Connecticut, Nebraska, Rhode Island, and Vermont).[7] For instance, New York fully exempts income from federal, military, and state–local government pensions from the state income tax and provides a $20,000 exemption for private pension income. Illinois, Mississippi, and Pennsylvania fully exempt all pension income—public or private—from state income taxation. Finally, some states provide exemptions or credits for interest or dividend income that reduce the effective tax rates on that income.

The combined effect of this special state income tax treatment for senior citizens can be dramatic. Paul Menchik (2003) discusses the generous advantages for seniors in the Michigan income tax, which include (1) exemption of social security benefits, (2) exemption of all public pension income, (3) an indexed exemption of $72,180 (joint return) for private pension and IRA income, (4) an indexed exemption of $16,095 (joint return) for investment income, (5) an additional senior personal exemption ($1,900, indexed), and (6) special, more advantageous property tax credit features. As a consequence of these factors,

---

[7]Baer, 2001.

Application 16.2 — State Income Taxation and an Aging Population

Menchik (p. 553) reports that ". . . taken as a whole, seniors on net pay no income tax. Indeed, the net amount contributed by all seniors [effective tax rate] is a *negative* 3.4%." Therefore, senior citizens in Michigan as a group actually receive net rebates through the state income tax system.

Four factors primarily contribute to the special tax treatment afforded to senior citizens. In the past (1950s and 1960s), the poverty rate among senior citizens was relatively high, encouraging public policy decisions to assist seniors. A series of Supreme Court decisions required states to treat federal and military pensions the same as they treat pensions from state and local employees in that state. Interstate competition and a concern about retirees moving to states without income taxes prompted some states to act. Finally, senior citizens are also powerful politically, both because a relatively large fraction of senior citizens vote and because of effective lobbying groups (such as the American Association of Retired Persons or AARP).

The current issue is whether this special treatment continues to be warranted and, if so, what the long-run effects will be. Census data for 2003 show that the poverty rate among those 65 years and older in the U.S. (about 10.2 percent) is lower than for the population in other age groups (17.6 percent for those under 18 and 10.8 percent for those 18–64 years of age). Special tax treatment for senior citizens also creates horizontal inequities in tax systems, as seniors with a specific income pay less tax than younger taxpayers with identical income. These special tax features also may create incentives for behavioral change, including earlier retirement than otherwise or decisions not to take part-time jobs. As noted previously, the relative importance of senior citizens in the population is growing, so the relative cost of these special state income tax features will continue to grow. Finally, to the extent that senior citizens contribute less through income taxes to pay for state and local government services, others have to pay higher taxes or expenditures on services have to be reduced.

THE CHOICE OF STATE TAX STRUCTURE

The diversity of state–local fiscal systems is continually stressed in this book, and the different state choices about tax structure are simply another example of this diversity. Examples of substantial differences in tax structure for states that otherwise seem similar abound. Oregon has no sales tax and relies on a state income tax, while Washington has no state income tax and relies heavily on sales taxes; Texas and Florida have no income tax but relatively high reliance on property taxes, while Oklahoma and Georgia make much more balanced used of all three major taxes (income, sales, and property); New Hampshire has neither a state sales nor broad personal income tax but very high property taxes, whereas all the other New England states use both state sales and income taxes.

Researchers have attempted to understand and explain these and similar different choices by analyzing how states make tax policy decisions. Nearly all the basic models of this choice assume that government needs to select a set of taxes to generate a fixed amount of revenue (to finance services), and that the government wants to find the set of taxes that imposes the lowest costs on residents. At least three types of costs are worth of consideration. First, as explained in Chapter 12, excess burden or the efficiency cost of taxes arises because individuals or firms change their behavior in response to the tax. One change in behavior that concerns many states is the relocation of economic activity, which refers to firms moving or workers out of the state. So states want tax structures that minimize the incentives for residents to change behavior (except for taxes designed to alter behavior, such as cigarette taxes perhaps). Second, administrative costs for some taxes can be high, so states want to avoid tax choices that have high collection costs in that state's situation. Finally, the direct revenue costs of the taxes are an issue. Finding the set of taxes that minimizes revenue costs to residents essentially is equivalent to exporting the maximum tax burden to nonresidents.

States can export tax burden in any ways, including ways that might look like exporting but really are not. First, federal tax deductibility (for both persons and corporations) of state–local taxes transfers part of the burden of deductible state–local taxes to all taxpayers nationally (by reducing federal revenue, which requires higher federal tax rates or cuts in federal services). Second, some taxes are exported directly to the extent that they are levied on nonresidents and cannot be shifted. This might include sales or excise taxes paid by visitors, property taxes paid by nonresident property owners, and income taxes on nonresident workers. Third, in some cases, taxes levied on businesses or business activity in a state may be shifted to consumers or suppliers in other states as a result of price changes.

This last possibility is somewhat limited, however. A state must have some unique feature or a monopoly position in some industry for a state's taxes to be shifted to consumers and firms in other states. Otherwise, consumers might simply switch to buying at lower prices from suppliers in lower-tax states; if that happens, producers in the state have the incentive to move their operations to the lower-tax states as well. For instance, states with some relatively unique features (sunshine and warmth in Florida and Hawaii or minerals in Alaska and other states) may be able to export taxes on those features (or economic activity related to those features) because the features themselves are immobile and consumers may have limited substitutes. On the other hand, taxes on manufacturing or commercial activity in a state may not be able to be exported if the producers easily can change the location of production to other states, or if consumers can buy from other suppliers (which prevents price increases by producers from the high-tax state).

Empirical studies of state tax policy decisions suggest that exporting as much state tax burden as possible goes a long way toward explaining many (but clearly not all) differences in state tax structures. In one such study, Daphne Kenyon (1986) examined the determinants of the mix of state taxes using fiscal year 1981 data, paying particular attention to whether differences among states in the average federal marginal income tax rate and the percentage of a state's taxpayers who itemize federal deductions influence how a state uses different taxes. The federal tax influences are captured by the **burden price** of the state income tax, which is defined as the cost of a $1 increase in state income tax after subtracting the amount offset by the federal deduction. Kenyon reports that a 1-percent increase in the net burden of state income taxes (for instance, from a lower-value federal deduction) leads to an 11-percent decrease in per-capita state income taxes.

In another more recent study, Mary Gade and Lee Adkins (1990) also examined the influence of tax exporting on the choice of state tax mix. In their model, state officials choose a state tax structure to minimize the net burden on residents (thus, maximize exporting), and given that structure, the state's median voter determines the level of state taxes and spending. Gade and Adkins find that shares for major state taxes are negatively related to the burden prices for those taxes and positively related to the prices for the other taxes. They conclude that ". . . as the . . . burden price associated with a particular tax rises [so that residents bear a larger fraction of that tax], states are expected to reduce their use of the offending tax and increase their reliance on substitute taxes." Importantly, Gade and Adkins also report that the relative size of a state's manufacturing base has no effect on the state's use of business (corporate income and severance) taxes, but that the relative importance of mining in a state's economy is associated with increasing use of severance, license, and selected excise taxes. Apparently, states believe that they can export taxes on mining activity (which is immobile), while they cannot export taxes on manufacturing activity, which is likely to be mobile in the long run.

Using their results to simulate the effects of the 1986 federal tax changes, Gade and Adkins estimate that responses are likely to differ greatly by state, with some states increasing use of sales taxes, excise taxes, and business taxes and decreasing use of income taxes, while other states do just the opposite and increase use of income taxes relative to sales taxes. In aggregate, however, their model (as did Kenyon's) overestimates the degree of tax structure change compared to the amount that actually occurred.

Finally, Gilbert Metcalf (1993) reports results similar to those of Gade and Adkins with two important differences. First, Metcalf finds that income taxes are sensitive to burden prices, but that sales taxes are not. In that case, changes in deductions, credits, or other features that allow a larger fraction of state income taxes to be exported lead to more use of that tax, but deductions and credits for sales taxes have no effect. Second, Metcalf finds that use of sales and corporate income taxes is greater in states that have relatively more purchases by nonresidents, suggesting that direct exporting may be important for decisions about the use of sales and business taxes.

The effect of federal income taxes on state–local tax structure has been of particular interest. Federal tax reform can affect state income taxes in two ways: (1) changes in federal definitions of income, exemptions, and deductions alter the base of state taxes that use those definitions, leading to changes in state income tax revenue if the state adopts the federal changes, and (2) changes in itemized deductions and tax rates alter the value of the federal deduction for state taxes, which changes the net cost of state taxes for those who itemize federal deductions.

Both occurred with the major revisions to the federal income tax in 1986. Marginal federal income tax rates were reduced substantially, while a number of exclusions, deductions, and credits were altered to expand the federal tax base in aggregate. The net effect was a small decrease in federal personal income taxes. Five particularly important changes were (1) increases in the personal exemption, standard deduction, and earned income credit (all of which *lowered* federal and conforming state taxes); (2) full taxation of all capital gains; (3) restrictions on the use of tax shelters to offset income; (4) ending of the deduction for Individual Retirement Accounts (IRAs) for many taxpayers; and (5) reductions in itemized deductions, including eliminating the federal itemized deduction for state–local sales taxes. These latter four elements *increased* the federal and potential state tax bases.

For those states that based their state tax on federal taxable income or adjusted gross income, the expanded federal base implied state income tax increases (windfall gains). States were expected to respond to these potential automatic changes in state income tax revenue, although the issue was to what degree states would act. Although state–local income and property taxes still were deductible, fewer taxpayers were expected to deduct income and property taxes because of the larger standard deduction. The lower federal marginal tax rates reduced the value of that deduction for those taxpayers who still use it. The combined effect of this and the ending of the deduction for sales taxes was an increase in the net burden of state income, sales, and property taxes—that is, the burden after the federal deduction—for many taxpayers, particularly higher-income taxpayers for whom the decrease in the value of the deduction was greatest. Many predicted that as a response to these changes, state governments might reduce reliance on general sales taxes (which were no longer deductible), reduce reliance on all deductible taxes (sales, income, and property) compared to other revenue sources, and/or reduce the progressivity of their state tax structures.

What actually happened? In aggregate, states tended to follow the federal government in reducing marginal income tax rates and broadening the tax base, particularly in accepting the federal changes that taxed capital gains fully and limited deductions for certain types of investments. Many states also took action to reduce revenue windfalls, often by raising personal exemptions and/or standard deductions. This reduced or eliminated income taxes for low-income taxpayers, as had the equivalent federal changes. In the end, then, state income taxes fell in many states and rose in some, but by less than they would have if structural changes had not offset some of the federal tax base changes.

Not surprisingly, state income taxes as a whole seem to have become less progressive as a result of these structural changes. The reduction in the value of the federal deduction made it difficult for states to maintain the prior level of progressivity. Marcus Berliant and Robert Strauss (1993, p. 35) reported that "Between 1985 and 1987, the . . . progressivity of 37 states' personal income taxes declined." Apparently, decreases in marginal tax rates offset the higher personal exemptions and standard deductions.[8]

Finally, despite the elimination of the deduction for state sales taxes, states did not make a major move away from using general sales taxes. General sales taxes accounted for 14.1 percent of state–local general revenue in 1986, and 13.4 percent in 1991, 13.9 percent in 1997, and 13.2 percent in 2002. In fact, over this period, a

---

[8]Even though state income taxes are less progressive than in the past, Berliant and Strauss still report that state income taxes increase the overall progressivity of the unified personal income tax system.

International Comparison

TYPES OF SUBNATIONAL GOVERNMENT TAXATION

Although governments in different nations use basically the same types of taxes, the importance of those various taxes differs substantially. The shares of state and local taxes in six main categories for the 24 industrialized nations that are members of the Organization for Economic Cooperation and Development (OECD) are shown in Figure 16.2. State and local governments in the United States use income, sales, and property taxes in a roughly balanced way. A similar balanced tax-use pattern also applies in the other major federal nations (Australia, Canada, Germany), although Germany has relatively high reliance on income taxes compared to the other three countries.

Substantially different subnational tax patterns apply in other sets of nations. Income taxes are clearly the dominant subnational (local) government tax in the Scandinavian nations (Denmark, Finland, Norway, Sweden), whereas property taxes are clearly the dominant local tax in Ireland, the Netherlands, New Zealand, and the United Kingdom. Most other nations use at least two subnational taxes.

The subnational tax pattern in Japan, for instance, is not substantially different from that in Germany; income taxes dominate, with Japan using property taxes a bit more and sales taxes a bit less than does Germany.

The data used to create Figure 16.2 combine states and localities, which present a somewhat distorted view for those nations that have more than one level of substantial government. Separate tax reliance data for state governments and local governments are shown in Table 16.8 for the four major federal nations. States in all four nations use income, sales, and property taxes, although the type of income tax used by Australian states is a payroll tax (a tax on wages only, rather than on all types of income). At the local level, property taxes are the most important tax by a wide margin in all these nations (except Germany) and the *only* local tax in Australia. Local governments in Germany, in contrast, rely heavily on income taxes, whereas the United States is the only one of this group where localities make substantial use of sales taxes.

Table 16.8

Percentage of Tax Revenue by Type of Tax, Federal Nations, 2002

	States				Localities			
Nation	Income	Goods & Services	Property	Other	Income	Goods & Services	Property	Other
Australia	—	33.0%	39.0%	28%[a]	—	—	100.0%	—
Canada	46.9	41.8	5.7	5.6	—	2.0	91.5	6.5
Germany	50.2	45.0	4.9	—	75.8	6.4	17.7	0.3
United States	39.5	57.5	3.1	—	5.2	22.2	72.6	—

[a]Australian states collect payroll taxes rather than broad-based income taxes.

SOURCE: OECD, *Revenue Statistics 1965–2003*, 2004.

International Comparison — Types of Subnational Government Taxation

Figure 16.2

The Structure of State and Local Government Tax Receipts

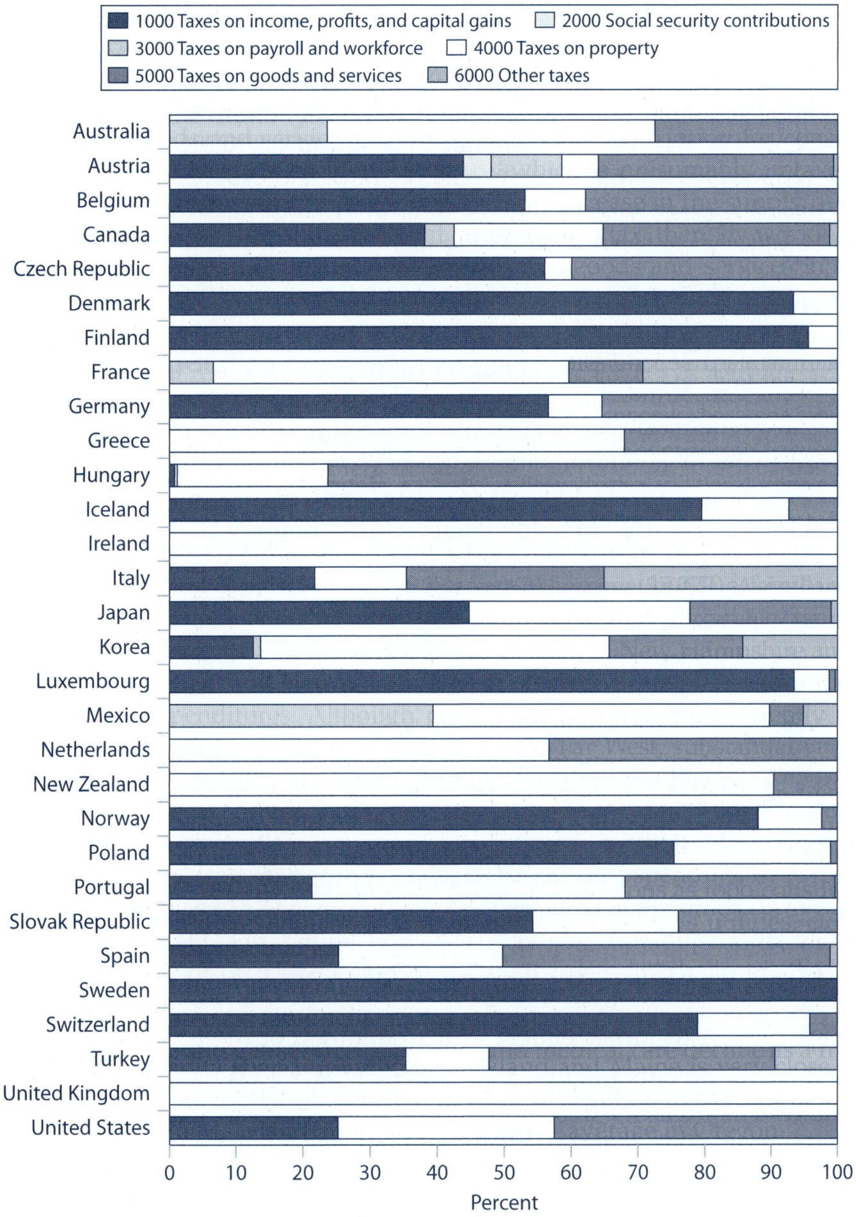

Legend:
- 1000 Taxes on income, profits, and capital gains
- 2000 Social security contributions
- 3000 Taxes on payroll and workforce
- 4000 Taxes on property
- 5000 Taxes on goods and services
- 6000 Other taxes

Countries (top to bottom): Australia, Austria, Belgium, Canada, Czech Republic, Denmark, Finland, France, Germany, Greece, Hungary, Iceland, Ireland, Italy, Japan, Korea, Luxembourg, Mexico, Netherlands, New Zealand, Norway, Poland, Portugal, Slovak Republic, Spain, Sweden, Switzerland, Turkey, United Kingdom, United States

X-axis: Percent (0 to 100)

1. This refers to only those taxes which are classified as sub-central government taxes. Social security contributions paid to social security funds are excluded.

SOURCE: OECD, *Revenue Statistics 1965–2003*, 2004.

number of states increased sales tax rates or expanded sales tax bases (refer to Chapter 15). Nor did states move away from income or property taxes, even though the value of the deduction for those taxes was reduced. Again, state–local reliance on personal income taxes increased, from 11.6 percent of revenue to 12.1, and changed little for property taxes, from 17.4 to 16.6 percent.[9]

Major federal income tax changes have happened several times since 1986, but none created the same degree of attention about the responses of state and local governments. For instance, the Economic Growth and Tax Relief Reconciliation Act of 2001 reduced federal marginal income tax rates and expanded limits for IRAs. Lower federal tax rates implied that the value of itemized deductions for state–local income and property taxes were reduced; increased opportunities to make tax-deferred contributions to IRAs reduced tax bases for states that follow the federal definitions. Neither effect on states and localities received much attention, however, and there seemed to be little in the way of dramatic state–local responses.[10]

Although none of the studies about states and localities choosing a tax structure is conclusive, all suggest that states consider their specific economic situation in selecting a tax structure best *for that state.* If so, trying to identify a "best" tax structure for all states or comparing one state's taxes to the average tax structure in all others is fruitless. In fact, different tax structures may be optimal for different states, at least in the sense of minimizing costs to residents.

SUMMARY

Currently, 41 state governments collect broad-based individual income taxes, and 2 states (New Hampshire and Tennessee) collect income tax on a narrow base of capital income only. Individual income taxes are also used by about 4,000 local governments spread over 11 states and the District of Columbia. In 2002, income taxes provided 17.5 percent of state government revenue on average, double the share provided by that tax in 1962.

The two principal issues when selecting an appropriate state income tax base are the degree of coordination between the federal-state income tax definitions and the treatment of income that crosses jurisdiction boundaries. State-federal income taxes also are related by deductions for income taxes paid to the other types of government.

State income taxes differ widely in the definition of the tax base and in rate structures. Only 6 of the 41 states with broad-based taxes (Colorado, Illinois, Indiana, Massachusetts, Michigan, and Pennsylvania) used flat rates in 2004. In the other states, the rate structure is progressive, although again to widely differing degrees.

---

[9]State–local reliance on federal aid, corporate income taxes, and other taxes (especially excise taxes) declined over this period, while reliance on user charges rose.

[10]EGTRRA also provided for repeal of the federal estate and gift tax and a phase out of the credit for state estate taxes. Most of the attention to state responses to federal tax reform in this instance focused on state responses in the area of estate taxation.

The marginal tax rate—that is, the tax rate that applies to the last dollar earned—determines the magnitude of the incentive effects of income taxes. Federal deductibility of the state tax reduces marginal tax rates and also narrows the difference in marginal rates between low-rate and high-rate states. Reciprocal deductibility—that is, simultaneous federal deductibility of the state tax and state deductibility of the federal tax—has much the same effect, although to a greater magnitude.

Intergovernmental income tax deductibility reduces the progressivity of the tax structure. As a result, states may choose more progressive income tax-rate structures than they would without those deductions, states may be able to collect more revenue and thus spend more than without deductibility, and interstate differences in taxes are less than are suggested by differences in income tax rates.

Empirical studies of state tax policy decisions suggest that exporting as much state tax burden as possible—indirectly through tax deductions or credits and directly through nonresident purchases—is an important factor in explaining many (but clearly not all) differences in state tax structures.

One potential effect of federal tax reform is change in state income tax revenue because of common income tax definitions. Estimates show that after the 1986 federal tax changes were adopted, states tended to follow the federal government in reducing marginal income tax rates and broadening the tax base. Despite changes to the federal deduction for state taxes, states did not move away from using income, sales, or property taxes.

DISCUSSION QUESTIONS

1. a. Does your state have an individual income tax? If so, how closely does it conform to the federal tax? Can one deduct the federal tax in computing the state income tax? List some specific ways that the federal and state tax bases differ. What problems, if any, do these differences create in computing your taxes?

   b. What is the rate structure of your state income tax? Are the rates progressive, and if so, how does that progressivity compare to the federal income tax rate structure?

   c. Use the information from parts a and b to estimate state income tax in your state for the families shown in the following table (assuming that all income is taxable and each takes the standard deduction if available):

Taxable Income	Marital Status	Number of Family Members	Estimated 2004 Federal Tax	Estimated State Tax
$20,000	Single	1	$1,454	
40,000	Single	1	4,756	
40,000	Married	2	2,904	
60,000	Married	4	2,974	
80,000	Married	4	5,974	

2. Suppose that a taxpayer is in the 15-percent tax-rate bracket for the federal individual income tax and faces a 5-percent state income tax rate.

   a. If the taxpayer cannot deduct either tax against the other, what is the taxpayer's combined marginal tax rate? What is the marginal rate if the taxpayer itemizes federal deductions and deducts the state tax? What if reciprocal deductibility is in effect?

   b. Now recalculate all three combined marginal tax rates assuming that the state tax rate is 10 percent. How do they change?

   c. Compute your combined marginal income tax rate (federal, state, and local, if appropriate) using your income last year or that expected this year.

3. Suppose a taxpayer faces a federal marginal income tax rate of 15 percent and pays local property taxes of $2,000 per year.

   a. Although the taxpayer itemizes federal deductions and thus deducts the local property tax in calculating federal income tax, suppose that no state income tax deduction for local taxes exists. What is the net, after-tax cost of property taxes to this taxpayer?

   b. Now suppose the state introduces an income tax *credit* for 25 percent of property taxes up to a maximum of $600. What is the taxpayer's net property tax cost now? (Remember that the state income tax is also deducted against the federal tax.) How much does the net cost fall because of the credit? How much more would this taxpayer pay (net) if property taxes were increased to $2,100?

4. The two most important state taxes are income and general sales taxes, although states also make substantial use of excise taxes, direct business taxes (usually a corporate income tax), and others. List and discuss briefly four factors that might influence a state in choosing between an income and general sales tax. What is the relative reliance in your state on these two taxes? If the relative reliance in your state is different than average, speculate about why that might be so.

SELECTED READINGS

Advisory Commission on Intergovernmental Relations. "Federal Income Tax Deductibility of State and Local Taxes: What Are Its Effects? Should It Be Modified or Eliminated?" In *Strengthening the Federal Revenue System: Implications for State and Local Taxing and Borrowing*, Report A-97. Washington, D.C.: Author, 1984, 37–66.

Break, George F. *Financing Government in a Federal System*. Washington, D.C.: The Brookings Institution, 1980. See Chapter 2, "Tax Coordination."

Chernick, Howard. "On the Determinants of Subnational Tax Progressivity in the U.S." *National Tax Journal* 57 No. 1 (March, 2005), 93–112.

Inman, Robert P. "State and Local Taxation Following TRA86: Introduction and Summary." *Journal of Policy Analysis and Management*, 12 (Winter 1993): 3–8. See also the other papers in this issue, which report the results of a conference focusing on changes in state and local taxation (particularly income taxation) after the federal tax reform in 1986.

Menchik, Paul. "Michigan's Personal Income Tax." In C. Ballard, et. al., editors, *Michigan at the Millennium*. East Lansing: Michigan State University Press, 2003, 535–557.

Mikesell, John L. "General sales, income, and other nonproperty taxes." In J. Richard Aronson and Eli Schwartz, editors, *Management Policies in Local Government Finance*. Washington, D.C.: International City/County Management Association, 2004.

BUSINESS TAXES

*The state corporation income tax does not do what many seem to
intend it to do, and it works only very clumsily and possibly at
considerable cost. . . . Any single state would seem to be well
advised at least to replace the corporation income tax with a tax
levied directly on corporate sales, payrolls, and property. . . .[1]*
—CHARLES E. MCLURE, JR.

HEADLINES

"WHEN HE TOOK OFFICE. . . , NEW JERSEY GOVERNOR JAMES MCGREEVEY NOTICED THAT
MANY OF THE COMPANIES DOING BUSINESS IN HIS STATE WERE NOT PAYING MUCH IN THE WAY
OF TAXES. MORE THAN 75 PERCENT OF NEW JERSEY COMPANIES, IN FACT, WERE PAYING ONLY
$200 APIECE IN STATE INCOME TAXES—THE BARE MINIMUM ALLOWED BY LAW. . . .

IT TOOK A SPECIAL SESSION, BUT MCGREEVY PERSUADED THE LEGISLATURE TO CLOSE A
NUMBER OF LOOPHOLES. AS A RESULT, NEW JERSEY CORPORATIONS PAID MORE THAN TWICE AS
MUCH IN STATE INCOME TAX LAST YEAR [2003] THAN THEY HAD IN 2002.

. . . TWENTY-FIVE YEARS AGO, CORPORATE INCOME TAXES ACCOUNTED FOR MORE THAN
10 PERCENT OF ALL STATE REVENUE. TODAY, WITHOUT LEGISLATION PURPOSELY REDUCING THAT
BURDEN, THE CORPORATE SHARE IS LESS. . . .

. . . MUCH OF THE LOST REVENUE FROM CORPORATE TAXES HAS LESS TO DO WITH INCEN-
TIVES OFFERED IN THE NAME OF JOB CREATION THAN WITH OUTRIGHT, IF LEGAL, EVASION."[2]

[1]"The State Corporate Income Tax: Lambs in Wolves' Clothing." In *The Economics of Taxation*, edited by H. Aaron
and M. Boskin. Washington, D.C.: The Brookings Institution, 1980, p. 342.

[2]Greenblatt, Alan. *Governing*, May, 2004, p. 42.

The two principal issues facing state and local governments in designing taxes to be collected directly from businesses are the choice of the *tax base*—that is, the type of tax—and the method for *apportioning that base* among the various subnational governments in which a firm does business. Both choices have important implications for the incidence and economic efficiency of the state–local tax structure. Various options states have for both choices and the economic implications of those options are considered in this chapter.

RELIANCE ON BUSINESS TAXES

All states have at least one major tax directly collected from businesses; most states use more than one. Among taxes generally applicable to most businesses, corporate income taxes are the most common, being used by 44 state governments and the District of Columbia. In addition, 4 states (Hawaii, Indiana, Washington, and West Virginia) use general gross receipts taxes, with Hawaii, Indiana, and West Virginia using both corporate income and gross receipts taxes. A value-added tax (VAT) is used only by Michigan. Other types of general business taxes are used by Nevada, South Dakota, Texas, and Wyoming.

State (and sometimes local) governments also commonly levy a set of different taxes on specific businesses, defined either by type or industry. Among the most important of these taxes are corporation license fees (used by 48 states), severance taxes—that is, excise taxes on the value of minerals extracted in the state—(used by 34 states), and special excise taxes on such industries as utilities, telephone, insurance, and financial institutions. For Texas and Wyoming, severance taxes are the primary business tax form and have provided such a substantial amount of revenue that the more general business tax types have not been required. Nevada, too, relies on a specialized source of revenue collected from business, that is, excise taxes and license fees related to gambling. A summary of the use of these business taxes is given in Table 17.1.

Table 17.1

State Business Tax Use, 2003

Type of Tax	Number of States	2003 Revenue (millions of dollars)	Percent of State General Revenue
Corporation Income	45	$26,541	2.4%
Gross Receipts[a]	4	n.a.	n.a.
Value-Added	1	1,843	0.2
Corporation License	48	6,129	0.6
Severance	34	5,322	0.5
Insurance Premiums	50	12,522	1.1

SOURCE: U.S. Census Bureau, *State Government Finances: 2003* and *State Government Tax Collections: 2003.*

[a]After 1992, the Census Bureau does not report data for gross receipts taxes separately from general sales taxes.

In 2003, state government corporate income taxes, including the one VAT, generated about $26.5 billion or 2.4 percent of state government general revenue, the lowest amount since World War II. That share had been relatively stable at around 5 percent over the 25 years up to the early 1980s and has been falling since. For the states using corporate income taxes, it provides between 0.8 percent (in Oklahoma) and 1.1 percent (in Louisiana, Missouri, Montana, and New Mexico) to 8.7 percent (in New Hampshire) of general revenue. Severance taxes provided about $5.3 billion and corporation license fees about $6.1 billion, as shown in Table 17.1.

Corporate income taxes easily represent the most important state–local business tax in aggregate. Of the 45 states plus the District of Columbia with corporate income taxes, 32 have a single flat tax rate with the other 14 using graduated rates. Most state corporate income taxes share a number of common tax definitions with the federal corporate income tax.

The relative importance of state corporate income tax revenue has declined substantially since the early 1980s. Cornia, Edmiston, Sjoquist, and Wallace (2005) report that state corporate income taxes declined from about 10 percent of state taxes in 1981 to only about 5 percent in 2002, although corporate profits rose as a share of national income over a similar period. Cornia and colleagues also note that state corporate income tax revenue grew more slowly than state economies, as measured by gross state product, since 1981.

What factors account for this slow growth or relative decline in revenue from state corporate income taxes? A number of studies identify five main possible factors: (1) changes in federal tax laws that affect state tax definitions, (2) adoption of new tax incentives by states, (3) changes in the legal form of business by firms, (4) aggressive tax avoidance measures by firms (often called *tax shelters*), and (5) movement of firms to states with lower corporate tax rates. Research by Fox and Luna (2002) and by Cornia, *et al.* (2005) suggests that the middle three factors have most likely had the greatest impact.

It certainly is possible that changes in federal tax laws that narrow the tax base could reduce state tax in states that adopt the federal tax definitions. Cornia, *et al.* (2005) show, however, that changes in federal tax laws since 1980 would have *increased* state corporate income tax bases and revenue. Similarly, Fisher (2002) shows that the states in which the manufacturing share of investment increased (suggesting a movement of manufacturing activity to those states) tended to have higher effective tax rates. Thus, these federal tax law changes do not seem to explain the long-run change in state corporate income tax revenue.

The other three factors reflect explicit changes by states to lower corporate taxes and action by firms to reduce tax liability by sheltering income. Certainly many states adopt a variety of special tax incentives to encourage economic development generally or to assist specific sets of firms, and such incentives obviously reduce state taxes. Cornia *et al.* (2005) estimate what corporate income tax revenue would have been in the absence of tax changes and compare that to actual revenue. They conclude that state tax changes account for only about a quarter of the revenue change.

This suggests that the change in the other three-quarters of the revenue is likely due to the other factors. Two trends seem particularly noteworthy. First, Limited

Liability Companies (LLC) are an increasingly popular form of business organization. LLCs have limited liability (like corporations) but are not subject to corporate taxation. Rather, for tax purposes, LLCs are treated as partnerships, with the owners paying individual income tax on the LLC profits. Cornia *et al.* (2005) report that the growth of LLCs may have reduced state corporate income tax revenue by as much as one-third. Second, some firms set up holding companies in states with no corporate income tax or low tax rates and arrange to have substantial amounts of business income transferred to the holding company. If successful, such passive investment mechanisms can shelter substantial amounts of corporate income. This method is described in Application 17.1.

Application 17.1

TAX AVOIDANCE THROUGH HOLDING COMPANIES

The method is relatively simple. Suppose that a business firm has a well-known trademarked name, symbol, formula, process, or service and transfers ownership of such to a holding company located in a state with no corporate income tax or a tax that would not apply to such a firm. The other divisions of this firm, which are located in states with corporate income taxes, pay royalties to the holding company for use of the trademarked name, process, or service, and those royalties, which are considered costs for those divisions, reduce profits of the divisions and add profits to the holding company. In that way, profits of the unified firm are "transferred" from states with effective corporate taxes to states without the tax. Importantly, this is done without moving any actual production (employees or capital) among the states.

Toys 'R' Us is one firm that uses this method (Greenblatt, 2004). A subsidiary called Geoffrey, Inc, was established in Delaware. Geoffrey, Inc. charges state Toys 'R' Us affiliates fees to use its intangible assets, which are the trademarked characters and names for Toys 'R' Us

(including Geoffrey the giraffe). In Delaware, "intangible assets" are not subject to tax. So, profits from the operation of Toys 'R' Us stores in other states with corporate income taxes are transferred to Delaware, where they are not taxed. Of course, Geoffrey, Inc. has exceptionally low costs (because it is not directly producing anything), so essentially all the fees it receives from the affiliates are profit. That is key to why such a large fraction of the unified firm's profits can be sheltered from taxation. The firm's costs are mostly in taxing states and the revenue mostly in a nontaxing state.

Although currently no hard data exist about the magnitude of growth in passive holding companies, firms seem to have many opportunities to engage in this type of income sheltering. The subsidiary located in a low- or no-tax state might handle all the firm's accounting, manage all the firm's real estate, or engage in any type of intangible service that the firm might purchase. All have the characteristic that revenue would be large in relation to costs, which provides the shelter. The difficulty is that these may be legitimate

Application 17.1 — Tax Avoidance Through Holding Companies

business expenses and even the type of services that some firms often purchase from an outside supplier. The problem for tax authorities is differentiating between actions taken essentially to avoid taxes and similar actions taken for legitimate business purposes.

States seem to have two policy options to attempt to counter these types of tax-avoidance transactions. One is to change state tax law so that these types of expenses, which are deductible for federal income taxes, must be added back in calculating tax bases for state income tax purposes; however, it may be difficult to define such expenses appropriately. The other option is to adopt so-called *combined reporting*, under which all revenue and costs for all related subsidiaries nationally (regardless of state location) are combined. The tax base for each state is then determined by a formula that allocates the combined profit among the states. Such allocation formulas are discussed later in this chapter. Greenblatt (2004) reports that 16 states have adopted combined reporting.

BUSINESS TAX STRUCTURE ISSUES

Alternative Business Tax Bases[3]

The three primary potential business tax bases are gross income or gross receipts, value-added—the increase in the value of goods caused by one stage in the production process—and net income or profits. A description of these bases (and several variations) is given in Table 17.2 and discussed next.

Gross Receipts Tax

A gross income tax collected from business is a tax on the total receipts or total revenue of a firm, with no deductions allowed for any type of expenses. Because revenue is, by definition, equal to costs plus profits, a gross receipts tax is the same as a tax on both profits and all types of costs (materials and supplies, labor, interest, rent, depreciation). If this type of gross receipts tax is applied to all firms, the total tax base for an economy is a multiple of the total value of production (GDP), because the tax applies to all business sales, including interbusiness sales, and those taxes are then added to the base for sales at later stages of production and distribution.

Commonly, however, when gross receipts taxes are used, sales of some commodities or sales by some types of firms are exempt from tax. For example, government and nonprofit entities almost always are tax-exempt. In that case, the aggregate base of a gross receipts tax is smaller and even could be less than GDP.

---

[3]This section draws upon material prepared for the U.S. Department of the Treasury and reported in *Economic Analysis of Gross Income Taxes*, 1986.

Table 17.2

Alternative Business Tax Bases

Type	Subtraction Base	Additive Base	Tax Base
Gross Receipts	Revenue	Purchases + Wages + Depreciation + Interest + Rent + Profits	a*GDP, a $>$ 1
Value Added, Gross Income	Revenue − Purchases of Materials	Wages + Depreciation + Interest + Rent + Profits	GDP
Value Added, Net Income	Revenue − Purchases of Materials − Depreciation	Wages + Interest + Rent + Profits	National Income
Value Added, Consumption	Revenue − Purchases of Materials − Capital Purchases	Wages + Interest + Rent + Profits − Net Investment	Consumption
Net Income or "Profits"	Revenue − Purchases of Materials − Wages − Interest − Rent − Depreciation	Profits	Profits or Return on Investment

Value-Added Taxes

Value added by a business is, in general, the difference between the sales of a firm and the cost of goods or services purchased from other firms that are used in production. The simple example outlined next illustrates the value-added concept.

Business: Bakery

Costs: Labor—Baker, salesclerk
          Materials—Flour, sugar, spices, utilities
          Capital—Mixer, utensils, oven
          Space—Building rent
          Credit—Interest paid on loans

Revenue = Wages + Purchases of Materials + Depreciation + Interest + Rent + Profit

Value Added = Revenue − Purchases of Materials
= Wages + Depreciation + Interest + Rent + Profit

The value added by the bakery is the difference between the sales value of the bakery's products and the value of the materials purchased to produce those products. There are two alternative but equivalent ways of calculating value added. One method is simply to subtract materials costs from sales. The alternative is to add labor costs plus depreciation plus interest paid plus rent plus profit. The two are equivalent.

Three variants of the VAT concept arise from different methods of treating capital-goods purchases, as shown in Table 17.2. If *no subtraction or deduction is allowed for capital expenditures* or capital depreciation, the tax is a **gross income-type VAT**, which is equivalent to a tax on the sum of wages plus interest plus rent plus depreciation plus profit, as shown previously. If all business entities were taxed, the aggregate base of the tax is the total value of final production (or GDP).

If *depreciation deductions are allowed*, then the tax is a **net income-type VAT**, with the base for the firm equal to wages plus interest plus rent plus profit, and the aggregate base equal to consumption plus net investment. In this case, deductions are allowed not only for the materials used in production but also for the capital goods "used-up" in production, that is, for the depreciation of capital goods during the production period. Because the aggregate base of this type of tax is total income if applied to all firms in a jurisdiction, the base is equivalent to that of a personal income tax.

The final VAT variant is a **consumption-type VAT**. In this case, *all capital expenditures are subtracted from revenue in addition to materials purchases*. The base of this tax is wages plus interest plus rent plus profit less net investment, which is equal to total consumption in a national economic accounting sense. In essence, capital income to individuals is not taxed unless consumed. This is now the predominant form of business taxation in Europe. The aggregate base of this tax is total consumption if levied on all firms in a jurisdiction and is thus equivalent to a retail sales tax or a personal consumption tax.

Net Income Tax

For the traditional net income or profits tax used by the federal government and most states, a business may deduct most business expenses—including costs for materials, labor, interest, rent, as well as depreciation of capital equipment—from gross income. The resulting tax base equals the return on investment to the business, that is, profits. No deductions are allowed for dividend payments out of profits to shareholders, so the business net income tax is independent of whether profits are distributed.

Illustration of Alternative Business Tax Bases

A numerical example of the bakery case, outlined in Table 17.3, illustrates how these alternative tax bases compare. A bakery purchases flour from a miller, who has purchased grain from a farmer. The bakery also purchases an oven, the only capital good in the example, from the oven manufacturer, who has purchased steel from a separate steel producer. Other capital goods or material inputs that might realistically be required have been left out to avoid cluttering the example.

The baker's revenue or retail sales are $2,000, which equals total consumption in this simple economy. The oven producer's sales are $500, which represents production of one oven, the only capital good (or investment) in this economy. GDP in this economy (consumption plus investment) therefore equals $2,500. In addition, the farmer makes $100 of sales to the miller, who makes $500 of sales to the baker, while a steel producer makes $200 of sales to the oven manufacturer.

The base of a gross receipts tax is the total sales of all firms, which equal $3,300 in the example, so that a 10-percent gross receipts tax generates $330 of revenue. In this case, the base of the gross receipts tax is 132 percent of GNP ($3,300/$2,500). The base of a gross income VAT is total sales minus purchases of materials from

Table 17.3

Tax Bases and Production Stages

	Farmer	Miller	Baker	Oven Producer	Steel Producer	Total
Sales	$100	$500	**$2,000**	$500	$200	$3,300
Purchases of Materials	0	100	**500**	200	0	800
Purchases of Capital Goods	0	0	**500**	0	0	500
Gross Receipts Tax @ 10%	10	50	**200**	50	20	330
Value Added, Gross Income	100	400	**1500**	300	200	2,500
Gross Income VAT @ 10%	10	40	**150**	30	20	250
Depreciation	0	0	**100**	0	0	100
Value Added, Net Income	100	400	**1400**	300	200	2,400
Net Income VAT @ 10%	10	40	**140**	30	20	240
Value Added, Consumption	100	400	**1000**	300	200	2,000
Consumption VAT @ 10%	10	40	**100**	30	20	200
Profit	8	40	**160**	40	16	264
Profit Tax @ 10%	.8	4	**16**	4	1.6	26.4

Value Added, Gross Income = Sales − Material Purchases

Value Added, Net Income = Sales − Material Purchases − Depreciation

Value Added, Consumption = Sales − Material Purchases − Capital Purchases

Profit = Sales − Material Purchases − Depreciation − Labor & Other Costs

other firms, which equals GDP, or $2,500 in the example. A 10-percent gross income VAT generates $250 of revenue, while a rate of 13.2 percent would be required to equal the gross receipts tax revenue. The net income VAT is based on sales minus purchases of materials *and* depreciation and generates $240 of revenue at a 10-percent rate. (The example uses straight-line depreciation over a five-year life for the oven, so the depreciation deduction is 1/5 of the price). The consumption-type VAT is based on sales minus purchases of materials *and* capital goods and provides $200 of revenue at 10 percent. Note that the consumption-type VAT generates revenue equal to a retail sales tax levied at the same 10-percent rate. The only retail sales in the example are by the bakery, equal to $2,000.

The base of a traditional net income or profits tax is sales minus purchases of materials and depreciation *minus other costs* such as those for labor, interest, and rent. The profits tax base equals the net income value-added base minus those other costs. Without specifying those other costs, sample profit figures, which are consistent with the ratio of corporate profits to net national income (GDP less depreciation) for the United States, are presented in the bottom row of Table 17.3. Total profits from these operations amount to $264. Therefore, a 10-percent profit tax rate generates only $26.40. A much higher rate is required to match the revenue from a 10-percent rate applied to the other tax bases.

Note that these tax equivalences (i.e., a consumption-type VAT is equivalent to a direct tax on consumption) strictly apply only for a closed economy. At the state–local level, however, many business and consumption transactions cross jurisdiction boundaries. For instance, suppose the farmer in the illustration of Table 17.3 is in a different state than the miller, oven producer, steel producer, baker, and consumer. Gross State Product in the latter state is then only $2,400. A gross-income VAT then is levied on a base of $2,400 if the miller could still deduct the $100 payment to the farmer in the other state, but the base is $2,500 if such a deduction is not allowed. Similarly, if some of the bread consumers are in other states, then a consumption-type VAT in the manufacturing state is not necessarily equivalent to a retail sales tax in that state. In practice, these issues usually are resolved by using some rules to allocate tax bases among states, as discussed next.

Allocating Tax Bases among Jurisdictions

If firms do business in more than one taxing jurisdiction, an additional issue is how to allocate that firm's tax base—whichever type of tax is used—among those juris-dictions. Using the bakery example, what if the bakery sells its products in more than one state, or for an even more complicated case, what if the bakery produces its products at two plants located in different states and sells those products in all states? And what if the bakery does business in another *nation*? Two issues must be resolved here: (1) Under what conditions should a business be taxed by a spe-cific jurisdiction, and if the business is taxable, (2) what share of the firm's business can reasonably be allocated to that jurisdiction?

Under the current procedures that are generally followed, a business is taxable in a state only if it has a "substantial business nexus or presence" in the state such that the business benefits from state activities. After a 1959 Supreme Court deci-sion, Congress "prohibited a state's taxing of income derived from sales within its borders when the only business activity in the state was the solicitation for orders to be sent outside the state for approval and shipment" (Break 1980, p. 61). This is the rule regarding mail-order and Internet sales discussed in Chapter 15. In prac-tice, therefore, interstate businesses often are taxable in a state only if they main-tain employees or property in the state.

If a business is to be taxed by a jurisdiction, three general methods may be used to apportion that firm's tax base among all taxing jurisdictions. One method requires **separate accounting** for some specific component of the business. Under this method, the firm's operations in different states or jurisdictions must be treat-ed as separate firms with calculation of the tax base separately for each one. It is often economically inappropriate and practically very difficult to do separate accounting in any convincing way for entire business entities. If an automobile manufacturer produces engines in one state, produces transmissions in another, and assembles the cars in still a third state, how can the profit made from selling a car be separately allocated to the engine production, transmission production, and vehicle assembly? The car as a final consumer product has very little value without any one of the three. The value of final product also includes the influence of nonmanufacturing operations of the firm, such as advertising and distribution. Implementing separate accounting requires that implicit or "transfer" prices be established for all the operations of the business. Essentially, one does accounting as if the division that produces engines actually sells them to the division that does assembly, and so forth.

Specific allocation is a second apportionment method that is sometimes effective for a firm's various kinds of subsidiary income. For instance, interest, or dividend income, for a manufacturer can be separated from the income for the whole entity, and that income may be specifically allocated to the state where the business is headquartered.

The third and most commonly used allocation method is to apportion tax base by **formula**. Historically, the most commonly used formula—called the "three-factor" formula—included three equally weighted factors: the firm's share of its (1) payroll, (2) property, and (3) sales in the state. In recent years, many states have switched to formulas that give added weight to sales in the formula. The allocation formulas used by states in 2005 are shown in Table 17.4.

If all three factors in the traditional formula are equally weighted (as is done currently by 12 states and the District of Columbia), the firms' allocation factor is the average of the payroll, property, and sales shares. Mathematically the formula is

$$A_i = \frac{1}{3}\left[\frac{W_i}{W} + \frac{P_i}{P} + \frac{S_i}{S}\right]$$

where

A_i = apportionment factor to state i for a firm

W_i = wages paid by the firm to employees in state i

W = total wages paid by the firm

P_i = value of property owned by the firm in state i

P = value of all property owned by the firm

S_i = dollar amount of sales by the firm in state i

S = total sales by the firm.

The operation of this formula is illustrated by two examples shown in Table 17.5. Firm I does all of its production in state A, and thus all of its employees and property are located there. Only 10 percent of firm I's sales take place in state A, however, as the rest of its production is sold to residents of other states (perhaps over the Internet, by mail order, or through independent manufacturers' representatives in those states). Because this firm has no property or employees in those other states, those other states most likely will not attempt or be able to levy tax on this firm. In that case, only $87,000 of the firm's total profit of $125,000, or 70 percent,

Table 17.4

State Apportionment of Corporate Income

(Formulas for tax year 2005—as of January 1, 2005)

Alabama[*]	3 Factor	Nebraska	Sales
Alaska[*]	3 Factor	Nevada	No State Income Tax
Arizona[*]	Double wtd. sales	New Hampshire	Double wtd. sales
Arkansas[*]	Double wtd. sales	New Jersey (1)	Double wtd. sales
California[*]	Double wtd. sales	New Mexico[*]	Double wtd. sales/3 Factor
Colorado[*]	3 Factor/Sales & Property	New York	Double wtd. sales
Connecticut	Double wtd. sales/Sales	North Carolina[*]	Double wtd. sales
Delaware	3 Factor	North Dakota[*]	3 Factor
Florida	Double wtd. sales	Ohio[*]	60% Sales, 20% Property & Payroll
Georgia	Double wtd. sales		
Hawaii[*]	3 Factor	Oklahoma	3 Factor
Idaho[*]	Double wtd. sales	Oregon[*]	80% Sales, 10% Property & Payroll
Illinois[*]	Sales		
Indiana	Double wtd. sales	Pennsylvania[*]	60% Sales, 20% Property & Payroll
Iowa	Sales		
Kansas[*]	3 Factor	Rhode Island	Double wtd. sales
Kentucky[*]	Double wtd. sales	South Carolina	Double wtd. sales/Sales
Louisiana	Double wtd. sales	South Dakota	No State Income Tax
Maine[*]	Double wtd. sales	Tennessee[*]	Double wtd. sales
Maryland	Double wtd. sales	Texas	Sales
Massachusetts	Double wtd. sales/Sales	Utah[*] (2)	3 Factor
Michigan	90% Sales, 5% Property & Payroll	Vermont (3)	3 Factor
		Virginia	Double wtd. sales
Minnesota	75% Sales,12.5% Property, and 12.5% Payroll	Washington	No State Income Tax
		West Virginia[*]	Double wtd. sales
Mississippi	Accounting/3 Factor	Wisconsin[*] (4)	Double wtd. sales
Missouri[*]	3 Factor/Sales	Wyoming	No State Income Tax
Montana[*]	3 Factor	Dist. of Columbia[*]	3 Factor

SOURCE: Federation of Tax Administrators, www.taxadmin.org

NOTE: The formulas listed are for general manufacturing businesses. Some industries have special formula different than those reported.

[*]State has adopted substantial portions of the UDITPA.

(1) A 3-factor formula is used for corporations not subject to the corporation business franchise tax.

(2) For tax years beginning in 2006, taxpayers may elect to double weighted sales factor.

(3) Effective for tax years beginning in 2006, a double weighted sales formula.

(4) Effective for tax years beginning in 2006, Wisconsin will be phasing in 100% sales factor by 2008.

is taxed by state A using the equally weighted three-factor formula. Because some part of this firm's net income goes untaxed by any state, some states have adopted rules that require that such untaxed sales be thrown back into calculation of the apportionment formula for the state (or states) where production occurs. If state A had such a **throwback provision**, then the entire $125,000 of the firm's profit would be taxable by state A.

Firm II both produces and sells in more than one state. In this example, 40 percent of both the firm's payroll and property are located in state A, although only 2 percent of the firm's sales volume arises in that state. Assuming that the other 98 percent of

Table 17.5

Tax Base Apportionment Example

Tax Component	Firm I		Firm II	
	State A	All States	State A	All States
Compensation	$ 500,000	$ 500,000	$2,000,000	$ 5,000,000
Property	$1,200,000	$1,200,000	$5,000,000	$12,500,000
Sales	$ 250,000	$2,500,000	$ 500,000	$25,000,000
Profit	—	$ 125,000	—	$ 1,250,000
Compensation Factor	1.00	—	0.40	—
Property Factor	1.00	—	0.40	—
Sales Factor	0.10	—	0.02	—
Three-Factor	0.70	—	0.27	—
Apportionment	[(1 + 1 + .1)/3]		[(.4 + .4 + .02)/3]	
Taxable Profit	$ 87,500 if other states tax remainder			$ 341,250
	$ 125,000 if sales in other states are "thrown back" to state A.			

sales are included in the allocation formulas for other states (no throwback), then 27 percent of the firm's total profits are subject to tax in state A.

One of the most controversial aspects of the three-factor apportionment formula is the inclusion of sales shares. Under current general practice, sales location is defined on a *destination basis*; the sale location is the location of the consumer. As a result, a business such as Firm I in Table 17.5 may avoid state taxation on some part of its total net income or sales, even though all its production and facilities are located in one state. If the allocation formula is to apportion a firm's tax base proportionate to the benefits received from state services, then the theoretical issue is whether those benefits better correspond to the location of production or the location of the consumers of the product. Because many economists believe that the benefits from the privilege of doing business in a state arise from the location of production, some suggest that a two-factor formula based on payroll and property is more appropriate for apportioning profits among states, if separate accounting or allocation is not feasible.

The sales-factor in the formula creates an opportunity for states to engage in strategic behavior in an attempt to stimulate economic development. All states could decrease effective tax rates on in-state production, and thus encourage more investment, by increasing the importance of sales in the formula. States with a substantial share of consumption but a lesser share of production (payroll and property) can increase tax bases (and revenue) by increasing the weight for destination-based sales in the formula. As a result of these incentives, a number of states have moved away from the traditional equally weighted three-factor formula and moved to formulas that weight sales more heavily (refer to Table 17.4). By 2005, 24 states used a four-factor formula that gives double weight to sales. Four states—Illinois, Iowa, Nebraska, and Texas—allocate tax bases based on the sales share only, using a single-factor formula that gives a 100 percent weight to sales. In addition, if *tax rates* differ among states as well, then the firms also may

Table 17.6

Illustration of Double-Weighted Sales Factor Apportionment

Tax Component	Firm II		
	State A	State B	All States
Compensation	$2,000,000	$ 50,000	$ 5,000,000
Property	$5,000,000	$ 125,000	$12,500,000
Sales	$ 500,000	$5,000,000	$25,000,000
Profit	—		$ 1,250,000
Compensation Factor	0.40	0.10	
Property Factor	0.40	0.10	
Sales Factor	0.02	0.20	
Three-Factor Formula	0.27	0.13	
	[(.4 + .4 + .02)/3]	[(.1 + .1 + .2)/3]	
Taxable Profit	$ 341,250	$ 166,625	
Double-weighted Sales Formula	0.21	0.15	
	[(.4 + .4 + .02 + .02)/4]	[(.1 + .1 + .2 + .2 +)/4]	
Taxable Profit	$ 262,500	$ 187,500	

have a preference for one formula over another as a way of minimizing total state tax burdens.[4]

The effects of weighting sales more heavily are shown by the illustration in Table 17.6. In state A, the sample firm has substantial production (40 percent of its payroll and property is in State A) but only a very small amount of sales (2 percent of its total sales). In contrast, this firm does little production in state B (only 10 percent of its payroll and property is there), but 20 percent of its sales are in state B. If state A switches from the traditional three-factor formula to one that gives double weight to sales, the share of the firm's profits taxed by state A falls from 27 percent to 21 percent. The firm's corporate tax liability in state A falls from $341,250 to $262,500. State A may hope that the reduction in state tax will induce the firm to expand production in the state (or at least not to move production from the state). State A does lose corporate income tax revenue in the short run, but may gain revenue (from personal income, property, and corporate income taxes) in the long run if investment and production increases. Essentially, weighting sales more in the allocation formula is a way for state A to assist a firm that has a major industrial presence and is important to the economy in that state.

If state B switches to a double-weighted sales formula, the share of the firm's profits taxed by state B rises from 13 percent to 15 percent, and the firm's corporate tax liability in state B increases from $166,625 to $187,500. State B has a relatively small amount of the firm's production (payroll and property) in the state. Weighting sales more in the allocation formula essentially allows state B to tax some of the production that occurs in state A. State B generates more revenue, even

---

[4]The use of formula apportionment creates a number of other incentives for firms to alter behavior. For a discussion, see Gordon and Wilson (1986).

though most of the production is elsewhere. If state A has a throwback provision, it actually loses revenue from state B's decision to weight sales more. That is, state B effectively takes revenue from state A.

Importantly, after state B increases the weight on sales in the formula, the firm can *reduce* its tax liability *overall* by moving production (payroll and property) to that state. Moving payroll or property to the state increases tax liability in state B, but reduces tax liability in state A more, so that overall taxes are reduced (Edmiston, 2002).

What happens if state B moves to a single-factor allocation formula that gives 100 percent weight to sales? Because the sample firm makes 20 percent of its sales in state B, that state could tax 20 percent of the firm's total profits, again generating an increase in revenue. If state A moved to a single-factor sales formula, the firm's taxes in the state would fall dramatically, providing an even stronger incentive for more investment in state A. This illustration shows, therefore, why even more states may move to greater and greater weighting of sales in the allocation formula in the future.

Another important aspect of formula apportionment is the degree of uniformity among states in the formula used. If all states use precisely the same formula, such as the equally weighted three-factor formula, then the sum of a firm's tax bases in all states exactly equals the total tax base for the firm. That is, the sum of all states' apportionment factors for the firm equals 1, as shown here:

$$\frac{\Sigma_i[W_i/W + P_i/P + S_i/S]}{3} = 1/3\{\Sigma_i[W_i/W] + \Sigma_i[P_i/P] + \Sigma_i[S_i/S]\}$$

$$= 1/3\left\{\frac{\Sigma_i W_i}{W} + \frac{\Sigma_i P_i}{P} + \frac{\Sigma_i S_i}{S}\right\}$$

$$= 1/3\{1 + 1 + 1\} = 1.$$

If, however, states use different formulas involving different factors or different weights, or if some states do not use formula apportionment in favor of some type of separate accounting, then the sum of a firm's tax bases in all states may be either greater than or less than the total base for the whole firm. In other words, either some of the firm's profit may be taxed by more than one state or some part is taxed by no state. The use of sales shares in the apportionment formula and the choice of the destination principle for defining sales is a major factor contributing to this possible inconsistency in apportionment.

ECONOMIC ANALYSIS

Incidence and Efficiency Effects of State Corporate Profit Taxes

The incidence and long-run economic effects of corporate income taxes is one of the most unresolved and controversial topics of public finance. The special aspects of state government use of corporate income taxes, especially formula allocation of the tax base, complicate matters still further. All the issues obviously cannot be resolved or even discussed carefully here. The approach therefore is to describe the potential effects of a national corporate income tax and then to consider how the special features of state use of the tax alter the story. The specific focus on state corporate income taxes also separately considers the aggregate effect of all state taxes together as opposed to the effect of a single state's tax from the viewpoint of that state.

A National Corporate Income Tax

The economic analysis of a national corporate income tax is essentially similar to the analysis of a national property tax discussed in Chapter 14. In the short run, a uniform national tax on the net income or profits of corporations that attempt to maximize profits is expected to reduce the return to corporate capital owners. This is based on the notion that firms are unlikely to be able to shift the tax to consumers or workers in the short run, either because of competitive pressures or because it would not be profit maximizing for them to do so (given that capital costs are fixed costs in the short run). Even this result is not guaranteed. Firms that have some objective other than maximizing profits, especially those operating in oligopolistic markets, may shift the corporate tax through higher prices or lower wages even in the short run.

If the tax is not shifted in the short run, corporate capital owners can avoid or shift the burden of the tax in the long run in at least two ways. First, tax burdens may be reduced by shifting capital from the corporate to noncorporate sector of the economy, because only corporations are subject to the corporate tax. The increase in supply of noncorporate capital reduces the return to owners of noncorporate capital as well. The tax on corporate capital is therefore shared by the owners of all types of capital. Second, if the tax reduces the return to capital ownership generally, then capital suppliers may respond by reducing the amount of capital accumulation in society. Over time, this means a smaller stock of capital will be available in the society than there would be without the tax, which causes labor productivity and thus real wages to be lower than they otherwise would be. In that case, part of the tax on corporate capital is shifted to labor in the long run.

State Corporate Taxation: Aggregate View

Two important features of state government corporate income taxation require this conventional national analysis to be altered. First, not all states use a corporate income tax, and among those that do, tax rates vary substantially. This creates an additional opportunity for shifting the corporate income tax by moving capital investment from high- to low- or no-tax states. Second, corporate net income of multistate firms is generally apportioned among the taxing states by an apportionment formula, as described previously. Charles McLure (1980, 1981) has carefully explained how this type of formula allocation effectively converts a state corporate income tax into a set of taxes on the formula's factors, usually, wages, sales, and property.

Following the discussion by McLure (1981), suppose that a state levies a tax at rate t on the national profits, denoted Y, of corporations. For multistate firms, the tax base is allocated among states according to the average of the share of the firm's wages W, sales S, and property P, in that state. With the equally weighted three-factor formula, the corporate income tax can be represented mathematically as

$$T = 1/3[S_i/S + W_i/W + P_i/P]tY \quad \text{or}$$

$$T = \frac{tY}{3S} S_i + \frac{tY}{3W} W_i + \frac{tY}{3P} P_i$$

where i represents sales, wages, or property in state i.

From this view, the tax is seen as a set of three taxes on sales, wages, and property in state i, with the tax rate for each equal to one-third the nominal rate multiplied by the firm's profit rate on sales, wages, and property, respectively. Therefore, not only might tax rates differ among states, but also the effective rate imposed by a single state on activity in that state may differ by firm, depending on that firm's national profit rate.

Just as with the analysis of property taxes, state corporate income taxes involve two effects—the effect of the average rate of tax in the nation and the effect of the differentials from that average. As with a national corporate tax, the average burden of state corporate income taxes represents a decrease in the return to owners of corporate capital, as demonstrated by Mieszkowski and Zodrow (1985). In the long run, that burden may be shifted to owners of all capital if activity is shifted from the corporate to the noncorporate sector, and the burden may also be partly shifted to labor in the long run if savings and capital investment are affected, as explained previously.

The effect from state tax-rate differentials around the national average is best seen in the context of the three separate taxes that arise from formula apportionment of the corporate income tax base. Transfer of sales, employment, or property from one state to another state with a lower tax rate reduces a firm's overall tax liability. In effect, it is as if states are imposing taxes on sales, payrolls, and property values in the state at differential rates. Therefore, each component of the formula provides an incentive for firms to move their economic activity to lower-tax rate states.

For instance, the effect of the allocation formula's property component is expected to be the same as the excise effects that result from a statewide property tax. If property owners move investment from higher- to lower-tax rate states, decreases in the prices of immobile capital, labor, and land are expected in the higher-tax states. Corresponding increases in the prices for those immobile factors are expected in the lower-tax rate states. Similarly, the sales component of the tax is expected to increase prices for consumers in the higher-tax states and lower prices in the lower-tax states, while the payroll tax component is expected to lower wages in the higher-tax states and raise wages in the lower-tax states if workers are largely immobile among states. In short, the excise effects from differentials in state corporate income tax rates are expected to impose relative burdens on immobile workers, consumers, and owners of land and immobile capital in the higher-tax states.

Mieszkowski and Zodrow (1985) have noted that the increased consumer prices and decreased wages and prices of immobile capital and land in the higher-tax states will be matched by decreased consumer prices and increased wages and prices of immobile capital and land in the lower-tax states. However, it is not clear whether these excise effects cancel out in any meaningful economic sense. If individuals' incomes are different in the higher- and lower-tax rate states, then these excise effects can have substantial effects on the distribution of tax burdens across income classes. The excise effects on different income groups can also have macroeconomic effects if marginal propensities to consume differ by income.

State Corporate Taxation: Single-State View

From the viewpoint of a single state, the effect of an increase in that state's corporate income tax is best represented by the effects from the implicit taxes on sales, payrolls, and property in the state. The national burden on all capital from the change in the average rate of tax is diffused among all states, and the gains to workers, consumers, and capital owners in the other states are of no concern to the state in question. Therefore, from the viewpoint of a single state, an increase in the state corporate income tax rate is expected to impose burdens on workers, consumers, and owners of immobile capital and land in that state. In other words, this tax increase generally is *not* exported to nonresidents, because changes in real income of residents do occur.

The perspective of thinking about implicit taxes on sales, payroll, and property also helps explain the incentive for a state to increase the weight on sales in the allocation formula. By doing so, a state effectively reduces taxes on payroll (labor) and property in the state and increases taxes on sales or consumption in the state. If labor and/or capital are mobile, then the reduced taxes on those inputs are expected to increase employment and income in the state (in the case of labor) or capital investment in the state (in the case of property). Of course, this change in the allocation formula also raises prices for consumption in the state. By weighting sales more in the allocation formula, a state effectively increases taxes on spending and reduces taxes on production.

A number of analysts have examined the economic effects of weighting sales more in the allocation formula. Kelly Edmiston (2002, p.249) concludes that ". . . the long-run economic development impact of independently moving from an equally weighted three-factor formula to a single-factor sales formula can be significant." Edmiston also shows, however, that if all states move to a single-factor sales formula, some states will gain and some will lose, as illustrated in Table 17.6. It turns out, however, that the losing states would lose even more investment and revenue if they did not use the single-factor sales formula. In other words, if many or most states move to weighting sales more in the allocation formula, other states seem to have an incentive to follow.

Incidence and Efficiency Implications of Gross Receipts Taxes

The use of gross receipts or gross income as the base of a general state tax collected from business creates a fundamental structural difficulty. Sales of all intermediate goods are taxed under a gross receipts tax, while sales of intermediate capital goods are taxed under a gross income VAT. Tax is levied on each of those transactions, and that tax *cascades* down into the price charged at the next production stage, on which tax is also levied. In that way, the tax is said to *pyramid* through the various stages of production, ending up larger than the single nominal rate might suggest.[5]

This factor underlies the three most fundamental criticisms of general gross income and gross receipts taxes:

(1) The effective tax rate will be greater than the nominal tax rate, with the difference depending on the number of stages of production.

(2) The effective rate will vary arbitrarily between economic sectors, depending on the number of stages of production.

(3) The tax creates an incentive for vertical integration to reduce taxes.

Returning to the numerical illustration shown earlier in Table 17.3, recall that total consumption is $2,000, although the gross receipts tax base is $3,300 and the gross income VAT base is $2,500. Therefore, the 10-percent nominal gross receipts tax has an effective tax rate of 16.5 percent of consumption; it generates the same amount of revenue as a 16.5-percent retail sales tax. Similarly, the gross income VAT nominally levied at a 10-percent rate has an effective rate of 12.5 percent on consumption. As noted earlier, effective rates exceed the nominal rates.

Also as noted previously, the baker can reduce gross receipts tax by integrating with any of the other firms in the production chain; the baker also can reduce gross income VAT by combining with the capital good supplier, the oven producer. If the baker integrates with the miller or the oven producer, gross receipts for the combined firm are $2,000 rather than $2,500 from the sum of the independent firms. If the baker integrates with the oven producer, aggregate gross income value added for the two is $1,300 rather than the $1,800 with separate firms. If this type of integration occurred in some sectors of the economy but not others, the tax burden would vary among those sectors even if the sectors are the same size economically.

Because gross receipts taxes are effectively taxes on consumption, they tend to be regressive with respect to current income, as described in Chapter 15. To alleviate both the potential regressivity and any differences that arise in effective rates among industries, exemptions from tax or differential rates for specific types of goods or industries are common.

Current State Gross Receipts Tax Use

Three states—Hawaii, Washington, and West Virginia—continue to use a gross receipts tax as a substantial general tax collected from businesses. The experience with those taxes in those states generally illustrates the difficulties noted earlier. As an illustration, one of those taxes is described next. In addition, many states apply gross receipts taxes to specific industries.[6]

The Hawaii General Excise Tax   Hawaii's General Excise Tax (GET) is a combination of gross receipts tax on all businesses and retail sales tax collected at a rate

---

[5]Such taxes are sometimes called "turnover" taxes because tax is collected at each stage of production.

[6]Gross income taxes also have been used by several other states on a more limited basis. A gross receipts tax was repealed by Alaska for all businesses but banks in 1979, with the tax on banks repealed in 1983.

of 4 percent on all "final" sales, including retail sales of goods and services (also medical and professional services) and intermediate sales of goods and services purchased by a business but not used directly in production. A rate of 0.5 percent is collected on nonretail sales of goods. Economically, this is equivalent to a 0.5-percent gross receipts tax on all businesses (including retail) and a very broad-based 3.5-percent general sales tax. For 2004, the GET generated about $1.9 billion of revenue, an amount equal to about 47 percent of state taxes in Hawaii. The non-retail component of the GET has provided about a quarter of state taxes in Hawaii.

In a report to the Hawaii Tax Review Commission, Bruce Billings (1984) esti-mated that pyramiding and taxation of intermediate sales increase the effective rate from the nominal 4-percent rate to an effective rate between 4.79 percent and 5.42 percent, an increase of about 25 percent. The Commission Report stated that "the 4 percent retail rate is actually about a 5 percent rate, on average, when the pre-retail general excise tax imbedded in the price is considered" (*Report of the First Tax Review Commission*, 1984, p. 8). It also appears that the gross excise tax may have contributed to vertical integration in the state. By comparing the ratio of value added to sales for specific industries across states (with the greater the ratio of value added to sales, the greater the degree of integration), Billings (1984) found statistically significant higher levels of integration in manufacturing industries in Hawaii when compared to all other states for 1972 and 1977 and compared to 15 selected states relatively similar to Hawaii for 1967, 1972, and 1977. On average, integration among Hawaiian manufacturing firms was 114.8 percent of that in all other states and 123.2 of the level in the 15 selected states. With respect to manu-facturing, Billings (1984, p. 37) concluded that "it appears that Hawaiian industry is somewhat more vertically integrated than the U.S. norm."

Even so, the Tax Review Commission recommended retention of the GET for three reasons: A single replacement tax on a narrower base would require a substan-tially higher rate; changeover to a different tax would alter the distribution of taxes among businesses; and the potential substitute taxes appeared to be administra-tively more complex. This illustrates an important feature of tax reform as opposed to tax design. After a tax has been in place for several years, the economic and busi-ness structure will have reacted to that structure so that any change to generate benefits in the long run must accommodate the short-run disruptions that result.[7]

State Value-Added Taxes: The Michigan Experience[8]

The Michigan state government's general business tax is a consumption-type VAT, called the Single Business Tax (SBT), which was adopted in 1975. The tax provided

---

[7]The state of Washington also levies a multistage gross receipts tax, called the Business and Occupation Tax (B&O Tax). The general rate is 0.484 percent. In concept, the combination of Washington's B&O and 6.5-percent retail sales taxes is very similar to Hawaii's GET; therefore, the Washington B&O Tax suffers from the same problems as Hawaii's GET.

[8]This section is based on Michigan Department of Treasury (2003) and Hines (2003).

about $2.2 billion in 2002, an amount equal to 10 percent of the state's tax revenue and about 0.7 percent of state personal income. Michigan has the only value-added tax in the United States, which it also used from 1953–1967 in the form of Michigan's Business Activity Tax (BAT). Michigan experimented with a state corporate profits tax during the intervening years. The base of a consumption-type VAT is revenue minus purchases of all intermediate goods and services, including capital goods. Therefore, the equity and efficiency problems caused by pyramiding gross income taxes do not occur with a consumption-type VAT. The SBT tax base, in theory, is computed by the equivalent approach of adding up wages plus interest plus rent plus profit and subtracting net investment. A set of adjustments to the SBT, which have changed over time, make the tax something less than an exact consumption-type VAT. The tax remains closer to a value-added tax than a traditional corporate income tax, however.

The Michigan SBT has a single rate (1.9 percent in 2002, but currently scheduled to fall to 0 by 2010) that is applied to a relatively broad spectrum of economic activities, with only government, nonprofit organizations, and agricultural firms exempt. The tax includes several exemptions, deductions, and credits that serve to reduce tax liability for smaller firms, for labor-intensive firms, for firms with negative profits, and for firms with certain other special characteristics. As a result of these adjustments, the average effective tax rate was 1.4 percent compared to the nominal statutory rate of 1.9 percent. Effective rates decline as the size of firms' tax bases decline. As a result, a relatively small number of larger firms pay the bulk of the tax. In 2000, the 94 firms with taxable Michigan value added exceeding $100 million represented only 0.06 percent of firms filing SBT returns, but more than 21 percent of tax liability. More than half of SBT revenue came from the 1.3 percent of SBT filers with value added (tax base) exceeding $10 million. When comparing firms of equal size (value added), however, effective tax rates vary little between different business sectors. For instance, among the largest firms, the average effective tax rate is 1.5 percent; it is 1.56 percent for retail businesses, 1.33 percent for transportation equipment (automobile) manufacturing, and 1.23 percent for businesses producing services. Because the tax applies to a broader set of firms than the corporations subject to most corporate income taxes, the Michigan Department of Treasury estimates that a corporate income tax rate of about 14.8 percent would have been necessary to generate the same revenue as the SBT since 1977. In contrast, the highest state corporate income tax rates are in the 10–12 percent range.

In effect, then, Michigan's tax structure has the advantages usually attributed to gross income taxes—broad-base, low-rate, and relatively stable revenue stream—without the efficiency and equity problems of gross income taxes. Because VATs are not common in the United States (although that is the standard business tax form in Europe), substantial confusion and many misconceptions exist about the SBT among the state's taxpayers. Common criticisms include the idea that taxes are positive even when profits are negative, and that value-added taxes discriminate against labor. Because the tax base is value added (wages + interest + rent + profit), the tax can be positive even if one component of the base is negative. Of course, business firms still use state services even when profits are negative. A consumption-type VAT, such as the SBT, taxes payments for *both* labor (wages) and capital (interest, rent, and profit) and thus is neutral with regard to input mix; in contrast, a corporate income tax is levied on the return to capital only and reduces rates of return to capital.

One potential economic advantage of a consumption-type VAT compared to a profits tax is a lower effective tax on capital income because capital expenditures are deducted immediately in the year the capital investment is made. In most corporate income taxes, in contrast, depreciation deductions for capital are spread over the life of the capital asset. If capital is mobile among states, then the substitution of a consumption-type VAT for a state profits tax is expected to increase the rate of return to capital in that state, thus stimulating an increase in investment in that state.

This aspect of the Michigan SBT has been one of the most vexing politically and legally, however. Originally when the tax was adopted, multistate firms allocated the tax base, including the deduction for real property investment, based on the standard three-factor formula—one-third based on sales location, one-third based on payroll, and one-third based on property. For deducting expenditures on personal property (equipment), however, multistate firms used a formula of half based on payroll and on the location of the property. As Hines (2003, p.611) notes, the effect of this provision was that ". . . Michigan's SBT offered a more generous treatment of investment expenditures than did the tax system of any other state . . . . The effect of this rule for apportioning deductions for personal property expenditures was to encourage investments by firms with significant production in Michigan." The concern on the part of the state was that investment expenditures anywhere in the United States reduced Michigan tax liability for these firms. The concern on the part of firms was that *all* capital expenditures were deductible by firms located entirely in Michigan.

Eventually, firms challenged these SBT allocation provisions by arguing that the provisions were unconstitutional because they discriminated against interstate commerce by giving more favorable tax treatment to capital investments in Michigan than those outside. As a result of the court challenges and continuing concern on the part of the state about subsidizing investment outside of Michigan, a number of changes were made in how the tax base and capital expenditures are apportioned for multistate firms. In 1999, the state substituted an investment tax credit for the apportioned investment deductions, moving the SBT further from the original concept of a consumption-type VAT. In addition, the magnitude of the credit was less than needed to make it equivalent to the capital expenditure deductions. At the time of this writing in 2005, Michigan continues to debate how to tax business activity effectively—whether to retain the SBT in some revised form or to replace it with some other set of taxes on business income or activity.

DISCRIMINATORY BUSINESS TAXES: THE INSURANCE CASE[9]

As the discussion of apportionment illustrates, the fundamental legal issue regarding taxation of business in a federal system is the degree to and manner in which subnational governments may tax economic activities that cross jurisdiction boundaries, which is usually called *interstate commerce* in the United States. The Commerce Clause of the United States Constitution prohibits states from enacting laws designed to restrict interstate commerce, while the Fourteenth Amendment's Equal Protection Clause prohibits states from enacting laws that do not give all individuals equal protection (treatment). In general, states have been prohibited from applying taxes that discriminate against out-of-state firms. We have already seen these issues arise in the application of state sales and use taxes and in the apportionment of business income among states.

Still another example of the complex interaction of the relevant economic and legal principles arises concerning state taxation of insurance companies. All 50 states levy specific sales taxes on insurance companies equal to some percentage tax rate multiplied by the amount of insurance premiums on contracts sold in the state. As of 1981, 34 of these state insurance premiums taxes provided lower taxes (usually through lower rates) for insurance companies headquartered in the state (domestic companies) than for insurance companies from other states (foreign companies). Typically, rates for domestic companies were 2 percent or less and rates for foreign

companies 1- or 2-percentage points higher. The states defended this discriminatory taxation on grounds of encouraging the expansion of the domestic insurance industry to ensure insurance for residents at the lowest cost and as a means of increasing investment in the state (because insurance companies use their cash flow to invest in many industrial and commercial projects).

The McCarran-Ferguson Act (1945) specifically gives states the authority to regulate and tax insurance activities, effectively limiting the Commerce Clause's application to the insurance industry. The insurance industry challenged these state domestic preference taxes on grounds that they violate the Equal Protection Clause, however, and in a 1985 decision (*Metropolitan Life Insurance Co. v. Ward*), the U.S. Supreme Court supported that view. The court rejected Alabama's domestic preference tax for insurance companies, arguing that the two reasons offered in support of the tax—to encourage the formation of insurance companies in the state and to encourage foreign insurance companies to increase investment in the state—were not legitimate constitutional reasons for state discriminatory taxation.

Subsequent to this Supreme Court decision, many states that previously had domestic preference taxes substituted premiums taxes with equal rates for domestic and foreign companies. A few states revised their insurance premiums taxes to levy equal tax rates on domestic and foreign insurers but

---

[9]For additional information on this topic, see Baldwin (1986).

Application 17.2 — Discriminatory Business Taxes: The Insurance Case

provide tax credits based on some other measure of the firm's activity in the state (such as investment, property value, or location of corporate headquarters).

Economically, some question remains as to whether these domestic preference taxes could, in practice, accomplish the basic objective of expanding the insurance industry within a state. The largest insurance companies that market nationally sell insurance in many or nearly all states. The lower premiums tax rate in such a company's home state applies only to insurance purchased by residents of that state, which typically would be a small fraction of the total insurance sold by a national firm. Thus, the differential rate for domestic and foreign insurers cannot be an advantage to an insurance company that desires to be national in scope (to lower taxes,

it would have to do most of its sales in its home state or move its headquarters to the state where it does most of its business).

The domestic preference is, therefore, likely to be an advantage only for smaller regional or state firms that sell a substantial part of their insurance in their home state. But for the domestic industry in a state to expand at the expense of the national companies, the domestic companies would have to offer insurance at lower prices than the national firms; that is, the lower state taxes would have to be at least partially passed on to consumers in the home state. But if entry of new insurance companies into a state can be limited by other means such as regulation or advertising, it seems more likely that the domestic preference tax would simply lead to higher profits for the domestic firms rather than lower prices.

SUMMARY

The two principal issues facing state–local governments in designing taxes to be collected directly from businesses are the choice of the tax base—that is the type of tax—and the method for apportioning that base among the various subnational governments in which a firm does business.

A gross income tax collected from business is a tax on the total receipts or total revenue of a firm, with no deductions for any type of expenses allowed. A VAT is a tax on the difference between the sales of a firm and the cost of goods or services purchased from other firms, which are used in production. The base for the traditional net income or profits tax is revenue minus most all business expenses, including costs for materials, labor, interest, rent, and depreciation of capital equipment.

The relative importance of state corporate income tax revenue has declined substantially since the early 1980s. Three factors: (1) adoption of new tax incentives by states, (2) changes in the legal form of business by firms, and (3) use of passive investment holding companies (often called tax shelters) seem to account for the bulk of the decline.

The most often used method to apportion a multistate firm's tax base among all taxing jurisdictions is formula allocation, historically involving the firm's share of its payroll, property, and sales in the state. If all are equally weighted, the firm's allocation factor is the average of the payroll, property, and sales shares. Recently, a number of states have moved away from the traditional equally weighted three-factor formula and moved to formulas that weight sales more heavily.

The three most fundamental criticisms of general gross receipts taxes are that the effective tax rate is greater than the nominal tax rate, depending on the number of stages of production; the effective rate arbitrarily varies between economic sectors; and the tax creates an incentive for vertical integration to reduce taxes.

The average burden of state corporate income taxes represents a decrease in the return of capital to owners just as with a national corporate tax. The excise effects from differentials in state corporate income tax rates among states are expected to impose relative burdens on immobile workers, consumers, and owners of land and immobile capital in the higher-tax states. From the viewpoint of a single state, an increase in the state corporate income tax rate is therefore expected to impose burdens on workers, consumers, and owners of immobile capital and land in that state.

Michigan is the only jurisdiction in the United States to use a VAT, although that is a common business tax in other parts of the world. VATs have many of the advantages of gross income taxes—broad-base, low-rate, and relatively stable revenue stream—without the efficiency and equity problems of gross income taxes. One additional potential economic advantage of a consumption-type VAT compared to a profits tax is a lower effective tax on capital income because capital expenditures are deducted.

DISCUSSION QUESTIONS

1. According to the "benefit principle" of taxation, a business's tax in a state should be related to the benefits to the business from services provided by the state and local governments. Practically, a firm's business activity or tax base is usually divided among states based on the state's share of the firm's capital, employment, and/or sales. Discuss how well each of those components of the allocation formula might correspond to service benefits. Does a firm with sales (through the Internet or mail-order, perhaps) but no employees or capital in a state benefit from any state or local government services?

2. Gross receipts, value-added, and net income are three different potential business tax bases. For each of three firms—an automobile manufacturer (assembly plant), a food retailer, and a private-practice physician—list the components of each potential tax base and describe how the bases differ among each other for one tax and among the three taxes.

3. A national consumption-type VAT has the same base as a national retail sales tax (assuming no exemptions or the same exceptions for each). If one state has a consumption-type VAT (similar to Michigan's SBT), is that tax on the same base as a state sales tax? Suppose that every state adopted a

consumption-type VAT. Would the cumulative effect of those taxes be the same as a national sales tax? How does the answer depend on how the tax base is allocated among states?

4. "If our state has to raise taxes, it should increase the corporate income tax. That way a good part of the tax will be paid by consumers in other states, not just taxpayers in this state." Evaluate this position.

SELECTED READINGS

Cornia, Gary, Kelly D. Edmiston, David L. Sjoquist, and Sally Wallace. "The Disappearing State Corporate Income Tax." *National Tax Journal*, 58 (March 2005): 115–138.

Hines, James. "Michigan's Flirtation with the Single Business Tax." In *Michigan at the Millennium*, ed. C. Ballard, *et al*. East Lansing, MI: Michigan State University Press, 2003.

McLure, Charles E. Jr. "The Elusive Incidence of the Corporate Income Tax: The State Case." *Public Finance Quarterly*, 9 (October 1981): 395–413.

Michigan Department of the Treasury, Taxation and Economic Policy Office. *The Michigan Single Business Tax, 1999-2000*. Lansing, August, 2003.

Mieszkowski, Peter and George R. Zodrow. "The Incidence of a Partial State Corporate Income Tax." *National Tax Journal*, 38 (December 1985): 489–96.

CHAPTER 18

REVENUE FROM GOVERNMENT MONOPOLY AND REGULATION

. . . Gambling is not a fiscal panacea, and we would be foolish, indeed, to expect it to provide much in the way of budgetary relief.[1]
—DANIEL B. SUITS

"THE SUPREME COURT GAVE A BOOST TO COMMERCE BETWEEN WINERIES AND THEIR FAR-FLUNG CUSTOMERS YESTERDAY, RULING THAT STATES THAT PERMIT IN-STATE VINTNERS TO SELL DIRECTLY TO CUSTOMERS MAY NOT DENY THAT RIGHT TO OUT-OF-STATE PRODUCERS.

RULING THAT INTERSTATE TRADE IN WINE TRUMPS THE STATES' RIGHTS TO REGULATE ALCO-HOL SALES, THE COURT STRUCK DOWN NEW YORK AND MICHIGAN LAWS UNDER WHICH WINER-IES FROM OTHER STATES HAD TO SELL THROUGH STATE-LICENSED WHOLESALERS, WHILE LOCAL WINERIES COULD DEAL WITH LOVERS OF THE GRAPE BY PHONE AND INTERNET.

'STATE POLICIES ARE PROTECTED UNDER THE TWENTY-FIRST AMENDMENT WHEN THEY TREAT LIQUOR PRODUCED OUT OF STATE THE SAME AS ITS DOMESTIC EQUIVALENT,' JUSTICE ANTHONY M. KENNEDY WROTE FOR THE MAJORITY. 'THE INSTANCE CASES, IN CONTRAST, INVOLVE STRAIGHTFORWARD ATTEMPTS TO DISCRIMINATE IN FAVOR OF LOCAL PRODUCERS. THE DISCRIMINATION IS CONTRARY TO THE COMMERCE CLAUSE AND IS NOT SAVED BY THE TWENTY-FIRST AMENDMENT.'"[2]

---

[1]"Gambling Taxes, Regressivity, and Revenue Potential." *National Tax Journal*, 30 (March 1977): 34.
[2]Lane, Charles "Justices Reject Curbs on Wine Sales." http://www.washingtonpost.com, May 17, 2005.

State–local governments may generate revenue by becoming the monopoly producer of a good or service and then charging prices for that good or service that are greater than costs. Three common examples of this behavior are considered in this chapter: operation of government-owned utilities, state government alcoholic beverage stores, and state lotteries and other forms of gambling. In all these cases, production by private firms is clearly an alternative and is used in some jurisdictions. Therefore, one issue is whether government production is desired, or whether the government should generate revenue from these activities by taxing the production or sale of the commodities by private producers. A separate but related issue is whether monopoly production is necessary, regardless of the choice between public and private production. As we will discover, if government production is selected to generate revenue, then the monopoly structure directly follows.

ECONOMICS OF GOVERNMENT MONOPOLY

Reasons for Government Monopoly

The issues considered in this chapter are different from the more general question of whether the characteristics of some goods and services lead the private market to an inefficient result, requiring government intervention (as discussed in Chapter 2). First, government can intervene in the market and even become a producer without becoming a monopoly—private schools typically coexist with public schools, for instance. Second, private production is not only feasible for the cases considered in this chapter, but is used in some states and localities. The issue, therefore, is how government can best regulate consumption and production of these goods and generate revenue from these specific economic activities.

Monopoly production is efficient when there are increasing returns to scale—that is, the average cost decreases as output rises. With those cost conditions, goods or services obviously can be produced at lower unit cost by a single firm than by a set of smaller, competing firms. Because of the relatively large fixed-cost component involved in producing and distributing utility services, such as electricity, natural gas, water, and mass transit, increasing returns to scale may be expected. Thus, monopoly production may be desired; in fact, these industries are sometimes referred to as *natural monopolies*. However, the existence of increasing returns does not require *government* monopoly. Instead, government may grant monopoly rights to a private producer subject to government regulation or taxation. Among these utility services, government monopoly is most common for water-sewer and local mass transit, whereas private, regulated monopoly is more common for electricity, natural gas, and intermetropolitan transit. Still, some electricity generation and distribution monopolies are owned and operated by state and local governments in a number of states.[3]

---

[3]These are monopolies only in their service areas. It is entirely possible to have private producers with exclusive rights to serve some areas of a state and government producers as the exclusive suppliers to other areas.

Some evidence of economies of scale in the administration of lotteries exists as well. Larry DeBoer (1985) reports that the administrative costs of state lotteries per dollar of sales decline as sales increase. DeBoer finds that this result apparently continues to be true even for those states with the largest lotteries, suggesting that producing lottery services is similar to producing utilities. This tendency is even reflected in the aggregate data in Table 18.3 (later in this chapter), which show that administrative costs as a fraction of sales tend to be lower in those states with a larger dollar volume of sales. But even with economies of scale, why should the government operate the monopoly? Presumably, a state could grant the lottery monopoly to a private firm similar to a private utility and then regulate and tax that entity.

Using a monopoly for the distribution or sale of alcoholic beverages seems more problematic. Economies of scale are not expected to be important in this industry; in fact, (government) monopoly sale is used in only 18 states. Rather, the argument usually made for government monopoly in providing lotteries and sale of alcoholic beverages concerns controlling the externalities associated with these types of consumption. The idea is that because sales are made only through the government, regulations such as those regarding underage consumption can be enforced more easily.

Thinking about for all these cases, there is no completely convincing argument why government monopoly is required in any of them. Cost considerations may favor monopoly, as noted in the discussion about economic efficiency in Chapter 2, but do not necessarily *require* government monopoly. If externalities associated with these activities imply that marginal social cost is greater than private cost, then raising private costs (through taxes or monopoly prices) or regulating the activity is called for. Taxes often work well for this purpose (also discussed in Chapter 2), so again government monopoly may not be required. Finally, both taxes and monopoly production can be used to generate revenue.

Economic Objectives

Whatever theoretical arguments are offered to support government monopoly provision of these services, the political fact is that these monopolies often are effective ways for states and localities to generate revenue. Again, this is not to imply that government monopoly exists *only, or even,* to produce revenue. Monopoly may provide a service that would otherwise not exist, as in the case of goods and services whose production exhibits increasing returns to scale, or monopoly provision may serve other objectives of government. Generating revenue is only one reason, but it is the main focus of this chapter.

The economic options to a government monopoly in terms of pricing and sales, which determine revenue for the government, are no different from those for private-sector monopolists. The standard economic analysis is shown in Figure 18.1. The monopolist faces a downward sloping demand for its product, which implies that additional sales can be achieved by reducing the price. Consequently, the **marginal revenue**—that is, the *additional revenue from selling one more unit of the good or service*—is always less than the price charged for that last unit. Selling more output

Figure 18.1

Monopoly pricing

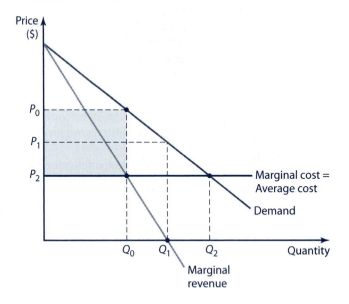

entails reducing prices for all units of output sold. Graphically, this is reflected by the fact that the marginal revenue curve lies below the demand curve (for any given quantity, marginal revenue is less than the price determined from demand). In general, the equation for marginal revenue for any given output is

$$MR = P\left[1 - 1/E_p^d\right]$$

where

   P = Price so that the output is demanded.

   E_p^d = The (absolute value) of the price elasticity of demand at that output.

If the price elasticity of demand equals one, then marginal revenue equals zero—increases or decreases in price do not generate any additional revenue for the monopolist. An increase in price causes fewer units to be sold, with both effects exactly offsetting. If demand is price-elastic (the price elasticity of demand is greater than one), then marginal revenue is positive but less than price. In that case, a decrease in price causes an increase in sales revenue for the monopolist—the price decrease is more than offset by an increase in the number of units sold. Finally, if the price elasticity of demand is less than one (demand is price-inelastic), then marginal revenue is negative. Any increase in the number of units sold from lowering the price is not sufficient to offset the lower price, so sales revenue would decline.[4]

   To illustrate the monopolist's pricing options, the cost per unit of production is assumed constant in this case, so that marginal cost and average cost are equal. The

---

[4]If you are confused by these uses of price elasticity, refer to the review in Chapter 4.

price the monopolist should charge to get the highest possible profit corresponds to the *output where marginal cost and marginal revenue are equal*, quantity Q_0 in Figure 18.1. Recall from microeconomics that as long as the extra revenue from selling one more unit (marginal revenue) is greater than the extra cost (marginal cost), more production will generate more profit. The maximum profit is attained when all those opportunities are taken, that is, when marginal revenue and marginal cost are equal. So a price of P_0 and the resulting quantity of Q_0 provide the highest possible profit to a monopolist with these demand and cost functions. That profit is the difference between sales revenue and cost, which is shown as the shaded area in the Figure 18.1.

Maximizing profits by a monopolist is generally not the same as attempting to maximize the dollar volume of sales. Maximum sales revenue results when marginal revenue is zero, that is, at price P_1 and quantity Q_1 as shown in Figure 18.1. Of course, the difference between the two is that sales revenue alone takes no account of production cost. Lowering price to increase quantity sold beyond Q_0 simply does not pay off in increased profits because the marginal revenue from those transactions is less than marginal cost. Finally, if this product were produced by a competitive industry or if the government provider was trying to maximize consumer surplus, the price would equal P_2, and the quantity sold would be Q_2. Competition drives prices down to just cover costs (including the opportunity costs of the investors). At quantity Q_2, price equals marginal and average costs.

The economic opportunity for a monopolist should now be clear. By increasing price above the level that would be charged by a competitive industry, the monopolist sells fewer units of product but may earn returns above those available in other industries if price is greater than average costs. A limit exists, however, to how high the price should be. If the monopolist sets the price too high, the amount sold may decline so drastically that some potential profit may be missed. The trick is to balance marginal revenue and marginal cost, which depends on how sensitive consumers are to price. For any given production cost, the price the monopolist should charge to maximize profits is higher, the less price elastic is demand.

The analysis is only slightly different if production exhibits increasing returns to scale, as shown in Figure 18.2. Because average cost decreases as quantity rises, marginal cost is always less than average cost. It follows that if price is set equal to marginal cost at any output, financial losses result because the price (revenue per unit) is less than average cost (cost per unit). This is implicitly why these situations are called natural monopoly; competitive market prices always generate losses. If the price is set equal to average cost at price P_1 and quantity Q_1, profits are zero. Because all costs are covered, the monopolist could continue to operate at this position, but no revenue above costs would be generated either for the private or public (government) monopoly owners. As before, profit-maximizing output occurs when marginal revenue and marginal cost are equal, which occurs at price P_0 and quantity Q_0. Again, the profit earned by the monopolist is indicated by the shaded area of Figure 18.2.

This analysis explains how a government monopoly can generate revenue for the government for general purposes. As long as the government charges a price

Figure 18.2

Monopoly pricing
with increasing
returns to scale

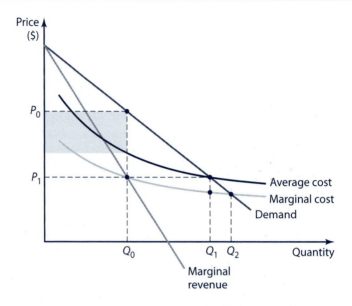

above average cost, economic profits result. In other words, the government monopoly would earn profits beyond the normal rate of return on its investment in the business. Those profits could be used as revenue for general purposes or some specific earmarked purpose.

Even if government uses a monopoly position to generate general revenue, it does not necessarily follow that the government will—or should—set prices to maximize profits, thus maximizing general revenue to the government. The monopoly profits are only one of many sources of revenue to state or local government and should be evaluated by the same economic criteria applied to all revenue sources—equity, efficiency, and administration cost. Just as state–local governments may choose to set less than revenue-maximizing tax rates on some activities because of equity or efficiency factors, so too might the government choose to set less than revenue-maximizing prices for goods produced by government monopoly. For instance, recall from Chapter 15 that many states exempt food sales from the sales tax to reduce regressivity of the state's tax structure; but a zero state tax rate on food is surely less than the revenue-maximizing rate. The appropriate price for goods produced by government monopoly must be evaluated in a similar manner, depending on whether the objective for having government monopoly is to generate revenue and depending on the equity and efficiency implications of raising revenue in that way.[5]

---

[5]Jeff Biddle has pointed out to me that states can gain monopoly power through their sovereignty. For instance, states require all drivers to have licenses that are provided only by the state. Theoretically states could charge relatively high fees for those licenses, but do not.

Figure 18.3

Monopoly pricing
and taxation of
competitive prices
are equivalent

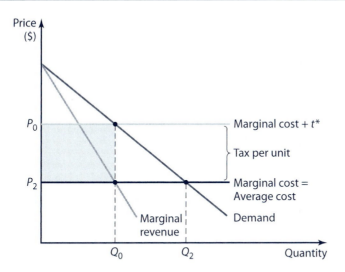

Monopoly versus Taxation

Any general government revenue generated through a government monopoly also could be obtained through taxing private producers, regardless of whether the market is served by a monopoly or competitive firms. This point is illustrated by Figure 18.3, which compares a profit-maximizing government monopoly to a profit-maximizing private competitive industry that is taxed by the government. With the government monopoly, the profit-maximizing price of P_0 and quantity Q_0 generate economic profits or revenue to the government, represented by the shaded area. If a set of private competitive firms produced this good or service, the price would be P_2, equal to marginal cost. An excise tax levied on sales by those private firms would increase marginal cost; if the tax rate is t^*, the new marginal cost is $MC(1 + t^*)$. If t^* is chosen so that the new competitive market price is P_0, the quantity sold equals Q_0, and the tax revenue generated again equals the shaded area. Obviously, both the monopoly profits and the excise tax revenue can be equal. If economic conditions call for monopoly production, whether by government or a private firm, taxes and government production can again be equivalent. If private monopoly production is called for, the government can just tax away all or part of the private firm's profits.[6]

From this viewpoint, it is clear that a government monopoly price that is above average cost is implicitly a tax that generates revenue. If the government monopoly sets prices above average cost, the same good or service could be provided by the government firm at lower prices. This is essentially equivalent to taxing the production or distribution of the service by a private firm. Although these two

---

[6]It is a standard microeconomic result that a proportional tax on true economic profits (excluding the normal return to capital) will have no effect on the monopolist's choice of price and output.

sources may be called and classified differently—one as revenue from government production and the other as revenue from a tax—economically this is a distinction without a difference. In both cases, government has intervened in the economy to increase the price of a good or service to generate government revenue. Important political distinctions may exist between a "tax" and "monopoly revenue," however. A monopoly may permit the government to gain revenue without anyone having to vote for higher taxes, the monopoly revenues may not be subject to constitutional or statutory revenue limitations, and monopoly revenue may be perceived as a type of user charge paid only by consumers of particular services.[7]

Application 18.1

YOUR CITY: BROUGHT TO YOU BY ALL EVERYTHING CORP.

Over the past 10 years or so, localities and some states have increasingly sought revenue by using their monopoly provision of services or facilities as opportunities for private marketing. Some examples are common and well established—advertising billboards on or inside buses and subway trains have been in use for years. Other examples, however, are more recent and unusual—firms acquiring the naming rights to city streets or parks, for instance. How substantial are the revenue opportunities for states and localities from assisting private sector marketing? What problems do these public-private sector relationships create? How will citizens view this marketing expansion through the public sector?

Public-private marketing arrangements fall into three general categories: (1) private advertising on public facilities, (2) exclusive contracts between governments and private firms, and (3) the selling of naming rights for public facilities. An article by Christopher

Swope (2004) provides the following examples of all three. General Motors contracted with the Port Authority of New York/New Jersey to put images on the walls of a subway tunnel that runs under the Hudson River, which give riders the impression that they are watching a video as they ride by. In 1999, San Diego entered into an exclusive contract with the Pepsi Bottling Group, Inc. through which Pepsi vending machines are located on city property, Pepsi was granted the designation "Proud Sponsor of the City of San Diego," and the city receives a marketing fee, commissions, and merchandise for city programs. Finally, Las Vegas sold the name of a key station in its new monorail system to Nextel (reportedly for $50 million).

In most instances so far, the revenue from such public-private marketing arrangements appears to be relatively minor; however, the potential is unclear. One can only speculate about the potential for private naming of

---

[7]However, it is not correct to state that the government monopoly is generating consumer surplus by producing a good or service that is valued by consumers. Such an argument presumes that this good or service would not be provided by private firms in the absence of the government production. But if the government monopoly was created by first prohibiting private production or sale, government has created the possibility of providing a demanded service to consumers. That demand can be satisfied either by allowing private firms to operate or by government production.

Application 18.1 — Your City: Brought to You by All Everything Corp.

Central Park in New York City, for instance (Central Park by Disney?). How citizens view the expansion of private marketing through the public sector also is not clear. Citizens may see marketing revenue as a desirable alternative to taxes or user charges, partly because citizens do not directly pay for that revenue, which comes indirectly from the consumers, workers, and investors of the private firms. Thus, citizens may also see marketing revenue as a way of exporting public sector costs to nonresidents. On the other hand, citizens may worry whether the contract or advertising is affecting quality of service. For instance, locating soft drink machines in public schools has become controversial, with concerns about the potential effects on students and learning. Some may worry that governments might accept inferior products because of marketing arrangements. Issues of image, taste, and morality are even more problematical. According to Swope (2004), Dallas rejected a naming offer from the parent company of Jose Cuervo tequila for a performance hall at a new Latino Cultural Center.

Some of the other main concerns about public-private marketing arrangements relate to the contract or negotiation process. States and localities need to identify correctly the market value of these opportunities, which often is not easy because there may be few comparable markets. If some company wanted to purchase naming rights for New York City's Central Park, for instance, how would the city go about determining the value to name such a unique asset? Competitiveness in the bidding or negotiation process is also considered important, as it usually provides maximum revenue and helps people perceive the process as fair. As a result, some cities—New York and San Diego among them—have hired marketing professionals to coordinate this process. In fact, San Diego has an official "Corporate Partnership Program," with a separate office and page on the city's web site. So far, San Diego has official partnerships with six private entities: Cardiac Science, Inc. (for defibrillators); General Motors; MCHune Chrysler-Jeep; Pepsi Bottling Group; Qualcomm; and Verizon Wireless (see http://www.sandiego.gov/corporatepartnership/exist.shtml).

Public-private marketing arrangements represent another way that states and localities may generate revenue through monopoly power—in this case, by providing public services or owning public facilities. How far this trend might go is just speculation at present. It is not at all clear that the forecast of one marketing industry—"I'm sure one day that Yellowstone will be named Tostitos Park" (Blackmon, 1996)—will ever materialize.

OPERATION OF GOVERNMENT MONOPOLY

Utilities

Although government production of utility services is most common for water-sewer and urban mass transit, government monopolies also produce and distribute electricity and natural gas in a number of states, as noted previously. Municipalities most commonly own and operate these utilities, although some states also use

Table 18.1

Operation of Utilities Owned by Subnational Governments, 1997

(Net Income in Millions of Dollars)

	States		Counties		Cities	
Utility	**Net Income**[a]	**Income/ Sales**[b] **(%)**	**Net Income**	**Income/ Sales (%)**	**Net Income**	**Income/ Sales (%)**
Water	−$3.0	−28.6%	$279.0	12.7%	$2800.0	16.9%
Transit	−1684.0	−125.7	−735.0	−257.9	−2339.0	−92.0
Electric	335.0	12.9	17.0	12.1	3303.0	15.6
Natural Gas	4.0	50.0	−2.0	−12.5	444.0	14.7

[a]Revenue minus expenditure excluding capital expenditure equals revenue minus operating expenses minus debt service, in millions of dollars.

[b]Net income as a percent of revenue.

SOURCE: U.S. Census Bureau, *Government Finances, 1996–97*, 1998.

special districts. Cities in 46 different states operate electric utilities, and city-owned gas utilities operate in 34 states. In contrast, a few states have county-owned electric utilities and state-owned utilities. Similarly, a few states have county-owned natural gas distribution facilities, but no state-owned facilities. In those states where cities own the electric and gas utilities, they typically serve only a limited geographic area. In most cases, city utilities can buy power from or sell power to the private electric firms as production and market conditions warrant. If a municipal utility does not own generating or production facilities, it enters into a long-term contract with a private provider or another municipal utility. Thus, the city monopoly exists more in distribution than production.

Some economic information about the operation of these government-owned utilities, at least in aggregate, is given in Table 18.1. Both net income (sales minus operating and debt expenses) and net income as a fraction of sales are shown for each of the four main types of utilities owned by states, counties, or cities. Several implications follow. First, net income of the transit utilities is negative in each instance, showing that the consumers of these services do not pay enough in prices to cover the costs of the service. Not only are transit monopolies not sources of other revenue for the operating governments, they, in fact, require subsidy from other sources, which are discussed in more detail in Chapter 20. Second, county- and city-owned electric, gas, and water utilities do provide positive net income—that is, revenue beyond operating costs and debt service. However, the positive net income does not guarantee that the utility is generating economic profits because all the opportunity costs to the government of owning the utility are not measured. Specifically, the operating costs do not include any measure of depreciation. Because the government has a large investment in capital goods in the utility, part of the net income is simply the normal or average return on that investment, equivalent to what the city could have earned by investing those funds elsewhere.

The question of whether these utilities earn economic profits is better shown by the ratio of net income to sales, the "profit" rate on sales, if you will. For city utilities, the highest ratio of net income to sales is for water service, at about 17 percent. This means for every $1 of water sales, $.17 remains after operating costs and interest charges are paid, which is a larger amount than for city electric and gas utilities. This suggests that the water company is the most likely city-owned utility to be generating economic profits or revenue for other purposes. Such a result is not surprising economically because usually few private firms provide this service for comparison. Thus, consumers may not be aware that a government water monopoly is earning economic profits through its pricing policies. On the other hand, if the city electric company attempted to generate large profits, it would be relatively easy to compare that firm's prices and rate of return to those of private utilities serving neighboring areas.

Alcoholic Beverages

States follow one of two general methods for regulating the sale of alcoholic beverages. Under the so-called **control method** used by 18 states, the state government has a monopoly on at least the wholesale distribution of distilled liquor. In some cases, the state wholesale monopoly also extends to beer and/or wine. Control states operate at least the wholesale system directly. Some control states with a wholesale-distribution monopoly also impose one or more restrictions on retail sale, varying from limiting retail sale of alcoholic beverages in state liquor stores (exclusively or in competition with private retailers) to establishing minimum retail prices to imposing limitations on the number and business hours of retail outlets to making restrictions on advertising about the retail sale of alcoholic beverages. In the control states, the state government wholesale monopoly allows the state to set wholesale prices to generate revenue for the state government, although state taxes on the sale of alcoholic beverages may be levied in addition.

The alternative **open method** used by the other states involves wholesale and retail sale of alcoholic beverages by private firms, usually a large number, so that the market is relatively competitive. In these states, the sellers are licensed by the state government (thus, the method is sometimes referred to as a **license system**), with the licensed private sellers also sometimes constrained by sales rules setting minimum prices or restricting business hours or advertising. In some license states, a limited number of wholesalers are licensed, and all alcoholic beverages must be distributed through those wholesalers. These states levy excise taxes on the sale of alcoholic beverages, typically collected at the wholesale level; in contrast to the control states, these wholesale taxes are the main source of revenue from alcohol for open method states. Examination of these state systems by Barbara Weinstein (1982) and others shows a great variety of regulatory systems used by states of both general types.

These two systems of state involvement in the sale of alcoholic beverages clearly show that state taxation and regulation of private firms is an alternative to state monopoly production. The history of the two systems is that states adopted one or the other at the time of the Twenty-first Amendment to the U.S. Constitution, which repealed Prohibition in 1933 and gave states authority to regulate the sale and distribution of alcoholic beverages. No state has since switched from one general

Table 18.2

Operations of State Alcoholic Beverage Monopolies, 1992

State[a]	Sales (millions of dollars)	Net Income[b] (millions of dollars)	Net Income as Percentage of Sales	Per Capita Net Income
Alabama	$ 152.6	$ 18.1	11.8%	$ 4.37
Idaho	43.6	9.9	22.7	8.53
Iowa	84.1	25.8	30.6	9.17
Maine	72.5	21.5	29.6	17.4
Michigan	444.3	62.5	14.0	6.62
Mississippi	122.8	25.5	20.7	9.75
Montana	36.4	2.3	6.3	2.79
New Hampshire	204.6	42.9	20.9	38.61
Ohio	354.7	81.8	23.0	7.42
Oregon	168.6	64.5	38.2	21.66
Pennsylvania	667.2	44.4	6.6	3.69
Utah	69.3	16.9	24.3	9.32
Vermont	28.3	.9	3.1	1.57
Virginia	258.9	35.3	13.6	5.53
Washington	259.4	24.0	9.2	4.67
West Virginia	45.1	4.8	10.6	2.64
Wyoming	31.7	3.8	11.9	8.15
Total	$3,044.7	$485.6	15.9%	$ 7.42

[a]North Carolina is also a controlled state, with the state government contracting with a private firm to operate the state wholesale distribution of liquor at prices set by the state. North Carolina is not included in the Census list of state liquor stores, however.

[b]Net income equals sales of state stores excluding taxes and discounts minus costs of goods sold minus operating expenses plus other income minus other expense.

SOURCE: U.S. Bureau of the Census, *State Government Finances*, 1992.

method to the other (although states have altered the rules and restrictions used within their system to bring about more or less economic competition).[8]

Some historical information about the operation of the state alcoholic beverage monopolies in 17 states is reported in Table 18.2 (the Bureau of the Census does not report data for North Carolina, a control state, evidently because North Carolina contracts with a private firm to operate the state wholesale-distribution monopoly). The state monopolies in these 17 states generated about $486 million of income above operating and debt expenses in 1992, which represents a return of about 16 percent of sales. In per-capita terms, state alcoholic beverage monopoly net income equaled $7.42, on average. Remember, however, that depreciation, capital opportunity costs, and capital construction costs are not included.

The monopoly states vary widely in the magnitude of per-capita net income generated. Although most of these states fall in the $4 to $8 range, Vermont ($1.57), West Virginia ($2.64), and Montana ($2.79) generated substantially smaller

---

[8]For instance, Iowa, Michigan, and West Virginia ceased state *retail* sales operations since 1987, but all three states maintained *wholesale* liquor monopolies.

amounts of net income per person while New Hampshire ($31.61), Oregon ($21.66), and Maine ($17.40), had substantially larger amounts of net income from alcoholic beverage sales than average. Such differences in per-capita net income from alcoholic beverages could arise from differences in the level of per-capita alcoholic beverage consumption by residents of these states, the costs of operating state liquor monopolies, the pricing policies, or interstate transactions (residents of one state buying liquor from stores in a different, probably neighboring, state). Evidence and experience seem to suggest that the last of the three is the dominant explanation. The policy of the New Hampshire liquor monopoly to seek purchases from residents in the surrounding states is well known, as described in Application 18.2; in fact, New Hampshire generates the highest per-capita income from liquor sales while the neighboring state of Vermont has the lowest. Similarly, per-capita income from state liquor sales in Oregon is high, although per-capita net income from the state monopoly in Washington is lower than average (at $4.67).

Control and Licensing Compared

The potential effects in a state from switching from one regulatory system to another are uncertain because no states have changed systems. However, research comparing the open and control states suggests some potential economic differences between the two methods. First, state wholesale-liquor monopolies not only control the sale of liquor in a state but also the purchase of liquor from the manufacturers. As the single buyer from the distillers for all retail establishments in the state, the state monopoly may also have **monopsony power.** A **monopsony,** the parallel of monopoly but from the demanders' side of the market, is defined as a *single buyer of a commodity.* Just as monopolies can use their market power on the supply side to charge higher prices than would prevail in competition, so too monopsonies can use their market power on the demand side to pay lower prices for the product they are purchasing than they would in a competitive market. Weinstein (1982, p. 726) reported, for instance, that at that time, the Michigan Liquor Control Commission "is the world's largest single purchaser of distilled spirits. . . ." Although state laws generally prohibit distillers from explicit price discrimination among the states, some large state government buyers may still be able to pay lower prices in effect by altering the timing of purchases from and payments to the manufacturers. To the extent that the state monopoly distributors can exercise monopsony power over the distillers, the wholesale cost of liquor would be lower in the control states.

Second, several studies have shown that retail liquor prices tend to be slightly lower in the control states when compared to the open states, but not always by a substantial amount. Weinstein (1982) reports, for instance, that the retail price in 1980 for a fifth of Seagram's 7 averaged $6.12 in the 18 control states and $6.37 in the other open states, although an average price for nine different brands was $7.36 in the control states and $7.57 in the others. More variation in prices appears, however, within open-system states than in the control states, which may reflect more direct restrictions on retail prices in the control states, more restrictions on advertising, or fewer retail outlets.

In the cases of specific states, however, pricing differences can be substantial. Reporting data from the American Chamber of Commerce Research Association, Young and Bielinska-Kwapisz (2002) note that the price of a 750 ml bottle of J&B Scotch varied among the states in 1997 from a low of $15.07 to a high of $22.05. *The Detroit News* reported in 1994 that prices in Michigan and Ohio, both control states that set retail prices, are much higher than in Illinois and Indiana, both open states in which private retailers set their own prices. A half-gallon bottle of Tanqueray gin, for instance cost $34.95 in Michigan and $34.45 in Ohio, but only $30.17 in Illinois and $26.24 in Indiana. Not surprisingly, therefore, consumers from Michigan and Ohio sometimes travel to Indiana to purchase alcoholic beverages, even though laws limit interstate importing of liquor in those states. Similarly, the *Los Angeles Times* (Hirsh, 2005) reported that a bottle of Charles Shaw wine that sells for $1.99 in California (an open state) goes for $3.39 in Columbus, Ohio (a control state).

A third, related observation is that per-capita consumption of liquor tends to be greater in the open states as compared to the control states. Jon Nelson (2003) provides a careful analysis of this issue and reports (p. 21) that ". . . monopoly control of retail sales of spirits reduces consumption of spirits and increases consumption of wine. . . . The net effect of monopoly on total alcohol demand is significantly negative." Thus, the higher prices for distilled liquor in the control states reduce liquor consumption. Although these higher liquor prices also induce some consumers to substitute wine for liquor, total alcoholic beverage consumption is reduced.[9]

The full cost of consuming liquor to a consumer includes not only the retail price charged by the store or bar but also the time and out-of-pocket costs of going to the sales outlet. If few retail outlets are available or they have limited hours, this second component of the cost of liquor consumption could be substantial. Even if retail prices are the same in two states, the full consumers' price will be higher in states that limit retail competition. If control states limit retail competition more than the open-system states, then the lower alcohol-consumption levels in the control states are consistent with economic expectations about demand (that is, higher costs). Data tabulated by the Distilled Spirits Council of the United States (DISCUS) for 1991 showed that 1.18 retail outlets are selling liquor (including both on-premises and off-premises consumption) per 1,000 people in the open states, on average, compared to 1.09 outlets per 1,000 population in the control states. This is equivalent to about 1 outlet for each 845 people in the open states and 1 outlet for 915 people in the control states. The difference between the two groups of states is most apparent for retail stores selling for off-premises consumption only: There was 1 store for every 700 people in the open states, but only 1 store for every 8,100 people in the control states (DISCUS, 1991). Of course, a state's residents' attitudes about alcohol also simultaneously determine the level of consumption and the type of distribution system.

---

[9]Interestingly, Nelson (2003) also reports that bans on billboard advertising for alcoholic beverages do not seem to reduce overall consumption, although the effects vary by type of beverage.

The fourth observation from comparing control and open states is that per-capita state liquor revenue (from sales and taxes) tends to be greater in the monopoly-control states. That this results despite lower per-capita consumption suggests that the source is higher explicit taxes or higher implicit taxes through the state monopoly. As previously explained, however, the revenue generated by the state monopoly includes both the normal return to investment and the true economic profits. Thus, the apparently higher state government revenue from the control system may be partly an illusion, given that the state also incurs a substantial capital and inventory cost from operating the state stores. Thus, after reviewing all the available information from several studies, Weinstein (1982, p. 738) could only conclude that "there is not enough evidence regarding the relative efficiency of public and private liquor distribution systems to shed much additional light on" the economic advantages of one method over the other.

Application 18.2

NEW HAMPSHIRE SELLS LIQUOR[10]

Although 18 states generate revenue from the monopoly sale of liquor in their states, at least at the wholesale level, New Hampshire, a state with neither a personal income tax nor sales tax, relies on this revenue source more than any of the others. The state's liquor store sales of more than $326 million in 2003 accounted for about 5 percent of the state government's general revenue, compared to a ratio of less then one-half of 1 percent nationally. Data reported by DISCUS show that per-capita sales of distilled spirits in New Hampshire in 2003 was about 3.3 gallons, compared to about 1.3 gallons per capita nationally. Data from the Beer Institute show that New Hampshire had the second highest per-capita beer sales among the states (second to Nevada).

New Hampshire, a state with about 1.3 million residents, achieves such a high level of sales and income by setting prices lower than in the surrounding states, aggressively advertising those bargains, and then locating state liquor outlets along major highways just over the state border. For instance, according to a survey conducted by DISCUS, the price for a 750 ml bottle of Smirnoff 8.0 vodka at the New Hampshire stores was $6.90 in 1993 compared to a price of $7.91 in Maine and $8.45 in Vermont (both monopoly states) and $8.18 in Massachusetts (an open state). According to *The Wall Street Journal*, about 80 percent of the advertising expenditures by the New Hampshire Liquor Commission go for ads in those other states. As a result, the state estimates that about 55 percent of its liquor sales are made to out-of-state residents, mostly from Connecticut, Maine, Massachusetts, New York, Rhode Island, and Vermont. In essence, the state government in New Hampshire is in the business of marketing and selling wine and liquor throughout the New England region.

Not surprisingly, this behavior by New Hampshire is not appreciated by the

---

[10] For background information see *The Wall Street Journal* (1985b).

Application 18.2 — New Hampshire Sells Liquor

governments in the neighboring states, which receive less revenue from their own alcohol monopolies and taxes because their residents purchase liquor in New Hampshire. In fact, most states have laws limiting the amount of wine and liquor individuals are allowed to transport from other states in an attempt to protect the state's monopoly and collect the state's taxes. Although those laws are difficult and expensive to enforce effectively, New Hampshire's neighboring states do sometimes identify their residents at New Hampshire stores and then stop them for inspection after they leave the state. Of course, an alternative is for the other states to lower prices to compete with New Hampshire. For example, in November 1994, Maine opened a large discount liquor store along the interstate highway about 30 miles from the New Hampshire border in a direct attempt to draw business from New Hampshire.[11]

This interstate purchase and transport of wine and liquor because of state government-induced price differentials is no different economically than interstate cigarette purchases to take advantage of state excise tax differences or interstate and mail-order purchases because of state sales tax differences, which were considered in Chapter 15. This emphasizes the point that state monopoly and state taxation can be equivalent ways of raising revenue through higher prices. The only possible political difference is that New Hampshire's policy is to create and

exploit liquor-price differences. Recall that the federal government intervened in the case of cigarette sales, making interstate transmission a federal crime and helping states enforce their cigarette taxes. In the case of e-commerce, however, the federal government has not acted to help states collect use taxes. Nor has the federal government helped states enforce liquor taxes.

Is there any economic reason why New Hampshire should be prohibited from undertaking this activity? Theoretically, a state could monopolize the sale of any good (say automobile tires) on grounds of ensuring public safety and use the advantages of government monopoly to undercut the prices of private sellers in other states. The result would be redistributed sales and resources from one state to another. Of course, if all states followed this strategy—for the same commodity or for different ones—there would not necessarily be any interstate redistribution. Exporting state taxes in this way could lead to inefficient public-goods provision because residents do not perceive the correct cost of financing government. Another potential problem is that the capability of a state to regulate the sale and consumption of a commodity for safety or externality reasons is affected by other states' provision.[12] If such externality problems do not exist, however, restricting interstate competition reduces consumers' welfare and provides no corresponding increase in public welfare.

---

[11] See MacTaggert (1994).

[12] Liquor provides a clear example. One state may set a high legal drinking age for highway safety reasons and enforce it partly through state monopoly sale. If another nearby state makes liquor easily available to younger drivers, the state's capability to regulate public safety is diminished. Partly for this reason, the national government created incentives for all states to adopt a legal drinking age of 21.

Gambling and Lotteries

Although states have generated revenue from gambling activities for many years, mostly from taxes on betting at horse and dog races, states have increased their reliance on gambling revenue and changed the nature of their involvement substantially over the past 30 years. Current types of legal gambling by state are shown in Figure 18.4. Only two states—Hawaii and Utah—do not have some form of legalized gambling (excluding bingo).

First came the growth of state lotteries. In 2003, 38 states and the District of Columbia operated lotteries, as shown in Table 18.3. Two more states—Tennessee and North Dakota—added lotteries in 2004. The first state lottery was adopted by New Hampshire in 1963; by 1975, 13 states had begun lotteries, there were 22 state lotteries in 1986, and 32 in 1992. In 2003, the lotteries in those 38 states generated an average of 1.1 percent of state governments' total revenue and 1.2 percent of the states' general revenue. These state lotteries are operated as state government monopolies (with potential competing private lotteries made illegal by the states). This stands in contrast to the more traditional way states have generated revenue from gambling, that is, by taxing gambling provided by private firms on such activities as racing, casino games, and sporting events. Even though state governments have always closely regulated these private gambling activities, it was generally not until lotteries that the states directly operated, and encouraged, gambling.[13]

The second and more recent increase in gambling activity is the explosion of casinos owned and operated by Indian tribes, casinos on riverboats, and commercial casinos as tourist attractions in other locations, as shown in Figure 18.4. A federal government law adopted in 1988, the Indian Gaming Regulatory Act, made it clear that Native-American tribes have a right to operate casinos on their lands offering games that are legal in those states, subject to agreements with the state governments. By 2004, more than 350 gambling casinos on Indian tribal lands were operating in some 30 states. By 2005, nearly 400 commercial casinos—either riverboat casino gambling (in 6 states—Illinois, Indiana, Iowa, Louisiana, Mississippi, and Missouri) or private, commercial land-based casinos—were operating in a total of 15 states. Kearney (2005, p. 281) reports that "Gambling in some form [including race tracks, bingo and other forms] is now legal in every state except Hawaii and Utah."

Lotteries

State lotteries are not homogeneous goods, with lottery bureaus or commissions typically operating several types of games simultaneously. The most common types of games include instant lotteries, for which the player buys a ticket and scratches off a covering surface to reveal the prize, if any; numbers games or the daily lottery, for which the player chooses a three- or four-digit number and a fixed payoff is made daily on a randomly selected winning number; and lotto, involving parimutuel betting in which the player selects a number (usually 6 or 7 digits) from

---

[13]One other example of a state-operated gambling monopoly is offtrack betting.

Figure 18.4

State gambling activities

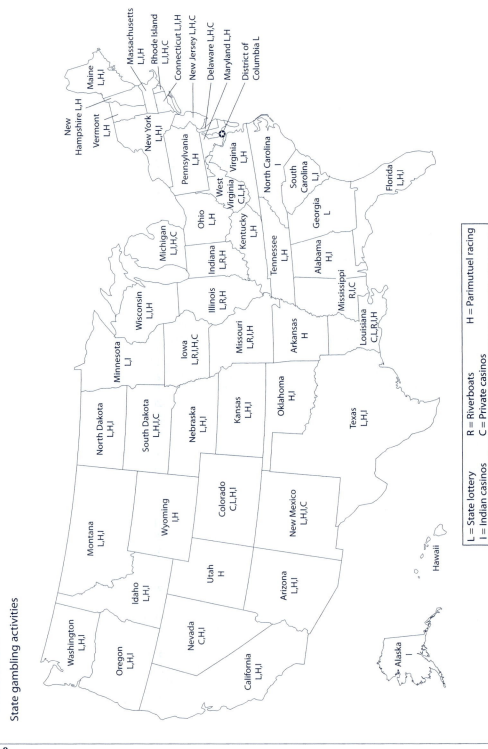

Montana L,H,I
Idaho L,H,I
Washington L,H,I
Oregon L,H,I
Nevada C,H,I
California L,H,I
Utah H
Arizona L,H,I
Wyoming I,H
Colorado C,L,H,I
New Mexico L,H,I,C
North Dakota L,H,I
South Dakota L,H,I,C
Nebraska L,H,I
Kansas L,H,I
Oklahoma H,I
Texas L,H,I
Minnesota L,I
Iowa L,R,I,H,C
Missouri L,R,I,H
Arkansas H
Louisiana C,L,R,I,H
Wisconsin L,I,H
Illinois L,R,H
Michigan L,I,H,C
Indiana L,R,H
Kentucky L,H
Ohio L,H
Tennessee L,H
Mississippi R,I,C
Alabama H,I
Georgia L
South Carolina L,I
North Carolina I
West Virginia C,L,H
Virginia L,H
Florida L,H,I
Pennsylvania L,H
New Hampshire L,H
Vermont L,H
Maine L,H,I
New York L,H,I
Massachusetts L,I,H
Rhode Island L,I,H,C
Connecticut L,I,H
New Jersey L,H,C
Delaware L,H,C
Maryland L,H
District of Columbia L
Hawaii
Alaska I

L = State lottery   R = Riverboats   H = Parimutuel racing

I = Indian casinos   C = Private casinos

Table 18.3

Operation of State Lotteries, 2003

State	Ticket Sales, Excluding Commissions (millions)	Percentage of Sales to:		Net Revenue	Implicit Tax Rates	Net Lottery Revenue as a Percentage of Total State Revenue
		Prizes	Administration			
United States	$41,886.3	60.5%	6.6%	32.9%	49.0%	1.1%
Alabama	—	—	—	—	—	—
Alaska	—	—	—	—	—	—
Arizona	300.8	57.8	10.3	31.9	46.8	0.5
Arkansas	—	—	—	—	—	—
California	2,592.0	56.0	6.3	37.6	60.4	0.5
Colorado	361.9	62.9	8.8	28.3	39.6	0.7
Connecticut	867.4	60.4	10.1	29.5	41.8	1.4
Delaware	367.1	14.4	1.7	83.9	521.0	6.1
Florida	2,712.3	57.4	4.8	37.8	60.8	1.9
Georgia	2,284.1	60.8	6.3	32.9	49.0	2.5
Hawaii	—	—	—	—	—	—
Idaho	90.8	62.3	11.3	26.3	35.8	0.4
Illinois	1,458.5	60.7	4.3	35.0	54.0	1.2
Indiana	604.4	65.6	5.6	28.9	40.6	0.7
Iowa	176.1	59.2	14.9	25.9	34.9	0.4
Kansas	192.2	56.0	10.7	33.3	50.0	0.6
Kentucky	632.0	63.6	7.3	29.0	40.9	1.0
Louisiana	284.9	54.7	6.9	38.4	62.4	0.6
Maine	159.5	62.6	11.6	25.8	34.7	0.6
Maryland	1,322.2	56.2	10.5	33.3	50.0	2.0
Massachusetts	4,202.1	71.6	1.6	26.8	36.6	3.7
Michigan	1,563.2	57.6	4.4	38.1	61.4	1.2
Minnesota	313.4	65.4	14.3	20.3	25.4	0.2
Mississippi	—	—	—	—	—	—
Missouri	664.1	65.4	6.1	28.5	39.9	0.9
Montana	32.7	53.8	20.2	26.1	35.2	0.2
Nebraska	80.9	53.1	22.7	24.1	31.8	0.3
Nevada	—	—	—	—	—	—
New Hampshire	211.2	61.5	7.0	31.4	45.8	1.3
New Jersey	1,959.0	57.8	3.8	38.3	62.2	1.6
New Mexico	128.6	60.4	13.0	26.6	36.2	0.3
New York	5,071.1	60.4	4.3	35.3	54.6	1.5
North Carolina	—	—	—	—	—	—
North Dakota	—	—	—	—	—	—
Ohio	2,078.3	58.1	14.3	27.6	38.1	1.1
Oklahoma	—	—	—	—	—	—
Oregon	1,523.6	72.7	16.9	10.5	11.7	0.8
Pennsylvania	1,958.9	57.4	2.4	40.1	67.1	1.6
Rhode Island	1,119.9	78.7	0.6	20.7	26.1	4.0
South Carolina	673.2	61.8	5.5	32.8	48.7	1.1
South Dakota	136.0	11.7	4.6	83.8	515.9	3.8
Tennessee	—	—	—	—	—	—
Texas	3,130.7	58.9	10.1	30.9	44.8	1.2
Utah	—	—	—	—	—	—
Vermont	74.8	68.7	10.2	21.1	26.8	0.4

Table 18.3

(continued)

State	Ticket Sales, Excluding Commissions (millions)	Percentage of Sales to:				Net Lottery Revenue as a Percentage of Total State Revenue
		Prizes	Administration	Net Revenue	Implicit Tax Rates	
Virginia	$1,137.4	61.1	10.3	28.6	40.0	1.2
Washington	460.4	64.7	14.1	21.2	26.9	0.3
West Virginia	556.3	20.6	5.0	74.4	291.2	4.2
Wisconsin	404.5	61.4	8.3	30.3	43.5	0.5
Wyoming	—	—	—	—	—	—

[a]Net revenue as a percentage of prizes plus administration costs.

SOURCE: U.S. Census Bureau, *State Government Finances 2003*, February 2005.

a choice of possibilities (usually 40–60 different numbers). The winning number is selected randomly weekly or semiweekly, and if no winner is selected in one period, the money pool rolls over into the next game period. Most recently, some states have begun offering video lottery games, where individuals can play various lottery-type games on electronic machines. According to John Mikesell and Kurt Zorn (1986), the numbers games historically provided the largest percentage of sales on average and in most states, with the lotto games second in significance, but growing in importance. States typically use a particular game only for a limited period and then switch to a "different" game, even though it may be of the same generic type. The state lottery bureaus or commissions usually contract with one of only a few private firms that design the different state games. The state lottery industry even has its own trade magazine, *Public Gaming International.*

Although the lottery games differ somewhat financially, an overall picture of the economics of state lottery operations is shown by the data in Table 18.3. For these 38 states, the lottery pays out $.60 in prizes for each $1 of sales, on average, with another $.07 going for administration costs. This understates the size of operation costs because the Census reports lottery sales net of sales commissions. Private retailers typically sell lottery tickets and are allowed to retain a percentage, often 5–8 percent, as compensation. If commissions are included, then, operation costs are closer to $.10 per $1 of sales, with the shares for prizes and state revenue correspondingly lower. Understanding this complication, the Census data show that about $.33 of every lottery-sale dollar ends up as revenue for the state government, on average.[14]

State monopoly pricing of lotteries is economically equivalent to state taxation of lotteries. The implicit tax rate embodied in lottery prices is the ratio of the

---

[14]In contrast to the lottery, bettors at a thoroughbred race track get back $.80 to $.85 in winnings per $1 bet. The remainder goes to the track (usually private) and to state taxes. At a Las Vegas or Atlantic City casino, the "house cut" is perhaps only 5 to 10 percent.

revenue share per $1 of sales to the sum of the prize and cost shares. For these 38 states, the average lottery tax rate is about 49 percent. In other words, only $.67 of each sale dollar is used to operate the lottery and pay out prizes, but the ticket price is $1, about 49 percent greater.[15]

Why states have chosen to levy such high implicit tax rates (high prices) on lottery tickets is not clear. States clearly levy higher tax rates on lotteries than cigarettes, alcoholic beverages, hotel/motel stays, gasoline, and other forms of gambling, not to mention traditional consumer goods. One possibility is that these high tax rates create small efficient costs if demand is very price inelastic, as explained in Chapter 15. However, it seems unlikely that the demand for lotteries is that much less elastic than the demand for other forms of gambling or commodities that may be addictive. Even if there are efficiency reasons for the high tax rates, there may be conflicting equity effects (as discussed later in this chapter). Of course, it may just be that it has been politically easier to collect these lottery taxes, perhaps because consumers are not aware of the rates.

Revenue significance varies substantially among these states with lotteries. The six state lotteries with the largest sales—in New York, Massachusetts, Florida, California, Georgia, and Ohio—account for more than 45 percent of total national lottery sales. If the next five largest lotteries are added—from New Jersey, Pennsylvania, Michigan, Oregon, and Illinois—then 65 percent of total sales is represented. Obviously, the economic characteristics of these lotteries dominate the national average. As previously noted, however, the administrative cost share is substantially greater than average in several states with small or recently enacted lotteries. Prize shares are especially high in Rhode Island, Oregon, and Massachusetts; whereas prize shares are especially low in South Dakota, Delaware, and West Virginia.

Largely as a result of these higher administration costs and because of lower than average shares for prizes, the implicit tax rates on lotteries also vary substantially among the states. The highest tax rates are the 521 percent in Delaware (only $.14 to prizes and $.02 to administration), 516 percent in South Dakota (only $.12 per $1 goes to prizes and $.05 to administration), and 291 percent in West Virginia ($.21 to prizes and $.05 to administration). Implicit taxes are between 60 and 70 percent in six other states (Pennsylvania, Louisiana, New Jersey, Michigan, Florida, and California). In contrast, the lowest tax rates are 12 percent in Oregon ($.73 to prizes and $.17 to administration), 25 percent in Minnesota ($.65 to prizes and $.14 to administration), 26 percent in Rhode Island ($.79 to prizes and $.01 to administration), and 27 percent in Vermont ($.69 to prizes and $.10 to administration) and Washington ($.65 to prizes and $.14 to administration).

Finally, the state lottery provides 3 percent or more of state government revenue only in 5 states: Delaware (6.1 percent), West Virginia (4.2 percent), Rhode Island (4.0 percent), South Dakota (3.8 percent), and Massachusetts (3.7 percent). On the other end of the spectrum, the state lottery provides 0.5 percent or less of state revenue in 11 states.

---

[15]If a lottery ticket sold for $.67 and was taxed at a rate of 50 percent, the tax would be $.33, giving a total ticket cost of $1.00.

Although this analysis shows that on average about $.33 per dollar bet in lotteries becomes state revenue, this revenue gain is overestimated for at least two reasons. First, some of the money spent on lotteries would have been spent on other taxable activities (such as going to the movies) if there were no lottery, which also would have generated state revenue. Research by Mary Borg, Paul Mason, and Stephen Shapiro (1993) suggests that 15–20 percent of net lottery revenue is offset by loss of other state taxes as a result of decreases in consumer purchases. In addition, Daniel Gulley and Frank Scott (1989) report evidence showing that each additional dollar spent on lotteries reduces the amount spent betting on horse races, an activity that states also tax. Gulley and Scott estimate that each dollar spent on lotteries reduces attendance at racing tracks and reduces the amount bet at the track by $.18 per person. Thus, the decreased tax revenue from betting on horse races partly reduces the revenue the state gains from the lottery sale.

What are the economic gains from lotteries and what are the economic reasons for governments to provide lotteries? Although these two questions are often considered together, they are logically separate. The economic gain from providing lotteries is the same as the gain from providing any service, consumers get happiness or economic welfare from consuming the service, in this case, either because of the potential for winning, because of the entertainment value, or both. After all, why do consumers get pleasure from watching hockey games or going to the theater or anything else? Some do. If individuals voluntarily spend resources to consume those services, they must receive some pleasure. So providing lottery services does increase consumer welfare because consumers are willing to pay to have that service; however, this is not a reason why the government must or should provide lotteries. Private firms could provide this service just as easily—as private firms provide horse racing and casino gambling—with government taxation if revenue collection from those activities is desired. In fact, private firms as well as states have provided numbers games (one of the most common and largest types of state lottery games) in the past and continue to provide them, by all reports. Of course, the states argue that criminals run these private firms, but that is partly circular logic given that the state declared private numbers games illegal (although these firms may also be involved in other illegal activities).

Economic arguments for government-provided as opposed to private-provided lotteries could be that the state revenue can be collected at lower administration cost with government provision rather than taxation, that providing lotteries either creates or generates opportunities for other effects that require regulation, and that lotteries can be more efficiently regulated by state provision. The case for the first argument seems weak; Mikesell and Zorn (1986) have noted that the administrative cost of broad-based state taxes is usually estimated to be less than 5 percent of tax revenue collected, which is less than the corresponding cost ratio for lotteries. The common version of the second argument regarding lotteries is that gambling can be complementary with other types of criminal activity, as a source of cash, as a way of transferring funds gained illicitly to legal uses, or as a means of fraud or extortion. By the government providing the gambling service, these potential secondary activities presumably can be limited. This argument is problematic, at best, because it presumes that legal state-provided gambling reduces demand for illegal private gambling; but if state gambling and the attendant advertising increases the overall demand for gambling, the opposite is possible.

One economic fact about state government revenue generated by lotteries, whether from government production of lotteries or taxation of private lotteries, is that the revenue comes disproportionately from lower-income households. A number of studies based on data from different sources and states shows uniformly that low-income households spend a larger fraction of their income on lotteries than do high-income households, so that state lotteries are a regressive source of revenue. These results are summarized in Rubinstein and Scafidi (2002) and Oster (2004). One analysis based on a nationwide survey of gambling behavior (Suits, 1977) showed that in 1974, about 25 percent of state lottery revenue came from families with incomes below $10,000, although those families represented only about 11 percent of total income in 1974. By some measures, lottery revenues appear to be twice as regressive as state sales taxes.

Such results are supported by subsequent studies. Charles Clotfelter and Phillip Cook (1987) collected data on lottery expenditures by players in California, Maryland, and Massachusetts for a variety of current games, including instant games, numbers games, and lotto. The authors (1987, p. 544) conclude that "The evidence presented here demonstrates that the incidence of the implicit tax on lottery products in the 1980s is decidedly regressive, as it was in the 1970s." The regressivity of lottery revenue is so dominant that a regressive pattern emerges even when considering the benefits of education that is financed by the lottery. Mary Borg and Paul Mason (1988) estimated the **budget incidence** of the lottery in Illinois, which is earmarked to education, and conclude that "deducting the benefits of education . . . received by the average lottery playing household in Illinois from their lottery ticket expenditures reduces the regressivity [of the tax] but falls far short of eliminating it" (1988, p. 75). Similarly, a budget incidence analysis of the Georgia lottery and HOPE scholarships, which it funds, by Rubinstein and Scafidi (2002, p. 236) finds ". . . a highly regressive pattern of net benefits. Lower income households (those reporting under $25,000 annual income) spend more on the lottery than they receive in benefits, while higher income households (those reporting over $50,000 in annual income) receive a positive net benefit."

Clotfelter and Cook also report that purchase of lottery products tends to be concentrated in a relatively small sector of the population, even within income classes, and that lottery products tend to be consumed relatively more by blacks, males, and individuals with less education. Clotfelter and Cook (1990b) report that although 60 percent of adults in a lottery state may play at least once a year, the top 20 percent of lottery players (about 12 percent of the population) account for about two-thirds of the money spent on lotteries. Lottery play, therefore, and the state revenue that results from that play depends mostly on the behavior of this group of heavy players. State lotto games with exceptionally large jackpots may represent one exception to this idea of concentrated lottery purchasing. Oster (2004) presents evidence that the regressivity of the multistate *Powerball* lotto game decreases as the jackpot size increases, essentially because the large jackpots attract higher-income individuals who are usually not lotto players. In fact, Oster suggests that at *Powerball* jackpots around $800 million, the incidence of that lotto game might become progressive. However, the largest *Powerball* jackpots to date have been in the neighborhood of $300 million.

Increased state reliance on lotteries for revenue is equivalent, in an equity sense, to increased state taxation of any good that is consumed relatively more heavily by lower-income households. The curious difference about lotteries, of course, is that states promote and encourage consumption of this service so that additional revenue can be generated. Through advertising, expanding distribution networks, and lottery product packaging, state lottery agencies try both to attract new players and to increase sales to regular players. Would the public be equally tolerant of *state government* advertising to encourage cigarette smoking or liquor consumption so that state excise taxes would generate more revenue? As Daniel Suits argued in 1975 regarding state-run gambling, "the government has become a pusher. And they're not pushing fire or police protection—only dreams" (*Business Week* 1975, p. 68). Clotfelter and Cook (1990a) have suggested that lotteries might be run instead either to favor lottery players (the "Consumer Lottery" with much higher payout rates than currently) or to recognize the social costs of gambling (the "Sumptuary Lottery" without the current promotional advertising). Favoring the Sumptuary Lottery, the authors argue that some people's interest in betting could be accommodated without encouraging or expanding that interest *as government policy*.

Casinos

Casino gambling, including nonbanking (poker) and banking (blackjack) card games, slot machines, roulette, and electronic games such as video poker, originally followed the state monopoly model. Illegal in most places (or allowed only in a very limited way for special charity "Las Vegas Nights"), casino gambling was monopolized first in Nevada, followed by Atlantic City. Although the government did not own the casinos (unlike the lottery) and several licensed private firms were at each location, the governments that regulated the activity and received a share of the take essentially had monopoly power.

This situation changed dramatically starting in the late 1980s. In a 1987 decision involving California and the Cabazon Band of Indians, the U.S. Supreme Court recognized the right of Native Americans to offer on their land any form of gambling legal in that state. The Indian Gaming and Regulatory Act, passed by Congress in 1988, set rules and procedures to govern such gambling. Under that law, tribes could operate traditional Indian games and such games as bingo and poker (Class II games) if legal in the state. In addition, Indian casinos could offer such games as video poker, slot machines, blackjack, roulette, baccarat, and so on (Class III games), if such games were used at all in a state (including by charities), and the state and tribe entered into a compact negotiated in good faith. Following a series of court cases involving disputes between states and tribes, a large number of Indian casinos now operate (or are approved) in 30 states. Most of these casinos offer the full range of Class III games.

While the Indian Gaming Act was being implemented, several states along the Mississippi River followed Iowa's lead in 1991 in approving casino gambling on riverboats. The initial idea was to allow very limited gambling in a strictly regulated fashion on a few boats. Apparently, state and local officials believed that some of the potential negative effects of casinos could be controlled if the activity was only on riverboats. This type of activity proved very popular, however, so that now more than 20 riverboat casinos operate in 6 states offering, in many cases, a full range of casino games.

Finally, as a tourism and economic development move, a number of cities (including Detroit and New Orleans) among 12 states have joined Las Vegas and Atlantic City in licensing major private, commercial casinos.

A demand for gambling activities has driven this expansion. Total expenditures on legal gambling are estimated at approximately $79 billion in 2003 (Kearney, 2005). Expenditures on illegal sports betting are further estimated to fall between $80 and $380 billion annually. Both have been increasing at a fast pace. Kearney (2005) reports gambling expenditure or revenue for 2003 as nearly $29 billion in private, commercial casinos (including riverboats and $17 billion at Indian casinos). Casino gambling is estimated to generate almost $3 billion in public revenue annually. However, one should distinguish the economic effects of casino expansion from the fiscal effects.

Casino gambling is different from state lotteries in two important ways. First and most obviously, states generally have not directly operated the casinos as they have lotteries, and in some cases, the states do not even derive tax revenue from casino gambling. States do tax riverboat and private casino gambling at rates that vary from about 6 to 35 percent. However, states do not necessarily receive revenue from some Indian casinos. States cannot tax tribal businesses, according to federal law. As a result of agreements between the tribes operating casinos and state governments in five states (California, Connecticut, Michigan, New Mexico, and Wisconsin), the tribes make annual payments to the states for the rights to operate their casinos with limited competition. Those payments amounted to about $760 million in 2003, which translates to an effective tax rate of less then 5 percent. Thus, effective state tax rates on casino gambling are lower than the implicit tax rates on state-owned and state-operated lotteries (about 49 percent).

Secondly, besides ownership, casinos generally do not enjoy the same degree of monopoly power as state lotteries. Although numerous states, including neighboring ones, operate lotteries, purchasing lottery tickets through the mail is not allowed so state governments essentially operate monopoly lotteries (except for tourists or those who live near state boundaries). As casinos have increased in number, however, the monopoly once enjoyed by Las Vegas (and then Atlantic City) has eroded. Individuals commonly cross state boundaries to visit casinos, and consumers have multiple choices in some states and regions of the country. If the number of casinos continues to grow, the monopoly power (and revenue potential) of each will decline. In fact, if the original idea of state-sponsored casinos was to attract business and state tax revenue from nonresidents, the proliferation of casinos in most states makes it less likely that a casino will serve nonresidents. Rather, each casino mostly will register business from residents.

Also, the expansion of all forms of gambling has increased competition and reduced the monopoly power of each gambling form. Tosun and Skidmore (2004) report that competition among state lotteries across state borders is important.

They report that "Lottery and lottery game adoptions in West Virginia's contiguous states have had statistically and economically significant negative effects on West Virginia border county lottery sales" (p. 176). Elliot and Navin (2002) report evidence that both casino and parimutuel betting are substitutes for state lotteries, with increases in either leading to reductions in state lottery sales. In addition to offering alternative forms of gambling, many casinos offer lotteries or lottery-type games, such as video poker or keno. In some cases, these are the exact games that state lotteries are moving to adopt. This may be one reason a number of states resisted the creation of Indian casinos by way of changes in state law and challenges in court. The growth of spending and revenue from state lotteries declined substantially in recent years so that lotteries already provide a smaller fraction of state revenue than in the mid-1980s.

Finally, some states and localities have been concerned about substitution between expenditures on gambling activity and purchases of other consumer goods. If increased expenditure on gambling is offset by reduced expenditure on other commodities whose sales are taxable, then the actual, net increase in government revenue from gambling is less than it appears. Research by Anders, Siegel, and Yacoub (1998) and by Popp and Stehwien (2002) suggest that such substitution may occur, causing decreases in state–local income or sales tax revenue as a result of new Indian casinos. This is another reason to be cautious about the state–local revenue potential from gambling.

Application 18.3

BEATING THE ODDS: BETTING SYNDICATES

In a one state lotto game, players pick a six-number sequence using the numbers between 1 and 40 once (for instance, 6-9-24-26-27-32) and buy a $1 ticket for that number. Such a game has about 3.5 million possible number combinations, so a player or group of players could guarantee winning by purchasing a ticket for each of the possible combinations (which costs about $3.5 million). Would this ever make sense? Interestingly, the answer may be yes, because lotto is a parimutuel game with the pot growing until someone wins. If there was no winner in such a lotto game for several weeks, the prize pool might grow to $10 or $15 million. If someone or some group spent $3.5 million on all ticket

combinations, a win is guaranteed. The possibility of winning less than $3.5 million arises only if there are a sufficient number of multiple winners. For instance, if the pot is $15 million, there would have to be more than four winners for the group betting all combinations to lose.

Gary Cohn (1986) described just such a bet on a series of jai alai games at a Miami, Florida fronton (arena). Four individuals spent $524,288 to bet every possible combination of winners in six jai alai games involving eight players each. Their guaranteed winning bets paid $752,778, so the four pocketed a total of more than $228,000 for a night's work and investment of over half

Application 18.3 — Beating the Odds: Betting Syndicates

a million dollars. The four were gambling because it was possible that another bettor could also have picked the winning combination, requiring that the winnings be split. By betting all the combinations, however, the four had clearly substantially increased their odds of winning.

The same *Wall Street Journal* story reported that a number of private betting syndicates had been formed around the country to follow this betting strategy for horse and dog racing as well as jai alai. The syndicates would typically bet exclusively on so-called exotic wagers, those requiring selection of a series of winners in order of finish, which often have a very high payoff. For instance, in a "pick-six" bet, which is the one used by the jai alai syndicate noted in the preceding paragraph and is also widely used for racing, the object is to pick the winners of six consecutive events. Syndicate betting is even more attractive if the betting pool rolls over to the next game or day should there be no winner, like in lotto and many exotic race games. In that case, the players can know ahead of time the

maximum amount to be won by covering the board.

The potential effects of betting syndicates are unclear. On the one hand, it is possible that smaller regular bettors may be discouraged by the large syndicates, which may be perceived as unfair competition. On the other hand, the large amounts of wagering required by syndicate bets may increase interest and excitement in the game and stimulate more small bets. It is interesting, however, that a number of state lotto games were changed in 1985 and 1986 to picking a series of six numbers from the set of 1 to 44 (rather than 40). That seemingly insignificant change increased the number of possible combinations from about 3.5 million to about 7 million, greatly reducing the opportunity for a winning syndicate bet on state lotto. Currently, many state lotto games involve picking six numbers from even larger sets of numbers—47 or 52 are common. The large multistate lotteries—such as *Powerball* and *Megamillions*—typically pick at least five of the six winning numbers from sets of 52 or 53 options.

Application 18.4

METOO-1: PERSONALIZED AND SPECIALTY LICENSE PLATES

Although state–local governments are the exclusive providers of many services, they have generally used their monopoly power to set high prices to generate surplus revenue only in cases where the government can justify a strong regulatory role, such as those already described in this chapter. One other similar case is the sale of both personalized

and specialty (or affinity) license plates. Personalized license plates, which have characters selected by the buyer to indicate a specific message, are sold by all states for an additional fee beyond that for regular automobile registration. Most commonly, the additional fee is a fixed amount charged annually, although some states charge both

Application 18.4 — METOO-1: Personalized and Specialty License Plates

an initial fee and a lower renewal fee for subsequent years (which may even be zero).

Specialty or affinity license plates provide buyers the opportunity to purchase plates with special backgrounds recognizing an institution (such as colleges or universities) or cause (Save the Bay, and so on) or experience (military service, and so on). Specialty plates are sold by all but one state (Louisiana). States charge an additional fee for the specialty plates, with the revenue shared in a variety of ways between the state government and the recognized organization or cause. According to 1999 data compiled by the Association of Motor Vehicle Administrators and reported by NCSL, the number of specialty plates available averaged more than 80 per state! In most instances, individuals also can choose to personalize a specialty plate, effectively increasing the plate combinations available in any state.

One study by Erik Craft (2002) shows that the fees charged for personalized plates vary from $7.50 to $50 annualized over a four-year period, with initial charges averaging about $30 and renewal fees about $20 (above that charged by the state for automobile registration generally). According to Craft, only about 3.5 percent of all automobile plates were personalized in 1997, substantially greater than the 2 percent reported by Alper, *et al.* (1987) for 1983. Among the 37 states in the 1997 data set, the share of personalized plates in 1997 was substantially greater than average in five states—Virginia (9.8 percent), Nevada (9.0 percent), Montana (8.7 percent), Maine (8.0 percent), and Vermont (8.0 percent). Using similar but less specific data, Craft estimated that about 5 percent of all license plates in 1997 were specialty or affinity plates.

Specialty plates were a relatively new phenomenon in 1987; casual observation suggests that the use of specialty or affinity plates has proliferated in recent years. At this writing, the share is much greater than 5 percent.

Economic analysis can help explain just what factors influence people to buy personalized or specialty plates and thus why personalized-plate usage differs among different states' residents. Economic studies by Alper and his colleagues, by Jeff Biddle (1991), and by Craft show that the use of personalized plates is negatively related to price and positively related to income, as economists expect. Aggressive marketing also seems to increase demand. This research also shows that the demand for personalized plates is price elastic, at least in a number of states. When combined with information about the marginal cost of the plates (expected to be between $2 and $10, depending on whether it is an initial or renewal sale), the estimated demand curves suggest that some states are charging less than profit-maximizing prices for personalized plates, while a few states charge too much. Craft (2002, p. 143) reports that 10 of the 37 states in his sample "...charge such a high price for personalized license plates that net revenues would rise by lowering the fees." Similarly, the demand results reported by Craft suggest that prices may be substantially less than revenue-maximizing in 15 states. Craft's results show revenue-maximizing (four-year annualized) prices that vary among states from about $20 to $65. Biddle suggests that the profit-maximizing price may average about $40 if fixed annual charges are used, although the figure varies by state. Harrington and

Application 18.4 — METOO-1: Personalized and Specialty License Plates

Krynski (1989) estimate that profit-maximizing prices vary from about $44 to $63.

Biddle also reports that the demand for personalized plates differs in at least one important way from the standard economic concept of demand. He notes that typically sales of personalized plates increase substantially in the years immediately following the start of a program, which are not explained by changes in prices or income. Apparently, the purchase of personalized plates by some individuals causes an increase in demand by others. Biddle offers two possible explanations for this behavior: The use of the plates by some is a type of advertising, conveying information about the existence of the program to individuals who are not aware of it, or the use of personalized plates by some people makes them more attractive to others who also want to be part of the fad, called the *bandwagon effect*. In fact, Biddle's research shows that sales of personalized plates in one year are positively related to sales in the prior year, after accounting for other demand factors. One important

implication of Biddle's observation, regardless of which of the two possible explanations cause it, is that it may be attractive for states to maintain relatively low prices for personalized plates in the early years of the program if they want to generate as much state revenue as possible. The initial lower prices are expected to attract consumers whose use of the plates would then attract even more consumers in subsequent years.

Craft also reports that the use of specialty or affinity plates seems to increase the use of personalized plates. This suggests either that personalized and specialty license plates are complementary consumer goods for individuals, or that the purchase of a specialty or affinity plate lowers the cost to an individual of also purchasing a personalized plate. This in turn implies that the optimal prices for either special service need to be lower than one would otherwise expect. States might be able to generate even more revenue from selling personalized license plates if they also can sell more specialty plates.

SUMMARY

State–local governments may generate revenue by becoming the monopoly producer of a good or service and then charging prices that are greater than costs for that good or service. Three common examples of this behavior are operating government-owned utilities, state government alcoholic beverage stores, and state lotteries or other forms of gambling.

Monopoly production is efficient when there are increasing returns to scale—that is, average cost decreasing as output rises—because goods or services obviously can be produced at lower unit cost by a single firm than by a set of smaller, competing firms. The existence of increasing returns does not require government monopoly, however. Instead, government may grant monopoly rights to a private producer subject to government regulation or taxation.

The political fact is that these monopolies often are effective ways for states and localities to generate revenue, although raising revenue is not the only reason for government monopoly. As long as the government charges a price above average cost, the economic profits beyond the normal rate of return on investment represent potential government revenue.

Government revenue generated from government monopoly prices above average cost is implicitly a tax because the same good or service could be provided by the government at lower prices. Although these two sources may be classified differently—one as revenue from government production and the other as revenue from a tax—and have different political implications; economically, this is a distinction without a difference. The monopoly profits should be evaluated by the same economic criteria applied to all revenue sources—equity, efficiency, and administration cost.

States follow one of two general methods for regulating the sale of alcoholic beverages. Under the control method used by 18 states, the state government has a monopoly on at least the wholesale distribution of distilled liquor. In some cases, the state monopoly also extends to beer and/or wine or to retail sales. The open method used by the other states involves wholesale and retail sale of alcoholic beverages by private firms, which are licensed by the state government and sometimes constrained by sales rules. These states levy excise taxes on the sale of alcoholic beverages, typically collected at the wholesale level.

In 2003, 38 states and the District of Columbia operated lotteries as state government monopolies (with potential competing private lotteries made illegal by the states). These lotteries generated an average of 1.1 percent of the states' general revenue. These lotteries pay out, on average, $.60 in prizes for each $1 of sales, with another $.07 going for administration costs, so that about $.33 of every lottery-sale dollar ends up as revenue for the state government.

One economic fact about state government revenue generated by lotteries, whether from government production of lotteries or taxation of private lotteries, is that the revenue comes disproportionately from lower-income households. By some measures, lottery revenues appear to be twice as regressive as state sales taxes. Lottery sales also are concentrated, with the top 20 percent of players accounting for almost two-thirds of the total revenue.

Casino gambling initially followed the monopoly model also, with the activity limited to just a few states, although those states licensed private firms to run the casinos and received tax revenue in return. As casinos have proliferated, however, on Indian land, on river boats, and with approval in new states, state monopoly power for casino gambling as well as other forms of gambling is being reduced. Gambling of at least some type is now available in all but two states. Increasingly, states receive smaller (and sometimes zero) net revenue benefits from the expansion of gambling activities.

DISCUSSION QUESTIONS

1. Some 38 states now operate state lotteries. In most of those states, the lottery was approved by a majority vote of the residents in a statewide election. States operate lotteries as a revenue source to finance state services. A number

of studies also show that the state revenue generated by lotteries comes disproportionately from lower-income people—in other words, the lottery is a regressive revenue source. Do you think that concern about the incidence of lottery revenue is irrelevant because it was approved by the voters? If you were someone who never (or seldom) intends to buy lottery tickets (not because you are morally opposed to gambling, but because you simply do not choose to gamble in this way), how would you have voted on the lottery? What would you consider in making that decision?

2. It is sometimes argued that state revenue generated by lotteries is different from tax revenue because people choose to buy lottery tickets. Compare three state-revenue sources—cigarette excise taxes, personal income taxes, and state lotteries—in terms of the usual economic criteria of economic efficiency, equity, and administrative cost. Do all three arise from voluntary acts of taxpayers and does that matter for the economic analysis?

3. States can generate revenue either by becoming the sole producer of a good or service and retaining the monopoly profits as revenue or by taxing goods or services provided by private competitive firms. One such case is the choice between a state monopoly for liquor sales and state taxation of private sellers. Another is the different treatment of lotteries and horse racing. Can you think of any reasons why states decided not to make lotteries legal and tax the private firms, or why states generally decided against state-owned and -operated race tracks?

4. Suppose the demand for personalized license plates and the marginal cost of production in a state is as shown earlier in Figure 18.1. If all the profits go to the government and the state wants to maximize revenue, what price should the state charge for the plates, and how many will be sold? Suppose the state actually sets a price 10 percent lower than is profit-maximizing. Show graphically how much profits are reduced. Does the incorrect pricing cost the state very much? What might the state gain by setting the price a bit lower than the immediate profit-maximizing level?

SELECTED READINGS

Clotfelter, Charles T. and Phillip J. Cook. *Selling Hope, State Lotteries in America*. Cambridge, Massachusetts: Harvard University Press, 1989.

Clotfelter, Charles T. and Phillip J. Cook. "On the Economics of State Lotteries." *Journal of Economic Perspectives*, 4 (Fall 1990): 105–119.

Kearney, Melissa Schettini. "The Economic Losers and Winners of Legalized Gambling." *National Tax Journal*, 57 (June 2005): 281–302.

Martin, Lawrence. "Miscellaneous Taxes in Michigan: Sin, Death, and Recreation." In C. Ballard, et. al., editors, *Michigan at the Millennium*. East Lansing: Michigan State University Press, 2003, 667–680.

Suits, Daniel B. "Gambling Taxes: Regressivity and Revenue Potential." *National Tax Journal* 30 (March 1977): 19–35.

APPLICATIONS AND POLICY ANALYSIS

WHILE THE EARLIER PARTS OF THIS BOOK FOCUS ON DETAILED ANALYSIS AND EXPLANATION OF SPECIFIC ASPECTS OF STATE AND LOCAL GOVERNMENT EXPENDITURE, REVENUE, AND ORGANIZATION, CHAPTERS 19–22 FOCUS ON SPECIFIC GOVERNMENT RESPONSIBILITIES THAT ARE OF SUBSTANTIAL POLICY INTEREST. The four issues selected are provision of education, transportation, health and welfare services, and the relationship between state and local fiscal policies and economic activity in the jurisdiction. Although this is clearly not an exhaustive list of important fiscal policy issues among subnational governments, these four represent the largest amounts of state–local expenditure and have continued over a long period to be among the most controversial and topical fiscal policy issues. All also involve substantial economic aspects that can be analyzed with the information and tools presented in the book. The discussion in these final four chapters draws on the theory and evidence discussed in previous chapters and tends to be less conclusive, reporting what is known about these complex policy questions as well as factual matters that are as yet unresolved.

Spending for education, transportation, and health and welfare services together accounts for almost 65 percent of state–local general expenditure. Moreover, these are perhaps the most apparent state–local services, the ones that directly affect the greatest number of people on a day-to-day basis and can be most controversial. For all three, the discussion in these chapters is intended to report both how those services currently are financed and produced as well as what the expected effects of proposed changes in production and finance may be.

The last chapter does not involve specific services or expenditures, but rather focuses on the overall economic and fiscal effects of individual state and local government fiscal behavior. Although economic conditions in a jurisdiction are different and separate from fiscal conditions of the government for that jurisdiction, it is important to consider the relationship between economic and fiscal conditions. That states compete for economic activity is obvious; whether that competition is effective in increasing welfare is not.

CHAPTER 19

EDUCATION

An Act

To close the achievement gap with accountability, flexibility, and choice, so that no child is left behind. . . . Each State plan shall demonstrate that the State has adopted challenging academic content standards and challenging student academic achievement standards . . . Each State plan shall demonstrate that the State educational agency, in consultation with local educational agencies, has implemented a set of high-quality, yearly student academic assessments . . .[1]

—NO CHILD LEFT BEHIND ACT OF 2001

HEADLINES

"A STATE JUDGE RULED LAST NIGHT THAT AN ADDITIONAL $5.6 BILLION MUST BE SPENT ON [NEW YORK CITY'S] PUBLIC SCHOOLCHILDREN EVERY YEAR TO ENSURE THEM THE OPPORTUNITY FOR A SOUND BASIC EDUCATION THAT THEY ARE GUARANTEED UNDER THE STATE CONSTITUTION.

BEYOND THAT, ANOTHER $9.2 BILLION MUST BE SPENT OVER THE NEXT FIVE YEARS TO SHRINK CLASS SIZES, RELIEVE OVERCROWDING, AND PROVIDE THE CITY'S 1.1 MILLION STUDENTS WITH ENOUGH LABORATORIES, LIBRARIES, AND OTHER PLACES IN WHICH TO LEARN.

THE DECISION IS A LANDMARK IN ONE OF THE NATION'S BIGGEST SCHOOL-FINANCE CASES. . . . THOUGH VIRTUALLY EVERY STATE IN THE NATION HAS BEEN EMBROILED IN LAWSUITS OVER SCHOOL SPENDING, THE NEW YORK SUIT HAS BEEN MORE CLOSELY WATCHED, IN PART BECAUSE OF THE NUMBER OF STUDENTS AND THE DOLLAR FIGURES AT STAKE.[2]"

---

[1]U.S. Department of Education. Public Law print of PL 197-110, the *No Child Left Behind Act of 2001,* http://www.ed.gov/policy/elsec/leg/esea02/index.html.

[2]Winter, Greg. "Judge Orders Billions in Aid to City Schools." *The New York Times,* http://nytimes.com, February 15, 2005.

Table 19.1

Overview Of Public Elementary and Secondary Education, Various Years

Year	Spending (billion $)	Pupils[a] (thousands)	Spending as a Percentage of GDP	Spending per Pupil[b] (current $)	Spending per Pupil (2001–2002$)[b]	Teachers (thousands)	Pupil– Teacher Ratio
2002	$430.6	47,688	4.3%	$8,203	$8,203	2,998	16:1
2000	381.8	46,857	4.1	7,394	7,782	2,911	17:1
1995	279.0	44,111	4.0	5,989	7,095	2,552	18:1
1990	212.8	40,543	3.9	4,980	6,988	2,357	17:1
1985	137.0	39,208	3.5	3,470	5,847	2,168	18:1
1980	96.0	41,651	3.7	2,272	5,214	2,162	19:1
1970	40.7	45,550	4.1	816	3,849	2,055	22:1
1960	15.6	35,182	3.1	375	2,275	1,408	26:1

[a]Total enrollment in fall of that school year.

[b]Current expenditures per pupil in average daily attendance.

SOURCE: U.S. Department of Education. *Digest of Education Statistics*, 2003, 2004.

Education is, by almost any measure, the primary service provided by state–local governments in the United States. You have already learned that expenditures on elementary and secondary education represent the single largest category of state–local government spending, equal to nearly a quarter of aggregate subnational government direct general expenditure in 2003. Elementary and secondary education is an even larger fraction of local government spending, nearly 41 percent in 2003. This is five times as great as local spending for police and fire protection and about nine times as great as local spending on roads. Public elementary and secondary education teachers represent about 15 percent of total state–local employees and about 25 percent of local government employees.

In the 2001–2002 academic year, expenditures for public elementary and secondary schools were nearly $431 billion, equal to about 4.3 percent of GNP and $8,203 per student in average daily attendance at those schools, as shown in Table 19.1. Public-school expenditures have increased substantially over this period—by more than 100 percent just since 1990—but generally remained between 3.5 and 4.0 percent of GDP during this time. Expenditures per pupil also have increased substantially over the past 40 years, even in real terms (after adjustment for inflation). In fact, real expenditures per pupil by public elementary and secondary schools were about three and one-half times as great in 2002 than in 1960 (see Figure 19.1).

In Fall of 2001, 47.7 million students were enrolled in these public schools. Public-school enrollment generally increased in the 1950s and 1960s—peaking in elementary schools in the late 1960s and in secondary schools in the mid-1970s, as shown in Figure 19.2. After that time, public- (and private-) school enrollment decreased, largely because of demographic factors, until the mid-1980s. Elementary school enrollment began to increase again in 1985 and secondary school enrollment increased starting in 1991. Even more importantly, the fraction of the

Figure 19.1

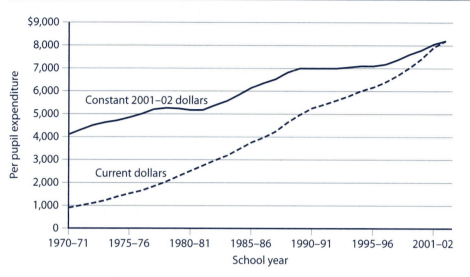

SOURCE: U.S. Department of Education. *Digest of Education Statistics,* 2004.

Current expendi-
ture per pupil in
average daily
attendance in
public elementary
and secondary
schools:
1970–1971 to
2001–2002

Figure 19.2

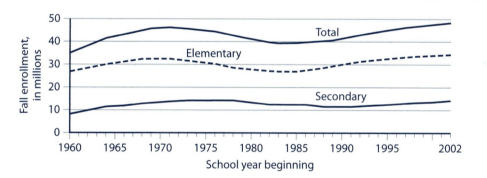

Enrollment,
number of
teachers, and
pupil/teacher ratio
in public schools:
1960–1961 to
2002–2003

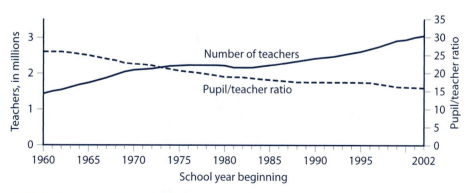

SOURCE: U.S. Department of Education. *Digest of Education Statistics,* 2004.

Table 19.2

Governmental Organization of Public Schools

Year	Number of School Districts[a]	Percent of Independent Districts[a]	Number of Public Elementary Schools	Number of Public Secondary Schools
2001	15,014	90.0%	65,228	22,180
2000	15,178	90.4	64,601	21,994
1995	15,834	91.1	60,808	20,904
1990[b]	15,367	90.8	59,015	21,135
1985	15,747	90.6	58,827	23,916
1980	15,912	91.7	59,326	22,619
1970	17,995	91.5	65,800	25,352
1960	40,520	93.7	91,853	25,784

[a]For the Census of Governments years: 1962, 1972, 1977, 1982, 1987, 1992, 1997, 2002.

[b]Data since 1990 are not strictly comparable to earlier years; different survey coverage.

SOURCES: U.S. Department of Education, *Digest of Education Statistics,* various years; U.S. Bureau of the Census, *Governmental Organization*, various years.

population aged five and under began to rise in 1988, suggesting that the number of students enrolled in elementary schools would continue to rise. Importantly, total expenditures by these schools, per-pupil expenditures, and even real per-pupil expenditures continued to increase in the 1970 to 1985 period when school enrollment was declining.

Salaries for teachers and other workers (administrators, librarians, counselors, maintenance persons, bus drivers) comprise the bulk of the expenditures by public schools. Recall from Chapter 7 that employee compensation represented about 63 percent of the noncapital direct expenditure of school districts in 2002. The number of public elementary and secondary school teachers also has increased over the past 40 years, including the period between 1970 and 1985 when the number of students was decreasing. As a consequence, the pupil-teacher ratio also decreased over the past 40 years, from nearly 26 students per teacher in 1960 to about 16 in 2002, a decrease of about 40 percent (see Figure 19.2).

Public-school services in the United States are provided both by independent school districts and by dependent school systems that are part of general-purpose local governments such as cities, townships, or counties. The number of school districts decreased substantially over the past 40 years and particularly between 1960 and 1970, as shown in Table 19.2.[3] Also, substantial decreases occurred in the number of public elementary schools until 1980. At the same time, the number of public secondary schools decreased slightly. Since 1995, the

---

[3]The decreases in the 1960s were a continuation of the trend operating at least since 1930. See U.S. Department of Education (May 1987).

number of secondary schools has been increasing again, reflecting growth in the number of students. Thus, the picture that emerges of the provision of public education since 1960 is one of increasing spending per pupil, largely because of decreases in class sizes and consolidation of both school districts and elementary schools within districts.

Budgetary data about education spending really do not capture the importance placed on public education and state–local government educational institutions. Education has been identified as an important means of altering the income distribution, generating social mobility, improving economic growth, increasing the "international competitiveness" of firms in the United States, and even improving the operation of the political public-choice system in a democratic society. A substantial economic literature shows that the perception of local schools is an important factor influencing locational choices of both individuals and firms, and through that, perception also influences property values in specific jurisdictions. And perhaps no local government fiscal or political issue generates as much or as intense public interest and comment as consideration of closing or consolidating local public schools or the results of educational assessment tests.

State and local governments continue to debate and experiment with three broad and important public policy issues regarding education: (1) How should public education be financed, including the relative role for state as opposed to local governments, the appropriate structure for state aid to local schools, and the relative roles for various taxes and charges; (2) How can education be produced most effectively and efficiently, including questions about school and class size, teacher compensation and training, and the role of technology; and (3) How to measure and assess educational results and enforce accountability, including issues about the appropriate structure and uses for student testing, the use of incentives or penalties for school systems, and the role of the federal as opposed to state–local government.

FINANCING EDUCATION

Current Practice

Nearly half of the revenue for financing public elementary and secondary schools in 2002 was provided by state governments, on average; local governments—the school districts—generated a slightly smaller share from their own sources at about 43 percent of public-school spending. The federal government has a relatively minor role in financing elementary and secondary education, providing only 8.4 percent of public school spending in 2002, and even private sources of spending (for private schools) represented only about 8 percent of total school spending in that year. This division of revenue sources for 2002–2003 is shown in Figure 19.3a. Importantly, local taxes (mostly property taxes) constitute the bulk of local revenue for schools and amount to 37 percent of total revenue. Also, fees and charges represent a very small fraction of revenue for public education. As shown

Figure 19.3

Distribution of
public elementary-
secondary
education revenue
and expenditure,
2002–2003

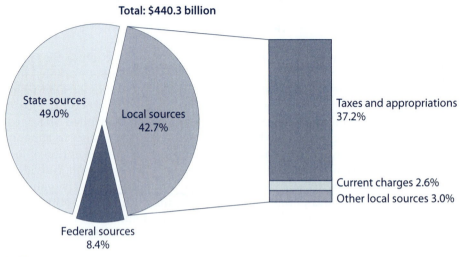

Total: $440.3 billion

State sources
49.0%

Local sources
42.7%

Taxes and appropriations
37.2%

Current charges 2.6%
Other local sources 3.0%

Federal sources
8.4%

(a) Revenue

Total: $453.6 billion

Other expenditure 2.9%

Current spending
86.0%

Instruction
52.0%

Support services
29.3%

Other 4.6%

Capital outlay 11.1%

(b) Expenditure

SOURCE: U.S. Census Bureau.

by the data in Table 19.3, the federal government's role has always been relatively
small, increasing a bit from 1960 to 1980 but relatively constant since.

The relative roles of state compared to local governments in financing education changed dramatically in the 1970s, with the two levels of government effectively switching positions, as shown in Figure 19.4. Prior to the 1970s, state
governments provided about 40 percent of school revenue, on average, and local

Table 19.3

Sources of Elementary and Secondary School Funding

	All Schools Percent Financed By				Public Schools Percent Financed By		
Year	Federal	State	Local	Private	Federal	State	Local
2001	6.8	46.2	40.1	7.0	7.3	49.7	43.1
2000	6.8	45.9	40.1	7.2	7.3	49.5	43.2
1995	6.2	43.2	42.8	7.7	6.8	46.8	46.4
1990	5.6	43.5	40.7	10.1	6.1	47.3	46.6
1985	6.1	44.7	40.7	8.6	6.6	48.9	44.4
1980	9.1	43.3	40.3	7.3	9.8	46.8	43.4
1970	7.4	34.6	47.5	10.5	7.2	40.9	51.8
1960	3.9	31.1	52.8	12.3	3.7	39.5	56.8

SOURCE: U.S. Department of Education, *Digest of Education Statistics*, various years.

Figure 19.4

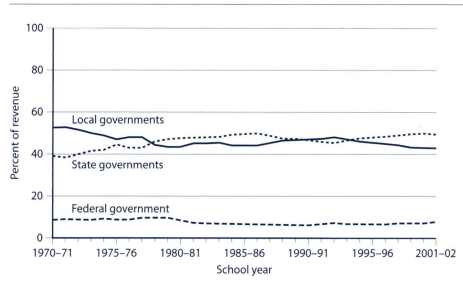

Sources of revenue for public elementary and secondary schools: 1970–1971 to 2001–2002

SOURCE: U.S. Department of Education. *Digest of Education Statistics,* 2004.

governments provided more than 50 percent. Responding to a number of forces, state governments attempted to equalize educational opportunity across districts in the 1970s, which resulted in increased state financial commitments and corresponding decreases in local financial responsibility. The increased state share was accomplished both by changing the magnitude and type of state grants to school districts, discussed in detail later. Because the primary local revenue source for schools (and only source in many states) is the property tax, the increased state

Table 19.4

State Government Percentage of Public Elementary-Secondary School Revenue, 2002–03

South Dakota	34.1	Massachusetts	41.4	Wyoming	50.9	North Carolina	60.3	New Mexico	72.6	Hawaii	90.1
Nebraska	34.5	Rhode Island	41.5	Oregon	51.3	West Virginia	60.9	Minnesota	73.7		
Illinois	35.6	Maine	42.1	Oklahoma.	51.4	Washington	62.4	Arkansas	74.2		
Connecticut	36.3	New Jersey	42.5	Mississippi	53.9	Michigan	63.2				
North Dakota	36.5	Colorado	43.4	Wisconsin	54.8	Delaware	65.8				
Pennsylvania	36.7	Ohio	44.1	Utah	55.9	Vermont	69.3				
Maryland	38.2	Tennessee	44.4	Alaska	57.0						
Texas	39.1	Florida	44.5	Alabama	57.1						
Virginia	39.6	Arizona	44.9	Indiana	57.1						
		Missouri	45.4	California	58.0						
		Montana	46.2	Idaho	59.0						
		New York	46.2	Kansas	59.0						
		Iowa	46.8	Kentucky	59.6						
		Louisiana	48.2	Nevada	59.9						
		South Carolina	48.4								
		Georgia	48.5								
		New Hampshire	49.0								

U.S. average = 49.0 %
Median states are New Hampshire (49.0) and Georgia (48.5)

SOURCE: U.S. Census Bureau. 2003 Public Elementary-Secondary Education Finance Data.

role in financing education reduced the demand for property tax increases in these years and, in some cases, resulted in property tax reductions. For a number of years, the state government share of school finance was a bit larger than the local share. After being about equal in the first half of the 1990s, the state share has again exceeded the local share since.

Great diversity exists among states in the relative role of the state government in financing education. In fact, the varied roles that state governments play in education are even greater than for most other services. The distribution of states by the state government's share of public-school expenditures in 2002 is shown in Table 19.4. State government provides more than 60 percent of revenue in ten states and less than 40 percent in another nine states. At the opposite extreme, the public schools are substantially financed by local governments in South Dakota (the state share is 34.1 percent of revenue), Nebraska (34.5 percent), Illinois (35.6 percent), Connecticut (36.3 percent), North Dakota (36.5 percent), and Pennsylvania (36.7 percent). In contrast, elementary and secondary education is a state government function in Hawaii where local school districts do not exist, and the state generates 90.1 percent of revenue for school expenditures (the federal share is relatively large in Hawaii because of the substantial U.S. military presence in the state). Other states with a substantial state share include Arkansas (74.2 percent), Minnesota (73.7 percent), and New Mexico (72.6 percent). The U.S. average is 49.0 percent, and the median states are Georgia (48.5 percent) and New Hampshire (49.0 percent).

States that are considered similar in many other ways have a number of interesting differences in the state government role in financing education. In Michigan, the state share of school revenue is 63.2 percent, but only 35.6 percent in neighboring Illinois. Texas has a low state share (at 39.1 percent), and Louisiana and Oklahoma are about at the national average (48.2 and 51.4), however, Arkansas has the second highest state share (74.2). Vermont is another state with a large state share (69.3), whereas Connecticut has one of the lowest state shares (36.3). Major changes have occurred over time in the role of state governments in many of these states as new financing systems were put in place. For instance, in 1992, Michigan had among the lowest state shares (at 26.6 percent), but had the seventh highest in 2002 (at 63.2 percent). Similarly, New Hampshire had the lowest state share at only 8.5 percent in 1992; by 2002, New Hampshire was at the national average. The obvious conclusion is that there is no one or even typical way that states finance elementary and secondary education. As you will discover in this chapter, the economic, political, and social factors that underlie these financial differences extend as well to the states' role in regulating education.

Just as differences exist among states in how elementary and secondary education is financed, substantial differences also exist among the states in the level of educational spending, as demonstrated in Figure 19.5. Per-pupil spending on current services by all public schools in aggregate was $8,019 in the 2002–2003 school year, but per-pupil spending averaged less than $6,500 in ten states and more than $9,500 in seven states and the District of Columbia. At the extremes, per-pupil spending was $4,840 in Utah but $12,202 in New Jersey. The **coefficient of variation**, a comparative measure of variation in distributions equal to the **standard deviation divided by the mean**, was .22 for 2002–2003, meaning that among the states, there was an average of about 22 percent variation in per-pupil spending around the mean. There has been little long run change in the degree of difference among states in the level of education spending over the past 40 years, as the interstate coefficient of variation for per-pupil spending was .25 in 1992 and 1980, .21 in 1970, and .22 in 1960.

The differences in per-pupil spending among different school districts within states appear to be about as large as the differences among states. Wayne Riddle and Liane White (1994, p. 358–62) report, for example, that the ratio of per-pupil expenditures for districts at the 95th percentile to those at the 5th percentile had a median value of about 1.5 in 1990 for those states with local school districts and varied from 3.1 to 1.3. (The ratio is 1 in Hawaii, which has a state school system.) Similarly, Linda Hertent *et al.* (1994) report the coefficient of variation for per-pupil revenues among districts within states varied from .07 (West Virginia) to .35 (Montana) in 1990, with a median of about .175. Seventeen states had coefficients exceeding .20. Recall from Chapter 7 that differences in expenditures can result from differences in input prices and environmental conditions as well as from differences in demand, so that these differences in per-pupil spending may not correspond to equivalent differences in educational results.

Eighty-six percent of spending by public elementary and secondary schools in 2002–2003 was for current services to students, as shown earlier in Figure 19.3b.

Figure 19.5

Current spending per pupil in public elementary and secondary schools, 2002–2003

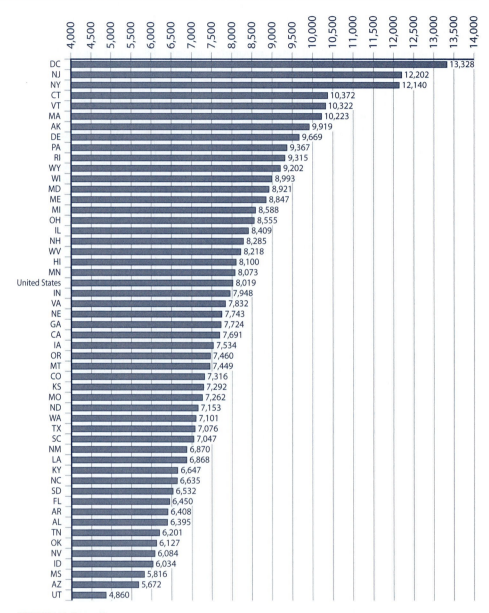

SOURCE: U.S. Census Bureau.

The bulk of current spending was for direct instructional expenses, which represented 52 percent of total spending, while support services accounted for another 30 percent of total spending. In contrast, capital expenditure on such things as buildings, technology, and transportation equipment represented only about 11 percent of total spending by public elementary and secondary schools.

Types of State Aid

Unless state governments want to operate the public-school system directly (as in Hawaii), states have to rely on intergovernmental grants to assist local governments in financing public education, and those grants must be one of the two general forms—lump-sum or matching—as described in Chapter 9.

Foundation Aid

Lump-sum school grants are usually referred to as **foundation aid** because *the per-pupil grant represents a minimum expenditure level*; the state aid is thought of as providing a basic foundation on top of which local revenue supplements may be added. Prior to the 1970s and then starting again in the 1990s, states generally used lump-sum per-pupil grants to support local education. Those grants were sometimes equal per-pupil amounts provided to all school districts, but more commonly the amount of the per-pupil grant for each district was directly related to educational costs in the district or inversely related to some measure of district wealth. Still, the grant is lump-sum because the size of the grant (per pupil) is independent of the district's choice about the level of spending (and thus taxes).

In general, a foundation aid program requires a basic grant per pupil and perhaps a way of reducing the grant for richer districts. A generic formula for a foundation aid grant is

$$G_i = F[1 + C_i] - [R^*][V_i]$$

where

G_i = per-pupil grant to district i

F = basic per-pupil grant or foundation level

C_i = cost index for district i

R^* = basic property tax rate set in the formula

V_i = per-pupil property tax base in district i

Suppose, for instance, that a state establishes such a program with $F = \$5,000$ and $R^* = \$10$ per $\$1,000$ of taxable property value (assuming all $C_i = 1$ for a moment). The largest (per-pupil) grant any district could receive is $\$5,000$, but only if V_i is zero. Compare two school districts, one with per-pupil property value of $\$50,000$ and the other $\$100,000$. The first would receive a per-pupil grant of $\$4,500$ [$\$5,000 - (\$10 \times 50)$] and the second $\$4,000$ [$\$5,000 - (\$10 \times 100)$]. Because the only district-specific factor in the formula is the property tax base per pupil, which is outside the direct control of the district, these are lump-sum grants. If both districts had identical property tax rates equal to the basic rate in the formula ($\$10$), both would end up with $\$5,000$ per student to spend. The first would collect $\$500$ in property taxes per pupil and receive $\$4,500$ in grant funds; the second would generate $\$1,000$ from property taxes and $\$4,000$ from the grant program. Thus, all districts are guaranteed $\$5,000$ per pupil, which is the foundation amount. If districts want to spend more than the guaranteed $\$5,000$ per pupil, they must collect local taxes to finance all the additional spending.

In states where costs among districts are substantially different, the *nominal* foundation level must be greater in districts with relatively higher costs to ensure equal *real* foundation spending. For instance, if costs are 10 percent greater than average in one district (so $C_i = .10$), and that district has a per-pupil property value of $100,000, the district's per-pupil grant would be $4,500 [$(1.1 \times \$5,000) - (\$10 \times 100)$]. This grant, combined with $1,000 of local property tax, would provide $5,500 per student to spend. A similar-wealth district with average costs would receive only $4,000 in grants. When combined with $1,000 of local property tax, this district has $5,000 per student to spend. Per-student spending is 10 percent greater in the first case because costs are 10 percent greater. In implementing such a formula, one might adjust for two types of cost differences—differences in input prices (especially for labor) and differences in environment (such as the nature of the students who are to be educated), as discussed in Chapter 7.[4]

Under what conditions would a district's grant be $0? A district gets no grant if its per-pupil property tax base is equal to or greater than $(F/R^*)/(1 + C_i)$. If a district's per-pupil property value is $500,000 and $C_i = 1$ for the example, then the per-pupil grant is $0 [$\$5,000 - (\$10 \times 500)$]. The reason is simple: With a per-pupil tax base of at least $500,000 and standard costs, the basic tax rate of $10 would generate the full foundation amount in taxes; no grant is required to bring such a district up to the foundation level.[5]

Under foundation aid programs, however, districts often may choose tax rates greater (but often not less) than the basic rate in the formula. Again, compare two districts with $50,000 and $100,000 property tax bases per pupil. If they both select property tax rates of $40 per $1,000 of taxable value, the first collects $2,000 of property taxes per pupil and receives a grant of $4,500, allowing spending equal to $6,500 per pupil. The second collects $4,000 per pupil in property taxes and receives a grant of $4,000, allowing spending of $8,000 per pupil. The difference in grant amounts does not fully offset the difference in property taxes. Equal property tax rates do not generate equal amounts of per-pupil spending if those tax rates are greater than the basic rate in the aid formula. These two districts are not required or expected to select equal tax rates. In fact, the wealthier district might even select a *higher* tax rate.

Guaranteed Tax Base Aid

An entirely different type of state aid to education, called the **Guaranteed Tax Base (GTB) or District Power Equalizing** plan, is intended to provide an equal, basic per-pupil property tax *base* to each district, rather than basic per-pupil minimum expenditure level of the foundation program. Per-pupil spending may still differ among school districts if they choose different property tax rates, but the aid program effectively provides the same basic tax base to which the selected rate is

---

[4]But the "costs" must not be determined solely by the recipient government. With respect to labor, for instance, the index might be based upon average wages for all jobs in the region of the school district.

[5]Note that districts with per-pupil tax bases greater than $(F/R^*)/(1 + C_i)$ will generate more than $5,000 per-pupil in real revenue and will be able to spend more than the foundation.

applied. A GTB plan involves matching grants that reduce the price of education to the school districts, which is the important economic difference from foundation grants.

A GTB grant formula requires, at least, that the GTB and the allowed tax rate be specified. The general formula for grants of this type is

$$G_i = B + (V^* - V_i)R_i$$

where

B = basic or foundation grant

V^* = guaranteed per-pupil tax base

V_i = per-pupil tax base in district i

R_i = property tax rate in district i or maximum rate allowed for the guarantee

In a pure GTB program, $B = 0$, and R_i is the local tax rate without any maximum. In that case, districts receive positive grants if their per-pupil tax base (V_i) is less than the GTB (V^*), with the grants being positively related to the tax rate selected by the district. Although theoretically these grants could be negative, requiring that districts with $V_i > V^*$ transfer funds to the state for redistribution, only in a few cases has such **recapture** of funds been tried. In one variation on this program, some states mix the foundation and GTB styles by providing a basic per-pupil grant in addition to the guaranteed base, that is, they set $B > 0$. These are sometimes called *two-tier* programs. In that case, a district receives a per-pupil grant exactly equal to the foundation amount if $V_i = V^*$, with that grant being reduced if $V_i > V^*$ until G is zero (negative grants again are not used). In one other variation, the guaranteed base V^* applies only to some maximum, state-specified tax rate; districts may set a higher rate, but it generates only more local tax revenue and not additional grant funds.

To illustrate the operation of the basic GTB formula, suppose that a state program guarantees a tax base of $200,000 per pupil ($V^*$ = $200,000) and sets no maximum on the tax rate that is eligible for that guarantee. Districts with a per-pupil property tax base of $200,000 or more would receive no education grants from the state government. For districts with $V_i < \$200,000$, the grant is inversely related to per-pupil wealth. For instance, a district with a per-pupil property tax base of $50,000 and a tax rate of $40 per $1,000 of taxable value would collect $2,000 per pupil [$50,000 × ($40/$1,000)] from property taxes and receive $6,000 per pupil [$150,000 × ($40/$1000)] from the state grant program. A district with a per-pupil tax base of $80,000 and the same tax rate would collect $3,200 per pupil [$80,000 × ($40/$1,000)] from property taxes and $4,800 per pupil [$120,000 × ($40/$1,000)] in state aid. Both receive $8,000 per pupil in total, which is the revenue generated from a base of $200,000 and a tax rate of $40. In essence, all districts are guaranteed $200 per pupil for each $1 of property tax rate selected. Any portion of that amount that is not provided by the local property tax base is made up by a state grant.

It follows from this discussion that an increase in a district's tax rate also leads to a larger grant per pupil for districts with $V_i < V^*$. Continuing the numerical illustration, suppose that the district with a per-pupil tax base of $50,000 increases its property tax rate to $41 per $1,000 of taxable value. That additional $1 in the tax rate generates an additional $50 per pupil from local property taxes and $150 per pupil from state aid; again, the net effect is an increase of $200 per pupil for each $1 of tax rate, the guarantee amount. The local district's share of the additional per-pupil revenue is V_i/V^*, generally, and 0.25 in this specific example. The district with a per-pupil value of $50,000 pays only 25 percent of the cost of increased school expenditures per pupil; the remainder is financed by the aid program. In contrast, the district with per-pupil value of $80,000 would pay 40 percent of the cost of increasing per-pupil spending ($80,000/$200,000). As previously mentioned, one effect of a GTB aid program is to reduce the local price of providing education. The marginal cost or price to the local district of increasing per-pupil spending by $1 is V_i/V^* if $V_i < V^*$, and $1 otherwise.

Economic Effects of Equalizing State Aid

An important economic and policy issue about different state aid programs is their expected influence on recipient school districts to alter educational expenditures. Do state education grants induce school districts to spend more on education, and if so, by how much? This was the rationale for why many states adopted guaranteed tax-base systems in the 1970s. Perhaps the best way to understand the potential economic effects of different grant types is to actually work through the responses of specific districts given some assumptions about economic and fiscal conditions. The following educational grant simulation does just that. Information about the demand for educational service and the initial expenditure choices of several representative schools is first presented, and then a new proposed state education grant program is described. The effect of that grant program on each school district's behavior is then analyzed, given the demand restrictions. The simulation will be most useful if *you* attempt to analyze the expected outcomes before reading the analysis in the text. Some suggestions about how you might proceed to do that are offered after the simulation is set up.

Education Grant Simulation

Suppose a state consists of four school districts, denoted A through D, each financing education solely with local property taxes. The initial fiscal situation in each of those districts is shown in the following table, with V equaling the per-pupil taxable property value in each district, R equaling the property tax rate in each district specified in dollars of tax per $1,000 of taxable value, and E equaling the per-pupil school expenditure in each district:

A	B	C	D
$V = \$100,000$	$V = \$130,000$	$V = \$200,000$	$V = \$225,000$
$R = \$55$	$R = \$53.85$	$R = \$45$	$R = \$60$
$E = \$5,500$	$E = \$7,000$	$E = \$9,000$	$E = \$13,500$

Thus, district A is the low-wealth, low-spending district, while D is the opposite—high-wealth, high-spending district. Note that the product of the per-pupil value and tax rate equals the per-pupil expenditure in each district, which is required if local property taxes fully finance the schools.

Suppose the (absolute value of the) price elasticity of demand for educational spending is known to be the same in each district and equal to .5, so that demand for education is price inelastic. This value is consistent with the evidence reported in Chapter 4; if anything, it may be relatively high. Similarly, suppose that the income elasticity of demand for education in each district is 1.0, and that the average family income in each district is half as large as the per-pupil property value (such would be the case if all the property is residential and consumers buy houses valued at twice their income, so a consumer with a $50,000 income has a $100,000 house).

The state government is considering introducing a program of state education grants to these school districts, to be determined by

$$\text{Grant per Pupil} = \$500 + (\$200,\!000 - V)R$$

where V and R correspond to the per-pupil value and tax rate in each district, and the per-pupil grant may not be smaller than zero (no recapture). The policy question is to analyze what the expected effect of such a grant program would be on educational spending and property taxes in each district, and given that, what the potential advantages might be from the state's point of view.

At this point you should stop reading and think about how you would do such an analysis if you were assigned this task as an economic or policy analyst for the state. Consider the following suggestions:

1. Determine whether the grant for each separate district is matching or lump sum. Lump-sum grants are fixed amounts that do not change in response to a recipient government's fiscal reactions, whereas matching grants explicitly depend on the fiscal decisions of those governments.

2. If the grant is lump sum, use the income elasticity to determine the effect on per-pupil spending and the required local property tax rate.

3. If the grant is matching, determine the marginal cost or "price" to the locality of increasing education spending and note how the grant has changed that "price." Use the price elasticity to compute the expected effect on per-pupil spending and the tax rate in the district.

4. If you follow steps 1–3, you will estimate new levels of spending and taxes in each district. Now evaluate those changes. Has education spending increased on average? Has spending become more equal? To what degree? Have local taxes decreased on average? What has happened to the distribution of tax rates? Has the state received a good return on the use of its funds? Would you recommend the adoption of this grant program?

Now let's see how you did. Consider the districts in order of ease of the analysis. **District D** receives no grant because its per-pupil value is greater than the $200,000 base guaranteed in the grant formula (D's grant from the formula is negative, but the smallest a grant can be is $0). Therefore, the grant program is expected to have no effect on education spending or property taxes in district D.[6]

District C receives a lump-sum grant of $500 per pupil because its per-pupil value exactly equals the guarantee amount [$G = \$500 + (0)R$]. Thus, district C receives the foundation amount but no matching aid from the GTB component of the formula. The lump-sum aid means that this district now has $500 more per pupil in income, which can be spent to buy more education services or other things. The per-pupil income in district C is $100,000, so the $500 grant represents an income increase of 0.5 percent [($500/$100,000) × 100%]. With an income elasticity of demand for education equal to 1, an increase in income of .5 percent causes an increase in educational spending of .5 percent. Thus, per-pupil spending is expected to increase by $45, from $9,000 to $9,045. Although the district receives a grant of $500 per pupil, only $45 of that amount gets spent on more educational spending. What happens to the rest of the grant? It goes for lower local property taxes and thus more private spending by taxpayers. The new level of spending is financed both by property taxes and the grant, so that

$$E' = \$500 + (V)R'$$

$$\$9,045 = \$500 + \$200,000 \times R'$$

$$R' = \$42.725 \text{ per } \$1,000 \text{ of taxable property value}$$

The grant allows district C to lower its property tax rate to $42.725 from $45.00. The district collects $8,545 per pupil in property taxes and receives $500 per pupil in state aid for per-pupil education expenditures of $9,045. Spending rises slightly, but local property taxes decline by a greater amount.

District A receives both the full foundation amount of $500 per pupil and matching aid from the GTB part of the formula because its per-pupil value is less than the guaranteed amount. The grant to district A given the initial conditions would be $6,000 [$500 + ($100,000)($55/$1000)], but that grant amount will change as district A changes its property tax rate in response to the grant itself. First, district A receives the $500 of foundation aid, which it would continue to receive even if its property tax rate (and spending) was $0. That $500 grant represents a 1 percent increase in per-pupil income [($500/$50,000) × 100%], which is expected to increase per-pupil spending by 1 percent or $55 because the income elasticity of demand for education spending is assumed to be 1.[7]

---

[6]D would get a positive grant if it lowered its tax rate to less than $20 per $1,000 of value, but education spending per pupil would fall drastically.

[7]Douglas Wills has pointed out to me that there is some ambiguity about this example because the analysis of the lump-sum component of the grant assumes a tax price of one, even though the matching component of the GTB grant reduces the tax price. The analysis presented here is equivalent to assuming that the lump-sum grant occurs first. This seems appropriate because if a district selects a tax rate (R) equal to zero, it still receives the lump-sum grant.

In addition, the matching grant from the GTB formula reduces the "price" of educational spending to the residents of district A. Following the discussion of the previous section, the new price is $V_A/\$200,000$, or 0.50. To increase per-pupil spending by \$1, district A must collect an additional \$.50 in local property taxes per pupil and would receive an additional \$.50 per pupil in state aid. Without the grant program, the local price was \$1, so that the effect of the grant is to lower the education price in A by 50 percent. If the price elasticity of demand for education spending is .5, then per-pupil spending is expected to increase by 25 percent as a result of the matching grant. Through this effect, per-pupil spending in district A would increase by \$1,388.75. Thus, the new level of per-pupil education spending in district A is expected to be about \$6,944, an increase of about \$1,444 due to the grant. Again, district A finances that expenditure with property taxes and the grant, so that

$$\$6,944 = (\$100,000)R' + \$500 + (\$100,000)R'$$

$$R' = \$32.22 \text{ per } \$1,000 \text{ of taxable value}$$

District A lowers its property tax rate to \$32.22 from \$55.00 as a result of the grant. The district collects \$3,222 per pupil in property taxes and receives \$3,722 per pupil in state aid, allowing spending of \$6,944 per pupil. Of the total education grant of about \$3,722, only about \$1,444 goes for higher-education spending and the rest into lower taxes. The grant causes a larger expenditure increase in district A than district C because district A receives a matching grant in addition to the foundation amount.

District B also receives both the full foundation amount of \$500 per pupil and matching aid from the GTB part of the formula. First, district B receives \$500 of lump-sum foundation aid, which it would continue to receive even if its property tax rate (and spending) was zero. This component of the grant increases income by .77 percent [(\$500/\$65,000) $\times$ 100%] and desired spending by an additional .77 percent, or \$53.90.

In addition, district B faces a price effect from the matching component. In this case, the price effect is smaller because the district's per-pupil tax base is larger. Because district B has a per-pupil tax base of \$130,000, its price for additional school spending is \$0.65 [\$130,000/\$200,000]; district B can increase spending by \$1 by collecting an additional \$.65 in property taxes and receiving, as a result, an additional \$.35 in state aid per pupil. The grant has lowered the tax price by 35 percent (from \$1 to \$.65), which is expected to increase desired spending by 17.5 percent given the price elasticity. This represents an increase of \$1,234 [.25 x \$7,053.90]. Thus, the new level of per-pupil education spending in district B is expected to be about \$8,288, an increase of about \$1,288 due to the grant. The new property tax rate is determined by

$$\$8,288 = (\$130,000)R' + \$500 + (\$70,000)R'$$

$$R' = \$38.94 \text{ per } \$1,000 \text{ of taxable value}$$

District B collects \$5,062 per pupil in property taxes and receives \$3,226 per pupil in state aid to fund spending of \$8,288.

The expected effects of the grant program on these school districts are summarized in the following table:

	A	B	C	D	Average
Initial Spending	$5,500	$7,000	$9,000	$13,500	$8,750
New Spending	6,944	8,288	9,045	13,500	9,444.25
Per-Pupil Grant	3,722	3,226	500	0	1,862
Initial Tax	5,500	7,000	9,000	13,500	8,750
New Tax	3,222	5,062	8,545	13,500	7,583.63
Initial Tax Rate	55.00	53.85	45.00	60.00	53.46
New Tax Rate	32.22	38.94	42.725	60.00	46.66

On the basis of this analysis, the proposed education grant program is expected to have the following effects in the state:

- Per-pupil education spending increases slightly by about 7.9 percent, on average, although spending rises in only three of the districts. A little less than 40 percent of the state grant funds go for higher spending on education.

- The variance in per-pupil spending among the districts in the state is reduced only slightly. The ratio of the highest- to lowest-spending level is reduced to 1.94 from 2.45, about a 21-percent change; however,the dollar difference between those districts is still nearly $6,556.

- Property taxes are reduced in all districts that receive state grants, resulting in about a 13 percent decrease in property tax rates, on average. About 60 percent of the state education grant funds go to reduce local property taxes.

- Property tax rates are reduced more in districts with lower per-pupil property values, so that effective tax rates now increase with property value. The ratio of tax rate to per-pupil expenditure—which represents the tax rate required to provide per-pupil spending of $1—is made much more equal across the districts. Without the grants, those ratios were .01 for district A, .0077 for district B, .005 for district C, and .0044 for district D. Thus, a tax rate of $.01 per $1,000 of taxable value was required in order to spend $1 per pupil in district A, but a rate of only about $.005 was required in district C. With the grants, the required rates are $.0046 in district A, and $.0047 in districts B and C.

It is also interesting to note what the effect would have been on district D if recapture—that is, negative grants—were allowed. In that case, the price to local residents per dollar of per-pupil spending would have been $1.125 ($225,000/ $200,000). Residents of district D would have had to increase local property taxes by $1.125 per pupil to increase spending by $1 per pupil because the district would also have to pay additional funds to the state. Thus, the price of education to residents of district D rises by 12.5 percent, which is expected to cause a 6.25 percent *decrease* in per-pupil spending if the price elasticity is .5. Thus, per-pupil spending in district D would have fallen to $12,656. Although that would have generated more spending equality than without recapture, the interdistrict differences would still be large, and the increased equality would be achieved by worsening educational opportunity in one district.

Policy Implications

One of the traditional criticisms of foundation grants is that such aid programs do not equalize resources across districts and thus are not expected to equalize spending unless the basic tax rate in the foundation aid formula is set high relative to the actual rates employed by school districts (which requires that the foundation level of spending also be set high) or unless district choice of R is limited. Beginning in the late 1960s and early 1970s, this effect of the traditional foundation aid programs used by states led to a series of court challenges in various states to the educational systems in place. In these cases, plaintiffs argued that per-pupil spending on local education was dependent on and generally varied by the per-pupil taxable wealth of the school district and not exclusively on the wealth or income of the family. Because state aid programs did not offset this dependence, those bringing the cases argued that students were being denied equal protection under the law. These cases were successful in a number of states, the courts finding that the state aid systems violated the equal protection clause of the Fourteenth Amendment to the U.S. Constitution or similar equal protection provisions in state constitutions. The *Serrano* decision in California in 1971 was the most influential and often cited. The courts ordered the states to devise state aid programs that would eliminate (or at least reduce) the relationship between property wealth and per-pupil spending in school districts.[8]

As a result of these decisions and other forces encouraging states to equalize educational opportunities, some states increased the basic grant amount in their foundation programs, while many others switched to forms of guaranteed tax-base aid programs because those programs provided the wealth neutrality that the courts had demanded. That is, with GTB aid, each district is guaranteed a minimum tax base, usually property value per student, so that spending need not depend on district property wealth.

However, the results of the grant simulation that you completed previously represent accurately the actual results obtained in many states that adopted grant programs of this type. Often substantial equalization of per-pupil spending among school districts did not occur. The economic reasons for this are clear. Because the demand for education spending is price inelastic, the price reductions that are caused by the matching grants do not influence consumption very much. Similarly, given the magnitude of income effects, lump-sum grants also do not influence education-spending levels substantially. As a result, most of these state education grant funds went to reduce local property taxes rather than to increase education spending. Therefore, the wide differences in educational spending between

---

[8]For more detail about these court challenges and decisions, see Lukemeyer (2004) and Huang, Lukemeyer, and Yinger (2004).

districts within states were not reduced substantially. As Richard Murnane (1985, p. 133) has noted:

> ... It seems clear that the main lesson from the first ten years of school finance [reform] is that GTB finance plans which lower the price of education to property-poor communities, but leave the communities free to choose between more spending on education or lower tax rates, will not produce an equalization of per-pupil spending levels across school districts and will not result in districts spending enough to provide their students with a strong basic academic program.

This difficulty cannot be changed by increasing the size of state aid programs if the structure of those programs remains the same. If demand is price inelastic, a substantial portion of the grants will go to reduce taxes regardless of how much the price of education spending is reduced. The simulation understates the magnitude of the problem in several ways. If incomes are increasing over time, then the demand for education spending is also rising in many and perhaps all districts. Many states provide education grants for purposes other than equalization—such as grants for special education or transportation—and these often increase spending in all districts. As you learned in Chapter 14, state property tax credits can induce tax and spending increases in high-tax jurisdictions. Those economic forces may serve to widen the spending disparities, so that the modest equalizing force from state aid may serve only to preserve the existing distribution and prevent the increased variance that would otherwise occur.

Therefore, even though many states adopted GTB aid programs at one point, which are theoretically wealth neutral, court challenges to state education finance systems have continued. Huang, Lukemeyer, and Yinger (2004) report that as of 2003, only 5 states (Delaware, Hawaii, Mississippi, Nevada, and Utah) had not faced any litigation regarding education finance. State education finance systems have been rejected or overturned by the courts in 18 states, and systems have been upheld in 16 states, although litigation continues at this writing in a number of cases. Thus, Huang, Lukemeyer, and Yinger (2004, p. 329) report "Of these thirty-four states, at least eleven have ongoing litigation in which plaintiffs are seeking further reform or ... presenting new evidence or legal theories. In an additional four states, state supreme courts have issued interim decisions favorable to plaintiffs and litigation continues. Finally, suits are pending in three states. . . ."

Anna Lukemeyer (2004) reports that the basis for continuing court challenges to state education finance systems has changed over time. Many challenges still focus on the wide differences in educational spending per student that exist within states, although often no longer using an "equal protection" argument, but rather based on clauses in state constitutions about the required state role in providing or guaranteeing adequate or appropriate education for all students. Cases taking this approach are essentially arguing on equity grounds that education differences should be reduced. The most recent set of court challenges focus on a different issue, however: whether or not the education system in a state serves to provide an "adequate" or "efficient" education to students in aggregate. In such cases, plaintiffs are less concerned about spending differences, per se, and more about the level of education spending, services, and outcomes in the state overall. For instance, Lukemeyer (2004) notes the 1989 Kentucky Supreme Court decision in which the court found that the constitution's requirement of "an efficient system of common schools throughout the state" was not being met and ordered changes to provide each student "an equal opportunity to have an adequate education" and then defined an "adequate education" at a quite high level.[9]

Summarizing the actual types of aid programs used by the states is difficult because each state typically has a number of different components, and the structure of the aid programs often includes fiscal features specific to each state. For a conference held at Syracuse University in 2002, Yao Huang (2004) summarized state aid systems for education for all states in 2001. Focusing only on general aid for schools (ignoring specific categories such as transportation or capital investment), Huang reports that 30 states were using foundation aid programs, all but two of which included some type of adjustment for cost differences. Three states used a GTB aid system exclusively and another 11 states used a GTB system in addition to a foundation level, to create an incentive for equalization. The remaining states used other systems, including flat per-student grants in North Carolina, Pennsylvania, and Rhode Island, and full state funding in Hawaii. Whatever system is used, limits on spending or revenue are common. Three states effectively permit no local supplementation of revenue beyond that in the state formula, with another 25 states limiting local supplementation by setting maximum tax rates, by setting limits on the per-student amount of supplemental funds that can be collected, by limiting the growth of revenue or spending, or by requiring that part of any local supplemental revenue be recaptured by reducing state aid.

Thus, most states that switched from GTB aid programs back to foundation aid coupled the foundation level with caps on spending or revenue. The simplest foundation plan, of course, is one that sets equal spending in all districts. Such a plan could set targeted per-pupil spending in each district at F and pay state grants to each district equal to the difference between F and the local property tax collected at some mandated level. Other options include foundation amounts (F) that vary with district costs, again with some maximum allowed expenditure or limit on local supplements to the foundation. These spending caps essentially are necessary to prevent growing spending differences among districts (or to bring about additional equalization) if the foundation is to be below the highest district spending levels.

What are the options for state policymakers who want to equalize education opportunities or spending among school systems in their state or who want to increase the level of spending throughout the state? In general, there are three approaches. First, a state government can assume the responsibility for directly providing elementary and secondary education, effectively having a single state school district, as in Hawaii. This would certainly involve the most dramatic and traumatic change to the fiscal system among the alternatives. There are at least two economic reasons why this alternative may not be desirable. If cost differences exist among different school districts, then equal per-pupil expenditures

---

[9]See Lukemeyer (2004) and Flanagan and Murray (2004).

may not generate equal educational service. And politically, it would likely be very difficult not to have equal per-pupil spending in all areas with a state system. The advantage of local districts is that such cost differences as well as differences in individual desires about emphasis in education can be recognized and acted on.

The second option is for states to mandate a minimum amount of per-pupil spending through their aid programs and to set that minimum relatively high compared to actual spending levels in that state. The second prescription is crucial because unless the minimum applies to a number of school districts, little equalization will occur. States can do this using either a foundation or GTB program. With foundation aid, the state can require that districts at least levy the specified tax rate in the formula, with both that rate and the foundation amount set relatively high. For instance, if the foundation amount is set at $5,000 per pupil and the required tax rate is $50 per $1,000 of taxable value, districts with per-pupil values less than $100,000 per pupil ($5,000/($50/$1,000)) would receive foundation grants. But the minimum any district could spend is $5,000 per pupil. With GTB aid, this result can similarly be accomplished by setting a relatively high minimum required tax rate. Returning to the simulation, if the minimum were set equal to the average rate of about $47 that prevailed after the grants were received, districts A, B, and C would have to increase their tax rates and per-pupil spending. By requiring a number of local districts to increase spending up to the minimum amount, the state government is restricting local choice but to a lesser extent than results from direct state provision of education.

This second option, to narrow school spending differences by raising the minimum allowed spending or tax rate, often is accompanied by limits on maximum allowed spending (or maximum allowed growth of spending) for high-spending districts. Such spending limits are intended to prevent or reduce spending increases that would occur in these districts (due to income growth or other factors) to assist in narrowing the differences. Such spending limits have at least three difficulties. By preventing some districts from raising local taxes to support additional desired education service, states may reduce support for the education finance system overall. In addition, such spending caps may reduce the overall level of spending on education. And finally, these limits might induce residents of the limited districts simply to purchase more education service in a different way—from the private market or through school-parent associations or foundations, for instance. Of course, this last difficulty is the ultimate reason why it is impossible to cap spending by higher-income families; the state may limit school spending, but not spending on education.

Evidence reported by William Evans, Sheila Murray, and Robert Schwab (1999) and by Caroline Hoxby (2001) suggests that states have in fact pursued this second option, so that court-ordered changes in state systems to finance education did lead to equalization of education resources among districts. Evans, Murray, and Schwab examined education provision in 46 states during the period from 1972 to 1992; 11 of those states experienced court-ordered school finance reform in those years. They report that those education finance reforms, all of which involved increases in the state government role in financing schools, reduced spending differences between districts in those states substantially—on average about 20 to 30 percent. Evans and colleagues also report that for these cases, the reduced differences between districts occurred as a result of the lowest-spending districts increasing spending substantially—what is called *leveling up*. Hoxby modeled the state education finance systems in every state in 1990 and then related the characteristics of each state's financing system to actual education spending in the state. She reports that spending is increased by high foundation levels and by GTB programs that reduce tax prices substantially for low-wealth, low-spending districts. But Hoxby also finds that a substantial amount of the equalization of spending among districts arises by limiting or restricting spending by the highest-spending districts—what is called *leveling down*.

A final alternative is for states to mandate minimum educational conditions but not minimum spending levels in local school systems. For instance, a state might set minimum standards all teachers must satisfy, or a state might establish minimum course requirements that students must satisfy to graduate. If those minimum standards are set relatively high compared to the actual performance of many districts in the state, then those local districts will be required to adjust the educational service provided, which might require increased per-pupil expenditures in some districts. The difficulty with this alternative, as we will examine next, is discovering just what conditions matter for educational results and thus how to set the minimum standards.

Application 19.1

STATE ATTEMPTS TO REFORM EDUCATION FINANCE:
THE CASES OF CALIFORNIA AND MICHIGAN

Many states have continued to wrestle with the fundamental policy problem of providing for an equitable and efficient level of education to all children in the state, while recognizing the role for local school districts and differences between districts in educational costs and demands. In most states, this has been a continual process involving interaction between state government, the courts, and the local districts. Occasionally, states make radical or dramatic changes in the educational system, but smaller marginal changes occur almost continuously. The experiences in California and Michigan are particularly illuminating in showing both the forces that have operated over the past 30 years and those that are likely to continue into the future.

California was among the first states in recent years to have the courts find that the state system of financing and providing education was unconstitutional and order specific changes in that system.[10] In a series of legal decisions between 1969 and 1976

---

[10]This section draws heavily from Thomas A. Downes, "Evaluating the Impact of School Finance Reform on the Provision of Public Education: The California Case," *National Tax Journal*, 45, (December 1992): 405–19.

Application 19.1 — State Attempts to Reform Education Finance

(the *Serrano v. Priest* cases), state courts essentially found that "any education financing scheme that allowed for a positive correlation between a district's taxable wealth [property tax base] and per-pupil expenditures would be unconstitutional" (Downes, 1992, p. 406). In response to these decisions, the state adopted a financing system providing a foundation level of spending to districts and limits on revenue per student excluding categorical aid and local property taxes. These changes alone were not sufficient to bring the state's school finance system into compliance with the court mandate because local districts still had the option to collect local taxes to exceed the spending limits.

But in 1976, California voters adopted a major tax limitation proposal (Proposition 13) that, among many things, imposed tight limits on both the level and growth of local property taxes. Compliance with the new limits required large reductions in property taxes and effectively prevented schools (and other localities) from replacing those property tax revenues in the future. As a result, the local government share of school revenue fell in 1978–1979 (the first year Proposition 13 was in effect) to about 30 percent from about 54 percent in prior years. Because the state government replaced much of the lost property tax revenue for schools (from state surpluses initially and general state taxes later), the state's share of education revenue rose from less than 40 percent to about 60 percent in 1978–1979, where it has essentially remained since.

These changes had a number of important effects in California. First, the property tax limit meant that the state and revenue limit for school districts, exclusive of categorical aid, was tight and became a force for equalizing spending differences between districts. Downes (1992) reports substantial reductions in the differences between districts in both the revenue limit per student and total expenditures per student. Second, the state government became the dominant level for financing education, especially for any growth of spending. As a result, the relative level of school spending in California declined. Fabio Silva and Jon Sonstelie (1993) report per-pupil spending in California went from 13 percent above the U.S. average in 1970 to about 10 percent below average in 1990. Per-student spending remained 5 percent below the national average in 2002–2003. Third, because districts have been prevented from using local taxes to increase school spending to desired levels, many districts have instead turned to increased fees, parent contributions to schools or fundraising by school associations or foundations, and generation of school revenue in other ways, such as renting out school facilities.

A disappointing aspect of the changes in California is that even though per-student spending differences between districts have been reduced substantially, there has not been a corresponding equalization of student performance, at least as measured by test scores. This failure to affect performance as much as spending seems to result from three factors: (1) wealthier districts used nontax sources to maintain spending, (2) low-wealth districts used the increased resources to lower dropout rates (which may actually cause test scores to fall, if the retained students are worse-than-average academically, (3) costs of educating students increased relatively in the low-wealth districts, partly due

Application 19.1 — State Attempts to Reform Education Finance

to demographic changes in the student population.

Michigan also made fundamental changes to its school finance system in the early 1970s, but because the subsequent developments in Michigan were different than in California, a completely new and radically different financing system was put in place in 1994. Beginning with 1974, Michigan had changed its state aid program for schools from a foundation program to a power-equalizing/GTB plan, which then was continued with only minor modification until 1993. Under the state's GTB aid plan, the aid formula parameters were altered each year so that between 50 and 65 percent of the local school districts received aid and had a marginal reduction in tax prices. Districts generated local revenue from property taxes, which were limited only slightly, and there were no limits on school spending.

The results of the new (1974) financing system in Michigan were disappointing on at least two fronts. Differences in spending among districts were not reduced (although differences in local taxes per pupil were reduced); in fact, spending differences increased over time. Prior to 1974, the coefficient of variation for operating expenditures per pupil among Michigan districts was about 0.16; by 1980, it was about 0.17 and by 1994, it had increased to 0.23. Spending differences increased rather than decreased due to continued use of state categorical aid (which was not equalizing), state property tax credits that applied to wealthy as well as poor localities, local tax increases adopted by voters in districts who wanted to increase spending (because of income increases or other personal influences), and lack of response to the price

incentives of the GTB plan (demand was very price inelastic) by residents of low-spending districts. In addition, state equalizing aid did not increase sufficiently to fund local desired spending on education, so local property taxes provided an increasing share of local school revenue. In 1978, local property taxes provided about half of school revenue; by 1994, this share had increased to about 66 percent. Property tax burden in Michigan relative to income was seventh highest in the nation.

As a consequence of high property taxes and growing spending disparities among districts, Michigan changed its system entirely again in 1994. The new system is based on a *foundation guarantee* for each district, which is the allowed per-student spending, determined by spending in 1993–1994, plus allowed annual increases. Districts above the state's *basic foundation* (initially $5,000 per student in 1994–1995) receive annual lump-sum per-student increases equal to the percentage growth of state school aid revenue multiplied by the basic foundation. Districts spending less than the basic foundation receive up to double those annual per-student amounts. To finance the districts' foundation guarantee, each district receives a lump-sum per-student grant from the state equal to the difference between that district's guarantee and an 18 mill local tax on non-homestead taxable property. Districts spending more than $6,500 per student in 1994–1995 (the highest 6 or 7 percent) also levied an additional local property tax on homesteads only to fund the differences between $6,500 and the district's guarantee. Over time, the foundation amount grows, so that the minimum level of per-student spending also

Application 19.1 — State Attempts to Reform Education Finance

rises. For 2003, the basic foundation was $6,700. The maximum foundation grant was $8,000, and only 45 school districts levied local taxes to spend more than that amount.

Michigan's new financing system has had four primary long-run effects, as noted by Julie Cullen and Susanna Loeb (2004). First, the state government generates more than 75 percent of funding for schools, more than double its share before the change. Second, as the state funding comes mostly from state sales taxes, a state property tax, and the state income tax, the importance of property taxes (and especially local property taxes) was substantially reduced. Third, the level of educational spending has increased substantially, by more than 9 percent in real terms between 1990 and 1998. Average real revenue per student grew from about $5,700 in 1991 to more than $7,200 in 2000. Finally, relative spending differences between districts have been reduced as low-spending districts were raised to the basic foundation level, which is indexed annually, and as the growth of spending in high-spending districts was limited. The coefficient of variation for per-student revenue fell from 0.22 in 1991 to 0.13 in 2000.

Even with these changes, a number of concerns and controversies remain. Although spending differences have narrowed (as in California), it is not clear that corresponding educational outcomes have equalized as well (California did not see an equalization, for instance). Because the state sets allowed spending in each district, some high-spending districts have not been allowed to raise local taxes to spend as much as is demanded. These high-spending districts seem unwilling to accept the restriction on new education spending and have worked to eliminate the restrictions or seek new nontax methods to fund additional services (as also happened in California). Some of the previously low-spending districts that received substantial amounts of new funds are essentially forced to spend more than what the voters selected. Some of these districts may now use the general spending funds for capital projects rather than collecting separate revenue for that purpose. Because the grants are in per-student terms, decreases in enrollment cause proportionate decreases in state funding, but costs may not fall proportionately. Finally, with the state government providing nearly 80 percent of revenue for schools, K-12 education must compete with other state services for the available state revenues.

PRODUCING EDUCATION

The Paradox of Declining Performance

We have learned that per-pupil spending in real terms by public schools increased nearly continuously over the past 40 years, in part because average class sizes declined. The paradox, however, is that student performance, at least as measured by a variety of average test scores, has not increased proportionately.

Changes in the scores on the Scholastic Aptitude Test (SAT)—a test purporting to measure preparation for college given to high school seniors and with which many of the readers of this book are intimately familiar—have been given prominent attention. The now well-known story is that those average scores, for both verbal and mathematics skills, declined from 1963 to 1980. Over that period, the average SAT verbal score declined by more than 11 percent from 478 to 424, and the average math score declined by more than 7 percent from 502 to 466 (possible SAT scores range from 200 to 800 on each component of the test). Since 1980, average SAT verbal scores have remained about the same, whereas average math scores have increased modestly. Similarly, American College Testing Program (ACT) average scores also declined from 1966 to 1975 and have remained about constant since 1995.

Although not as widely reported, the SAT score changes also were being reflected by changes in scores of other standardized tests given to students at various grade levels over that period. For instance, Hanushek (1986) noted that scores on the Iowa Tests (standardized tests used in many states and given to students in grades 5, 8, and 12) also declined beginning in the mid-1960s through the 1970s. Interestingly, Hanushek also noted that the timing of improvements in those test scores and others he discusses are consistent: Fifth-grade scores started to rise in 1975, eighth-grade scores in 1977, and twelfth-grade scores in 1980. These average scores do mask some differences by subject matter. Murnane (1985) discussed a set of tests sponsored by the national government called the National Assessment of Educational Progress (NAEP) given to students aged 9, 13, and 17 in various years. Those results show that reading skills have remained essentially constant since 1971 for 13- and 17- year olds and improved for 9-year-olds. Over the same period, students' mathematics skills remained stable for 17-year-olds but have improved substantially for 9- and 15-year-olds. More recently, attention has focused on a set of student assessments used internationally. By those measures, achievement by students in the United States remains below that of students in many other nations that have lower educational spending (see the "International Comparison" section later in this chapter).

What are the possible explanations for why student-achievement test scores did not keep pace with increases in public school spending relative to both enrollment and inflation? Part of the explanation for the change in college-entrance test scores lies in changes in the number and mix of students who were taking the test and going on to college, which was important in the 1960s but not the 1970s. Some of the explanations offered for the broader trend include shortages of qualified teachers, especially in mathematics and science, the nature of teacher-training programs emphasizing education over academic classes, social factors that altered interest or participation in education, and changes in the characteristics of schools and public-school programs themselves, such as the introduction of broader, less academic curricula or new teaching methods. But the evidence is inconclusive or even negative on some of these factors.

The real task in resolving the paradox is discovering in a general sense just what inputs into the education process affect educational outcomes and by what magnitude. With that information, it may be possible both to understand what happened in the 1960s and early 1970s and to improve the provision of education in all types of schools.

A Production Function Approach to Education

A production function characterizes the relationship between inputs and the range of possible outputs that can be produced with each input combination (as discussed in Chapter 7). If that technology of producing "education" can be identified and quantified—that is, if the effect of different educational inputs on educational results can be determined—then a mechanism is revealed to evaluate how different schools go about educating and why educational results differ for different students or at different times. The concept of education production analysis by economists, then, is to statistically relate education outputs to education inputs. Mathematically,

$$Q = q(I_1, I_2, I_3, \ldots)$$

where

Q = the educational outcome

I = educational inputs

Although it seems natural to economists to examine the production of education in the same way that one might study the production of automobiles, computers, or agricultural products, this approach when applied to education remains somewhat controversial.

Measuring Outcomes

The necessary first step in analyzing and evaluating production decisions is identifying both the *objective* of the organization and some way of *measuring output*. As discussed in Chapter 7, neither of these decisions is straightforward in the case of many services provided by governments, including, and perhaps especially for, education. Moreover, the appropriate way to measure output depends on the government's objective in providing the service. For instance, a discovery that schools do not do a good job of improving students' scores on standardized tests may not be surprising or very useful if, in fact, schools do not care about test scores and thus do not try to improve them.

In doing production analysis for private firms, particularly those in manufacturing, these decisions seem clearer. Economists typically assume that the objective of the firms is to produce the amount of product that generates the highest possible profit. Output can either be measured by the number of physical units produced or by the dollar volume of sales. If profit rises, then the firm is moving in the direction of achieving its goal. Production changes that increase profits are deemed desirable. Economists also sometimes consider objectives other than maximizing profit, such as increasing market share or maximizing sales subject to a minimum-profit restriction, but even in those cases, the objective is clear and easily quantifiable.

With respect to government services and education particularly, the government's objective is not so easily defined. Even if an objective can be agreed on, the measures of output and thus success in meeting the objective are imprecise. The output or result of education is usually measured in one of four ways: by scores on standardized tests, by numbers of students achieving a particular level of education (number graduating from high school and number entering college, for example), by economic achievements such as rate of employment or level of income, or by subjective measures (often through surveys) of individual satisfaction. Among the numerous studies attempting to relate education inputs and methods to educational results, test scores are easily the most commonly used measure of performance or output, partly because they are readily available for many students and because they make comparisons over time relatively easy.

Analyses relating economic achievements to education level certainly suggest, at least on the surface, that more education leads to economic gains. For instance, the basic data shown in Figure 19.6 indicate that unemployment rates are lower and incomes higher among those who have completed more years of school. These correlations have two qualifications, however. First, some have argued that rather than producing education, the primary effect of the school system is to serve as a *screening device*, identifying more able individuals by the fact that they are allowed to pursue more education. By this viewpoint, the role of schools is to select the more able and provide that information to the market. If that is the case, those with more education do better economically because they are more able, not because additional years of school made them more skilled.

Second, these correlations do not distinguish the *quantity* of education from the *quality* of result. Measures of numbers of students graduating on time, the percentage entering college, the number of school years completed, or the number who are employed x years after graduating are predominately quantity measures, which do not distinguish very well the quality of education. After all, there are different types of colleges, and the fact that someone is employed does not indicate the type of job or level of satisfaction. This is, of course, another reason for the attractiveness of test scores that can be interpreted as reflecting an entire range of outcomes. Whether test scores do, in fact, reflect educational quality is controversial and problematic. The evidence shows, for instance, that test scores do not necessarily correlate with later economic success by students.

Even if a measure (or several measures) of educational output from this list can be agreed on, however, it is not clear what the objective of the school system is or should be. This difficulty arises because there is typically a wide range of students in any school system, so that one might be interested in the distribution of results among those students as well as the average result. This point has been emphasized by Byron Brown and Daniel Saks (1975) who suggest that schools might be interested in both the mean and variance of test scores, for instance. Suppose that

Figure 19.6

The relationship between education level attained and economic status, 2001–2002

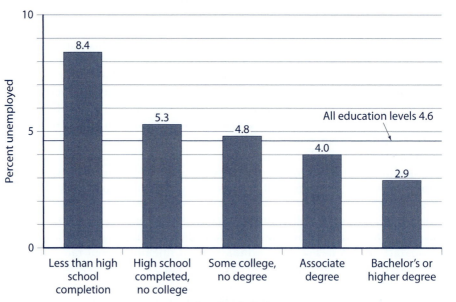

(a) Unemployment rates of persons 25-years-old and over by highest degree attained.

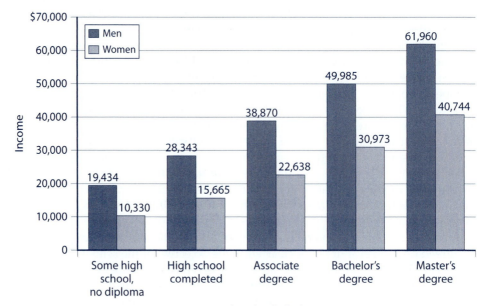

(b) Median annual earnings of workers 25-years-old and over by years of schooling completed and sex.

Table 19.5

Sample Alternative Test Score Distributions

Student	Case A	Case B	A−B	Percent Change
1	700	600	−100	−14.3%
2	650	570	−80	−12.3
3	600	550	−50	−8.3
4	550	520	−30	−5.5
5	500	490	−10	−2.0
6	450	450	0	0.0
7	400	410	+10	+2.5
8	350	380	+30	+8.6
9	300	350	+50	+16.7
10	250	320	+70	+28.0
Average	475	464	−11	(Loss) −2.3
Standard Deviation	143.6	92.1	−51.5	(Gain) −35.9
Std. Dev./Ave.	30.2	19.8	−10.4	−34.4

the two alternative sets of test scores shown in Table 19.5 are both possible outcomes that arise from different allocations of the teacher's time and other resources, for a school or class. The average test score (or equivalently, the sum of scores) is maximized in case A by applying more of the educational resources to the better students. Although the resulting average score is high, the variation among the students is also very large; the coefficient of variation is 30.2, meaning an average of 30.2-percent variation in scores around the mean score. Case B represents the results of an alternative application of the same educational resources, perhaps applying those resources more evenly among the students. The result is a 2-percent lower average score but much less variation among the students (about 20 percent around the mean). In essence, what has happened is that the top scores have fallen by more than the bottom scores have risen, but the percentage gains by the students at the bottom of the distribution outweigh the percentage decreases by those at the top.

Which distribution is better? Which do *you* prefer? There may be no clear answer. One often hears about equal opportunity in education or society, and an explicit economic objective of government is to alter the distribution of income or resources in society. If that is the case, then individuals and government may be willing to accept lower average test scores or educational outcomes in exchange for a more even distribution of those outcomes. This issue implies one of the difficulties in evaluating teachers or schools. If teachers are evaluated or paid, or are if districts are rewarded with state aid, based on the average score of their students on some standardized test, then there is an incentive to maximize those average scores by allocating teaching time or resources to those students whose test scores improve the most; however, the resulting distribution of student performance may not be that which is most desired.

Measuring Inputs

The second requirement for analyzing educational production is to identify and measure the inputs into the production process, which are those factors that are expected to influence educational results. In general, three types of inputs are identified: those provided by the schools, those provided by society (broadly defined), and those provided by the student. The following equation reflects these inputs:

$$Q = q(\text{School Inputs, Social Inputs, Student Inputs})$$

Examples of each type of input are listed here:

School Inputs	Social Inputs	Student Inputs
Teachers	Family Experiences	Innate Ability
Books	Cultural Factors	Effort
Computers	Nonschool Learning	
Classroom Hours	Books at Home	
Curricula		
Other Students		

At least three important issues must be resolved before this general model can be applied. First, one factor that differentiates the production of education from the production of many other commodities is that the inputs are expected to have a cumulative effect. The educational achievement of a student at a particular grade or age is expected to depend on all the previous education inputs applied to that person, not just on the most recent or those from a particular grade. In other words, for a statistical analysis based on test scores, one should not relate the score at a particular grade to the inputs provided by that year's class, but rather to all past education received by that student. This is another difficulty in using test scores or achievement results to evaluate teachers or school systems because a student's achievement at one time may depend on the work of past teachers or other schools. This is another reason why focusing on the change in achievement in a particular period may be more useful.

Second, the school inputs either can be measured by the actual numbers of inputs used (number of teachers per student, number or percentage of teachers with a Master's degree, number or percentage of teachers with more than five years' experience, number of school days or hours per year, types of subjects taught) or by the amount of money spent by the school on those inputs (instructional expenditures per student). However, it may be that additional spending will improve educational outcomes only if those resources are applied in particular ways. Finally, it must be decided whether the unit of analysis is to be the classroom, thus focusing on specific teachers, or the school or school system.

Evidence on Educational Production: What Matters?

Hanushek (1986) has identified about 150 different studies—prepared over the past 20 years using the basic approach outlined previously—of the factors influencing educational production. Although these studies use different data sources and different theoretical and statistical models, some relationships among inputs and results have been noted consistently, although other hypotheses about relationships have consistently not been supported by the research. Accordingly, a consensus has developed about what factors appear to be important in improving educational results.

First is a surprising result about some factors that apparently have not been associated with improved educational outcomes. As stated by Hanushek (1986, p. 1162), "There appears to be no strong or systematic relationship between school expenditures and student performance." As stated previously, the instructional expenditures of schools are largely composed of the costs of teachers. So higher per-pupil expenditures most likely arise from smaller class sizes, paying all teachers higher salaries, or hiring teachers with more education (which requires higher salaries). The absence of a relationship between per-pupil expenditures and student performance is also found when expenditures are decomposed into these characteristics. So there also appears to be no strong or systematic relationship between student performance and smaller class sizes, teachers with more graduate education, or higher teacher salaries generally.

That per-pupil expenditures *per se* do not appear to matter for student performance is certainly surprising, at least to economists, because it implies that additional inputs do not lead to additional output. It is important to note, however, that although the result suggests that increased per-pupil expenditures *have not* led to improved performance, increased spending still *might* lead to improved performance if those additional resources were spent differently, that is, on different inputs that do affect performance. For instance, smaller classes might improve performance if the time in those classes was used differently than it is in larger ones, whereas the finding that graduate education of teachers does not improve performance may say more about the current nature of graduate education than it does about the value of more training generally. Therefore, what these studies suggest about how to improve educational performance is particularly important.

Second, the "skill" of the teacher is one factor that apparently is related to student performance. As Murnane has noted (quoted in Brown and Saks 1981, p. 222), "Virtually every study of school effectiveness finds that some attributes of teachers are significantly related to student achievement. . . . In particular, the intellectual skills of a teacher as measured by a verbal ability test or the quality of college the teacher attended tend to be significant." A similar theme is cited by Hanushek (1986, p. 1164) who writes that "The closest thing to a consistent finding among the studies is that 'smarter' teachers, ones who perform well on verbal ability tests, do better in the classroom. . . ." The practical difficulty with this finding is that it may not always be easy to identify ahead of time "more skilled" or "smarter" people and then to induce more of those people into teaching. In fact, it may be that there are several ways for individuals to be successful teachers, so identifying a single characteristic as indicative of whether someone will be a "good" teacher is not feasible.

The third general conclusion of these studies is that the school curriculum can be related to student performance, at least on standardized tests. As noted by

Murnane (1985, p. 120), "The best documented schooling change contributing to the [SAT] score decline is a reduction in the number of academic courses students take. . . . Subsequent research supports the link between the number of academic courses students take and their scores on standardized tests." By "academic courses," this finding refers to the basics—reading and writing, mathematics, science, social studies—as opposed to vocational and other courses students can select (the arts, sports, and so on). This finding should not be surprising because these academic skills are primarily tested by standardized tests. Nonetheless, it is comforting that the statistical studies come to such a common sense conclusion: If one wants students to read and write well and do mathematics, then those are the courses students must take and the skills they must practice in school.

Policy Implications

In large measure, these results have spurred many of the actual and proposed changes in state education policies in recent years. Most of these changes and proposals focus on teachers and courses. Regarding teachers, the policy issues concern how teachers are trained, certified and evaluated, and paid. A number of colleges and universities have now agreed that students working to become teachers will take fewer education classes and more classes in the specific disciplines they plan to teach. Thus, for example, someone who plans to be a high school math teacher might major in mathematics in college and take some specialized education classes in addition (rather than majoring in education and taking a few math classes). All states have some procedure to certify teachers as eligible to teach in that state. A number of states have acted to toughen certification requirements by raising the basic education requirement, creating certification exams, and/or using a probation period coupled with an on-the-job evaluation. In 1991, 40 states required teachers to pass specific tests for initial certification, all but 3 of which took effect since 1980.

Regarding teacher pay, the two common proposals are for higher teacher salaries generally and for the adoption of a merit-pay system for salary increases, with those increases depending on some measure of a teacher's "success." The first is intended to attract more skilled people into teaching, whereas the second is intended both as an incentive for teachers to be more successful and as a reward for teachers who are. The average annual salary of public elementary and secondary school teachers was $45,822 in 2002–2003 (U.S. Department of Education, 2003).[11] Although the average nominal salary of teachers has increased essentially continually since 1960, real average salaries have risen and fallen over this period. For instance, real salaries in 1985 ($40,636 in 2002–2003 dollars) were less than in 1970 ($41,587). Of course, the average real salary of all workers declined some in the 1970s, although Hanushek (1986) presents evidence that suggests that the real salaries of teachers declined slightly more than those of all workers in those years.

---

[11]In contrast, the median annual earnings in 2001 of workers 25-years-old and over with at least a Bachelor's degree was about $55,930 for men and $40,995 for women.

Since 1985, real average salaries increased in the period 1985 to 1991, fell from 1991 to 1997, and have increased again after 1997. Still, real average teacher salaries have increased by only about 13 percent in the 20 years since 1985, less than 1 percent per year.

There seem to be at least three important economic issues about these proposals to alter teacher pay. First, increased salaries may not be successful in attracting more skilled people into teaching soon if no mechanism is in place to create job vacancies for these individuals, and if teacher certification requirements prevent some people from moving into teaching without additional specialized training. Second, increases in teacher pay generally may not succeed in attracting more of the scarcest teachers, those in mathematics and science. The opportunity costs for people trained in those disciplines may require paying different salaries to teachers of different subjects, even if they have the same education and experience. Third, although merit pay is likely to induce teachers to spend more time generating the results on which the merit evaluation is based, that will improve education only to the extent that the performance test is valuable or appropriate. If the merit pay is based on the average performance of students, then teachers have an incentive to maximize test scores and may be less concerned with the distribution of those scores, as previously discussed.

Application 19.2

SCHOOL SIZE AND PERFORMANCE[12]

Although the number of school districts in the United States has decreased substantially as a result of consolidations, the structure of school districts has not changed substantially. The Census Bureau reported that in 2002, 77 percent of independent school districts and 71 percent of dependent (city or county) districts provided both elementary and secondary grades. The great bulk of high schools—nearly 14,000 representing about 75 percent of all secondary schools—cover three or four years involving grades 10 to 12 or 9 to 12. Another set of approximately 4,000 schools comprising 18 percent of all secondary schools covers five or six years of grades, essentially combining the junior and senior high school grades. The U.S. Department of Education further reports that of all the regular junior- and senior high schools (18,456 in number), about 8 percent had enrollment of less than 100 students, 27 percent enrollment of less than 300 students, and 50 percent enrollment of less than 600.

A substantial number of economies of scale or size studies in the U.S. context have

[12]This section draws from Ronald C. Fisher, "Organization of Educational Production: Schools, School Districts, and Consolidation." Working paper presented at the annual conference of the International Institute of Public Finance, Milan, 2004.

Application 19.2 — School Size and Performance

been conducted to examine both size effects for local school districts as well as individual schools. That research was initially reviewed and summarized by Fox (1981) and most recently by Andrews, Duncombe, and Yinger (2002). In some cases, these studies examine the effects of size (enrollment) on costs, holding output constant, whereas other studies examine the effect of size on output (student performance), holding cost constant.

In their review of production function studies, Andrews *et al.* (2002, p. 258) conclude that ". . . decreasing returns to size may begin to emerge for high schools above 1,000 students and elementary schools above 600 students." Lee and Smith (1997) find that high schools of between 600 and 900 students maximize student performance, while Eberts *et al.* (1984) find that elementary schools of between 300 and 500 students seem optimal. Taking all the studies into account, Andrews *et al.* (2002, p. 246) conclude that there likely are ". . . potentially sizeable cost savings up to district enrollment levels between 2,000 and 4,000 students" and that " . . . moderately sized elementary schools (300–500 students) and high schools (600–900 students) may optimally balance economies of size with negative effects of large schools."

Monk and Haller (1993) carefully examine the effect of high school size on the variety of classes in the high school curriculum, disaggregating effects both by academic discipline and by the target audience (advanced vs. remedial). They report that ". . . there are stronger positive relationships between

school size and course offerings in foreign languages and the performing and visual arts than in mathematics and social studies" and practically no relationship in English and science. Specifically, their results show that ". . . the largest schools offer more than fifteen additional foreign language and more than sixteen additional . . . arts courses than do the smallest schools." Focusing on the fraction of classes in each disciplinary area that are "specialized," that is targeted either to advanced or remedial students, Monk and Haller find that "the percentage share of the courses earmarked for either remedial or advanced students increases with school size." A particularly striking pattern emerges for mathematics, which is the area with the least degree of class specialization in the smaller schools but the area of greatest specialization in the largest schools.[13]

A substantial number of studies have emerged recently in the education literature suggesting that large high schools can have substantial negative effects on student performance (and/or cost), especially for disadvantaged students. The issues usually include concern about an environment that effectively discourages student and staff motivation and effort in large schools, the potential for less parental involvement, the potential for higher labor costs, and possibly greater opportunity costs for students due to greater transportation distances. Many of these studies seem to focus on large high schools with enrollments of approximately 1,500 students or more. From this perspective,

---

[13]Interestingly, Monk and Haller find that the increased specialization in mathematics classes in larger high schools arise primarily because of the offering of more remedial classes. Thus, the students needing the most help may be most disadvantaged in mathematics by small schools.

Application 19.2 — School Size and Performance

the result in a variety of statistical studies that an optimal size high school is between 600 and 1,000 students seems reasonable and understandable.

Evidence also shows that the cost structure for providing primary education is different from that for providing secondary education, as the optimal size elementary school (300 to 500) is about half that of the optimal size high school (600 to 1,000). Unless a highly skewed age-distribution of children exists in a school district, there is a standard relationship between district and school size at each level. For districts that provide both elementary and secondary education, elementary students represent about 54 percent of the total (7 out of 13 grades) and high school students about 31 percent (4 out of 13). Districts with 2,000 to 3,500 students are expected to have approximately 1,100 to 1,900 elementary students and 600 to 1,000 high school students, permitting an "optimal" size high school and multiple "optimal" size elementary schools. After districts exceed 4,000 students or so, single high schools may become too large, or it may be efficient to operate multiple high schools. Districts with fewer than 2,000 students, on

the other hand, may be too small to operate an efficient size high school.

The situation in Michigan illustrates the difficulties posed by district and school organization. Of the approximately 550 independent public school districts in Michigan, 95 percent provide both elementary and secondary education. The enrollment in these districts varies dramatically. The resulting size distribution for the approximately 460 public high schools that cover grades 9 through 12 is shown in Table 19.6. About 40 percent of Michigan's traditional high schools are smaller than the optimal size range for high schools (less than 600 students) and about 40 percent are larger than the optimal size range (more than 900 to 1,000 students). Similar circumstances exist in other states, as well.

This suggests a whole range of school organization options—including separate primary and secondary districts, small primary districts contracting with larger integrated districts for high school service, high schools that are jointly operated by separate K-8 districts, and a possible increased state role for secondary as opposed to primary education.

Table 19.6

Michigan Public High Schools, Grades 9—12*

Rank/Percentile	Enrollment
Minimum	127
20th Percentile	406
40th Percentile	624
Median	769
60th Percentile	951
80th Percentile	1,416
Maximum	2,596

*461 total schools with mean enrollment of 897

Assessment and Accountability

You have learned previously in this chapter about the changes many states have made in their financing systems in an attempt to improve education or to meet court-ordered expectations. The other major development in education policy in the past decade has been an increased focus on evaluating students, schools, and educational results. State governments initiated the emphasis on accountability during the 1990s, which in many ways was the natural result of those legal decisions that forced states to take more fiscal responsibility for distributing educational resources and for ensuring adequate educational production. The state emphasis on accountability also arose from the now well-documented long-run trend of increasing real per-student spending by public schools and decreasing average class sizes, which is coupled with student performance that—as measured by a wide variety of tests comparing students in the United States as well as comparing U.S. students internationally—either declined or did not improve nearly as fast as spending grew. This fact has induced states to want to improve the results of public education systems and to find ways to ensure that the increasing state spending is being used in the most effective manner.

With the approval of the No Child Left Behind Act in 2002, advocated by the Bush administration, the federal government became an additional force encouraging educational assessment and accountability. The act requires states to adopt education-assessment systems and accountability measures that impose consequences—such as denying federal education grants—on school systems that show poor assessment results.

"No Child Left Behind"

Even before the No Child Left Behind Act was passed and signed in 2002, many states had adopted and implemented new educational standards and assessment mechanisms. Ladd (2001, p. 385) reported that "Forty-five states now [in 2001] have report cards on schools, and 27 of them rate schools or identify low performing schools." Hanushek and Raymond (2001, p. 369) noted that "The basic skeleton of accountability systems involves goals, standards for performance, measurement, and consequences. . . ." They further reported that although few states had set clear goals for their accountability systems, essentially all states had established standards for performance and tested students in some form. In addition, most of the states also evaluated and reported on the performance of schools, but perhaps only about half of the states had explicit consequences for poor performance by either students or schools. The No Child Left Behind Act put the force of the federal government behind this trend and made inescapable the increased focus by states on educational performance.

The No Child Left Behind Act established a series of assessment provisions and procedures that states are to pursue, as follows:

■ Each state identifies an assessment mechanism (usually some test or set of tests) and sets specific academic achievement levels (called "proficiency levels") for reading and mathematics based on the state's assessment method.

- Each state sets performance goals, measured as the percentage of students, by grade level and for both reading and mathematics, who meet the proficiency level on the state assessment mechanism. The performance goals are to be increased each year so that all students are at the proficient level by the end of the 2013–2014 school year.

- The results of the state assessment (test scores or the percentage of students achieving the proficient level) are to be reported for all schools and for specific subgroups of students in each school, including low-income students, racial or ethnic minorities, students with disabilities, students with limited English language capability, and others.

- By the 2005–2006 school year, states are to have a system in place to test every student in grades 3 through 8 annually and students in grades 10 through 12 once in both reading and mathematics. Testing in science must be added by the following year.

- Schools and school districts will be evaluated each year as to whether they are making "adequate yearly progress" toward the ultimate goal of full proficiency for all students by 2014. Adequate yearly progress is defined as all student groups (including each subgroup) in that school or district meeting the proficiency level percentage goal for that year. If the percentage of students in any group failing to achieve a proficiency level score on the test exceeds that year's goal, then the entire school and district are deemed to be not making adequate yearly progress.

- At least 95 percent of the students in a school and in each subgroup must take the assessment test for that school to be deemed as making adequate yearly progress.

- Schools that fail to make adequate yearly progress face a number of special requirements and procedures, including such things as developing and implementing a school improvement plan, allocating additional federal funds to teacher improvement, providing the opportunity for students to transfer to other schools, provide special tutoring assistance to selected students, and ultimately facing the possibility of school staff replacement, consolidation with other schools, state takeover, or private firm management.

The NCLB act has a number of other provisions and expectations concerning testing students with disabilities, testing students with limited proficiency in the English language, measuring and certifying teacher quality, and applying the schedule and set of required remedies and actions to schools that fail to make adequate yearly progress, called "schools in need of improvement." The carrot or stick, depending on one's point of view, that enforces NCLB is the $33 billion of federal government support for public primary and secondary education in 2002. Although only about 8 percent of total revenue for public K-12 education, this is still an amount of funds that provides the federal government substantial clout.

NCLB is controversial, to say the least. States have expressed concern about a variety of issues, most notably the costs associated with implementing and operating such an extensive assessment system, the seeming rigidity of requiring annual improvements for all groups of students in all tested areas, the complicated procedures for dealing with students with special circumstances, the costs associated with educational improvements needed to make adequate yearly progress, the notion of 100 percent proficiency as the ultimate goal (almost assuring that every school system will fail), and what some see as an unwarranted and heavy-handed intrusion by the federal government into matters that traditionally have been the responsibility and purview of state and local governments. All these issues cannot be resolved here, and likely will not in practice for several years at least, but the economic and fiscal analysis presented in this chapter can be used to clarify these issues.

Assessing and Accountability Issues

Four issues about educational accountability seem to be the most difficult and contentious: (1) who should be evaluated—students, teachers, schools, or school districts; (2) how should the evaluation be structured—that is, what are the relative advantages of various evaluation methods; (3) what level of government should be primarily responsible for setting standards, conducting the evaluation, and paying the costs—states or the federal government; and (4) what remedies or consequences should apply to schools or students who fail to meet assessment standards. Each is considered next.

Unit of Evaluation

The production function approach to education presented earlier in this chapter can be used to illustrate the difficulties of using districts, schools, teachers, or students as the unit of evaluation. Districts and teachers clearly seem the worst options. Education is produced in schools, not districts, and focusing on district average results would allow poorly performing schools to be hidden by other schools that perform well. A given teacher in a single grade is but one input among many that affect a student's learning, and thus it would seem nearly impossible to attribute a student's score on an assessment test to one single teacher.

Between students and schools, Ladd (2001, p. 398) argues that "schools are the most logical starting point for a top-down accountability system...." First, schools are the production unit that controls educational resources and can act to reallocate those resources in an attempt to improve educational performance. Second, what school to attend is the educational unit that families most directly select and that families can change if performance is unacceptable. Third, poorly performing schools cannot escape notice and attention if schools are the focus of assessment. Finally, as Ladd (p. 389) puts it, "school-based incentive rewards provide an incentive for all school personnel to work cooperatively toward a well-specified goal."

The concerns about focusing on schools also are easy to note. Student learning and knowledge, either that which students actually possess or that which may be represented or measured by test scores, is a cumulative result both of learning done in *all* schools attended and of learning done *outside of school* through personal or family experiences and activities. Scores on tests administered in the middle of the 8th grade, for example, can hardly be attributed only to the 15 months that the student attended that particular middle school. Certainly the elementary schools that the students attended, which might be in a different district, different state, or even a different country, is expected to have had an impact. In addition, one cannot minimize the importance of the learning that students achieve through interactions with their fellow students as well the learning that arises from private activity—parental reading or teaching, books in the home, family travel or other experiences, athletics, music, and so on. Finally, not all students are in a personal or community environment that places equal value on education or provides equal motivation. Surely, the score a student achieves on a test in the 3rd grade, 8th grade, or 11th grade reflects the combined effects of *all* of these influences. Why, then, should those scores be attributed solely to the contribution of the last school?

In the end, one of the strongest arguments for assessing schools may be the difficulties with assessing and penalizing only students. Although students certainly influence their own educations by their behavior, they have little direct control or influence over the allocation of educational resources; students do not control curricula, hire teachers, maintain facilities, and so on. Some of the potential problems of focusing assessment on schools may be mitigated by appropriately structuring the assessment instrument and information, as discussed next.

Methods of Evaluation

A host of controversial and well-known issues exist about student testing. However, assuming that one believes in the value of a particular test, results may be used to shed light on the school contribution. One option is to compare schools only with the same populations—schools in rural, low-income communities to those in similar communities; predominately minority, central city schools to the same; and so on. A second option is to correct, using statistical methods, for different student populations. Usually this involves comparing the results in a particular school or district to the results that might be expected or predicted for the population of students in that district. A third possibility is to look only at the *improvement* of students in a particular district. If a district's average score is at the 50th percentile of the statewide average for students in 3rd grade, say, but at the 75th percentile for that same group of students in the 11th grade, then the district would seem to have made relative improvement in the students' performance. Which is having a greater impact—such a district or one that has students who perform at the 85th percentile in both grades?

The issue, then, is whether to focus on the *level* of outcome or result by a student or school or on the *change in that level* by a student or school over some time. The distinction is important because factors specific to a student (innate ability, effort, family circumstances, social environment) are expected to influence the student's level of achievement, and those factors may be difficult to measure and thus control for in studies of educational outcomes. By focusing on the change in achievement for a given student or set of students over time, those other student-specific factors are held constant, so that the change in achievement may reflect the *value added* by the educational system.

Many times, the same standardized test is given to students at different times—for instance, in grades 5, 8, and 12—and the scores at each grade level compared to some average or norm for that level. The student's score relative to the norm at one grade level (90 percent of the norm in grade 5) compared to the same student's score in a later grade (110 percent of the norm in grade 12) may reflect the improvement caused by the school system. The fact that the average 12th-grade score for two schools is both 110 percent of the norm may not mean that both schools are doing an equally good educational job if the students in one school started at a lower level. The change in scores for the same students may be the preferable measure. In fact, it may be that a school with a lower average 12th-grade score has a greater value added than some other school with a higher average score, but one whose students started at a higher level.

A preference for measuring educational performance by value added led the state of Utah to adopt legislation in 2005 giving Utah's state education evaluation system priority over the procedures specified in NCLB, even at the risk of losing $76 million of federal education aid to the state. Utah measures student achievement by value added, comparing achievement for the same set of students as they progress from grade to grade. NCLB, on the other hand, requires states to compare test scores for one set of students in a given grade to scores for a different group of students in that grade the following year. By one report, as many as half the states have been considering legislation urging changes in NCLB or permitting state officials not to follow its requirements (and risk losing federal aid). Vermont has adopted a law that gives local school districts that option.[14]

Local, State, or National Responsibility

States remain concerned about the federal government imposing a single evaluation mechanism on all schools regardless of differences in circumstances or expectations of state residents. Many state officials have argued that state assessment systems are better able to accommodate differences among states and differences among districts within states. Alternatively, state officials have asked the federal government to build in more flexibility to the NCLB system. You have seen evidence earlier in this chapter about the substantial variation in educational levels and emphasis between states and even between districts within states. A report of a task force on the NCLB act composed of state officials and organized through the National Conference of State Legislatures (NCSL) even questions the constitutionality of NCLB because the conditions that the federal government imposes through NCLB on receipt of federal

---

[14]See Alan Greenblatt. "The Left Behind Syndrome." *Governing*, September 2004.

education grants may violate the 10th Amendment, which reserves certain powers to the states, because it uses coercion to attain state participation.[15]

States also are extremely concerned about the costs of administering the assessments required by NCLB as well as the costs that schools will face to improve achievement toward the 100-percent proficiency goal. The NCSL Task Force notes that the federal government's share of K-12 education funding has risen by about 2 percentage points (to 8 percent of total education revenue) since adoption of NCLB. Estimates of the administrative costs to schools of implementing the assessment procedures of NCLB seems to be have about the same magnitude. So, one can argue that the federal government has provided roughly sufficient additional funds to cover the administrative costs of NCLB. Additional state and local government costs to bring all students to a proficiency level are likely to be of much greater magnitude, however, which the federal government seems unwilling to provide. The NCSL Task Force therefore questions whether NCLB should be evaluated as an unfounded mandate imposed by the federal government on states, which would require additional federal action by federal law.

Consequences and Remedies

Assessment consequences can include releasing information about the performance of schools, providing rewards (perhaps in the form of additional resources) to schools that meet specific performance objectives, or imposing penalties on schools that do not meet assessment standards. Some states have incorporated reward/penalty provisions in their education grant systems, essentially threatening to reduce resources to poorly performing schools. This might be seen as counterproductive by some, although the concept is that resource reductions would induce additional students to leave poorly performing schools and to move to other schools with better performance ratings, which would then receive additional resources.

Perhaps the most important long-run issue is how students, teachers, schools, school districts, states, and the federal government will respond to cases where schools are found to be performing poorly, whether measured by adequate yearly progress as mandated by NCLB or by some other standard. The options through NCLB are relatively limited. Students can switch schools, low-achieving students may receive additional tutoring, school staff can be changed, the school day can be lengthened, or curricula can be revised. Unfortunately, the economic research about education production discussed earlier in this chapter does not provide much guidance. That research, as well as the body of research by educational specialists, has identified only a limited number of curriculum, teacher, and technology options that clearly seem to improve educational results.

The fact that research about education production has not identified many specific factors that can be used to boost teacher productivity and educational results has caused a number of states to experiment with entirely new approaches. Some

---

[15]See "Final Report of the Task Force on No Child Left Behind." National Conference of State Legislatures, February 2005.

states, such as Kentucky, have experimented with grouping students differently (eliminating traditional elementary grades) and less-structured classroom activity. Other states are experimenting with changes to the length of both the school day and school year; perhaps it would be preferable if students attended school for fewer hours (providing time for more personal study and work) but more days (eliminating long breaks away from school). The results of these and other experiments are likely to be important in improving education in the future.

States also have acted to change school curricula and the types of courses students take, largely by altering graduation requirements imposed by state governments. According to the U.S. Department of Education (2005), all but six states (Colorado, Iowa, Massachusetts, Michigan, Nebraska, and Pennsylvania) have substantial state-set academic requirements for high school graduation. Many of those state standards have been established or strengthened since 1985. The other six states essentially leave those standards as an option for local districts. Among those states with course requirements imposed by the state government, common requirements are three to four units (years) of English and two to three units of mathematics, science, and social studies each. One of the most dramatic changes occurred in Florida, which now has among the most stringent requirements. Local school districts previously determined requirements, but now all high school graduates are required to have four units of English; have three units each of social studies, mathematics, and science; and pass a minimum competency test. Indeed, 20 states now require students to pass a competency test to graduate.

Therefore, schools already have incentives to use any new methods or technologies known to improve educational performance, although they may not always have sufficient resources to apply all of them effectively. In addition, in the cases of some students, it just may not be possible through the application of additional school resources to offset a variety of environmental factors—the social inputs and peer effects in the educational production function—that work against those students' educational achievements. Therefore, simply identifying that a school (and its students) is performing poorly and not meeting assessment standards is not particularly helpful unless some clear mechanisms are known that will improve education results for that particular group of students, and unless adequate resources are available to implement those mechanisms.

INTERNATIONAL COMPARISON

Not surprisingly, the structure and financing of primary and secondary education varies greatly among industrialized nations. Comparisons are difficult because of differences in the structure of government generally, because of problems in converting financial amounts to comparable units, and because of obvious cultural differences. Still, comparing primary and secondary education in the United States to other nations both illustrates many of the issues discussed in this chapter and suggests options that the United States might consider for altering its educational system.

Table 19.7

Secondary Education Comparisons, Selected Nations

	Percentage of 15-Year-Olds in Secondary School 1999	Pupils Per Teacher in Upper-Secondary Education 2001	Secondary Education Expenditure Per Student 2000	Average Literacy Score* for 15-Year-Olds in Reading 2000	Average Literacy Score* for 15-Year-Olds in Mathematics 2000	Average Literacy Score* for 15-Year-Olds in Science 2000
Australia	92.0%	10.8	$6,894	528	533	528
Austria	91.9	9.9	8,578	507	515	519
Canada	93.4	17.2	5,947	534	533	529
Denmark	92.8	13.9	7,726	497	514	481
France	95.3	11.2	7,636	505	517	500
Germany	96.7	13.7	6,826	484	490	487
Ireland	91.5	—	4,638	527	503	513
Italy	78.7	10.4	7,218	487	457	478
Japan	95.1	14.0	6,266	522	557	550
Norway	94.2	9.2	8,476	505	499	500
Spain	85.4	—	5,185	493	476	491
Sweden	96.8	16.6	6,339	516	510	512
Switzerland	90.5		9,780	494	529	496
United Kingdom	84.5	12.3	5,991	523	529	532
United States	88.5	14.8	8,855	504	493	499

*Scales were designed to have an average score of 500 points and standard deviation of 100.

SOURCE: U.S. Department of Education. *Digest of Education Statistics.* 2003.

The information reported in Table 19.7 and Figures 19.7 and 19.8 (and other background data from the same sources) suggest the following comparative observations about primary and secondary education in the United States:

- The United States spends about 4 percent of GDP on primary and secondary education, which is about average among the developed nations represented by the Organization for Economic Cooperation and Development (OECD).

- Expenditure per student is relatively high in the United States (second only to Luxembourg for primary education and fourth behind Luxembourg, Switzerland, and Norway for secondary education).

- The United States is about average in terms of the percentage of students attending or graduating from secondary schools, with about 89 percent of 16-year-olds in school (but compared to 97 percent in Germany and Sweden, 95 percent in France and Japan, and 94 percent in Canada) and about 75 percent of students graduating from secondary school at the typical age (compared to an OECD average of 78 percent).

- Typical class sizes in the United States also are about average, substantially smaller than in such nations as Canada and Japan, but larger than in such nations as Denmark and Switzerland.

Figure 19.7

Expenditure on
primary and
secondary
education as a
percentage of
GDP, 2002

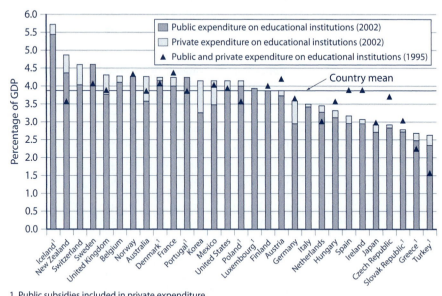

Primary, secondary, and post-secondary non-tertiary education

1. Public subsidies included in private expenditure.

SOURCE: OECD, *Education at a Glance*, 2005.

Figure 19.8

Average class
size in educational
institutions
by level of
education, 2003

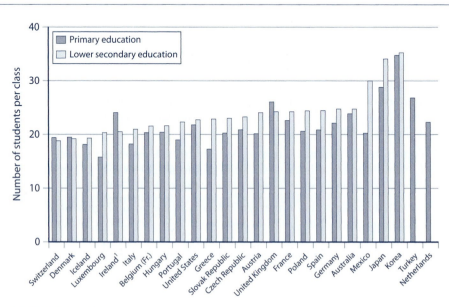

1. Public institutions only.

SOURCE: OECD, *Education at a Glance*, 2005.

■ Students in the United States attend school for more hours per year (about 1,150) than in any other nation.

■ Teacher salaries in the United States relative to per-capita GDP are lower than average at about 130 percent of per-capita GDP, compared to 180 percent in Germany, 160 percent in Japan, and 140 percent in Australia, for instance.

■ Scores of U.S. students on standardized tests administered specifically for international comparisons are about average, but substantially lower than for students from Australia, Canada, Japan, and the United Kingdom, for instance.

The picture that emerges for the United States is a nation that spends an average fraction of its income on education, but because income (GDP) is very high, spending per student is also very high. Data reported by the OECD show clearly that education spending per student is positively related to national income, as measured by GDP per capita. That relatively high spending in the United States funds a larger than average amount of time in school for students rather than substantially smaller than average class sizes or higher than average teacher salaries (which could be alternative uses of the funds). The longer time in school per year by U.S. students arises not because U.S. students go to school more days per year, generally, but rather because of more hours per day. The comparison with Japan is particularly dramatic. Japan spends roughly 25 percent less on education than does the United States (3 percent of GDP in Japan compared to 4 percent in the U.S) and has roughly 25 percent larger classes (at least in primary and lower secondary schools). Students in Japan attend school fewer hours per year than in the United States, but teachers are paid more relative to national GDP.

Two other important structural differences in the educational system in the United States become clear when compared to most other nations not illustrated by the data. First, the United States uses one of the most decentralized systems to provide education of all nations, even compared to the other nations with federal systems of government (having federal, state, and local governments, such as in Australia, Canada, and Germany). Local school districts in the United States generate about 43 percent of revenue for primary and secondary education and are responsible for spending essentially 100 percent. In comparison, reliance on local finance is substantially lower in Germany, and state governments in Australia govern, finance, and operate the schools (as is done only in Hawaii in the United States). Second, U.S. primary and secondary education is a uniform or nonstratified system, with students at any given age and location all participating in the single-school system and taking a similar curriculum. A number of other nations, notably most European nations, operate stratified systems, with students sorted into various educational tracks at relatively young ages (as young as 10 years of age in Austria and Germany).

Interestingly, there seems to be no clear overall relationship between these characteristics of educational production systems and educational results, at least as measured by standardized tests. As noted previously, U.S. students perform about average on these tests, although there is some variation by subject area; U.S. students score relatively better in reading than mathematics. The OECD reports that although students in stratified educational systems tend to perform relatively less well, this tendency is small and not statistically significant. However, the OECD also concludes "in countries that separate students at an early age into schools of different types, students' social background tends to be relatively strongly related to their performance. Disadvantaged students are more likely to be placed in low-status schools with less demanding curricula... and then to end up with relatively poor performance. Socially advantaged students are more likely to be placed in high-status schools with demanding curricula and then to end up with relatively high quality performance.... In countries that keep students together in comprehensive schools, the relationship between social background and educational performance is weaker...." (OECD, *Education at a Glance, 2005 Edition*, p. 399).

SUMMARY

In 2002, public elementary and secondary schools served about 48 million students. Public school spending amounted to about $8,200 per student, 4.3 percent of GDP and 40 percent of local government spending. Expenditures per pupil, even after adjustment for inflation, increased substantially in the past 40 years.

State governments generated about half of the revenue for financing public elementary and secondary schools in 2001–2002, and local governments generated about 43 percent. The federal government provided the remaining 7 percent. Since 1995, the relative role of state governments has increased, and the relative role of local governments has decreased.

Lump-sum per-pupil grants to support local education are referred to as foundation aid because the per-pupil grant represents a minimum expenditure level; the state aid is intended to provide a basic foundation on top of which local revenue supplements may be added.

Guaranteed Tax Base (GTB) or District Power Equalizing aid plans are intended to provide an equal, basic per-pupil property tax base to each district, rather than basic per-pupil minimum expenditure level. A GTB plan involves matching grants that reduce the price of education to the school districts. Because the demand for education spending is price inelastic, the price reductions that are caused by the matching grants generally did not influence education spending very much.

Little relationship appears to exist between rising school expenditures and improved student performance, given how those funds have been used, including spending for smaller classes or higher teacher salaries. The intellectual skills of a teacher as measured by a verbal ability test or the quality of college the teacher attended tend to have a significant effect on student performance. A third general conclusion is that the school curriculum can matter because of the link between the number of academic courses students take and their scores on standardized tests.

In the 1970s, the primary educational policy issue concerned the differences in per-pupil spending among districts. States altered their educational grant programs and spent more money on education, but spending differences among districts were not reduced and educational performance generally did not improve. Recently, the primary issue moved from focusing on educational spending to educational results. Expenditures are a very imperfect measure of the output of government in providing services, and consistent with that observation, increasing expenditures may be necessary, but certainly are not sufficient, for improving service results.

DISCUSSION QUESTIONS

1. Per-pupil spending often varies among school districts in a given state. Suppose that one district spends $5,000 per pupil for instruction (excluding transportation, lunches, administration, and so on), while another district of about the same size spends $8,000 per pupil. What could account for this difference? Consider factors in the categories of the quantity of inputs, the type of inputs, the prices of inputs, and the type of output.

2. The role of state governments in providing public primary and secondary education varies greatly. In one case, the state government operates the school system; in a number of others, the state government provides a substantial amount of the revenue for local schools (half or more) and sets minimum graduation or teacher requirements; and in other cases, the state provides either a relatively small amount of revenue or sets few standards or both. What are the economic arguments for and against state involvement in financing and producing education? What social and economic characteristics of a state might influence the choice of how to produce education? Do these help explain the cases of Hawaii and New Hampshire or Washington compared to Oregon?

3. Refer to the "Education Grant Simulation" section earlier in this chapter. In that illustration, a program of matching grants was not effective in equalizing per-pupil spending because demand was relatively inelastic. What other means might be used to narrow these spending differences? Outline the specifics of a state program that you believe would be successful in setting a minimum per-pupil spending level of $9,444, the average level in the illustration. Explain the effect of that program on each district and discuss whether you would support such a change in your state.

4. Suppose your college or university decides to evaluate its undergraduate program to determine how successful it is at educating students. How should the output of a university be measured? In terms of education only, what characteristics do you think show how good of a job a college does? How should the teaching output or quality of individual professors be measured? Does your university attempt to measure education output or teaching success? Does your university have a merit pay system for faculty, and if so, what role does education output or teaching quality play?

SELECTED READINGS

Fisher, Ronald C. and Leslie Papke. "Local Government Responses to Education Grants." *National Tax Journal*, 53 (March 2000): 153–168.

"Forum on School Accountability Programs." *National Tax Journal* 54, (June 2001). This Forum includes three papers, by Eric Hanushek and Margaret Raymond; by Helen Ladd; and by Richard Murnane and Frank Levy.

Hanushek, Eric A. "The Economics of Schooling." *Journal of Economic Literature* 24 (September 1986): 1141–77.

Hanushek, Eric A. *Making Schools Work*. Washington, D.C.: Brookings Institution, 1994.

Ladd, Helen F. and Janet S. Hansen, eds. *Making Money Matter: Financing America's Schools*. Committee on Education Finance, Commission on Behavioral and Social Sciences and Education, National Research Council. Washington, D.C.: National Academy Press, 1999.

Murnane, Richard J. "An Economist's Look at Federal and State Education Policies." In J. Quigley and D. Rubinfeld, eds., *American Domestic Priorities: An Economic Appraisal*. Berkeley: University of California Press, 1985, 118–47.

Yinger, John, ed. *Helping Children Left Behind: State Aid and the Pursuit of Educational Equity*. Cambridge MA: The MIT Press, 2004.

CHAPTER 20

TRANSPORTATION

*. . . In no other major area are pricing practices so
irrational, so out of date, and so conducive to waste as
in urban transportation.*[1]

—WILLIAM S. VICKREY

HEADLINES

"CONGESTION CONTINUES TO GROW IN AMERICA'S URBAN AREAS. DESPITE A SLOW GROWTH IN JOBS AND TRAVEL IN 2003, CONGESTION CAUSED 3.7 BILLION HOURS OF TRAVEL DELAY AND 2.3 BILLION GALLONS OF WASTED FUEL . . . TO A TOTAL COST OF MORE THAN $63 BILLION.

IN GENERAL, TRAFFIC CONGESTION IS WORSE IN THE LARGER URBAN AREAS THAN IN THE SMALLER ONES. TRAFFIC CONGESTION LEVELS HAVE INCREASED IN EVERY AREA SINCE 1982. CONGESTION EXTENDS TO MORE TIME OF THE DAY, MORE ROADS, AFFECTS MORE OF THE TRAVEL AND CREATES MORE EXTRA TRAVEL TIME THAN IN THE PAST. AND CONGESTION LEVELS HAVE RISEN IN ALL SIZE CATEGORIES, INDICATING THAT EVEN THE SMALLER AREAS ARE NOT ABLE TO KEEP PACE WITH RISING DEMAND.

THE AVERAGE COST PER TRAVELER IN THE 85 URBAN AREAS WAS $794 IN 2003 . . . 2.3 BILLION GALLONS OF FUEL WERE WASTED IN THE 85 URBAN AREAS. THE AVERAGE DELAY PER PEAK TRAVELER IN THE 85 URBAN AREAS IS 47 HOURS. [2]"

---

[1]"Pricing in Urban and Suburban Transport." *American Economic Review* (May 1963): p. 452.

[2]Schrank, David and Tim Lomax. *The Urban Mobility Report.* Texas Transportation Institute, The Texas A&M University System, http://mobility.tamu.edu, May, 2005.

CONGESTION EFFECTS ON THE AVERAGE TRAVELER—2003

Congestion Statistics per Traveler Population Group	Average Cost ($)	Average Delay (hours)	Average Fuel (gallons)
VERY LARGE AREAS	$1,038	61	36
LARGE AREAS	620	37	23
MEDIUM AREAS	418	25	15
SMALL AREAS	222	13	8
85 AREA AVERAGE	794	47	28
85 AREA TOTAL	$63.1 BILLION	3.7 BILLION	2.3 BILLION

Although education may be the dominant single service provided by subnational governments, transportation is surely the most apparent service, the one more individuals directly interact with on a day-to-day basis. In fact, transportation facilities provided by state and local governments may be so apparent that they are sometimes taken for granted, without an understanding of what they cost or how they are financed. Once while making a presentation about state government spending to a local citizens group, I was confronted by an individual who asserted that he did not get any benefits from state taxes. I asked the fellow how he had gotten to the meeting that day. He responded that he had driven and then said "Well, obviously I use the roads, but except for that. . . ." Except for the roads? It is estimated that in 2002, one mile of interstate highway cost between $3.5 and $5.0 million for construction alone, plus the cost of engineering and acquisition of land. And even though primary, secondary, and most urban roads cost less, clearly even a short automobile trip requires the use of many millions of dollars worth of capital infrastructure provided through governments.[3]

Transportation is also somewhat of a unique service because inputs provided publicly and privately usually are combined to produce transportation service. Individuals own private automobiles, which they drive on public roads and bridges. Private airline firms fly privately owned airplanes among publicly provided airports using a publicly provided air traffic control system. Privately owned and operated boats travel on publicly owned and maintained waterways and harbors. In essence, the private and public sectors jointly provide transportation service, with the public sector primarily responsible for providing and maintaining transportation routes. The demand for transportation service—both for routes and vehicles—arises almost entirely from private choice, however. As a result of the complementary nature of the public- and private-transportation

---

[3]It is estimated that it cost about $14 billion over some 10 years to replace and rebuild the 7.5 miles of Boston's Central Artery, converting it into an underground highway. See "Massachusetts Governor Signs Big Dig Bailout Bill," CNN.com, May 18, 2000.

inputs, government must consider private demand for transportation in providing facilities. However, it is also true that those publicly provided facilities—and their prices—can influence private decisions about the amount and type of transportation individuals demand.

The emphasis in this chapter is on the role of government in providing and financing those public facilities. Roads and highways are the largest category, measured both by dollars and use, of transportation facilities provided by government. In the provision of highways, state governments play the dominant role by receiving aid funds from the federal government, collecting substantial own-source revenues, spending directly on the construction and maintenance of roads, and transferring aid funds to local governments for their direct spending.

FINANCING TRANSPORTATION: CURRENT PRACTICE

Types of Transportation Service

Governments provide transportation facilities or service for air, rail, road, and water transit. Of the total expenditures by all levels of government on these transportation services in 2001, about 60 percent (more than $110 billion) went for highways, as shown in Table 20.1. In contrast, about 15 percent of government transportation spending went for air transit and about 18 percent for mass transit. Of the $110 billion spent on highways, more than half—$60 billion or 55 percent—represented capital expenditure, that is, construction of roads and highways. From 1991 to 2001, transportation spending increased by 69 percent, as shown in both Table 20.1 and Figure 20.1. Not surprisingly, the fastest growing category of spending among major transportation modes was for air transportation; in contrast, government expenditure for rail transportation declined.

The dominance of spending on highways among all government transportation spending is certainly not surprising because it reflects the dominance of the automobile and the scope of highway transportation in general. In 2003 in the

Table 20.1

Federal, State, and Local Transportation Expenditures by Mode, 1991 and 2001

	1991 (millions of current dollars)	Percentage of Total	2001 (millions of current dollars)	Percentage of Total	Percentage Change
Highway	$66,588	61.5%	$110,465	60.3%	66%
Transit	20,848	19.2	33,590	18.3	61
Air	13,978	12.9	27,404	15.0	96
Water	5,847	5.4	10,469	5.7	79
Rail	781	0.7	737	0.4	−6
Pipeline	28	0.0	29	0.0	4
General Support	270	0.2	364	0.2	35
Total	**$108,338**	**100.0%**	**$183,057**	**100.0%**	**69%**

SOURCE: U.S. Department of Transportation. *National Transportation Statistics, 2004,* January 2005

United States, 190 million licensed drivers drove approximately 230 million registered motor vehicles about 2.9 trillion vehicle-miles on about 4 million miles of roads. The 2000 National Household Travel Survey showed that about one-third of households in the United States have one motor vehicle, about 60 percent have at least two vehicles, although only about 8 percent have none. The share of households with more than one vehicle has increased essentially continually since 1960, and survey data suggest that travel per vehicle remains constant as the number of vehicles grows (see Figure 20.2). More vehicles, then, means more highway travel. The main purposes for automobile travel by individuals are for travel to work (16 percent of trips and 27 percent of vehicle-miles), for family and personal business (45 percent of trips and 33 percent of vehicle miles),

Figure 20.1

Transportation expenditures and user charges in current dollars

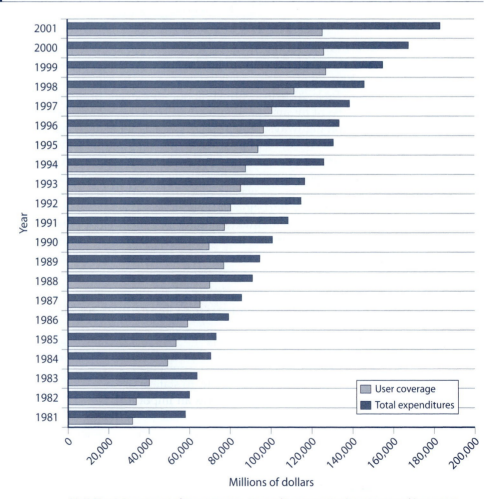

SOURCE: U.S. Department of Transportation, *National Transportation Statistics: Annual Report 1994.*

Figure 20.2

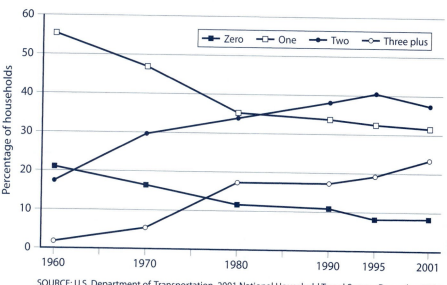

SOURCE: U.S. Department of Transportation, 2001 National Household Travel Survey, December 2004.

and for social and recreational trips (20 percent of trips and 25 percent of vehicle miles).

The Role of the National and Subnational Governments

The general pattern for financing transportation services involves both direct spending on purchases and payment of intergovernmental aid by each of the three primary levels of government. Total spending and intergovernmental aid payments by each level of government for various categories of transportation service are shown in Tables 20.2a and 20.2b.[4] The federal government's role concerning highways and public transit is primarily in providing grants to subnational governments. However, for air and water transportation, the federal government has a substantial role in directly purchasing and providing services and facilities. For instance, of the approximately $30 billion spent by the federal government for highways in 2001, about $27.7 billion, or 93 percent, was composed of highway grants paid to state–local governments. Ninety-nine percent of federal government spending for public transit is in the form of grants to state and local governments. Therefore, although the federal government plays an important role in financing highway and transit transportation, almost all of that role is generating funds to be spent by states and localities. The federal government spends very little directly purchasing highway or transit facilities.

---

[4]The state and local data are for 1997 because the corresponding data from the 2002 Census of Governments are not generally available at the time this is being written.

Table 20.2a

Composition of Federal Transportation Expenditure, 2001 (millions of dollars)

Transportation Mode	Total Spending	Grants to States and Localities	Direct Spending
Highways	$29,950	$27,749	$ 2,201
Transit	7,048	6,965	83
Air	13,889	2,017	11,872
Water	4,475	1	4,474
Rail	722	35	687

SOURCE: U.S. Department of Transportation. *National Transportation Statistics, 2004,* January 2005

Table 20.2b

Transportation Expenditure By States and Localities, 1997 (millions of dollars)

	States		Local Governments	
Function	Total Spending	Intergovernmental Aid Paid	Total Spending	Intergovernmental Aid Paid
Highways	$60,204	$11,431	$33,352	$63
Air Transp.	1,413	531	9,249	4
Water	747	8	2,071	1
Transit Subsidies	127	—	228	—
Parking Facilities	—	—	812	—

SOURCE: U.S. Bureau of the Census, *Compendium of Government Finances, 1997,* December 2000

State governments, on the other hand, are both substantial direct purchasers of highway and air transportation services and facilities and transmitters of aid to local governments. In the case of highways, for instance, state transportation departments engage in highway construction and maintenance directly (or through contracts) on the roads for which each state government has responsibility. State governments also make substantial intergovernmental grants (that is, transfer state highway funds) to local governments for road construction and maintenance. Local governments mostly serve as direct purchasers and providers of facilities and services using both their own revenues and the intergovernmental aid they receive from states and directly from the federal government. In 1997, for example, state governments spent about $60 billion on highways with about 19 percent ($11.4 billion) representing grants paid to local governments, whereas nearly all the approximately $33 billion spent by local governments went for direct purchases of facilities and services.

A truly accurate picture of the roles of the different levels of government in financing transportation requires both the distribution of final spending and the distribution of own-source revenue used for purchases and intergovernmental grants in each transportation category. State–local governments are responsible for about 98 percent of the actual spending on highway facilities and services; states alone accounting for nearly 60 percent. States also generate about 60 percent of the revenue spent on highways. The federal government provided about 27 percent of the funds spent on highways in 2001 but spent only about 2 percent directly itself. Local governments generated about 8 percent of revenues spent on highways but accounted for about 38 percent of direct spending. The conclusion from these analyses is that state governments are dominant in both generating and spending funds for highways. For air and water transportation, in contrast, about half of the spending is done directly by the federal government and the other half by subnational governments; for other transportation categories, the states and localities are dominant.

The central role of state governments in financing highways is reflected in Figure 20.3. States receive substantial amounts of federal aid, which accounts for 30 percent of state highway revenue, and pay substantial grants to local governments, which represent about 12 percent of state highway-related expenditures. On the revenue side, about 50 percent of state receipts is user revenue and tolls. On the spending side, about half of state disbursements goes for direct capital expenditure, compared to only about 31 percent for local governments. However, states

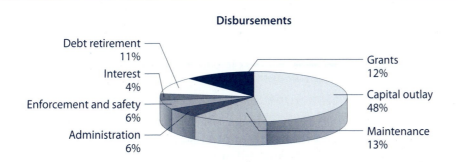

Figure 20.3

State receipts and disbursements for highways, 2003

Disbursements

Debt retirement 11%
Interest 4%
Enforcement and safety 6%
Administration 6%

Grants 12%
Capital outlay 48%
Maintenance 13%

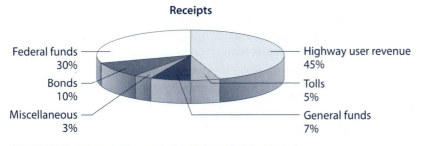

Receipts

Federal funds 30%
Bonds 10%
Miscellaneous 3%

Highway user revenue 45%
Tolls 5%
General funds 7%

SOURCE: U.S. Department of Transportation, Highway Statistics 2004.

Table 20.3	

Transportation Revenue Sources, 2005

Source	Tax Rate
Federal Government	
Motor Fuel Tax	$.184/gal. (gasoline)
	$.244/gal. (diesel fuel)
Aviation Gasoline	$.194/gallon
Truck and Trailer Tax	12% retail price
Tire Tax	$.0945/10 pounds
Road Use Charges for Trucks	$100–$550/truck
Air Transportation Tax (passengers)	7.5% of ticket price
	$3.20 per domestic segment
Air Transportation Tax (property)	6.25% of price
Airport Charges	
Water Transport Use Charges	
State–Local Governments	
Motor Fuel Tax[a]	$.075–$.32/gal. (gasoline)
Motor Vehicle License Fees	
Motor Vehicle Operator License Fees	
Highway Use and Toll Charges	
Parking Charges	
Airport Use Charges—Landing Fees; Passenger Facility Charges ($1, $2, $3)	
Water Transport Use Charges	

[a]Does not include state and local general sales taxes on gasoline and motor vehicles.

SOURCE: U.S. Department of Transportation (2005).

spend a smaller fraction of disbursements on highway maintenance (13 percent) when compared to local governments (41 percent of spending).

Transportation Revenues

Although governments generate revenues for transportation spending from a variety of sources, taxes and tolls collected from users are the major component. As shown earlier in Figure 20.1, transportation revenue from users increased faster than total spending during the 1980s and 1990s. For instance, revenue from users covered about 75 percent of transportation spending in 2000 compared to only about 70 percent in 1990 and 60 percent in 1980. The tax rates for the larger transportation taxes and charges are shown in Table 20.3. The federal government levies excise taxes on the sale of motor fuels ($.184 per gallon of gasoline and $.244 per gallon for diesel fuel), tires, trucks and trailers, and airline tickets and also collects user charges for road use (from trucks weighing more than 55,000 pounds) as well as for airport and waterway use. State governments and some local governments also levy excise taxes on the sale of motor fuels (varying from $.075 to $.31 per gallon of gasoline for the states only, in 2005), as shown in Figure 20.4; some states apply their general sales tax to the sale of gasoline as well, often with that revenue

Figure 20.4

State gasoline excise tax rates, 2005

Federal Rate: $.184   Lowest: $.075 (Georgia)
Median State Rate: $.21   Highest: $.31 (Rhode Island)

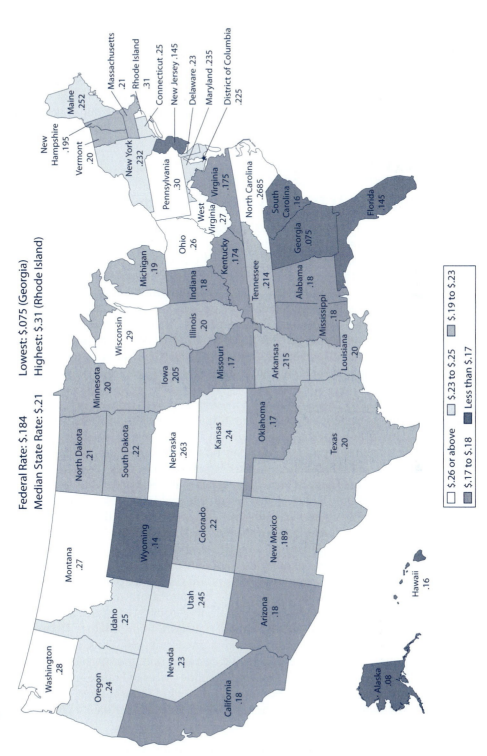

Legend:
- $.26 or above
- $.23 to $.25
- $.19 to $.23
- $.17 to $.18
- $.17 to $.17
- Less than $.17

State rates shown on map:
- Massachusetts .21
- Rhode Island .31
- Connecticut .25
- New Jersey .145
- Delaware .23
- Maryland .235
- District of Columbia .225
- New Hampshire .195
- Maine .252
- Vermont .20
- New York .232
- Pennsylvania .30
- West Virginia .27
- Virginia .175
- North Carolina .2685
- South Carolina .16
- Georgia .075
- Florida .145
- Ohio .26
- Kentucky .174
- Tennessee .214
- Alabama .18
- Mississippi .18
- Louisiana .20
- Michigan .19
- Indiana .18
- Illinois .20
- Wisconsin .29
- Minnesota .20
- Iowa .205
- Missouri .17
- Arkansas .215
- North Dakota .21
- South Dakota .22
- Nebraska .263
- Kansas .24
- Oklahoma .17
- Texas .20
- Montana .27
- Wyoming .14
- Colorado .22
- New Mexico .189
- Idaho .25
- Utah .245
- Arizona .18
- Washington .28
- Oregon .24
- Nevada .23
- California .18
- Alaska .08
- Hawaii .16

earmarked for transportation. State–local governments collect fees, which serve both a regulation function and as transportation revenue source, for licensing both vehicles and drivers. State–local governments also collect tolls and charges for use of highways, airports, and waterways and for parking. Even if the notion of transportation-user taxes and charges is broadly defined to include all these, motor fuel taxes comprise at least 60 percent of the revenue collected from users.

INTERNATIONAL COMPARISON

Differences in Transportation Modes and Facilities

Passenger transportation methods and finance vary substantially among industrialized nations. Personal automobiles and public highways dominate transportation in the United States. For ground passenger travel, the people of the United States rely more on personal vehicles and roads and less on rail transportation than any of the other major industrialized nations. Use of personal vehicles and roads accounts for more than 96 percent of ground transport passenger-miles in the United States, but it represents only about 87 percent in France, 84 percent in Germany and 62 percent in Japan. In contrast, rail transportation, which provides less than 1 percent of ground transit in the United States, accounts for about 9 percent of ground travel in France, 8 percent in Germany and nearly 32 percent in Japan.[5]

These differences in transportation approach reflect or result from several government policy decisions. First, government in the United States has invested relatively more in roads and highways and less in rail facilities compared to these other nations. Second, excise taxes on gasoline are substantially less in the United States than in most other industrialized nations, which largely explains why gasoline prices are lower in the United States than elsewhere. Thus, the story seems to be that because the United States has maintained low taxes on gasoline, U.S. residents choose to own more personal vehicles and drive more than residents of these other nations, which requires government to invest more in road facilities. In other nations, such as Japan, gasoline taxes and prices are relatively high, consumers choose relatively more rail travel, and government invests more in rail facilities.

This story misses an important point; consumer preferences influence government's fiscal choices, including the decision about the level of gasoline taxation. Due to preferences or other economic and social factors (area and income perhaps), U.S. consumers have chosen road transportation, whereas Japanese consumers have selected rail transportation to a greater degree. Thus, it is not clear that consumers in the United States would respond to higher gasoline prices in the same way as the Japanese. For instance, gasoline prices in France are essentially the same as in Japan, but the reliance on road travel in France is more similar to the United States than Japan. Noting the relatively high miles per gallon of vehicles in France,

---

[5]Bus transportation represents the remainder, varying from 8 percent in Germany to 3 percent in the U.S.

it seems that the preferred response of French consumers to high gasoline taxes and prices has been to change the nature of their vehicles rather than the mode or amount of travel. In short, the transportation systems selected by residents in these various nations vary dramatically and reflect the combination of economic, geographic, and cultural factors.

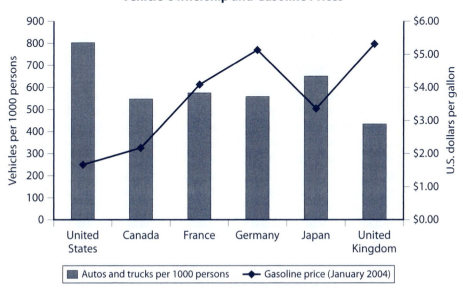

Vehicle Ownership and Gasoline Prices

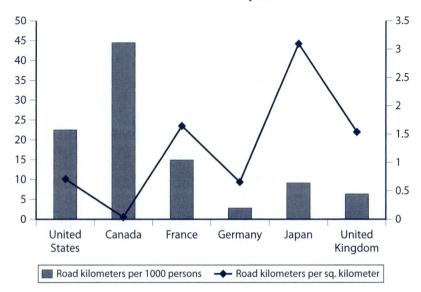

Road Kilometers Relative to Population and Area

SOURCE: U.S. Department of Transportation. *Highway Statistics,* 2002.

FINANCING TRANSPORTATION: THEORETICAL ISSUES AND ALTERNATIVE PRACTICES

Role for User Charges

Recall from Chapter 8 that user-charge financing is attractive if the share of marginal benefits accruing to direct users is relatively large, the users can be identified easily, and the direct users can be excluded (at reasonable cost) from consuming the service unless the charge is paid. Does it seem that these conditions are satisfied by transportation facilities and services provided by state–local governments? Typically the answer is yes, with one qualification. Although external benefits from transportation systems undoubtedly exist, they may be swamped by the substantial demand by and benefits to direct users. Direct users identify themselves by purchasing and registering vehicles, by purchasing fuel and other supplies, and by taking trips. The potential qualification is that while excluding users who do not pay is possible, it may be costly, particularly for some forms of transportation user charges. This suggests that transportation user charges are attractive only when they can be collected and enforced in a relatively low-cost manner.

One issue in applying user charges to transportation is whether users—through direct charges—should pay part or all of the capital cost of facilities. The answer depends on the distribution of *marginal benefits* between those who are direct users and those who are not, rather than simply on the existence of benefits to nonusers. Surely benefits from the transportation network provided by state–local governments do flow to individuals for reasons other than their direct use of those networks. The transportation networks are used to bring individuals and goods to those who are not direct users, that is, there are general social benefits from a transportation system. In general, a basic transportation network enables the economy to function smoothly and assists government in carrying out its defense and public safety responsibilities; however, the relevant question is whether those social purposes are enhanced by expanding the transportation network. Are there social or external benefits at the margin?

The possibilities are illustrated in Figure 20.5a. Demand curve A_0 represents the private marginal benefits that go to individuals as a result of their direct use of the transportation network and B_0 represents the general social marginal benefits that go to all of society. Remember that marginal benefit means the additional gain from an additional unit of transportation facility, perhaps another mile of highway. The efficient amount of this transportation facility is T_0, where the marginal cost of another unit of the facility equals the sum of the marginal benefits that go to direct users and generally to society. At that size transportation system, however, there are no additional benefits to society generally, only additional benefits for direct users. Apparently, a smaller transportation network would be sufficient to allow the economy and government to function as well, at least in providing general benefits to all of society. Expanding the transportation network beyond that size benefits specific individuals due to their use of that facility but does not provide any additional general benefits to all. In that case, those direct users who benefit from expanding the transportation facility should pay all the capital cost.

Figure 20.5

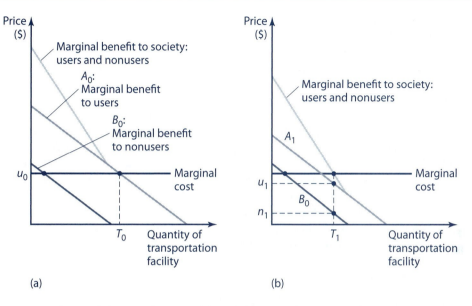

Allocation of
transportation
costs to users
and nonusers

(a)

(b)

A second possibility, perhaps representing an earlier time or the case for a different transportation mode, is shown in Figure 20.5b. Although the general social marginal benefits from this transportation facility are the same as in Figure 20.5a, the private, direct benefits to users are lower; that is, the private demand for this transportation facility is less than in Figure 20.5a. In this case, marginal gains exist for both direct users and generally the society at the efficient amount of the facility, T_1. Appropriate financing in this case requires that direct user charges be u_1 per unit of the facility, with the remainder of the cost, $MC - u_1$, coming from general taxes paid by all of society. User charges are still appropriate but only to cover a portion rather than all the capital costs.

In other words, if the transportation system is already large enough to provide all the general benefits that arise from having a transportation network, than any further expansion of that system only generates private benefits and should be financed entirely by users of that expansion. It is often suggested that this is the current situation regarding highways, so that it is appropriate to finance more road building entirely from user charges. If full user-charge financing is used when additional social benefits are still to be had, however, society ends up underinvesting in transportation facilities. If users were charged the full marginal cost in Figure 20.5b, they would demand less than the efficient amount of facility. In short, user charges should cover the same portion of costs equal to the share of direct-user benefits in aggregate marginal benefits.

How well does the actual transportation financing system correspond to this theory? For highways, at least, it seems fairly well. According to DOT, about 75 percent of the revenue for highway expenditures for all purposes in 2003 came from highway user taxes and tolls (56 percent), income from invested funds and reserves (9 percent), and proceeds of transportation bond sales (10 percent). The latter two primarily represent past and future highway-user taxes and tolls, respectively. The other 25 percent of highway revenues came from other taxes, fees, and assessments, especially property taxes. In fact, most of the highway revenue not collected directly from users arose at the local government level. Some local government property taxes were special assessments for streets and roads. When coupled with the fact that not all total highway expenditures actually go for the facilities (some of the money goes for law enforcement and safety programs, for instance), it seems clear that funds collected directly from highway users account for almost all expenditures on road and highway facilities.

Motor fuel taxes on gasoline and diesel fuel account for the great bulk of highway-user taxes and tolls, about 90 percent of charges to users in 2003. Thus, motor fuel taxes represent a bit more than half of total highway spending for all purposes. It is important to ask therefore how well motor fuel taxes work as user charges. Most importantly, motor fuel taxes do vary by the amount and type of road use. The more miles an individual goes, the more gasoline is required and thus the more gasoline excise tax is implicitly paid. Similarly, larger or heavier vehicles generally require more gasoline than smaller or lighter ones to travel a given distance, which corresponds to road "use" if larger and heavier vehicles impose greater maintenance or safety costs on the highway system. Collecting motor fuel taxes also entails relatively low administration costs, partly because they are usually collected at the wholesale or distributor level where there are fewer firms than at retail.

However, motor fuel taxes are imperfect user charges for at least three reasons. First, all gasoline and diesel fuel is not used on highways; some is used for boats, airplanes, agricultural machinery, off-road vehicles, and lawnmowers, for example. Because of this, some motor fuel taxes often are earmarked for waterway or natural resources uses, and some states exempt fuel for agricultural purposes from taxation. Second, fuel usage is not expected to correspond perfectly to road and highway use because vehicles (and drivers) differ in their fuel economy and because different vehicles impose varying maintenance costs on the roads. Third, fuel taxes do not do a good job of differentiating highway use by location and time, so they do not adequately represent congestion costs created by highway users. Fuel taxes may have to be supplemented with some form of congestion charge, therefore, as discussed later in this chapter. Despite these difficulties, motor fuel taxes have come to be accepted and used as the primary highway user charge.

Note that many of the other fees and taxes collected from highway users do not correspond to use nearly as well as fuel taxes. Driver's license and vehicle registration fees, for instance, are usually not based on any accurate measure of road use. Driver's license fees are usually lump-sum charges, and vehicle registration fees are usually based either on vehicle value or weight, neither of which correspond to actual road use. These fees are intended more as a regulatory device than as a source of revenue for highway facilities. A similar argument also applies to road-use fees for trucks and excise taxes on tires, which are also based on weight. On the other hand, road tolls can be tailored to road use, differentiating by distance traveled, vehicle type, and time and place of trips, although tolls sometimes entail high administrative and compliance costs, depending on the toll collection mechanism.

Spending on transportation facilities for air and water travel is also heavily financed through taxes and charges collected from direct users. On the other hand, spending on mass-transit services—urban bus, rail, and subway systems—does not rely as heavily on user taxes and charges. According to Jose Gomez-Ibanez (1985, p. 191),

> Passenger fares had been enough to cover operating costs and make a small contri-
> bution to capital expenses through the 1950s, despite the fact that the [mass-transit]
> industry was contracting. In 1964, passenger receipts fell below operating expenses
> for the industry as a whole and by the 1980s covered only about 40 percent of oper-
> ating costs and made no contribution to capital expenses.

Data for 2003 show that the share of operating costs covered by passenger fares had fallen to about 32.6 percent. Mass-transit expenditures, which are almost all made by local governments, are financed by substantial amounts of federal and state aid and by local taxes. Among transit revenue for operating purposes, state and general local government grants for operations have increased faster than passenger revenue, as shown in Figure 20.6. In 2003, general local government aid for operations represented about 20 percent of operating revenue, state aid 24 percent, and federal aid 6 percent; fares accounted for 32.6 percent of operations. Capital expenditures for transit infrastructure (rail lines, cars, and buses) are financed separately. In 2003, federal grants provided about 40 percent of transit capital revenues, and state and general local government aid about 31 percent, with about

Figure 20.6

Trend of transit operating revenue

Excludes commuter railroad and most rural transit systems before 1984.

SOURCE: American Public Transit Association (2005).

29 percent being generated by the transit system from transit taxes and tolls.[6] For the federal government and many states, gasoline taxes are a major source for at least part of the mass-transit grant funds. This may serve as an indirect form of benefit charge if highway users do in fact benefit from the existence of mass-transit systems, an issue considered in the later section on transportation pricing.

Role for Federal Aid

Even if the share of transportation costs to be born directly by users has been determined, the appropriate level of government to collect those user taxes and charges and the appropriate level to provide any general funds also must be resolved. Recall that federal aid plays an important role in financing transportation, particularly for highways and investment in mass-transit facilities. The federal government finances more than one-fifth of all expenditures on highways, almost all through grants to the states, and 40 percent of new capital expenditures on mass-transit facilities. What economic rationale is there for the federal government's role in financing transportation facilities and services, and does the federal aid system as structured correspond to that theory?

Recall from Chapter 9 that a chief economic rationale for intergovernmental grants is to correct for inefficient service choices by subnational governments, which arise because consideration is given only to local or state benefits. If there are benefits external to the government providing a service and those benefits are not considered, then too little of the service is provided from the broader viewpoint of the entire society. One way to correct that problem is to provide a matching grant for the service, which reduces the cost of the service to the providing government and thus induces an increase in the amount provided. The matching rate should correspond to the ratio of nonresident to resident benefits at the margin. A matching grant also achieves a degree of fairness by effectively requiring nonresidents of a jurisdiction to help finance services provided by that jurisdiction from which they benefit.

In theory, this notion also provides a reason for federal government involvement in transportation finance. There are presumably national reasons for wanting to have a relatively uniform transportation network covering the breadth of the nation and connecting various metropolitan areas and states. At the very least, such a transportation network has been argued as necessary for the federal government to carry out its national defense responsibilities. To the extent that the benefits of interstate transport are underestimated or neglected by the states or to the extent that intrastate transport is underappreciated by local governments, the federal government has the responsibility of resolving those externality problems. Because nonresidents substantially use transportation facilities directly provided by states and localities, some nonresident contributions—through federal and state aid—are called for.

Initially at least, these reasons did seem to correspond closely to the structure of federal aid for transportation, and especially for highways, as suggested by the abbreviated history of federal transportation aid in Table 20.4. Federal aid initially

---

[6]For those transit capital projects that receive federal support, the federal grant share is 80 percent.

Table 20.4

History of Federal Transportation Aid to States and Localities

Year	Federal Aid Structure And Uses
Early 1900s	Federal highway aid begins.
1921	Federal aid restricted to principal roads connecting states or counties within states.
1944	Rural secondary roads and principal urban highways added to federal aid system by Federal Highway Aid Act. Matching grants used with 75% federal and 25% state–local shares. Federal aid road system includes rural primary roads, rural secondary roads, and urban extensions of rural primary roads.
1954	Urban extensions of rural secondary roads added to federal aid system.
1956	Substantial grants for Interstate and Defense Highway System begun with 90% federal and 10% state shares. Highway Trust Fund created by the Highway Revenue Act to receive transportation-related taxes and charges.
1964	Grants for mass transit capital costs instituted, to cover up to two-thirds of the cost.
1970	Separate grants for bridge rehabilitation and replacement instituted.
1973	Maximum federal grant share for mass transit capital costs increased to 80%, still the current rate.
1974	Grants for mass transit operating costs at a 50/50 share instituted.
1976	Specific grants for resurfacing, restoration, and rehabilitation of interstate highways provided.
1983	Surface Transportation Assistance Act increased federal gasoline tax from $.04 to $.09 per gallon with $.04 of the increase restricted to aid for interstate and rural primary roads only and $.01 earmarked for mass transit capital grants.
1991	Intermodal Surface Transportation Efficiency Act (ISTEA) revamped the federal aid system, creating a new National Highway System to include Interstate highways, most urban and rural principal arterials, and strategic connectors. The Interstate System is to be completed by 1995, with continuing funds for interstate resurfacing and rehabilitation at a 90% federal share. The Surface Transportation Program provides grants for local or rural roads, bridges, and mass transit capital projects.
1993	Federal gasoline tax increased to $.184 with $.10 for highway aid, $.015 earmarked for mass transit capital grants, and $.068 for deficit reduction. In October 1995, the division changes to $.12 for highways, $.02 for mass transit, and $.043 for deficit reduction.
1998	Transportation Equity Act for the 21st Century (TEA-21) extended most transportation user taxes and allocations through September 30, 2005. Federal aid for highways was increased and allocation formulas changed to direct more revenue to growing states, essentially those in the Sun Belt. The transit share of the gasoline tax was increased to $.0286.
2005	Safe, Accountable, Flexible, and Efficient Transportation Equity Act: A Legacy for Users (SAFETEA-LU) adopted just before provisions of TEA-21 were to expire. It extends highway-user taxes at current rates through September 30, 2011. States will be guaranteed a minimum 92% return on contributions to the Highway Trust Fund. States receive increased flexibility to use tolls and other forms of road pricing to manage congestion and to finance infrastructure improvements.

SOURCE: U.S. Department of Transportation (1986a), (1994), and (2005); Gomez-Ibanez, 1985.

was limited to principal roads connecting states or counties within states, and even until 1954, the roads eligible for federal highway grants were limited to rural primary and rural secondary roads and urban extensions of rural primary roads. For those types of roads, federal matching grants resulting in a 75-percent federal cost share and 25-percent state share were available. Urban extensions of rural secondary roads were added to the federal aid highway system in 1954, and financing of the Interstate and Defense Highway System began in 1956, with federal grants covering 90 percent of capital costs. Even then, the focus of federal transportation grants remained on transport among states or regions within states.

The role of federal aid was expanded somewhat in the 1960s and 1970s, however, by the creation or expansion of grant programs for road maintenance and mass-transit services. A separate grant program for bridge repair and replacement was instituted in 1970, and specific grants for resurfacing, restoring, and rehabilitating interstate highways were first offered in 1976. As more and more of the primary and interstate highway system was in place, a change in spending away from additional construction and toward maintaining the existing structure is certainly expected. The issue, however, is whether the federal government should play a similar role for maintenance as it did for construction. The federal government also began to support mass-transit services in this period. Grants for up to two-thirds of capital expenses were started in 1964, with the federal share increased to 80 percent in 1973. Matching grants for mass-transit operating costs at a 50-percent federal share were started in 1974. Thus, a federal aid system that had started out to assist states in financing the construction of major roads connecting states and population centers was, by the late 1970s, also substantially assisting in the construction and operation of roads and transit systems mostly used for transport within metropolitan areas.

Although the Reagan administration proposed a major restructuring of federal transportation aid in 1981 in the direction of the original notion of financing transport only among states and regions, a less radical alteration was adopted. With the Surface Transportation Assistance Act of 1982, the federal gasoline tax was increased from $.04 to $.09 per gallon with all the $.05 per-gallon increase in the tax earmarked for limited purposes. The additional revenue from $.04 of the increase was restricted for aid for interstate and rural primary roads only, while the revenue from the additional $.01 increase was earmarked for the Federal Mass Transportation Trust Fund to be used for mass-transit capital expenses only. As a result, the portion of federal aid going for highways used for transport among states and areas was substantially increased, consistent with the original intent of federal transportation aid.

In 1991, the entire federal grant system for roads was changed with the passage of the Intermodal Surface Transportation Efficiency Act (ISTEA), which eliminated the old federal-aid highway definitions and replaced them with a National Highway System (NHS). The NHS includes interstates, with grants for interstate maintenance at a 90 percent federal share, and most principal urban and rural arterial roads. A companion Surface Transportation Program provides grants for other local roads, for highways, and for mass-transit capital projects at an 80 percent federal share.

In 1990, federal gasoline excise taxes were increased to $.14 per gallon, with $.10 earmarked for highway aid, an increase from $.08 previously. Then in 1993, gasoline tax rates were increased further to $.184 per gallon, with $.10 for highway aid, $.015 earmarked for mass-transit capital grants, and $.068 for deficit reduction. In October 1995, the division changed to $.12 for highways, $.02 for mass transit, and $.043 for deficit reduction. With this change, federal motor fuel taxes were being used for general federal services, not just those related to transportation.

The federal transportation funding bills in 1998 (TEA-21) and 2005 (SAFETEA-LU) increased the amount of federal funding for transportation purposes substantially. The transit share of the federal gasoline tax was increased to $.0286 in 1998. The

Table 20.5

Public Road System in the United States, 2003

Type of Road	Miles (millions)	Percentage of Total Miles	Vehicle-Miles (millions)	Percentage of Vehicle-Miles
Rural Mileage, Total	3,033,138	76.3%	1,085,385	37.5%
Interstate	32,048	0.8	269,945	9.3
Other Principal Arterial	97,038	2.4	245,345	8.5
Minor Arterial	135,596	3.4	171,251	5.9
Major Collector	424,288	10.7	203,368	7.0
Minor Collector	267,524	6.7	60,294	2.1
Local	2,076,644	52.3	135,182	4.7
Urban Mileage, Total	940,969	23.7	1,805,508	62.5
Interstate	14,460	0.4	432,633	15.0
Other Freeways and Expressways	9,870	0.2	199,520	6.9
Other Principal Arterial	56,870	1.4	425,622	14.7
Minor Arterial	93,888	2.4	348,794	12.1
Collector	97,114	2.4	153,751	5.3
Local	668,767	16.8	245,188	8.5

SOURCE: Department of Transportation. *National Transportation Statistics*, 2003.

major issue in these recent years has not been the division of the gasoline tax among the various purposes, but rather the allocation formulas for federal aid, which determine how federal support is divided among the states. The changes in allocation formulas in 1998 had the effect of directing more aid to the Sun Belt states, mostly at the expense of the older states in the North. With the adoption of SAFETEA-LU in 2005, a compromise was reached guaranteeing states that at least 92 percent of gasoline taxes collected in a state will be returned through federal grants.

The structure and effects of federal highway aid can be seen by examining both the road system in the United States and the distribution of aid dollars among various types of roads. In 2003, urban roads represented slightly less than a quarter of all road miles, but accounted for more than 62 percent of travel (measured in vehicle miles), as shown in Table 20.5. In contrast, rural roads represented more than three-quarters of all road miles, but handled only about a third of travel or traffic. The concentration of travel on certain types of roads certainly is illustrated by the interstate highways, which represent only about 1 percent of road miles but handle almost one-quarter of all vehicle-miles of travel. At the opposite end of the spectrum, the great majority of road miles are in the form of local roads (69 percent of road miles), but those local streets account for only about 13 percent of travel.

Despite the expansion in scope of federal highway aid over the years, federal highway aid remains primarily directed toward roads used for interstate and interregional travel, as shown by the comparison of the distribution of federal highway funds to the distribution of vehicle miles traveled by type of road in Table 20.6. For instance, in 2003, 28 percent of federal aid highway funds were used for interstate highways although they accounted for only about 24 percent of the total vehicle miles traveled. The categories of roads for which the share of aid is greater than the share

Table 20.6

Comparison of Federal Aid and Vehicle Travel by Type of Road, 2003

	Percentage of Vehicle-Miles	Percentage of Federal Highway Funds	Ratio of Aid Share to Travel Share
Rural Mileage, Total	37.5%		
Interstate	9.3	9.0%	0.97
Other Principal Arterial	8.5	13.1	1.54
Minor Arterial	5.9	6.3	1.06
Major Collector	7.0	5.7	0.81
Minor Collector	2.1	0.7	0.34
Local	4.7	1.6	0.34
Urban Mileage, Total	62.5		
Interstate	15.0	18.6	1.24
Other Freeways and Expressways	6.9	5.1	0.73
Other Principal Arterial	14.7	15.9	1.08
Minor Arterial	12.1	6.8	0.57
Collector	5.3	2.8	0.52
Local	8.5	1.7	0.20

SOURCE: U.S. Department of Transportation. *Highway Statistics*, 2003.

of vehicle miles are rural principal arterials (major rural roads connecting cities; aid share is 1.54 times the share of vehicle miles), urban interstate highways (1.24 ratio), urban principal arterial roads (1.08 ratio), and rural minor arterial roads (1.06 ratio).

For all other categories of roads, the share of aid is less than the share of travel. Moreover, the share of aid relative to travel declines as one goes from interstate highways to arterial (primary) roads to collector roads and then to local roads. The ratio of aid share to travel share is only .34 for rural local roads (1.6 percent of aid but 4.7 percent of vehicle miles) and .20 for urban local roads (1.7 percent of aid but 8.5 percent of vehicle miles).

It is important to remember, of course, that this is only the distribution of the nominal or intended categories of grant funds. Recall from Chapter 9 that the actual effect of categorical grants on spending may differ from the specified categories. For instance, even though almost 30 percent of federal highway aid goes for interstate highways, that does not mean all those funds represent spending that states would not otherwise undertake. If a state spends $50 million on resurfacing interstate highways involving $45 million of federal funds and $5 million of state money but would have spent, say, $30 million without the federal aid, then the $45 million federal grant increased spending on interstate resurfacing by only $20 million ($50 − $30). Still, because the matching grant involves a 90-percent federal government share and thus a 90-percent decrease in the price of interstate construction and maintenance to states, a substantial increase in spending is possible even if demand is relatively price inelastic. (If the elasticity is −.5, a 45-percent increase in spending results.) In fact, the evidence from demand studies shows price elasticities between −.5 and −1.

The notion that federal transportation aid is intended to offset interstate or inter-regional benefit externalities is still the reason usually cited by economists opposed to federal aid for urban mass transit at current levels. As noted, the federal government pays 80 percent of the capital costs of local mass-transit systems and for a time paid up to 50 percent of operating costs. Because these urban (rail and subway) mass-transit systems largely transport individuals only within metropolitan areas, the nature of the national interest in these systems is problematic, at best. There may well be interjurisdictional spillovers from mass-transit systems, but because they are nearly all contained within specific metropolitan areas, perhaps state governments could better address these issues. On the other hand, another benefit from mass transit is reduced air pollution from automobile transportation, which may benefit individuals across states.

Although economists cite externalities as a theoretical reason for federal grants, more often the actual political reason for grants may be distributional. Federal mass-transit aid is justified because aid is implicitly given to individuals who use other transport modes (cars), because the central cities where most mass-transit systems are located may have fiscal or economic difficulties and because certain states or localities are perceived as being "shortchanged" in receipt of federal government spending. Certainly, the federal government has distributional responsibilities, and those are legitimate concerns. It is also important, however, to explicitly recognize that those are the reasons for federal mass-transit aid rather than the national interest arguments that are more appropriate for highways.

When interstate or regional transportation externalities justify federal grants for efficiency reasons, the second economic issue concerns the appropriate matching rate for those grants. The theoretical answer is that the grant should cover that fraction of marginal benefits that spill over to nonresidents. If, for instance, 30 percent of the benefits from a new highway project in one state will go directly to nonresidents of that state or to society generally, then a federal matching grant with a 30-percent federal share and 70-percent state share is appropriate. By focusing only on direct benefits to residents, the state underestimates aggregate benefits by 30 percent, which then can be offset by a grant that reduces the price to the state also by 30 percent. If the grant-matching rate is set above the share of marginal external benefits, then the price reduction to the state or local government causes overinvestment in that transportation facility.

The current federal government share for the major transportation grants is 90 percent for both construction and maintenance of interstate highways, 80 percent for other roads eligible for support, and 80 percent for the capital costs of new or expanded urban mass-transit systems. It seems unlikely, however, that the share of general social and nonresident benefits is anywhere near that high. In fact, if the federal government pays 90 percent of the cost of interstate highways and 80 percent of the cost of subways, you might wonder why states and cities are not building new highways and transit systems all over the place.

The answer, of course, is that these are not open-ended grants; the matching rates do not apply to any-and-all expenditures on these services by states and localities, only those approved by the granting federal agencies. Proposals for federal support for some roads and projects will not be approved. Similarly, the Interstate and Defense Highway System begun in 1956 includes only a planned set of interconnected highways. Other divided, four-lane, or larger highways, some of which predate the interstate system and some of which are toll roads, are not part of the interstate system and not eligible for the matching grants at the 90-percent rate.[7] For mass-transit systems, cities must apply to the Federal Transit Administration and satisfy a number of federal regulations concerning the cost of potential alternatives to the proposed transit system, treatment of potential cost overruns, and timing of the development.

Because of the limitations on the magnitude of these transportation grants, the full effect of the large price reductions is not expected to be realized. If the grant to a state is capped at an expenditure level below that which the state actually selects, then the last dollar spent by the state is not matched and the price of the marginal expenditure is not reduced. For those states, these are effectively lump-sum rather than matching grants. The irony is that the caps are required because of the very high matching rates, rates well beyond the expected magnitude of external benefits. However, the caps also negate the spending effect that the high matching rates are intended to bring about.

The common prescription of economists for this problem is to return to the original notion of matching grants to offset only benefit spillovers. As proposed by Edward Gramlich (1985b, p. 57),

> . . . if there is a valid spillover rationale for categorical grants, a better way to improve the grant than by simply converting it to block form . . . is simply to lower federal matching shares until the ratio of internal to total program costs at the margin equals the ratio of internal to total program benefits at the margin. . . . My own preference would be to assume an internal share of 80 percent unless it could be shown to be significantly lower.

If Gramlich's prescription were applied to transportation grants, the relative cost shares of the federal and state governments effectively would be reversed from the current status. Paradoxically, such a change could actually *increase spending* on these transportation services, however. In at least some cases, the caps on the current transportation grants mean that they have no effect on the marginal cost of transportation facilities in some states; the price of the marginal dollar spent is $1. If a 20-percent federal grant *without any spending limits* were substituted, the marginal cost or price to states of these transportation facilities would be reduced by 20 percent. Because a small price reduction is expected to have more effect than no price reduction, state–local spending on these transportation facilities could be expected to rise in those cases. On the other hand, the amount of federal aid would fall, and states would pay a larger share of the average cost of these facilities than now. In other words, the appropriate role for the federal government in financing transportation is reflected not just by the *amount* of federal aid but also by the *structure* of those grant programs.

---

[7]These are likely to be eligible for matching grants at the 80-percent rate.

Application 20.1

GASOLINE PRICES, CONSUMPTION, AND TAXES

The bulk of state–local own-source revenues spent on transportation comes from state excise taxes on the sale of motor fuels, especially gasoline. Because each of those states' taxes is a specific tax at a rate of so many cents per gallon, the revenue generated by those taxes for any set of rates depends on the number of gallons consumed. As gasoline prices increased in the 1970s after OPEC-led moves to hold down world oil output, consumers eventually responded by altering behavior in a number of ways to hold down their consumption of gasoline. Those changes put a squeeze on highway and other transportation funds in a number of states because reductions or slow growth in the *gallons of fuel* consumed directly affected excise tax revenues.

The average price of gasoline in the United States more than tripled between 1970 and 1980, with the largest increases coming in 1973 and 1979. As a result, the price of gasoline was increasing much faster than the average level of prices; the price of gasoline in "real terms" (after adjustment for inflation) rose nearly 65 percent in that decade. Consumer use of gasoline proved to be more sensitive to the price than was often believed. After the large price increases in 1973 and 1979, both highway use of gasoline and consumption of all motor fuels (diesel fuel, gasohol, as well as gasoline) actually declined in the next several years. Gasoline consumption for highway use in 1980—about 101 billion gallons—was not substantially different from the 100.6 billion gallons consumed in 1973 despite increases in population, income, and highway travel over those years. Part of the explanation lies in a switch to more fuel-efficient vehicles and part in a switch to other fuels. The first effect dominated, however, as shown by the information about highway use and fuel consumption since 1973 in Table 20.7. Between 1973 and 1992, a 71-percent increase in the number of vehicle miles traveled on highways was

Table 20.7

Highway Travel and Fuel Consumption, 1973–2002[a]

Year	Vehicle Miles of Travel (billions)	Fuel Consumption (billions of gallons)	Average Miles Per Gallon
1973	1,313	110.5	11.89
1975	1,328	109.0	12.18
1979	1,529	122.1	12.52
1981	1,553	116.1	13.57
1985	1,774	121.3	14.62
1990	2,147	131.6	16.32
1992	2,240	132.9	16.85
2002	2,856	167.7	17.10
Percentage Change			
1973–92	71	20	42
1992–2002	28	26	2

[a]Travel and consumption for all vehicles, including passenger cars, motorcycles, buses, and trucks.
SOURCE: U.S. Department of Transportation.

Application 20.1 — Gasoline Prices, Consumption, and Taxes

Figure 20.7

Highway use and fuel consumption

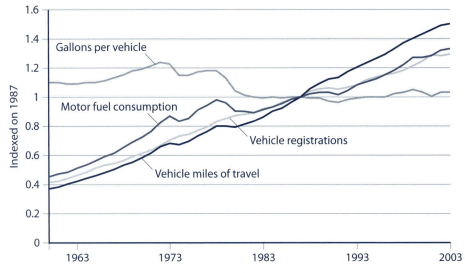

SOURCE: U.S. Department of Transportation, Highway Statistics, 2005.

accomplished with only a 20-percent increase in fuel consumption due to a substantial increase in fuel efficiency. From the early 1980s until 2002, the real price of gasoline declined and fuel consumption increased again. Since 2002, real gasoline prices have increased substantially, again raising the issue of whether gasoline consumption will decline. The long run trends are shown in Figure 20.7. Fuel consumption has generally increased, but fell in several periods: 1973–1974; 1979–1981; and 1991. Although vehicle miles of travel continue to increase, gallons of fuel used per vehicle is essentially unchanged since 1980.

State highway funds felt the effect of these changes. The number of gallons of motor fuel taxed by states was lower in 1974 and 1975 than in 1973 and was lower in all the years 1980 through 1984 than in 1979. By 1985, slightly more than 123 billion gallons of motor fuel were taxed by the states, about the same as the 122.7 billion in 1979. Clearly,

unless motor fuel tax *rates* were increased, reductions in motor fuel consumption would lead to reductions in state transportation revenue. In fact, state motor fuel tax collections remained about constant from 1973 to 1975 and went down in the 1980–1981 period. Yet over these years, the amount of highway use and the cost of highway construction and maintenance continued to increase, creating something of a crisis in some states. State governments reacted to this financial problem in several ways. Many states simply increased, some more than once, the magnitude of their motor fuel tax rate. A few states adopted a variable motor fuel tax rate that automatically increases if fuel consumption decreases or prices rise. Some states considered switching from a specific per-gallon tax structure to an *ad valorem*, or percentage tax, system; because the prices were rising faster than consumption was falling, total expenditure on fuels was rising.

Application 20.1 — Gasoline Prices, Consumption, and Taxes

Table 20.8

State Motor Fuel Taxes and Highway Costs, 1973–2002

Year	Average State Motor Fuel Tax (cents per gallon)	State Motor Fuel Tax Revenue (billion dollars)	Cost Index for Highway Construction[a]
1973	7.53	8.1	42.5
1975	7.65	8.3	58.1
1979	8.01	10.0	85.5
1981	9.11	9.7	94.2
1985	11.11	13.4	102.0
1990	14.74	19.4	108.5
1992	16.78	22.3	105.1
2002	19.13	32.0	147.9
Percentage Change			
1973–1985	48	65	140
1985–1992	51	66	3
1992–2002	14	43	41

[a]1987 Base Year = 100.

SOURCES: U.S. Department of Transportation, *National Transportation Statistics*, various years.

U.S. Department of Commerce. *State and Local Government Finances*, various years.

The overall effects of changes in fuel consumption and state tax rates for state highway finance since 1973 are shown in Table 20.8. The average state tax rate on all motor fuels increased continually over these years, rising about 48 percent from 1973 to 1985, 51 percent from 1985 to 1992, and by 14 percent from 1992 to 2002. In each of the three periods identified in the table, state motor fuel revenues increase more than state motor fuel tax rates due to growth in fuel consumption. In the first period (1973 to 1985), the increase in revenue was dwarfed by the increase in the cost of road construction, about 140 percent over these years. In the 1985 to 1992 period, however, tax rate increases allowed revenue growth to be much greater than cost increases. Essentially, states were catching up for the earlier revenue shortfall. In the last period from 1992 to 2002, revenue increases essentially matched cost increases. Gasoline prices have increased substantially in 2004 and 2005 as this is being written. If gasoline consumption subsequently declines, as happened in the 1970s, then states may again see motor fuel revenue not keeping up construction and maintenance cost increases.

This situation illustrates two important features about government finance. Earmarking revenues reduces budget flexibility for government and can create short-run disruptions. Because highway finance is tied to motor fuel taxes, other revenues often are not readily available. Fuel tax rates had to be increased, but in some cases not before a highway finance crisis resulted. Second, focusing on tax rates alone can be misleading because the change in the rates *and* base determines what happens to the amount of tax revenue. In this case, holding tax rates constant would have meant decreases in revenue and an even wider gap between the growth of revenue and costs.

Optimal Transportation Pricing

Although the use of charges and taxes to finance construction and maintenance of transportation facilities has been considered, user charges also may be appropriate to bring about *efficient use* of public facilities after they have been constructed, if those facilities experience congestion. If a facility is congested, an additional consumer imposes extra costs on all other users. The purpose of use fees or prices for those facilities is to make those costs apparent to potential users, that is, to allocate the scarce facility among competing demands. In fact, congestion on roads and in mass-transit systems and airports is common. Estimates for 2003 (see *The Urban Mobility Report,* http://mobility.tamu.edu, May, 2005) show that highway congestion in the 85 large urban areas causes 3.7 billion hours of travel delay and 2.3 billion gallons of wasted fuel, which translates to an annual cost of about $63 billion or $794 per traveler. Much of the delay due to congestion occurs in the five cities with the worst congestion—Los Angeles (average of 93 hours of delay per traveler per year), San Francisco (72 hours), Washington, D.C. (69 hours), Atlanta (67 hours), and Houston (63 hours). Among the 85 large urban areas, the average delay per traveler is 47 hours—more than a full week of work.

The Department of Transportation has explained the circumstance as follows: "Because the next user of a congested system bears only a small fraction of the additional delays he or she causes, transport systems with essentially free access are unable to ration their use efficiently and are thus prone to congestion." The DOT concludes, "Traffic congestion problems have steadily worsened, thereby increasing traffic delays, fuel consumption, and air pollution while decreasing productivity. . . . These increases have prompted federal, state, and local highway agencies to rank urban traffic congestion as a top priority" (*National Transportation Statistics: Annual Report 1994*, p. 89). Thus economists have long suggested that a more efficient transportation system would result if users were charged prices for transportation services that reflected congestion costs. One important aspect of SAFETEA-LU is that states receive increased flexibility to use tolls and other forms of road pricing to manage congestion.

Congestion Prices

A facility is said to be congested when an additional user reduces the benefits for all other users. In the case of transportation, this usually means that it takes more time to travel between two given points. As a road or highway becomes congested, for instance, the traffic speed is reduced, increasing the travel time required for a given trip. That increase in travel time, rather than an increase in vehicle-operating costs, accounts for most of the increase in travel cost to users due to congestion.

This notion of highway congestion is represented in Figure 20.8. Up to traffic quantity T_c, sometimes called the travel "capacity" of the road, there is no congestion. The operating and time costs for one vehicle to travel one mile are constant at C_0, assuming some value of time. If traffic exceeds T_c, congestion begins. The operating and time costs for one vehicle to travel one mile, the average cost which each individual driver faces, increase as the amount of traffic increases—travel speed

Figure 20.8

Pricing traffic
congestion

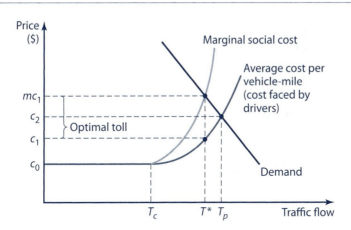

goes down and travel time increases the more traffic there is. The marginal social cost, on the other hand, represents the extra cost to all travelers from one more vehicle using the road: it is the extra time cost imposed on all travelers because the additional vehicle slows traffic. As with all marginal and average cost curves, for average cost per vehicle to increase requires that the extra cost created by each additional vehicle be greater than the old average (the marginal cost is above the average cost in Figure 20.8).

The existence of congestion creates inefficiency because each user is concerned only with his or her travel costs and does not consider the costs imposed on other travelers by the additional congestion. Because users perceive the costs to be lower than they truly are, the road is overused or too crowded. If the demand for this road is as shown, then T_p vehicles would use this road at an average cost of C_2, although the cost imposed on all users by the last vehicle to enter this road, the marginal cost, is much greater. Thus, use of this road at peak demand is ineffi- ciently too high—the marginal cost imposed by the last vehicle is greater than the marginal benefit to that user, as shown by the demand curve. The efficient amount of use of this road is T^*, where marginal cost equals marginal benefit or demand. Reducing the number of vehicles on this road from T_p to T^* reduces travel time, and the gains to the remaining users are greater than the loss to those who no longer use the road at this time.

Efficient use of this road requires that all potential users fully perceive all the costs of their road use, including the congestion costs imposed on others. In short, users must face a price that reflects all costs. The economic solution to this conges- tion problem is to levy a congestion fee or toll equal to the difference between aver- age and marginal cost at the efficient quantity. For the case in Figure 20.8, a con- gestion fee equal to $mc_1 - C_1$ would mean that users face a price per vehicle-mile of mc_1 at quantity T^*. A price equal to true marginal cost would result in T^* vehicles using the road at this demand time. Note first that with the efficient price, conges- tion is not necessarily eliminated, but it is reduced until the benefits from the use of this road are in line with the true costs. Second, because the optimal congestion fee equals the difference between average and marginal cost, the fee should be greater for facilities or times when the congestion is worse. If demand is such that road use is below T_c, no congestion toll is required because no congestion exists.

Application of this transit-pricing theory to real situations is obvious. Many roads, highways, and bridges are very congested during the work commuting periods in the morning and early evening but not crowded during other parts of the day. Roads in some parts of urban areas seem congested all day—midtown Manhattan, the Loop in Chicago, or the Central Artery in Boston come to mind—although roads in other parts of those metropolitan areas are congested only at some times or perhaps not at all. Public, mass-transit systems may be congested during commuting periods, and airports may be congested during certain times of day and during holiday periods. All these situations might be resolved by using congestion pricing, but actual use of that tool so beloved by economists remains relatively rare.

Four reasons seem to account for the general absence of congestion pricing in transportation. The first is public opposition to "paying twice" for facilities, a misperception because the costs of construction and the costs from congestion are separate and different. As noted by William Vickrey (1963, p. 455) more than 25 years ago, "The delusion still persists that the primary role of pricing should always be that of financing the service rather than that of promoting economy in its use." The second reason is that consumers often see the congestion tolls as a new immediate cost, whereas the benefits of reduced congestion or expansion of the transportation facility are received only in the future. Third, sometimes it is difficult to measure just what the marginal congestion cost is and thus what the appropriate congestion charge should be. The last reason arises from difficulties in administering and enforcing congestion charges, the issue to which we now turn.

Methods of Levying Congestion Charges

The most obvious way to levy a congestion charge is by a road or bridge toll paid at a booth either just before or just after traveling on the facility. Such use tolls can reflect both the costs of construction and maintenance as well as congestion and can vary by vehicle type, place, time of day, and time of year. The disadvantage of tollbooths is that they traditionally entail both high administration costs (wages of collectors) and high compliance costs (delay). Use of tollbooths to relieve congestion can be counterproductive because stopping to pay the toll may only create more congestion. On the other hand, where tolls are already being collected, such as for buses, subways, and airports, changing the structure of those tolls to levy congestion charges may not increase collection costs much, if at all. For example, if the usual or regular bus or subway price is $1.00 per trip, it would not cost more administratively to charge $2.00 per trip during congested periods.

Motor fuel taxes, although a relatively good way of collecting charges for construction and maintenance of roads, do not make very good congestion charges. If gasoline taxes were increased so that drivers faced the full costs of travel, including congestion costs at the most congested time of day, then the cost of travel would be inefficiently too high for uncongested times. This simply substitutes a new efficiency problem for the other. Also, it would be nearly impossible to enforce higher gasoline prices in congested areas than in uncongested ones, because individuals may simply adjust where they buy gasoline.

A third alternative, one often favored by economists, is metered usage, which entails some method of measuring and recording the use of transit facilities coupled with a billing or paying procedure. A number of variations of this alternative have been suggested, but one of the first and still among the most interesting is that proposed by Vickrey in 1963:

> My own fairly elaborate scheme involves equipping all cars with an electronic identifier. . . . [which] would be scanned by roadside equipment at a fairly dense network of cordon points, making a record of the identity of the car; these records would then be taken to a central processing plant once a month and the records assembled on electronic digital computers and bills sent out. Preliminary estimates indicate . . . the operating cost would be approximately that involved in sending out telephone bills. Bills could be itemized to whatever extent is desired to furnish the owner with a record that would guide him in the further use of his car. In addition, roadside signals could be installed to indicate the current level of charge. . . .

Writing in the early 1960s—before personal computers, digital electronics, microchips, and microwave transmission—Vickery envisioned receiving a monthly bill for road or transit use, just as we are billed for our metered use of electricity, natural gas, water, and telephone. The charge for traveling on a particular segment of a particular road could vary by vehicle type and time of day or year, although any differences in prices for different times would have to be known by the users so that travel decisions can be altered. Individual drivers could use congested roads at congested times if they were willing to pay the full price, or they would have the option of using a less congested (and thus lower-priced) alternative road, changing to a mass-transit system, changing the time of their trip, or foregoing the trip altogether.

When Vickery advanced this idea more than 30 years ago, questions about technological feasibility and cost were a legitimate concern, but no longer. The *Wall Street Journal* reported in 1994 that there was a $225 million market for electronic toll-collection systems already. Today, a number of "smart highway" systems allow drivers to pay tolls with a prepaid toll credit card. Electronic toll-collection systems, such as E-Z*Pass*—used in New York and other places—are now commonplace. Concern about government acquiring and using travel records of individuals is one potential difficulty with this version of metered usage, although it is not clear that those records would be any more sensitive than the telephone and tax records maintained now and available to the government.

A simplified version of metered usage involves selling travel permits for driving in a specific area during congested hours. Under such a system, any vehicle entering the restricted zone during established hours would have to display a nonremovable sticker purchased by the operator. In effect, anyone wanting to drive anywhere in the zone for any period would have to pay the single extra charge for the permit. Such a system was adopted in 1975 in Singapore. Windshield stickers were required to enter a restricted zone between 7:30 A.M. and 9:30 A.M. from any of 22 entry points. The price of the dated stickers was about $1.30 (U.S.) per day or $26 per month. Cars with at least four occupants and public-transit vehicles were exempt, and 14 park-and-ride lots were established just outside the zone for transfer to relatively inexpensive minibuses. Guards located at the 22 entry points to the zone enforced the requirement by recording the license numbers of vehicles violating the rules for subsequent arrest.

According to a World Bank study reported by K. J. Button and A. D. Pearman (1986), the Singapore congestion-pricing scheme had dramatic immediate effects. After about one month, the number of vehicles entering the zone during the two-hour period decreased by about 45 percent and average speeds increased by about 22 percent. The reduction in vehicles resulted from a large increase in the use of car pools, a shift to travel routes just outside the zone (which increased traffic congestion in those areas), and an expansion of commuting into the 7:00 A.M. to 7:30 A.M. period (eventually the time a permit was required was expanded to include this half-hour as well). In contrast, very few individuals switched from cars to the buses, so the park-and-ride lots were eventually largely abandoned. The travel-permit system generated substantial revenue for the government, so much so that fees were substantially increased in early 1976 to levels that may not have been justified purely on congestion grounds. Although it is not clear that this particular method could be applied equally effectively in larger or more diverse urban areas, the responses to congestion prices in Singapore suggest that there is substantial elasticity to commuting travel demand.

An alternative to travel permits for congestion pricing in urban areas is to use toll collection before entering the congested area, as used in Bergen, Oslo, and Trondheim, Norway. For example, since 1986, a ring of tollgates around Bergen are used to collect tolls during rush hours. After just one year, traffic was reduced by 7 percent, with the revenue used for road improvements and construction of bus-only lanes.[8] Apparently, consumers do respond to prices by altering their travel behavior.

Pricing of Competing Transportation Facilities

An alternative to direct congestion pricing is available if consumers have the choice of a competing mass-transit system or uncongested road as an alternative to a congested road. If it is technologically or politically infeasible to levy a congestion charge on the congested road, a reduction in the cost of the competing transit mode may have an equivalent effect. In both cases, the relative cost of the congested road *rises*. This possibility is illustrated in Figure 20.9, which shows T_0 use of the uncongested transit mode at an average cost of C_0 and T_p use of the congested road at the peak travel time. The efficient use of the congested road is T^*, which could be accomplished by an efficient congestion charge, as previously argued. If the congestion charge is not feasible, however, a similar effect can be accomplished if the modes are substitutes by lowering the cost of the uncongested

---

[8]Ingersoll, 1993.

Figure 20.9

Pricing of substi-
tute transit modes

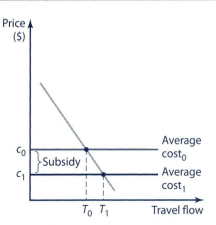

(a) **Uncongested transit mode**

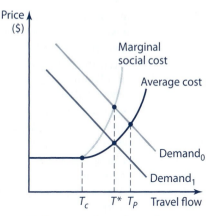

(b) **Congested transit mode**

travel mode. If travel on mode *I* is subsidized so that the cost falls to C_1, the demand for the now relatively more expensive mode *II* is reduced. Theoretically, some subsidy would reduce demand for mode *II* just enough so that use falls to T^*.

This argument has been applied to justify the use of gasoline excise tax revenue to subsidize mass-transit costs. If lower transit fares induce travelers to switch from cars to transit, then the remaining drivers who pay the gasoline tax benefit from the reduced highway congestion. In essence, the share of the gasoline tax that goes for mass transit is a type of congestion charge. Of course, the validity of this argument depends on the willingness of some travelers to switch from cars to mass transit. The evidence is not encouraging, as it suggests that very large subsidies—sometimes even larger than the transit fares—are often required to induce a substantial switch to transit.

If the competing mode *I* is an uncongested road, the switch may be easier. To induce travelers to switch to the uncongested road (even though it may require a longer distance trip), the cost might be reduced by raising the speed limit, removing some traffic lights, and resurfacing, for example. It is important to understand why transferring travelers from an existing congested to uncongested transportation facility increases economic efficiency. Because the uncongested road already exists, more vehicles can be accommodated there at no additional cost, whereas less use of the congested road reduces social costs. Not using the uncongested road up to capacity means that society is effectively wasting resources invested in that facility.

Airport Congestion and Airline Delays

The nature of airport congestion is remarkably similar to that of highways. The large airports in major metropolitan areas and a few others that the airlines use as hubs are very congested, especially at certain hours of the day, although most other airports in smaller cities are never congested. Thus, crowded facilities in some places are balanced by an excess capacity at others. Where congestion does exist, typically there are peak and off-peak periods.

Since federal government deregulation of airline routes and fares in 1978, there has been an increase in the number of airline firms, general decreases in air travel prices, and a resulting substantial increase in the amount of airline travel, with more passengers traveling more miles. Airlines carried nearly 630 million passengers in the United States in 2004 compared to 475 million in 1992 and only 275 million in 1978. Thus, passengers carried increased by 130 percent since 1978. The number of passenger miles in 2004 is about four times that in 1978. In contrast to the increase in air travel, the number and size of airports has not increased comparably since deregulation. Airports serving commercial airline flights are owned and operated by local governments and financed by a combination of federal government grants and locally generated revenues. The federal government levies an 8-percent tax on the price of domestic airline tickets with the revenue earmarked for the aviation trust fund and used for airport construction grants as well as other air services. Local airports generate revenue from aircraft-landing (or takeoff) fees; "passenger facility charges (PFCs)" of $1, $2, or $3 per ticket; parking and concession charges; and sometimes property taxes. Revenue from PFCs is intended for capital projects to expand, to improve safety or security, to increase competition, or to reduce noise.

Just as with highways, there are two major economic issues. The short-run issue concerns the efficient use of all existing facilities. All airlines tend to want to offer flights to the major metropolitan areas at the same times because those are the areas and times of greatest demand. But the peak-time-and-place users are not charged fees for the congestion they create because landing fees are not higher at those congested times or even at the more congested airports. The solution proposed by economists should not be surprising: congestion tolls. Specifically, it is argued that landing fees should be higher at congested than uncongested airports and at those crowded airports, higher at the more congested times. Such a pricing strategy would create an incentive for the airlines to schedule and consumers to prefer more flights at the less congested times and airports, making better use of the existing airport capacity.

The long-run issue concerns the appropriate amount and location of new investment in airport facilities. The optimal amount of airport investment in an area depends on the cost of construction compared to the benefits from reduced delays. Because both the cost of airport construction (largely due to land price differences) and the benefits from reduced congestion vary for different areas, some of the congested airports should be expanded more than others, and some of the uncongested airports should be closed or allowed to depreciate.

Optimal Transportation Investment

One alternative for dealing with a congested transportation facility, which was not discussed previously, is simply to expand that facility. If a two-lane road is crowded, build a four-lane road; if that becomes crowded, expand it to six lanes; if that becomes congested, build a new road parallel. More often than not that has been the approach to transportation investment in the United States; however, this

Figure 20.10

The relation
between highway
capacity and use

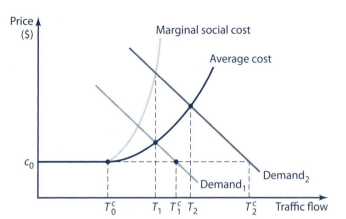

concept raises the issues of just what determines the optimal amount of investment
in transportation facilities by the society and how that determination is related to
the use (or absence) of efficient transportation prices.

The simplistic and standard economic answer to the question about the optimal
amount of investment in transportation facilities is that more facilities should be
built if the marginal benefit to society exceeds the marginal cost. The marginal cost
includes the cost of the land for the facility and the actual cost of construction. The
marginal benefit includes both the amount of time that would be saved in making
current trips and the value of any new trips that would be made on the expanded
facility. The difficulty in applying this rule is knowing what the marginal benefit of
road or transit expansion is if individuals are not charged the true cost of using
those facilities now. Thus, the first step in determining the optimal investment in
transportation facilities is setting an efficient price for the current capacity.

The cost curves in Figure 20.10 represent a transportation facility, say a road,
with a "capacity" of T_0^c; that is, no congestion occurs until use rises above that
quantity. If demand is D_1 and there is no congestion pricing, the amount of traffic
using the road is T_1, so the road is congested. How much would the road have to
be expanded to eliminate congestion given $Demand_1$? The road would have to be
expanded so that it has capacity T_1^c; that amount of traffic could use the road at the
constant average cost of C_0. Note that the amount of traffic using the road after
expansion, T_1^c, is greater than the amount using the road before expansion, T_1. The
expansion of the road itself lowers travel costs and attracts more traffic.

A similar argument applies if an expansion is justified by a forecast increase
in demand to $Demand_2$. To maintain the target average travel cost of C_0 with the
higher demand, the road capacity must be increased to T^{2c}. But if demand
increased and the road was not expanded, average travel cost would rise due to
the congestion, and use of the road would stop at T_2. The congestion serves to hold
down use of the road, while expansion of the road attracts more traffic by reducing congestion and thus lowering travel costs. Note that if an efficient congestion

charge were levied (price equals marginal social cost), use of this road would stop at T_1 even if demand rises to the higher-level *Demand₂*. The basic point is that *use of a road or other facility is not an appropriate measure of the "need" for or benefits from expansion of that facility if users do not pay the full costs.*

This point emphasizes again why efficient use charges are important. If use and congestion of a transportation facility continue to increase even when the consumers are paying charges reflecting all the costs, then there is evidence of substantial benefits from additional investment in those facilities. Herbert Mohring and Mitchell Harwitz (1962) have shown that if the production of the transportation facility exhibits constant returns to scale (the cost of producing another unit of the facility is constant), and if users are charged the full costs including congestion costs, then the revenue generated by the congestion tolls will be exactly sufficient to pay the cost of an efficient-size facility. Under those conditions, if revenues greater than costs are being generated, then the facility should be expanded using those surplus funds. When the facility is at the efficient size, toll revenues will just cover costs. If production of the facility exhibits increasing or decreasing returns, the results of this type of analysis are different although the concept is the same. If consumers are charged appropriate congestion fees and if the cost conditions for expansion of the facility are known, then the revenue from the congestion charge can be a guide to the efficient amount of investment. Without efficient congestion fees, government officials are effectively flying blind in trying to evaluate the demand for expanding transportation facilities.

Application 20.2

EVALUATING STATE TRANSPORTATION POLICY: THE MICHIGAN CASE[9]

As you have learned in this chapter, state and local governments almost exclusively provide transportation services and facilities (although admittedly using some revenue generated by the federal government). State governments take direct responsibility for constructing and maintaining some roads and provide the bulk of resources that local governments use to build and maintain the other roads in the state. Local governments also own, operate, and finance airports as well as operate public transit systems (buses, subways, etc.). State and local governments share

responsibility for public safety services related to transportation.

Therefore, any careful evaluation of transportation facilities and policy needs to be done on a state-by-state basis. In 2001 and 2002, as part of a larger examination of the state's economy and fiscal policy, Kenneth Boyer completed just such an analysis of Michigan's transportation system. That study serves both as a guide to the type of analysis that might be done in each state and also illustrates many of the transportation issues discussed previously in this chapter.

[9]This section is based on Boyer, Kenneth D. "Michigan's Transportation System and Transportation Policy." In *Michigan at the Millennium*, eds. C. Ballard, *et al.* East Lansing, MI: Michigan State University Press, 2003.

Application 20.2 — Evaluating State Transportation Policy: The Michigan Case

Professor Boyer's analysis shows, first, that Michigan is rather typical among the states in terms of the quantity of roads in the state relative to land area and population. Among states, increases in both area and population lead to an increase in lane miles of roadway, but less than proportionally. The elasticity of lane miles of road with respect to area is 0.3 to 0.5, whereas the elasticity of lane miles of road with respect to population is 0.5 to 0.7.

The road structure in Michigan is different from other similar states in two important ways, however. The state government in Michigan "owns" (is responsible for) a much smaller fraction of major roads in Michigan than is true in most other states. Focusing on highways that carry significant amounts of interstate traffic or traffic between regions in the state, he notes "The Michigan Department of Transportation owns only 29.2 percent of through roads, compared to Ohio's 64.6 percent and the national average of 57.6 percent" (Boyer, 2003, p. 326). Thus, local governments in Michigan are responsible for an unusually large fraction of roads and highways, including those that are major through routes. As a consequence of this local ownership, it appears that Michigan has invested in far fewer multilane roads other than limited access freeways—particularly in rural areas—when compared to other states. Also, Michigan seems to have a different pattern of road-construction techniques than in comparable states.

Professor Boyer's analysis also showed that all classes of major urban roads and rural interstate highways in Michigan are of poor quality compared to similar roads in other states, as measured by the International Roughness Index, an index that varies from 60 (very smooth) to 220 (very rough). For instance, among urban arterial roads that are not freeways or interstates (that is, most major urban roads), only about 14 percent of Michigan roads meet a medium roughness standard (index of 120) compared to 44.4 percent in the Great Lakes states and 41.4 percent nationally. For urban interstates, the comparison is 61.5 percent meeting a medium roughness standard in Michigan compared to 83.3 percent in the Great Lakes states.

Therefore, the most important policy question is: Why are roads in Michigan of such poor quality compared to other similar states? It is not because Michigan has more roads relative to area or population compared to other states; as noted Michigan is typical. It is also not due to more driving or use of roads in Michigan compared to other places; vehicle miles of travel per person in Michigan is almost exactly the national average. Finally, it turns out that the poor quality of Michigan roads is also not because Michigan spends less on roads and highways than other states; per-capita revenue for highways in Michigan is similar to other states in the Great Lakes region. So why?

Four factors seem to account for the relative poor quality of roads, and especially urban roads, in Michigan. First, as noted earlier, local governments own an unusually large fraction of major roads in Michigan. Those local governments receive a portion of Michigan Transportation Fund revenue generated by state fuel taxes to pay for road construction and maintenance. The allocation formulas used, however, direct a disproportionate amount of that revenue to rural as opposed to urban areas. Counties in Michigan with population of more than 100,000 received $44.59 per capita in 1999, whereas counties with fewer than 20,000 people received

Application 20.2 — Evaluating State Transportation Policy: The Michigan Case

$199.74. Especially because a very large share of traffic in Michigan travels on urban roads, it is not surprising, therefore, that major roads in urban areas of Michigan are of such poor quality.

A second factor is state regulations that effectively permit much heavier trucks on Michigan highways than are allowed in most any other state. Consequently, nearly 11,000 trucks weighing more than 80,000 pounds are registered in Michigan and essentially none in the other Great Lakes states. The scientific relationship between truck weights and road wear is not clear cut and depends not only on truck weight, but also the number of axles and the road material. Still, it is striking that Michigan has the most liberal truck weight laws in the nation and a relatively large fraction of poor quality roads. Third, public transportation systems in Michigan's major urban areas are far less developed than in other comparable urban areas; Detroit is very unusual among major U.S. cities in having no rail-based commuter transit. This puts correspondingly heavier pressure on major urban roads, which again are not favored by

the highway fund allocation formula. Finally, Michigan is also unusual in that it has essentially no toll roads (tolls from some bridges amount to less than 2 percent of state highway funds compared to 15 percent of highway revenue from tolls nationally), and Michigan is one of only a handful of states in which the tax rate on diesel fuel ($.15) is less than that for gasoline ($.19). These latter two factors suggest that changes in the way Michigan funds roads might affect the nature of traffic and thus the quality of roads.

The Michigan story is interesting in itself, of course, but the way it illustrates the complicated relationship between state–local fiscal policy and public service is more relevant to you as a student of government finance. The fundamental choice of which government level will be responsible for a public service, the choice of revenue sources and relative tax rates, the option for direct user fees, the allocation mechanism for state grants to localities, and state regulations all combine to determine the resulting "produced output"— that is the benefit or level of service of a public good that consumers receive.

SUMMARY

Of the total expenditures by all levels of government on transportation facilities or service for air, rail, road, and water transit in 2001, about 60 percent (about $110 billion) went for highways.

Taxes and tolls collected from users, including motor fuel taxes, vehicle and driver license fees, taxes on airline ticket prices, aircraft-landing fees, and a variety of user tolls, are the major component of revenues for transportation spending.

The federal government provided about 27 percent of the funds spent on highways in 2001 but spent less than 2 percent directly itself. States generated about 60 percent of the revenue spent on highways and accounted for nearly 60 percent of direct spending on highways. Local governments generated about 8 percent of revenues spent on highways but accounted for about 38 percent of direct spending.

If the transportation system is already large enough to provide all the general benefits that arise from having a transportation network, then any further expansion of that system will only generate private benefits and should be entirely financed by users of that expansion. About 75 percent of the revenue for highway expenditures for all purposes in 2003 came from highway users, with motor fuel taxes representing a bit more than half of total highway spending.

Motor fuel taxes are good proxies for highway-user charges because motor fuel taxes vary by the amount and type of road use, and they can be collected at relatively low administration costs. However, motor fuel taxes are imperfect user charges because all gasoline and diesel fuel is not used on highways, vehicles (and drivers) differ in their fuel economy, and fuel taxes do not differentiate highway use by location and time.

The argument for federal highway aid is that nonresidents substantially use transportation facilities directly provided by states and localities. And despite the expansion in scope of federal highway aid over the years, federal highway aid is still heavily skewed toward roads used for interstate and interregional travel.

The appropriate matching rate for federal grants should cover that fraction of marginal benefits that spill over to nonresidents. The current federal government share for the major transportation grants is 90 percent for both construction and maintenance of interstate highways; 80 percent for other roads eligible for federal aid; and 80 percent for the capital costs of new or expanded urban mass-transit systems.

The existence of congestion creates inefficiency because each user is concerned only with his or her travel costs (the average cost) and does not consider the costs imposed on other travelers by the additional congestion (the marginal cost). The economic solution to any traffic-congestion problem is to levy a congestion fee or toll equal to the difference between average and marginal cost at the efficient quantity. The congestion fee can be levied through tolls, fuel taxes, or metered usage.

The degree of congestion of a road or other facility is not an appropriate measure of the "need" for or benefits from expansion of that facility if users do not pay the full costs. Thus, the first step in determining the optimal investment in transportation facilities is setting an efficient price for the current capacity. The facility should then be expanded if that price generates sufficient revenue.

DISCUSSION QUESTIONS

1. Congestion is a common problem on roads and other transportation systems. Carefully explain what an economist means by *congestion* and why it is an economic problem. What type of user charge can "solve" a congestion problem?

2. "If a road is congested, then it is too small for the demand. The road should be expanded or replaced." True, false, or uncertain? Explain.

3. Suppose that Your College Town has two parallel four-lane roads connecting the college to the rest of the city. One goes from the college

directly into the heart of town and is usually congested, particularly so at rush hours and other times when there are special activities on campus (such as a concert or athletic event). The road requires no special tolls or charges. The other runs two miles south of the first with a number of connecting streets and is seldom crowded. The state highway department would like to use the revenue from a gasoline tax increase to expand the first road to six lanes. Would such an expansion be called for on economic efficiency grounds? Does society lose anything if the second road is not used to capacity? How else might the congestion on the first road be alleviated? What if congestion tolls were not feasible?

4. Besides gasoline taxes, most states also generate revenue from vehicle registration fees and drivers' license charges. If these are to serve as user charges, what types of transportation service should be financed by the gas tax and what types by these fees? Recently, some states have considered levying special-use fees on each driving infraction conviction. For instance, in addition to the existing fines, there could be an additional $5 charge for each case of speeding. If this was to be a user charge, what type of service might it finance?

SELECTED READING

Boyer, Kenneth D. *Principles of Transportation Economics,* (Reading, MA: Addison Wesley, 1998.)

Boyer, Kenneth D. "Michigan's Transportation System and Transportation Policy." In *Michigan at the Millennium, eds.* C. Ballard, *et al.* East Lansing, MI: Michigan State University Press, 2003.

Downs, Anthony. *Stuck in Traffic: Coping with Peak-Hour Traffic Congestion.* Washington, DC: Brookings Institution, 1992.

Gomez-Ibanez, Jose A. "The Federal Role in Urban Transportation." In *American Domestic Priorities: An Economic Appraisal, ed.* J. Quigley and D. Rubinfeld. Berkeley: University of California Press, 1985, 183–223.

Vickrey, William S. "Pricing in Urban and Suburban Transport." *American Economic Review* (May 1963): 452–65.

CHAPTER 21

HEALTH AND WELFARE

The purpose of this part is to increase the flexibility of States in operating a program designed to

(1) provide assistance to needy families so that children may be cared for in their own homes or in the homes of relatives;

(2) end the dependence of needy parents on government benefits by promoting job preparation, work, and marriage;

(3) prevent and reduce the incidence of out-of-wedlock pregnancies and establish annual numerical goals for preventing and reducing the incidence of these pregnancies; and

(4) encourage the formation and maintenance of two-parent families.

PERSONAL RESPONSIBILITY AND WORK OPPORTUNITY
RECONCILIATION ACT OF 1996[1]

HEADLINES

"A GROWING INABILITY TO PAY EVER-INCREASING MEDICAID COSTS HAS FORCED VERMONT INTO AN INNOVATIVE DEAL WITH THE FEDERAL GOVERNMENT . . .

. . . THE STATE HAS AGREED TO ACCEPT CAPS TO FEDERAL MEDICAID FUNDING OVER THE NEXT FIVE YEARS, . . . STATE OFFICIALS [WILL BE GIVEN] UNPRECEDENTED FLEXIBILITY TO MANAGE THE HEALTH INSURANCE PROGRAM FOR THE POOR AND BEGIN TO CONTROL COSTS.

STATES ACROSS THE COUNTRY . . . ARE WATCHING VERMONT'S APPROACH BECAUSE IT COULD PROVIDE A ROAD MAP FOR REFORMING AN ENTITLEMENT PROGRAM WHOSE COSTS HAVE RISEN BEYOND MOST GOVERNMENTS' ABILITY TO PAY.

VERMONT WAS ONE OF THE FIRST STATES TO EXPAND MEDICAID AMBITIOUSLY . . . ROUGHLY ONE OF EVERY FOUR VERMONTERS IS COVERED.

OTHER STATES ALREADY ARE LOOKING AT CAPS OF THEIR OWN . . . OTHER STATES [ARE] CONSIDERING SOME KIND OF REFORM, ALTHOUGH NOT NECESSARILY SPENDING CAPS.

(continues on next page)

---

[1]H.R.3734. Personal Responsibility and Work Opportunity Reconciliation Act of 1996 (Enrolled as Agreed to or Passed by Both House and Senate). Section 401. Purpose.

> . . . CONGRESS AND THE BUSH ADMINISTRATION ALSO HAVE BEEN LOOKING FOR WAYS TO CURB MEDICAID INFLATION THAT HAS BEEN RUNNING AROUND 20 PERCENT A YEAR. THE FEDERAL GOVERNMENT PAYS ROUGHLY 60 PERCENT OF THE COSTS . . . AND STATE GOVERNMENTS PAY THE REST.
>
> STATES ADMINISTER MEDICAID, BUT MUST DO SO UNDER STRINGENT FEDERAL RULES . . . . STATES SAY THE 40-YEAR-OLD RULES OFTEN STIFLE CREATIVITY AND INNOVATION THAT MIGHT MAKE MEDICAID CHEAPER OR . . . EASIER TO RUN."[2]
>
> ---
>
> [2]"Vermont Tests Reformed Medicaid Plan." The Associated Press. Published on cnn.com, October 3, 2005.

The provision of health and welfare services in the United States is the combined responsibility of the federal government, state–local governments, a variety of charitable nongovernmental organizations, religious groups and organizations, and private-sector service providers. Regarding the public-sector role, the federal government has had primary responsibility for financing programs and services and establishing minimum requirements. State governments have had a substantial responsibility for operating a variety of these programs that are designed to deliver health and welfare services, in addition to providing financing. This joint responsibility generates an inherent tension between the level of government that primarily finances services and the level that determines and delivers them, on the one hand, and between achieving national objectives for citizen welfare and alleviating poverty and allowing state choice about the level and structure of support programs, on the other.

When President Clinton signed the Personal Responsibility and Work Opportunity Reconciliation Act in 1996 to reform welfare, dramatic changes were fostered in the health and welfare support system. There were major changes to the objectives, methods, and relative roles of government in promoting health and welfare. Welfare was to become a path to work, rather than an end in itself. States were to be rewarded for preparing and moving welfare recipients into jobs. States were to have both greater responsibility and more flexibility to accomplish these goals. In part, all these things have happened. However, several tensions remain. One concerns establishing a fiscal structure to combine national standards and expectations about health and welfare with differences among states in needs, resources, and interests. A second is the conflict between the conventional policy wisdom, which suggests that states cannot effectively conduct redistributive policy because of interstate mobility, and actual practice in providing welfare services, where states have substantial options in determining eligibility and benefit levels. These issues are covered in this chapter.[3]

---

[3]This chapter cannot cover all the numerous issues about the design of appropriate welfare programs; rather, the focus is on those issues that involve interaction between the federal and state–local sector or interaction among various subnational governments. Issues not considered in detail, for instance, include the labor supply effects of different welfare structures and the effects on family composition.

Table 21.1

Poverty in the United States, 1960—2004

| | Poverty Thresholds | | Number of Poor Persons (millions) | | Percentage of Group Who Is Poor | |
| | | | | | | |
Year	Individual	3-Person Family		All Ages	Children Under 18	Adults 65 or Older
1960	$1,490	$2,359	39.5	22.4%	26.9%	35.2%
1965	1,582	2,514	33.2	17.3	21.0	28.5
1970	1,954	3,099	25.3	12.6	15.0	24.6
1975	2,724	4,293	25.9	12.3	16.8	15.3
1980	4,190	6,565	29.3	13.0	17.9	15.7
1985	5,469	8,573	33.1	14.0	20.1	12.6
1990	6,652	10,419	33.6	13.5	20.5	12.2
1995	7,929	12,158	36.4	13.8	20.8	10.5
2000	8,959	13,740	31.6	11.3	16.2	9.9
2004	9,827	15,205	37.0	12.7	17.8	9.8

SOURCE: U.S. Census Bureau, *Income, Poverty, and Health Care Coverage in the United States: 2004*, 2005.

POVERTY AND HEALTH CARE IN THE UNITED STATES

About 37 million people in the United States in 2004, including some 8 million families as well as single individuals, were deemed to be living in poverty, which represents about 13 percent of individuals and 10 percent of families (see Table 21.1). Individuals and families are considered officially to be "poor" if the income of their household or family is below a threshold level based on the age of the householder and the number of people in the household. For instance, in 2004, the overall individual poverty threshold was an income of $9,827, while the poverty threshold for a household with three persons, including one child, was $15,205.[4]

Both the number of persons and families living in poverty and the fraction of poor persons and families have risen and fallen over time, due to changes in economic conditions and changes to antipoverty programs, as shown in Figure 21.1. Since 1990, the fraction of the population who that is poor has varied from a low of 11.1 percent (in 2000) to a high of 15.2 percent (in 1993); the poverty rate rose in the early 1990s following the recession in the 1990–1991 period, then declined throughout the remainder of the 1990s as the national economy grew substantially, and has increased again since 2000. The degree of poverty in the United States currently is substantially less than in 1960, before the expansion of federal welfare programs. In 1960, nearly 40 million people, or about 22 percent of individuals, were classified as poor.

Among poor individuals or families, poverty is most prevalent among children under the age of 18, as shown in Figure 21.2. In 2004, there were about

---

[4]For individuals under 65, the threshold was $8,827; for those over 65, the level was $9,060. For families, the four-person threshold was $19,484; the six-person level was $27,025.

Figure 21.1

Number in poverty
and poverty rate:
1959 to 2004

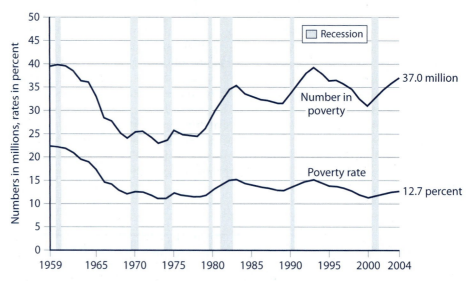

Note: The data points are placed at the midpoints of the respective years.
SOURCE: U.S. Census Bureau, Current Population Survey, 1960 to 2005 Annual Social and Economic Supplements.

Figure 21.2

Poverty rates by
age: 1959 to 2004

Note: The data points are placed at the midpoints of the respective years.
Data for people 18 to 64 and 65 and older are not available from 1960 to 1965.
SOURCE: U.S. Census Bureau, Current Population Survey, 1960 to 2005 Annual Social and Economic Supplements.

13 million children in poor households, which made up almost 18 percent of all children of that age and about 35 percent of all poor people in 2004. Although the fraction of children who lived in poverty was lower in 2004 than 1960, the decline in poverty rates among children has been much less than for the entire population. The poverty status of these children is explicitly intertwined with the economic status of those children's families. Of all children living in female-headed households (17.0 million total), about 42 percent live in poverty (7.1 million). In contrast, only about 10 percent of adults 65 years of age and older were poor in 2004 compared to more than 35 percent in 1960. The relative welfare of older, often retired adults has improved substantially since 1960, partly because of private pensions and improvements in Social Security and other programs for the aged.

Economic conditions and poverty rates differ substantially among the states and also geographically within states, as shown in Figure 21.3. (Additional information about state incomes and economic conditions is also presented in Figure 22.1, Figure 22.2, and Table 22.1 in Chapter 22.) State poverty rates for individuals (measured by three-year averages for 2002 to 2004) varied from 5.7 percent of the population in New Hampshire and 7.0 percent in Minnesota to at least 17 percent of the population in Louisiana (17.0 percent), New Mexico (17.5 percent), Arkansas (17.6), and Mississippi (17.7 percent). Obviously, state poverty rates are related to average state incomes, with the higher-income states (such as Connecticut, Maryland, New Jersey, and Minnesota) having relatively low poverty rates and the lower-income states (such as Mississippi, Arkansas, New Mexico, and Louisiana) having among the highest poverty rates.

Actual differences in poverty among the states are overstated somewhat by the data in Figure 21.3 because the same poverty income thresholds are used for all states and regions; no adjustments are made to the poverty thresholds for regional cost-of-living differences. Thus, in 2004, all three-person, one-child families with income less than $15,205 were classified as poor. If the prices of some consumer goods are higher in higher-income states, however, then that fixed amount of $15,205 will buy more goods and services in some locations than others. In fact, competitive-market analysis suggests that prices for some locally produced goods, especially housing and some services such as medical care, are likely to be higher in high-income states than low-income states. However, differences in cost of living are not large enough to account for all the differences in poverty rates. For instance, the poverty rate in Mississippi is three times that in New Hampshire, but cost-of-living differences between those states are not nearly large enough to account for the poverty difference.[5]

---

[5]For instance, suppose the family poverty level is $15,205. If living costs were 20 percent higher in Hew Hampshire than in Mississippi, the relevant comparison would be the percentage of families in Mississippi with income less than $15,205 compared to the percentage of families in New Hampshire with income less than $18,246, which is a 20 percent higher poverty level than in Mississippi. That is, $15,205 in Mississippi would buy the same consumption as $18,246 in New Hampshire. But if 6 percent of families in New Hampshire have income less than $15,205, it is unlikely that anywhere near 18 percent would have incomes below $18,246.

Figure 21.3

Three-year average poverty rate by state: 2002 to 2004

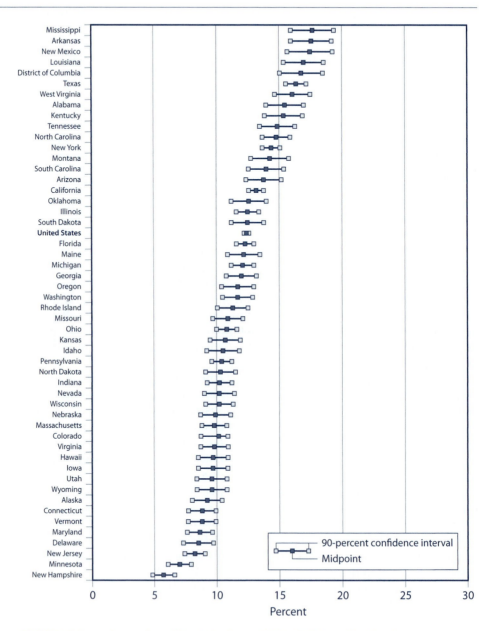

SOURCE: U.S. Census Bureau, Current Population Survey, 2003 to 2005 Annual Social and Economic Supplements.

Table 21.2

Health Insurance Coverage, 2004

Type of Health Insurance	Number of People (millions)	Percentage of People
Employment-based Private Plan	174.2	59.8%
Direct-purchase Private Plan	27.0	9.3
Medicare	39.7	13.7
Medicaid	37.5	12.9
Military Health Care	10.7	3.7
Uninsured	45.8	15.7

SOURCE: U.S. Census Bureau. Health Insurance Coverage, 2004.

The seemingly obvious point that poverty rates tend to be higher in lower-income states is central to determining to what degree and which welfare programs should be the responsibility of state government as opposed to federal government. If income redistribution or welfare programs were to be financed entirely by states, then redistribution occurs only from higher-income individuals *in that state* to poorer persons in the state. Because income is not uniformly distributed among the states, lower-income states could "afford" less redistribution—that is less income support—than higher-income states. In the limit, if one state had only poor people and another only rich people, then no redistribution occurs if welfare is entirely a state responsibility.

Welfare or antipoverty issues in states cannot be separated from health-care issues, mainly because Medicaid is by far the largest "welfare" or low-income support program in the United States, and the absence of health insurance is clearly related to poverty. In 2004, more than 30 percent of people in the United States received health insurance coverage as a result of government programs, as shown in Table 21.2. Medicare (health care for senior citizens) provided health insurance coverage to about 14 percent of the population, Medicaid (health care for low-income individuals) covered another 13 percent, and health insurance to military personnel covered another 4 percent. About 46 million people, representing about 16 percent of the population, had no health insurance coverage.

Very large variation exists among the states in the share of population without health insurance coverage, as shown in Figure 21.4. On average over the period from 2002 to 2004, the largest share of people without health insurance coverage occurred in Texas (25.1 percent) and New Mexico (21.4 percent). At the opposite end of the spectrum, fewer than 10 percent of people were without health insurance in Hawaii (9.9 percent) and Minnesota (8.5 percent). Not surprisingly, the share of people without health insurance coverage nationally declines as family income rises, as shown in Table 21.3. The states with a large fraction of people without health insurance tend to be lower-income states, although that relationship is not nearly as strong or clear as for the percentage of the population in poverty. For instance, California is a state with above-average income, but also a high fraction of people without health insurance, perhaps partly due to migration and

Figure 21.4

Percentage of people without health insurance by state, three-year average: 2002 to 2004

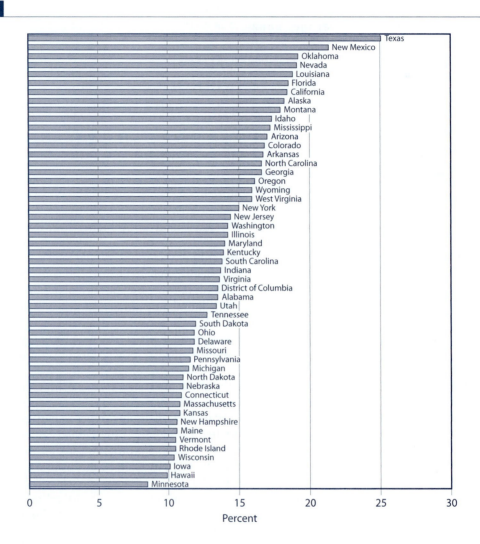

Table 21.3

Uninsured Health Coverage by Family Income, 2004

Family Income	Number of People (millions)	Number Uninsured (millions)	Percentage Uninsured
All	291.2	45.8	15.7%
Less than $25,000	73.0	19.4	26.6
$25,000 to $49,999	73.8	13.6	18.4
$50,000 to $74,999	55.0	6.4	11.6
$75,000 or More	89.4	6.4	7.2

SOURCE: U.S. Census Bureau. Health Insurance Coverage, 2004.

the relative importance of agricultural jobs in the state. Some regional differences also exist, as the absence of health insurance is relatively low among all the New England states.

FINANCING WELFARE AND HEALTH-CARE SERVICES: MAJOR PROGRAMS

The public sector in the United States engages in a variety of activities to improve social welfare, including programs providing direct cash payments, subsidies for purchases of specific goods and services, provision of in-kind benefits for specific services to specific groups, services to improve the skills and income-earning ability of individuals, as well as a variety of insurance, research, and public information efforts. Total government expenditures for education, health, and income security amounted to about $2.09 trillion in 2004, an amount equal to about 58 percent of total government spending and 18 percent of GDP. In addition to these amounts, a number of private-sector organizations, especially nonprofit ones, provide additional social welfare services.

The focus in this chapter is on a subset of health and social welfare services that provides cash payments or in-kind benefits to particular needy individuals or families, programs that are typically referred to as *public welfare programs*. Thus, each of the programs discussed in this chapter includes a specific means test so they are targeted to individuals or families based on income and/or wealth.[6] As a consequence, many other important government programs that support subsets of the population who are in special circumstances, but not based directly on income or wealth, are not considered in this chapter. These latter cases include Social Security, Medicare (health care for the aged), unemployment compensation, workers' compensation (for injured or disabled workers), and veterans' benefits.

Five major welfare or support programs represent the bulk of public aid spending and thus are the programs focused on in this chapter. Temporary Assistance to Needy Families (TANF) and Supplemental Security Income (SSI) provide monthly cash payments to individuals and families with low incomes, disabilities, or other special circumstances. Medicaid finances health care for low-income individuals and families who do not have other health insurance or health benefits. The Food Stamp program allows low-income individuals and families to purchase food using coupons or credit provided by government. Federal and some state governments provide Earned Income Tax Credits (EITC) to subsidize the earnings of low-income workers, so that the total income of these workers is increased. In addition to these

---

[6]Herbert Stein (1994) noted how welfare is but only one way government supports specific groups: ". . . welfare . . . is money paid by the federal government to people because they are poor. It does not include money paid to people because they are over 65 years of age, or because they are farmers or because they are veterans, or the special benefits provided because they have health coverage provided by their employers or because they are in the business of producing textiles."

Table 21.4

Participation and Expenditure for Major Health and Welfare Programs

Year	TANF/AFDC[a]		SSI		Medicaid[b]		Food Stamps	
	Number of Recipients[c]	Amount[d]	Number of Recipients[c]	Amount[d]	Number of Recipients[c]	Amount[d]	Number of Recipients[c]	Amount[d]
1970	8.5	$ 4.9	na	na	17.6[e]	$ 5	4.3	$ 0.6
1975	11.3	9.2	4.4	$ 5.9	22.0	12.2	17.1	4.4
1980	10.8	12.5	4.2	7.9	21.6	23.3	21.1	8.7
1985	10.9	15.2	4.2	11.1	21.8	37.5	19.9	10.8
1990	11.7	19.1	4.9	16.6	25.3	64.9	20.0	14.2
1995	13.4	21.6	6.6	27.6	36.3	120.1	26.6	22.8
2000	5.8	24.8 (12.1)	6.7	31.6	44.5	194.7	17.2	15.0
2003	4.9	26.3 (11.0)	7.1	35.6	53.3	235.7	21.3	21.4
Percentage Change								
1995–2003	−63.4%	n.a.	7.8%	29.0%	46.8%	96.3%	−19.9%	−6.1%

[a]AFDC through 1995; TANF for 2000 and 2003. Amount is total TANF expenditures. Federal block grant amount for 2003 including bonuses is $17.2 billion. TANF payments for cash assistance only were $12.1 billion in 2000 and $11.0 billion in 2003.

[b]Vendor payments only from Medicaid Statistical Information System.

[c]Number of recipients in millions.

[d]Amounts in billions of dollars.

[e]1972

SOURCE: Social Security Administration, *Annual Statistical Supplement to the Social Security Bulletin, 2004*. U.S. Department of Health and Human Services, Administration for Children & Families, FY 2003 TANF Financial Data, http://www.acf.hhs.gov/programs/ofs/data/tanf_2003.html.

major programs, various other federal and/or state programs provide public or subsidized housing, health and nutritional services, and energy assistance.

Of these five major public welfare or support programs, Medicaid is by far the largest, both in terms of the magnitude of spending and the number of recipients, as shown in Table 21.4. Total Medicaid expenditures were $275.3 billion in 2003, including $235.7 billion spent on direct health-care services (vendor payments) and $11.8 billion payments for health insurance premiums. This amount is essentially double the *sum* of amounts spent through the other four programs in 2003 (about $26.3 billion for AFDC, $35.6 billion for SSI, about $21 billion for Food Stamps, and $38.7 billion through the federal EITC). Nearly 50 million persons received direct medical care paid for by Medicaid in 2002, and on average during 2003, about 21 million people received food stamp support, about 5 million were in families receiving TANF payments, and about 7 million received SSI payments. Slightly more than 22 million federal tax returns for 2003 included earned income tax credits. Obviously, many individuals benefited from more than one of these programs. For instance, AFDC and SSI recipients automatically are eligible for Medicaid, and many AFDC and SSI recipients also may receive food stamps.

Medicaid also has been the fastest growing of these major welfare or support programs and the fastest growing component overall of state and local government spending. Expenditure rose by more than 96 percent just in the 1995 to 2003 period, an average rate of about 12 percent annually. Less than half of the increase in Medicaid expenditures is attributable to increases in eligibility and participation, as the number of recipients increased by about 47 percent, with the remainder due to higher health-care costs or coverage of new medical procedures for people who already were participants.

TANF—Temporary Assistance for Needy Families

With the passage and adoption of the Personal Responsibility and Work Opportunity Reconciliation Act of 1996, Temporary Assistance for Needy Families (TANF) replaced Aid to Families with Dependent Children (AFDC) and two other smaller programs as the government's direct welfare or cash-assistance programs.[7] TANF is designed for states to provide financial assistance for individuals mostly for limited time periods in exchange for those individuals either working or preparing for work. State governments have wide latitude to establish and operate TANF programs that meet the four goals identified in the act and listed in the introductory quote to this chapter. State governments receive block grants from the federal government to finance their TANF programs, although states are required to maintain a minimum level of state funding—related to its AFDC expenditures in 1994—to receive the federal block grant funds. The federal block grants to states also impose certain programmatic constraints on the states' TANF choices.

AFDC, the program most often thought of as "welfare" for many years, was instituted in 1935 as part of the Social Security Act to provide monthly cash payments to families (with children) who had income and assets below certain limits and where there was an absent, incapacitated, or unemployed parent. The program was operated by state governments, which established eligibility requirements and benefit levels subject to a number of federal regulations. AFDC was financed by a combination of state revenues and federal open-ended matching grants to the states.

A number of important differences exist between TANF and the AFDC program that it replaced. Following are several of the most significant differences:

- *TANF includes federal requirements that recipients must work or engage in work-related activity as soon as they are ready for a job and no more than two years after beginning to receive assistance.* For 2004, states were required to show that 50 percent of all families and 90 percent of two-parent families receiving assistance through TANF were engaging in work-related activities. Single parents are expected to engage in those activities at least 30 hours per week, and two-parent families at least 35 to 55 hours per week depending on circumstances. Besides direct employment, work-related activities include on-the-job training, community service, secondary school attendance, vocational training (for up to 12 months), and job searching (for up to

---

[7]TANF also replaced the Job Opportunities and Basic Skills Training program and the Emergency Assistance program.

6 weeks).[8] States may use federal TANF funds to create community service jobs or provide hiring incentives for private employers.

- *Generally, there is a time limit as to how long individuals or families may receive assistance through TANF.* A family that includes any adult who has received federally funded assistance for five years, or a shorter time period set by state option, is not eligible for cash assistance through TANF. The idea is that there is a maximum lifetime five-year limit on TANF benefits for any individual. States have the option of extending TANF benefits beyond five years to no more than 20 percent of the beneficiaries, and states may provide benefits beyond five years using state-only funds.

- *Federal financial support of TANF is through a lump-sum, block grant to states with a requirement for a minimum state financing amount, whereas AFDC was financed by an open-ended matching grant to states.* Each state receives a lump-sum grant annually to finance administrative expenses, benefits, and other services to recipient families. The amount of the federal grant was set at $16.5 billion annually for the years 1997 to 2002. Subsequently, TANF has been extended through a series of continuing approvals, with formal reauthorization of the act pending in Congress at this writing. Each state's allocation from the TANF grant is based on the amount that state received during the mid-1990s in federal support for AFDC. In addition to programmatic requirements, state governments are required to spend an amount of state funds on TANF each year; states must spend 75 percent of the amount it spent on AFDC in 1994 if the work requirements of recipients are met and 80 percent if those work requirements are not met. States that make improvement in the work requirements and other goals of TANF can receive "bonus" payments from the federal government.[9]

- *Under TANF, states have substantial flexibility in how to allocate federal block grant funds and the required state "maintenance of effort" funds and are not limited to making cash-assistance payments.* States are expected to use TANF funds in a manner "reasonably calculated to accomplish the purposes of TANF." For instance, substantial amounts of TANF funds are used to pay child care expenses for working parents, to pay for transportation to work or school, to fund programs targeted at pregnancy prevention and family formation, and to cover the administrative costs of the programs. States also can allocate TANF funds to cover the costs of refundable Earned Income Tax Credits, which create cash assistance payments to low-income workers indirectly.

These last two differences between the programs have important economic implications, as you should realize from the discussion about the expenditure effects of intergovernmental grants in Chapter 9. The federal share of state expenditure in the open-ended matching grants that funded AFDC was determined by

---

[8]Single parents with a child under one and single parents with a child under six and who cannot obtain child care are exceptions.

[9]For more information about the block grant issues, see Weaver, 2002.

a formula based on state per-capita income over a three-year period, similar to the continuing grants that fund Medicaid. Thus, the federal grant share of state expenditure varied between 65 and 50 percent among the states, without any limit on the amount. The federal government paid half of AFDC expenditures in states with per-capita income equal or greater than that for the nation, and it paid a larger percentage of expenditures in states with lower than average per-capita incomes, up to a maximum of 65 percent. These matching grants therefore reduced the "tax price" or marginal cost to states of spending on AFDC benefits below a price of $1.00. The block grants that fund TANF are lump-sum grants, however. States are required to allocate an amount of state government funds equal to a percentage of state AFDC spending in 1994. If states elect to spend more than those amounts, however, the amount of federal grant funds does not increase. Thus, the tax price or marginal cost to states of increasing state spending on cash-assistance benefits now is equal to $1.00, which is higher than under the old AFDC program.

In 2003, about 4.9 million individuals, or 1.7 percent of the population, in slightly more than 2 million families received direct assistance or benefits through state programs related to TANF. Total TANF-related expenditures by states were about $26.3 billion in 2003, although cash-assistance payments were only about $11 billion of that total. The financial structure of TANF for five years starting in fiscal year 2000 is shown in Table 21.5. In each of these years, state governments received about $17 billion in federal TANF grant funds, including the basic TANF block grant and various bonuses. States also had to allocate state government *maintenance of effort* funds toward achieving the goals of TANF. Thus, state aggregate spending related to TANF from both sources of funds was about $25 to $26 billion in each of these years.[10]

Table 21.5

TANF Program Finances, Fiscal Years 2000–2004

Fiscal Year	Federal TANF Grants to States[a] (billions of dollars)	Total State TANF Expenditure[b] (billions of dollars)	Percentage for Basic Cash Assistance	Child Care	Transportation	Cash Assistance, Prior Law	Expenditures for Other Than Cash Assistance
2000	$17.007	$24.758	45%	0%	2%	4%	49%
2001	17.033	25.667	40	2	2	4	53
2002	17.004	25.414	37	2	1	4	56
2003	17.198	26.340	39	1	1	3	56
2004	16.977	25.821	40	2	1	3	53

[a]Federal grants received by states in that fiscal year.

[b]State expenditure in that fiscal year using both federal funds and state maintenance of effort funds.

SOURCE: U.S. Department of Health and Human Services, Administration for Children & Families, TANF Financial Data, Tables A1 and F, http://www.acf.hhs.gov/programs/ofs/data/index.html.

---

[10]In the initial years of TANF, state spending was less than the federal grants, as states adjusted to the new structure. Similarly, in any given year, states may not spend all federal funds received, putting the remainder into reserves for spending in subsequent years.

Table 21.6

State Program Parameters, TANF Cash Assistance, 2002

State	Earnings Limit, Applicants, 1-Parent Family of 3	Asset Limit, Recipient	Monthly Maximum Benefit, Family of 3	Lifetime Time Limit per Recipient	Benefits Continue to Children After Time Limit
Alabama	$2,460/year	$2,000[1]	$164/month	60 months	No
Alaska	15,312/year	2,000[1]	923/month	60 months	No
Arizona	7,032/year	2,000	347/month	None	Not applicable
Arkansas	3,348/year	3,000	204/month	24 months	No
California	11,388/year	2,000[1]	679/month	60 months	Yes
Colorado	6,132/year	2,000	356/month	60 months	No
Connecticut	10,020/year	3,000	543/month	60 months	No
Delaware	5,136/year	1,000	338/month	36 months	No
District of Columbia	6,468/year	2,000[1]	379/month	60 months	Yes
Florida	4,716/year	2,000	303/month	48 months	No
Georgia	6,168/year	1,000	280/month	48 months	No
Hawaii	19,692/year	5,000	570/month	60 months	No
Idaho	7,776/year	2,000	309/month	24 months	No
Illinois	5,832/year	3,000	396/month	60 months	No
Indiana	4,536/year	1,500	288/month	24 months	Yes
Iowa	12,732/year	5,000	426/month	60 months	No
Kansas	6,228/year	2,000	429/month	60 months	No
Kentucky	10,908/year	2,000	262/month	60 months	No
Louisiana	4,320/year	2,000	240/month	60 months[2]	No
Maine	12,276/year	2,000	485/month	60 months	No
Maryland	7,080/year	2,000	472/month	60 months	No
Massachusetts	8,496/year	2,500	618/month	None[2]	Not applicable[3]
Michigan	9,288/year	3,000	459/month	None	Not applicable
Minnesota	12,156/year	5,000	532/month	60 months	No
Mississippi	5,496/year	2,000	170/month	60 months	No
Missouri	6,696/year	5,000	292/month	60 months	No
Montana	10,512/year	3,000	507/month	60 months	No
Nebraska	8,784/year	6,000	364/month	None	Not applicable[3]
Nevada	13,440/year	2,000	348/month	60 months	No
New Hampshire	9,372/year	2,000	625/month	60 months	No
New Jersey	7,632/year	2,000	424/month	60 months	No
New Mexico	12,732/year	3,500	389/month	60 months	No
New York	8,004/year	2,000[1]	577/month	60 months	No
North Carolina	9,000/year	3,000	272/month	60 months	No
North Dakota	15,024/year	6,000	477/month	60 months	No
Ohio	11,760/year	No limit	373/month	60 months	No
Oklahoma	8,448/year	1,000	292/month	60 months	No
Oregon	7,392/year	10,000	503/month	None	No
Pennsylvania	8,124/year	1,000	403/month	60 months	No
Rhode Island	15,336/year	1,000	554/month	60 months	Yes
South Carolina	7,308/year	2,500	204/month	60 months	No
South Dakota	8,316/year	2,000	483/month	60 months	No
Tennessee	12,096/year	2,000	185/month	60 months	No
Texas	4,812/year	2,000[1]	208/month	60 months	No
Utah	6,876/year	2,000	474/month	36 months	No
Vermont	12,000/year	1,000	638/month	None	Not applicable
Virginia	15,024/year	1,000	320/month	60 months	No
Washington	13,104/year	1,000	546/month	60 months	Yes

Table 21.6

(continued)

State	Earnings Limit, Applicants, 1-Parent Family of 3	Asset Limit, Recipient	Monthly Maximum Benefit, Family of 3	Lifetime Time Limit per Recipient	Benefits Continue to Children After Time Limit
West Virginia	9,036/year	2,000	453/month	60 months	No
Wisconsin	17,280/year	2,500	673/month	60 months	No
Wyoming	6,480/year	2,500	340/month	60 months	No

[1]Households that include a member age 60 and older may exempt $3,000.

[2]There is a fixed-period time limit of 24 in 60 months.

[3]Benefits do not continue to children after reaching a fixed-period time limit.

SOURCE: National Center for Children in Poverty, Columbia University, http://www.nccp.org

States can spend both the federal grant funds and the required state resources in a variety of ways to meet the objectives of the Personal Responsibility and Work Opportunity Reconciliation Act of 1996. Only about 40 to 45 percent of total spending is allocated to cash-assistance payments, including both basic cash assistance under TANF and cash-assistance payments required under prior law. Cash-assistance payments have varied between $10 and $12 billion during these years. A small amount of funds is used to pay child care expenses for working parents and job-related transportation costs. A bit more than half of total TANF-related spending goes for other than direct cash assistance. For instance, federal TANF funds to states may be transferred to the Social Services Block Grant program, which is used to provide a variety of social services related to adoption, child/adult protective care, foster care, family planning, counseling, day care, and recreation, among others. TANF funds also can be used to provide community service opportunities and to cover administration costs.

For 2003, cash-assistance payments through TANF averaged about $163 per individual recipient per month ($1,956 annually) and $393 per family per month ($4,716 annually). In contrast, in 1992 about 14 million people or about 5.4 percent of the total population were in families receiving AFDC benefits that totaled $21.9 billion and averaged about $131 per person, per month ($1,572 annually) or $374 per family, per month ($4,488 annually). This comparison illustrates that one major effect of the transition to TANF from AFDC is coverage of far fewer individuals and families, partly because of the work requirements and time limits. On the other hand, average payments per recipient have remained about constant in real terms. With essentially the same payments per recipient as in AFDC but fewer recipients, state expenditures for TANF programs are much less in aggregate than for the previous AFDC programs.

Given that a major objective of TANF was to permit state governments substantial flexibility in designing programs, it is not surprising that very large differences have evolved among the states in the TANF programs. The structural characteristics of state cash-assistance programs operated as part of TANF are shown in Table 21.6. The annual earnings eligibility limit for a single-parent family of three people varies from \$2,460 in Alabama to \$19,692 in Hawaii; the highest earnings limit among mainland states is \$17,280 in Wisconsin. Almost all the states also use an asset limit for eligibility, typically on the order of \$2,000 or \$3,000. Most of the states have adopted the maximum federal time limit of 60 months; 7 have a lower limit and 6 have no time limit (requiring the use of state funds only after 60 months). The maximum monthly benefit for a family of three people varies from \$164 in Alabama to \$923 in Alaska; the highest monthly benefit among mainland states is \$679 in California.

Some of the outcomes of the state cash-assistance programs operated through TANF are shown in Table 21.7. About 1.7 percent of the population was in

Table 21.7

TANF Program Results by State, 2003

Jurisdiction	Number of Families	Number of Recipients	Recipients as a Percentage of Population	Children as a Percentage of Recipients	TANF Expenditure as a Percentage State Expenditure (1)	Monthly Average Amount per Family	Monthly Average Amount per Recipient
United States	2,020,819	4,918,783	1.7%	75.4%	1.28%	$393.18	$161.53
Alabama	19,158	45,541	1.0	78.5	0.38	198.73	83.6
Alaska	5,211	14,749	2.3	66.5	0.74	671.31	237.19
Arizona	49,434	116,478	2.1	73.1	1.81	282.36	119.84
Arkansas	10,906	24,770	0.9	74.3	0.41	235.92	103.87
California	449,698	1,106,544	3.1	80.7	4.16	644.04	261.74
Colorado	13,968	36,528	0.8	72.9	0.55	343	131.16
Connecticut	20,634	43,441	1.2	71.5	0.76	424.85	201.8
Delaware	5,626	12,732	1.6	76.0	0.49	247.72	109.47
District of Columbia	16,741	42,731	7.7	74.8	1.08	331.34	129.81
Florida	57,986	119,545	0.7	80.8	0.53	253.82	123.12
Georgia	56,153	134,014	1.5	77.0	0.82	224.48	94.06
Hawaii	9,529	24,918	2.0	70.3	0.93	532.83	203.77
Idaho	1,737	3,233	0.2	79.2	0.19	299.97	161.21
Illinois	36,189	92,157	0.7	82.3	0.20	134.81	52.94
Indiana	52,357	138,281	2.2	75.9	0.91	202.44	76.65
Iowa	19,558	50,404	1.7	67.4	0.95	327.96	127.26
Kansas	15,642	40,707	1.5	69.2	0.86	303.7	116.7
Kentucky	35,065	77,222	1.9	74.1	0.79	241.04	109.45
Louisiana	22,501	56,746	1.3	80.2	0.57	251.5	99.72
Maine	9,926	27,503	2.1	64.1	0.93	362.69	130.9
Maryland	26,055	62,123	1.1	73.8	0.71	351.62	147.48
Massachusetts	49,760	109,398	1.7	69.9	1.41	525.61	239.07
Michigan	76,944	205,634	2.0	73.5	1.48	397.34	148.68
Minnesota	36,196	93,569	1.8	71.7	1.05	368.56	142.57
Mississippi	19,748	45,407	1.6	73.4	0.43	143.97	62.61
Missouri	40,678	100,602	1.8	71.5	0.86	241.51	97.66
Montana	5,988	16,698	1.8	66.1	1.00	399.97	143.43
Nebraska	10,966	27,071	1.6	71.9	1.03	345.64	140.02
Nevada	10,150	24,114	1.1	76.3	1.02	319.04	134.28
New Hampshire	6,072	14,090	1.1	68.7	1.23	504.49	217.4

Table 21.7

(continued)

Jurisdiction	Number of Families	Number of Recipients	Recipients as a Percentage of Population	Children as a Percentage of Recipients	TANF Expenditure as a Percentage State Expenditure (1)	Monthly Average Amount per Family	Monthly Average Amount per Recipient
New Jersey	42,921	103,646	1.2	75.1	0.81	369.54	153.03
New Mexico	16,858	44,523	2.4	70.8	0.96	305.99	115.86
New York	147,805	335,924	1.7	71.8	1.78	576.08	253.47
North Carolina	39,843	82,614	1.0	77.8	0.51	215.36	103.86
North Dakota	3,351	8,619	1.4	69.6	0.71	395.31	153.67
Ohio	84,434	187,284	1.6	74.2	1.18	317.88	143.31
Oklahoma	14,956	36,504	1.0	76.5	0.37	198.37	81.27
Oregon	18,659	42,599	1.2	74.0	0.97	464.33	203.38
Pennsylvania	82,182	213,990	1.7	72.8	0.93	323.37	124.19
Rhode Island	13,131	34,747	3.2	69.8	1.63	424.54	160.43
South Carolina	19,639	47,376	1.1	73.3	0.30	162.26	67.26
South Dakota	2,774	6,189	0.8	82.4	0.53	328.17	147.09
Tennessee	70,143	185,114	3.2	71.6	1.02	170.27	64.52
Texas	128,590	318,295	1.4	78.1	0.64	187.59	75.79
Utah	8,745	22,309	0.9	71.6	0.60	397.27	155.72
Vermont	4,865	12,510	2.0	64.0	1.32	534.65	207.91
Virginia	19,748	47,154	0.6	70.3	0.27	195.86	82.02
Washington	54,836	135,469	2.2	69.9	1.52	425	172.03
West Virginia	16,052	41,129	2.3	67.9	1.15	366.08	142.88
Wisconsin	20,998	50,280	0.9	79.8	0.83	447.02	186.69
Wyoming	400	712	0.1	86.8	0.06	195.06	109.49

(1) State government direct general expenditure.

SOURCES: *Social Security Bulletin. Annual Statistical Supplement, 2004.* U.S. Census Bureau. *State and Local Government Finances, 2002–2003.*

families receiving TANF benefits during 2003, varying from highs of 3.2 percent in Rhode Island and Tennessee and 3.1 percent in California to lows of less than 1 percent of the population in Wyoming (0.1 percent), Virginia (0.6 percent), Florida and Illinois (0.7 percent), South Dakota (0.8 percent), and Utah and Wisconsin (0.9 percent). Children represented more than 75 percent of individuals in recipient families nationally. Average actual monthly benefits received per participating family varied from $671 in Alaska and $644 in California to $135 in Illinois and $144 in Mississippi. State government expenditure on TANF programs represented slightly more than 1 percent of state direct general expenditure in 2003, varying from more than 4 percent in California to less than one-tenth of 1 percent in Wyoming. Looking at the overall picture, it seems that California ran the largest program in 2003 (on average over the year, 3.1 percent of the population received benefits that accounted for 4.16 percent of state spending), whereas Wyoming had the smallest program (only 712 individuals received benefits on average over the year that accounted for 0.06 percent of state spending).

Medicaid—Health Care for Low-Income Persons

Medicaid, instituted in 1965, is a joint federal-state program partly financed with federal open-ended grants to the states to provide medical care to individuals and families with low incomes and resources. States have substantial latitude in setting eligibility and benefits subject to federal restrictions and requirements. For medical care received by recipients, states pay Medicaid funds directly to providers (vendors) so that individuals never receive the cash. In addition to direct provider payments for services, Medicaid also pays some health insurance premiums and makes payments to some hospitals (usually in inner-city areas) that provide care, especially emergency care, to unusually large numbers of Medicaid recipients.

Regarding eligibility, states are required to cover certain individuals: individuals eligible for AFDC payments based on rules in effect on July 16, 1996; recipients of SSI payments; generally all children in families with income below the official poverty thresholds (at least children under 19 and some up to 21); pregnant women and children under 6 in families with income less than 133 percent of the poverty level; and certain other specific groups. States have an option to provide Medicaid coverage to broader groups and receive federal matching funds, such as infants and pregnant women in families with income under 185 percent of the poverty level; certain aged, blind, or disabled individuals with low incomes; some institutionalized individuals; and others.

Regarding benefits, states determine the types of medical services to be covered, the duration of coverage, and the rate of payment to providers for each type of covered service. Certain services are mandated in order for states to receive federal funds, including inpatient and outpatient hospital services, physician services, prenatal care, vaccinations for children, laboratory and X-ray testing, and others. Optional coverages for state choice include prescription drugs, eyeglasses and optometrist services, dental services, prosthetic devices, and others. For both required and optional services, states determine the duration of coverage, such as a limited number of days of hospital care or number of physician visits or tests. Finally, states set the payment rates to health-care providers, which they must accept, for all covered services, and states also determine any deductibles or copayments that recipients must pay.[11]

States receive open-ended matching grant funds from the federal government to help finance Medicaid payments. The federal grant share of state expenditure is determined by the formula

$$100 - \left\{ \frac{\text{State Per Capita Income}^2}{\text{National Per Capita Income}^2} \right\} \times 45$$

with per-capita income measured as the average over a three-year period. However, the maximum allowed federal share is 83 percent, and the minimum is 50 percent. Thus, the federal government pays half of Medicaid expenditures in states

---

[11]States must set payment rates so that health-care service supply is available to Medicaid recipients to the same extent that services are available to the general population.

with per-capita income equal or greater than that for the nation; it pays a larger percentage of expenditures in states with lower than average per-capita incomes, up to a maximum of 83 percent. The federal shares for 2005 are shown in the far-right column of Table 21.8. The largest federal government Medicaid shares are 77 percent in Mississippi, 75 percent in Arkansas and West Virginia, and 74 percent in New Mexico; the federal share is the minimum 50 percent in 11 states.

Table 21.8

Medicaid Programs by State, 2002

Jurisdiction	Number of Recipients 2002	Recipients as a Percentage of State Population	Vendor Payments 2002 (billions of dollars)	Vendor Payments as a Percentage of Total State Expenditure 2002	Average Vendor Payment per Recipient 2002 (dollars)	Federal Share 2005 (percentage)
United States	49,754,619	17.5%	$213.491	16.7%	$4,291	59.0
Alabama	765,328	17.1	3.204	17.8	4,187	70.83
Alaska	109,641	17.3	0.686	9.3	6,264	57.58
Arizona	878,362	16.6	2.881	15.9	3,281	67.45
Arkansas	579,278	21.5	2.015	17.5	3,479	74.75
California	9,301,001	26.9	23.636	12.8	2,541	50
Colorado	425,878	9.6	2.166	12.9	5,086	50
Connecticut	479,051	14.0	3.245	16.1	6,774	50
Delaware	167,162	21.0	0.651	14.0	3,897	50.38
District of Columbia	193,494	34.0	1.027	13.1	5,308	70
Florida	2,676,235	16.4	9.827	19.0	3,672	58.9
Georgia	1,637,329	19.5	4.796	16.0	2,929	60.44
Hawaii	199,966	16.4	0.695	9.3	3,477	58.47
Idaho	176,499	13.4	0.791	15.1	4,487	70.62
Illinois	1,731,398	13.8	9.121	18.6	5,268	50
Indiana	849,427	13.9	3.725	16.8	4,386	62.78
Iowa	352,635	12.0	1.855	14.6	5,263	63.55
Kansas	289,349	10.7	1.501	14.2	5,188	61.01
Kentucky	808,294	19.9	3.459	18.8	4,280	69.6
Louisiana	898,824	20.1	3.234	17.7	3,599	71.04
Maine	275,826	21.4	1.716	27.4	6,223	64.89
Maryland	692,539	12.9	3.662	15.7	5,288	50
Massachusetts	1,065,636	16.7	6.387	19.4	5,994	50
Michigan	1,449,915	14.5	5.918	12.0	4,082	56.71
Minnesota	620,652	12.4	4.439	16.6	7,153	50
Mississippi	712,457	24.9	2.499	19.6	3,508	77.08
Missouri	1,036,150	18.4	4.071	19.5	3,929	61.15
Montana	103,617	11.4	0.532	12.5	5,143	71.9
Nebraska	255,771	14.9	1.255	19.2	4,907	59.64
Nevada	202,306	9.7	0.723	9.8	3,579	55.9
New Hampshire	104,138	8.3	0.745	15.4	7,161	50
New Jersey	954,491	11.2	5.497	13.1	5,759	50
New Mexico	798,665	43.6	1.796	17.8	2,250	74.3
New York	3,920,718	20.5	31.488	26.4	8,031	50
North Carolina	1,355,269	16.5	6.041	18.2	4,457	63.63

Table 21.8

(continued)

Jurisdiction	Number of Recipients 2002	Recipients as a Percentage of State Population	Vendor Payments 2002 (billions of dollars)	Vendor Payments as a Percentage of Total State Expenditure 2002	Average Vendor Payment per Recipient 2002 (dollars)	Federal Share 2005 (percentage)
North Dakota	70,132	11.0	0.422	14.0	6,028	67.49
Ohio	1,656,124	14.5	9.186	17.5	5,547	59.68
Oklahoma	631,498	18.2	2.238	15.2	3,544	70.18
Oregon	621,462	17.9	2.136	11.8	3,438	61.12
Pennsylvania	1,627,261	13.2	8.523	15.4	5,238	53.84
Rhode Island	199,014	18.8	1.251	21.7	6,288	55.38
South Carolina	809,136	19.9	3.382	16.9	4,181	69.89
South Dakota	117,631	15.5	0.503	18.1	4,284	66.03
Tennessee	1,732,381	30.1	4.747	23.7	2,740	64.81
Texas	2,952,569	13.8	11.121	15.8	3,767	60.87
Utah	274,707	12.0	1.215	12.0	4,425	72.14
Vermont	153,731	25.1	0.607	17.3	3,950	60.11
Virginia	665,203	9.3	3.017	10.8	4,537	50
Washington	1,039,070	17.3	4.373	14.4	4,209	50
West Virginia	362,030	20.1	1.577	16.8	4,358	74.65
Wisconsin	716,298	13.3	3.605	13.5	5,034	58.31
Wyoming	59,071	12.0	0.280	9.5	4,748	57.9

SOURCES: *Social Security Bulletin, Annual Statistical Supplement, 2004.* U.S. Bureau of the Census. *State and Local Government Finances,* 2001–02.

Slightly more than 53 million people received direct health-care services in fiscal year 2003 through Medicaid (about 18 percent of the population).[12] Total Medicaid expenditures were $275.3 billion and included $235.7 billion for direct medical services, $11.8 billion for health insurance premiums, $14.3 billion for hospital subsidies (disproportionate share hospital payments), and $13.5 billion for administration. The federal government provided revenue for 59 percent of all Medicaid expenditures, with the remainder financed by state and local governments. The average payment per recipient for direct medical services and insurance was $4,643.

The largest group of Medicaid recipients is children in low-income families, who represented nearly 49 percent of all recipients in 2003. Other recipient groups include adults (26 percent), blind or disabled individuals (16 percent), and seniors (9 percent). Although children are the largest group of recipients, they account for a relative small fraction of health-care expenditures financed by Medicaid, as

[12]Tritz, Karen. "Medicaid Expenditures, FY 2002 and FY 2003." Congressional Research Service Report for Congress, 2005. Centers for Medicare and Medicaid Services, 2003 Data Compendium.

Figure 21.5

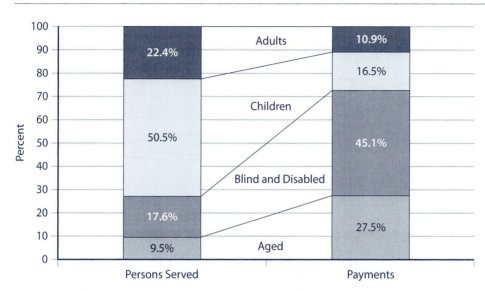

Distribution of persons served through Medicaid and payments by basis of eligibility, fiscal year 2000

Note: (1) "Payments" describe direct Medicaid provider payments and Medicaid program expenditures for premium payments to third parties for managed care, as well as cost sharing on behalf of persons served who are dually enrolled in Medicaid and Medicare, but exclude DSH payments and Medicare premiums. (2) This chart excludes 3.7 million persons served with "unknown" basis of eligibility and 6.5 billion expenditures on behalf of persons served with "unknown" basis of eligibility in FY 2000.

SOURCE: Centers for Medicare and Medicaid Services.

shown in Figure 21.5. In fiscal year 2000, children represented about half of the recipients but accounted for only 16.5 percent of payments. On the other hand, aged beneficiaries represented 9.5 of all recipients and 27.5 percent of payments, and the blind and disabled were 17.6 percent of recipients but accounted for more than 45 percent of total payments. Thus, more than 72 percent of Medicaid expenditures for direct medical care went for aged, blind, or disabled recipients, even though they represented only about one-quarter of beneficiaries.

Medicaid not only is the single largest welfare program, but also the fastest growing, and the fastest growing component of state budgets. The share of personal health-care expenditures covered by Medicaid has increased from about 11 percent in 1990 to more than 17 percent in 2003, as shown in Figure 21.6. That figure also illustrates the great long-run change in health-care financing in the United States, as the share of health-care expenditures paid directly by patients has fallen from 40 percent in 1970 to about 16 percent in 2003, whereas the shares covered by private and government insurance have risen substantially during the same period. This means that Medicaid expenditures are growing much faster than overall health-care expenditures. Since 1990, personal health-care expenditures in the United States have increased at an average annual rate of 10.5 percent; Medicaid expenditures have grown at an average annual rate of 19.7 percent, almost twice as fast. Therefore, state government costs for Medicare expenditures also

Figure 21.6

Share of personal
health-care
expenditure by
type of payment

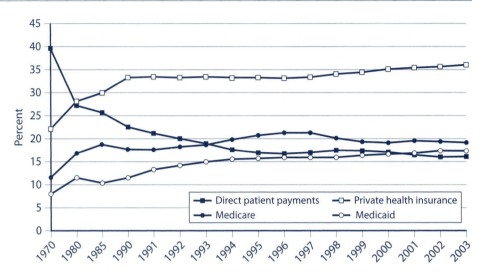

SOURCE: National Center for Health Statistics, Health, 2004.

have been growing substantially faster than aggregate state government spending, so that Medicare is becoming a larger and larger share of state budgets. According to the National Association of State Budget Officers, Medicaid expenditures represented about 21 percent of state spending in fiscal year 2003, up from only about 7 percent in 1990.[13]

States differ substantially in regard to Medicaid eligibility, coverage, and benefits, as shown previously in Table 21.8. Medicaid recipients varied from 8.3 percent of the population in New Hampshire to 43.6 percent in New Mexico, an enrollment rate nearly five times as great in one state compared to the other. Medicaid expenditures for vendor payments only (not counting insurance premiums, disproportionate share hospital payments, and administration costs) in 2002 averaged nearly 17 percent of total state government spending, but varied from less than 10 percent of state spending in Alaska (9.3 percent), Hawaii (9.3), Wyoming (9.5), and Nevada (9.8) to more than 20 percent in Maine (27.4 percent), New York (26.4), Tennessee (23.7), and Rhode Island (21.7). If the other components of Medicaid spending (for administration and disproportionate share hospital payments are included), the Medicaid share of state spending is obviously higher, closer to 20 percent on average. The average amount paid for direct medical care per recipient varied from less than $3,000 in New Mexico ($2,250), California ($2,541), Tennessee ($2,740), and Georgia ($2,929) to more than $7,000 in New Hampshire ($7,161) and Minnesota ($7,153).

In 1997, the State Children's Health Insurance Program (SCHIP) was established as a complement to Medicaid to assist states in expanding health insurance to

[13]NASBO, Chapter 4, "Medicaid Expenditures," 2003 State Expenditure Report.

children in families with income too high to qualify for Medicaid, but who also do not have private- or employment-based health insurance. State governments are given the option of using SCHIP to expand Medicaid coverage for children, create a children's health-insurance program separate from Medicaid, or use both approaches simultaneously. All states have established SCHIP programs. Although state plans differ, generally coverage is provided to children under age 19 in families with income less than 200 percent of the poverty level or up to 50 percent greater than the Medicaid eligibility level. As with Medicaid, states receive matching grants with a federal matching rate that is slightly higher than that for Medicaid, although the total appropriation for SCHIP in any year is fixed (so it is not an open-ended grant). In fiscal year 2002, the federal government allocated $3.8 billion to SCHIP, which, when augmented by state funds, was used to provide benefits to 5.3 million children.

Food Stamps

The Food Stamp program provides low-income individuals and households with coupons or credit that can be redeemed for food at retail stores. Like Medicaid, then, this program provides in-kind benefits (quantities of a specific good, food) rather than cash payments, but the national government operates and finances the program with nationally uniform eligibility and benefit standards, similar to SSI.[14]

When the program was fully instituted in 1964, recipients purchased coupons at a discount—a family might purchase $100 worth of coupons for $50—so that effectively the program reduced the price of food purchases. To purchase a food item that cost $1.00 in the store, an individual needed to spend $.50 of private income to buy the coupons worth $1.00. The rate of price reduction was related to income, with bigger price decreases for those with lower incomes. Beginning in 1977, the program was changed so that individuals did not pay for the "free" value of coupons for which they were eligible. Rather than paying $50 for $100 worth of coupons, an individual in the same economic circumstances would just receive $50 worth of coupons as a grant. Economically, this change is expected to be significant, as now the coupons do not reduce the price (marginal cost) of food, but rather give recipients more resources that must be spent on food. Beginning in 1996, states began switching from paper coupons to electronic benefit transfer systems through which recipients essentially receive a debit card for the amount of their benefits. Recipients may purchase only prescribed food items with coupons or credit, and coupons may not be sold.

To be eligible to receive food stamps in most cases, a household must have less than $2,000 of assets, total income less than 130 percent of the poverty threshold for a household of that size, and net income (income minus specific deductions)

---

[14]The federal government operates several additional programs besides food stamps to assist low-income individuals or those in special circumstances with food and nutrition. The largest among these are Women, Infants, and Children (WIC), which provided a total of $4.9 billion of benefits to nearly 8 million pregnant women and children under 5 in 2004; school meals programs (lunches, breakfasts, milk), which provided more than $9 billion of benefits to some 29 million children in 2004.

less than the poverty threshold.[15] Net income is 80 percent of gross income minus a standard deduction and a portion of costs for shelter, medical care, and child care expenses. Households with individuals receiving TANF or SSI payments are automatically eligible for food stamps independent of the above tests. The amount of coupons or credit a household receives is the difference between the cost of a nutritionally adequate diet for a household of that size (which is determined annually by the national government based on food prices) and 30 percent of net income. In October 2004, for instance, a four-person household with no income would receive $499 per month in food stamp benefits; if income is positive, benefits are reduced. The implicit assumption is that households should spend no more than 30 percent of their net income (as defined previously) on food.

In fiscal year 2004, an average of nearly 24 million people received food stamp coupons or credit worth an average of $86 per month. Total program expenditure for 2004 was $27.1 billion. As noted previously, the maximum monthly food stamp amount for a four-person family with no income (the cost of a nutritionally adequate diet) was $499. The number of food stamp recipients grew pretty much continually until the early 1980s, when program changes reduced eligibility to some extent, as shown in Figure 21.7. The number of recipients increased

Figure 21.7

Food Stamp recipients and benefits, 1969 to 2004

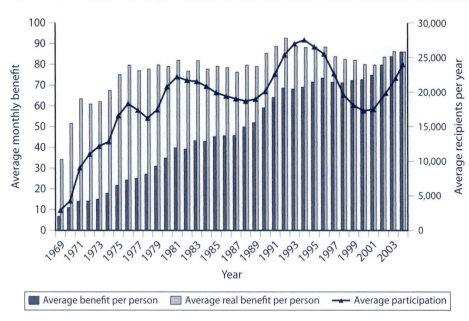

SOURCE: Food and Nutrition Service, U.S. Department of Agriculture, 2005.

[15]A household with someone who is age 60 or older or with a disabled person receiving Social Security, SSI payments, or other specific benefits may have higher income.

substantially in the first half of the 1990s, declined in the latter half of the 1990s, and has been increasing since. Average monthly benefits remained constant in real terms from about 1975 until the late 1980s, after which they have also fluctuated in real value.

Perhaps the most contentious participation issue in recent years has concerned *legal* immigrants. In 1996, legal immigrants were made ineligible for food stamp benefits unless they became citizens, worked and paid taxes for a total of 40 quarters (10 years), served in the U.S. armed forces, or had special refugee status. Food-stamp benefits were restored to some legal immigrants (disabled, over 65, or under 18) in 1998. In 2003, eligibility for food stamps was returned to all legal immigrants under the age of 18 and other legal immigrants after residing in the United States for five years.

State differences in food-stamp payments and participation reflect differences in the number of eligible persons (state income or poverty relative to the national poverty threshold), as was the case for SSI. For fiscal year 2004, Texas operated the largest program in absolute size involving 2.3 million people in more than 864,000 households. Not surprisingly, the smallest program was in Wyoming (about 26,000 people in 10,000 households). Relative to population, Louisiana has the largest fraction of people receiving benefits (15.6 percent), and New Hampshire has the smallest fraction (3.7 percent). Average benefit levels are highest in Hawaii ($128 per recipient per month) and Alaska ($109) and lowest in New Hampshire ($75). Among mainland states, benefits are highest in New York ($98).

EITC—Earned Income Tax Credit

The federal government, 17 states, and the District of Columbia provide an income tax credit for low-income workers that either reduces income taxes owed or, in the case of the federal government and 12 states, can be refunded if the credit is more than tax liability. In this latter case, the EITC becomes a mechanism to make cash payments to low-income workers. The federal EITC was established in 1975, initially as a means of encouraging work by AFDC recipients. It has become a substantial income-support program that also includes a powerful incentive for recipients to work. The various EITCs together represent the largest cash-assistance program for low-income families operated by government and the second largest welfare or support program overall (after Medicaid).

The federal EITC is based on earnings, marital status, and family size, with separate credit parameters for taxpayers with no children, one child, or two or more children. To be eligible, taxpayers must have a Social Security number allowing them to work in the United States, have earned income less than certain thresholds, have investment income (interest, dividends, and so on) of less than $2,650, and not be claimed as a dependent by another taxpayer. For each class of taxpayer, earnings are matched at a constant credit rate up to a threshold earnings level. After reaching that earnings amount, the credit remains a constant dollar amount for an additional range of earnings. At a second threshold level, the credit begins to be reduced until falling to zero. The operation of the credit based on 2004 law for a single-parent household with two children is illustrated in the following table.

Federal Earned Income Tax Credit, Head of Household, Two Children, 2004

	First Threshold	Second Threshold	Third Threshold
Earnings Range	$0 to $10,750	$10,751 to $14,050	$14,051 to $34,500
Credit Rate	40%	Varies	Varies; falls to zero
EITC	.40* Earnings	$4,300	$4,299 to 0
Sample calculation			
Earnings	$7,000	$12,500	$21,000
EITC	$2,800	$4,300	$2,839
Total Income	$9,800	$16,300	$23,839
Credit Rate	40% (2,800/7,000)	34.4% (4,300/12,500)	13.5% (2,839/20,000)

Taxpayers receive a credit equal to 40 percent of earnings up to earnings of $10,750. Consequently, total income increases by $1.40 for every $1.00 the taxpayer earns. Put another way, if a taxpayer is offered a job paying $5 per hour, the taxpayer effectively earns $7 per hour ($5 + .40 * $5). For earnings between $10,750 and $14,050, the EITC is a constant $4,300, so the credit rate continuously falls. Finally, when earnings exceed $14,050, the credit amount is reduced as earnings rise, until the EITC is zero at earnings of $34,500. As shown by the illustration, at earnings of $21,000, this taxpayer receives an EITC of $2,839, which is a credit of 13.5 percent of earnings. If the taxpayer with earnings of $21,000 is paid $10 per hour, the effective wage per hour, including the EITC, is $11.35 ($10 + .135 * $10).

The EITC parameters in 2004 for married taxpayers with zero, one, or two children are shown in the following table.

EITC Parameters, Married Filing Jointly, 2004

	No Children	One Child	Two Children
Initial Credit Rate	7.65%	34%	40%
First Threshold	$5,100	$7,700	$10,750
Constant EITC	390	2,604	4,300
Second Threshold	7,400	15,050	15,050
EITC = 0	12,500	31,350	35,460

Several important features of the EITC are apparent. Unlike other welfare programs that provide support if income is zero, individuals must work and have earnings to receive any EITC. The initial credit rates are substantial for taxpayers with children, augmenting earnings substantially and creating a stronger incentive to work. For families with children, the credit falls to zero at an earnings amount about twice the federal poverty level. The importance of having the credits be refundable is also clear. A married couple with one child and earnings of $15,000 would owe no federal income tax, so by making the credit refundable, the taxpayer

Table 21.9

Federal Earned Income Tax Credit

	1990	1995	2000	2001	2002	2003
Percentage of all Returns with EITC	11.0%	16.4%	14.9%	15.0%	16.7%	16.9%
Number of Returns with EITC (millions)	12.6	19.3	19.3	19.6	21.7	22.0
Amount of EITC (billions of dollars)	$7.5	$26.0	$32.3	$33.4	$38.2	$38.7
Refundable EITC (billions of dollars)	$5.3	$20.8	$27.8	$29.0	$33.7	$34.0
Percentage of EITC that was Refunded	70.1%	80.2%	86.1%	87.0%	88.3%	88.0%
Percentage of EITC Returns, Families with Children	na	81.8%	82.3%	82.0%	81.4%	80.1%
Percentage of EITC Amount, Families with Children	na	97.6%	97.8%	97.8%	97.8%	97.6%
Percentage of EITC Refunds, Families with Children	na	98.0%	98.2%	98.3%	98.3%	98.1%

SOURCE: U.S. Internal Revenue Service. *Individual Income Tax Statistics, Publication 1304, 2003.*

receives the credit amount as a cash supplement to income. One aspect about EITCs is that taxpayers need to file a tax return to claim the credit and receive the refund, even if tax liability is zero. This has led to a concern that substantial numbers of eligible taxpayers may not receive the EITC benefits.

For tax year 2003, 22.2 million federal individual income tax returns included an EITC, and the total amount of credits was $38.7 billion. Obviously, state EITCs were claimed in addition to this federal amount. About 17 percent of federal tax returns for 2003 included an EITC, which averaged about $1,760 (see Table 21.9). Not surprisingly given the credit structure, families with children accounted for 80 percent of tax returns with an EITC and nearly 98 percent of the EITC amount. Reflecting the importance of the refundable nature of the credit, 88 percent of the total EITC amount was refunded, with the other 12 percent going to reduce income tax owed. The fraction of tax returns with an EITC has remained essentially the same for the past 10 years, so the number and dollar amount of credits has been increasing.

The states with a state EITC are Colorado[16] Illinois, Indiana, Iowa, Kansas, Maine, Maryland, Massachusetts, Minnesota, New Jersey, New Mexico, New York, Oklahoma, Oregon, Rhode Island, Vermont, Wisconsin, and the District of Columbia. All state government EITCs are based on the federal credit, except for New Mexico, which offers a separate state credit. All states except Iowa, Maine, Oregon, and Rhode Island permit the credit to be refunded if it is greater than taxes owed. Typically, the income limits for eligibility for the state credits are the same as for the federal EITC. The state credits are a fixed percentage of the federal EITC, varying between 4 percent and 46 percent, although most states also specify maximum credit amounts. In Kansas, for instance, the state credit is 15 percent of the federal EITC, with maximums of $391 for families with one child and $645 for families with two.[17]

---

[16]Colorado's EITC applies only if the state ends its year with a fiscal surplus.

[17]Detailed information about the state credits is available at the Web site of the National Center for Children in Poverty at Columbia University, http://www.nccp.org/

SSI—Supplemental Security Income

The second major means-tested program providing cash payments is Supplemental Security Income (SSI), administered by the federal Social Security Administration and instituted in 1974. SSI provides monthly payments to persons aged 65 and older, blind or disabled adults, and disabled children with low incomes and assets. SSI eligibility standards and benefit levels are set by the federal government and are uniform nationally, with benefits indexed for cost-of-living increases in the same way that Social Security payments are. States may supplement the federal SSI benefit amounts. In 1994, 27 states plus the District of Columbia did so, adding about 18 percent to federal SSI expenditures.

For 2004, the basic monthly federal SSI benefit for an eligible person with no income was $564 ($6,768 annually). This benefit is reduced if the individual has other income (including from Social Security). The benefit is reduced by one-half of monthly earnings above $85 and by all Social Security or unearned income above $20. For instance, a disabled person who earns $180 per month would have benefits reduced by $47.50 [($180 − $85) * .5] and would receive a monthly SSI payment of $516.50 ($564 − $47.50). Similarly, a retired person with a monthly Social Security benefit of $300 would receive an SSI payment of $284 [$564 − ($300 − $20)]. To be eligible, individuals must have assets totally less than $2,000, excluding a home, car, household goods, burial plots, and $1,500 of life insurance.

In December 2003, about 7.1 million people received some form of SSI payments that totaled $35.6 billion for all of 2003 and averaged about $418 per month ($5,016 annually). Of this total amount, $30.7 billion (86 percent) represented basic federal SSI payments and $4.9 billion represented state supplementation. Some 3 million individuals received state supplement amounts. The largest category of SSI recipients and payments by far is for disabled persons, who accounted for 80 percent of the recipients and 84 percent of expenditures in December 2003. Recipients over the age of 65 but not disabled make up the next largest group, accounting for about 18 percent of persons and 14.5 percent of payments. Because eligibility and federal benefits are uniform nationally, differences in SSI payments by state arise either due to differences in the number of people who are eligible or differences in income for recipients.

FINANCING HEALTH AND WELFARE SERVICES: POLICY AND STRUCTURAL ISSUES

Role of Federal Compared to State—Local Government

The conventional economic wisdom for many years was that subnational governments had limited capability to provide income redistribution because individuals and firms might move among jurisdictions to frustrate any intended redistribution. For instance, a local welfare program that redistributes resources to the jurisdiction's low-income residents would create incentives for high-income residents to leave (to avoid the taxation) and low-income residents to move in (to receive the transfer). Similar incentives, although perhaps to a weaker degree, were expected to operate among states. Interjurisdictional mobility suggests, therefore, that redistribution is more appropriately carried out by the national government. As summarized by Oates (1972, p. 8):

> The scope for redistributive programs is thus limited to some extent by the potential mobility of residents, which tends to be greater the smaller the jurisdiction under consideration. This suggests that, since mobility across national boundaries is much less than that within a nation, a policy of income redistribution has a much greater promise of success if carried out at the national level.

Essentially, income redistribution has a number of public-good characteristics. Welfare or redistributive programs provide benefits not just to direct recipients, but to all in society.—Redistributive programs operate as social insurance against an economic calamity for any person. They also provide altruistic benefits to taxpayers for helping the needy simply because they are needy. And redistribution may be a means of reducing social unrest and related destructive behavior. Because everyone benefits if anyone provides some redistribution, wealthy individuals have an incentive to want others to make the contributions, that is to be "free riders," even if everyone in society benefits from and thus desires real redistribution. Moving is just a form of that free-riding behavior that is eliminated if redistribution is provided nationally (so that all wealthy individuals must contribute).

The idea that redistribution provides social benefits suggests a different perspective for thinking about the appropriate role for the national as opposed to state–local government. If the externalities associated with redistributive services are local or regional, that is, if the *social* benefits from redistribution to a particular population are confined only to other people in that area, then redistribution should be a local or regional service. Whether this is true depends somewhat on the type of social benefit. The concept of social insurance—the social safety net—almost must be national, as it should apply no matter where one moves in the nation. But altruistic benefits and concern about social unrest might be local, if individuals care only about people in their state, city, or neighborhood. On the other hand, if individuals care about poverty wherever it occurs, this becomes an additional argument for national provision.[18]

Finally, a number of people have argued that because states and localities are smaller than the nation, and it is easier to focus on specific conditions, they might serve as effective laboratories for trying new policies that might eventually be adopted by other states or even the nation. As you have learned previously in this chapter, increasing flexibility for states to develop and operate different approaches to health and welfare programs has been a theme of policy and legislative change in the past 15 years. Of course, this does not suggest that all those experiments will be successful or that welfare services should necessarily be provided exclusively by states.

Over the past 45 years, substantial changes have been made in the responsibilities of the federal government and state–local government in providing social

---

[18]It is particularly difficult to assess people's attitudes about this issue. If people accept the idea that one should help only those one wants to help personally, the result is redistribution only through private charity.

Figure 21.8

Federal government share of social welfare expenditure: 1960 to 2004

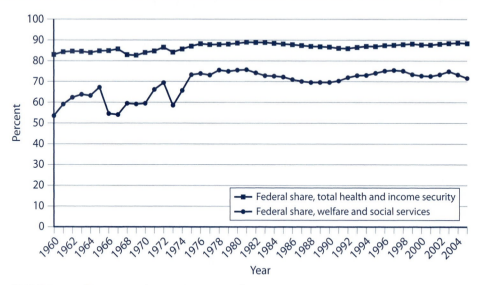

SOURCE: Bureau of Economic Analysis, U.S. Department of Commerce, 2005.

welfare programs in the U.S. federal system. The federal government's responsibility for financing these programs has always been dominant, but it also increased substantially, especially between 1960 and 1980, when the basic structure of most current public-aid programs was established. As shown in Figure 21.8, the federal share of expenditures for the broad category of all health and income security programs (including Social Security and Medicare as well as AFDC/TANF, SSI, Medicaid, Food Stamps, state general-assistance programs, and other social services and work incentives) remained between 80 and 90 percent over this period. The federal government's share of spending on a narrower set of welfare and social service programs (the means-tested programs, including AFDC/TANF, SSI, Medicaid, Food Stamps, state general-assistance programs) rose from about 54 percent in 1960 to 72 percent in 2004, with the major growth before 1980.

The dominance of federal financing is also illustrated by examining the individual programs. The federal government financed about 59 percent of Medicaid expenditures in 2003, and total Medicaid spending was about 70 percent of spending on the five main programs discussed in this chapter. The federal government pays essentially 100 percent of the costs of the Food Stamp program and funded about 86 percent of SSI expenditures in 2003 (the other 14 percent represented state supplements). Although data about aggregate amounts of state EITCs are not available, a basic estimate suggests that the federal EITC provides about 88 percent of total EITC benefits.[19] The federal block grant for TANF programs (including

---

[19]State EITCs are a percentage of the federal EITC, up to a maximum set in each state. The state credit rate averages about 15 percent of the federal EITC, which suggests that state EITC amounts in 2003 were about $5.8 billion compared to the federal EITC amount of $38.7 billion.

state bonuses) was about 70 percent of aggregate state spending on TANF. Aggregating these five together, the result is that the federal government provides nearly 70 percent of the financing.

From a programmatic perspective, however, the state governments have taken on additional responsibility for designing and operating welfare programs in the United States. Given the uncertainty about whether to provide uniform aid to everyone or to base aid on differential regional preferences, the country does some of both. As you learned, the SSI and Food Stamp programs (as well as Social Security and Medicare for the aged) provide essentially uniform national benefits, except for the small state supplements as part of SSI, and the national government operates these programs. Although many states offer EITCs, all but one state EITC are calculated as a fraction of the federal EITC; thus the federal government has essentially determined the structure of those tax credits. On the other hand, state governments have substantial flexibility to determine eligibility and benefit levels for the TANF and Medicaid programs, with the resulting substantial differences among the states in both eligibility conditions and benefits, as you have seen. Clearly, state autonomy in implementing welfare plans has increased with the switch to TANF after the adoption of the Personal Responsibility and Work Opportunity Reconciliation Act of 1996 and increasing use of waivers in Medicaid.

Money vs. In-Kind Support (or Subsidies)

When choosing between providing cash or amounts of specific goods or services to welfare recipients, policy makers face a difficult tradeoff. It is a standard and important microeconomic result that cash grants improve the welfare (utility) of recipients the most per dollar spent because cash provides the greatest flexibility to recipients and allows them to spend the welfare payments in ways that are best for each person's circumstances. On the other hand, providing specific goods or services to recipients (such as food or housing or medical care), or subsidizing the purchase of those commodities, usually increases consumption of the targeted commodity more, restricts the ability of recipients to use welfare funds for less-preferred consumption, and may be more acceptable to taxpayers who fund the welfare programs.

An illustrative comparison between a cash grant (equal to CG dollars) and a food grant (equal to FG units of food) is shown in Figure 21.9. A low-income household with income I^0 chooses to consume at bundle Z on the initial budget line; this household buys F^0 units of food, which costs 25 percent of the household's income, leaving 75 percent of income for consumption of other things. If this household receives a cash grant of CG dollars, the new budget is line YU. The household can consume the same amount of food and spend all the cash on other things (bundle X), spend all the cash grant on more food (bundle V), or buy more food and other things (bundle W). Essentially, the household can select any consumption option on the new budget—whatever serves them best.

Alternatively, the household could receive a grant of FG units of food, with FG equaling the amount of food that can be purchased with CG dollars, so both programs cost the same. However, recipients may not sell the food they receive; that is, recipients must consume at least FG units of food. In this case, the household

Figure 21.9

Assisting
low-income
consumers with
cash grants or
food grants

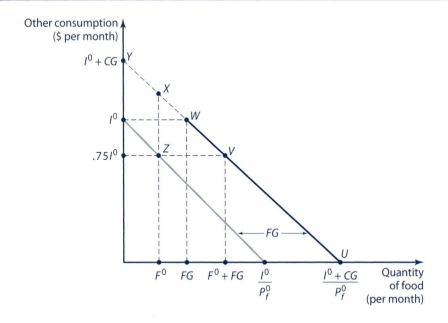

can choose any bundle on the budget line *WU;* any consumption option on the seg-ment *YW* (such as bundle *X*) is prohibited by the restriction against selling the food grant. So the food grant reduces the consumption options for the recipients and makes them potentially worse off than with the cash grant.

Note that neither program insures (or requires) that all the grant is spent on food, which occurs if the household selects bundle *V* on the new budget. Although this is possible with either the cash or food grant, it is an unlikely choice. With the cash grant, the expectation is that the household will spend some of the cash on additional food and some on other things (such as clothing, housing, or personal care), perhaps selecting bundle *W*. With the food grant, the household can use the food grant instead of food that it otherwise would have purchased, which frees up income to be spent on other things. Again, a bundle such as *W* seems most likely.

In-kind benefits historically have been more important than cash payments in the U.S. welfare system. In fiscal year 2003, the two major means-tested, in-kind benefit programs (Medicaid and Food Stamps) swamped the three major cash-payment programs (TANF, SSI, and the EITC) by $299.2 billion in health care and food subsidy to about $90 billion of cash assistance payments, a ratio of more than three to one.[20] As a result of program changes and the relative growth of different types of welfare spending, the importance of cash assistance in state budgets has declined over time, and the importance of in-kind benefits has increased

---

[20]This computation does not include other in-kind welfare-related services, including noncash assistance through
TANF, school meals programs, housing subsidies and programs, and so on.

Figure 21.10

State–local welfare expenditure relative to general expenditure

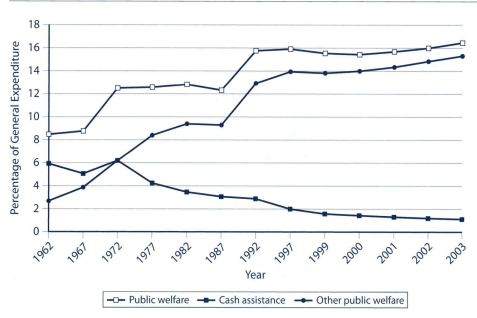

SOURCE: U.S. Census Bureau, 2003.

correspondingly, as shown in Figure 21.10. By 2003, state cash-assistance payments were less than 2 percent of state spending, whereas expenditures on noncash welfare services were at least 16 percent of state spending. Vendor payments by Medicaid (direct payments to medical care providers) accounted for about 46 percent of state–local welfare expenditures in 1985, but had risen to be more than 60 percent by 1992, making it the largest single program.

Interstate Differences in Services: Structure of Federal Grants to States

One of the most difficult and fundamental issues about welfare policy is the degree to which geographic differences in benefits or support are tolerated (or are desirable, depending on your point of view). Differences among states are substantial for those programs in which states have leeway in setting eligibility and benefits. A first step in dealing with this issue is to consider why different states choose different types and levels of welfare support. The structure of federal grants for health and welfare programs is the first factor to consider.

As you have learned, the federal grant to the states for Medicaid is an open-ended matching grant, with the federal government share for any state inversely related to the state's per-capita income. On the other hand, the federal grant to states to fund TANF is a lump-sum, block grant, with a condition that states also continue to spend a fixed amount of state funds. Importantly, the federal grant for AFDC, the welfare program that preceded TANF, was similar to that for

Medicaid—an open-ended matching grant with greater federal shares in lower-income states. In addition, many other federal categorical grants—some lump-sum and some close-ended matching—for other social or redistributive services, especially in the areas of education, health, and nutrition. The broad policy issue is whether this structure of grants is appropriate or whether an alternative structure of grants might be better. A more specific issue is the effect on state health and welfare spending of the change in grants when TANF replaced AFDC.

The average matching rate for the previous AFDC grants was 50 to 60 percent, so the state tax price per dollar of benefit was only $.40 to $.50. When those grants were replaced with the TANF block grant, the state tax price for welfare expenditures rose to $1.00. Even if demand for welfare services is price inelastic, several possible consequences of this change cause concern. First, the increase in the marginal cost of providing welfare services in all states could lead to a lower level of support overall. Second, the cost of financing welfare services increased more in low-income states when compared to high-income states, because the matching grants that were replaced provided larger federal shares for lower-income states. Because benefits were lower in low-income states initially, the concern is that the differences in benefit levels between states could increase, at least initially.

Under the welfare structure before 1996 (AFDC), cash-assistance benefits were substantially lower in low-income states, even though states received matching federal grants with a larger federal share for low-income states. Similarly, Medicaid expenditures tend to be lower in low-income states, again with federal matching grants and greater federal financing shares for low-come states (refer to Table 21.8). This is expected if there is a lower desired level of health or welfare service in lower-income states and if residents' willingness to fund health and welfare is price inelastic. Such a circumstance is shown in Figure 21.11. The "demand" for providing health or welfare service (that is the willingness to pay for the service)

Figure 21.11

State differences in demand for providing welfare service

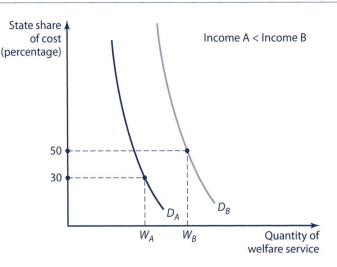

is lower in lower-income state A than in higher-income state B. This reflects the idea that typical or median residents of a higher-income state would be willing to spend more on health or welfare both because they can afford more and because they may receive more benefit.[21] In addition, both demands are inelastic with respect to the state share of costs (the state's price).

Suppose the state share of health or welfare costs after federal grants is 30 percent in state A and 50 percent in state B. State A selects welfare level W_A, while state B selects the higher welfare level W_B. The lower state cost (price) in A due to a larger federal grant share is not great enough to offset the lower willingness to provide service in state A, which resulted from the lower income in A. Even more importantly, decreasing the state's cost share further (increasing the federal grant share) still leaves a welfare service difference if the willingness to provide service (demand) is insensitive (inelastic) to the state cost.

Research suggests that this illustration is a realistic representation of the circumstances surrounding AFDC. Robert Moffitt (1984) estimated that the elasticity of state per-capita AFDC benefits with respect to the subsidy rate (federal share) was about .15, which means that a 10-percent increase in the subsidy rate would increase per-capita benefits by only 1.5 percent. For instance, if the federal share per dollar spent for state A was increased to $.80 from $.70, the subsidy rate rises by about 14 percent (.10 / .70). If the elasticity is .15, then per-capita expenditure rises by about 2 percent (.15 * 14). So if the monthly per-capita benefit was $100 initially, the new benefit would be $102. Benefits change only a little, even though the federal government is now paying 80 percent of the cost. In these circumstances, increasing the federal grants does little to equalize welfare services among states because the willingness to provide those services is so different. Essentially, residents of lower-income states prefer and can afford less redistribution. Therefore, only two broad ways exist to equalize welfare services: either make the services a federal government responsibility with uniform eligibility and benefit levels, as with Food Stamps and SSI, or mandate more uniform state services by federal regulations.

Some also were concerned that the substitution of the TANF block grant might reduce welfare services, especially in low-income states, because the tax price of welfare services increased. Certainly the number of people receiving cash assistance through TANF is much fewer than under AFDC previously, but that change may be do as much to economic conditions or the work and time limit conditions in TANF as to the change in grant structure. Two pieces of evidence suggest why the change in federal grant structure has not and may not greatly reduce welfare benefit levels, at least in the short run. Surveys by David Ribar and Mark Wilhelm (1999) and by Robert Moffitt (2003) of recent studies of elasticities of welfare benefits continue to show small effects, such as price elasticities between -0.2 and 0 and income elasticities between 0.2 and 0.8. With these elasticities, increases in tax prices have little effect on reducing benefits (just as decreases in prices have little effect on increasing benefits, as described in the preceding paragraph).

---

[21]For instance, higher-income residents might have more to lose if widespread poverty leads to civil disruption or collapse of the political structure. Alternatively, higher-income individuals might be more altruistic.

Howard Chernick (2000) suggests another reason the expenditure effects of the switch from a matching grant to a block grant may have been minor so far. Chernick suggests that some substitutability may exist between cash assistance (through AFDC or TANF) and Food Stamps. Food Stamps are essentially funded fully by the federal government, whereas the cost of cash assistance is shared between the states and federal government. Also, increases in income reduce the amount of Food Stamp support a family is eligible to receive. If a state reduces cash assistance, families can receive more Food Stamp support—the state saves state resources in providing less cash assistance while the federal government pays all the increased Food Stamp costs. To the extent that this cross-program incentive has been important, states would already have reduced cash assistance even before the switch to the TANF block grant.

In contrast to cash-assistance programs, the available evidence suggests that state funding for Medicaid is substantially more price sensitive than for cash assistance—with price elasticities in the range of 0.6 to 0.8.[22] These estimates imply, for instance, that if the federal share of Medicaid costs in a state was reduced from 70 percent (state tax price = .3) to 50 percent (state tax price = .5), the resulting 67 percent increase in tax price could induce something on the order of a 40-percent reduction in Medicaid spending.[23] Thus, Chernick (2000, p. 150) argues "... that efforts to cap Medicaid, or convert it to a block grant, would lead to very large reductions in Medicaid spending." Some evidence also suggests that Medicaid benefits are seen by states as substitutes for cash assistance, so that incentives that cause states to reduce cash payments may simultaneously induce states to increase Medicaid benefits. Some believe that this was part of the reason AFDC benefits declined in the 1980s as Medicaid rules were changed to expand Medicaid eligibility.

Interstate Differences in Services: Interstate Mobility and Migration

One reason to be concerned about state differences in welfare eligibility and benefits is that the differences might induce some individuals to relocate among states; the possibility of low-income individuals moving to a state to receive greater benefits gets the most attention. Welfare lore is full of anecdotes about "welfare mothers" who move (or pretend to move) to a particular city or state just to become eligible for larger benefits. Some states in the past enacted residency time requirements for welfare eligibility to reduce the potential for this problem, although such waiting times or differential benefits were subsequently prohibited by the Supreme Court.

This type of mobility poses two potential problems for fiscal federalism and welfare policy. First, if migration to receive benefits occurs, the willingness and ability

[22]See Chernick (2000).

[23]Tax price rises from 0.3 to 0.5, a 67 percent increase (.2/.3). If the price elasticity is 0.6, benefits fall by about 40 percent (.67 * .6).

to provide sufficient welfare support in some states is reduced. To the extreme, if all welfare recipients moved to the highest-benefit state, the other residents of that state could not afford and likely would not be willing to continue that level of support. Substantial recipient migration would tend to equalize benefit levels, frustrating some residents' desires to provide a particular degree of redistribution. Second, if migration occurs, some high-income residents can avoid contributing to national income redistribution. This would result if most recipients were located in only a few states or if higher-income taxpayers migrated to low-benefit states to avoid taxes.

Finally, interstate migration *solely for redistributive factors* may be inefficient because that migration can impose external costs on other residents of the state. For instance, if many low-income welfare recipients moved to one state that had relatively high welfare benefits initially, the increase in population could create congestion for some current public services (schools, transportation, parks) causing a loss of benefits or higher costs to other residents, driving up land prices (imposing a cost on current housing consumers or other land users), or decreasing wages for some types of work by increasing the supply of workers (assuming some welfare recipients work). Note that these problems arise if welfare benefits are the only reason for the migration, because no economic benefits are provided to offset these problems.[24]

The evidence about interstate migration for welfare purposes (or other economic purposes for that matter) is largely ambiguous. For instance, Edward Gramlich and Deborah Laren (1984) reported that only a small number of AFDC recipients (3 to 7 percent) moved among states over a five-year period; however, when moves do occur, they tend to be toward higher-benefit states. Over a very long period of time (the authors' results imply some 45 years for half of all moves to occur), the cumulative effect of these few short-run moves could be a major reallocation of welfare recipients toward higher-benefit states. Rebecca Blank (1988) used data from 1979 to examine interregional migration decisions of female-headed households with children compared to their locations in 1975. She reported that three factors—expected wage income, expected welfare benefits, and migration distance—have a statistically significant effect on moving decisions by these families, although wage income seems to have the greatest effect. Phil Levine and David Zimmerman (1995) used 1979 to 1992 data to examine whether high welfare benefits in a state seem to restrain the out migration of poor, female-headed households with children relative to other groups. They reported no statistically significant difference between the groups, suggesting that single mothers do not tend to remain in states with high welfare benefits. Finally, Gordon DeJong, Deborah Graefe, and Tanja St. Pierre (2005) used data from 1996 to 1999 (after TANF) to examine migration behavior. They reported evidence suggesting that poor families do tend to move *from* states with more stringent welfare eligibility or work rules. They also reported evidence, however,

---

[24]For instance, if a state had a serious shortage of unskilled labor, then migration would create an economic benefit for that state and the national economy. That benefit could then offset the costs from the migration.

that when poor families move, they often move to other states with stringent welfare policies. The location to move toward seemed influenced as much by employment opportunities and the availability of social support networks of family and friends as welfare rules, however. Therefore, the evidence supports no single, clear conclusion.

It is difficult to use statistical methods to study migration that is undertaken in an effort to receive welfare benefits or escape redistributive taxation, and thus results of statistical studies are sometimes contradictory. First, as you learned earlier in the chapter, characterizing the breadth of state differences in health or welfare programs is often difficult. One state may have restrictive eligibility rules but high benefits for participants, whereas another state might do the opposite. How do you determine which might be more attractive? Second, individuals may make location choices—moving or not moving—based on factors other than welfare services and taxes, including such issues as job prospects, family connections, or noneconomic preferences, so it is often difficult to separate those influences statistically. If a poor or unemployed welfare recipient moves to a state with better employment prospects or higher wages, the welfare benefits in such a state are likely to be higher also, although welfare was not the primary reason for the move. Third, the number of people moving between states in any given year is relatively small, in any case. For instance, Gramlich (1987, p. 17) reports generally that "... only a tiny fraction of unemployed workers in high unemployment states leave their states for better job markets in low unemployment states. There is very little labor mobility in the short run."

Concerns about interstate mobility, then, should not prevent states from adopting different health and welfare policies if residents desire those policies. However, over a long period of time, those persisting differences in policies may affect the geographic population distribution. It seems unlikely, however, that interstate migration by itself would be substantial enough to drive a "race to the bottom" in income-support services.

Welfare to Work

The relationship between welfare support and employment has been a continual theme in social welfare policy in the United States. A basic concern is whether welfare programs create incentives that discourage work. To counter such incentives, attempts have been made to develop training programs to increase the employability of welfare recipients and to craft assistance programs that also encourage work (such as the EITC). Most recently, of course, requiring assistance recipients to work is a fundamental characteristic of TANF.

The AFDC program that existed from 1935 until just after 1996 included relatively high effective tax rates on earnings, including effective tax rates of 100 percent in some years. In other words, when earnings of AFDC recipients increased by $1, cash assistance benefits were reduced by $1. As a consequence, effective wage rates were zero and work disincentives were high. To counter this, the federal government instituted mandatory job training and education programs. The Family Support Act adopted in 1988 required states to implement by 1990 a Job

Opportunities and Basic Skills Program (JOBS), which was financed by a federal matching grant to the states, although these grants were close-ended (meaning there is a maximum amount). These JOBS programs were to be state-designed efforts at education, training, work experience, or job search assistance, particularly for AFDC recipients. Obviously, the success of these plans depends on two factors: the ability to develop marketable skills in current welfare recipients and the ability to place such people in appropriate jobs that provide sufficient income. The difficulty of achieving both should not be underestimated. Follow-up studies of a number of past job-training programs found that they often fell below expectations. In some cases, individuals required basic education before they could succeed in specific training programs; in other cases, the training was not tied to specific future likely job requirements; and in still other cases, an absence of skills or training was not the problem that contributed to welfare participation in the first place.

A second approach has been to use tax credits to encourage work. The EITC, discussed previously in this chapter, is used to supplement income for low-income workers. The EITC effectively increases net wages for many workers or imposes lower effective tax rates than otherwise, both of which create incentives to work compared to the absence of the credit.[25] The federal personal income tax (and some state income taxes) also includes a nonrefundable child-care tax credit that effectively partly offsets child-care costs so that parents may work. The child-care credit reduces income taxes for families whose income rises high enough that tax liability, even after the EITC, becomes positive.

Finally, the current programs operated through TANF include several work incentives, as discussed previously. In general, cash-assistance recipients are required to engage in work-related activity, including employment, on-the-job training, community service, secondary school attendance, vocational training, or job searching. In addition, states can use funds from the TANF block grant to pay work-related child-care and transportation expenses, to fund public service work opportunities for recipients, and to provide hiring incentives to private firms. Public-sector work can be a long-term solution if the public-sector jobs would have been filled in any case (not make-work efforts) or if the process of working at any public-sector job helps develops work habits and practices that eventually make the recipient more attractive to other employers. If neither occurs, then welfare recipients at least provide some public-sector services, even if the marginal value of those services is less than the payments to the recipients.[26]

The effect of these policy changes on the labor market activity of low-income individuals, especially those who are recipients of benefits through these health and welfare programs, has been examined in a number of recent studies with

---

[25]Changes in the EITC and Medicaid decreased work incentives for married women with children whose husbands also work.

[26]If the marginal social benefit of the public-sector service is greater than the payments made to recipients, then this should be a "real" public or private job. The wages paid, equal to marginal benefit, would provide more income than welfare or the welfare-replacement payments.

remarkably consistent conclusions. David Ellwood (2000, p. 1,100) concluded "The combination of the higher EITC, welfare reform, and a strong economy has led to a truly unprecedented increase in labor market activity by low-income single parents." Bruce Meyer and Dan Rosenbaum (2000, p. 1,057) reported "Between 1984 and 1996, . . . the Earned Income Tax Credit was expanded, welfare benefits were cut, welfare time limits were added and cases were terminated, Medicaid for the working poor was expanded, training programs were redirected, and programs providing subsidized or free child care were expanded . . . . These changes were followed by large increases in the employment rates of single mothers." And Joseph Hotz and John Karl Scholz (2003, p. 183, 191–192) note "Over the last twenty-five years, the EITC has become, by a considerable margin, the country's largest cash or near-cash program directed at low-income families . . . . based on evidence from many studies, the EITC positively affects the labor force participation of single-parent households . . . . in aggregate, the positive participation effects appear to be fairly substantial."

Ellwood's (2000) analysis shows clearly why this happened. In 1986, an unmarried woman with children who worked and earned $10,000 would have ended up with total disposable income of $10,644 after accounting for income and Social Security taxes, AFDC and Food Stamp benefits, the EITC amount, the Dependent Care Tax Credit amount, and child-care expenses that the woman would pay. This family also would not have been covered by Medicaid. If the woman did not work at all, the family would have received net disposable income of $8,804 plus Medicaid coverage. Working increased income by $1,800 but lost Medicaid coverage, creating little incentive to work. In 1998, the situation was dramatically different. That same unmarried woman with children who earns $10,000 by working receives net disposable income (after all the costs and programmatic benefits) of $14,593 and Medicaid coverage for the children, at least. If she did not work at all, net disposable income is $7,717 plus Medicaid. Working and earning $10,000 added almost $7,000 to net disposable income without the substantial loss of Medicaid coverage. Obviously, the combination of welfare, health, and tax programs in 1998 created a much stronger incentive to work than did the program structure in 1986. In Ellwood's simulation, the greatest changes between the situation in 1986 and 1998 were for the EITC and the Dependent Care Tax Credit, which had been expanded between that time, and Medicaid, for which eligibility had been expanded to include more working families.[27] Presumably with TANF now fully implemented, the incentive to work is even stronger.

Even with these incentives, individuals must be able to find and hold jobs paying sufficient income to support their families. Thus, the strong national economy during the 1990s provided an ideal time to make changes to health and welfare programs, as the number of jobs and national employment increased substantially.

---

[27]The changes in the EITC and other programs created a modest negative effect on labor participation of some married mothers. If the husband also works, additional earnings by the wife can move the family into the range of the EITC where benefits fall as earnings rise. This effectively imposes a tax on earnings by the woman, reducing the gains from work. See Ellwood (2000).

The job situation was more problematic during the national recession from 2000 to 2001 and the period of slow economic growth since. Even if jobs are available, they might be in different geographic locations (even different states) than the concentration of past welfare recipients (what has come to be called the *spatial mismatch factor*).

Finally, one hopes that the jobs available to former welfare recipients, coupled with the benefits from health, welfare, and tax credit programs, will provide sufficient income to support the family. For instance, a full-time job paying $5.15 per hour (the current minimum wage) generates annual income of about $10,300.[28] Using Ellwood's simulation, a single mother working full-time at the minimum wage might receive total income plus benefits of about $15,000 annually plus Medicaid coverage for the children. The 2004 poverty threshold for a two-person family with one child was $13,020 and for a three-person family with two children was $15,219. In the early 1990s, President Clinton set the goal that full-time work at the minimum wage plus the benefits of the EITC and other programs should be sufficient to move the family out of poverty. It appears that this goal is achieved only in some cases. Even a wage 25 percent higher ($6.50 per hour) provides annual income of only about $13,000 and aggregate disposable income only slightly above the poverty thresholds.

Improving Medicaid's Health

Health-care financing, and Medicaid specifically, is arguably the most serious and vexing fiscal issue facing state governments currently. Mark McClellan, the Administrator for the Centers for Medicare and Medicaid Services in the U.S. Department of Health and Human Services, stated recently "Medicaid is facing a lot of challenges today. Everyone agrees that it is not sustainable in its current form."[29] At about 20 percent of state spending, Medicaid is the second largest category of state expenditure, after education. Medicaid also is the fastest growing component of state–local spending, more than doubling in amount in the past 10 years (1995 to 2005). As noted earlier and shown in Table 21.4, about half of the growth in Medicaid spending in the past decade was due to more people participating in the program; the other half of the growth resulted from increased health-care costs. State and local governments also have faced substantial and increasing costs for health care of state–local government employees, as has been the case for private employers, as well.

The growth of Medicaid and other state–local health-care expenditures is part of a national trend of increasing relative expenditure on health care generally. Health care spending in the United States rose from 8.8 percent of GDP in 1980 to 12 percent in 1990 and to nearly 15 percent in 2002. Total private and public health-care expenditures increased by 123 percent between 1990 and 2002, more than 10 percent per year, a rate of growth that is persisting since 2000. A major factor is that

---

[28]Full-time work is defined as 2,000 hours per year; 50 weeks at 40 hours per week.

[29]"A Conversation with Mark McClellan." *Governing*, June 2005, p. 30.

growth in spending for prescription drugs continues to outpace growth of spending for health-care services in general. In 2002, spending for prescription drugs accounted for about 11 percent of all health-care expenditures, but spending for prescription drugs increased at an average rate of 15 percent per year from 1995 to 2002.[30] Since 2002, prescription drug spending has been growing at a rate of more than 16 percent per year.

Although Medicaid expenditure is often identified as a major policy issue for state–local government, health-care spending in general remains a major issue in the economy affecting essentially all individuals and industries, both private and public. As such, this issue is much broader than a limited state–local fiscal matter, but one that has continued to occupy state–local officials. Not surprisingly, therefore, states continue to explore options to restrain Medicaid and other health-care expenditures. States are following three approaches:

1. States are simply altering the parameters of their existing programs.

2. States are attempting to develop entirely new programs, often with programmatic waivers for Medicaid.

3. States are seeking new revenues and to alter behavior that leads to health-care expenditures.

In the first instance, the National Association of State Budget Officers (NASBO) (2004) reported that state government Medicaid expenditures exceeded amounts initially budgeted in about half of the states for fiscal years 2003 and 2004. As a consequence, all states reduced or froze reimbursement fees to health-care providers for services; all states introduced policies, such as requiring prior authorization or limiting prescriptions to preferred drug lists, to reduce spending for prescription drugs; 34 states reduced or limited Medicaid eligibility; 35 states reduced maximum benefits; and 32 states increased the copayments required of participants for some services. NASBO also reported that about half of the states were attempting to generate additional revenue for Medicaid by increasing fees or taxes on health-care providers, increasing cigarette and tobacco taxes, and reallocating funds states receive as a result of lawsuits against the tobacco companies and the resulting settlements.

Second, to contain costs and maintain services, some states have sought and received federal waivers to implement state programs to substitute for Medicaid. The details of these state experiments are less important than the fact that they are occurring. Essentially, states are operating as laboratories and conducting experiments on alternative ways of delivering health-care services, generally, and especially to low-income individuals and those with other health insurance coverage. In many of these cases, states are developing forms of managed-care plans, in which care is overseen by a single organization such as a Health Maintenance Organization (HMO); some states are using waivers to expand health-care financing

---

[30]Other major components of health-care spending in 2002 were hospital care (31 percent), physician services (22 percent), and nursing home care (7 percent). See National Center for Health Statistics. *Health, United States, 2004, With Chartbook on Trends in the Health of Americans.* Hyattsville, Maryland: 2004.

through government to others not covered by insurance plans. For instance, Arizona, Florida, and Tennessee all operate forms of managed-care programs as alternatives to traditional Medicaid, while Oregon received a federal waiver to implement a rationing plan, in which benefits are limited to specific prescribed lists of health services, with expanded preventive care. The common theme of these and other state experiments—including the two discussed next—is finding some way to limit services to beneficiaries.

In 2002, Utah used a waiver to institute a substitute plan that added additional beneficiaries by eliminating some benefits and instituting copayments for previous beneficiaries.[31] Under this experiment, the basic program provided as an alternative to traditional Medicaid includes only primary care, drugs, and emergency services—inpatient hospitalization is not included. The expansion plan that is available to a broader set of individuals than through Medicaid does cover hospitalization, but also includes an enrollment fee, substantial copayments, and an annual limit of $1,000 that individuals must pay out-of pocket. Utah therefore elected to use the resources available for Medicaid to finance some health-care services for individuals who were not eligible for Medicaid and to reduce services for previous recipients.

As noted in the *Headlines* introduction to this chapter, in 2005, Vermont entered into a Medicaid agreement with the federal government to (1) put a limit on the magnitude of federal Medicaid grants to the state and to (2) give the state authority to operate Medicaid through a managed-care organization. The limit on the federal grant to Vermont essentially converts it to a block grant similar to that for TANF, rather than the open-ended matching grant that other states receive for Medicaid. The managed-care organization receives a fixed amount per recipient and agrees to provide health services for that amount. This different financing system transfers the incentive for containing costs from the state government to the private managed-care organization and the health-care providers who work with them. Of course, it is not clear what happens if that per-recipient fee to the managed-care organization is not sufficient to cover costs; health benefits to recipients could be reduced, reimbursement payments to health-care providers could be reduced, or the state would have to allocate more resources. More federal funds will not be available.

Finally, in a completely different direction, states have directed attention at activities or organizations that contribute to the states' health-care costs. The best known of these may be the lawsuits filed by states against the tobacco products companies seeking reimbursement from those firms for state health-care costs associated with smoking and other uses of tobacco products. Initial lawsuits were filed in 1994 and 1995; in 1998, the attorneys general of 46 states settled most of those cases by approving the Master Settlement Agreement (MSA) with the four largest tobacco companies in the United States. Under that agreement, the tobacco industry is projected to pay the settling states in excess of $200 billion over the next 25 years. Four other states—Florida, Minnesota, Texas, and Mississippi—settled

---

[31]See Anderson, 2005.

their tobacco cases separately from the MSA and will also receive payments from the tobacco companies. Total payments to the 50 states are expected to be about $246 billion.

Three other examples of recent state action of this type should be noted. First, similar to the tobacco experience, recent government attention has been focused on issues of obesity, including the potential effects of making soft drinks and "fast foods" available to students in schools.[32] Second, a number of states have taken action to impose limitations on elderly people who transfer assets to heirs to become eligible for long-term nursing home care funded through Medicaid. Finally, states have begun to focus on major business firms that do not provide health-care insurance coverage or options for substantial numbers of employees, especially Wal-Mart. The Maryland legislature passed a bill in 2005 requiring firms with at least 10,000 employees to spend at least 8 percent of payroll on health-care coverage for employees or pay directly to help fund state Medicaid expenditures. Reportedly, Wal-Mart is the only firm in the state to which the bill would apply. Other states are apparently considering similar action directed at all firms in this circumstance.[33]

It seems likely that no one of these actions being pursued by states will be sufficient to resolve the broad set of public-policy issues raised by rising health-care expenditures and the resulting substantial and growing Medicaid costs for states. In fact, it is not clear that the fiscal issues arising from Medicaid can ultimately be resolved by the states at all, as the fundamental issues are broad social questions about what types of health care will be provided to low-income children and families, how that care will be funded, and who will deliver the care.

INTERNATIONAL COMPARISON: PROVIDING HEALTH-CARE SERVICES

As you have learned, financing health-care expenditures has become a crucial issue facing all governments—federal and state–local—in the United States. This component of government spending depends both on the magnitude of health-care spending generally and the role of government or public programs funding that care. As with most components of social welfare services, substantial differences exist among industrialized nations in both the magnitude and role of the public sector in financing health-care services. The relative situation for the United States is easily summarized: health-care spending is substantially higher in the United States than in other industrialized nations, whereas the share of health expenditures financed publicly is lowest in the United States among these nations.

In 2001, health-care expenditures in the United States were nearly 14 percent of GDP.[34] The nations closest in the magnitude of health-care spending were

---

[32]At least one study suggests that perhaps 11 percent of state Medicaid costs are related to obesity (Lemov, 2004).

[33]See Lemov, 2005.

[34]For 2002, health expenditures in the United States had risen to 14.9 percent of GDP.

Switzerland (10.9 percent) and Germany (10.7 percent). Among other major federal nations, spending was lower in Canada (9.7 percent) and Australia (8.9 percent). Health-care expenditures were even lower in Japan and the United Kingdom, at 7.6 percent of GDP. Even larger differences in magnitude apply to per-capita health expenditures, which were $4,867 in the United States, but only $2,808 in Germany, $2,792 in Canada, $2,350 in Australia, $1,992 in the United Kingdom, and $1,984 in Japan. It may not seem surprising that consumers in the United States spend more on health care than people in the other nations because income is also higher in the United States. But U.S. consumers also spend a substantially larger *fraction* of income on health care, about 43 percent more than consumers in Canada, for instance.

In the United States in 2001, about 44 percent of health expenditure was funded by the public sector (including Medicare, Medicaid, public health services, and so on), whereas about 34 percent was funded by private health insurance, as shown in Figure 21.12. In contrast, the public sector accounted for 78 percent of health-care spending in Japan, 75 percent in Germany, 71 percent in Canada, and 69 percent in Australia. The relatively small role of government in funding health care in the United States is matched, at least among these nations, only by Mexico (46 percent) and Korea (44 percent). Another interesting fact of the data in Figure 21.12 is that the share of health expenditures financed from private, out-of-pocket

Figure 21.12

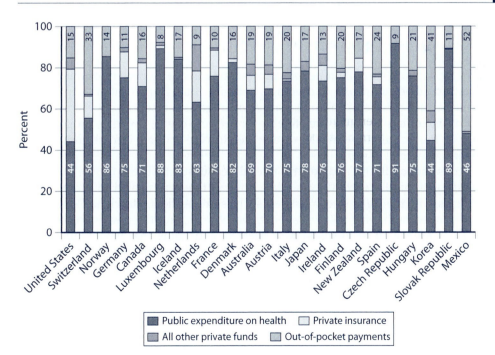

Health expenditure by source of funding, 2000

SOURCE: OECD Health Data 2003.

payments by individuals is about the same in these other nations. Thus, the greater role for the public sector in such places as Japan, Germany, Canada, and Australia substitutes for the role of private health-care insurance in the United States.

These differences reflect, of course, the fact that each of these other nations has a national, public health-care system that provides the great bulk of health-care services in those countries. In contrast, the system of health-care providers in the United States is predominantly private, with the role of government to ensure care for low-income individuals and children in families without access to health care. This fundamental difference is a major source of the Medicaid financing issue facing state governments. Prices for health care are set in the private sector, individuals in consultation with private health-care providers determine what health-care services to consume, but government funds a substantial portion of the cost of services for the target population. Many of the policy adjustments to state Medicaid plans are intended to limit prices paid to providers or to limit choices about covered services by consumers.

SUMMARY

The adoption of the Personal Responsibility and Work Opportunity Reconciliation Act in 1996 brought major changes to the objectives, methods, and relative roles of government in promoting health and welfare.

About 37 million people in the United States in 2004, including some 8 million families as well as single individuals, were deemed to be living in poverty, which represents about 13 percent of individuals and 10 percent of families. Among poor individuals or families, poverty is most prevalent among children under the age of 18.

In 2004, about 46 million people, representing about 16 percent of the population, had no health insurance coverage, and more than 30 percent of people in the United States received health insurance coverage as a result of government programs, including Medicare (health care for senior citizens, covering about 14 percent of the population) and Medicaid (health care for low-income individuals, covering another 13 percent).

Economic conditions and poverty rates differ substantially among the states and also geographically within states. State poverty rates are related to average state incomes, with the higher-income states (such as Connecticut, Maryland, New Jersey, and Minnesota) having relatively low poverty rates, and the lower-income states (such as Mississippi, Arkansas, New Mexico, and Louisiana) having among the highest poverty rates. On average over the period from 2002 to 2004, the largest share of people without health insurance coverage was in Texas (25.1 percent) and New Mexico (21.4 percent), whereas fewer than 10 percent of people are without health insurance in Hawaii (9.9 percent) and Minnesota (8.5 percent).

Five major welfare or support programs represent the bulk of public-aid spending. Temporary Assistance to Needy Families (TANF) and Supplemental Security Income (SSI) provide monthly cash payments to individuals and families with low income, disability, or other special circumstances. Medicaid finances health care for low-income individuals and families who do not have other health insurance or health benefits. The Food Stamp program allows low-income individuals and families to purchase food using coupons or credit provided by the government. Federal and some state governments provide Earned Income Tax Credits (EITC) to subsidize earnings of low-income workers.

Of these five major programs, Medicaid is by far the largest, both in terms of the magnitude of spending and the number of recipients, and is also the fastest growing welfare program and fastest growing component of state budgets. The $275.3 billion spent on Medicaid in 2003 is essentially double the *sum* of amounts spent through the other four programs in 2003 (about $26.3 billion for AFDC, $35.6 billion for SSI, about $21 billion for Food Stamps, and $38.7 billion through the federal EITC).

In-kind benefits historically have been more important than cash payments in the U.S. welfare system. In fiscal year 2003, the two major means-tested, in-kind benefit programs (Medicaid and Food Stamps) swamped the three major cash-payment programs (TANF, SSI, and the EITC) by $299.2 billion in health care and food subsidy to about $90 billion of cash-assistance payments, a ratio of more than three to one.

The federal government finances and establishes uniform national standards and benefits for SSI and Food Stamps. States have substantial policy discretion in determining eligibility and benefits for TANF and Medicaid, which are jointly financed by the federal government and the states. As a result, substantial differences exist among states in eligibility standards and benefit levels for TANF and Medicaid.

Studies of elasticities of welfare benefits show small effects—price elasticities between 0.2 and 0 and income elasticities between 0.2 and 0.8. With these elasticities, increases in tax prices have little effect on reducing benefits (just as decreases in prices have little effect on increasing benefits. The available evidence suggests that state funding for Medicaid is substantially more price sensitive than for cash assistance—with price elasticities in the range of 0.6 to 0.8.

The evidence about interstate migration for welfare purposes (or other economic purposes for that matter) is ambiguous. Some studies show low-income individuals moving toward higher-benefit states, whereas others show no difference in moving patterns between low-income mothers and others. The location to move toward seems influenced as much by employment opportunities, the availability of social support networks, and distance as welfare policies. It seems unlikely, therefore, that interstate migration by itself is substantial enough to drive a "race to the bottom" in income-support services.

The set of health and welfare policy changes in the 1980s and 1990s—growth of earned income and dependent care tax credits, expansion of Medicaid eligibility, and increased use of work requirements for cash assistance—contributed to major increases in labor market participation by low-income single parents.

States are following three approaches to restrain Medicaid spending, which has doubled in the past form1995 to 2005. States are altering the parameters of their existing programs, using Medicaid waivers to develop entirely new programs and altering behavior that leads to health-care expenditures.

DISCUSSION QUESTIONS

1. States select welfare benefit levels for low-income state residents, subject to federal rules. Suppose that the demands (marginal benefits) for welfare services by poor and nonpoor state residents are shown in the following figure. State and discuss three possible components of the benefits to the nonpoor from welfare services. To what extent does each type of benefit arise from helping poor people in the state or helping poor people in all states?

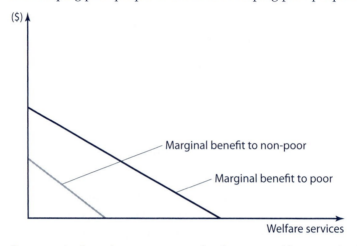

2. Suppose, in fact, that taxpayers who finance welfare care both about poor state residents and the poor who live in other states, but to different degrees. Thus, when the residents of Your State (YS) select the level of welfare benefits, all residents of YS (both the poor and nonpoor) benefit, but residents of other states also benefit because the poor in YS are being helped. (For instance, because of the assistance in YS, poor residents may be less likely to migrate to other states.) Both the marginal benefits to all residents from welfare payments in YS and the marginal benefits to residents of other states are shown in the following figure.

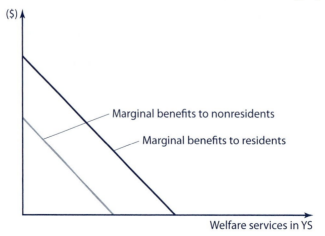

a. If your state must pay all welfare costs (the marginal cost of a dollar of benefit is $1.00), what level of service is selected?

b. What level of welfare service in YS is efficient from a national viewpoint, taking into account the benefits to residents of other states?

c. How might the federal government use intergovernmental grants to induce YS to select the amount of welfare benefits that is efficient from a national perspective?

d. If the federal government used grants for this purpose, under what conditions would it make sense for the federal grant share to be greater for low-income states as opposed to high-income states? Explain.

3. Old State (OS) receives an open-ended matching grant from the federal government to finance Medicaid services to state residents. The federal grant covers 50 percent of state expenditures, and the state has selected a program that provides $4,000 of medical services per recipient per year, on average.

a. Suppose that the (absolute value of the) price elasticity for Medicaid services in OS is 0.5. If the federal matching grant were eliminated so that OS had to pay $1.00 for each dollar of Medicaid expenditures, what is expected to happen to the average level of Medicaid services selected in OS? Estimate the new expected average benefit amount.

b. Now suppose the national government gives OS a lump-sum block grant to replace the previous matching grant. OS receives lump-sum grant funds equal to $2,000 times the initial number of recipients, which is the same amount of funds as was paid before. If the total lump-sum grant equals 5 percent of total income in Old State, and the income elasticity of demand for Medicaid services is 0.6, estimate how much average Medicaid spending will now increase.

c. After the grant substitution—replacing the matching grant with an equal-amount lump-sum grant—is Medicaid spending in OS expected to be the same, larger, or smaller? Explain why.

4. Look at Figure 22.1 in Chapter 22 to find per-capita income in your state. Suppose then that a single parent with one child works in your state and earns income equal to one-third of the state per-capita income (for instance, earnings of $10,485 in Florida where per-capita income is $31,455). Use the information in this book and your own research about programs through your state government's Web site to estimate the effect of each of the following fiscal factors for this family:

a. Federal and state income and Social Security taxes

b. EITC

c. TANF cash-assistance payments

d. Food Stamp benefits

e. Medicaid eligibility and coverage

What is the net economic position for such a family in your state? Assuming full-time work (2,000 hours per year), what is the equivalent hourly wage that such a single parent earns, including all benefits?

SELECTED READINGS

Burtless, Gary. "The Economist's Lament: Public Assistance in America." *Journal of Economic Perspectives*, 4 (Winter 1990), 57–78.

Ellwood, David T. "Anti-Poverty Policy for Families in the Next Century: From Welfare to Work—and Worries." *Journal of Economic Perspectives* 14, No. 1 (Winter, 2000), 189–198.

Ellwood, David T. "The Impact of the Earned Income Tax Credit and Social Policy Reforms on Work, Marriage, and Living Arrangements." *National Tax Journal* 53, No. 4, Part 2, (December, 2000), 1063–1105.

Moffitt, Robert A. *Incentive Effects of the U.S. Welfare System*. Madison: The University of Wisconsin, Institute for Research on Poverty, 1990.

Moffitt, Robert A., editor. *Means-Tested Transfer Programs in the United States*. A National Bureau of Economic Research Conference Report. Chicago: The University of Chicago Press, 2003. See especially Chapter 1, "Medicaid" by Jonathan Gruber; Chapter 3, "The Earned Income Tax Credit" by V. Joseph Hotz and John Karl Scholz; and Chapter 5, "The Temporary Assistance for Needy Families Program" by Robert A. Moffitt.

CHAPTER 22

ECONOMIC DEVELOPMENT

. . . State and local governments have been engaged
for some time in an increasingly active competition
among themselves for new business[1].
—GEORGE F. BREAK

"IT'S BEEN FETED BY THE STATE, CELEBRATED BY THE UNIVERSITY OF MICHIGAN, EVEN FEATURED IN A WALL STREET JOURNAL ARTICLE. . . . A YOUNG PERSON (IN THIS CASE, A UNIVERSITY STUDENT) HAS AN IDEA FOR A COMPANY, FINDS SUPPORT FOR IT WITHIN THE UNIVERSITY SETTING, STARTS A FIRM, TAKES IT TO MARKET, AND VOILA, A SUCCESSFUL HIGH-TECH FIRM IS BORN. AND THAT'S BEEN THE STORY THUS FAR OF DETROIT-BASED MOBIUS MICROSYSTEMS INC.

DESPITE THE ACCOLADES, [THE CEO AND COFOUNDER] ASSUMES THE COMPANY WILL LIKELY BE FORCED TO . . . MOVE OPERATIONS TO SILICON VALLEY, WHERE . . . THE DOLLARS ARE CERTAINLY MORE FLUSH . . . SPECIFICALLY, MORE FLUSH WITH VENTURE CAPITAL DOLLARS AVAILABLE FOR SEMICONDUCTOR BUSINESSES. . .

THE FIRM HAS BEEN WINED AND DINED RECENTLY BY OTHER STATES LIKE CALIFORNIA, ILLINOIS AND OHIO—ALL ANXIOUS TO PERSUADE IT TO RELOCATE. THE STATE OF MICHIGAN . . . GRANTED MOBIUS A \$4.4- MILLION, 10-YEAR TAX ABATEMENT TO STAY PUT. AS A RESULT, THE FIRM MOVED FROM ANN ARBOR TO . . . DETROIT.

WHEN ASKED FOR HIS ASSESSMENT OF MOBIUS'S SITUATION, [THE CEO] SAYS: 'I STILL THINK IT'S LIKELY WE'LL BE FORCED TO MOVE.'[2]"

---

[1]*Intergovernmental Fiscal Relations in the United States.* Washington, D.C.: The Brookings Institution, 1967, 23.
[2]Cain, Carol. "Silicon Valley Tempts Detroit Firm." *Detroit Free Press,* May 23, 2005.

Competition among states and localities for new investment or business expansion is hardly new (as reflected by George Break's comment from 1967), but seems to have intensified and received more public attention in recent years. Perhaps this is both because the range of incentives offered to potential investors has grown (to include tax-exempt financing and government provision of special services to businesses as well as the more traditional business tax incentives) and because the magnitude of incentives is rising. Timothy Bartik (1994) reports survey evidence from the 1990s suggesting that state and local direct expenditures on economic development are in the neighborhood of $8 per capita annually. In addition to this direct spending, state–local governments also incur costs from tax incentives ($16–$60 per capita per year) and from financial guarantees or low-interest loans.

The controversy about the equity and efficiency of these policies for influencing business investment decisions is particularly important given the increased use of investment incentives due to the heightened competition among subnational governments. Do business incentives influence economic activity at all; if so, which types of activity—investment, employment, wages, incomes, land prices—are affected to the greatest degree? Do incentives discriminate among businesses, treating new businesses differently from existing ones and some industries different from others? And how should one evaluate the success of business incentives, by short-run local economic effects or by long-run changes to overall economic welfare?

Substantial differences have always existed among states and different localities in economic conditions. Differences in fiscal policies—taxes and spending—carried out by those governments may be part of the reason for the differences in employment and income. However, you have learned in this book that the opposite is also true: economic conditions influence the demand for state–local government services, as well. Moreover, differences in economic conditions among states or regions may themselves influence business investment and location decisions and thus cause changes in future economic conditions. For instance, a firm might be attracted to an area with relatively high unemployment because of the availability of workers at lower wages than in other places.

The fundamental question, then, is what accounts for differences in economic conditions such as employment and income among different states and regions? With some understanding of that issue, it is possible to examine why and how economic conditions in various places change over time. Understanding that issue directly leads to a series of questions concerning the appropriate policy of state-local governments toward economic development. Do firms and consumers change the location of their economic activity because of general state-local government fiscal policies? Do specific state-local business investment incentives "succeed" in attracting new businesses or investment? If so, who receives the bulk of the final economic benefit of that new investment? And if tax and financial incentives do "succeed" in attracting new investment, are they cost-effective and fair? These are the public policy issues being debated by the business community and government officials and the issues considered in this chapter.

INTERSTATE DIFFERENCES IN ECONOMIC CONDITIONS

In any given year, substantial differences exist in incomes and unemployment rates among the states, as shown in Figures 22.1 and 22.2. In 2004, state per-capita incomes varied from $45,398 in Connecticut to $24,650 in Mississippi, with the average for the nation at $32,937. The coefficient of variation (standard deviation/ mean) for state per-capita income is 0.14, meaning that state per capita income varies 14 percent on average around the mean. Similar differences among the states exist in family incomes as with per-capita incomes. In 2003, median family income—that is the income level at which half of families are higher and half lower—was greatest in Connecticut at $69,917 and smallest in West Virginia at $38,568. Relatively big income differences remain even if states are grouped together in regions, with regional per-capita income varying from $40,206 in New England to $28,282 in the Southwestern states, although in some cases as much variation exists within those regions as among them.

Remember that personal income includes all income regularly received by persons, including wages, salaries, and other labor income; rent; interest; dividends; and transfer payments. The last means that personal income may be maintained or even increase in periods when economic activity declines because of transfer payments such as Social Security, unemployment compensation, welfare programs, and government subsidy payments. In essence, those transfer payments reduce income differences that would otherwise occur.

Of course, these differences in nominal incomes may overstate the real differences in purchasing power if the prices of consumer goods (the cost of living) are generally higher in higher-income states and regions. Not surprisingly, that seems to be the case. An analysis of that issue by Peter Mieszkowski (1979) suggests that regional per-capita income differences are reduced by about one-third because of cost-of-living differences. Even with that adjustment, regional income differences still exist, and the state-by-state differences are not reduced nearly as much as differences between regions by considering price differences for consumer goods.

The variation in state and regional unemployment rates is similar to that for income. In July 2005, state unemployment rates varied from 2.7 percent in Hawaii to 7.0 percent in Michigan, with the national average at 5.0 percent. Among the Census regions, both the highest and lowest unemployment rates are in the Midwest. Unemployment was lowest in the West North Central states (4.5 percent among Iowa, Kansas, Minnesota, Missouri, Nebraska, North Dakota, and South Dakota) and highest among the East North Central states (5.9 percent among Illinois, Indiana, Michigan, Ohio, and Wisconsin). You should recall that the unemployment rate is the ratio of the number of unemployed persons (those not working but looking for work) to the number of unemployed plus employed persons (what is called the labor force). The unemployment rate therefore reflects both the supply of labor in each market and the demand for workers in those markets. Although demand for workers depends on the economic conditions of the industries and the wages in each region, the supply of workers reflects demographic

Figure 22.1

State per-capita income, 2004

United States: $32,937   Low: $24,650 (Mississippi)   Median: $31,322 (Ohio)   High: $45,398 (Connecticut)
$31,339 (Nebraska)

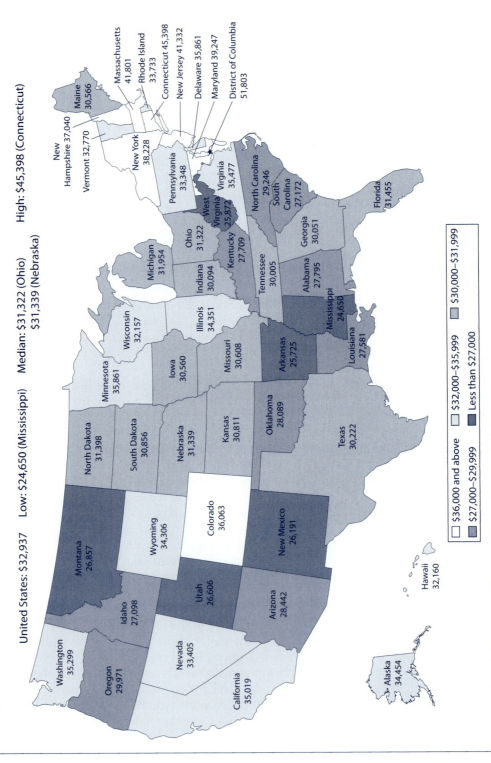

SOURCE: U.S. Department of Commerce, Bureau of Economic Analysis.

Figure 22.2

State unemployment rates, July 2005

| United States: 5.0 | Low: 2.7 (Hawaii) | Median: 5.0 (Maine, Texas) | High: 7.0 (Michigan) |

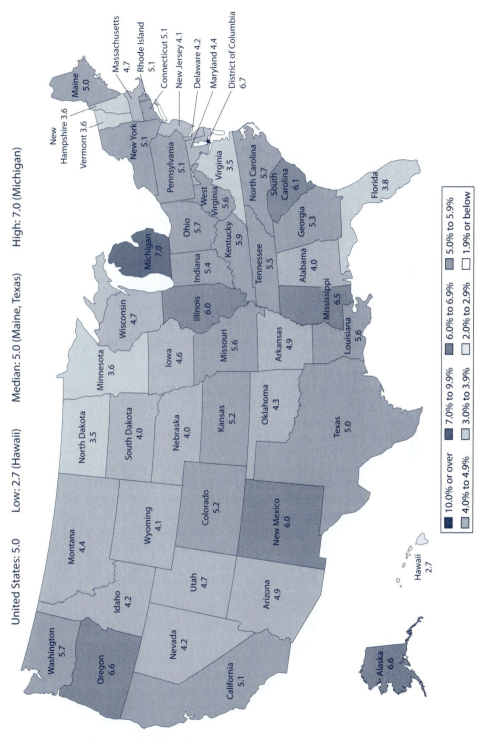

Massachusetts 4.7
Rhode Island 5.1
Connecticut 5.1
New Jersey 4.1
Delaware 4.2
Maryland 4.4
District of Columbia 6.7

New Hampshire 3.6
Vermont 3.6
Maine 5.0

New York 5.1
Pennsylvania 5.1
West Virginia 5.6
Virginia 3.5
North Carolina 5.7
South Carolina 6.1
Florida 3.8
Ohio 5.7
Kentucky 5.9
Tennessee 5.5
Georgia 5.3
Alabama 4.0
Mississippi 6.5
Louisiana 5.6
Michigan 7.0
Indiana 5.4
Illinois 6.0
Wisconsin 4.7
Minnesota 3.6
Iowa 4.6
Missouri 5.6
Arkansas 4.9
North Dakota 3.5
South Dakota 4.0
Nebraska 4.0
Kansas 5.2
Oklahoma 4.3
Texas 5.0
Montana 4.4
Wyoming 4.1
Colorado 5.2
New Mexico 6.0
Washington 5.7
Oregon 6.6
Idaho 4.2
Nevada 4.2
Utah 4.7
Arizona 4.9
California 5.1
Alaska 6.6
Hawaii 2.7

10.0% or over
7.0% to 9.9%
6.0% to 6.9%
5.0% to 5.9%
4.0% to 4.9%
3.0% to 3.9%
2.0% to 2.9%
1.9% or below

SOURCE: Bureau of Labor Statistics. Local Area Unemployment Statistics.

Regional per-
capita income as
a percentage of
the U.S. average,
selected year,
1900–2003

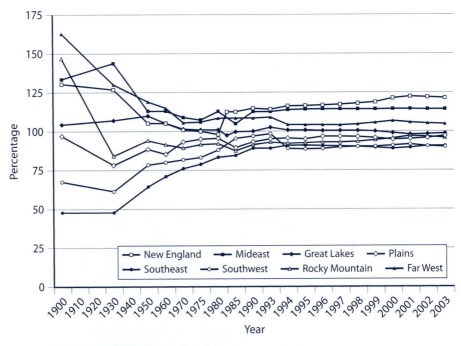

SOURCE: ACIR (1981b) updated by author.

characteristics of the population as well as economic opportunities. Thus, economic growth and higher incomes in a region might not lead to substantial
decreases in the unemployment rate if more people begin looking for work or
migrate to the region, thus increasing the size of the labor force.

Throughout this century, the differences in per-capita income among the states
and regions generally have been reduced continually, dramatically between 1930
and the mid 1970s, as depicted in Figure 22.3. This narrowing of income differences
has been accompanied by a general realignment of population and economic activity. Although per-capita income in the Southeast was less than half of the national
average in 1930, it is about 90 percent of the national average today. At the other
end of the distribution, per-capita income in the Mideast states was about 40 percent greater than the national average in 1930 but only about 14 percent higher
today. Although the income differences have narrowed substantially, the relative
position of the various regions has remained fairly stable. The New England,
Mideast, and Far West regions have generally had above-average income,
although the Southeast, Southwest, Rocky Mountain, and Plains regions have had
below-average incomes (and the Great Lakes states about average income).

This narrowing of income differences is undoubtedly due to a number of factors.
Because wages and salaries account for about 60 percent of personal income, one
attractive economic explanation might be a flow of new investment to regions with

relatively low wages, resulting in an increase in economic activity, population, and ultimately wages and incomes. At the same time, workers may migrate from low-wage to high-wage regions, reducing the supply of labor in the lower-wage areas. This is certainly what would be expected in the standard competitive economic model, with investors allocating mobile capital to those regions where the highest returns are possible and where workers are moving, perhaps to a lesser degree, to take advantage of job opportunities. If low wages in a region truly mean low costs (that is, the workers are equally productive as in higher-wage areas), then capitalists who invest in those low-wage areas might be able to earn higher profits.

The evidence on this theory is somewhat inconclusive, however. George Borts and Jerome Stein (1964) examined the growth of employment and capital investment among states for the periods 1918–1929, 1929–1948, and 1948–1953 and found that wage differences were only weakly related to changes in investment and not at all related to employment growth. The first issue is more important because a constant level of employment is still consistent with rising wages (and incomes) if the demand for labor is increasing due to new investment. More recently, Timothy Bartik (1991) reported on 42 different studies completed since 1979 on the effect of wage differences on business location or employment among states. He reports that 62 percent of these studies find a statistically significant negative effect of higher wages on economic activity, with an average long-run elasticity of business activity with respect to wages of about −0.7; that is, 10-percent higher wages lead to about a 7-percent decline in economic activity. Again, the combined effect of an out migration of workers from low-wage areas (a decrease in labor supply) coupled with new investment in the region (an increase in the demand for labor) is expected to be an increase in wages, although employment (the quantity of labor) may rise or fall. From this viewpoint, a narrowing of income differences is the natural result of economic forces.

Among the other factors that have likely contributed to this narrowing of income differences are differences in the prices of other important inputs into production, especially land, energy, and transportation services. As with labor, areas with little development and thus relatively low prices for these goods may be attractive to some investors. Capital movements in response to those price differences would again naturally serve to equalize those price differences and thus income differences. Some fiscal policies of the federal government are also thought to have played a role in promoting economic growth in various regions of the country. On one hand, the growth of transfer programs such as Social Security, health insurance, and welfare payments, which stimulate economic growth through demand, has added income in some areas. On the other hand, attention has also been directed at federal decisions about the location of federal (especially military) installations as well as federal government purchases of goods and materials. The regional pattern of federal government expenditures is believed to have particularly stimulated growth in the Southeast and Southwest states. Finally, some analysts have suggested that various social and historical changes, such as changes in the pattern of immigration to the United States, the introduction of air conditioning, and improvement in racial relations, also have contributed to the dispersion of economic activity.

Note that substantial differences in economic conditions also exist among various regions or areas within states. This is demonstrated by the 2005 unemployment rates and 2003 per-capita incomes for metropolitan areas in California, Michigan, and New York, shown in Table 22.1. In such a large and diverse state as California, unemployment rates varied from 4.0 percent in the Santa Barbara area to 8.4 percent in Fresno. Although the variation is smaller in Michigan and New York, it is still substantial, from 4.4 to 7.9 percent in Michigan and 3.8 to 5.3 percent in New York. Substantial differences also exist in per-capita income within states, from nearly $46,958 per person in San Francisco to less than $22,947 in Bakersfield, for instance. As with differences among states, the mobility of capital and labor is apparently not sufficient to fully eliminate economic differences among regions within states.

The long-term dispersion of population and economic activity in the United States from the older industrialized areas to regions that were primarily rural and

Table 22.1

Variation of Per-Capita Income and Unemployment Rates Among Metropolitan Areas Within Selected States

	California			Michigan			New York	
Area	Unemployment[a]	Income[b]	Area	Unemployment[a]	Income[b]	Area	Unemployment[a]	Income[b]
Bakersfield	8.3%	$22,947	Ann Arbor	4.4	38,323	Albany	3.8	32,208
Fresno	8.4	24,277	Benton Harbor	7.0	na	Binghampton	4.7	25,747
Los Angeles-Long Beach	5.2	33,347	Detroit	7.7	35,972	Buffalo	5.2	29,145
			Flint	7.8	27,521	Elmira	5.3	23,349
Modesto	8.1	24,276	Grand Rapids	6.1	29,188	Glens Falls	3.9	25,275
Riverside-San Bernadino	5.2	24,526	Jackson	6.6	25,712	New York	4.6	40,899
			Kalamazoo-Battle Creek	5.7	28,947	Rochester	4.7	31,057
Sacramento	4.7	31,425			28,671	Syracuse	4.8	28,429
Salinas	5.6	31,801	Lansing	6.3	26,454	Utica	4.8	26,554
San Diego	4.4	35,841	Saginaw	7.9				
San Francisco	4.9	46,958						
San Jose	5.6	46,072						
Santa Barbara	4.0	33,624						
Santa Rosa	4.4	36,466						
Stockton	7.5	24,397						
Vallejo-Fairfield-Napa	5.5	30,259						
State	5.4	33,415	State	7.2	31,178	State	4.9	36,112

[a]June 2005

[b]2003

SOURCES: U.S. Department of Labor, Bureau of Labor Statistics, 2005; U.S. Department of Commerce, Bureau of Economic Analysis, 2005.

the resulting narrowing of income differences serves as a background against which the role of state fiscal policies can be examined. The issue in the remainder of this chapter is whether state–local taxes and services contribute to interstate reallocations of economic activity, and if so, how states might alter their fiscal decisions to induce more investment.

INTERSTATE DIFFERENCES IN FISCAL POLICY

Magnitude of Tax Costs

To evaluate whether tax differences among the states influence investment decisions, it is first necessary to determine the magnitude of those tax differences. The degree of business taxation in different states has been measured in three primary ways: by the share of total taxes collected from businesses, by the ratio of total business taxes in a state to some measure of total business size or income for a particular year, and by the comparative profitability of "identical" firms located in different states and thus paying different taxes. Each method has advantages and disadvantages, so that the information conveyed by each measurement is different and often not consistent with the results of the other methods.

Business Tax Share

ACIR (1981a) estimated the state–local government taxes with "an initial impact on business" for each state for 1977 and then calculated the **share of state–local taxes initially collected from business.** The list of taxes with "an initial impact on business" included business property taxes, sales taxes collected on business purchases of goods and services, gross receipts taxes, business income and value-added taxes, license fees, and taxes on specific business activities, such as severance taxes. ACIR reported that these "business" taxes represented about 31 percent of total state–local taxes (34 percent if unemployment insurance taxes were included), and that the business tax share of total taxes had declined steadily from 1957, when taxes with an initial impact on business represented about 37 percent of total state–local taxes. Among the various regions, business taxes were relied on relatively most heavily in the Southwest (41 percent) and least heavily in the Plains states and New England (27 percent).

Tannenwald (2004) reports two sets of estimates for the business share of state and local taxes for 2000. Taxes assumed in these studies to be nominally borne at least partly by businesses include the property tax, sales and gross receipts tax, motor fuels tax, business license taxes, severance taxes, workers compensation and unemployment insurance taxes, and corporate net income taxes. In cases where the tax is collected both from businesses and individuals (such as property and sales tax), an attempt is made to determine the appropriate division. One tax that might have been included, but is not, is personal income tax on business income from partnerships, limited liability companies, and similar entities. Estimates from work compiled by Ernst and Young and discussed in Cline *et al.* (2004) suggest that these taxes collected from business amounted to about 42 percent of total state–local taxes, varying from 81 percent in Alaska to 31 percent in Maryland. Tannenwald's similar calculations put the average share of state–local taxes collected from business at 44 percent, again with large variation from 80 percent in Alaska to 33 percent in Maryland.

Hines (2003) focused on state corporate income taxes only and calculated the variation in corporate income tax as a share of total state taxes for each state from 1977 to 1997. In many states, the level and importance of state corporate income taxes varied substantially from year to year. For instance, from 1977 to 1997, state corporate income tax revenue per capita varied by more than 35 percent, on average, around the mean. This suggests first that the state tax burden on corporations measured in this way is highly time dependent and that state corporate income taxes are highly sensitive to economic conditions.

The "tax share" approach shares one problem common to many business tax studies, the inability to distinguish between the initial and final burden of a tax. If the ability of businesses to alter behavior and thus shift taxes to consumers or factor suppliers differs among states, then the share of taxes with an initial impact on business will be misleading as to the final tax burdens on business from a state's taxes. This is clearly illustrated in the business tax share data reported by Tannenwald (2004). The states with the highest share of taxes collected from business include Alaska, Wyoming, Texas, and Louisiana, all of which collect a substantial share of their taxes from extracted energy. However, much of that tax burden is then shifted to consumers in other states.

In addition, the *share* of taxes with an impact on business does not necessarily correspond to the *level* of taxes on business. Obviously, even if a state collects a large share of its taxes from businesses, the tax burden on businesses with a low level of total taxes may be smaller than that in some other state with higher taxes generally, but with a smaller business share. But if the share of state service benefits enjoyed by businesses is known or at least similar in different states, then the share of taxes does convey information about the potential fiscal advantage of businesses in some states. If businesses "pay" 40 percent of taxes in a state and receive benefits from only 30 percent of state–local expenditures, they may not care that the level of business taxes in that state is low.

Business Taxes Compared to Business Income

An alternative approach is taken by William Wheaton (1983), who estimates the level of business tax collections from a set of specific taxes compared to the level of net business income in the state. Net business income is sales less expenses but before federal taxes. Wheaton includes all tax payments for which a business is legally liable—including property, corporate income, unemployment insurance, and specific output taxes—except for sales taxes on business purchases. The last taxes were excluded because he believed that no reliable estimate exists of the fraction of state sales taxes that arise from intermediate goods transactions, even though it makes sense to include those taxes. The estimates are made for both all business taxes and all business income in each state (which requires an estimate of total net business income) and for taxes and income of manufacturing firms only (which requires an estimate of manufacturing taxes only but not manufacturing net business income, available from the Census of Manufacturing). The estimates are based on 1977 data.

Wheaton reports that state–local taxes collected from business represented 7.7 percent of net income for all firms in 1977, on average, and 7.9 percent for manufacturing firms alone. Wheaton also found substantial interstate variation in business tax levels. For all businesses, the level of taxation varied from 20.2 percent of net income (in Delaware) to 4.8 percent (in Utah), with an average of about 36-percent variation in state business tax levels around the median level. On a regional basis, the highest level of business taxation occurred in New England (10.2 percent), the Mid-Atlantic states (9.5), and the Pacific Coast (8.7), while the lowest levels were in the East South Central (5.6 percent) and South Atlantic (5.7) states. The pattern for manufacturing firms alone was similar, although the degree of interstate and regional variation in effective business tax rates was greater for manufacturing firms than for all businesses. For instance, manufacturing taxes varied from 14.8 percent of net income in New England to 3.8 percent in the East South Central states.

Hines (2003) provides a similar, but more limited measure, calculating state corporate income taxes as a share of Gross State Product (the total value of final production in a state). From 1977 through 1996, state corporate income taxes in aggregate varied from a high of about 1.0 percent of GSP to a low of about 0.7 percent. The variation in this measure of business taxes among states is greater than the aggregate variation over time, however. For instance, corporate income tax in Michigan averaged about 1.3 percent of GSP over these years and varied from 1.2 percent to 1.6 percent.

Tannenwald (2004) presents estimates, similar to those of Wheaton from an earlier period, of taxes initially collected from business as a percentage of both business profits (net income) and state personal income for 2000. A major difference from Wheaton's analysis is that Tannenwald includes estimates of both general and specific sales taxes on business purchases. The data for 2000 suggest that business taxes represented about 36 percent of business profits and about 4.7 percent of state personal income. As with all these studies, substantial differences exist among the states. Business taxes were lowest in Maryland, North Carolina, Virginia, and Massachusetts (3.4 to 3.7 percent of personal income); they were highest in Alaska, Wyoming, West Virginia, and North Dakota (7 to 10 percent of personal income).

Again, these estimates also are based on the initial magnitude of taxes collected from business rather than the final burden of those taxes. In addition, it is not clear what measure of business activity—net income (profits), sales, personal income, or GSP—is best to compare against taxes. Because sales equals the total costs of a firm plus profits, sales might be the most appropriate base against which to compare taxes, particularly if firms can shift business taxes to suppliers, for instance, by paying lower wages. Because net income is usually between 5 and 10 percent of sales, and given Wheaton's estimate that business taxes are about 8 percent of net income, state–local business taxes would amount to less than 1 percent of total sales, on average. Even using Tannenwald's broader measure of business taxes at 36 percent of net income, this suggests business taxes at about 2 to 4 percent of sales. This is consistent with Hines' result that corporate income taxes averaged about 0.8 percent of GSP.

Comparing these business tax estimates shows how difficult it is to draw clear conclusions. One issue again is the direction of causation for tax rates; do low tax rates contribute to business growth or does business growth contribute to an increased demand for government services? Another issue is the *share* of the taxes from business compared to the *level* of business taxes. According to Tannenwald's computations, Texas was fourth highest in the share of taxes collected from business (at 59 percent), but only twentieth among the states in business taxes as a percentage of profits. In contrast, New York is twentieth in the share of taxes collected from business, but eighth in terms of business taxes as a percentage of personal income. The high level of business taxes in New York resulted from the high level of taxes and expenditures generally, rather than any decision to adopt a tax structure designed to impose a relatively heavy tax burden on business.

Business Taxes and Profitability

A third approach to measuring interstate tax differentials does not focus on the tax differences *per se* but rather on the profit differences that result from operating in different places with different taxes. One common method of doing this is to create some hypothetical firms and then calculate their profitability under some assumptions about operating procedures for sets of different states' taxes. Most often these calculations are made for a single year. The single-year tax differences for these representative firms may not be very accurate measures of profit differences over the life of a capital investment, however, because many state and local taxes have time-dependent features that vary from place to place.

A more sophisticated approach to measuring business profitability at various locations has been developed by James Papke and Leslie Papke (1984). The Papkes focus on the *profitability of a new investment* at various locations *over the entire productive lifetime* of that investment. For an assumed set of characteristics of a representative firm, Papke and Papke compute the change in profitability that results from a new investment at one location, which allows calculation of the rate of return on that new investment. Because the taxes at that location are carefully modeled, the rate of return from investment at one location can be compared to the return from investment at another, with any difference arising from the tax differences.

Because the Papke measure of the rate of return depends on the assumed characteristics of the sample firm, it is not possible to get one single estimate for each state, but rather a different estimate for a given type of firm in different states. For illustration, Leslie Papke (1987) reported the after-tax rates of return on new investment for both the furniture and electric components industries in 20 different states. For furniture, the rates of return varied from 11.9 percent (in New Jersey) to 13.7 percent (in Texas), an average difference of about 14 percent from the highest to lowest. Thus, it does seem that interstate tax differences can result in different profits on new investments in different states, even for similar firms, although those differences are not huge and could easily be offset by differences in other costs or government services. Also, because state–local taxes are a relatively small fraction of a firm's total costs, relatively large differences or changes in state–local taxes are required to bring about even small differences or changes in after-tax rates of return.

In terms of reflecting the relative degree of business taxation in different states, the Papke measures of profitability tell a somewhat different story than the ACIR, Hines, or Wheaton measures. For instance, among the 20 states examined by Papke, Michigan had the highest level of business taxes according to the Wheaton measure but the fifth highest return on new investment. On the other side, Tennessee had the fourth lowest level of business taxes by the Wheaton measure but the seventh highest by the Papke measure. A large part of the difference in these two measures of comparative business taxes arises from a fundamental difference in concept, which is emphasized in every introductory economics class and should be familiar. Wheaton's method measures the *average cost* imposed by state–local taxes because it compares all business taxes to net income. In contrast, Papke's method reflects the influence of taxes on the *marginal cost* of investment, that is, how much taxes would increase as a result of new investment.

Business Taxes and Government Services

Of course, government taxes are used to provide public services, and many public services provide direct benefits to businesses, such as infrastructure, education services, and public safety services. If state differences in business taxes are offset by state differences in public services important to businesses, then some measure of net burden or benefit (taxes minus service benefits) might be a more appropriate measure of a state's fiscal policy toward business. In practice, such calculations are difficult and thus rare, because one must determine which services provide benefits to business and then assign a value to those benefits.

One attempt at comparing state taxes and service benefits was made by *Worth* magazine.[3] Although this comparison applies to all state taxes and services, not just those related to business, it suggests the degree to which results can change when taxes are not examined in isolation from the services they finance. For the *Worth* analysis, tax burden is measured by state and local taxes as a percentage of personal income. A state service or benefit index was calculated based on the state's value in 14 different public service/benefit categories, including such measures as the student-teacher ratio, average SAT/ACT scores, high school graduation rate, the arrest rate for violent crimes, the infant-mortality rate, and a measure of the quality of roads, among others. When the scores were combined, some interesting changes occurred in state rankings. Although Wisconsin had the fourth highest tax burden by the measure used, Wisconsin was rated the tenth best state

---

[3]Blyskal, Jeff, "The State of State Taxes," *Worth,* November 1994, 82–86.

overall fiscally when the service benefits in the state were added. From the opposite viewpoint, Georgia, which had a below average tax burden, ended up as third worst ranked state overall after the service benefits in the state were taken into consideration. High taxes in Wisconsin were offset by unusually strong services and benefits, while the low taxes in Georgia still seemed unreasonable given the relatively low services. Similarly, two states with equal tax burdens (Massachusetts and Nebraska) ended up with very different overall rankings (Nebraska as the third best state and Massachusetts as the ninth worst) because of differences in service levels and results.[4]

Obviously, one might think that the measures of service levels and benefits used in this study and the weights used in creating the benefit index are not the correct ones. As noted in Chapter 7, costs of producing government services can vary among states and a number of factors outside the control of governments can influence the results in public-service categories. But the main point remains; however public expenditures are measured and valued, as long as benefits are positive, the notion of taxes as net costs rather than prices can be misleading.

Effect of Federal Taxes on Interstate Tax Differences

The magnitude of nominal interstate tax differences shown by some measures greatly overstates the effective differences because state–local business taxes are a deductible expense for firms in computing their federal income tax liability. As a result of the deductibility of state–local taxes, part of any difference in state–local taxes in different locations is offset by higher federal taxes for firms in the lower state–local tax areas. This point is demonstrated in Table 22.2, which shows a

Table 22.2

Effect of the Federal Tax Deduction for State—Local Taxes on Interstate Tax Differences

Property Value, Taxes, and Profits for an Identical Firm in Two States

Fiscal Characteristic	State A	State B
Property value	$1,000,000	$1,000,000
Property tax rate	$50 per $1,000	$30 per $1,000
Property tax	50,000	30,000
Profit before property tax	200,000	200,000
Federal taxable income	150,000	170,000
Federal income tax (35% rate)	52,500	59,500
Net after-tax income	97,500	110,500
Difference in property tax	+$ 20,000	
Difference in federal tax		+$ 7,000
Difference in after-tax income		+$ 13,000

---

[4]The state with the highest tax burden, New York, also ended up with the lowest overall rating even after service benefits were included. But the lowest tax state, Tennessee, finished in the middle of the pack, rated 22nd overall.

comparison of the net income after local property taxes and federal income taxes for two identical firms located in different states. The firm in state A pays $50,000 in property taxes, which is then deducted from the $200,000 of operating profits to compute federal taxable income, resulting in a federal income tax liability of $52,500 (at a rate of 35 percent and ignoring exemptions and credits). The same firm in state B pays only $30,000 in property taxes but then has a federal tax liability of $59,500. The net effect is that although there is a $20,000 difference in property taxes, there is only a $13,000 difference in net after-tax income. Fully 35 percent of the property tax difference has been offset by the additional federal income tax deduction.

As part of the Tax Reform Act of 1986, the maximum federal corporate income tax rate was reduced from 46 percent to 34 percent, which had the effect of reducing the value of the federal deduction for state–local taxes and increasing the effective difference in state taxes. Steven Galante reported in *The Wall Street Journal* (1987) that as a result, more and more firms were focusing on their state income tax liability. Galante quoted Joseph J. Nugent, the regional director for state and local taxes in Coopers and Lybrand's Philadelphia office, as stating "A dollar in state taxes used to cost you 54 cents out of pocket. Now it's going to cost 66 cents."

Not only does federal tax deductibility of state–local business taxes reduce effective interstate tax differences, but it also works to negate some of the benefits of state or local tax incentives. In Table 22.2, if state A gave this firm a property tax abatement reducing taxes from $50,000 to $30,000, the firm's federal income tax would increase from $52,500 to $59,500. Thus, the state or local government would have given up $20,000 of property tax revenue, but the firm would only have gained $13,000 in net income; the remaining $7,000 goes to the federal government in the form of a larger federal tax payment. The magnitude of the effect of federal income tax deductibility of state–local business taxes depends directly on the federal marginal tax rate; the higher the rate, the more federal deductibility offsets interstate tax differences and reduces the value of state and local tax incentives.

Types of Fiscal Incentives

The fiscal incentives offered by state–local governments to offset real or perceived business cost differences—whether they arise from tax differences or other factors such as energy or transportation cost differences—are of three basic types: financial incentives, such as loans at below-market interest rates, direct grants, or loan guarantees; tax reductions through the use of credits, deductions, abatements, or specialized rates; and sometimes direct grants of goods or services, such as land, labor training, or infrastructure. Most states offer all these incentives in one way or another, developing a package of specific incentives from the general list for each potential investment project. Each of these general types of incentives is briefly described next, and a selected list of specific types of incentives is shown in Table 22.3.[5] The 2002 survey of state development agencies by the National

---

[5]For more detail on the specific incentives available in each state, see the *Directory of State Business Incentives,* National Association of State Development Agencies, 2002.

Table 22.3

State Economic Development Incentives, 2002

Type of Incentive	Number of States Offering	Number of Incentive Programs
Non-Tax Incentives	50	643
Loans	50	242
Grants	46	194
Bond issuance	44	75
Loan guarantees	22	36
Equity investments	20	26
Other	27	70
Tax Incentives	48	445
Tax credits	46	258
Tax exemptions	40	101
Tax abatement	18	32
Tax refunds	10	20
Other	21	34
Other Types	10	17
Enterprise Zones	40	3000

SOURCES: National Association of State Development Agencies. *Directory of State Business Development Incentives,* 2002; Alan Peters and Peter Fisher. *State Enterprise Zone Programs: Have They Worked?,* 2002.

Association of State Development Agencies reveals that all states provide some form of financing incentive spread among more than 640 different programs. Of these, loans by government to private firms are most common. Tax incentives are used by 48 states (not in Alaska and Wyoming), with various forms of tax credits most common.

Financing

Recall from Chapter 10 that nearly all state–local governments use their capability to sell tax-exempt revenue bonds to provide low-interest loans to private investors. State or local governments or their development agencies sell bonds at relatively low tax-exempt rates and provide those funds to private firms at either a slightly higher rate (although still less than the firm would pay if it borrowed in the private market on its own) or in exchange for some service fee. Although the capability of state–local governments to issue these "private-purpose revenue bonds" was reduced by the Tax Reform Act of 1986, it was not eliminated, at least for many purposes. In 2002, all states had programs to make direct loans to businesses, and 44 states had programs to issue bonds on behalf of firms.

Another form of subnational government financial assistance to investors takes advantage of the fact that most states and localities have major pension funds to finance retirement benefits for government employees. In some cases, both employees and the employer governments contribute toward future retirement benefits; in other cases, the funds are established entirely by employer contributions. Some state retirement funds are managed by the states themselves; others are managed by private financial investment firms hired by the states. In either case, the pension fund monies are invested in bonds (both government and corporate), stocks, bank certificates of deposit, money market funds, and other investments; the idea being to earn a reasonable return on the funds so that the planned retirement benefits can be paid without incurring inordinate risk of loss of the funds. A number of states have now specified that a certain percentage of the pension fund money may be used to finance new businesses in that state or locality. The pension fund either loans the money to the potential investor in the state or exchanges it for an equity position in the firm. At least in those states with relatively large pension funds, the idea is to increase the available money for new investment in that state. In 2002, 20 states had programs through which the state or some public entity could take an equity position in private firms.

Government loans to or investment in a new business venture is attractive to the firm if the loan is at a low interest rate or if the government will accept a lower return on investment than in the private market or if private loans or investment are simply not available to this firm. In the last instance, a firm may have difficulty getting private financing because the management has little experience, insufficient collateral, or the product is so new that it has no track record. In essence, the venture is judged too risky by private investors. As a result, 22 states provide loan guarantees to private firms, essentially reducing the risk of the loan and permitting the firm lower interest costs. For all these types of financing assistance, however, there is a real cost to the government, either in the form of foregone income (a lower return than available elsewhere) or additional risk.

Tax Incentives

Tax incentives are offered to at least certain types of businesses in 48 states. The most common form of tax incentive is a tax credit of some form, used by 46 states. Tax credits often are used for personal or corporate income taxes as well as property taxes and apply to capital investment, increases in employment, or research and development expenses. Tax exemptions often apply to sales taxes or to local property taxes. Tax abatement usually refers to property tax reductions for firms building new facilities or rehabilitating existing ones. Commonly, the approach is a reduction in property taxes of some specified percentage for a certain number of years. Decision about granting tax incentives and the ultimate financing of their cost may be the responsibility of state government, local governments, or both.

A traditional criticism of tax incentives is that most, such as property tax abatements and corporate income tax credits, serve to reduce capital costs (or equivalently, increase the return to capital owners). Consequently, the tax reductions are relatively more valuable for capital-intensive firms and provide an incentive for all firms to increase the amount of capital used in production compared to other inputs, particularly labor. This potential problem is a particular concern if one of the main objectives of the incentives is to increase employment in the state or locality. As a consequence of this concern, some states have turned to offering tax credits tied to employment increases by firms. Obviously, these credits reduce labor costs relatively in an attempt to encourage larger increases in employment than would otherwise occur. For instance, Faulk (2002) analyzed the corporate income tax credit available to firms in Georgia for creation of new full-time jobs. Firms may receive tax credits of between $500 and $2,500 per job depending on location and the number of jobs created. Faulk reports that about one-quarter of the increased employment by firms participating in the credit program could be attributed to the tax credits.

One possible fiscal incentive, of course, is a reduction in the overall level of business taxes in a state for all businesses, for instance, by the substitution of a personal tax (on consumption or income) for those collected from businesses. More commonly, however, states offer *targeted tax incentives*, which are available only for specific types of firms or firms in specific circumstances. The idea is that general business tax reductions provide benefits to some firms that have no intention of either expanding or relocating their business; thus, some of the tax reduction is considered wasted as an economic development device. Understand, however, that targeting tax incentives requires government and the political process to make decisions about what firms are to receive the incentives. Because officials never have complete information about investment options, those governmental decisions may also entail "waste" or error of two types. Government officials may decide to grant tax reductions to firms that would invest in the state or locality anyway, and tax reductions may be denied to firms when the incentive would have influenced the investment location decision. It is not clear, therefore, that targeted tax incentives are any different or any more efficient than general business tax reductions.

Direct Grants

States and localities also may provide direct grants of goods or services to firms specific to a firm's production requirements. Governments have long used their eminent-domain power to assemble tracts of land for public projects, such as roads; however, in recent years, governments have also done so to provide large blocks of land for commercial or industrial development. In some of these urban renewal projects, the government acquires the land and then gives it or sells it to the private investor at a below-market price (see Application 22.3 later in this chapter). State and local governments sometimes build public infrastructure—such as roads, water and sewer systems, or public facilities—that will assist a private development. State or local governments also may provide or finance specific training for the new employees of a business willing to invest, expand, or remain in the state or area. Because of a number of studies suggesting that many new small businesses lack managerial or financial experience, some states and localities have started *incubators*, which are facilities that house new businesses and provide technical or management assistance for all the firms. The idea is that after the firms are established and the operators gain experience, they have greater likelihood of success on their own.

Incentives for Existing Businesses

Bartik (1991, 1994) has reported on a number of new incentives, what he calls "new wave policies," which are intended to encourage innovation and expansion by existing businesses. Such policies include Small Business Development Centers (now more than 500) that provide management and financial advice to small business owners and operators, export assistance programs and financing to encourage firms to enter and be successful in foreign markets, and university/business interaction involving targeted university research or technology transfer programs from universities or industrial extension services providing management, marketing, or financial advice and assistance. These new policies are intended to help existing firms become more competitive and successful rather than attempting to attract new investment or jobs from other actual or potential locations.

Clawbacks

A number of states have begun attaching conditions to fiscal incentives, essentially requiring firms that receive incentives to repay the government if the business fails to achieve targeted economic growth projections or promises. For instance, a business might receive a five-year tax reduction in exchange for new investment that promises to generate 1,000 new jobs over those years. If those jobs do not materialize, then the business might have to pay the amount of reduced taxes. Although such provisions are attempts by governments to avoid using public funds to support unsuccessful business ventures, implementation and enforcement is difficult. Many clawback provisions include escape clauses that relieve the business of liability if the problems are due to market forces outside of the business's control. And if a firm ends up having serious financial problems, it may be counterproductive or even impossible to collect repayment for past public incentives.

Application 22.1

ENTERPRISE ZONES (EZs)[6]

As part of the targeting of fiscal incentives, many states also have identified specific areas within states where the incentives are to be used particularly intensively. Since 1982, some 40 states and the District of Columbia created about 3,000 *enterprise zones (EZs)*, areas where special tax, service, or regulatory incentives are available or where greater incentives are available than elsewhere in the state. In 1993, the federal government entered the fray, partnering with states in creating a small number of *empowerment zones*. The 11 federal zones, each no more than 20 square miles, are eligible for a substantial amount of focused federal economic development and financial assistance. Most EZs are small, about 2 square miles and 4,500 persons at the median, and areas generally have population and economic characteristics suggesting distress—population loss,

---

[6]This application draws heavily from the following: Papke, Leslie. "What Do We Know About Enterprise Zones?" In J. Poterba, editor, *Tax Policy and the Economy.* Cambridge: MIT Press, 1993, 37–72; Peters, Alan H. and Peter S. Fisher. *State Enterprise Zone Programs: Have They Worked?* Kalamazoo, MI: W.E. Upjohn Institute for Employment Research, 2002.

Application 22.1 — Enterprise Zones (EZs)

high unemployment, low incomes (60 percent of the national average for the median zone), or high poverty rates. Thus, EZs are an attempt to increase economic activity in a state and to influence the location of that activity toward economically depressed areas.

Different states offer a variety of incentives in zones. Tax reductions are most common; for instance, up to full property tax abatement in Ohio, elimination of property taxes on inventories in Indiana, a reduced state sales tax rate from 6 to 3 percent in New Jersey, and personal income tax deductions for zone residents in Indiana. In many states, employers can receive a direct subsidy or tax credit equal to a percentage of wages for new employees who are zone residents. Other common incentives include subsidies for loans to or investments in zone businesses, special job training, reductions in utility prices, and relaxation of environmental or safety regulations. As this list makes clear, some of the incentives are focused particularly on reducing labor costs for firms in the zones (such as employment tax credits), whereas others primarily reduce capital costs (such as property tax abatements).

Evaluating the success of EZs is difficult for several reasons. First, the intent of the states establishing the zones is not always clear. Second, determining carefully the magnitude or importance of the tax incentives offered in zones is sometimes difficult; that is, the magnitude of cost reductions is sometimes unclear. Third, economic changes within zones often are accompanied by changes in the areas surrounding zones, and relating or separating the two often is difficult. Therefore, there may be new investment or employment in zones, but some of that

investment might have occurred anyway and some might have moved or otherwise would have been located in other areas of the state or even the same metropolitan area. There may be an increase in employment in the zones, but only a fraction of that employment might go to zone residents. And the new employment may offer only relatively low wages. All these potential difficulties with EZs have been experienced in practice.

The United Kingdom had created 24 EZs by 1983 in small areas with vacant or deteriorating industrial land (but existing businesses were excluded). Although ten-year tax incentives were offered, the great bulk of new businesses operating in the zones relocated from nearby areas, thus creating no *new* economic activity. In the United States, a 1989 survey of state EZs found that 55 percent of new investment was expansion of existing firms, many of which were retail or service firms largely serving the zone. About 17 percent of new investment was relocated from outside the zone or was a new branch of a nonzone business. Only about 26 percent of zone investment represented new businesses.

Alan Peters and Peter Fisher (2002) examined the average effects of 75 EZs located in 13 states from 1989 to 1995. Using a model of a hypothetical firm to compute the expected cost reduction from the incentives offered in the zones, they estimate that about 10 percent of the increase in employment in the zones was "induced" by the economic development incentives. In contrast, they believe that 90 percent of the job growth would have occurred anyway. As a consequence of these estimates, they argue that EZs have a net

Application 22.1 — Enterprise Zones (EZs)

negative reduction on state revenue. The gain in revenue from the induced jobs in not sufficient to offset the revenue incentives for jobs that they believe would have arisen anyway.

Even if the EZs cost states revenue in aggregate, they may still be valuable tools if the increase in employment in the economically depressed zones areas is particularly important. One important rationale that has been offered in support of zones is the idea that the location of jobs in a metropolitan area may be inaccessible to many unemployed and disadvantaged workers—called the *spatial mismatch hypothesis*. One idea behind EZs then, is to move jobs to the area where the unemployed, disadvantaged population resides. Peters and Fisher suggest, however, that in light of their estimated revenue results from EZs, it might be more cost effective for government to create incentives to move the workers to the jobs rather than the opposite.

Perhaps the most studied EZ program in the United States is that in Indiana.[7] Since 1984, 23 zones have been created offering a range of incentives, including elimination of the business property tax on inventories, a business credit equal to 10 percent of wages paid to zone residents, a tax credit for interest on loans to zone businesses and residents, and a personal income tax deduction for zone residents. Zones in Indiana are small, have high unemployment (1.5 times the state average), and substantial poverty (a poverty rate one-quarter greater then the US average). Surveys of the zones show that a number of new jobs have been established, with about 15 to 20 percent of new jobs in the zones going to zone residents. About one-third of zone businesses are retailers, 30 percent provide business or professional services, and about 19 percent are in manufacturing, although the manufacturers received the bulk of the tax savings.

Although relative unemployment fell in Indiana EZs, relative income per person and population also declined, suggesting that many of the jobs offered low wages. Most significantly, Papke (2000) finds substantial changes in the nature of capital investment in the zones. Inventories held in the EZs increased substantially in both the short and long runs, which is not surprising because the largest tax incentive provided was exemption from the property tax on inventories. On the other hand, the value of manufacturing machinery and equipment of firms in the zones declined both short term and long term. Finally, Papke (2000, p. 87) finds "... there is no strong effect of zone designation on the value of real estate." At the most, real estate values may have increased by a very modest amount. In essence then, the Indiana EZs induced firms to expand their holding of inventories in the zones but reduce the amount of productive machinery and equipment. Papke notes that the future of the Indiana EZs is unclear because the state began in 2000 a ten-year phase out of the property tax on inventories, which will make the major incentive provided in the zones irrelevant.

---

[7]For the latest information about the Indiana experience, see Papke, Leslie. "The Indiana Enterprise Zone Revisited: Effects on Capital Investment and Land Values." *Proceedings of the Ninety-Third Annual Conference on Taxation.* Washington, D.C.: National Tax Association, 2000.

EFFECTS OF FISCAL FACTORS: THEORY

Intergovernmental Interaction

One fundamental fact about fiscal incentives is that they are offered by most states and at least most of the larger counties and municipalities. If fiscal incentives are available in most locations, however, they do not affect the *relative* cost for businesses in those different locations. Rather, the cost *differences* among locations that existed without incentives are preserved, although the level of business tax and financing costs is decreased at all locations. The fact that similar fiscal incentives for business come to be offered by nearly all states seems a natural result of interstate competition. The number of states is large enough that collusion among states not to offer fiscal incentives is difficult, but not so large that states are unaware of the nature and magnitude of incentives offered by competitors. The result seems to be equivalent to an oligopolistic market in which a competitor's offers of lower prices (fiscal incentives) are always matched.

A simplified version of the process as it seems to have worked is shown in Figure 22.4. Beginning in Figure 22.4a, state A offers some set of business incentives

Figure 22.4

State interaction in offering investment incentives (the diagram is arranged in a cyclical, clockwise format).

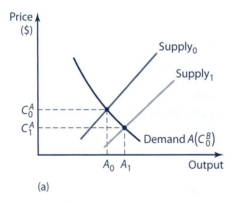

(a)

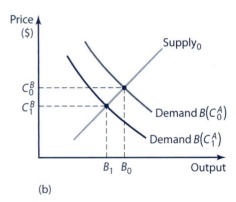

(b)

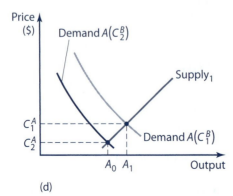

(d)

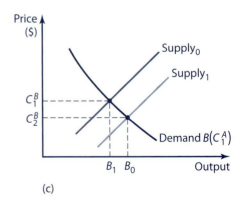

(c)

that lowers business costs in the state, shown by a downward shift in the supply curve (recall that supply represents marginal costs). If the incentives are successful and capital is mobile, production costs in A decrease, and output in the state increases. The effect of the lower costs and prices of production in state A is to lessen the demand for production in state B, causing a corresponding decrease in output there. In essence, if state A's incentives are successful, they move economic activity from the competitor state B to state A.

But state B is expected to either respond to the effect of the incentives offered by state A or to see the same opportunity in incentives as state A did. The result, shown in Figure 22.4c, is that state B also offers fiscal incentives that reduce business costs in that state. Thus, the supply curve in B is shifted downward and production rises. In Figure 22.4c, the incentives offered by B exactly offset those offered by A, so that output in B returns to the level that existed before the incentives were offered. In addition, the cost reduction caused by B's fiscal incentives reduces the relative attractiveness of production in state A, causing output in A to also return to its original level. Before the process began, costs in B were higher than in A (C_0^B is greater than C_0^A); after the incentives are offered, costs in B are still higher than in A (C_2^B is greater than C_2^A). Neither state has gained a *relative advantage*, although business costs have been lowered in both states. Both states were forced to adopt incentives to avoid losing economic activity to the other, however.

It might be incorrect to conclude, however, that nothing has changed in the world depicted by Figure 22.4. If these governments are providing the same amount of government services after the incentives as before, the tax burden has been redistributed; direct business taxes account for a smaller share of total taxes than previously. That redistribution of tax burden could alter economic decisions in the overall society. Suppose, for instance, that the tax burden on capital ownership has been reduced, and that the tax burden on consumption has increased. The expected result is a modest increase in saving and thus a larger capital stock in the future than would have been the case without the tax redistribution. In that case, the subnational government fiscal incentives, which resulted from interstate tax competition, would have been equivalent to a federal reduction in capital taxes, such as a reduction in the federal corporate income tax. Although each state acted to improve its competitive position compared to the other states, the result is maintenance of relative costs but a reduction in national business costs. The combined reactions of all the states and localities effectively comprise a national policy of providing business incentives.

Role of Consumer and Factor Mobility

If individual states or localities are successful in using fiscal incentives to reduce the *relative cost* of investment or business in those locations, the ultimate economic effects and beneficiaries of the incentives depend mostly on the mobility of consumers and factor suppliers.

The mobility case most often considered by economists, at least theoretically, is that suppliers of capital (investors) are fully mobile among different locations, whereas suppliers of other factors, especially labor, and consumers do not move among locations in response to economic differences. In this special case, the expected effects of fiscal incentives that lower investment or capital costs in one location compared to others are straightforward. The incentive increases the rate of return to investment in that location and thus attracts more capital. Because the increased supply of capital investment at that location reduces the rate of return, the capital inflow continues until the rate of return is reduced to that available at those other locations without any incentives. The obvious result of the incentive is an increased amount of investment in the jurisdiction offering the incentive and a decrease in the quantity of investment at the other locations. The increased amount of investment in the jurisdiction is expected to increase the demand for other factors of production such as labor, which increases the wage in that jurisdiction. If *workers are not mobile*, then those wage differences persist. If *workers are mobile*, then the higher wages in the jurisdiction attract new workers from other locations until wages are equalized. Because of the increased investment and production in the jurisdiction with the incentive, the prices of local consumer goods are expected to decrease. If *consumers are not mobile*, then local consumers benefit from these lower prices.

Suppose, for instance, that one locality provides a property tax reduction that is not matched by surrounding communities for new commercial investment. The new lower taxes on new commercial buildings make it more attractive than previously to build in that locality, so an increase in the supply of apartment buildings, retail store space, and office buildings is expected. The increase in commercial building has two subsequent effects. First, there is more demand for workers, which results in an increase in wages if more workers do not appear (labor is immobile). Second, the increase in commercial building is expected to reduce commercial rents if more consumers of commercial space do not appear (consumers are immobile). So if apartments and office buildings rented for equal amounts in all the communities before the tax abatement, rents are now lower in the community with the abatement.

This story shows why assuming workers and consumers are immobile is implausible, at least for regions within states or for metropolitan areas. If apartment and office building rents are reduced in one location because of new construction or conversion from other uses, one certainly expects that some individual renters of housing or businesses that lease office space will move to the locality offering lower rents; that is, consumers are mobile. But as consumers move to take advantage of the lower rents, the demand for the apartments and office space increases, driving rents up. The movement of consumers is expected to continue until rents are again equal in all locations.

If consumers move to take advantage of the lower rents, what does that do to the profit position of the investors? If investors or owners of the buildings charge the same rent at all locations, then those in the higher-tax areas (those without abatements) must be earning lower rates of return than those in the lower-tax areas (those with the abatement). That difference in profitability should start another round of capital movement, again toward the jurisdiction with the tax incentive. That increases the supply of capital and reduces rents, which should then start another round of consumer moves.

What force exists that might stop this process before all the investment and economic activity is in one locality? Land is the one factor of production that is generally very immobile. The increase in the amount of investment in the jurisdiction with the tax incentive and any subsequent increase in demand for space by mobile consumers both serve to increase the demand for the available land in the jurisdiction, thus increasing the price of that land. Eventually, land becomes so expensive that additional investment and location in the locality is unattractive, even with the tax abatement.

Who benefits, then, from this process that was instituted by granting tax abatements in one locality? Clearly, those who own land in the jurisdiction at the time the tax abatement is granted (regardless of where they live) benefit from the increase in the value of their land. Whether consumers of local goods in that jurisdiction, such as individual tenants in rental housing and commercial tenants in office buildings, benefit depends on the mobility of those consumers. If new tenants move into the jurisdiction, then rents are not lowered by the abatement. (Similarly, if tenants move out of the jurisdictions without the abatement, then those that remain are not hurt by the relatively higher taxes that exist in those locations.) Aside from the benefits to landowners, whether benefits go to property owners or property consumers depends on which group is relatively more mobile.

This story of the **capitalization of the fiscal incentive** should be familiar to you because it is the same one discussed in Chapter 14 concerning property tax incidence. It doesn't matter what the source of the higher cost is in some localities— higher property tax rates, lack of a tax-abatement program, an absence of a subsidized interest rate for borrowing, or higher costs for worker training—the process of reaction and adjustment to those cost differences is the same. But remember two warnings about this analysis. First, the process starts only if some jurisdictions obtain a cost advantage over others and if investors respond to that advantage, which might not happen if all communities offer equivalent incentives or if the incentives generate only relatively small cost differences. Second, how smoothly the process actually proceeds compared to the theory depends on many other factors, including moving costs, perceptions of market conditions for buyers of a firm's product, the public services available at different locations, the accuracy and cost of information about cost and market differences at various locations, the personal preferences of business owners and managers, and perhaps even inertia. The degree to which investors, workers, and consumers actually respond to regional or interstate fiscal differences is uncertain and can be resolved only by looking at some evidence.

Before we turn to that review of the evidence about fiscal differences and incentives, it may be helpful to review the theoretical possibilities again by referring to Figures 22.5 through 22.7. The effect of a capital subsidy, either from a tax abatement or a tax-exempt revenue bond, is shown in Figure 22.5. If the rate of return available in the economy is r_0, the subsidy increases the return available in this jurisdiction to r_1. The higher rate of return available in this jurisdiction attracts more investment, so the amount of capital increases from K_0 to K_1 until the rate of return in the jurisdiction returns to the average level of r_0. (This is equivalent to the analysis of a property tax decrease by one locality discussed in Chapter 14.)

Figure 22.5

Effect of a capital
investment
subsidy

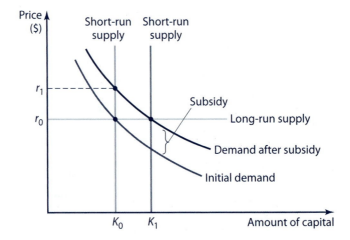

Figure 22.6

Effect of an
increase in
investment in
markets for
other inputs

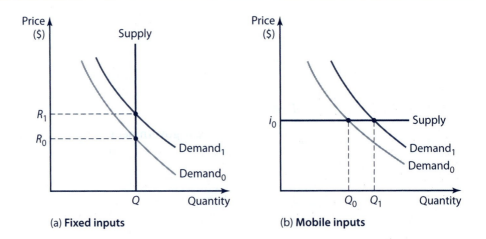

(a) **Fixed inputs**   (b) **Mobile inputs**

The expected effect of the capital subsidy on the markets for other inputs is shown in Figure 22.6. The increased investment is expected to increase the demand for other inputs, which increases the price of other inputs that are not mobile—that is, those with a fixed quantity in the jurisdiction—and increases the quantity of those other inputs that are mobile. For instance, if labor is mobile, then an increase in employment is expected to accompany the increase in investment, whereas because land is not mobile, the rents on land are expected to increase because of the new investment.

If the net effect of the capital subsidy and related input market changes is a reduction in production costs, as intended, then the effects on the prices and quantities of outputs are shown in Figure 22.7. For nationally traded goods—those sold

Figure 22.7

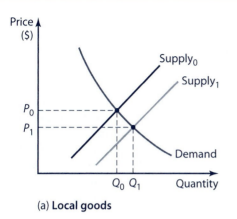

(a) **Local goods**

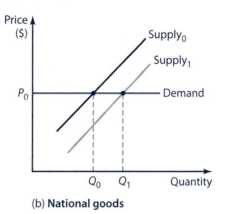

(b) **National goods**

Effect of an investment subsidy on prices of consumer goods

outside the local jurisdiction with a price determined in a broader market—the cost decrease causes an increase in production in the jurisdiction but no decrease in price. For local goods, those whose price is determined entirely in the jurisdiction, the cost decrease is expected to induce both an increase in production and a decrease in the price of these local goods.

EFFECTS OF FISCAL FACTORS: EVIDENCE

Investment Among Regions

The evidence concerning the effect of state–local government fiscal policies on investment among states or regions is mixed, with the one consistent conclusion perhaps being that there is no general result—fiscal policies have very different effects for industries with different characteristics. Most of the research on this issue has been focused on manufacturing industries, and it has been carried out by relating variation in the number of firms or amount of employment or changes in those measures across states to variations in market, cost, and fiscal factors among the states. Most of the earlier studies of these issues, such as those by John Due (1961), Dennis Carlton (1979), and Roger Schmenner (1982), found that differences in wages, energy costs, labor skills, and the amount of manufacturing already carried out in a state influenced firms' decisions to locate or expand in a state, but the level of state and local taxes did not have much influence. The amount of a specific economic activity already being carried out represents **agglomeration economies**, cost advantages that arise when firms producing the same thing are located near each other. For instance, it may be possible to have inputs delivered at lower cost if the supplier can deliver to several firms in one trip.

Other more recent studies have found that subnational government taxes do influence business decisions among states or regions. Summarizing 99 studies carried out between 1979 and 1991, Bartik (1991, 43) argues that "The long-run elasticity of business activity with respect to state and local taxes appears to lie in the range of -0.1 to -0.6 for intermetropolitan or interstate business location decisions. . . ." This suggests that a 10-percent reduction in state business taxes, accompanied by no change in state services and no changes in other states' taxes or services, could lead to a 1 to 6 percent increase in investment, in the number of firms, or in employment, depending on how business activity is measured. Still, the results of these studies are not unequivocal. About 75 percent of the studies find a statistically significant negative effect of taxes on economic activity, but then 25 percent find no effect or even a positive one. And the range of measured elasticities is quite large. Still, it seems a reasonable conclusion from this research that taxes can exert a small effect on business decisions and activity (with an expected elasticity of about -0.3), but that the effect will be substantially smaller or larger in different cases.

Incorporating studies since Bartik's review, Michael Wasylenko (1997) finds less of an effect of interregional taxes on business activity than reported by Bartik, concluding "Taxes do not seem to have a substantial effect on economic activity among states" (p. 47). Wasylenko's review of the literature shows "For the total tax responsiveness of economic activity . . . the median values of the estimates [of elasticities] range from -0.58 to -0.02, with most of the medians clustering around -0.1. Of the 34 studies examining business tax elasticities . . . the median values of these elasticity estimates cluster between 0.0 and -0.26, indicating not much responsiveness of economic activity among regions to business taxes" (p. 45). One reason for such findings, Wasylenko suggests, is when states adopt tax structures that are similar to each other. If tax systems are similar among competing states, then taxes cannot be important in affecting business location decisions. However, if a state's taxes deviate substantially from those in competitor states, then taxes may affect economic activity in those states.

Substantial evidence also supports the idea that state–local government spending, particularly on education, worker training, or infrastructure, may attract new investment to a state. Among 30 studies reviewed by Bartik, 60 percent find statistically significant positive effects on business activity from measures of state–local public services. A subsequent review by Fisher (1997, p. 54) concludes that ". . . *some* public services clearly have a positive effect on some measures of economic development in *some* cases." The most substantial evidence of an effect on economic activity exists for transportation facilities and public-safety services, with much greater variability in the research results concerning education services. For instance, Bartik (1989) finds that increased spending for local education and fire protection is positively related to subsequent economic growth; Garcia-Mila and McGuire (1992) find that highway miles per square mile of state area has a positive effect on growth of GSP; Tannenwald (1996) finds that increases in per-capita spending on public safety increases business capital investment among states; and Munnell (1990) reports that increased public capital raises the growth rate of private employment.

These results suggest that it is entirely possible for simultaneous increases in state–local taxes and particular public services to lead to increased business investment, employment, or output. For instance, Luce (1994) suggests that increased local taxes to fund additional public-safety or public-works spending would increase employment among manufacturing, service, and wholesale trade industries, but not for all industries (especially finance and retail trade). On the other hand, a number of studies find a negative effect of higher welfare spending on business growth. This second result is serious, because it implies that if a state with a substantial poor population attempts to help that group with welfare programs, it creates a disincentive to the economic growth that might cure the poverty problem in the long run.

Examples from specific studies show how sensitive the results can be to different conditions. Michael Wasylenko and Therese McGuire (1985) examined the percentage change in employment in states from 1973 to 1980 for six industries—manufacturing, wholesale trade, retail trade, utilities, finance, and services. They report that the wage level, electricity prices, and the educational attainment of workers generally affected investment in these industries. Among fiscal factors, the overall level of state–local taxes seemed to influence employment growth negatively for manufacturing, retail trade, and services (although the level of any particular tax had no effect), whereas the level of state–local spending on education seemed to affect employment growth positively for the retail trade and financial industries. These results certainly suggest that the magnitude of the effect of fiscal policies on investment will vary by industry, although it is not clear why the level of state–local taxes would influence retail and service investment, industries that are generally dependent on local markets, but not investment in wholesale trade and finance, where more flexibility in locations is expected.

Leslie Papke (1987) examined the relationship between the after-tax rate-of-return on new investment in a state and the amount of new capital expenditure per worker in the state for a number of different industries in 1978. The effect of state–local taxes is to reduce the rate of return available in a state. She reported that a "significant part of the geographic pattern in investment across industries and states can be accounted for by differences in net profit rates," that is, returns net of state–local and federal taxes. On average, a 1-percent variation in after-tax rate-of-return is expected to cause about a 2-percent difference in new investment per worker. The sensitivity of new investment to the net return varies greatly by industry, with manufacturing of drugs (elasticity of .75) and blast furnaces (elasticity of 1.08) being relatively insensitive and manufacturing of furniture (elasticity of 3.91) and apparel (elasticity of 4.1) being very sensitive.

Because higher state–local taxes are expected to reduce net profits, Papke's results suggest that higher state–local taxes are expected to reduce new investment also. But Papke cautions that large changes in state–local tax rates are required to bring about even modest changes in rates of return. For instance, her computations suggest that a 1-percent reduction in the rate of return would require an increase in a state corporate income tax rate from 7 to 15 percent or an increase in effective property tax rates from .7 percent to 5.0 percent (assuming a 7-percent corporate income tax rate). And even those large state tax-rate differences would reduce new investment per worker by only about 2 percent in the higher-tax state, on average.

It appears, therefore, that interstate tax differences may influence new investment decisions for branch plants or expansions in some industries. For other industries, interstate tax differences are just too small to have any substantial effect on net profitability in different states, or tax differences are simply not as important as differences in other cost or market factors. Spending on public services and facilities important to business also can influence investment decisions, this time positively, at least for some types of industries in some locations. Other than the direct fiscal policies of state–local governments, relatively consistent evidence supports that labor costs and skills, energy costs, and advantages brought about by a concentration of manufacturing in a location all are important factors in influencing interstate manufacturing investment decisions.

Investment within Regions

Studies of business investment decisions within states or metropolitan areas are more consistent in finding that local fiscal policies, and especially property taxes, influence the location of new investment. As stated by Michael Wasylenko (1986) in a review of the evidence concerning intraurban location of business, "Tax differentials probably have significant effects on the location of firms and differences in intraregional employment growth" (p. 227). Moreover, Bartik (1991) reports that tax differences have substantially larger effects on economic growth within areas than among them. He suggests that the elasticity of intrametropolitan area business location with respect to taxes ranges from -1.0 to -3.0, so that a 10-percent tax difference could translate into a 10 to 30 percent change in economic activity. Wasylenko (1997) notes that the smaller the area in which a business is choosing a location, the more similar nontax factors (such as labor costs) should be, and thus a greater effect from taxes is expected. He concludes (p.47) "The tax elasticities within a region appear to be at least four times the interregional elasticities." John Anderson and Robert Wassmer (2000) agree that local taxes and local economic development incentives often influence, sometimes substantially, the intrametropolitan location of business activity; however, they also note that those local government tax incentives may operate by lowering costs and stimulating development in the metropolitan area without affecting the specific jurisdiction in the area chosen for location.

The other (nontax) factors that are consistently found to affect business location decisions within metropolitan areas, at least for manufacturing firms, are the availability of labor with suitable skills, the availability of sufficient quantities of (usually vacant) land, the quality of the transportation network for transporting both goods and workers, and agglomeration economies.

Analyzing the effect of local tax differentials on business investment decisions is complicated by the fact that some communities in almost every metropolitan area choose to effectively zone out some types of industry. Those communities may find any noise, congestion, or environmental pollution, which accompanies industrial development, to be particularly undesirable and thus respond by not supplying many or any industrial development sites. Other communities may allow industrial development but not encourage it by offering tax or other incentives. If communities that effectively preclude development are included with those seeking development in studies of the effect of tax differentials, biased results are expected. If the communities that exclude industrial development by zoning have high tax rates, for instance, statistical studies might attribute the lack of investment to the tax rates, even though the actual cause is the community's unwillingness to allow development.

To correct for this problem, studies of business investment within an area must consider the supply of land by a community for industrial development in addition to the demand for locations or land for development by business firms. This adjustment may be accomplished either by excluding those communities that do not allow development from the studies or by explicitly modeling a community's decision about the amount of development to allow. When either of these adjustments are made in studies of intraurban location decisions, local tax differences are consistently found to be even more important factors in influencing business investment decisions within areas.

For instance, Robert Wassmer (1990, 1992) reports estimates of the effects of property tax abatements offered by localities in the Detroit metropolitan area, taking account of different choices by communities about offering abatements. Communities with higher property taxes and more crime tend to offer more or larger tax abatements to offset these characteristics that otherwise might reduce potential profits for the businesses. After the choice of abatements is allowed for, Wassmer estimates that additional property tax abatements in those cases attract sufficient investment to increase the local tax base and local property tax revenue.

Besides any direct effects of local business taxes on business location, local taxes may have indirect effects by affecting population and local labor markets. A number of studies, starting with that by Wallace Oates (1969) and followed by many others, have found a negative relationship between local property tax rates and residential housing values and a positive relationship between local government services (especially education) and housing values. These studies have been interpreted as confirming at least the process envisioned by Tiebout where individuals move among communities based on fiscal packages. Put another way, the results of these studies are consistent with an outflow of population and thus a decrease in demand for housing in relatively high-tax communities. The results of local business location studies show that firms are attracted to communities where labor is readily available. Relatively high property or personal income taxes may therefore reduce the available supply of labor in a region or raise the wage that employers must pay for a given quantity or quality of workers. In either case, the local personal taxes may indirectly influence business location decisions in that manner.

The results of the studies about housing values suggest that consumers move among communities within a region in response to price differences caused by tax differences. Consumers of capital, such as renters, homeowners, and commercial tenants, were also found to be mobile in research by William Wheaton (1984), who examined the relationship between rental rates for space in commercial buildings in the Boston metropolitan area in 1980 and community effective property tax rates; John McDonald (1993) examined the same issue using 1991 data from Chicago.

Wheaton reported that differences in tax rates had no effect on the relative level of commercial rents in the Boston-area communities. In other words, it appears that if landlords attempted to charge higher rents for commercial space in communities with higher taxes, tenants were willing to move to lower-tax, and thus lower-rent, communities. Although Wheaton's research showed that tax-rate differences did not affect rents, differences in building characteristics (age, size, whether located in a complex) and community characteristics (public transit, highways, labor skills) did affect commercial rents in the ways expected.

McDonald reported that only about 45 percent of property tax differences among downtown Chicago commercial office buildings were shifted forward to tenants in the form of higher rents. Again, landlords could not charge sufficiently higher rents to offset property tax differences. If rents are the same for similar buildings in high- and low property tax communities or if rent differences are smaller than tax differences, then the tax difference is being born at least partly by owners—landlords earn lower rates of return in higher-tax communities. For that to occur, commercial office space consumers must be more willing to move within the region than owners of capital are willing to relocate their investments.

POLICY ISSUES

Even if fiscal incentives are effective in attracting new investment to a state or locality, several other issues should be considered to fully evaluate incentives. First, the use of targeted fiscal incentives rather than general business-tax decreases means that some businesses in a jurisdiction will be taxed at lower effective rates than others. If the incentives are applied on a case-by-case basis, likely even otherwise similar businesses—for instance, similar size firms in the same business area—will pay different taxes if one is granted an incentive to avoid a threatened move or to retain an expansion. Although it is a fundamental principle of optimal tax theory that taxpayers who respond to taxes differently should be taxed at different rates, differential taxation of similar businesses creates difficult equity and political concerns.

Second, granting tax reductions to some or even all businesses may create an external cost to other taxpayers. If those businesses consume government-provided goods or services that are not pure public goods—that is, that require additional cost to provide—then the tax structure is moved further away from a benefit tax. Essentially, other taxpayers must bear the marginal costs of services that exclusively benefit the firm's owners. This means that the tax costs imposed on the other taxpayers—individuals only or individuals and some businesses—must be greater than the marginal benefits received by those taxpayers. The external cost therefore leads to inefficient decisions about the amount and mix of government services to provide.

Third, some states and localities elect to offer fiscal incentives because other competing jurisdictions are doing so. By acting to counteract others' fiscal incentives, a state or locality intends to maintain relative business costs at the level before any incentives were granted. As previously discussed, this intergovernmental competition leads to a lowering of overall business costs but does not create any incentive for the pattern of investment among the jurisdictions to change. (Businesses may invest more because of the lower taxes but not change the location of the investment because no relative change in taxes occurs among jurisdictions.) One option for states and localities to consider in this case is collusion—mutual agreements not to offer certain types of incentives to certain types of businesses. Such collusion could improve economic efficiency if it prevents the kind of external cost effects noted previously without altering the relative costs of business in different jurisdictions. Of course, as with all attempts at collusion when there are more than just a few players, enforcing the agreements is nearly impossible. And given some recent antitrust decisions concerning the market power and actions of subnational governments, such agreements might be found to be illegal.

Finally, even if incentives increase business investment, employment, or land prices, it is not clear that overall welfare is improved because these incentives involve costs. For instance, if an incentive-induced increase in investment raises land prices, a transfer has occurred from the taxpayers who financed the incentive to landowners, but everyone is not likely to be better off. What if the incentives increase the demand for labor? An increase in wages is likely in the short run, and a permanent increase in employment is likely in the long run, as supply adjusts. If there was local unemployment initially and workers are not perfectly mobile (perhaps due to moving costs), then the increase in employment *can* represent an increase in overall economic welfare, but not in all cases. Evidence suggests that in many cases only a fraction of the increased employment goes to local residents who previously were unemployed; some goes to new workers who move to the area. An increase in employment of local residents entails the loss of whatever other activity occupied their time. And the new jobs to local residents may not go to the low-income, low-skilled workers who might have been the target of the policy. Finally, an increase in business investment may bring an increase in congestion, a worsening of air pollution, and new challenges to public safety.

For all these reasons (and others), Paul Courant (1994) argues emphatically that what is needed is solid benefit-cost analysis of economic development policies, including the distributional effects of those policies. What matters, Courant argues, is not whether tax incentives or greater public spending increase business investment or employment, but rather whether those fiscal changes make the residents of a jurisdiction better off.

What is the likely long-run effect on overall state fiscal policy of the continuing interstate competition for economic activity? Some have suggested that the increased magnitude of interstate fiscal competition will make it more difficult to maintain state fiscal differences; essentially, if higher taxes drive away business activity and relatively lower taxes attract it, then in the long, run all states will have to have similar tax burdens (or at least similar *net* burdens, after the benefits of public services are considered). As discussed in Chapter 1, fiscal differences among the states have narrowed substantially over the past 20 years. Some of the narrowing of fiscal differences over this period is the result of growth and changes in the structure of intergovernmental grants and some from the narrowing of regional economic differences (that is, convergence of state personal income), which has translated into a corresponding narrowing of fiscal differences as well. It also seems likely, however, that interstate competition for economic activity has contributed to the narrowing of tax and spending differences. It seems unlikely that interstate competition will ever fully eliminate interstate fiscal differences because residents of different states are likely to continue expressing different demands for public services.

BUSINESS CLIMATE STUDIES AND RANKINGS[8]

As a result of the increased attention to state–local taxes and their effect on economic development by both business and government, a number of attempts have been made to evaluate and compare business costs—or what is often called the *business environment*—in the various states. Over the years, a number of state *business climate* rankings or indexes have been produced. For instance, in the late 1970s and 1980s, Grant Thornton, an accounting and management consulting firm, weighted factors thought to be important for manufacturing investment decisions to compute an overall index of manufacturing business climate for each state. After substantial criticism (including some in an earlier edition of this book), that index was abandoned. Peter Fisher (2005) reports that at least eight other indexes about state business, investment, or living climates have recently been published, including the "State Business Tax Climate Index" published by the Tax Foundation, which is based largely on tax levels and *Forbes* magazine's "Best Places" rating, which focuses on a broad set of economic and social factors.

For the last Grant Thornton study[9], 21 different factors were measured representing the 5 major categories of state–local government fiscal policies, state-regulated employment costs (unemployment and workers' compensation), labor costs, availability and productivity of resources, and quality of life (education, health care, cost of living, transportation).

The heaviest weighted factors of the 21—all reflecting the labor market in the state—were the average annual hourly manufacturing wage (7.14 percent of the total index), the percentage of manufacturing workers who were unionized (6.81 percent), an index representing the size and education level of the labor force (5.78 percent), the average workers' compensation insurance rate per $100 of payroll (5.38 percent), and the percentage change in the average hourly manufacturing wage over the previous 5 years (5.36 percent). These factors accounted for more than 30 percent of the overall manufacturing climate index of a state. The 5 state fiscal policy factors—the level of taxes; the change in taxes, expenditures, and debt over the previous 5 years; and the level of state business incentives—represented about 20 percent of the overall index. Other major factors included the educational level of the population, energy costs, and the productivity of manufacturing workers.

The states ranked as having the best manufacturing climate by this process for 1986 were North Dakota and Nebraska, while the two with the supposedly worst manufacturing climate were Michigan and Ohio. Interestingly, the states with supposedly the best manufacturing climates actually had little manufacturing activity and weak state economies, while some of the states with the supposedly worst climates were the manufacturing centers in the United States and

---

[8]For more information, see Fisher, Peter. *Grading Places*. Washington, D.C.: Economic Policy Institute, 2005; Tannenwald, Robert. "Business Tax Climate: How Should It Be Measured and How Important Is It?" *State Tax Notes*, May 13, 1996, 1459–1471.

[9]*The Eighth Annual Study of General Manufacturing Climates of the Forty-Eight Contiguous States of America* (1987).

Application 22.2 — Business Climate Studies and Rankings

had relatively strong economies at the time of the study. This is not surprising. In a state with little economic activity and substantial unemployment, the demand for labor is relatively low, and thus one expects wages and other labor costs to be relatively low and perhaps even falling. For instance, Eugene Carlson reported in *The Wall Street Journal* (1987a) that both North Dakota and Nebraska had lost manufacturing jobs since 1980.

The same economic argument helps to explain why states with a large amount of manufacturing activity and relatively high incomes show up with an unfavorable manufacturing business climate. Where there is substantial manufacturing activity, demand for labor is high and thus wages and other labor costs are expected to be relatively high and perhaps even rising. In addition, workers in the larger manufacturing firms are more likely to be unionized than in smaller firms, and manufacturing workers in many cases tend to have a lower overall level of education than in other commercial activities. Not surprisingly, with high wages and incomes, these states appear as high-cost states.

In short, the Grant Thornton index had the direction of causation reversed. Business investment (because of some factor) caused an increase in demand for labor and wages, rather than low labor costs attracting more investment. Some other reasons must have been responsible for manufacturing employment to continue to decline in North Dakota and Nebraska and increase in Michigan and Ohio. The answer is that some other factors not captured by the index, perhaps the location of production compared to the location of markets (transportation costs) and to the location of financial market centers, were more important for some types of manufacturing.

Peter Fisher's examination of the other recent indexes suggests several other difficulties common to many "climate" measures, other than the correct relationship between economic growth and the variables in the index. Indexes may include variables that are not important or not related to business investment or location decisions, some variables may not measure what they are intended to measure correctly, and the weights assigned to components of the index may reflect a desired outcome of the measure rather than the actual relative importance of that factor to businesses or individuals. As a consequence, Fisher shows that the various climate indexes produce conclusions that are often contradictory to each other and that many of the climate measures may be poor predictors of actual economic changes.

For instance, the Tax Foundation's "State Business Tax Climate Index" (Tax Foundation, 2004) includes a large number of measures of tax rates and bases for corporate income, individual income, sales, and unemployment taxes, as well as measures of aggregate state taxes per capita and relative to income. Although the index is complicated, Fisher argues that lower tax rates, less progressive rates, and narrower tax bases are favored by the weighting mechanism. For instance, regarding the corporate income tax component of the index, the Tax Foundation argues that "States that do not impose a corporate income tax . . . receive a perfect score. States that do impose a corporate income tax generally will score well if they have a flat, low tax rate system." Fisher argues that this index overemphasizes the economic importance of tax levels for economic growth, in some cases measures tax levels incorrectly, and ignores other fiscal and economic factors that may be

Application 22.2 — Business Climate Studies and Rankings

equally or even more important for growth. For instance, taxes go to finance public services, so it is difficult to understand how a zero tax rate would create a "good" business climate if accompanied by no public education, no public roads, no public safety service, and so on. Fisher also notes that states rated as having a favorable business tax climate by the Tax Foundation measure are in some cases rated as high-tax states by other measures, or vice versa. Minnesota has one of the five worst business tax climates according to the Tax Foundation index, but the tenth lowest overall business tax burden relative to profits (according to Tannenwald, 2004).

In contrast to the Tax Foundation measure that focuses rather narrowly on taxes, *Forbes* magazine produces a set of "Best Places" ratings for metropolitan areas. The *Forbes* measure includes cost factors (business costs—including labor costs and taxes—as well as living costs); public and private environmental factors (education levels, crime rate, an index of cultural and leisure activity opportunities); and evidence about changing conditions (income, employment, and migration change

over the past five years). Obviously, this measure is not just about taxes and not even just about the public sector. Rather, it is used to attempt to measure many factors that may contribute to business or individual location or investment decisions. Even such a broad-based measure is controversial, however. For instance, it may be appropriate to include the growth of income in the index if individuals or business are attracted to areas where income is growing. On the other hand, it may be inappropriate to include income growth if that change in income was caused by population or business growth for other reasons; in that case, those other reasons should be measured.

Given the discussion about the evidence concerning business investment decisions and economic growth provided earlier in this chapter, the controversy and contradictory nature of economic climate indexes are not surprising. That research has not been able to identify a few key factors influencing economic growth broadly in all areas and for all industries. Thus, be suspicious about any measure that purports to measure economic attractiveness with a single index number or rating.

Application 22.3

ASSEMBLING LAND FOR PUBLIC USE[10]

Governments, including the federal government as well as states and localities, have legal authority to acquire private property from private owners to use the property or land for public purposes. This authority follows from

the "Takings Clause" of the Fifth Amendment to the U.S. Constitution, which says, in part, "Nor shall private property be taken for public use, without just compensation." The Fourteenth Amendment extends this provision to

[10]See *Kelo v. New London, Wikipedia,* http://en.wikipedia.org; and Mears, Bill, "Supreme Court Backs Municipal Land Grabs", http://www.CNN.com/.

Application 22.3 — Assembling Land for Public Use

the behavior of state and local governments. Called *eminent domain*, a series of legislative and court actions have permitted government to "condemn" private property, purchase the property for a fair market price, and then use the land for an alternate public use.

Historically, this power has been used to acquire and assemble land to build highways, schools, parks, or other public works. One can understand the importance of this power; without it a single private landowner could, for example, force a highway project to be rerouted or even stopped simply by not selling the property. Past court cases extended the eminent domain power to acquiring private property for the purpose of eliminating slums and blight. In recent years, states and localities have increasingly used the eminent domain power to acquire property for economic development purposes, including such projects as convention centers, sports stadiums, corporate parks, and the like. Effectively, the issue concerns determining what exactly constitutes "public use."

In 2000, the city of New London, Connecticut identified plans to develop a hotel, conference center, residences, office and retail space, and park land in an industrial and residential neighborhood that was near a new research facility built by the pharmaceutical firm, Pfizer. The city argued that this plan would provide substantial benefits to the community from new jobs, increased revenue, and a stronger local economy. New London had experienced substantial economic and population decline, although the neighborhood itself was not considered "blighted." Rather than pursuing the project itself, however, the city transferred its eminent domain authority to the New London Development Corporation, which is a

nonprofit group of private citizens operating under the authority of the city government, to pursue the project. The Development Corporation attempted to purchase 115 property lots for the project, but 15 owners refused to sell. The Development Corporation then condemned those lots, compelling the owners to sell and move. Those owners filed suit to stop the action of the Development Corporation, arguing both that general economic development does not qualify as a "public use" authorized by the Constitution, and that the city was effectively using its eminent domain power to assist private individuals and firms rather than for public benefit.

The U.S. Supreme Court decided *Kelo v. New London* in June 2005, by a 5-4 decision. In a majority opinion written by Justice Stevens, the Court upheld the prior decision of the Supreme Court of Connecticut in finding that "the city's proposed disposition of this property qualifies as a 'public use' within the meanings of the Takings Clause of the Fifth Amendment."

In reaching this opinion, the Justices in the majority apparently believed that there would be "appreciable benefits to the community" from the project and that the primary benefit was not going to the developer. However, the Court also noted that state governments have the authority to set limits or constraints on the use of eminent domain by local governments.

The decision by the Court in *Kelo* has raised a number of issues relevant to economic development. Some critics of the decision think that one needs to distinguish a "public use" from a "public purpose": a road or school clearly seems to be public use, but economic redevelopment of an area may be closer to

Application 22.3 — Assembling Land for Public Use

"public purpose." Others are concerned that this decision will encourage governments to expand the use of eminent domain power even further, potentially leading to government serving as the agent for transferring property from one set of owners to another, if the government believed that the new owners would be better for the community. Imagine, for instance, a government using eminent domain to acquire a neighborhood of small, inexpensive houses and then giving the land to a developer who would build large, expensive houses. Most analysts and legal scholars would see this type of transfer as an abuse of the authority. Finally, some political officials are proposing changes in state laws to greatly restrict the use of eminent domain authority in light of *Kelo*, which might be a serious problem for legitimate public-use projects, as explained next.

Independent of the legal question in the *Kelo* case as to whether this particular project involved an appropriate "public use," eminent domain power clearly serves at least one important economic purpose. As noted by Richard Posner, without this authority, individual property owners can take a "holdout" position and either extract an extraordinary, above-market price for a property or even prevent a legitimate public project from going forward.[11] For instance, if one owner of a key parcel of property waits until all other parcels have been acquired, that owner essentially acquires monopoly power over the proposed public project and can use that power as a "holdout" to receive a higher payment than otherwise. The "holdout" owner's action creates an externality; that action imposes costs on other residents of the jurisdiction or users of the proposed public facility.

---

[11]Posner, Richard. "The Kelo Case, Public Use, and Eminent Domain–Posner Comment." The Becker-Posner Blog. http://www.becker-posner-blog.com

SUMMARY

Differences in per-capita income among the states and regions have been continually reduced, dramatically since 1930. This change has been accompanied by a general realignment of population and economic activity from the urban industrialized areas to more rural regions. One possible economic explanation for these changes is a flow of new investment to regions with relatively low wages, resulting in an increase in economic activity, population, and, ultimately, wages and incomes.

State–local taxes with an initial impact on business represented about 40 percent of total state–local taxes in 2000. State–local taxes collected from business also represented about 4.5 percent of state personal income in 2000 and seem likely to represent about 2 to 4 percent of total business sales revenue. Although all measures of state–local business taxes show substantial interstate differences, the magnitude of those nominal differences overstates the effective differences because state and local business taxes are a deductible expense for firms in computing their federal income tax liability.

Fiscal incentives for investment are offered by most states and at least most of the larger counties and municipalities, so they often do not affect the relative cost for businesses in those different locations.

The evidence concerning the effect of state–local government fiscal policies on investment *among* states or regions is mixed, with the one consistent conclusion perhaps being that there is no general result—fiscal policies have very different effects for industries with different characteristics. Relatively consistent evidence exists that labor costs and skills, energy costs, and advantages brought about by a concentration of manufacturing in a location are generally important factors in influencing interstate manufacturing investment decisions.

Studies of business investment decisions *within* states or metropolitan areas are more consistent in finding that local fiscal policies, and especially property taxes, influence the location of new investment. Relatively high property taxes or personal income taxes may also reduce the available supply of labor in a region or raise the wage that employers must pay for a given quantity of workers, thereby indirectly influencing business location decisions.

DISCUSSION QUESTIONS

1. In thinking about the effects of state–local government fiscal policy on economic development, attention is usually focused on what government can do to attract economic activity; however, some communities actually discourage or prohibit new industrial or commercial investment. What are the gains to the community from new business investment? What are the costs or problems to a community from a new shopping center, for instance? What about a new manufacturing plant? When would a community discourage these types of activities?

2. If localities offer incentives such as tax breaks or tax-exempt financing to firms that provide new investment in the community, a common complaint is that this disadvantages existing firms that receive no similar incentives and yet may be in the same business. Is this correct? Suppose that one community offers an incentive for new investment that is successful in actually attracting new investment. Work through the effects on the return to capital in the community, on the local labor market, and on the land market in the community.

3. If all states offer essentially the same economic development incentives, then no state gains an advantage. Yet this is exactly what seems to happen in many cases. Why might states continue to offer these incentives when it is not to their collective advantage or when the overall effects on economic welfare are negative?

4. The evidence about interstate investment decisions seems to show that state incentives have very different effects for different industries. In some

industries, investment is greatly influenced by state incentives; in others, state incentives seem to have little effect. What types of industry would seem to be most likely to have investment decisions easily influenced by tax or financing incentives?

SELECTED READING

Anderson, John E. and Robert W. Wassmer. *Bidding for Business*. Kalamazoo, MI: W.E. Upjohn Institute for Employment Research, 2000.

Bartik, Timothy J. *Who Benefits from State and Local Economic Development Policies?* Kalamazoo, MI: W.E. Upjohn Institute for Employment Research, 1991.

Bartik, Timothy J. "Jobs, Productivity, and Local Economic Development: What Implications Does Economic Research Have for the Role of Government?" *National Tax Journal*, 47, (December 1994), 847–61.

Courant, Paul N. "How Would You Know a Good Economic Development Policy if You Tripped Over One? Hint: Don't Just Count Jobs." *National Tax Journal*, 47, (December 1994), 863–81.

New England Economic Review, Proceedings of a Symposium on The Effects of State and Local Policies on Economic Development, March/April 1997. This issue includes seven articles and a number of comments about interjurisdictional competition and fiscal effects on economic development. See particularly the articles "Theories of Interjurisdictional Competition" by Daphne Kenyon; "Taxation and Economic Development: The State of the Economic Literature" by Michael Wasylenko; and "The Effects of State and Local Public Services on Economic Development" by Ronald C. Fisher.

Papke, Leslie E. "What Do We Know About Enterprise Zones?" In J. Poterba, editor, *Tax Policy and the Economy*. Cambridge: MIT Press, 1993, 37–72.

Papke, Leslie E. "The Indiana Enterprise Zone Revisited: Effects on Capital Investment and Land Values". *Proceedings of the Ninety-Third Annual Conference on Taxation*. Washington, D.C.: National Tax Association, 2000.

Peters, Alan H. and Peter S. Fisher. *State Enterprise Zone Programs: Have They Worked?* Kalamazoo, MI: W.E. Upjohn Institute for Employment Research, 2002.

Tannenwald, Robert. *Massachusetts Business Taxes: Unfair? Inadequate? Uncompetitive?* Boston: Federal Reserve Bank of Boston, Discussion Paper No. 04-4, 2004.

REFERENCES

Aaron, Henry J. *Who Pays the Property Tax.* Washington, D.C.: The Brookings Institution, 1975.

_____. "What Do Circuit-Breaker Laws Accomplish?" In *Property Tax Reform*, edited by G. Peterson, 53–64. Washington D.C.: The Urban Institute, 1973.

Addonizio, Michael F. "Intergovernmental Grants and the Demand for Local Educational Expenditures." *Public Finance Quarterly* 19 (April 1991): 209–32.

Advisory Commission on Intergovernmental Relations. *State Limitations on Local Taxes and Expenditures*, Washington, D.C.: Advisory Commission on Intergovernmental Relations, February 1977.

_____. *Regional Growth: Historic Perspective*, Washington, D.C.: Advisory Commission on Intergovernmental Relations, 1980.

_____. *Regional Growth: Interstate Tax Competition*, Washington, D.C.: Advisory Commission on Intergovernmental Relations, 1981.

_____. *Changing Attitudes on Governments and Taxes*, Washington, D.C.: Advisory Commission on Intergovernmental Relations, 1984.

_____. *A Catalog of Federal Grant-in-Aid Programs to State and Local Governments.* Washington, D.C.: Advisory Commission on Intergovernmental Relations, 1984.

_____. *Strengthening the Federal Revenue System: Implications for State and Local Taxing and Borrowing*, Report A–97. Washington, D.C.: Advisory Commission on Intergovernmental Relations, 1984.

_____. *Intergovernmental Service Arrangements for Delivering Local Public Services: Update 1983.* Washington, D.C.: Advisory Commission on Intergovernmental Relations, October 1985.

_____. *Cigarette Tax Evasion: A Second Look*, Report A–100. Washington, D.C.: Advisory Commission on Intergovernmental Relations, March 1985.

_____. *State and Local Taxation of Out-of-State Mail Order Sales*, Report A-105. Washington, D.C.: Advisory Commission on Intergovernmental Relations, April 1986.

_____. *Preliminary Estimates of the Effect of the 1986 Federal Tax Reform Act on State Personal Income Tax Liabilities.* Washington, D.C.: Advisory Commission on Intergovernmental Relations, December, 1986.

_____. *Fiscal Discipline in the Federal System: National Reform and the Experience of the States.* Washington, D.C.: Advisory Commission on Intergovernmental Relations, July 1987.

_____. *Significant Features of Fiscal Federalism.* Washington, D.C.: Advisory Commission on Intergovernmental Relations, various years.

_____. "Public Attitudes on Governments and Taxes 1994," *Intergovernmental Perspective* 20 (Summer/Fall 1994): 29.

Alamar, Benjamin, Leila Mahmoud, and Stanton Glantz. *Cigarette Smuggling in California: Fact and Fiction.* San Francisco: Center for Tobacco Control Research and Education, University of California at San Francisco, October 2003.

Alper, Neil O., Robert B. Archibald, and Eric Jensen. "At What Price Vanity?: An Econometric Model of the Demand for Personalized License Plates." *National Tax Journal* 40 (March 1987): 103–109.

American Public Transit Association. *2005 Public Transportation Fact Book.* Washington, D.C.: American Public Transit Association, 2005.

Anders, Gary C., Donald Siegel, and Munther Yacoub. "Does Indian Casino Gambling Reduce State Revenues? Evidence from Arizona." *Contemporary Economic Policy* 16 (July 1998): 347–356.

Anderson, Carol. "Squeeze Play." *Governing* (June 2005): 24–26.

Anderson, John E. "Two-Rate Property Taxes and Urban Development." *Intergovernmental Perspective* 19 (Summer 1993): 19–28.

Anderson, John E., ed. *Fiscal Equalization for State and Local Government Finance.* Westport, Conn. Praeger Publishers, 1994.

Anderson, John E., and Robert W. Wassmer. *Bidding for Business.* Kalamazoo, Mich.: W.E. Upjohn Institute for Employment Research, 2000.

Andrews, M., William Duncombe, and John Yinger. "Revisiting Economies of Size in American Education: Are We Any Closer to a Consensus?" *Economics of Education Review* 21 (June 2002): 245–262.

Aronson, J., Richard and John L. Hilley. *Financing State and Local Governments.* Washington, D.C.: The Brookings Institution, 1986.

Aronson, J. Richard and Eli Schwartz. *Management Policies in Local Government Finance.* Washington, D.C.: International City/County Management Association, 2004.

Bahl, Roy W. *Financing State and Local Government in the 1980s.* New York: Oxford University Press, 1984.

Bahl, Roy W., and Johannes F. Linn. *Urban Public Finance in Developing Countries.* New York: Oxford University Press, 1992.

Bahl, Roy W., and Walter Vogt. *Fiscal Centralization and Tax Burdens: State and Regional Financing of City Services.,* Cambridge, Mass: Ballinger Publishing Company, 1975.

Baker, Bruce E. "Receipts and Expenditures of State Governments and of Local Governments, 1959–2001." *Survey of Current Business* (June 2003): 36–53.

Baldwin, Robert R., "Domestic Preference Litigation: A Review of Developments Since the Decision in *Metropolitan Life Insurance Company v. Ward.*" Paper presented at the National Tax Association-Tax Institute of America conference in Hartford, Conn., November 1986.

Ballard, Charles L., and John B. Shoven. "The V.A.T.: The Efficiency Cost of Achieving Progressivity by Using Exemptions." In *Modern Developments in Public Finance: Essays in Honor of Arnold Harberger,* edited by M. Boskin, 109–29, Oxford: Basil Blackwell, 1985.

Ballard, Charles L., Paul N. Courant, Douglas C. Drake, Ronald C. Fisher, and Elisabeth R. Gerber, eds. *Michigan at the Millennium.* East Lansing, Mich.: Michigan State University Press, 2003.

Barr, James L., and Otto A. Davis. "An Elementary Political and Economic Theory of Local Governments." *Southern Economic Journal* 33 (October 1966): 149–165.

Bartik, Timothy J. "Business Location Decisions in the U.S.: Estimates of the Effects of Unionization, Taxes, and Other Characteristics of States." *Journal of Business and Economic Statistics* 3 (1985): 14–22.

———. "Jobs, Productivity, and Local Economic Development: What Implications Does Economic Research Have for the Role of Government?" *National Tax Journal* 47 (December 1994): 847–61.

———. *Who Benefits from State and Local Economic Development Policies?* Kalamazoo, Mich.: W.E. Upjohn Institute, 1991.

Baumol, William J. "Macroeconomics of Unbalanced Growth: The Anatomy of the Urban Crisis." *American Economic Review* 62 (June 1967): 415–426.

Beaton, W. Patrick, ed. *Municipal Expenditures, Revenues, and Services.* New Brunswick: Rutgers University, 1983.

Beck, John H. "Nonmonotonic Demand for Municipal Services." *National Tax Journal* 37 (March 1984): 55–68.

Beckmann, Martin. *Location Theory.* New York: Random House, 1968.

Bell, Michael E., and Ronald C. Fisher. "State Limitations on Local Taxing and Spending Powers: Comment and Re-evaluation. *National Tax Journal* 31 (December 1978): 391–95.

Bell, Michael E., and John H. Bowman. "The Effect of Various Intergovernmental Aid Types on Local Own-Source Revenues: The Case of Property Taxes in Minnesota Cities." *Public Finance Quarterly* 15 (July 1987): 282–297.

Bergstrom, Theodore C., and Robert P. Goodman. "Private Demand for Public Goods." *American Economic Review* 63 (June 1973): 280–296.

Berliant, Marcus C. and Robert P. Strauss. "State and Federal Tax Equity: Estimates Before and After the Tax Reform Act of 1986." *Journal of Policy Analysis and Management* 12 (Winter 1993): 9–43.

Biddle, Jeff. "A Bandwagon Effect in Personalized License Plates." *Economic Inquiry* 29 (April 1991): 375–88.

Billings, R. Bruce. *Report of the First Review Commission.* Hawaii Tax Review Commission, 1984.

Blackmon, Douglas A. "New Ad Vehicles: Police Car, School Bus, Garbage Truck." *The Wall Street Journal* (February 20, 1996): B1.

Blyskal, Jeff. "The State of State Taxes." *Worth* (November 1994): 82–86.

Board of Governors of the Federal Reserve System. *Flow of Funds Accounts.* Washington, D.C.: Board of Governors of the Federal Reserve System, various years.

———. *Federal Reserve Bulletin.* Washington, D.C.: Board of Governors of the Federal Reserve System, various years.

Borcherding, Thomas E., and Robert T. Deacon. "The Demand for the Services of Non-Federal Governments." *American Economic Review* 62 (December 1972): 891–906.

Borg, Mary O., and Paul M. Mason. "The Budgetary Incidence of a Lottery to Support Education." *National Tax Journal* 41 (March 1988): 75–85.

Borg, Mary O., Paul M. Mason, and Stephen L. Shapiro. "The Cross Effects of Lottery Taxes on Alternative State Tax Revenue." *Public Finance Quarterly* 21 (April 1993): 123–140.

Bowen, Howard R. "The Interpretation of Voting in the Allocation of Economic Resources." *The Quarterly Journal of Economics* 58 (November 1943): 27–64.

Boyer, Kenneth D. *Principles of Transportation Economics*. Reading, Mass.: Addison Wesley, 1998.

———. "Michigan's Transportation System and Transportation Policy." In *Michigan at the Millennium,* edited by C. Ballard, *et al.* East Lansing: Michigan State University Press, 2003.

Bradbury, Katherine L., *et al.* "State Aid to Offset Fiscal Disparities Across Communities." *National Tax Journal* 37 (June 1984): 151–170.

Bradford, David F., R. A. Malt, and Wallace E. Oates. "The Rising Cost of Local Public Services: Some Evidence and Reflections." *National Tax Journal* 22 (June 1969): 185–202.

Bradford, David F., and Harvey S. Rosen. "The Optimal Taxation of Commodities and Income." *American Economic Review* (May 1976): 94–101.

Brazer, Harvey E., ed. *Michigan's Fiscal and Economic Structure*. Ann Arbor: University of Michigan Press, 1982.

Brazer, Harvey E., Deborah S. Laren, and Frank Yu-Hsieh Sung. "Elementary and Secondary School Financing." In *Michigan's Fiscal and Economic Structure,* edited by H. Brazer, 411–46. Ann Arbor: University of Michigan Press, 1982.

Break, George F. *Intergovernmental Fiscal Relations in the United States*. Washington, D.C.: The Brookings Institution, 1967.

———, ed. *Metropolitan Financing and Growth Management Policies*. Madison: The University of Wisconsin Press, 1978.

———. *Financing Government Expenditure in a Federal System*. Washington D.C.: The Brookings Institution, 1980.

Brennan, Geoffrey, and James Buchanan. "The Logic of Tax Limits: Alternative Constitutional Constraints of the Power to Tax." *National Tax Journal Supplement* 32 (June 1979): 11–22.

Brokaw, Alan J., James R. Gale, and Thomas E. Merz. "The Effect of Tax Price on Voter Choice in Local School Referenda: Some New Evidence from Michigan." *National Tax Journal* 43 (March 1990): 53–60.

Brown, Byron W., and Daniel H. Saks. "The Production and Distribution of Cognitive Skills." *Journal of Political Economy* 83 (June 1975): 571–93.

———. "The Microeconomics of Schooling." In *Review of Research in Education* 9, edited by D. Berliner. Washington, D.C.: American Educational Research Association, 1981.

———. "Spending for Local Public Education: Income Distribution and the Aggregation of Private Demands." *Public Finance Quarterly* 11 (January 1983): 21–45.

Brueckner, Jan K. "A Modern Analysis of the Effects of Site Value Taxation." *National Tax Journal* 39 (January 1986): 49–58.

———. "Welfare Reform and Interstate Welfare Competition." Washington, D.C.: Urban Institute, December 1998.

Brunori, David, ed. *The Future of State Taxation*. Washington, D.C.: Urban Institute Press, 1998.

Buchanan, James M. "The Economics of Earmarked Taxes." *Journal of Political Economy* 71 (October 1963): 457–69.

———. "An Economic Theory of Clubs." *Economica* 32 (February 1965): 1–14.

———. *Public Finance in Democratic Process: Fiscal Institutions and Individual Choice*. Chapel Hill: University of North Carolina Press, 1967.

Buchanan, James M., and Charles J. Goetz. "Efficiency Limits of Fiscal Mobility: An Assessment of the Tiebout Model." *Journal of Public Economics* 1 (1972): 25–45.

Buchanan, James M., and Gordon Tullock. *The Calculus of Consent*. Ann Arbor: University of Michigan Press, 1962.

Burtless, Gary. "The Economist's Lament: Public Assistance in America." *Journal of Economic Perspectives* 4 (Winter 1990): 57–78.

Button, K. J., and A. D. Pearman. *Applied Transport Economics*. Amsterdam: Gordon and Breach Science Publishers, 1985.

Carlson, Eugene. "Los Angeles County Discovers Benefits in Taxable Securities." *Wall Street Journal* (1986): 33.

———. "Manufacturing-Climate Rating Sparks Usual Storm in States." *Wall Street Journal* (June 23, 1987): 33.

Carlton, Dennis. "The Location and Employment Choices of New Firms: An Econometric Model with Discrete and Continuous Endogenous Variables." *The Review of Economics and Statistics* 65 (1983): 440–449.

Carroll, Robert J., and John Yinger. "Is the Property Tax a Benefit Tax? The Case of Rental Housing." *National Tax Journal* 47 (June 1994): 295–316.

Chernick, Howard A. "An Econometric Model of the Distribution of Project Grants." In *Fiscal Federalism and Grantsin-aid*, edited by P. Mieszkowski and W.H. Oakland. Washington, D.C.: The Urban Institute, 1979.

———. "Federal Grants and Social Welfare Spending: Do State Responses Matter?" *National Tax Journal* 53 (March 2000): 125–152.

———. "On the Determinants of Subnational Tax Progressivity in the U.S." *National Tax Journal* 57, no. 1 (March, 2005): 93–112.

Citrin, Jack. "Do People Want Something for Nothing: Public Opinion on Taxes and Government Spending." *National Tax Journal Supplement* 32 (June 1979): 113–29.

Cline, Robert J., and Thomas S. Neubig. "The Sky is Not Falling: Why State and Local Revenues Were Not Significantly Impacted by the Internet in 1988." *State Tax Notes* (July 5, 1999): 43.

Cline, Robert, William Fox, Thomas S. Neubig, and Andrew Phillips. "Total State and Local Business Taxes: A 50-State Study of the Taxes Paid By Business in FY2003." *State Tax Notes* (March 1, 2004): 737–750.

CNN. "Massachusetts Governor Signs Big Dig Bailout Bill," CNN, http://www.CNN.com, May 18, 2000.

CNN. "Utah Governor Snubs 'No Child' requirements," CNN, http://www.CNN.com, May 3, 2005.

Clotfelter, Charles T. "Public Services, Private Substitutes, and the Demand for Protection Against Crime." *American Economic Review* 67 (December 1977): 867–877.

Clotfelter, Charles T., and Phillip J. Cook. *Selling Hope, State Lotteries in America*. Cambridge, Mass.: Harvard University Press, 1989.

_____. "Redefining 'Success' in the State Lottery Business." *Journal of Policy Analysis and Management* 9 (Winter 1990): 99–104.

_____. "On the Economics of State Lotteries." *Journal of Economic Perspectives* 4 (Fall 1990): 105–119.

Coase, Ronald H. "The Lighthouse in Economics." *Journal of Law and Economics* 17 (October 1974): 357–376.

Cohn, Gary. "As Jackpots Grow at Tracks and Frontons, Bettors Form Syndicates to Even the Odds." *The Wall Street Journal*, 1986: B3.

Collins, David J., ed. *Vertical Fiscal Imbalance and the Allocation of Tax Powers*. Sydney: Australian Tax Research Foundation, 1993.

Cordes, Joseph J., Robert D. Ebel, and Jane G. Gravelle, eds. *The Encyclopedia of Taxation and Tax Policy*. Washington, D.C.: Urban Institute Press, 2005.

Container Corporation of America v. Francise Tax Board, 463 US 159 (1983).

"A Conversation with Mark McClellan." *Governing* (June 2005): 30.

Cornia, Gary, Kelly D. Edmiston, David L. Sjoquist, and Sally Wallace. "The Disappearing State Corporate Income Tax." *National Tax Journal* 58 (March 2005): 115–138.

"Costing and Pricing for Local Governmental Services." *Governmental Finance* 11 (March 1982): 3–27.

Council of Economic Advisers. *Economic Report of the President*. Washington, D.C.: Council of Economic Advisers, various years.

Courant, Paul N. "How Would You Know A Good Economic Development Policy if You Tripped Over One? Hint: Don't Just Count Jobs." *National Tax Journal* 47 (December 1994): 863–81.

Courant, Paul N., Edward M. Gramlich, and Daniel L. Rubinfeld. "Why Voters Support Tax Limitation Amendments: The Michigan Case." *National Tax Journal* 33 (March 1980): 1–20.

Craft, Erik D. "The Demand for Vanity (Plates): Elasticities, Net Revenue Maximization, and Deadweight Loss." *Contemporary Economic Policy* 20 (April 2002): 133–144.

Craig, Steven, and Robert P. Inman. "Federal Aid and Public Education: An Empirical Look at the New Fiscal Federalism." *Review of Economics and Statistics* (November 1982): 541–552.

_____. "Education, Welfare, and the 'New' Federalism." In *Studies in State and Local Public Finances*, edited by Harvey Rosen. Chicago: University of Chicago Press, 1985.

Cullen, Julie Berry, and Susanna Loeb. "School Finance Reform in Michigan: Evaluating Proposal A." In *Helping Children Left Behind*, edited by J. Yinger. Cambridge, Mass.: MIT Press, 2004.

"Chairman Hits Out at Water Cost." *The Daily Mercury* (September 26, 1992): 9.

Davies, Daniel G. "The Significance of Taxation of Services for the Pattern of Distribution of Tax Burden by Income Class." In *Proceedings of the 52th Annual Conference*, 138–146. Columbus, Ohio: National Tax Association, 1969.

Deasey Jr., John A. "An Update on National Survey of Production Exemptions Under Sales and Use Tax Laws." In *Proceedings of the Seventy-Ninth Annual Conference*, 296–310. Columbus, Ohio: National Tax Association, 1987.

DeBoer, Larry. "Administrative Costs of State Lotteries." *National Tax Journal* 38 (December 1985): 479–487.

DeJong, Gordon F., Deborah Roempke Graefe, and Tanja St. Pierre. "Welfare Reform and Interstate Migration of Poor Families." *Demography* 42 (August 2005): 469–496.

DiMassi, Joseph A. "The Effects of Site Value Taxation in an Urban Area: A general Equilibrium Computational Approach." *National Tax Journal* 40 (December 1987): 577–590.

Donahue, John D. *The Privatization Decision: Public Ends, Private Means*. New York: Basic Books, 1989.

Downes, Thomas A. "Evaluating the Impact of School Finance Reform on the Provision of Public Education: The California Case." *National Tax Journal* 45 (December 1992): 405–419.

Downes, Thomas A., and Thomas F. Pogue. "Accounting for Fiscal Capacity and Need in the Design of School Aid Formulas." In *Fiscal Equalization for State and Local Government Finance*, edited by J. Anderson. Westport, Conn. Praeger Publishers, 1994.

Downing, Paul B., and Thomas J. DiLorenzo. "User Charges and Special Districts." In *Management Policies in Local Government Finance*, edited by J. R. Aronson and E. Schwartz, 184–210. Washington, D.C.: International City Management Association, 1981.

Downs, Anthony. *Stuck in Traffic: Coping with Peak-Hour Traffic Congestion*. Washington, D.C.: The Brookings Institution, 1992.

Due, John F. *State and Local Sales Taxation*. Chicago: Public Administration Service, 1971.

Due, John F., and John L. Mikesell. *Sales Taxation: State and Local Structure and Administration*. Washington, D.C.: Urban Institute Press, 1994.

Duncombe, William. "Demand for Local Public Services Revisited: The Case of Fire Protection." *Public Finance Quarterly* 19 (October 1991): 412–436.

Duncombe, William, and John Yinger. "Alternative Paths to Property Tax Relief." Chap. 9 in *Property Taxation and Local Government Finance*, edited by W. Oates. Cambridge, Mass.: Lincoln Institute of Land Policy, 2001.

———. "Does School District Consolidation Cut Costs?" Working paper, Center for Policy Research, New York: Syracuse University, 2003.

Duncombe, William, Jerry Miner, and John Ruggiero. "Potential Cost Savings from School District Consolidation: A Case Study of New York." *Economics of Education Review* 14, no. 3 (1995): 265–284.

Dye, Richard F., and Therese McGuire. "Growth and Variability of State Individual Income and General Sales Taxes." *National Tax Journal* 44 (March 1991): 55–66.

Edmiston, Kelly. "Strategic Apportionment of the State Corporate Income Tax." *National Tax Journal* 55 (June 2002): 239–262.

The Eighth Annual Study of General Manufacturing Climates of the Forty-Eight Contiguous States of America. Chicago: Grant Thornton Accountants, June 1987.

Elliott, Donald S., and John C. Navin. "Has Riverboat Gambling Reduced State Lottery Revenue?" *Public Finance Review* 30 (May 2002): 235–247.

Ellwood, David T. "Anti-Poverty Policy for Families in the Next Century: From Welfare to Work—and Worries." *Journal of Economic Perspectives* 14, no. 1 (Winter, 2000): 189–198.

———. "The Impact of the Earned Income Tax Credit and Social Policy Reforms on Work, Marriage, and Living Arrangements." *National Tax Journal* 53, no. 4, Part 2 (December, 2000): 1063–1105.

Evans, William N., Sheila E. Murray, and Robert M. Schwab. "Schoolhouses, Courthouses, and Statehouses After Serrano." *Journal of Policy Analysis and Management* 16 (Winter 1997): 10–31.

———. "The Impact of Court Mandated School Finance Reform." In *Equity and Adequacy in Education Finance: Issues and Perspectives*, edited by H. F. Ladd, R. Chalk, and J. S. Hansen. Washington, D.C.: National Academy Press, 1999.

———. "The Property Tax and Education Finance: Uneasy Compromises." In *Property Taxation and Local Government Finance*, edited by W. Oates. Cambridge, Mass.: Lincoln Institute of Land Policy, 2001.

Faulk, Dagney. "Do State Economic Development Incentives Create Jobs? An Analysis of State Employment Tax Credits." *National Tax Journal* 55 (June 2002): 263–280.

Federation of Tax Administrators, "Sales Taxation of Services," Federation of Tax Administrators, http://www.taxadmin.org/

Feenberg, Daniel R., and James M. Poterba. "Which Households Own Municipal Bonds? Evidence from Tax Returns." *National Tax Journal* 44 (December 1991): 93–103.

Feldstein, Martin. "Wealth Neutrality and Local Choice in Public Education." *American Economic Review* 65 (1975): 75–89.

Fischel, William A. "A Property Rights Approach to Municipal Zoning." *Land Economics* 54 (1978): 64–81.

———. "Property Taxation and the Tiebout Model: Evidence for the Benefit View from Zoning and Voting." *Journal of Economic Literature* 30 (March 1992): 171–77.

———. "Municipal Corporations, Homeowners and the Benefit View of the Property Tax." In *Property Taxation and Local Government Finance*, edited by W. Oates. Cambridge, Mass.: Lincoln Institute of Land Policy, 2001.

———. "Homevoters, Municipal Corporate Governance, and the Benefit View of the Property Tax." *National Tax Journal* 54, no. 1 (March 2001): 157–173.

Fisher, Peter. *Grading Places, What Do the Business Climate Rankings Really Tell Us?* Washington, D.C.: Economic Policy Institute, 2005.

Fisher, Ronald C. "The Combined State and Federal Income Tax Treatment of Charitable Contributions. In *Proceedings of the 70th Annual Conference*. Columbus, Ohio: National Tax Association-Tax Institute of America, 1978.

———. "A Theoretical View of Revenue-Sharing Grants." *National Tax Journal* 32 (June 1979): 173–184.

———. "Expenditure Incentives of Intergovernmental Grants: Revenue Sharing and Matching Grants." *Research in Urban Economics* 1 (1980): 201–218.

———. "Local Sales Taxes: Tax Rate Differentials, Sales Loss, and Revenue Estimation." *Public Finance Quarterly* 8 (April 1980): 171–188.

———. "Income and Grant Effects on Local Expenditure: The Flypaper Effect and Other Difficulties." *Journal of Urban Economics* 12 (1982): 324–345.

———. "The Effects of State and Local Public Services on Economic Development." *New England Economic Review, Proceedings of a Symposium on the Effects of State and Local Policies on Economic Development* (March/April 1997): 53–67.

———. "Taxes and Expenditures in the U.S.: Public Opinion Surveys and Incidence Analysis Compared." *Economic Inquiry* 23 (July 1985): 525–550.

———. "Macroeconomic Implications of Subnational Fiscal Policy: The Oversees Experience." In *Vertical Fiscal Imbalance and the Allocation of Tax Powers*, edited by David J. Collins. Sydney: Australian Tax Research Foundation, 1993.

_____. "The Changing State-Local Fiscal Environment: A 25-year Retrospective." In *State and Local Finances Under Pressure*, edited by D. Sjoquist. Cheltenham, U.K. Edward Elgar, 2003.

Fisher, Ronald C., and Leslie Papke. "Local Government Responses to Education Grants." *National Tax Journal* 53 (March 2000): 153–168.

Fisher, Ronald C., and Robert H. Rasche. "The Incidence and Incentive Effects of Property Tax Credits: Evidence from Michigan." *Public Finance Quarterly* 12 (July 1984): 291–319.

Fisher, Ronald C., and Robert W. Wassmer. "An Evaluation of the Recent Move to Centralize the Funding of Public Schools in Michigan." *Public Budgeting and Finance* 16 (Fall 1996): 90–112.

_____. "Economic Influences on the Structure of Local Government in Metropolitan Areas." *Journal of Urban Economics* 43 (1998); 444–470.

_____. "Interstate Variation in the Use of Fees to Fund K–12 Public Education." *Economics of Education Review* 21 (2002): 87–100.

Flanagan, Ann E., and Sheila E. Murray. "A Decade of Reform: The Impact of School Reform in Kentucky." In *Helping Children Left Behind*, edited by J. Yinger. Cambridge, Mass.: MIT Press, 2004.

Flatters, Frank, J., Vernon Henderson, and Peter Mieskowski. "Public Goods, Efficiency, and Regional Fiscal Equalization." *Journal of Public Economics* 3 (1974): 99–112.

"Best Places." *Forbes*, http://www.forbes.com/2004/05/05/04bestplacesland.html

Fox, William F. "Reviewing Economies of Size in Education." *Journal of Educational Finance* 6 (1981): 273–296.

_____. "Tax Structure and the Location of Economic Activity Along State Borders." *National Tax Journal* 39 (December 1986): 387–401.

_____, ed. *Sales Taxation: Critical Issues in Policy and Administration*. Westport, Conn.: Praeger, 1992.

_____. "Can the Sales Tax Survive a Future Like Its Past?" In *The Future of State Taxation*, edited by D. Brunori. Washington, D.C.: The Urban Institute Press, 1998.

Fox, William F., and Matthew Murray. "Economic Aspects of Taxing Services." *National Tax Journal* 41 (March 1988): 19–36.

Fox, William F., LeAnn Luna, and Matthew N. Murray. "How Should a Subnational Corporate Income Tax on Multistate Businesses Be Structured?" *National Tax Journal* 57 (March 2005): 139 D. Brunori, ed., 159.

Freedman, Eric. "Some State Residents Heading South to Save on Liquor." *The Detroit News* (November 13, 1994): C1.

Friedman, Lewis. "Budgeting." In *Management Policies in Local Government Finance*, edited by J. R. Aronson and E. Schwartz, 91–119. Washington, D.C.: International City Management Association, 1981.

Gade, Mary N., and Lee C. Adkins. "Tax Exporting and State Revenue Structures." *National Tax Journal* 43 (March 1990): 39–52.

Galante, Steven P. "Companies Shifting Tax Focus as State Levies Loom Larger." *The Wall Street Journal* (April 20, 1987): 25.

Galligan, Brian, ed. *Federalism and the Economy: International, National, and State Issues.* Canberra: Federalism Research Centre, Australian National University, 1993.

Garcia-Mila, Teresa, and Therese J. McGuire. "The Contribution of Publicly Provided Inputs to States' Economies." *Regional Science and Urban Economics* 22 (1992): 229–241.

Garcia-Mila, Teresa, Therese J. McGuire, and Robert H. Porter. "The Effect of Public Capital in State-Level Production Functions Reconsidered." *The Review of Economics and Statistics* 78 (February 1996): 177–180.

Getz, Malcolm. *The Economics of the Urban Fire Department.* The Johns Hopkins University Press, 1979.

Giertz, J. Fred, and Seth Giertz. "The 2002 Downturn in State Revenues: A Comparative Review and Analysis." *National Tax Journal* 57, no. 1 (March 2004): 111–132.

Goddeeris, John. "User Charges as Revenue Sources." In *Michigan's Fiscal and Economic Structure*, edited by Harvey E. Brazer, 765–787. Ann Arbor: University of Michigan Press, 1982.

Gold, Steven D. *Property Tax Relief.* Lexington, Mass.: Lexington Books, 1979.

———. "Contingency Measures and Fiscal Limitations: The Real World Significance of Some Recent State Budget Innovations." *National Tax Journal* 37 (September 1984): 421–32.

———, ed. *Reforming State Tax Systems.* Denver: National Conference of State Legislatures, 1986.

Gomez-Ibanez, Jose A. "The Federal Role in Urban Transportation." In *American Domestic Priorities: An Economic Appraisal*, edited by J. Quigley and D. Rubinfeld. Berkeley: University of California Press, (1985): 183–223.

Gordon, Roger H., and Joel Slemrod. "An Empirical Examination of Municipal Financial Policy." In *Studies in State and Local Finance*, edited by H. Rosen. Chicago: University of Chicago Press, 1986.

Gordon Roger H., and John D. Wilson. "An Examination of Multijurisdictional Corporate Income Taxation Under Formula Apportionment." *Econometrica* 54 (1986): 1357–73.

Gramlich, Edward M. "Alternative Federal Policies for Stimulating State and Local Expenditures: A Comparison of Their Effects." *National Tax Journal* 21 (June 1968): 119–29.

———. "Intergovernmental Grants: A Review of the Empirical Literature." In *The Political Economy of Fiscal Federalism*, edited by W. Oates. Lexington, Mass.: Lexington Books, 1976.

———. "Deductibility of State and Local Taxes." *National Tax Journal* 38 (December 1985): 447–466.

———. "Reforming U.S. Federal Fiscal Arrangements." In *American Domestic Priorities: An Economic Appraisal*, edited by J. Quigley and D. Rubinfeld, 34–69. Berkeley and Los Angeles: University of California Press, 1985.

———. "Subnational Fiscal Policy." *Perspectives on Local Public Finance and Public Policy* 3 (1987): 3–27.

———. "The 1991 State and Local Fiscal Crisis." *Brookings Papers on Economic Activity* 2 (1991): 249–75.

Gramlich, Edward M., and Harvey Galper. "State and Local Fiscal Behavior and Federal Grant Policy." *Brookings Papers on Economic Activity* (1973): 15–58.

Gramlich, Edward M., and Daniel L. Rubinfeld. "Micro Estimates of Public Spending Demand Functions and Tests of the Tiebout and Median-Voter Hypotheses." *Journal of Political Economy* 90 (1982): 536–560.

Gramlich, Edward M., and Deborah S. Laren. "Migration and Income Redistribution Responsibilities." *Journal of Human Resources* 19 (1984): 489–511.

Grasha, Kevin. "Eaton County Passes Juvenile Millage." *Lansing State Journal* (November 3, 2004).

Greenblatt, Alan. "The Left Behind Syndrome." *Governing* (September 2004): 38–43.

Greene, Kenneth V., and Thomas J. Parliament. "Political Externalities, Efficiency, and the Welfare Losses from Consolidation." *National Tax Journal* 33 (June 1980): 209–217.

Greenstein, Robert. "The Earned Income Tax Credit: Boosting Employment, Aiding the Working Poor." Washington, D.C.: Center on Budget and Policy Priorities, August 2005.

Gulley, O. David, and Frank A. Scott Jr. "The Demand for Wagering on State-Operated Lotto Games." *National Tax Journal* 46 (March 1993): 13–22.

Hales, David F. Letter to the Editor. *Lansing State Journal* (April 25, 1989): 10A.

Hamilton, Bruce W. "Zoning and Property Taxation in a System of Local Governments." *Urban Studies* 12 (June 1975): 205–211.

_____. "The Effects of Property Taxes and Local Public Spending on Property Values: A Theoretical Comment." *Journal of Political Economy* 84 (June 1976): 647–650.

_____. "Capitalization of Interjurisdictional Differences in Local Tax Prices." *American Economic Review* 66 (December 1976): 743–753.

_____. "The Flypaper Effect and Other Anomalies." *Journal of Public Economics* 22 (December 1983): 347–361.

Hansen, W. Lee, and Burton A. Weisbrod. "The Distribution of Costs and Direct Benefits of Public Higher Education: The Case of California." *Journal of Human Resources* 4 (Spring 1969): 176–191.

Hanushek, Eric A. "The Economics of Schooling." *Journal of Economic Literature* 24 (September 1986): 1141–77.

_____. *Making Schools Work*. Washington, D.C.: The Brookings Institution, 1994.

Hanushek, Eric A., and Margaret E. Raymond. "The Confusing World of Educational Accountability." *National Tax Journal* 54 (June 2001): 365–384.

Harrington, David E., and Kathy J. Krynski. "State Pricing of Vanity License Plates." *National Tax Journal* 42 (March 1989): 95–99.

Hellerstein, Jerome R. "The *Quill* Case: What States Can Do to Undo the Effects of the Decision." *State Tax Notes* (February 8, 1993): 273–275.

Henderson, J. Vernon. "The Tiebout Model: Bring Back the Entrepreneurs." *Journal of Political Economy* 93 (April 1985): 248–264.

_____. "Property Tax Incidence with a Public Sector." *Journal of Political Economy* 93 (August 1985): 648–665.

Hendrix, Michelle E., and George R. Zodrow. "Sales Taxation of Services: An Economic Perspective." *State Tax Notes* (February 23, 2004): 641.

Hertert, Linda, Carolyn Busch, and Allan Odden. "School Finance Inequities Among the States: The Problem from a National Perspective." *Journal of Education Finance* 19 (Winter 1994): 231–255.

Hettich, Walter, and Stanley Winer. "A Positive Model of Fiscal Structure." *Journal of Public Economics* 24 (1984): 67–87.

Hines, James. "Michigan's Flirtation with the Single Business Tax." In *Michigan at the Millennium*, edited by C. Ballard, *et al.* East Lansing: Michigan State University Press, 2003.

Hirsch, Jerry. "Is Wholesale Change in Alcohol Pricing on Tap?," *Los Angeles Times*, http://www.latimes.com, April 10, 2005.

Hirsch, Werner Z. *The Economics of State and Local Government.* New York: McGraw-Hill, 1970.

Hodge, Scott A., J. Scott Moody, and Wendy P. Warcholik. *State Business Tax Climate Index.* Washington, D.C.: Tax Foundation, 2004. Available at: http://www.taxfoundation.org/sbtci.html

Holcombe, Randall G. "Concepts of Public Sector Equilibrium." *National Tax Journal* 34, (March 1980): 77–80.

Holtz-Eakin, Douglas, and Harvey S. Rosen. "Tax Deductibility and Municipal Budget Structure." In *Fiscal Federalism: Quantitative Studies*, edited by H. Rosen. Chicago: University of Chicago Press, 1988.

Horwitz, Sari. "Cigarette Smuggling Linked to Terrorism," *Washington Post*, http://www.washingtonpost.com, June 8, 2004.

Hoxby, Caroline M. "All School Finance Equalizations Are Not Created Equal." *Quarterly Journal of Economics* 66 (November 2001): 1189–1232.

Hu, Patricia S., and Timothy R. Reuscher. "Summary of Travel Trends, 2001 National Household Travel Survey." Washington, D.C.: U.S. Department of Transportation, December 2004.

Huang, Yao. "A Guide to State Operating Aid Programs for Elementary and Secondary Education." In *Helping Children Left Behind*, edited by J. Yinger. Cambridge, Mass.: MIT Press, 2004.

Huang, Yao, Anna Lukemeyer, and John Yinger. "A Guide to State Court Decisions on Educational Finance." In *Helping Children Left Behind*, edited by J. Yinger. Cambridge, Mass.: MIT Press, 2004.

Hulten, Charles R. "Productivity Change in State and Local Governments." *Review of Economics and Statistics,* 66 (1984): 256–266.

Humphrey, Tom. "Tennessee Lawmakers OK Two-Year delay for Sales Tax Streamlining." *State Tax Notes* (May 30, 2005): 634.

Ingersoll, Bruce. "Keep It Moving." *The Wall Street Journal* (January 20, 1993): R12.

Inman, Robert P. "Testing Political Economy's 'As If' Proposition: Is the Median Voter Really Decisive?" *Public Choice* 33 (Winter 1978): 45–65.

———. "The Fiscal Performance of Local Governments: An Interpretive Review." In *Current Issues in Urban Economics*, edited by P. Mieskowski and M. Strasheim. Baltimore: The Johns Hopkins University Press, 1979.

———. "Subsidies, Regulations, and the Taxation of Property in Large U.S. Cities." *National Tax Journal* 32 (June 1979): 159–168.

———. "Federal Assistance and Local Services in the United States: The Evolution of a New Federalist Fiscal Order." In *Fiscal Federalism: Quantitative Studies*, edited by H. Rosen. Chicago: University of Chicago Press, 1988.

_____. "State and Local Taxation Following TRA86: Introduction and Summary." *Journal of Policy Analysis and Management* 12 (Winter 1993): 3–8.

International Monetary Fund. *Government Finance Statistics Yearbook 2003*. Washington, D.C.: International Monetary Fund, 2003.

Jackson, E. Donley. State taxation of endorsement and royalty income of nonresident professional athletes. *Journal of State Taxation* 16, no. 4 (April 1998): 1–14. Retrieved July 19, 2005, from ABI/INFORM Global database. (Document ID: 28519230).

Jay, Christopher. "NSW Crackdown on Bootleg Cigarettes." *Financial Review* (August 6, 1987): 6.

Johnson, David. *Public Choice, An Introduction to the New Political Economy*. Mountain View, Calif.: Bristlecome Books, 1991.

Kaufman, George, C. "Debt Management." In *Management Policies in Local Government Finance*, edited by J. R. Aronson and E. Schwartz, 302–327. Washington, D.C.: International City Management Association, 1981.

Kearney, Melissa Schettini. "The Economic Losers and Winners of Legalized Gambling." *National Tax Journal* 57 (June 2005): 281–302.

Kenyon, Daphne A. "Implicit Aid to State and Local Governments Through Federal Deductibility." In *Intergovernmental Fiscal Relations in an Era of New Federalism,* edited by M. Bell. Greenwich, Conn.: JAI Press, 1988.

_____. "Effects of Federal Volume Caps on State and Local Borrowing." *National Tax Journal* 44 (December 1991): 81–92.

_____. "Private Activity Bond Cap: Effects Among the States." *Intergovernmental Perspective* 19 (Winter 1993): 25–33.

_____. "Theories of Interjurisdictional Competition." *New England Economic Review, Proceedings of a Symposium on the Effects of State and Local Policies on Economic Development*, March/April 1997.

Kenyon, Daphne A., and Karen M. Benker. "Fiscal Discipline: Lessons from the State Experience." *National Tax Journal* 37 (September 1984): 433–46.

Kenyon, Daphne A., and John Kincaid, eds. *Competition Among States and Local Governments*. Washington, D.C.: Urban Institute Press, 1991.

Kettl, Donald F. *Sharing Power: Public Governance and Private Markets*. Washington, D.C.: The Brookings Institution, 1993.

King, A. Thomas. "Estimating Property Tax Capitalization: A Critical Comment." *Journal of Political Economy* 85 (April 1977): 425–432.

King, David. *Fiscal Tiers*. London: George Allen & Unwin, 1984.

_____. "Intergovernmental Fiscal Relations: Concepts and Models." In *Intergovernmental Fiscal Relations*, edited by R. Fisher. Boston: Kluwer Academic Publishers, 1997.

Kmitch, Janet H., and Bruce E. Baker. "State and Local Government Fiscal Position in 1999." *Survey of Current Business* 80 (May 2000): 6–13.

Ladd, Helen F. "Local Education Expenditures, Fiscal Capacity, and the Composition of the Property Tax Base." *National Tax Journal* 28 (June 1975): 145–158.

_____. "An Economic Evaluation of State Limitations on Local Taxing and Spending Powers." *National Tax Journal* 31 (March 1978): 1–18.

_____. "State Responses to the TRA86 Revenue Windfalls: A New Test of the Flypaper Effect." *Journal of Policy Analysis and Management* 12 (Winter 1993): 82–103.

————, ed. *Local Government Tax and Land Use Policies in the United States*. Cheltenham, U.K.: Edward Elgar, 1998.

————. "School-Based Educational Accountability Systems: The Promise and the Pitfalls." *National Tax Journal* 54 (June 2001): 385–400.

Ladd, Helen F., and Janet S. Hansen, eds. *Making Money Matter: Financing America's Schools*. Committee on Education Finance, Commission on Behavioral and Social Sciences and Education, National Research Council. Washington, D.C.: National Academy Press, 1999.

Lankford, R. Hamilton. "Efficiency and Equity in the Provision of Public Education." *The Review of Economics and Statistics* 67 (February 1985): 70–80.

Lee, Valerie E., and Julia B. Smith. "High School Size: Which Works Best and for Whom?" *Educational Evaluation and Policy Analysis* 19, no. 3 (Fall 1997): 205–227.

Lemov, Penelope. "Is There Anything Left to Tax?" *Governing* (August 1993): 26.

————. "The Weight Line." *Governing* (March 2004): 49.

————. "My Big Fat Insurance Premium." *Governing* (June 2005): 8.

Leonard, Paul A. "Debt Management." In *Management Policies in Local Government Finance*, edited by J. Aronson and E. Schwartz. Washington, D.C.: International City/County Management Association, 2004.

Luce, Thomas F., Jr. "Local Taxes, Public Services, and the Intrametropolitan Location of Firms and Households." *Public Finance Quarterly* 22 (April 1994): 139–167.

Lukemeyer, Anna. "Financing a Constitutional Education: Views from the Bench." In *Helping Children Left Behind*, edited by J. Yinger. Cambridge, Mass.: MIT Press, 2004.

Lynch, Carolyn D. "The Treasury II Tax Reform Proposal: Its Impact on State Personal Income Tax Liabilities." In *Proceedings of the Seventy-Ninth Annual Conference*, 310–16. Columbus, Ohio: National Tax Association, 1987.

MacTaggert, Stacy. "The Neverending Whiskey Wars." *Governing* (November 1994): 36–40.

Marshall, Jonathan. "How to Break Up Traffic Jams." *Wall Street Journal* (September 15, 1986).

Martin, Lawrence. "Miscellaneous Taxes in Michigan: Sin, Death, and Recreation." In *Michigan at the Millennium*, edited by C. Ballard, 667–680. East Lansing: Michigan State University Press, 2003.

Martinez-Vasquez, Jorge. "Selfishness Versus Public 'Regardingness' in Voting Behavior." *Journal of Public Economics* 15 (June 1981): 349–361.

Martinez-Vazquez, Jorge, Mark Rider, and Mary Beth Walker. "Race and the Structure of Local Government." *Journal of Urban Economics* 41 (1997): 281–300.

Maxwell, James A. *Financing State and Local Governments*. Washington, D.C.: The Brookings Institution, 1965.

Mazerov, Michael. "Expanding Sales Taxation of Services: Options and Issues." *State Tax Notes* (July 21, 2003): 183.

McDonald John. "Incidence of the Property Tax on Commercial Real Estate: The Case of Downtown Chicago." *National Tax Journal* 46 (June 1993): 109–120.

McEachern, William A. "Collective Decision Rules and Local Debt Choice: A Test of the Median-Voter Hypothesis." *National Tax Journal* 31 (June 1978): 129–36.

McGuire, Therese J., and C. Eugene Steuerle. "A Summary of What We Know—and Don't—About State Fiscal Crises." *State Tax Notes* (August 4, 2003): 357–361.

McLure, Charles E. "Commodity Tax incidence in Open Economies." *National Tax Journal* 17 (June 1964): 187–204.

_____. "Tax Exporting in the U.S.: Estimates for 1962." *National Tax Journal* 20 (March 1967): 49–77.

_____. "The 'New View' of the Property Tax: A Cavea." *National Tax Journal* 30 (March 1977): 69–75.

_____. "Taxation of Multijurisdictional Corporate Income: Lessons of the U.S. Experience." In *The Political Economy of Fiscal Federalism*, edited by W. Oates, 241–59. Lexington, Mass.: Lexington Books, 1977.

_____. "The State Corporate Income Tax: Lamb in Wolves Clothing." In *The Economics of Taxation*, edited by H. J. Aaron and M. J. Boskin. Washington, D.C.: The Brookings Institution, 1980.

_____. "The Elusive Incidence of Corporate Income Tax: The State Case." *Public Finance Quarterly* (October 1981): 395–413.

Mears, Bill. "Supreme Court Backs Municipal Land Grabs," CNN, http://www.CNN.com/ 2005

Megdal, Sharon B. "A Model of Local Demand for Education." *Journal of Urban Economics* 16 (1984): 13–30.

_____. "The Flypaper Effect Revisited: An Econometric Explanation." *The Review of Economics and Statistics* 69 (May 1987): 347–51.

Menchik, Paul. "Michigan's Personal Income Tax." In *Michigan at the Millennium,* edited by C. Ballard, *et al.,* 535–557. East Lansing: Michigan State University Press, 2003.

Metcalf, Gilbert E. "Tax Exporting, Federal Deductibility, and State Tax Structure." *Journal of Policy Analysis and Management* 12 (Winter 1993): 109–126.

Meyer, Bruce D., and Dan T. Rosenbaum. "Making Single Mothers Work: Recent Tax and Welfare Policy and Its Effects." *National Tax Journal* 53 (December 2000): 1027–1061.

Michigan Department of the Treasury, Taxation and Economic Policy Office. *The Michigan Single Business Tax, 1999–2000.* Lansing: Taxation and Economic Policy Office, August, 2003.

Mieskowski, Peter M. "The Property Tax: An Excise Tax or a Profits Tax?" *Journal of Public Economics* 1 (1972): 73–96.

_____. "Recent Trends in Urban And Regional Development." In *Current Issues In Urban Economics*, edited by P. Mieszkowski and M. Straszheim, 3–39. Baltimore: The Johns Hopkins University Press, 1979.

Mieskowski, Peter M., and George R. Zodrow. "The Incidence of a Partial State Corporate Income Tax." *National Tax Journal* 38 (December 1985): 489–496.

_____. "Taxation and the Tiebout Model." *Journal of Economic Literature* 27 (September 1989): 1098–1146.

Mikesell, John L. "Patterns of Exclusion of Personal Property from American Property Tax Systems." *Public Finance Quarterly* 20 (October 1992): 528–542.

_____. "The Future of American Sales and Use Taxation." In *The Future of State Taxation,* edited by D. Brunori. Washington, D.C.: The Urban Institute Press, 1998.

Mikesell, John L., and C. Kurt Zorn. "Impact of the Sales Tax Rate on Its Base: Evidence from a Small Town." Working paper, Bloomington, Indiana University, 1985.

———. "Revenue Performance of State Lotteries." In *Proceedings of the 78th Annual Conference,* 159–169. Columbus, Ohio: National Tax Association-Tax Institute of America, 1986.

Miller, Merton H. "Debt and Taxes." *Journal of Finance* 32 (1977): 261–275.

Moffitt, Robert A. "The Effects of Grants-in-Aid on State and Local Expenditures: The Case of AFDC." *Journal of Public Economics* 23 (April 1984): 279–305.

———. *Incentive Effects of the U.S. Welfare System.* Madison: The University of Wisconsin, Institute for Research on Poverty, 1990.

———. "Has State Redistribution Policy Grown More Conservative?" *National Tax Journal* 43 (June 1990): 123–142.

———, ed. *Means-Tested Transfer Programs in the United States.* A National Bureau of Economic Research Conference Report. Chicago: The University of Chicago Press, 2003.

Mohring, Herbert, and Mitchell Harwitz. *Highway Benefits: An Analytical Framework.* Evanston, Ill.: Northwestern University, 1962.

Monk, David H., and Emil J. Haller. "Predictors of High School Academic Course Offerings: The Role of School Size." *American Educational Research Journal* 30 no. 1 (Spring 1993): 3–21.

Morgan, William E., and John H. Mutti. "The Exportation of State and Local Taxes in a Multilateral Framework: The Case of Business Taxes." *National Tax Journal* 38 (June 1985): 191–208.

Moulder, Evelina. *Financing Parks and Recreation: User Fees and Fund-Raising as Revenue Sources.* Washington, D.C.: International City/County Management Association, 2002.

———. *Contracting for Service Delivery: Local Government Choices.* Washington, D.C.: International City/County Management Association, 2004.

Mueller, Dennis C. *Public Choice II.* Cambridge: Cambridge University Press, 1989.

Munnell, Alicia H. "Why Has Productivity Growth Declined? Productivity and Public Investment." *New England Economic Review* (January/February 1990): 3–22.

———. "Infrastructure Invest and Economic Growth." *Journal of Economic Perspectives* 6 (1992): 189–198.

Murnane, Richard J. "An Economist's Look at Federal and State Education Policies." In *American Domestic Priorities: An Economic Appraisal,* edited by J. Quigley and D. Rubinfeld, 118–147. Berkeley: University of California Press, 1985.

Murnane, Richard J., and Frank Levy. "Will Standards-Based Reforms Improve the Education of Students of Color?" *National Tax Journal* 54 (June 2001): 401–415.

Mushkin, Selma, ed. *Public Prices for Public Products.* Washington, D.C.: The Urban Institute, 1972.

Mutti, John H., and William E. Morgan. "The Exportation of State and Local Taxes in a Multilateral Framework: The Case of Household Type Taxes." *National Tax Journal* 36 (December 1983): 459–476.

National Association of State Budget Officers. *Budget Processes in the States.* Washington, D.C.: National Association of State Budget Officers, January 2002.

_____. *2003 State Expenditure Report*. Washington, D.C.: National Association of State Budget Officers, 2004.

National Association of State Development Agencies. *Directory of Incentives for Business Investment and Development in the United States: A State by State Guide*. Washington, D.C.: National Association of State Development Agencies, 2002.

National Bellas Hess v. Illinois Department of Revenue, 386 US 753 (1967).

National Center for Health Statistics. *Health, United States, 2004, with Chartbook on Trends in the Health of Americans*. Hyattsville, Md.: U.S. Government Printing Office, 2004.

National Conference of State Legislatures. *Final Report, Task Force on No Child Left Behind*. Denver: National Conference of State Legislatures, February 2005.

National Governor's Association and National Association of State Budget Officers. *The Fiscal Survey of States*. Washington, D.C.: National Governor's Association and National Association of State Budget Officers, December 2004.

Neenan, William B. *Urban Public Economics*. Belmont, Calif.: Wadsworth Publishing, 1981.

Nelson, Jon P. "Advertising Bans, Monopoly, and Alcohol Demand: Testing for Substitution Effects Using State Panel Data." *Review of Industrial Organization* 22 (2003): 1–25.

Nelson, Michael A. "Decentralization of the Subnational Public Sector: An Empirical Analysis of the Determinants of Local Government Structure in Metropolitan Areas of the U.S." *Southern Economic Journal* 57 (October 1990): 443–457.

Nelson, Richard R. "Roles of Government in a Mixed Economy." *Journal of Policy Analysis and Management* 6 (Summer 1987): 541–57.

Netzer, Dick. *Economics of the Property Tax*. Washington, D.C.: The Brookings Institution, 1966.

_____. "Differences in Reliance on User Charges by American State and Local Governments." *Public Finance Quarterly* 20 (October 1992): 499–511.

"New Hampshire Tries Harder Marketing Liquor with Spirit." *Wall Street Journal* (October 8, 1985): 33.

Niskanen, William A. "The Peculiar Economics of Bureaucracy." *American Economic Review* 58 (May 1968): 293–305.

Oakland, William H. "Earmarking and Decentralization." In *Proceedings of the Seventy-Seventh Annual Conference*, 274–277. Columbus, Ohio: National Tax Association, 1985.

Oates, Wallace E. "The Effects of Property Taxes and Local Public Spending on Property Values: An Empirical Study of Tax Capitalization and the Tiebout Hypothesis." *Journal of Political Economy* 77 (November 1969): 957–971.

_____. *Fiscal Federalism*. New York: Harcourt Brace Jovanovich, 1972.

_____. "The Effects of Property Taxes and Local Public Spending on Property Values: A Reply and Yet Further Results." *Journal of Political Economy* 81 (July 1973): 1004–1008.

_____, ed. *The Political Economy of Fiscal Federalism*. Lexington, Mass.: Lexington Books, 1977.

_____. "Fiscal Decentralization and Economic Development." *National Tax Journal* 46 (June 1993): 237–243.

Oates, Wallace E., ed. *The Economics of Fiscal Federalism and Local Finance*. Northampton, Mass.: Edward Elgar Publishing, 1998.

————, ed. *Property Taxation and Local Government Finance*. Cambridge, Mass.: Lincoln Institute of Land Policy, 2001.

————, and Robert M. Schwab. "Land Taxes and Urban Development." *National Tax Journal* 50 (March 1997): 1–21.

Organisation for Economic Co-operation and Development. *OECD in Figures, 2004 Edition*. Paris: Organisation for Economic Co-operation and Development, 2005.

————. *Education at a Glance*. Paris: Organisation for Economic Co-operation and Development, 2005.

Oster, Emily. "Are All Lotteries Regressive? Evidence from the Powerball." *National Tax Journal* 57 (June 2004): 179–187.

O'Sullivan, Arthur, Terri A. Sexton, and Steven M. Sheffrin. " Differential Burdens from the Assessment Provisions of Proposition 13." *National Tax Journal* 47 (December 1994): 721–729.

Pack, Janet Rothenberg. "Privatization of Public-Sector Services in Theory and Practice." *Journal of Policy Analysis and Management* 6 (Summer 1987): 523–40.

Papke, Leslie. "Subnational Taxation and Capital Mobility: Estimates of Tax-Price Elasticities." *National Tax Journal* 40 (June 1987): 191–203.

————. "Interstate Business Tax Differentials and New Firm Location." *Journal of Public Economics* 45 (1991): 47–68.

————. "What Do We Know About Enterprise Zones?" In *Tax Policy and the Economy*, edited by J. Poterba. Cambridge, Mass.: MIT Press, 1993.

————. "Tax Policy and Urban Development: Evidence from the Indiana Enterprise Zone Program." *Journal of Public Economics* 54 (May 1994): 37–49.

————. "The Indiana Enterprise Zone Revisited: Effects on Capital Investment and Land Values." In *Proceedings of the Ninety-Third Annual Conference on Taxation*. Washington, D.C.: National Tax Association, 2000.

Papke, James A., and Leslie E. Papke. "State Tax Incentives and Investment Location Decisions." In *Indiana's Revenue Structure: Major Components and Issues, Part II*, edited by J. Papke. West Lafayette, Ind.: Purdue University Press, 1984.

Pechman, Joseph A. *Who Paid the Taxes, 1966–85*. Washington, D.C.: The Brookings Institution, 1985.

Peters, Alan H., and Peter S. Fisher. *State Enterprise Zone Programs: Have They Worked?* Kalamazoo, Mich.: W.E. Upjohn Institute for Employment Research, 2002.

Phares, Donald. *Who Pays State and Local Taxes*. Cambridge: Oelgeschlager, Gunn, and Hain, 1980.

Plummer, Elizabeth. "Evidence on the Incidence of Residential Property Taxes Across Households." *National Tax Journal* 56 (December 2003): 739–753.

Poole, Robert W., Jr., and Philip E. Fixler, Jr. "Privatization of Public-Sector Services in Practice: Experience and Potential." *Journal of Policy Analysis and Management* 6 (Summer 1987): 612–25.

Popp, Anthony V., and Charles Stehwien. "Indian Casino Gambling and State Revenue: Some Further Evidence." *Public Finance Review* 30 (July 2002): 320–330.

Posner, Richard. "The Kelo Case, Public Use, and Eminent Domain—Posner Comment," The Becker-Posner Blog, http://www.becker-posner-blog.com

Poterba, James J. "Explaining the Yield Spread Between Taxable and Tax-Exempt Bonds: The Role of Expected Tax Policy." In *Studies in State and Local Public Finance*, edited by H. Rosen, 5–49. Chicago: University of Chicago Press, 1986.

Preston, Anne E., and Casey Ichniowski. "A National Perspective on the Nature and Effects of the Local Property Tax Revolt, 1976–1986." *National Tax Journal* 44 (June 1991): 123–146.

Ramsey, Frank P. "A Contribution to the Theory of Taxation." *Economic Journal* 37 (1927): 47–61.

Raphaelson, Arnold H. "The Property Tax." Chap. 10 in *Management Policies in Local Government Finance*, edited by J. R. Aronson and E. Schwartz. Washington, D.C.: International City/County Management Association, Washington, 2004.

Reischauer, Robert P. "General Revenue Sharing—The Program's Incentives." In *Financing the New Federalism*. Baltimore: The Johns Hopkins University Press, 1975.

Reschovsky, Andrew, and Michael Wiseman. "How Can States Most Effectively Meet Their School Financing Responsibilities?" In *Fiscal Equalization for State and Local Government Finance*, edited by J. Anderson. Westport, Conn.: Praeger Publishers, 1994.

Ribar, David, and Mark Wilhelm. "The Demand for Welfare Generosity." *Review of Economics and Statistics*, no. 1 (February 1999): 81.

Riddle, Wayne, and Liane White. "Variations in Expenditures Per Pupil within the States: Evidence from Census Data for 1989–90." *Journal of Education Finance* 19 (Winter 1994): 358–362.

Rivlin, Alice. *Reviving the American Dream: The Economy, the States, and the Federal Government*. Washington, D.C.: The Brookings Institution, 1992.

Rodgers, James D. "Sales Taxes, Income Taxes, and Other Revenues." In *Management Policies in Local Government Finance*, edited by J. R. Aronson and E. Schwartz, 152–183. Washington, D.C.: International City Management Association, 1981.

Romer, Thomas, and Howard Rosenthal. "Bureaucrats versus Voters: On the Political Economy of Resource Allocation by Direct Democracy." *Quarterly Journal of Economics* 93 (1979): 563–587.

———. "The Elusive Median Voter." *Journal of Public Economics* 12 (1979): 143–170.

Rosen, Harvey S. *Public Finance*. 5th ed. Boston: Irwin/McGraw-Hill, 1999.

Rosen, Harvey S., and David J. Fullerton. "A Note on Local Tax Rates, Public Benefit Levels, and Property Values." *Journal of Political Economy* 85 (April 1977): 433–440.

Rubenstein, Ross, and Benjamin Scafidi. "Who Pays and Who Benefits? Examining the Distributional Consequences of the Georgia Lottery for Education." *National Tax Journal* 55 (June 2002): 223–238.

Rubinfeld, Daniel L. "The Economics of the Local Public Sector." In *Handbook of Public Economics*. Vol. 2. A. J. Auerbach and M. Feldstein, eds. New York: Elsevier Science Publishers B.V., 1987.

Samuelson, Paul A. "The Pure Theory of Public Expenditure." *Review of Economics and Statistics* 36 (November 1954): 387–389.

Sappington, David E. M., and Joseph E. Stiglitz. "Privatization, Information, and Incentives." *Journal of Policy Analysis and Management* 6 (Summer 1987): 567–82.

Savas, E.S. *The Organization and Efficiency of Solid Waste Collection.* Lexington, Mass.: Lexington Books, 1977.

————. *Privatization: The Key to Better Government.* Chatham, N. J.: Chatham House Publishers, 1987.

Schrank, David, and Tim Lomax. *The Urban Mobility Report.* College Station, Tex.: Texas Transportation Institute, The Texas A&M University System, May, 2005.

Scott, Charles E., and Robert K. Triest. "The Relationship Between Federal and State Individual Income Tax Progressivity." *National Tax Journal* 46 (June 1993): 95–108.

Shah, Anwar. *The Reform of Intergovernmental Fiscal Relations in Developing and Emerging Market Economies.* Washington, D.C.: The World Bank, 1994.

Shearing, Clifford D. "The Relation Between Public and Private Policing." In *Crime and Justice,* Vol. 15, edited by M. Tonry and N. Morris. Chicago: University of Chicago Press, 1993.

Shribman, David, "Colorado Business Groups Leave Ranks of Anti-Tax Forces, Urge Higher Taxes." *Wall Street Journal* (April 14, 1986): 60.

Siegfried, John J., and Paul A. Smith. "The Distributional Effects of a Sales Tax on Services." *National Tax Journal* 44 (March 1991): 41–53.

Silva, Fabio, and Jon Sonstelie. "Dis *Serrano* Cause a Decline in School Spending?" *National Tax Journal* 48 (June 1995): 199–215.

Sjoquist, David L., ed. *State and Local Finances Under Pressure.* Northampton, Mass.: Edward Elgar, 2003.

Sklansky, David. "The Private Police." *UCLA Law Review* 46 (April 1999): 1165–1287.

Slemrod, Joel. "The Optimal Progressivity of the Minnesota Tax System." In *Final Report of the Minnesota Tax Study Commission, Vol. 2,* 127–137. Minneapolis: Butterworth Legal Publishers, 1986.

Smith, James K, Ann T. King, Kathryn B. Reeves. "State Income Taxation of Nonresident Professional Athletes." *Journal of State Taxation* 16 (July 1997): 1–8.

Snell, Ronald K. "Earmarking State Tax Revenues." *Intergovernmental Perspective* 16 (Fall 1990): 12–16.

————. "State Balanced Budget Requirements: Provisions and Practice." Denver: National Conference of State Legislatures, March 2004.

Sostek, Anya. "Alarm Aggravation." *Governing* (October 1998).

Stein, Herbert. "Welfare Cutting as Welfare 'Reform'." *The Wall Street Journal* (December 5, 1994): A14.

Stein, Robert M. "Alternative Means of Delivering Municipal Services: 1982–1988." *Intergovernmental Perspective* 19 (Winter 1993): 27–30.

Steiner, Peter O. "The Public Sector and the Public Interest." In *Public Expenditure and Policy Analysis.* Boston: Houghton Mifflin Company, 1983.

Suits, Daniel B. "Gambling Taxes: Regressivity and Revenue Potential." *National Tax Journal* 30 (March 1977): 19–35.

————. "The Elasticity of Demand for Gambling." *Quarterly Journal of Economics* 93 (February 1979): 155–162.

Suits, Daniel B., and Ronald C. Fisher. "A Balanced Budget Constitutional Amendment: Economic Complexities and Uncertainties." *National Tax Journal* 38 (December 1985): 467–77.

Sunley, Emil. "State and Local Governments." In *Setting National Priorities, The Next Ten Years,* edited by H. Owen and C. Schultze, eds, 371–409. Washington, D.C.: The Brookings Institution, 1976.

Swope, Christopher. "Streamlining's Speed Bump." *Governing* (April 2004): 50.

———. "Brought To You By . . ." *Governing* (October 2004): 46–48.

Tannenwald, Robert. "Business Tax Climate: How Should It Be Measured and How Important Is It?" *State Tax Notes* (May 13, 1996): 1459–1471.

———. *Massachusetts Business Taxes: Unfair? Inadequate? Uncompetitive?* Boston, Mass.: Federal Reserve Bank of Boston, Discussion Paper No. 04–4, 2004.

Temple, Judy. "Limitations on State and Local Government Borrowing for Private Purposes." *National Tax Journal* 46 (March 1993): 41–52.

———. "The Debt/Tax Choice in the Financing of State and Local Capital Expenditures." *Journal of Regional Science* 34 (1994): 529–547.

Tideman, Deborah. "Pressure Mounts for User-Pays Water." *The Weekend Australian* (October 3–4, 1992): 9.

Tiebout, Charles M. "The Pure Theory of Local Expenditures." *Journal of Political Economy* 64 (1956): 416–424.

Toder, Eric, and Thomas S. Neubig. "Revenue Cost Estimates of Tax Expenditures: The Case of Tax-Exempt Bonds." *National Tax Journal* 38 (September 1985): 395–414.

Tosun, Mehmet Serken, and Mark Skidmore. "Interstate Competition and State Lottery Revenues." *National Tax Journal* 57 (June 2004): 163–178.

"Traverse City Whacks Washington." Editorial. Wall Street Journal (July 28, 1987): 28.

Tritz, Karen. "Medicaid Expenditures, FY 2002 and FY 2003." Congressional Research Service Report for Congress, 2005. Washington, D.C., Centers for Medicare and Medicaid Services.

U.S. Congress. *State Sales Taxation of Internet Transactions.* Congressional Research Service, Report for Congress, January 11, 2005.

U.S. Department of Commerce. *Survey of Current Business.* Washington, D.C.: U.S. Department of Commerce, various issues.

U.S. Department of Commerce, Bureau of the Census, Census of Governments. *Compendium of Government Finances.* Washington, D.C.: U.S. Department of Commerce, 1962, 1967, 1972, 1977, 1982, 1987, 1992, 1997.

U.S. Department of Commerce, Bureau of the Census, 1982 Census of Governments. *Taxable Property Values and Assessment-Sales Price Ratios.* Washington, D.C.: U.S. Department of Commerce, February 1984.

U.S. Department of Commerce, Bureau of the Census. *City Government Finances.* Washington, D.C.: U.S. Department of Commerce, various years.

———. *County Government Finances.* Washington, D.C.: U.S. Department of Commerce, various years.

———. *Current Population Reports,* P-60 series. Washington, D.C.: U.S. Department of Commerce, various years.

———. *Finances of School Districts.* Washington, D.C.: U.S. Department of Commerce, various years.

———. *Geographic Mobility: 2002 to 2003.* Washington, D.C.: U.S. Department of Commerce, March 2004.

_____. *Health Insurance Coverage: 2004.* Washington, D.C.: U.S. Department of Commerce, 2004.

_____. *Income, Poverty, and Health Care Coverage in the United States: 2004.* Washington, D.C.: U.S. Department of Commerce, 2005.

_____. *State Government Finances.* Washington, D.C.: U.S. Department of Commerce, various years.

_____. *State Government Tax Collections,* Series GF85. Washington, D.C.: U.S. Department of Commerce, various years.

_____. *U.S. Statistical Abstract.* Washington, D.C.: U.S. Department of Commerce, various years.

U.S. Department of Education. *Digest of Education Statistics.* Washington, D.C.: U.S. Department of Education, various years.

U.S. Department of Labor. *Consumer Expenditure Survey, Interview Survey.* Washington, D.C.: U.S. Department of Labor, various years.

_____. *Employment and Earnings.* Washington D.C.: U.S. Department of Labor, various issues.

U.S. Department of the Treasury. *Economic Analysis of Gross Income Taxes.* Washington, D.C.: U.S. Department of Treasury, 1986.

U.S. Department of Transportation, Federal Highway Administration. *Highway Statistics.* Washington, D.C.: U.S. Department of Transportation, Federal Highway Administration, various years.

_____. *National Transportation Statistics, 2004.* Washington, D.C.: U.S. Department of Transportation, January 2005.

U.S. Executive Office of the President, Office of Management and Budget. *Special Analyses, Budget of the U.S. Government, Fiscal Year 1986.* Washington, D.C.: U.S. Office of Management and Budget, 1985.

U. S. House Budget Committee. "State Government Experience with Balanced Budget Requirements: Relevance to Federal Proposals." Testimony of Steven D. Gold, May 13, 1992.

U.S. Internal Revenue Service. *Individual Income Tax Statistics, Publication 1304, 2003* Washington, D.C.: Internal Revenue Service, 2004.

U.S. Social Security Administration, *Annual Statistical Supplement to the Social Security Bulletin, 2004,* Washington, D.C.: Social Security Administration, 2004.

Vickrey, William S. "Pricing in Urban and Suburban Transport." *American Economic Review* (May 1963): 452–65.

Wallis, John J. "A History of the Property Tax in America." Chap. 5 in *Property Taxation and Local Government Finance,* edited by W. Oates. Cambridge, Mass.: Lincoln Institute of Land Policy, 2001.

Walsh, Michael J., and Jonathan D. Jones. "More Evidence on the 'Border Tax' Effect: The Case of West Virginia." *National Tax Journal* 41 (June 1988): 261–265.

Walters, Jonathan. "The Benchmarking Craze." *Governing* (April 1994): 33–37.

Wassmer, Robert M. "Local Fiscal Variables and Intra-Metropolitan Firm Location: Regression Evidence from the United States and Research Suggestions." *Environment and Planning C: Government and Policy* 8 (1990): 283–296.

———. "Property Tax Abatement and the Simultaneous Determination of Local Fiscal Variables in a Metropolitan Area." *Land Economics* 68 (1992): 263–282.

Wasylenko, Michael. "Local Tax Policy and Industry Location: A Review of the Evidence." In *Proceedings of the Seventy-Eighth Annual Conference*, 222–28. Columbus, Ohio: National Tax Association, 1986.

———. "Taxation and Economic Development: The State of the Economic Literature." *New England Economic Review, Proceedings of a Symposium on the Effects of State and Local Policies on Economic Development*, March/April 1997.

Wasylenko, Michael, and Therese McGuire. "Jobs and Taxes: The Effect of Business Climate on States' Employment Growth Rates." *National Tax Journal* 38 (December 1985): 497–512.

Weaver, R. Kent. "The Structure of the TANF Block Grant." Policy Brief # 22. Washington, D.C.: The Brookings Institution, 2002.

Weinstein, Barbara. "The Michigan Liquor Control Commission and the Taxation of Alcoholic Beverages." In *Michigan's Fiscal and Economic Structure*, edited by H. Brazer, 720–54. Ann Arbor: University of Michigan Press, 1982.

Wheaton, William C. "Interstate Differences in the Level of Business Taxation." *National Tax Journal* 36 (March 1983): 83–94.

———. "The Incidence of Interjurisdictional Differences in Commercial Property Taxes." *National Tax Journal* 37 (December 1984): 515–528.

White, Otis. "A Garden on Steriods." *Governing* (September 2004): 10.

Wicksell, Knut. "A New Principle of Just Taxation." In *Classics in the Theory of Public Finance*, edited by R. T. Musgrave and A. T. Peacock. New York: St. Martin's Press, 1967.

Wilde, James A. "The Expenditure Effects of Grants-in-Aid Programs." *National Tax Journal* 21 (September 1968): 340–348.

Wiseman, Michael. "Proposition 13 and Effective Property Tax Rates in San Francisco." *Research Papers in Economics*, no. 86–8. Berkeley: University of California at Berkeley, February 1986.

Wooldridge, Jeffrey M. *Introductory Econometrics, A Modern Approach*. Cincinnati: South-Western, 2003.

Yinger, John. "Capitalization and the Theory of Local Public Finance." *Journal of Political Economy* 90 (1982): 917–943.

———. "Inefficiency and the Median Voter." *Perspectives on Local Public Finance and Public Policy* 2. Greenwich, Conn.: JAI Press, 1985.

———, ed. *Helping Children Left Behind: State Aid and the Pursuit of Educational Equity*. Cambridge Mass.: The MIT Press, 2004.

Young, Douglas J., and Agnieska Bielinska-Kwapisz. "Alcohol Taxes and Beverage Prices." *National Tax Journal* 55 (March 2002): 57–73.

Zax, Jeffrey S. "The Effects of Jurisdiction Types and Numbers on Local Public Finance." In *Fiscal Federalism: Quantitative Studies*, edited by H. Rosen. Chicago: University of Chicago Press, 1988.

Zelio, Judy. *A Guide to Property Taxes: The Role of Property Taxes in State and Local Finances*. Denver, Col.: National Conference of State Legislatures, 2004.

Zimmerman, Dennis. "Resource Misallocation from Interstate Tax Exportation: Estimates of Excess Spending and Welfare Loss in a Median Voter Framework." *National Tax Journal* 36 (June 1983): 183–202.

_____. *The Private Use of Tax-Exempt Bonds.* Washington, D.C.: Urban Institute Press, 1991.

_____. "Tax-exempt Bonds." *The Encyclopedia of Taxation and Tax Policy,* edited by Joseph J. Cordes, Robert D. Ebel, and Jane G. Gravelle, 443–445. Washington, D.C.: Urban Institute Press, 1999.

Zodrow, George R. "The Property Tax as a Capital Tax: A Room with Three Views." *National Tax Journal* 54, no. 1 (March 2001): 139–156.

State–Local Fiscal Information and Data Sources

Information and statistics about state and local governments, economies, and finances are available from a wide variety of diverse sources. The fifteen organizations listed in this section are among the most often cited and most valuable sources for this information. The description for each major source includes a summary list of data available and titles of major publications each produces. To access the website of each source, go to the book's website at http://fisher.swlearning.com, and click on the link provided for each source.

U.S. Government Sources

Census Bureau, U.S. Department of Commerce
Annual statistical reports: revenue, expenditure, population, income
Census of Governments (for years ending in 2 and 7)

Bureau of Economic Analysis, U.S. Department of Commerce
National income accounts data
Survey of Current Business

National Center for Education Statistics, U.S. Department of Education
Education data
Digest of Education Statistics

Administration for Children & Families, U.S. Department of Health and Human Services
TANF information and data, Community Services Block Grant, Head Start

Centers for Medicare and Medicaid Services, U.S. Department of Health and Human Services
Legal and background information and data for Medicaid, Medicare, and other health care programs

Bureau of Labor Statistics, U.S. Department of Labor
Employment, unemployment, prices, wages, consumer expenditures

U.S. Social Security Administration
Information and data about Medicare and Supplemental Security Income
Social Security Bulletin
Annual Statistical Supplement to the Social Security Bulletin

Bureau of Transportation Statistics, U.S. Department of Transportation
Information and data for all transportation modes (highways, rail, airlines) and
  types (passengers, freight)

Federal Highway Administration, U.S. Department of Transportation
Highway transportation information and data
Highway Statistics

Professional Associations

Federation of Tax Administrators
State tax rates and bases, sales taxation of services, tax amnesty, state revenue

National Association of State Budget Officers
Budget processes, state expenditures, fiscal conditions of states

National Conference of State Legislatures
Fiscal outlook, budgets, tax actions, tax and spending limits, budget rules

National Tax Association
Links to a variety of sources
National Tax Journal
The Encyclopedia of Taxation and Tax Policy

International Organizations

International Monetary Fund
International data and comparisons
Government Finance Statistics Yearbook

Organisation for Economic Co-operation and Development (OECD)
International data and comparisons
OECD in Figures
Education at a Glance

SUBJECT INDEX

A

ability to pay, 410–411
access costs, allocating, 177–178
accountability in education.
   See assessment and
   accountability in education
accounting
  allocation of tax base among
   jurisdictions and, 444–445
  gimmicks to generate
   balanced budgets, 269
adjusted gross income, 411
adjustment to budgets, 273
administrative costs
  overview of, 123–124
  of user charges, 185
ad valorem tax, 304–305
advantage of joint
  consumption, 122
agglomeration economies, 659
aging population and state
  income taxation, 423–426
Aid to Families with Dependent
  Children (AFDC)
  description of, 593
  earnings and, 620
  as matching grant, 216, 617
  TANF compared to,
   593–595, 597
airport congestion and delays,
  575–576
alarm systems, 47
alcoholic beverages, monopoly
  distribution of, 463, 471–475
allocating tax bases among
  jurisdictions, 444–449
allocation policy, 28–29
allowed level of expenditure,
  maximum, 284
American College Testing
  Program (ACT), 521
arbitrage opportunities, 249, 251

Arizona, 162
assessed value of property,
  320–321
assessment and accountability
  in education
  consequences and remedies,
   537–538
  methods of evaluation and,
   535–536
  No Child Left Behind Act,
   495, 532–534, 536–537
  overview of, 532
  responsibility for, 536–537
  unit of evaluation and,
   534–535
assessment for property taxes
  evaluating results of,
   333–334
  leased commercial properties
   and, 332–333
  methods of, 328–331
  types, numbers, and values,
   324, 326–328
  use-value, of farmland, 344
assessment ratio rule, 321, 323
athletes, professional, taxation
  of, 406–407
Australia
  cigarette tax in, 395
  government spending in, 24
  government structure in, 129
  grants in, 224–225
  water service in, 193–194

B

balanced-budget incidence, 296
bandwagon effect, 489
Baumol hypothesis, 150–152, 166
Bay St. Louis, Mississippi, 393
benchmarking, 147
benefit tax equilibrium, 102

benefit view of property tax,
  110, 361–362
Bergen, Norway, 574
Bergstrom-Goodman study,
  88, 89
betting syndicates, 486–487
bidding, competitive, 160, 161
block grants, 206, 594–595
bond counsel, 236
bonded indebtedness, 268
bonds
  effect of federal income tax
   changes on, 254–257
  efficiency of tax exemption
   for, 250–252
  as fiscal incentive, 648
  general obligation, 235
  governmental, 245
  industrial development,
   244–245
  nonguaranteed, 235–236
  private-purpose, 237–238,
   244–246, 252–254
  selling, 234–237
  taxable municipal, 257–258
  taxes and, 240–243
  Treasury, 242–244
  trends in sale of, 237–240
  yield differential and,
   242–243, 249–250, 251
  See also investors, nature and
   behavior of
border effects of sales taxes,
  390–393
borrowing
  mechanisms for, 234–237
  reasons for, 231–234
budgetary model of expenditure
  behavior, 88–89
budget incidence of lottery, 483
budgeting and fiscal policy,
  macroeconomic results of,
  265–270

NAME INDEX